GENERATIVE GRAMMAR IN EUROPE

FOUNDATIONS OF LANGUAGE
SUPPLEMENTARY SERIES

VOLUME 13

GENERATIVE GRAMMAR
IN EUROPE

Edited by

F. KIEFER *and* N. RUWET

D. REIDEL PUBLISHING COMPANY/DORDRECHT-HOLLAND

Library of Congress Catalog Card Number 76-179893

ISBN 90 277 0218 7

FOREWORD

The present volume is intended to give an overall picture of research in progress in the field of generative grammar in various parts of Europe. The term 'generative grammar' must, however, be understood here rather broadly. What seemed to be an easily definable technical term several years ago is becoming more and more vague and imprecise. Research in generative grammar is carried on according to rather diversified methodological principles and being a generative grammarian is often more a matter of confession than any adherence to the common line of methodology which can be traced back to the conception of grammatical description initiated by Noam Chomsky. The direct or indirect influence of this conception is, however, clearly recognizable in most of the papers of this volume. The most difficult thing was, naturally enough, to select appropriate papers in the realm of semantics. Apart from the special trend in generative grammar referred to as 'generative semantics' (though here, too, we might ponder on what 'generative' really means) the term 'generative' is hardly employed in semantics. The search for semantic primes, the application of the methods of mathematical logic, the inquiry into the intricate relationships between syntax and semantics and the utilization of syntactic information in semantics are perhaps the most characteristic traits of contemporary semantics. All of this, of course, is at no variance with the principles of generative grammar, on the contrary, most of it has been made possible through the achievements of generative grammar.

This volume is representative in many but not all respects. The bulk of the papers are devoted to syntax and semantics; two papers deal with morphology, and only one with phonology. One paper is devoted to the history of universal grammar. The neglect of fields of research such as psycholinguistics, sociolinguistics and historical linguistics is deliberate. We thought that these branches of linguistics would deserve a separate volume.

The volume does not contain papers by scholars working in a framework different from that of generative transformational grammar. Thus, we have included no papers on the functional approach to grammar (Petr Sgall and his followers) and on the generative applicational model (S. K. Šaumjan and his followers) though these schools, too, apply the term 'generative'.

Unfortunately, not all of the scholars engaged in work on generative grammar were able to contribute (or not to the extent they would have liked to). A fact which we can only deeply deplore.

It should be made clear that the present collection of articles is not on European generative grammar but on generative grammar in Europe. There is nothing especially European about these papers. They could have been written in any other part of the world. One should not try to look for any special European tradition in this volume either, though it is apparent that the linguistic background with and against which European scholars have to work is in many respects essentially different from the American tradition. Unfortunately, much of the European linguistic tradition has not as yet been exploited for present day linguistic research. In this respect the present volume has not much to offer either.

We wish to express our gratitude to Dr. Manfred Bierwisch who has helped us in various ways in preparing this volume.

THE EDITORS

Paris/Stockholm, July 1, 1971

TABLE OF CONTENTS

WERNER ABRAHAM

THE ETHIC DATIVE IN GERMAN

In grammars of German, the ethic dative has been given the following descriptions: Behaghel (1923: 629) "The relation holding between the dative constituent and the verb is not one of reality; rather, it signifies the pragmatic constituent that participates in and assesses the event" (free translation from German).

(1) *Th. Corneille hat ihm* [Voltaire] *von der englischen Geschichte nur wenig gewußt.*

This dative structure, however, is not at all a good example of an ethic dative. Compare the much cited English and Latin utterances:

(2) *He plucket me ope his doublet* (Julius Caesar, Act I, Scene 1)
(3) *Quid mihi Fluvius agit?*

Both (2) and (3) are ambiguous and can be interpreted not only as ethic datives. The dative in (1), on the other hand, does not seem to be generally accepted and productive in modern German.

Havers (1931: 36) "... a true dative of affective participation is ... the dativus ethicus, frequent in popular usage". "In our area only occasional and somewhat arbitrary ...".

(4) *Du bist mir ein netter Kerl*
(5) *Gestern habe ich dir etwas Merkwürdiges erlebt*

Jung (1953: 48) "The ethic dative is exclusively a personal pronoun; it indicates a person not actively participating in the event but nevertheless involved emotionally".

Somewhat more explicit syntactic descriptions are given by Regula and Glinz.

As is propounded by Regula (1960: 11–12) there is a first person dative expressing interest:

(6) *Verachtet mir die Meister nicht*

Naturally, this interpretation fails in the case of the second person dative:

(7) *Das waren dir Kerle*

F. Kiefer and N. Ruwet (eds.), Generative Grammar in Europe, 1–19. All Rights Reserved.
Copyright © 1973 by D. Reidel Publishing Company, Dordrecht-Holland.

For (7) Regula assumes a parenthetical, elliptical *ich sage dir*; hence:

(8)   *Das waren – ich sage dir – Kerle*

While Regula separates the first person and second person datives, Glinz assumes one underlying structure.

(9)   *Nach deinen wie meinen Begriffen – Prachtkerle*

The trouble with Glinz' interpretation is that it is not identical with the ethic dative version in (7) in that *Prachtkerle* is only one meaning component of the *Kerle* in (7).

Regula's explanation, however, is not satisfactory, either, since first person and second person datives are described along different lines. However, there is no distribution to support such structuring: *mir* and *dir* are freely interchangeable. Furthermore, Regula's constraint to the effect that the ethic dative (ED) is bound to function in the context of an exclamation utterance deserves at least further commenting since it can also occur in questions.

(10)   *Habt ihr mir etwa die Blumen schon wieder gewässert?*

In addition to these arguments, Regula's description fails to account for a number of other characteristics of the ED. The investigations into the dative case that have been carried out so far can be characterized as follows: (1) They are almost exclusively attempts at semantic descriptions. This is elucidated by the names for the dative categories employed in grammars of German: the *dativus commodi/incommodi*; the *possessivus*; the *sympatheticus*; the *ethicus*; Behaghel, in addition to these, lists the classes not *expected* and *not unexpected* – classes that nowadays we tend to motivate syntactically; (2) The semantic categories of the dative case cannot be clearly separated from each other. There is much intersecting for which no distributional constraints have been propounded; (3) In traditional grammar, and, very infrequently, also in modern grammatical descriptions, the semantic observations have not been syntactically motivated. That is, no attempt has been made to locate the semantic dative categories within the framework of sentence patterns. Furthermore – and this holds equally for modern work on German case – the descriptions have not been pursued against the background of an explicit theory of semantics which delimits the range of semantic description from syntactic description.

Any attempt at a syntactic description of sentences with ED will have to include clarification as to how it can be set apart from the rest of the dative categories. (11) to (15) illustrate what have traditionally been called *dativus commodi/incommodi, Pertinenzdativ, dativus sympatheticus, dativus ethicus,* and the *obligatory (non free) dative category.*[1]

(11)	*Der Schlüssel fiel mir ins Wasser*	COMMODI/INCOMMODI
(12)	*Dem Mann zittern die Hände*	PERTINENZDATIV
(13)	*Ich blickte dem Mädchen ins Gesicht*	SYMPATHETICUS
(14)	*Du bist mir ein fauler Kerl*	ETHICUS
(15)	*Er gab dem Kind drei Maroni*	OBLIGATORY DATIVE OBJECT

When we suggest to motivate syntactically what has been given semantic interpretations so far we mean (1) testing the semantic differences on the syntactic level (commutation, deletion, contraction, etc.), and (2) describing the syntactic structure as such. This is achieved by means of a representation of the categorial sentence structure and through selection rules.

1. Let us look at the following sentences.

(16)   *Sie säubert mir den Anzug*

(17)   *Sie säubert meinen Anzug*

(16) is ambiguous in that the one reading (under normal intonation, or with primary accent on *mir*) is identical to that of (17). The second interpretation of (16) – *Sie säubert mir den Anzug aber* – is not included in (17). There is good reason to assume that the ambiguity of sentences like (16) is determined by the semantics of the verb. Compare with (18) where the same paraphrase is not possible.

(18)   *Sie lobt meinen Anzug*

(19)   **Sie lobt mir den Anzug*   (with the possessive reading)

Quite obviously, the utterance which places the primary accent on the dative constituent renders an acceptable reading which, however, is not the possessive meaning as in (16) and (17) relevant to this argumentation.

(20)   *Sie lobt mír den Anzug*   (reading: VOR MIR or FÜR MICH, respectively (*to make me buy the suit*))

(21)   *Er rühmt mír die Qualität*

(22)   *Sie tadelten íhr seine Leistungen*

(23)   *Sie machten íhr seine Leistungen schlecht*

---

[1] The class represented by (12) is also called *dativus possessivus.* The nomenclature for the different classes is by no means uniform in German grammar. Much rather, there are a host of class concepts which attempt to grasp the contents of the different dative classes. Cf. Polenz' notes 28; 33; and 40.

At present, it is not quite clear how this verbal class is to be characterized (perhaps *verba dicendi*). It is to be noted, however, that the verbs used above presuppose the presence of an addressee whereas this is not the case with the verbal class represented by *säubern*.

$$loben, rühmen, tadeln \quad \ldots \quad [+\text{Addr}]$$
$$säubern \qquad\qquad\qquad \ldots \quad [-\text{Addr}]$$

This classification receives further weight from the following observation (cf. also the conclusions that Isačenko (1965: 22) has drawn): The category represented by *säubern* ('clean' as a verb) is marked in the lexicon by the inherent feature $[+ \text{AFF}(+ \text{PHYS})]$ while the other category (*loben, rühmen, tadeln* 'approve, praise, disapprove') receives the feature $[+ \text{AFF}(- \text{PHYS})]$. (AFF = afficiens, PHYS = physical; ( ) means 'the relation defined by AFF is further characterized by PHYS'.)

$$säubern \quad \ldots \quad [+ \text{AFF}(+ \text{PHYS})]$$
$$loben \quad \ldots \quad [+ \text{AFF}(- \text{PHYS})]$$

Consequently, the sentence structures, or rather, the propositions of (16) and (17) can be represented by means of relational constants and arguments in the following manner (cf. Brekle, 1970; Abraham, 1970):

R(16)   CAUS [*sie*, AFF + PHYS (*säuber, mein Anzug*)]
R(17)   CAUS [*sie*, AFF − PHYS (*lob, mein Anzug*)]

In the case of the [AFF − PHYS]-verbs, then, the *mir*-equivalence (with the reading relevant here; cf. (19)) is not existent. The double reading (ED as well as possessive) as demonstrated by (16) is ruled out.

Verb class	Interpretation as	
	Ethic dative (ED)	Possessive dative
säubern $[+ \text{AFF}(+ \text{PHYS})]$	+	+
loben $[+ \text{AFF}(- \text{PHYS})]$	+	−

Fig. 1.

By making use of the feature [Addr] the distribution of interpretation can be sketched as in Figure 2.

Verb class	Logical presupposition	Interpretation of the dative constituent (realization of [+ Addr])
säubern	[− Addr]	+ ED
loben	[+ Addr]	− ED

See pp. 14–15 as to the constraints of the realizations of [Addr].

Fig. 2.

2. In Chapter (1) I have tried to atomize semantic differences and synthesize semantic components in an exemplary and by no means complete manner. I now turn to syntactic description.

2.1. *Obligatory Dative Object*

The obligatory object in the dative case is (syntactically) required by the verb. Compare the following sentences.

(24)   *Das Buch gefällt dem Kind*
(25)   *Ich gab dem Kind drei Maroni*

The verb phrases can be rewritten in the following form:

R(24)   VP →NP$_3$ + V
R(25)   VP →NP$_3$ + NP$_1$ + V
R'(25)

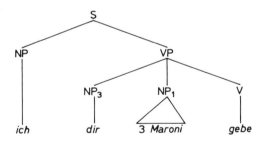

Rules R(24) and R(25) or R'(25), respectively, represent the categorial constraints characteristic of the verb classes which *gefallen* and *geben* stand for in our examples. They are not meant to be representations of the deepest (most universal) structures. To be quite clear, it is not my aim to set up deepest structures of the Fillmore type. On the other hand, it should be understood that the level of description used here is not of the *shallow* type (in the sense this term is used in (most) recent linguistic literature).

2.2. 'Pertinenzdativ'

The dative constituent is not required by the strict subcategorial frame of the verb. See the following sentences.

(26)   *Mir schmerzt der Rücken*

(26')   *Mein Rücken schmerzt*

(26'')   *Mir schmerzt mein Rücken*

(27)   *Dem Mann zittern die Hände*

(27')   *Die Hände des Mannes zittern*

(27'')   ?*Dem Mann zittern seine Hände*   (this structure may not be accepted generally; it is, however, widely used in colloquial German or dialect)

The paraphrases (26'), (26'') and (27'), (27''), respectively, provide a good motivation for expanding the dative constituents in (26) and (27) under the NP directly dominated by S:

R(26)

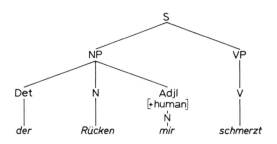

R(26) can be reinterpreted by means of a dependency grammar notation (cf. Polenz, 1969):

R'(26) $V(A^n, B^d$ [human]), [A pert B]

where V = verb, A = slot of the grammatical subject, B = slot of the dative object, n = nominative, d = dative, and pert = relation of pertinence. Here, also, the close relation between subject and dative object becomes obvious. *Adjl* is *adjectival* and indicates the class of elements possible at this node; cf. *mein, Jakobs, des Stabhochspringers*. According to the conventions of embedding in TG we rewrite R'(26) as R''(26).

R''(26)

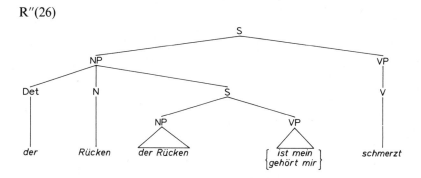

After passing the first transformational cycle S is realized as *mein* or *mir*. It is to be noted that the *mir*-transformation (more generally: whether the dative constituent rather than the possessive is realized) depends not on constraints imposed by the verb but, rather, on the semantics of the noun, in this case *Rücken* ('back'). Compare:

(28)   *Der Rücken brennt mir*
(29)   *Der Rücken ist mir kalt*
(30)   *Der Hut brennt mir*
(31)   *Der Hut, den ich auf dem Kopf trug, brannte mir*
(32)   **Der Hut, der auf dem Hutständer hing, brannte mir*
(33)   **Mein Hut, der auf dem Huständer hing, brannte mir*

The following observation is still fragmentary. It seems that the relation between the nominative constituent (grammatical subject) and the dative constituent – expressed syntactically by the embedded S – has to be interpreted as an INALIENATED-relation. (31)–(33) as well as the following sentences demonstrate that this relation is not covered by Fillmore's *inalienable*-feature.

(34)   *Die Hand brannte ihm wie Feuer*
(35)   **Die Hand, die der Scharfrichter ihm abgeschlagen hatte, brannte ihm wie Feuer*

There is one more point to be considered. The semantic feature [+anim] delimiting the class of objects under VP in the constituent sentence (R''(26)) or under Adjl (R(26)), respectively, is subject to certain constraints.

(36)   *Das Harz des Baumes tropft herunter*
(37)   *?Dem Baum tropft das Harz herunter*   (however, see (46))
(38)   *Die Blätter des Baumes zittern*
(39)   **Dem Baum zittern die Blätter*
(40)   *Das Moos des Steines schält sich ab*

(41)   *Dem Stein schält sich das Moos ab
(42)   Die Flanken des Tieres zittern
(43)   Dem Tier zittern die Flanken

If this observation proved to be of general relevance we would have to replace the feature [+ anim] by the feature composition [[+ human],
[+ animal]].

2.3. Sympathetic Dative

In contrast to the structure of the 'Pertinenzdativ', the Adjl in the structure
of the sympathetic dative is expanded under the prepositional object.

R(44)

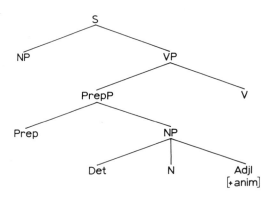

This is the structure underlying the sentences (44) and (45).

(44)   Ich blickte dem Mädchen ins Gesicht
(45)   Der Regen tropfte ihm in den Kragen

A structure like (46) provides an additional argument for abandoning the
selection constraint [+ human] in the adjectival.

(46)   Das Harz tropfte dem Baum vom Stamm

Note, however, that (46) is not in accordance with the decision about the
grammaticality of (37). At the moment, I do not know how to reconcile the
diverging conclusions to be drawn from (37) and (46). It is, however, to be
added that (46) was not accepted generally and without reservation, among a
number of people tested on this utterance.

2.4. Dativus Commodi/Incommodi

The dative constituent is free, i.e. not determined by strict subcategorization
of the verb. Compare again (11):

(11)   *Der Schlüssel fiel mir ins Wasser*

This dative constituent is clearly different from the 'Pertinenzdativ' described in 2.2. since there is no INALIENATE-relation or, specifically, no part-of-the-body relation as in (26) and (27).

However, the difference goes deeper still. Compare (11^I)–(11^V) which motivate the structural description in R(11).

R(11)

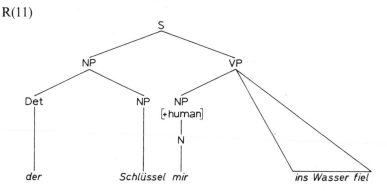

(11^I) *Der Fall des Schlüssels ins Wasser hat mich betroffen*
(11^{II}) *Der Fall des Schlüssels ins Wasser ist mir sehr unangenehm*
(11^{III}) *Der Fall des Schlüssels ins Wasser durch mich*
(11^{IV}) *Der von mir verschuldete Fall des Schlüssels ins Wasser*
(11^V) *Der Fall des Schlüssels ins Wasser, den ich verschuldete*

Note that there is agreement between the structural interpretation in R(11) and the observation made above that no part-of-the-subject relation holds.

(11) is structurally comparable to (47) and (48).

(47)   *Die Blumen verwelkten dem Gärtner*
(48)   *Der Ofen ist ihm ausgegangen*

It seems that only intransitive verbs are possible with this type of dative structure. This is supported by an additional observation.

(47′)   *Der Gärtner ließ die Blumen verwelken*
(48′)   *Er ließ den Ofen ausgehen*

Unambiguous *lassen*-paraphrases are yielded only if the subject constituent is marked with the feature [− Agentive] (in (47) and (48) it is the object constituent that has to be marked [− Agentive]). Compare:

(49′)   *Er ließ die Diebe laufen*
(49)   **Die Diebe liefen ihm davon*   (with the reading [+ Agentive])

Unlike (47), (48) and (47'), (48'), there is no true paraphrase relation between (49) and (49') since (49') covers the [+Agentive]-interpretation as well as the [−Agentive]-version whereas (49) has only the [−Agentive]-reading. For transitive verbs, this selectional constraint is not relevant at all. See (50) and (50'):

(50')   *Er läßt den Jungen arbeiten*

(50)   **Der Junge arbeitet ihm*

Consequently, the subclass of verbs occurring in the dative structure of the sympatheticus is characterized by the feature [+intransitive] and the selectional marker [−Agentive] for the dative constituent:

$$[+V_{intr}, +\underline{\quad\quad} [-Agentive]].$$

Back to (11). Expansions of the pronomial constituents in (11^I)–(11^V) by means of *trotz* ('despite') or *wegen* ('because of') yield grammatically well-formed structures.

(11^{VI})   *Der Fall des Schlüssels ins Wasser trotz meiner Vorsicht*

(11^{VII})   *Der Fall des Schlüssels ins Wasser wegen meiner Unachtsamkeit*

This *trotz* or *wegen* interpretation is possible in (47) and (48) as well as in all other cases that were tested. Steinitz (1969), has argued convincingly that this nominalization of a subordinate clause with causal interpretation is to be expanded directly under the VP dominated by S. The constituent structure underlying (11), (47), and (48), then, is as follows.

R(47)

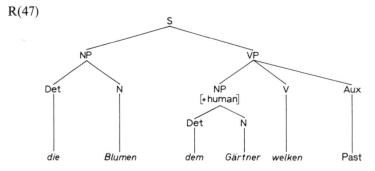

Thus, the P-marker which was motivated for (11) independently has received further support through Steinitz' findings. There is a residue of dative structures often labelled commodi/incommodi which I will not deal with here.

(51)   *Der Wein ist mir zu sauer*

(52)   *Sie schreibt mir zu schnell*

It is obvious that a syntactic description of such structures will have to be devised in connection with the syntax of the comparative.

2.5. *The Ethic Dative*

It is a characteristic feature of the ED constituent that it cannot carry primary sentence accent. If it receives the main accent – for example, through preposing *auch* – the result is an altogether ungrammatical (non-interpretable) structure or else a different interpretation of the dative constituent (possessive, commodi/incommodi). The decision as to whether a change of interpretation or total loss of interpretability takes place depends on the verb.

Structures with *haben* or *sein* cannot receive any other interpretation but the ED. The emphasis test in sentences with *haben* or *sein* yields ungrammatical structures. Cf. the following examples:

(51)   *Du bist mir ein fauler Kerl*   . . . ED

(52)   **Du bist auch mir ein fauler Kerl*

(53)   *Peter zerbrach mir die Vase*   . . . $\begin{cases} \text{. . . ED} \\ \text{. . . } meine \; Vase \end{cases}$

(54)   *Peter zerbrach auch mir die Vase*   . . . *meine Vase*

(55)   *Haut er mir* $\begin{cases} doch \\ nicht \end{cases}$ *den Hund*   . . . ED

(56)   *?Haut er auch mir* $\begin{cases} doch \\ nicht \end{cases}$ *den Hund*   (if at all possible then *meinen Hund*)

(57)   *Da vergeht dir immer die Zeit*   . . . $\begin{cases} \text{. . . ED} \\ \text{. . . } deine \; Zeit \end{cases}$

(58)   *Da vergeht dir uns immer die Zeit*   . . . only ED (dialect)

(59)   *Da vergeht auch dir immer die Zeit*   . . . *deine Zeit*

(60)   **Da vergeht auch dir uns immer die Zeit*

Primary accent is also entailed by placing *sogar* ('even') before the dative constituent.

(61)   *Das war sogar dir ein Hauptspaß*

As we have seen, primary accent on the dative constituent excludes the ED-interpretation (as in (52), (54), (56), (59), (60), and (61)) while any of the distributions of the accent in (62) is co-occurrent with the ED-reading.

(62)   *Dás wár dir ein Háuptspaß*

(61) and (62), then, render an argument for the structural distribution of the constituents: (61) means as much as *ein Spaß für dich, aber nicht für mich*.

Consequently, the constituent is to be expanded like the possessive pronoun
in *dein/mein Spaß.*

R(61)

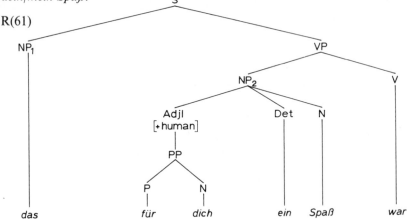

3.   The Underlying Structure of the Ethic Dative

In what follows an attempt is made to describe a deeper structure of (62).
Whether or not this structure is tenable on practical grounds depends essentially on whether or not the text categories introduced here will prove to be
tenable. One argument as to the structural description of (62) is provided by
the observation that the ED-constituent is optional for the sentence (in the
sense of a logical proposition).

(63)   *Das war ein Hauptspaß*

The amount of information that is lost in (63) as compared to (62) is its marking as a dialogue situation (including the 'inner' dialogue). Consequently, the
dative constituent is to be expanded *above* the domain of the sentence S.

R(62)

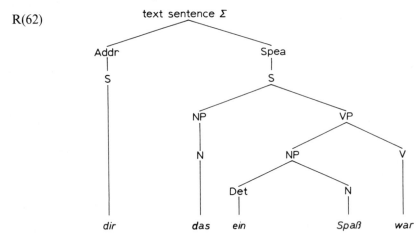

'text sentence' Σ is to be understood as a unit above the sentence unit. Its constituents are of a text-syntactic, text-semantic, and pragmatic nature.[2]

R'(62)

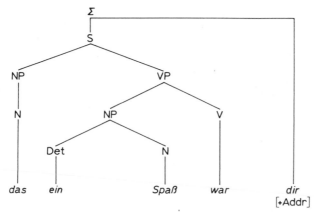

COMMENTS

1. It is no longer necessary to maintain the feature [human] in this constituent structure of a dialogue text, R'(62). On the contrary, it is made redundant by [Addr]. There is another reason why the [Addr]-marking is to be preferred. Provided we used a [+human]-marker we would be bound to exclude [−human]-objects to fill the constituent.

---

[2] Approaches such as those propounded by Lu (1965) and followed by Kiefer (1970), must be rejected since accent in this ED-structure is not to be explained along such lines as contrastive stress and, consequently, as comment. It may be worthwhile to consider another approach to the deep structure of (62).

R''(62)

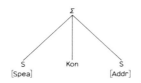

Σ is a unit of dialogue text, as before; *S*, with the pragmatic markers [*Spea*] and [*Addr*], are units of the sentence level. *Kon* is an argumentative as well as a syntactic *connective*. The logical-argumentative structure of this connective must include, among others, the following classes: *confirmatory-extending, confirmatory-restricting, confirmatory-paraphrasing*; *denying-extending, denying-restricting, denying-substituting*. In the case of (62), then, *S* [*Spea*] would have to be expanded to yield the structure of (63) (without the dative pronoun), S [*Addr*] would be reduced to represent the dative constituent, and *Kon* would be of a confirmatory character. It should be clear that R''(62) covers more general cases of the dialogue structure.

Such a description, then, would exclude metaphoric versions from the class of well-formed structures – definitely to its loss of descriptive power.

2. [Addr] is as much as [+m] for Heidolph, i.e. presupposition within the *linguistic* context. 'Context' is restricted to a dialogue form of the text, including, however, the 'situational' dialogue (i.e. presupposition also constituted by situational presence). Σ, then, has a pragmatic interpretation.

3. It may seem, that [Addr] marking *dir* in (62) is redundant, the argument being that the distinction between the interpretation as a reflexive pronoun and the pronoun as a dialogue category, in the case of MIR instead of DIR in (62), is necessary. See (64).

(64)   *Das war mir ein Hauptspaß*   . . . $\begin{cases} \ldots \text{FÜR MICH} \\ \ldots \text{ED} \end{cases}$

The decision has to be left to further discussion. It seems, however, that there are two possible approaches: (1) In order to motivate such a distinction it is necessary to provide a theory of reference in addition to the deep structure with syntactic and semantic information. Such reference approaches have been attempted by Karttunen (1968) and Postal (1968); (2) As Heidolph (1966) and, above all, Isenberg (1968) have done, one can also put the extra-linguistic information of the dialogue categorial part into the complex symbols of the base structure: specifically, for the above case, features like [+mentioned] (anaphoric function) or [+addressed] (personal deixis). The second approach, the one we have chosen here, may seem to be less problematical at first sight. However, there are theoretical hurdles behind it since it presupposes that we do not distinguish between semantics and reference, thereby entailing a number of weighty theoretical obstacles. Transformational generative grammar so far has vehemently refuted the proposal that the semantic component of its language description model must be considered to be a reference model as well (Pfeiffer, 1966; Katz, 1966). This much just to point out the problem.

If R′(62) is taken as the underlying structure – the one that I think I have better motivation for – the derivation to the surface structure is the following: S undergoes raising thereby replacing Σ; the [+ Addr]-constituent, consequently, will be directly dominated by S and will be subjected to the usual permutation transformations yielding the correct surface structure. There is one important rule in the process of this derivation: THE FINITE VERB FORM MUST DIRECTLY PRECEDE THE ED-PRONOUN. This constraint can be interpreted as a shallow structure interpretation rule (in the sense of Jackendoff (1969),

Chomsky (1969), and Perlmutter (1968), among others). This rule excludes other linear sequences from the ED-interpretation. More specifically, we can speak of a surface structure constraint since the ED-permutation which puts the ED-node directly behind the main verb must be the last in the derivational structure. In case this information were required already on a deeper level, one would have to introduce notions of predicate logic and, above all, the notion of scope – as has been done by Seuren. But I cannot see any advantage of this approach in this specific case since there is no such thing as a logical operator ranging over sentence constituents such as the ED-pronoun. The approach that we have sketched here leaves the rule mechanisms of the base structure intact and introduces extralinguistic (pragmatic) features like *speaker* (Spea) and *addressed person* (Addr). (I do not pursue R(62) any further where *Spea* and *Addr* appear as categories. *Spea* and *Addr* would have to be defined along lines such as: syntax and semantics of the textual unit Σ as functions of the speaker and the addressed person(s).)

4. *Constraints of Reference*

Let us look, then, at the following sentences.

(65)   *Ich bin mir ein Lehrer*
(66)   *Du bist mir ein Lehrer*
(67)   *Er ist mir ein Lehrer*
(68)   *Wir sind mir Lehrer*
(69)   *Ihr seid mir Lehrer*
(70)   *Sie/Die sind mir Lehrer*

From examples like these constraints of a lexical-referential sort with regard to the ED-constituent can be derived. (65)–(70) show that the realizations of the subject/ED-object relation like *ich/mir*, *wir/mir* yield ungrammatical structures.[3] It can be shown that the constraint is of a more general character: Once the person category of the subject is chosen the person category of the

---

[3] P. Trost pointed out to me the following sentence which seems to contradict this finding:

> *Da lob ich mir mein Leipzig*

This structure is not only well-known from literature (Goethe) and, therefore, a linguistic cliché, but is also productive. Compare:

> *Da lob ich mir schon meine eigenen Kartoffeln*

These sentences, however, are not EDs but must rather be interpreted in the sense of the afore-mentioned FÜR MICH or VOR MIR, respectively; cf. the discussion of *loben* vs. *säubern* on pp. 3–4. If, however, it were generally agreed that these structures are EDs we would have to clarify whether productivity also holds for other verbs beyond the verb *loben*. This is an interesting question for the grammarian only when such is the case.

dative object (pronoun) is determined as well. The relation is an exclusive one, that is to say, the person categories must be different. This relation can be formalized by R(65).

$$R(65) \quad \text{Subj.}\left\{i\binom{sg}{pl}\right\} \nsubseteq \text{Obj.}\left\{i\binom{sg}{pl}\right\}$$

Subj. { } means 'set of elements in the subject position'; *Obj.* { } is 'set of elements in the object position'; *i* specifies these two sets with regard to number: singular (*sg*) or plural (*pl*). The parenthesis indicates 'either-or'. R(65), then, is an abbreviation of four single rules excluding the following combinatory relations between subject and object elements: *ich/mir, ich/uns, wir/uns, du/dir, du/euch, ihr/dir, ihr/euch.* Compare (71)–(74):

(71)   *Ich verachte mir die Meister nicht*
(72)   *Wir sind uns Kerle*
(73)   *Du hast euch einen Rausch gehabt*
(74)   *Ihr seid euch Lehrer*

In accordance with R(65), the following sentences are correct.

(75)   *Verachtet mir nicht die Meister*
(76)   *Liebe mir nur keinen Hippie*
(77)   *Das ist dir ein Kerl*

(78)   *Spuckt er* $\left\{\begin{array}{l} dir \\ mir \end{array}\right\}$ *nicht auf die Hand*

(79)   *Da vergeht dir immer die Zeit*

Note that the structures (75) and (76) support the assumption made in gTG that for the imperative form, there is an underlying structure with a *du*-subject or an *ihr*-subject.

R(65) must be further qualified since it does not exclude ungrammatical structures such as (80) and (81).

(80)   *Ich bin ihm ein Lehrer*

(81)   *Sie hat ihnen eine Wut*

All cases with an ED-constituent realized as a third person prove to be ungrammatical. This must be taken care of by a further constraint.

$$R(80) \quad \text{Obj.}\{i\} \neq \text{Obj.}\{i_3\} \quad \text{where } i_3 \text{ is the third person category}$$

Among the subject referents, on the other hand, the third person category can be realized. See (82) and (83):

(82)   *Die sind mir Gauner*
(83)   *Der hat dir Mut*

Provided sentence (1) was really interpreted as an ED at one time R(80) could be taken to be a rule of diachronic change. Cf. again (1) which, for present-day German, is not interpreted as ED.

The conclusion to be drawn from these examples is this: There are constraints of a referential sort conditioning the realization of the ED-constituent. Rules R(65) and R(80), then, have the character of referential constraints of the dialogue constituents of Σ, *Spea* and *Addr* (be they features or categorial elements).

5. *A Type of Performance Strategy*

What, then, as to the following examples which obviously contradict R(65):

(84)   *? Ihr seid dir Kerle*   (? means 'there is reluctance to qualify the sentence as grammatical or ungrammatical'. This is not to be taken as a result with significant statistical value.)

(85)   *? Ihr habt euch einen Rausch*
(86)   *Du bist dir ein Lehrer*
(87)   *Du hast dir einen Rausch*

For me, (84)–(87), are partly opaque as far as acceptability goes, or they are wholly acceptable; none is to be rejected as altogether unacceptable. The key to an understanding of these 'deviations' from the rule lies in the colloquial speech of Austria and its dialectal usage. Compare (88) and (89), which are tne correspondent (translation) forms of the standard German utterances (84) and (85). It is to be noted that (88) and (89) are beyond any doubt correct.

(88)   *Es sads da keale*
(89)   *Es hapts da-r-an råsch*

Obviously, the formative *da* has taken over the function of the ED which includes both the first and second person categories, without, however, being subjected to the specific constraints holding between subject and object as is the case in standard German. In other words, this *da* is not interpreted as a dialectal (popular) reflex of *dir*. This is the reason why the structures are opaque or clearly unacceptable when translated back into standard German. This phenomenon is to be expected where more or less conscious changes between two linguistic competences are frequent (as is the case in Austria). A different strategy, however, may be responsible for the following (not generally accepted) structures.

(90) (?) *Ihr verachtet dir doch die Meister nicht*
(91)   *Du verachtest dir doch die Meister nicht*

It seems to be a plausible observation that this functional type, an exclamation, is used more frequently when addressing a single person than when
addressing several people. In all our examples and a lot more that have not
been listed here, the combinations *du/dir, ihr/dir* were invariably acceptable
or 'semi-acceptable' while *du/euch, ihr/euch* were not accepted at all.

(92)   **Du hast euch einen Rausch gehabt*
(93)   ?*Ihr habt dir einen Rausch gehabt*
(94)   *Du bist dir ein Lehrer*

I can see no other way of accounting for these 'deviations'. What has become
visible, then, is a particular strategy of performance whose reflex onto the
system, i.e. onto competence, has a rule-breaking effect or at least make the
border line between acceptability and non-acceptability opaque. This, to be
true, holds for speakers of German who have sociolectically internalized the
ED-morpheme *da*.

Germanistisch Instituut,
Rijksuniversiteit Groningen, The Netherlands

REFERENCES

Abraham, W.: 1969, 'Verbklassifikation und das Komplement "Indirekter Fragesatz"', *Die
    Sprache* **15**, 113–134.
Abraham, W.: 1970, 'Passiv und Verbableitung auf e. -able, dt. -bar', *Folia Linguistica* **4**, 15–29.
Behaghel, O.: 1923, *Deutsche Syntax*, I, Heidelberg.
Brekle, H. E.: 1970, *Generative Satzsemantik und transformationelle Syntax im System der
    englischen Nominalkomposition*, München.
Chomsky, N.: 1969, 'Deep Structure, Surface Structure, and Semantic Interpretation', *Indiana
    Linguistics Club* (mimeo).
Havers, W.: 1931, *Handbuch der erklärenden Syntax*, Heidelberg.
Heidolph, K. E.: 1966, 'Kontextbeziehungen zwischen Sätzen in einer generativen Grammatik',
    Kybernetika **3**, 274–281.
Isačenko, A. V.: 1965, 'Das syntaktische Verhältnis der Beziehungen von Körperteilen im
    Deutschen', *Studia Grammatica* **5**, 7–27.
Isenberg, H.: 1968, 'Uberlegungen zur Texttheorie', *ASG-Bericht* **2**, Berlin.
Jackendoff, R. S.: 1969, *Some Rules for Semantic Interpretation for English*, M.I.T. Dissertation.
Jung, W.: 1953, *Kleine Grammatik der deutschen Sprache*, Leipzig.
Karttunen, L.: 1968, 'What do Referential Indices Refer To?', *Indiana Linguistics Club*.
Katz, J. J.: 1966, 'Mr. Pfeifer on Questions of Reference', *Foundations of Language* **2**, 241–244.
Kiefer, F.: 1970, 'On the Problem of Word Order', *Progress in Linguistics* (Bierwisch and
    Heidolph, eds.), Mouton, pp. 127–142.
Lu, J. H.: 1965, *Contrastive Stress and Emphatic Stress*, The Ohio State University, Project
    Report 10.
Perlmutter, D.: 1968, *Deep and Surface Structure Constraints*, M.I.T. Dissertation.

Perlmutter, D.: 1970, 'Surface Structure Constraints in Syntax', *Linguistic Inquiry* **1**, 187–256.
Pfeifer, D. E.: 1966, 'The Question of Reference in the Writings of J. A. Fodor and J. J. Katz', *Foundations of Linguistics* **2**, 142–150.
Polenz, P. von:1969, 'Der Pertinenzdativ und seine Satzbaupläne', *Festschrift für Hugo Moser*, Düsseldorf, pp. 146–171.
Postal, P.: 1968, 'Cross-over Phenomena', IBM-report.
Regula, M.: 1960, 'Syntactica', *Indogermanische Forschungen* **65**, 11–12.
Seuren, A. M.: 1969, *Operators and Nucleus*, Cambridge University Press.

JOHN M. ANDERSON

MAXIMI PLANUDIS IN MEMORIAM

0. INTRODUCTION

The following remarks are not intended to constitute an argument that generative grammar originates with a thirteenth-fourteenth century Byzantine theologian or even that he represents the first European (?) generative grammarian.[1] I would indeed be somewhat perplexed as to how to interpret global claims of this kind – particularly in view of the ever-increasing diversity of current work that might be characterized in such terms (cf. e.g. Lyons, 1970a). Rather, it seems to me that, on the contrary, it is on account of its exploration of notions as yet ignored (or assumed to be irrelevant) by almost all present day grammarians that the tradition of which Planudes is, as far as I am aware, the earliest extant exemplar, demands our attention.

This situation is not unique. Our knowledge (and acknowledgement) of the work of previous centuries is intensely impoverished. Whole fertile traditions of concepts, hypotheses, arguments, protocols are either not now generally accessible, or, even where readily available, are assumed to be without current relevance.[2] This is particularly the case with traditions whose subsequent immediate influence has been small: such has been the fate of the Byzantine grammarians, and of the remarkable group of linguists who, in the mid nineteenth century, participated in the early meetings of the Philological Society of London. Something of the range of interests and speculations displayed by the latter can be discerned from the contents of the six volumes of the Society's *Proceedings* (1842–53). I am thinking in particular of the essays on general, or universal grammar. Key (1847), for instance, attempts to show the relatedness of demonstratives, definite articles, third person pronouns, and relative and interrogative pronouns,[3] and, incidentally (67–8), a connexion between relative clauses and co-ordinate conjoined sentences.[4]

---

[1] A brief account of the life and works of Maximus Planudes (together with some bibliographical information) is provided in Ziegler, 1950, 2202–53. Texts of two grammatical works are printed in Bachmann, 1828, 3–101, 105–66. I would like to acknowledge here my indebtedness to David Tittensor for his comments on an earlier version of this paper.

[2] It is particularly unfortunate that many such valuable investigations should be dismissed as irrelevant to 'scientific' linguistics (cf. e.g. Hall, 1969) on the basis of some eccentric delimitation of what constitutes science. See also note 7.

[3] Compare, for instance, Postal, 1966.

[4] Cf. Annear, 1967; Lakoff, 1967, Ch. 1.

F. Kiefer and N. Ruwet (eds.), Generative Grammar in Europe, 20–47. All Rights Reserved.
Copyright © 1973 by D. Reidel Publishing Company, Dordrecht-Holland.

Garnett (1846) discusses the phenomenon of morphological derivation by 'superdeclension', whereby in Basque, for instance, 'adjectives' can be formed from the oblique cases of nouns and thus become susceptible to bearing a second inflexion,[5] and proceeds (1847) to argue that many (at least) so-called 'participles' have their source in (the oblique case of) a verbal noun, his starting-point being the analysis of the Basque verb offered by Darrigol (1829).[6] In view of my preceding confession of ignorance, I am clearly not primarily concerned in asserting priority for these scholars with respect to all the various hypotheses and arguments they propose; in many instances this is clearly not the case, and they themselves are aware of at least contemporary work originating elsewhere, particularly in Germany. I merely want to indicate the existence of a relatively neglected tradition which generated or assimilated a large number of (what seem to me) insightful interpretations of a wide range of data drawn from a considerable variety of languages. We can benefit, I suggest, from a knowledge both of these hypotheses and of their associated protocols.[7]

It must be admitted that the arguments that could be constructed in the mid nineteenth century were of a limited kind: they were principally notional, morphological and historical. The semantic insights are of unquestionable value: this is what (it seems to me) is outstanding in these volumes of *Proceedings*. Semantic interpretations were supported with observations concerning morphological relationships, as when Garnett (1847) attempts to validate his interpretation of participles (as oblique verbal nouns) with reference to morphological evidence (suggestive of such a structure for participles) from a number of languages. Underlying such arguments is the quite proper assumption that the weakest hypothesis concerning morphological correspondences is the presupposition of coincidence (i.e. that it is accidental, for instance, that participles resemble oblique verbal nouns), and that alternative ('natural') hypotheses are supported by the recurrence of the correspondence in a number of languages. Present-day universal grammarians have been slow to utilize (or at least to explicitly recognize utilization of) this rich source of evidence (but cf. Zwicky, 1968) – and its potential extension outside the

---

[5] As an example, consider Basque *etche*, 'house'; *etcheko*, 'of/from the house'; *etchekoak*, 'the people from the house' (Lafitte, 1962, § 146).

[6] For further discussion, see Anderson, in preparation. Compare too the discussion in another paper by Key (1853, 69–72).

[7] Thus, it seems to me that books like Pedersen's (1931) render the present-day reader a distinct disservice in their interpretation of what developments in (in this instance) the nineteenth century are significant for posterity, depending (once again) as it does on an arbitrarily limited view of what constitutes 'scientific' linguistics. An almost exclusive concern with the development of methods for genetic comparison and reconstruction results in a misrepresentation of the achievements of the nineteenth century and of the relationship with earlier work.

strictly morphological domain. The following discussion presupposes in part some such assumption (as do a number of the arguments in Anderson, 1971b).

The proposals made by Key, Garnett etc. are at their weakest in the postulation of historical developments and relationships. In the pursuit of his hypothesis concerning the relatedness of articles and pronouns, Key is led to suggest some rather wild etymologies and suppose some far-reaching genetic relationships. This is, however, not uncharacteristic of their time.[8] Moreover, in discussing derivation or underlying relationships, only a diachronic and comparative interpretation for such notions was allowed as evidential within the then current methodological framework.[9] Nevertheless, it seems to me that the kind of evidence they adduced is not negligible (where well founded) and that it is unfortunate that the subsequent development of 'firmer' etymologies was not accompanied by the continuation of the universalist concerns espoused by these members of the early Philological Society.

This failure may be partly due to the fact that the increasing variety of evidence was difficult to reconcile with a universalist account which does not allow for a complex relation between semantic representations and their corresponding superficial syntactic structures. I have noted elsewhere (Anderson, 1971b, §1.3) the consequences of such difficulties for the localist tradition initiated by Planudes.

The localists (including Anderson, 1971b) also in many instances attempted to show the relevance of their claims concerning the character of grammatical relations to various historical (particularly morphological) developments. Such attempts have mainly been mere asides in an argument concerned with the primary, idiosynchronic (in Hjelmslev's sense) evidence. However, in §2 of the present discussion, I shall attempt to characterize something of the mechanism underlying certain changes in the Latin/Romance tense/aspect system with reference to the localistic proposals formulated in Anderson, 1971b, forthcoming. My assumption is that the elucidation of such changes would provide supporting evidence for a hypothesis consistent with the range of idiosynchronic data.[10]

Before turning to such questions, I intend in §1 to exemplify the consequences of a localistic conception of grammatical relations for a small set of

---

[8] Cf. e.g. Pedersen's (1931, 254–7) remarks on Bopp's etymologizing.

[9] In this respect at least, the sort of strictures formulated in, for instance, Harris's (1940, 216–7) review of Gray (1939) are appropriate (whatever one might think of the alternative envisaged by Harris).

[10] Kiparsky (1968, 1970) has attempted to show the relevance of diachronic considerations to certain theoretical issues. I would like to suggest that naturalness considerations with respect to grammatical change can be relevant to the evaluation of a synchronic hypothesis.

protocols. This draws upon the two works referred to immediately above, but I shall confine our attention to a certain limited area relevant to the concerns of the succeeding section. This involves the grammar of 'having' and 'giving'. Thus, in the following two sections, we shall be concerned with, in the first place, an attempt to re-establish the relevance for linguistic theory of certain traditional concepts, and secondly, with an examination of their pertinence with regard to certain problems of linguistic change. Apart from the overlap in relevant data alluded to above, these two discussions have in common their genesis in a concern deriving from the recent neglect by universal grammarians (in particular) of the content of both kinds of linguistic history, history of language(s) and history of linguistics.

1. 'DATIVES' AS LOCATIVE

I have tried to show in the course of other discussions (Anderson, 1968, 313–5; 1971b, 129–39, 190–5) that the function 'indirect object' is not relevant to underlying representations, and that in general they have their source in a (directional) locative, an allative (see, too, Lyons, 1968a, §8.4.6; Gruber, 1965, Ch. 3). Thus, the occurrence of both *to* and *from* in (1):

(1)   Egbert sent the bomb to Canada from Australia

and of *from* in (2):

(2)   Egbert sent Seymour the bomb from Australia

is not accidental. Their semantic representations involve in part a directional predication like that in (3):

(3)   The marble rolled from the door to the window

which contains an ablative phrase and an allative. (2) differs from (1) (and (3)) in that the allative phrase has undergone object-forming rules; and the passive in (4) shows the allative in subject position:

(4)   Seymour was sent the bomb from Australia

We shall return shortly to the processes involved in the relevant parts of the formation of (2) and (4).

Notice at this point, however, that the same directional relations are present in (5):

(5)   Egbert sold the bomb to Seymour

but the ablative is identical with the agent, which occupies subject position (as it does in (1) and (2)). This is also the case in (6):

(6)   Egbert sold Seymour the bomb

in which the allative has become the object; and in (7):

(7)   Seymour was sold the bomb

in which it is subject, and the agent/ablative phrase displaced as such (and deleted). Examples (5)–(7) differ from (1)–(4) in that the agent of the action is 'conflated' with the ablative. In a sentence like (8):

(8)   Seymour bought the bomb from Egbert

it is rather the allative and the agent that are identified; and there is no corresponding sentence with *Seymour* (the allative) as object.[11] In the passives corresponding to both (5) and (8), the phrase which I have described as 'conflating' a directional and an agentive function is marked with the *by* we would expect of a post-verbal agent: *The bomb was sold to Seymour by Egbert, The bomb was bought from Egbert by Seymour.*

Let us turn now to an attempt to characterize the underlying representations implied by the immediately preceding observations, and to a rather more careful examination of the processes of subject- and object-formation. In the first place, we shall be concerned with the establishment of the underlying relations involved.

I shall term the relation contracted by the noun phrase which becomes the (direct) object in (1)–(2) and (4)–(8) and the subject in the corresponding passives and in (3), the nominative (nom): it is neither directional nor agentive. The agentive subjects in (1)–(2), (5)–(6) and (8) are derived from underlying ergative (erg) phrases. I have already noted the various occurrences of the allative and ablative (abl). However, in the representations proposed below I shall substitute the term locative (loc) for allative. This depends on the assumptions that the allative simply equals loc in a directional predication, and that directional predications necessarily involve both loc and abl (cf. Anderson, 1971b, §8.2).

We can thus represent the relational structure of a sentence like (3) as in (9), which is a dependency tree with V as governor of and Ns as dependents of, the functional elements, nom, loc and abl.[12]

---

[11] However, if the agent and allative are distinct, object- and subject-formation for the allative are possible: *Seymour bought Plumtree the bomb, Plumtree was bought the bomb* (Anderson, 1971b, §§ 11.3–4). I shall not be concerned here with instances showing subjects and objects derived from underlying ablatives, as with the sentences containing *rob* (rather than *steal*) noted by Fillmore (1968b, 388); see too, Anderson, 1971b, 135.

[12] Each predication is a dependency structure with V as governor and immediately dependent case (functional) elements, each of which has in turn a N dependent on it: for discussion, see Anderson, 1971a, 1971b; and cf. Tesnière, 1959; Robinson, 1970; Sgall and Hajičová, 1970.

(9)

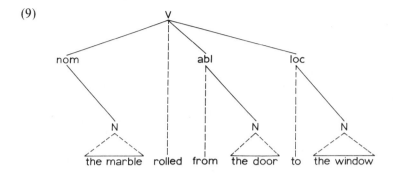

Nom is 'pruned' as part of the process of subject-formation.

Consider now the structure of (1). Clearly, . . . *the bomb to Canada from Australia* involves just such a directional predication as is represented in (9). (I ignore here differences in the superficial sequence of loc and abl). But in it there is also an erg present as subject, and there are passive forms in which erg is realized (in post-verbal position) as *by*. This can be allowed for if we propose that in the case of (1) the directional predication is subordinate to a causative one, containing erg and nom, as in (10).[13]

(10)

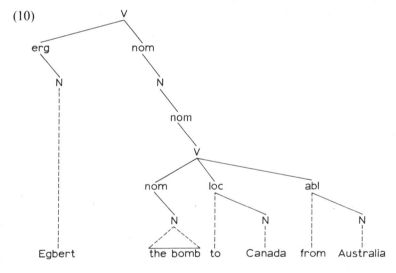

The N governed by the upper nom is semantically empty; and there is an intermediate stage at which the lower V comes (by abjunction – Anderson, forthcoming, §§ VIII–IX) to be governed directly by the upper V, as in (11).

[13] Complex predications are assumed to involve a V dependent on an adnominal case: see Anderson, forthcoming; in preparation. In this instance the adnominal case is nom; in sentences like *Lucinda prevented Boris from coming*, it is rather abl (*from*); *cause . . . to* involves loc.

(11)

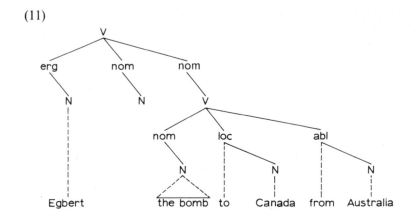

I have termed such a part representation as the upper predication in (11) a quasi-predication (Anderson, forthcoming): it contains an empty argument with no dependent, on to which a case phrase from the lower sentence can be copied. I shall refer to a non-quasi basic predication and its associated set of higher quasi-predications as a global predication. If the quasi-predication is simple (contains only one empty N) then it is the immediately lower subject that is copied. Thus, in this particular instance, the upper nominative N becomes free for the lower subject phrase to be copied on to it, and the original is deleted, to yield (12).[14]

(12)

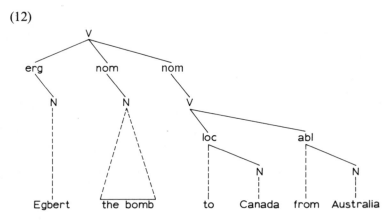

The originally lower nominative phrase can thus become the subject in the corresponding passive, since it is at this stage governed directly by the upper V. Finally (for our purposes), the lower V is subjoined to the upper: the con-

---

[14] I do not necessarily mean to suggest that the actual phonological specification is involved in copying, since these operations may be pre-lexical.

catenation relation between them is obliterated, and they form a single complex segment (see Anderson, 1971c; forthcoming). The result is (13).

(13)

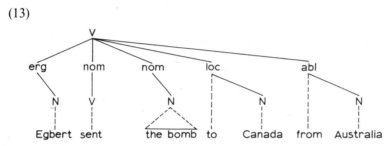

(I have ignored here the operation of the pruning rules associated with subject- and object-formation.)

We must now consider the derivations of the sentences with indirect objects or locative subjects. One or two preliminary observations are in order. Notice firstly that these phenomena are not independent: verbs which take an indirect object also allow the locative to be subject in passives. Compare the examples in (14):

(14)   (a)   (i) I said that to John
              (ii) *I said John that
             (iii) *John was said that

        (b)   (i) I told that to John
              (ii) I told John that
             (iii) John was told that

Secondly, observe that the locatives occur in subject position specifically in passives and as objects in the corresponding actives.[15] Now, this is exactly the distribution of nom in predications which also contain erg: subject if passive, object if active. (Erg, on the other hand, is subject in actives, and is not involved in subject- or object-formation in passives.)

Given these two observations, it would appear that it is the locative in the lower sentence that is copied on to the higher nominative phrase in sentences like (2), (4) and (6)–(7), and thus undergoes either subject- or object-formation (depending on whether the sentence is passive or active). And this suggests that the locative phrase (rather than the nominative) is originally in subject-position in the lower predication – as in (15).

[15] This account is very much oversimplified: see Anderson, 1971b, Ch. 10.

(15)

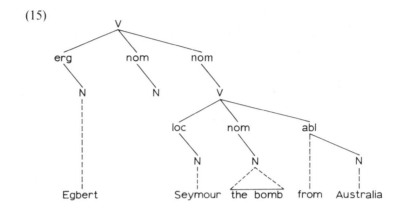

That is, the lower predication is like that required for *receive*, with locative subject and nominative object: *Seymour received a letter from Silvio.*

However, we also find passive sentences in which the loc with *receive* is post-verbal and is realized as *by* (and the nominative phrase is, as we would expect, the subject). *The letter was received by Seymour.* Once again, loc shows the distributional characteristics we have associated with another function, in this instance erg – which appears as subject in actives and post-verbal with *by* as its marker in passives. I suggest then that with such verbs the locative function is secondarily categorized as erg.[16] The structure under-lying *Seymour received a letter from Silvio* can therefore be represented as in (16).

(16)

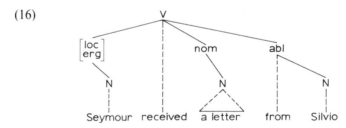

I presume a similar lower predication in (15). In this way, the occurrence of the locative phrase as subject in the lower predication and as object or subject in the upper is allowed for by its association with erg and nom. The rules for subject- and object-formation can thus be framed with reference to only these two latter functions: loc (and abl) become subject or object via erg and nom.[17]

---

[16] On this, see Anderson, 1971b, §11.44.

[17] Such an account does not allow without some qualification for subjectivization of the loc with verbs like *contain*, which do not have a corresponding *by*-form (unless they are causative). See also note 19.

In this fashion, even the most 'abstract', non-spatial instances of indirect objects can be allowed for as involving a directional predication embedded under a causative.

In certain instances, the ergative phrase as well as the nominative in the upper causative is also empty. Consider the structure in (17).

(17)

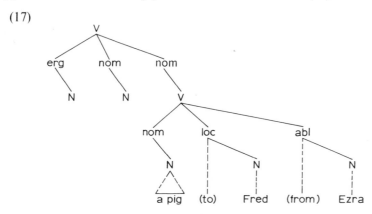

Such a structure underlies (in part) sentences containing *buy/sell*. Once more the lower subject is copied on to the upper nominative phrase. If the locative phrase is copied on to the ergative, then the verb is realized as *buy*; if the ablative is copied, then *sell* is the verb. Thus with *buy*, the resulting structure is as in (18) (after subjoining of the lower V).

(18)

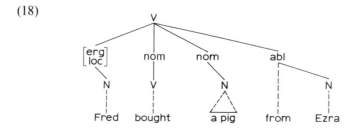

Compare the structure for *sell* in (19).

(19)

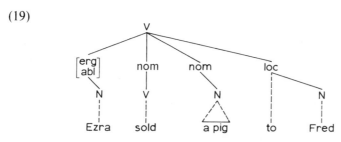

If the locative in the lower sentence is also erg, then the resulting structure is as in (20).

(20)

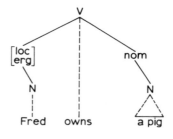

As the locative occupies the lower subject position, only the ablative phrase is available for copying on to the ergative in the higher predication.

Similar to *buy* and *sell* are *teach* and *learn*, *give* and *obtain*; and in some instances the same lexical items appear whether there is copying of the locative or of the ablative – as *hire* in English.[18]

In some languages, the locative phrase corresponding to the 'indirect object' in (15), (20) and the like has a distinctive superficial marker – the dative inflexion. Cf. Latin *Mihi librum dedit*. This same inflexion also characterizes the locative phrase in corresponding locationals: *Mihi est liber*. Compare English *Ezra has sold the pig to Fred* and *The pig belongs to Fred*. However, the locative in the non-directional instances can also (as in the directional – cf. (16)) be subjectivized. Compare *Habeo librum* or *Fred owns a pig*.[19]

(21)

```
                    V
           _____/|_____
          /         |         \
      [loc]          |          nom
      [erg]          |            \
          \          |             \
           N         |              N
           ¦         |             /‾\
           ¦         |            /___\
          Fred      owns         a pig
```

[18] See Anderson, 1971b, §§9.2, 11.3–4.
[19] I am ignoring here the distribution of 'definiteness', which is clearly crucial to a full account of such sentences. Observe too that (for the purposes of the present discussion) we are allowing throughout for the subjectivization of loc in *have*-predications in terms of its subcategorization as erg. However, there are considerable doubts concerning the appropriateness of this. *Have* is like *contain* in lacking a 'passive' with *by* . . . . . Further, with respect to such an interpretation, the occurrence of examples like *The table has a book lying on it* is in contravention of the principle governing the hierarchy of quasi-predications formulated in Anderson, forthcoming, §§ VI and X.

Consider too 'affective' verbs like *know* (compared with *teach/learn*) or *understand* (*explain*), which I would also interpret as taking a locative subject.

Have in English also occurs in a quasi-predication which allows for subjectivization of a non-dative locative. This is exemplified by a sentence like *The wall has a slogan on it*, for which I suggest an underlying structure like (22).

(22)

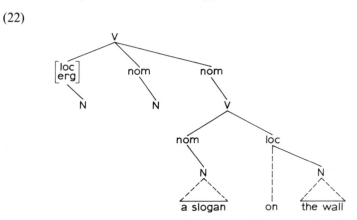

Both the upper locative and the upper nominative are empty, and (22) is derived from a more abstract structure in which the lower V is (before abjunction) dependent on the nominative N in the higher predication. Again, the subject of the lower predication is copied on to the upper nominative, and the lower locative assumes subject-position in the upper sentence. The lower nominative is deleted, and the locative pronominalized (in accordance with the principle proposed by Chapin, 1970, 376–8). The resulting structure, after subjunction of the lower V to the higher, is as in (23).[20]

(23)

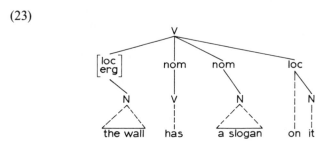

From the two instances of quasi-predications involving more than one empty argument that we have considered, it would appear that what determines the appropriate copyings is simply the requirement that the case phrase in subject

[20] This is a modification of the account of such sentences proposed in Anderson, forthcoming.

position in the lower predication be copied on to the upper empty nominative; a non-subjective phrase is copied on to the non-nominative empty argument. However, there are reasons for thinking that this is not the correct generalization. Consider, in particular, passive sentences. Passives involve a directional predication with locative subject superordinate to the basic predication, as in (24).

(24)

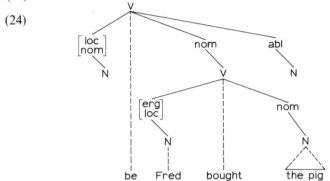

(Once again, the lower V has been moved out from dependence on the locative phrase to its left.)[21] In this instance, the lower subject is copied on to the ablative phrase in the quasi-predication. This, together with the copying of the lower nominative into subject position in the higher sentence, and deletion of both originals, accounts for the surface sequence of *The pig was bought by Fred*. Such a derivation is contrary to the generalization just sketched out.

Copying in complex quasi-predications appears then to be governed by some other principle. Namely, when a quasi-predication contains two empty arguments, the case phrases that are copied from the lower predication have their relative sequence reversed by the copying operation, as indicated in (25).

(25)

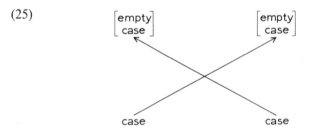

(We might term this the 'criss-cross-over principle' or 'X-principle'.) Consider in this regard (17) and (18), (22) and (23), and (24) and its surface structure. In the three instances we have looked at, the subject case-phrase in both

[21] *Suffer*, as in *Fred suffers from cold feet*, is a verb that appears in full predications with $\begin{bmatrix} \text{loc} \\ \text{nom} \end{bmatrix}$ subject and ablative phrase.

the upper and the lower predications is involved. Thus, the effect of copying in relation to such complex quasi-predications, as governed by the so-called 'criss-cross-over principle', is to displace from surface subject position the casephrase from the lower predication that would otherwise occupy it.

2. 'PERFECTS' AS DATIVE

In Anderson (forthcoming, § XII), it is argued that tense derives from a higher temporal locative predication (cf., too, Gallagher, 1970), as exemplified in (26).

(26)

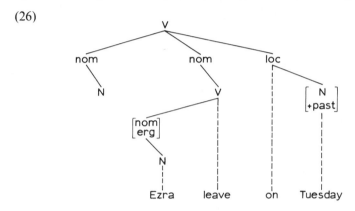

Again, the lower V has been separated from the empty case phrase to its left by abjunction, leaving the upper subject free for receiving a copy of the lower subject. The temporal deictic specification originates in the higher locative,[22] and this locative is subsequently copied as a subjunct to its governing V, as is the lower V. The result is as in (27).

(27)

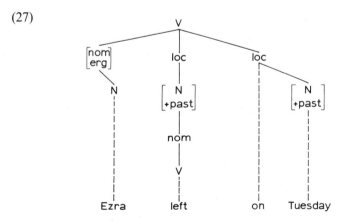

[22] '+past' etc. are abbreviations for whatever the appropriate specification may be.

The past tense inflexion is a morphological reflexion of the copied deictic specification.

Perfect forms involve the occurrence of two temporal quasi-predications above the 'basic proposition', non-past above past, or past above past (cf. Anderson, forthcoming, §XVI; in preparation). In a number of European languages such an underlying configuration entails the introduction of a *have*-predication (at least with a certain subset, including typically transitive, of 'main verbs'), just as in many languages an adjectival V requires a higher *be*-predication (see again Anderson, forthcoming). Thus, at some stage, underlying *Fred has bought a pig* is a structure like that abbreviated in (28).

(28)

Observe, however, that as it stands, the structure in (28) requires that, in accordance with the X-principle, *a pig* should become the surface subject. This is avoided if we assume that the *have*-predication entails the introduction below it of a locational predication of perhaps the form indicated in (29). This is in accordance with the typical occurrence of the *have* quasi-predication elsewhere, appearing as it does above locatives of the type of (22).

In this case, the reversals required by the X-principle will occur twice, and *Fred* will be placed as surface subject.

The placement of the locational predication containing two empty Ns can be argued for on various grounds. Notice firstly that the rules for subjunction are readily generalized in terms of such a placement: i.e. the degree of subjunction required is allowed for by processes of subjunction already formulated. A tense predication absorbs by subjunction the V immediately below it,

(29)

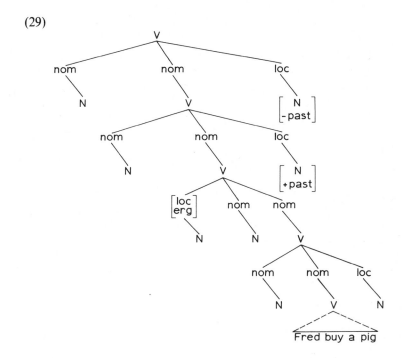

as does the *have*-predication. Thus, in terms of the vertical placement of the quasi-predications in (29), the higher tense predication will absorb the lower tense V, and it will absorb the V of the *have*-predication, which will in turn absorb the V in the locative above the basic predication. The whole complex segment is realized as *have* (as with other complex segments involving a quasi-predication of the type of that third from the top in (29)).

In the second place, observe that only if the *have*-predication and its associated locative come below the tense predications will the copying operations produce the correct results. If, say, one of the tense predications intervened between the locative-subject predication and the other non-tense construction, then the appropriate copyings would be blocked and incorrect arguments would be raised into surface subject position.

I have argued (Anderson, forthcoming, §§ XV–XVI) for a representation rather like that in (28) on the basis of the dual temporal deixis associated with perfects. The presence of the *have*-predication is allowed for by a more general requirement that also accounts for its presence below modals when past reference is involved, as in *He may have left last Tuesday*. Quite simply, the *have*-predication is introduced below a past temporal that is not the topmost quasi-predication. (I ignore here the question and characterization of performative and negative elements.) We also thus allow for *have* to appear in a uniform predication-type, in accordance with requirements of naturalness (cf. again Zwicky, 1968, §3). The modification introduced in (29) is entailed by our reinterpretation of the *have*-predication, which allows for a uniform distribution for *have*. Once again, the locative V below *have* undergoes subjunction. It is important to observe that both the *have*-predication and the locational predication immediately below it are semantically non-primitive. Their presence is required by the occurrence of a certain semantic configuration; the presence of the other quasi-predications we have discussed involves a semantic 'choice'; they may be absent from any particular global predication. I shall refer to these as secondary *vs* primary quasi-predications, respectively. I want now to show how such a representation may have been developed in one particular instance, and to try to demonstrate that such an interpretation of *have* perfects allows us to provide a very natural account of the historical processes involved.

Our instance concerns the development of the perfect in Latin and its descendants. In Classical Latin, there is a single verbal form expressing the perfect and the past tense. See, e.g. Ernout and Thomas, 1951, §§ 243–4. Thus, one underlying representation for *Julius epistolam scripsit* is (in the relevant respects) as in (30).

(30)

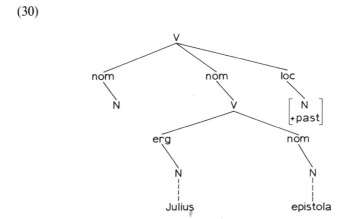

But it has an alternative source in the structure in (31).[23]

---

[23] The order of the elements in these dependency trees is not necessarily intended to be significant; certainly the order may be other than that suggested here. This is not crucial to the present discussion, and for the sake of exposition I retain the orders established for English. The copying rules, as formulated thus far, have assumed an ordering of the arguments; however, they could be framed with respect to the character of the arguments themselves (though this would entail a modification of the formulation of the X-principle).

(31)

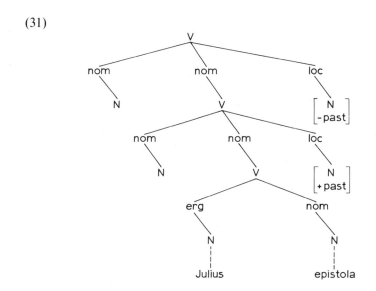

(30) is the 'perfectum historicum', (31) the 'perfectum praesens' (e.g. Kühner, 1912, §33). The verb in each of the tense predications in both (30) and (31) has the V below it subjoined to it, as well as the temporal locative. Thus, after the appropriate copying, deletion and subjunction, the structure in (30) is reduced to (32).

(32)

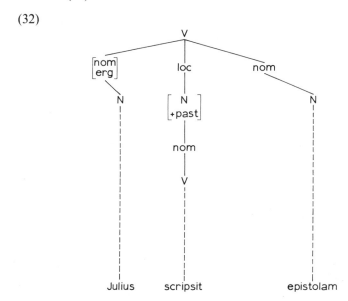

And (31) appears as in (33).

(33)

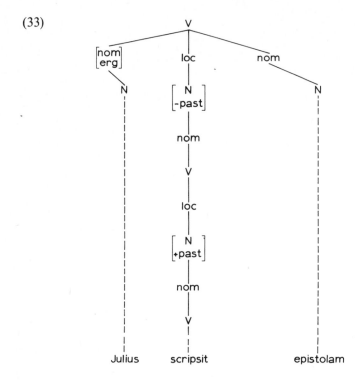

Corresponding to the (active) perfect is the passive *Epistola a Julio scripta est*. It involves two tense predications and a passive above the basic predication. After copying, deletion and subjunction of the appropriate elements, there is formed the structure represented in (34).

Once again, as is the case with the active in (33), subjunction results in a complex segment containing three Vs. The nom governing *scripta* is eventually pruned, thus ensuring an auxiliary status for *est* (as a V immediately governing another V – Anderson, forthcoming, §II).

However, we also find (particularly in poetry and apparently in the 'vulgar' language) a 'passive' construction with a dative rather than *a* + ablative, to indicate 'the person in whose interest an action is done' (Gildersleeve and Lodge, 1895, §215), where this is identical to the agent (in the absence of an indication to the contrary). Consider the example from Ovid cited by Gildersleeve and Lodge: *Carmina nulla mihi sunt scripta.*[24] This presumes a

---

[24] See too, Kühner, 1912, §76.8(d); Ernout and Thomas, 1951, 64. By 'passive', I intend to refer merely to the fact that in such sentences the 'agent' does not become subject. It is not my intention to contest the conclusions reached by Benveniste (1952), who has shown that these are 'possessive' (i.e. dative locative) rather than (true) passives of the kind represented in (34). See further Anderson, in preparation.

(34)

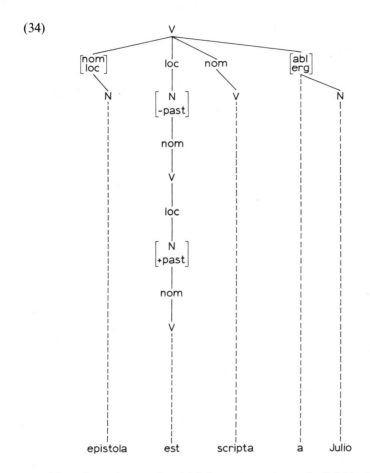

post-subjunction structure in which loc appears instead of abl in the segment in (34) which also contains erg.[25]

The development of the 'analytic' *habeo* perfect has been associated by a number of scholars with the existence of *habeo* as a dative-subject verb (as described above) corresponding to *esse* + dative. According to Lyons (1968a, 396–7; see too 1967, 1968b), "it is the same principle which explains both the diachronic development of the 'perfect with *have*' and the 'possessive *have*'. In both cases, the *have*-transformation became obligatory, its original function being to bring the 'person interested' (not necessarily the 'agent') into subject-position in surface structure". Similar proposals have been made by

---

[25] Alternatively, we could consider such sentences to involve both a passive and a 'dative of interest' predication, but this would result in incorrect surface representations (without modification of the copying rules), and I am unaware of any positive evidence for an alternative of this kind.

Kuryłowicz (1931), Benveniste (1968) and others, though these differ in the emphasis they give to particular aspects of the development.[26] Kuryłowicz, for instance, points to the causativizing function of the *habeo* perfect with otherwise intransitive verbs. I too would claim that the occurrence of *habeo* in both constructions is natural (not 'accidental'). But I want to suggest a rather different process of development and synchronic result for auxiliary *habeo* from that proposed by these particular scholars, though in a sense it represents a rather traditional position.

"Pour souligner la notion d'état acquis, le latin disposait d'une périphrase formée de habeo + un participe passé passif à l'accusatif" (Ernout and Thomas, 1951, 189–90). Ernout and Thomas are referring to a construction which apparently becomes widespread only in Low Latin, and in Classical Latin is limited to a certain subset of verbs.[27] This is involved in a sentence like *Julius epistolam scriptam habet*, which we might paraphrase as 'Julius has the letter written' (which has a similar derivation), and for which one can suggest an underlying structure like that in (35), in which a *habeo* quasi-predication is inserted in the structure I associated with *Carmina nulla mihi sunt scripta*.

The agreement between *epistola* and *scripta* suggests that *habeo* comes above a 'passive' structure (with *epistola* as subject), and its placement below the two tense predications is required for the correct operation of the copying rules. In such a structure, the *habeo* predication is thus clearly a device (in Lyons' formulation) 'to bring the "person interested" ... into subject-position in surface structure'.

Notice now that the vertical sequence of quasi-predications in (35) is identical to the representation suggested above in (29) for perfect *have*. Thus there are independent motivations for suggesting an identical underlying configuration for perfect *have/habeo* constructions and sentences involving periphrastic *have/habeo* illustrated in (35). Where they differ is that the quasi-predications with periphrastic *habeo* are all primary; the *habeo* and the 'dative of interest' predications are secondary in the case of the perfect, they are required by the presence of the two tense predications. What I want to suggest with respect to the development of the *habeo* perfect is that at some point in the history of languages which already possess the *habeo* periphrasis, there was added to the grammar the requirements that introduce the *habeo* and 'dative of interest' predications into the configurations for perfects. And

---

[26] Cf. Craddock, 1970, 692–3. On the development of *have*-constructions and related questions, see too Meillet, 1924; Vendryes, 1937; van Ginneken, 1939; Benveniste, 1960; Allen, 1964.

[27] On this restriction (which though important in implication, I shall be unable to pursue here), see, e.g. Benveniste, 1968, § 1. I ignore here, too, the development associated with 'intransitive' verbs, which involves a distinct template.

(35)

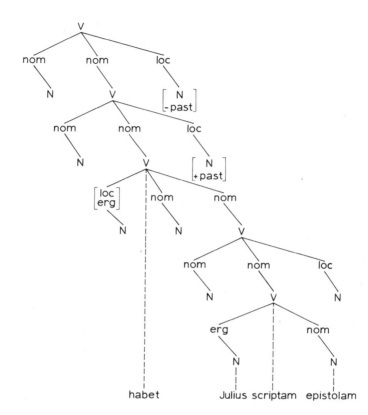

in this process the structure for the *habeo* periphrasis acted as a 'template'. Thus a new, analytic active perfect is created on the model of a periphrasis involving the 'passive' perfect in which the 'agent' occupies the surface sub-ject position it has in an active sentence. The *habeo* periphrasis possesses exactly the properties required for an 'analytic' perfect on the condition that the *habeo* and 'dative of interest' predications are demoted from primary to secondary. It thus fulfils the function of what I have termed a template.[28] I want now to consider the motivation for this modification to the grammar of such languages.

We noted above that the result of subjunction in the development of both active and passive perfects in Classical Latin is the formation of a complex segment containing two tense specifications and three Vs: consider (33) and

[28] As further examples of developments of this kind, consider the evolution of the *do*-periphrasis in English with causative *do* as template (Ellegård, 1953) and (analogously) the *faire*-periphrasis in Old French (Tobler, 1921, 20–4), which may indeed have reinforced the Middle English development (Orr, 1962, 20, 63–4); or the creation of 'reflexive passive' constructions (cf. Anderson, forthcoming, §II) with causative reflexives as template (as in e.g. Lappish).

(34). In particular, three non-secondary predications are collapsed. In comparison, the *habeo* perfect is apparently more complex: consider the post-subjunction form of (35) represented in (36).[29]

(36)

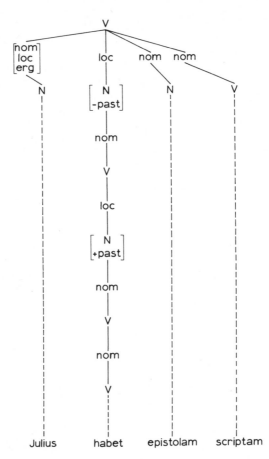

Observe, with regard to relative complexity, that the complex segment formed by subjunction now contains four Vs. However, only two of these Vs belong to primary quasi-predications. In the case of the Classical perfect, there are also two Vs from primary predications in the complex segment, plus the verb from the basic predication. Thus, the *habeo* perfect is less complex in terms of semantic 'information' (if secondary quasi-predications are excluded as such); it separates out the realization of the tense references from the 'main

[29] Pruning under subjectivization and objectivization will remove the case nodes governing the Ns realized as *Julius* and *epistolam* and the V realized as *scriptam*. The governing complex V is thus auxiliated.

verb'. I presume that this reduction in morphological complexity (i.e. the amount of 'semantic information' carried by a single syntactic segment) is a major motivation for the modification involved in the introduction of the *habeo* perfect.[30] We can formulate the initiating instruction in the form of a meta-rule (cf. Lass, 1969) like that informally expressed in (37).

(37)   Reduce segment complexity from three Vs to two
        (where secondary quasi-predications are excluded)

We shall return in the following section to a brief and rather speculative consideration of the motivation for the formation of such meta-rules at certain points in the development of a language. At this point, I merely want to suggest that the adoption of the *habeo* perfect (with the periphrastic *habeo* as template) in Latin is effected in response to a meta-rule of the type of (37); it is the particular interpretation of that instruction in this and similar instances.[31]

3. CONCLUSION

In §1 I attempted to show the relevance of the notions of location (and direction) to the characterization of the underlying functional relations appropriate to a certain set of closely connected sentences, and the relationship between various pairs in the set. This involved in particular the proposal of a locative source for 'indirect objects', and the subjects of 'affective' and 'possessive' verbs. This outline was intended as merely exemplificatory. I would claim that underlying all functional relations are the concepts of location (loc, abl *vs* nom, erg) and polarity (erg, abl *vs* nom, loc): for further discussions, see Anderson, 1971b; forthcoming. It is also hypothesized that these are universal. However, I would like to emphasize that this does not entail a claim

---

[30] Notice too, that the 'past'/'perfect' ('perfectum historicum' *vs* 'perfectum praesens') ambivalence of forms like *scripsit* contributes to morphological opacity in the sense of § 3, and may thus have contributed to the precipitation of the modification in the grammar involving the introduction of the *habeo* perfect. (Cf. e.g. Meillet, 1928, 260–2; Maurer, 1959, §93.) However, in Old French, for instance, the distinction between the perfect periphrasis and the past simple form is already sometimes difficult to demonstrate (Brunot, 1913, 240–1). On the restoration of the 'past'/'perfect' ambivalence with the periphrasis, see Meillet, 1958; Zieglschmid, 1930a (condensed as 1930b); and cf. note 31.

[31] The subsequent elimination of the 'synthetic' preterite (see the works referred to in note 30) in (for instance) colloquial French can perhaps be related to the formation of a subsequent even more restrictive condition on segment complexity such that only (non-secondary) predications of the same type (in terms of character of arguments) can undergo subjunction. Thus, the perfect periphrasis is extended to include the past. The perfect itself does not require further 'analysis', since the two primary quasi-predications realized as *habeo* (etc.) are of the same type. This same constraint perhaps also underlies the development of the French future with *habeo* + infinitive (though I shall not explore here the details of this development).

that such linguistic elements are genetically transmitted as such. On the contrary, the accumulation of support for localist (and thus notional) conceptions of case and other categories, and in particular for ontogenetic priority for the 'concrete' variants of these, would provide decisive counter-evidence to any claim of an innate status for these particular substantive universals of language. The essential determinant in such instances would be our perception of the physical environment.[32] Clearly, at this point in time, any suggested decision in such matters is premature in the extreme. My point is merely that innateness (with respect to certain linguistic elements) does not necessarily follow from universality in this instance, given our common environment.

We are at the very beginning of any careful and extensive investigation of such questions. However, this should not prevent us (to return to my initial plea) from acknowledging and profiting from those accounts of relevant phenomena that do exist. The long tradition of localist discussion of case, in particular, seems to me to merit more serious consideration than it has recently been accorded.

And it is once again with respect to some far from novel proposals that the appropriate account of the motivation for the introduction of meta-rules such as (37) may be formulated. In §2 I suggested that the development of the analytic *habeo* perfect is attributable to the formation of a meta-rule of the form of (37), which requires a reduction in the complexity of the segments formed by subjunction. However, what precipitates the formation of such a meta-rule? Clearly, the motivation is some kind of reduction in a certain type of complexity. I suggest that the particular precipitating factor involves some such notion as 'high morphological opacity'. What I intend by this is the degree to which the morphological realization of a syntactic segment reflects the underlying relational structure. Morphological opacity is increased with the number of primary predications subjoined if the morphological markers bear no resemblance to relevant parts of the underlying predications absorbed in a complex segment, or if, say, a relational element is provided with a number of distinct representations (depending on, e.g., cumulation with number, declension), or if, on the other hand, a certain morphological marker is systematically ambivalent. 'Agglutinative' languages are morphologically complex (i.e. there is considerable subjunction involving quasi-predications and relational elements) but relatively transparent; 'inflexional' languages are both complex and relatively opaque. Thus, I am suggesting that meta-

---

[32] Similarly, the establishment of a relationship between, say, certain transformational processes or constraints on these and various perceptual limitations (cf. e.g. Langendoen, 1970) suggests that, even though some of these processes may be recurrent (Bach, 1965), they do not necessarily constitute genetically determined aspects of linguistic competence as such.

rules like (37) are introduced as a means to reduce morphological opacity (particularly where this results from subjunction of Vs). Their implementation entails increased 'analysis' (via, in particular, the template mechanism). Why such a reduction in opacity is required at a certain point in the history of a language is another question. I suspect there may in general be a social motivation.[33]

Whatever may become of such speculations, it seems to me that the discussion in §2 has gone some way towards showing the kind of mutual support provided by synchronic and diachronic accounts of certain linguistic phenomena. In particular, I suggest that the naturalness of the explanation accorded to the development of the *habeo* perfect gives additional support to our synchronic, localistic analysis.

Department of English Language,
University of Edinburgh

BIBLIOGRAPHY

Allen, W. S.: 1964, 'Transitivity and Possession', *Lg* **40**, 337–43.
Anderson, J. M.: 1968, 'On the Status of "Lexical Formatives" ', *FL* **4**, 308–18.
Anderson, J. M.: 1971a, 'Dependency and Grammatical Functions', *FL* **7**, 30–7.
Anderson, J. M.: 1971b, *The Grammar of Case: Towards a Localistic Theory*, Cambridge University Press, London and New York.
Anderson, J. M.: 1971c, 'Outline of a Proposal for the Lexicalisation of Complex Structures', *SL* **25**, 8.
Anderson, J. M.: 'Remarks on the Hierarchy of Quasi-Predications', forthcoming.
Anderson, J. M.: 'Aspect: Some Considerations of a General Character Arising from the Abbé Darrigol's Analysis of the Basque Verb', in preparation.
Annear, S.: 1967, 'Relative Clauses and Conjunctions', in *Working Papers in Linguistics*, The Ohio State University Research Foundation, Columbus, Ohio, pp. 80–99.
Bach, E.: 1965, 'Some Recurrent Types of Transformations', *MSLL* **18**, 1–18.
Bach, E. and Harms, R. T., (eds.): 1968, *Universals in Linguistic Theory*, Holt, Rinehart and Winston, New York.

---

[33] We can perhaps view the 'synthetic'-to-'analytic' development that we have considered as an instance of one stage in a sort of neo-Boppian cycle of typological development, schematically formulated as follows:

inflexion ← agglutination
analysis

The development from 'analysis' through 'agglutination' to inflexion' involves increasing generalization of the process of lexicalization, whereby complex underlying configurations are reduced to single segments (cf. Anderson, 1971c). We might term this process syntagmatic simplification. This is basically Bopp's view of the source of inflexions, and we can perhaps regard it as the 'normal' development. However, in certain (? critical – e.g., say, bilingual) situations, it appears that the morphological opacity created by extensive 'agglutination' and 'inflexion' is reduced by the formation of, for instance, periphrastic constructions; that is, by morphological simplification.

Bachmann, L. (ed.): 1828, *Anecdota Graeca, II*, Leipzig; reprinted 1965, Georg Olms, Hildes-heim.

Benveniste, É.: 1952, 'La construction passive du parfait transitif', *BSL* **48**, 52–62.

Benveniste, É.: 1960, ' "Être" et "avoir" dans leurs fonctions linguistiques', *BSL* **55**, 113–34; reprinted in *Problèmes de linguistique générale*, Gallimard, Paris, 1966, Ch. 12.

Benveniste, É.: 1968, 'Mutations of Linguistic Categories', in W. P. Lehmann and Y. Malkiel (eds.), 83–94.

Brunot, F.: 1913, *Histoire de la langue française, I: De l'époque latine à la Renaissance*, Armand Colin, Paris.

Chapin, P. G.: 1970, 'Samoan Pronominalization', *Lg*.**46**, 366–78.

Craddock, J. R.: 1970, Review of W. P. Lehmann and Y. Malkiel (eds.), *Lg* **46**, 688–95.

[Darrigol, J.-P.]: 1829, *Dissertation critique et apologétique sur la langue basque*, Duhart-Fauvet, Bayonne.

Ellegård, A.: 1953, *The Auxiliary Do*, Gothenburg Studies in English II, Almqvist and Wiksell, Stockholm.

Ernout, A. and Thomas, F.: 1931, *Syntaxe latin*, Klincksieck, Paris.

Fillmore, C. J.: 1968a, 'The Case for Case', in E. Bach and R. T. Harms (eds.), 1–88.

Fillmore, C. J.: 1968b, 'Lexical Entries for Verbs', *FL* **4**, 373–93.

Gallagher, M.: 1970, 'Adverbs of Time and Tense', *Papers from the Sixth Regional Meeting, Chicago Linguistic Society*, Chicago Linguistic Society, Chicago, Ill., 220–5.

Garnett, R.: 1846, 'On the Formation of Words by the Further Modification of Inflected Cases, I', *PPhS* **3**, 9–15.

Garnett, R.: 1847, 'On the Formation of Words by the Further Modification of Inflected Cases, II', *PPhS* **3**, 19–29.

Gildersleeve, B. L. and Lodge, G.: 1895, *Latin Grammar*, Macmillan, London.

van Ginneken, J.: 1939, 'Avoir et être (du point de vue de la linguistique générale)', in *Mélanges de linguistique offerts à Charles Bally*, Georg, Geneva, pp. 83–92.

Gray, L. H.: 1939, *Foundations of Language*, Macmillan, New York.

Gruber, J. S.: 1965, *Studies in Lexical Relations*, M.I.T. Ph.D. Dissertation; duplicated 1970, Indiana University Linguistics Club, Bloomington, Indiana.

Hall, R. A.: 1969, 'Some Recent Studies of Port-Royal and Vaugelas', *AL* **12**, 207–33.

Harris, Z. S.: 1940, Review of Gray (1939), *Lg* **16**, 216–31.

Hjelmslev, L.: 1935, 'La catégorie des cas, I', *Acta Jutlandica* **7**, Part 1.

Key, T. H.: 1847, 'On the Origin of the Demonstrative Pronouns, the Definite Article, the Pronouns of the Third Person, the Relative, and the Interrogative', *PPhS* **3**, 57–70.

Key, T. H.: 1853, 'On the Imperfect Infinitive, Imperfect Participles, and those Substantives which Fall under the Definition *nomen actionis*', *PPhS* **6**, 63–72.

Kiparsky, P.: 1968, 'Linguistic Universals and Linguistic Change', in E. Bach and R. T. Harms (eds.), 170–202.

Kiparsky, P.: 1970, 'Historical Linguistics', Ch. 17 of J. Lyons (ed.).

Kühner, R.: 1912, *Ausführliche Grammatik der lateinischer Sprache, II*, Hahnsche Buchhand-lung, Hannover.

Kuryłowicz, J.: 1931, 'Les temps composés du roman', *PF* **15**, 448–53.

Lafitte, P.: 1962, *Grammaire basque (navarro-labourdin littéraire)*, Éditions des 'Amis du Musée Basque' et 'Ikas', Bayonne.

Lakoff, G. R.: 1967, *Deep and Surface Grammar*, duplicated, Indiana University Linguistics Club, Bloomington, Indiana.

Langendoen, D. T.: 1970, 'The Accessibility of Deep (Semantic) Structures', in R. A. Jacobs and P. S. Rosenbaum (eds.), *Readings in English Transformational Grammar*, Ginn-Blaisdell, Boston, Mass., pp. 99–104.

Lass, R.: 1969, *The Derivative Status of Phonological Rules: The Function of Meta-rules in Sound-change*, duplicated, Indiana University Linguistics Club, Bloomington, Indiana.

Lehmann, W. P. and Malkiel, Y. (eds.): 1968, *Directions for Historical Linguistics*, University of Texas Press, Austin, Texas.

Lyons, J.: 1967, 'A Note on Possessive, Existential and Locative Sentences', *FL* **3**, 390–6.
Lyons, J.: 1968a, *Introduction to Theoretical Linguistics*, Cambridge University Press, London and New York.
Lyons, J.: 1968b, 'Existence, Location, Possession and Transitivity', in B. van Rootselaar and J. F. Staal (eds.), *Logic, Methodology and Philosophy of Sciences III*, North-Holland Publ. Co., Amsterdam, 495–504.
Lyons, J.: 1970a, 'Generative Syntax', Ch. 6 of J. Lyons (ed.).
Lyons, J. (ed.): 1970b, *New Horizons in Linguistics*, Penguin, Harmondsworth, Middlesex.
Maurer, T. H.: 1959, *Gramática do Latim Vulgar*, Livraria Acadêmica, Rio de Janeiro.
Meillet, A.: 1924, 'Le développement du verbe *avoir*', in *Antidoron: Festschrift J. Wackernagel*, Vandenhoeck and Ruprecht, Göttingen, pp. 9–13.
Meillet, A.: 1928, *Esquisse d'une histoire de la langue latine*, Hachette, Paris.
Meillet, A.: 1958, 'Sur la disparition des formes simples du prétérit', in *Linguistique historique et linguistique générale*, Champion, Paris, pp. 149–58; reprinted from *Germanisch-Romanische Monatsschrift* **1** (1909).
Orr, J.: 1962, *Old French and Modern English Phrasing*, Blackwell, Oxford.
Pedersen, H.: 1931, *The Discovery of Language: Linguistic Science in the Nineteenth Century*, translated by J. W. Spargo, Harvard University Press, Boston, Mass.
Postal, P. M.: 1966, 'On So-Called "Pronouns" in English', *MSLL* **19**, 177–206; reprinted in D. A. Reibel and S. A. Schane (eds.), *Modern Studies in English: Readings in Transformational Grammar*, Prentice-Hall, Englewood Cliffs, New Jersey, 1969, pp. 201–24.
Robinson, J. J.: 1970, 'Case, Category and Configuration', *JL* **6**, 57–80.
Sgall, P. and Hajičová, E.: 1970, 'A "Functional" Generative Description', *PBML* **14**, 3–38.
Tesnière, L.: 1959, *Éléments de syntaxe structurale*, Klincksieck, Paris.
Tobler, A.: 1921, *Vermischte Beiträge zur französischen Grammatik*, *I*, 3rd ed., Hirzel, Leipzig.
Vendryes, J.: 1937, 'Sur l'emploi de l'auxiliaire "avoir" pour marquer le passé', in *Mélanges de linguistique et de philologie offerts à J. van Ginneken*, Klincksieck, Paris, pp. 85–92; reprinted in *Choix d'études linguistiques et celtiques*, Klincksieck, Paris, 1952, pp. 102–9.
Ziegler, K. (ed.): 1950, *Paulys Real-Encyclopädie der classischen Altertumswissenschaft* **20**, 2, Druckenmüller, Waldsee, Württ.
Zieglschmid, A. J. F.: 1930a, 'Der Untergang des einfachen Präteritums in verschiedenen indogermanischen Sprachen', in *Curme Volume of Linguistic Studies* (Language Monograph, 7), L.S.A., Baltimore, Md., pp. 169–78.
Zieglschmid, A. J. F.: 1930b, 'Concerning the Disappearance of the Simple Past in Various Indo-European Languages', *PQ* **9**, 153–7.
Zwicky, A. M.: 1968, 'Naturalness Arguments in Syntax', in B. J. Darden, C.-J. N. Bailey and A. Davison (eds.), *Papers from the Fourth Regional Meeting, Chicago Linguistic Society*, Department of Linguistics, University of Chicago, Chicago, Ill., pp. 94–102.

IRENA BELLERT

SETS OF IMPLICATIONS AS THE
INTERPRETATIVE COMPONENT OF A GRAMMAR*

Let us first consider what it is that is of interest in a grammar of a natural language conceived of as a system generating all and only sentences of that language together with their descriptions, and what can be verified in such a hypothesis.

A competent speaker of language is not always capable of deciding whether a given string of words in that language is a well formed sentence or not. There are countless boundary cases of strings which will be accepted as sentences by some speakers and rejected by others, or will be accepted only if the string of words is given in a specific context. If a competent speaker is unable to decide this in a non-arbitrary way, then a grammar generating all and only sentences of a language must be, in this respect, an arbitrary system of rules whose adequacy cannot be verified. All that can be proved is that a grammar is inadequate in clear cases: if it generates a string that doubtlessly is not a sentence, or if it does not generate a string that doubtlessly is one. In other words, a linguist writing a grammar has to decide arbitrarily whether certain strings will be generated by his rules or not.

Another aspect of a generative grammar which is of real interest, is its 'descriptional' aspect; given an ordered pair, a string of elements (say, morphemes or words) and its description, we may discuss whether the description is a proper basis for the semantic interpretation of the string (or can be accepted in itself as a semantic representation of the string). That is to say, we may consider whether the proposed deep structure description of the string gives an adequate interpretation, that is, one which is in agreement with what competent speakers always understand when the given string is used as an utterance. We may verify this by providing evidence or counter-evidence through proper 'testing texts' and eliciting competent speakers' judgements on the coherence or incoherence of such texts.

Most discussions on present day generative linguistics are thus centred around problems concerning the adequacy of deep structure representations.

* This paper was written at the University of Montreal while the author was working as a visiting professor in the Project of Professor Antonio Querido sponsored by the Ministry of Education, Quebec (Grant No. 88-28-546). I wish to express my indebtedness for the discussion on this paper I have had with Antonio Querido and his group. Moreover, I feel especially indebted to Brian Harris and Richard Kittredge for their comments and criticisms.

Deep structures become more and more complex as a result of linguistic evidence to the effect that certain significant components of meaning have not been, but should, be accounted for by the description of utterances. There are two main approaches to generative grammars, which can be referred to as generative syntax and generative semantics, respectively. Without going into the details of this well known controversy, we may say, roughly speaking, that in generative syntax the generated deep structures are assumed to serve as a basis for an interpretative component, which may, for instance, contain projection rules of the type proposed by Katz and Fodor, whereas in generative semantics the deep structures themselves are said to constitute the semantic representation of utterances. In the latter case interpretative projection rules are said to be unnecessary, since all the pertinent information contained in the lexical items is to be represented in the trees. Lexical items are thus derivable from trees, and as far as recent proposals suggest, the semantic structure of an utterance is assumed to be representable by a complex but single tree (a type of labelled graph with one highest node, which can be defined by ordering relations, and which is equivalent to a labelled and parenthesized string).

The interpretative component, as proposed by Katz and Fodor, has not been applied – as far as I know – in any detailed linguistic description; only some simple utterances have been interpreted according to the proposed theory by way of examples. The difficulties usually come up when one tries to apply a given theory to cases other than those shown as examples. However, Katz himself declared (during his lecture on generative syntax and semantics at the LSA Meeting in Washington, 1970) that he sees the proposal of generative semantics as an alternative method, equivalent to his own proposal (a tree-like description of a lexical item plus projection rules are considered by him equivalent to the representation of lexical items in deep structure trees plus the involved transformations). I will assume, then, that according to both methods the semantic representation of an utterance can be viewed as a complex tree. Let us now return to the problem concerning the adequacy of any description of utterances that is supposed to correlate 'sounds with meanings'.

If we ask a competent speaker what he gathers from a given string of words, he can give us a statement or statements that express the same meaning in a more explicit and expanded way. It seems thus plausible to search for rules that would interpret a string of words with its structural description in terms of some statements or propositions. A labelled tree is not a proposition in itself, neither is it equivalent to a proposition or statement, without some additional rules of interpretation applicable to labelled trees. We cannot say that a tree is true or false unless we understand what proposition it is equivalent to. What we should thus require of a grammar that is supposed 'to correlate sounds with meanings' is some rules that would relate the strings of elements through their descriptions with propositions which can be said to be true. Let us then consider such a proposal.

One aspect of linguistic competence which cannot be denied is a speaker's ability to draw conclusions from utterances[1] in his language and from some implicit rules of implication concerning those utterances. If someone understands an utterance he is capable of drawing conclusions from it; and vice versa, if someone is capable of drawing proper conclusions from an utterance, he gives proof of having understood it. Let us then make use of the above empirically justified two-way implication, and identify the semantic interpretation of an utterance with the set of conclusions that follow from its use and from some pertinent implicative statements that are tacitly employed by the speakers who produce or interpret an utterance or a discourse.

It is obvious that we draw conclusions from utterances not only through our knowledge of the language, but also by availing ourselves of our knowledge of the world and of the context or situation in which the utterances are produced. By explicitly interpreting any discourse (scientific, literary or every day discourse) it is not difficult to show that the speaker or author has taken advantage of the conclusions to be drawn from the preceding utterances and from some pertinent implicative statements concerning the extralinguistic world; and he does so in order to structure his text in such a way that the sequence of utterances may be understood as a coherent entity and not as a sequence of disjoined utterances (as might appear to be the case if we took only the surface elements of the utterances into account). It is not just a matter of the pronouns and other anaphora – most often some conclusions have to be drawn in order to interpret the text coherently, as it was intended by the author.[2]

In describing utterances of a language we must, however, distinguish between those conclusions that are derivable from the utterance by certain rules established by us from the remaining conclusions. It seems possible to give a description of lexical items and syntactic relations in the form of

---

[1] I employ here the term utterance when speaking of an entity used in the process of communication, and the term sentence when referring to an abstract entity, a result of a linguistic description, to which the category of sentence is assigned. I always refer, however, to an utterance as to a type, not a token.

[2] For more details concerning the interpretation of coherent texts, see my paper, 'On the Condition of the Coherence of Texts', *Semiotica* No. 4/1970, Mouton, The Hague.

implicative statements which constitute a set of sentences on the basis of which we will derive conclusions, provided that the utterance containing those items and relations is used appropriately.[3] In order to differentiate between the conclusions obtainable by such a description and all other conclusions, namely, those which could be drawn by a hearer who avails himself of his knowledge of the world and of the situation in which an utterance is produced, I shall refer to the former as consequences. Thus every consequence will correspond to a conclusion, but not every conclusion will correspond to a consequence. Obviously the set of consequences which can be drawn formally, if an explicit description is given, will account only partially for what goes on when we actually interpret natural language utterances in the process of communication.[4] In order to describe this process formally, we would have to provide all the pertinent information concerning the extralinguistic world and do so in the form of implicational statements – which of course is infeasible.[5]

For the sake of brevity we will speak about the consequences that follow from an utterance, and one may understand this intuitively, although the consequences do not follow from just one utterance, but from a set of sentences,[6] one of which is a statement concerning the appropriate use of the utterance in question, the others being implicational statements pertinent to the lexical items and syntactic rules employed in that utterance. Roughly speaking, the implicational statements would conform to the following scheme:

---

[3] When I say that a speaker uses an utterance appropriately, what I mean is simply that he uses it in accordance with the rules of language. In other words, a speaker uses an utterance appropriately if he knows the language and uses it in accordance with what he wants to express. Without such an assumption, obviously, no consistent semantic interpretation could be proposed.

[4] The conclusions we draw from utterances belonging to a discourse depend on the type of discourse. In everyday discourse we avail ourselves of encyclopaedic and factual knowledge of the world, and the situational context in particular; in a newspaper discourse we avail ourselves of encyclopaedic and factual knowledge of the world (events and characteristics concerning certain people, countries, etc.); in scientific discourse we avail ourselves of the encyclopaedic knowledge pertaining in particular to the given domain of science, well known theories, authors, etc. It can be easily shown that when we interpret a discourse, in drawing conclusions we have to make use of some additional premises relevant to the propositions expressed in the text, without which we would not be capable of properly understanding the information contained in the text; if we lack a certain factual knowledge that the author has assumed his readers have, we are unable to understand the text as coherent.

[5] This would be feasible only for a restricted domain, for instance, in constructing a question-answering system.

[6] In a formalized theory a conclusion (or consequence) of a set of sentences X is every sentence that can be derived from a number of sentences belonging to X by means of the rules of inference.

Antecedent: *Consequent:*

(1)   A speaker appropriately uses an $\begin{cases} \text{believes that} \\ \text{asserts that} \\ \text{denies that} \\ \to \text{he} \; \text{doubts if} \\ \text{wants that} \\ \text{assumes that} \\ \text{etc.} \end{cases} S$
         utterance whose structural des-
         cription satisfies the conditions
         specified in formula *F*

where *F* is a formula which indicates certain conditions concerning the
lexical items and syntactic relations occurring in the structural description
of the utterance, while *S* is a sentential form (propositional form) which –
together with one of the propositional attitudes (belief, assertion, denial,
etc.)[7] – interprets the use of a given lexical item or syntactic relation under
the specified conditions. Now if the structural description of an utterance
satisfies the conditions specified in a number of implications, we can, by the
rule of detachment, derive sentences corresponding to the consequents
since the antecedent is always accepted as true by the general assumption
that we interpret only utterances which are used appropriately (see footnote
3). We thus obtain a non-empty set of consequences from each utterance
whose structural description satisfies at least one formula *F*.

---

[7] The expression 'The speaker believes that' or 'The speaker wants that', etc. should be understood as an abbreviation of the respective expressions 'The speaker behaves linguistically as if
he believed that' or 'The speaker behaves linguistically as if he wanted that', etc. Thus all
propositional attitudes are meant here to be purported attitudes. The verb 'to believe' is ambiguous; I am using it only in the sense 'to accept as true'. The consequences hold true independently
of whether the speaker or author of a given utterance is telling the truth, is lying, is giving play
to his imagination or is expressing propositions which are not quite compatible with the actual
facts because the purported attitudes introduced into consequents do not express the actual
state of mind of the speaker.
      Compatibility between utterances and actual facts is of no relevance for the semantic inter-
pretation. It may be of interest to psychologists, moralists or policemen, but it is not a linguistic
problem.
      Under certain conditions, however, it is possible to interpret utterances in terms of sets of
sentences devoid of propositional attitudes. Such is the case when we accept an additional
assumption that the producer of an utterance is a reliable person speaking seriously about
factual matters. In such a case we may identify the assertions or beliefs concerning such or
other propositions with the propositions themselves. We may identify sentences of the form
'The speaker asserts that *S*' or 'The speaker believes that (accepts as true) *S*' with 'It is true that
S', 'The speaker denies that *S*' with 'It is not true that *S*', 'The speaker supposes that *S*' with
'It is possible that *S*'. There will be, however, consequences that cannot be devoid of propositional attitudes. For instance, those which follow from questions and commands and contain
the propositional attitudes 'The speaker wants the addressee to say (if) *S*' and 'The speaker
wants that *S*'.

There are evidently many ways of specifying formally the conditions in formula F. The general idea, however, is such that in formula F we specify the conditions concerning the items and relations present in the structural description of utterances, while the consequent containing the sentential form S gives explicitly the information that is always understood by a competent speaker from any utterance satisfying those conditions.

The term 'structural description' is used here in a very general sense. Before the matter is investigated in more detail, it is difficult to say what type of structural description will be the most convenient or economical to refer to in formula F. Those linguists who argue in favor of a generative semantics deny the need of interpretative rules. They want to include all the pertinent semantic information in the deep structure trees, which means that they will have to derive lexical items usually from two or more than two conjoined or embedded sentences (subtrees). To be consistent with their general principle, they would also have to derive n sentences differing only in the place of the main stress from n different deep structures. For instance, 'John married Ann', 'Jóhn married Ann' and 'John married Ánn' (the second utterance being a paraphrase of 'The person who married Ann is John', while the third is equivalent to 'The person whom John married is Ann'), as well as the corresponding three denials or questions would have to be derived from three different deep structures.[8] However, the shift of the main stress and the difference of interpretation which results is a general phenomenon which concerns almost all utterances, so that the problem becomes enormous. On the other hand, no matter how abstract and complex the deep structure trees become, it will be necessary to give some rules for interpreting those abstract objects in one way or another, and relate them to propositions with propositional attitudes, for reasons which remain to be discussed here. Thus, pursuing the principle of generative semantics results in no evident gain.

Let us now assume that we have a grammar which generates structural descriptions along the lines suggested by generative syntax. The lexical items (so-called derived nominals included), however, would have to be

---

[8] For a detailed discussion concerning the semantic differences following from the shift of the main stress see my paper 'On the Semantic Interpretation of Subject-Predicate Relations in Sentences of Particular Reference' delivered at the International Congress of Linguists in Bucharest, 1967, and published in an extended version in *Progress in Linguistics* (eds. M. Bierwisch and K. E. Heidolph), Mouton, The Hague, 1970. See also N. Chomsky, *Deep Structures, Surface Structures and Semantic Interpretation*, mimeographed, where the author suggests that the semantic differences following from the shift of stress could be accounted for in terms of surface structure considerations.

described in terms of implications.[9] Accordingly, utterances such as 'John kissed Mary' and 'John killed Mary', would have the same structural description, but the sets of their consequences would differ because of the implications associated with the verbs 'to kiss' and 'to kill', respectively. Sentences differing in the place of the main stress would also have the same structural description, but interpretative rules of implication would have to account for the differences involved. The formulas F in those implications would refer to the conditions of the surface structures; in this case the implications would not concern the lexical items, but would relate in a general way the shift of the main stress to a given constituent with the shift of the propositional attitudes, and the differences involved.

In general, it appears that both deep and surface structures may conveniently be used in interpretations, and thus both will be referred to in the implicational rules. There is nothing strange in this. As a matter of fact, we do interpret utterances only in terms of certain signals observable 'on the surface'. But the deep structures have been postulated only in order to account for the syntactic regularities of the surface structures, and in the corresponding cases it is simpler to give one interpretation for all surface structures which are equivalent to a given deep structure representation than to refer to each of the equivalent surface structures separately. In other cases, when the interpretation is dependent on some features pertinent to the surface structures which can more conveniently be generalized in terms of the surface structures (e.g. shift of the main stress), we should refer to the surface structures in Formula F. There may be rules of implication in which we will refer in formula F to both the deep and the surface structures. In general, formula F may be specified in terms of a Boolean function (as a combination of conjunction, disjunction and negation) of certain conditions concerning the deep and/or surface structures.

Let us now consider some examples. For the sake of convenience, we will abbreviate the antecedents of our implications to formula F alone, although the whole statement given in (1) will always be understood. Instead of writing down a propositional attitude, we will write 'A': for 'The speaker asserts that', 'B': for 'The speaker believes that', etc.

---

[9] Implicational rules constitute an alternative and convenient apparatus for accounting not only for the semantic description of a lexical item, but also for selectional restrictions, semantic roles of the corresponding arguments, converse, synonymous and inclusive predicates. For more details of the proposed description of verbs in terms of implicational rules, see I. Bellert and Z. Saloni, 'On the Description of Lexical Entries for Verbs', *The International Journal of Slavic Languages and Poetics,* forthcoming.

$$(2) \qquad NP_1 \ KILL_{t_i} \ NP_2 \rightarrow \begin{cases} A: \ NP_1 \ ACT_{t_i} \ \text{at time}_j \ \text{WITH THE EFFECT} \\ \text{THAT} \ [NP_2 \ BE_{t_i} \ \text{NOT ALIVE after time}_j] \\ B: \ NP_2 \ BE_{t_i} \ \text{ALIVE at time}_j {}^{10} \end{cases}$$

where the subscript t_i indicates a given tense as used with the verb *kill*, and time $_j$ indicates the time of reference, which may or may not be explicitly indicated in the context.

Notice now that if the verb *to kill* is used in the progressive tense, the interpretation is slightly different

$$(3) \qquad NP_1 \ KILL_{t_i \, pr} \ NP_2 \rightarrow \begin{cases} A: NP_1 \ ACT_{t_i \, pr} \ \text{at time}_j \ \text{WITH THE EFFECT} \\ \text{THAT} \ NP_2 \ BE_{t_i \, fut} \ \text{NOT ALIVE IF} \ NP_1 \\ \text{CONTINUE}_{t_i} \\ B: NP_2 \ BE_{t_i} \ \text{ALIVE at time}_j \end{cases}$$

Accordingly, if we have an utterance

(4)   John is killing Mary

where the time of reference is the time of speaking, we will interpret it as: The speaker asserts that John is acting with the effect that Mary will be not alive if he continues. The speaker believes that Mary is alive.

If we have an utterance

(5)   John was killing Mary (when the policeman came in)

we will interpret it as: The speaker asserts that (at the time the policeman came in) John was acting with the effect that Mary would not be alive, if he continued. The speaker believes that Mary was alive (at the time when the policeman came in).

The changes in the assertive consequent brought about by the use of progressive tense seem to be regular for all verbs expressing the cause and effect.

It is worth noticing in connexion with these considerations that the interpretation of the verb 'to kill' expressed by 'x_1 to cause x_2 to die' – which is accepted by many linguists – does not seem to be precise enough. In fact, a casual relation can hold true for two propositions, but not for an individual and a proposition. Accordingly, to say that an individual (or object) caused

[10] It may be worthwhile to mention here that I include among the consequences those sentences which correspond to what other linguists call presuppositions. A presupposition in the present approach is a consequence such that (1) it contains the propositional attitude: 'The speaker believes (accepts as true)', and (2) it holds true of an affirmation as well as of the corresponding negation, question, command, doubt, etc. I see no reason why the so called presuppositions should not be included in the semantic interpretation of utterances. If I hear someone say 'Ann's children have awakened', I understand from the utterance alone that the speaker believes (accepts as true) that Ann has children and also that Ann's children were sleeping before.

a state of affairs or an event is a concealed way of saying that a state of affairs or an event or action in which an individual (or object) was involved was the cause of another event, state of affairs etc.

It seems clear from the example of the verb 'to kill' that the interpretation of verbs also depends on whether they are used in a simple or a progressive tense. If we wanted to derive the verb 'to kill' from a tree, we would then have to account for the corresponding changes in the interpretation.

Let us now consider an example of an utterance in the form of a command-sentence, and present linguistic facts which would indicate that the given consequences do indeed constitute a necessary condition for the appropriate use of that utterance.

(6)   Open the door!

Consider now some of the consequences of the appropriate use of this utterance, or – in other words – what follows from the sentence:

(6')   The speaker has used the utterance 'Opên the door' appro-
           priately,

and from some implicit implications, which should therefore be made explicit in the description of the lexical item 'to open', the imperative mood and the linguistic index 'the door';

(a) The speaker wants (requires) the addressee to act so that the door will be open;

(b) The speaker believes that the door is closed (not open);

(c) The speaker believes that there is one and only one object referred to by him as 'the door' which the addressee can identify.

Consider now certain linguistic facts which might support the statement that (a), (b) and (c) are consequences of (6'). Notice, for instance, that the addressee can respond appropriately to (6) by using one of the following utterances:

(a') Why do you want me to do it? I can't move from my place;

(b') Do you really believe that the door is closed (not open)?;

(c') Can't you see there are three doors? Which one do you want me to
      open?

each of which is an appropriate response to one of the respective consequences (a), (b) and (c). If the set of conclusions from (6) had not included those sentences, then the answers above would have been inappropriate and strange. The fact that they are appropriate, that together with the utterance (6) each of them constitutes a coherent text (discourse), is a linguistic fact that empirically confirms that (a), (b) and (c) are in fact conclusions of (6').

This argument constitutes a sufficient condition for admitting (a), (b) and (c) as conclusions of (6), but it is not sufficient for admitting them as consequences (that is, as those sentences that follow directly from (6') and the rules which could be incorporated in the description of the language). For, in general, people may also react appropriately to those conclusions of an utterance which follow on the grounds of additional premises concerning the knowledge of a given extralinguistic situation. Thus, one of the possible replies to (6) could, for instance, also be the utterance: 'Do you really want to cool off?' It would be incorrect, however, to argue that the sentence 'The speaker wants to cool off' should belong to the set of consequences of (6'). It is obvious that such a sentence is not a necessary condition of the appropriate use of (6), there are only certain situations where it would follow from additional premises due to the knowledge of a given situation (in which just such a difference of temperatures occurs). A proper description of language, however, should seek to obtain as consequences only such sentences as can be justified by linguistic facts independent of the situation in which an utterance can be used. Let us present such facts for the discussed sentences (a), (b) and (c) above, which I claim should be derivable as consequences of (6'). Consider, for instance, utterances which are clearly anomalous and strange:

(a″) Open the door, I don't want you to do anything;
(b′) Open the door, I don't believe the door is closed (not open);
(c″) Open the door, there are two doors here.

The anomaly and strangeness of these utterances can be explained as a result of a contradiction between the consequence from the first clause and the proposition expressed explicitly by the second clause. This contradiction indicates that (a), (b) and (c) do, in fact, follow from (6') and from some implicit implications. We thus have empirical support for the correctness of the proposed description (for the necessity of introducing the corresponding implicational statements) through linguistic facts that are independent of the extralinguistic situation.

Let us observe here that analogous sentences which would not express these propositional attitudes could not be accepted as consequences. For instance, 'The door is closed' could not be said to be a consequence, for the truth of this sentence is by no means a necessary condition of (6'); it is clearly possible to say appropriately 'Open the door' (in the sense of the term 'appropriately' as defined in footnote 3) when speaking about a door that is not in the range of vision and being unaware that the said door is not closed. Such a state of affairs has no bearing whatsoever on the semantic interpretation of the discussed command-sentence.

Let us now present, as further examples, the utterances discussed by McCawley[11]

(7)   John and Harry went to New York
(8)   The 50 or 60 men I talked to went to New York
(9)   John and Harry are similar
(10)   The 50 or 60 men who I talked to are similar

First let us notice that (7) may cover different facts, but it is not linguistically ambiguous. John and Harry could participate in a single event of going to New York, or could go there separately, but I can think of no linguistic evidence which would justify two different deep structure descriptions for this type of utterance. To use McCawley's own criterion for deciding whether this is, or is not, a case of linguistic ambiguity,[12] let us consider a case in which John and Harry went together to New York, whereas Mary, George and Jim went there separately. We can very well say 'John and Harry went to New York and so did Mary, George and Jim'. The same will hold true *mutatis mutandis* of utterances such as 'John and Harry saw this play, and so did George and Mary', 'John and Harry have read this book, and so have George and Mary', etc. If we conclude anything about their seeing the play together, or reading the book separately, it is due to our additional knowledge of such activities (they can or cannot be done together, or are usually done together) or due to our additional knowledge of the relationship among the individuals in question and other extralinguistic facts concerning them. But this cannot be taken as part of the linguistic description.

The interpretations of (7) and (8) are parallel in that in each case the (distributive) predicate is asserted of each individual belonging to the set described as 'John and Harry' and 'The 50 or 60 men who I spoke to', respectively. The difference in the respective interpretations is due to two different linguistic facts, which, if described properly, will give grounds for different consequences. Namely, the set of individuals in (7) is given by enumeration, whereas the set in (8) is given by description.[13] Thus we will

[11] J. McCawley, *The Annotated Respective*, University of Chicago, mimeographed.
[12] McCawley proposed a criterion for deciding whether a sentence should be considered as ambiguous or not in his paper at the LSA Meeting, Washington, 1970. I am here following his line of reasoning.
[13] McCawley is right in saying that in one case the elements of the set are enumerated, in the other case the set is given by description. But he concludes that in the case when the set is given by enumeration of n elements, the surface structure is derived from n conjoined sentences. To be consistent, we would have to agree that the sentence 'Jim, George, Dick and Robert are similar to each other' should be derived from twelve sentences. This seems terrifying if we increase the number of conjoined nouns in a sentence. For five conjoined nouns we would have twenty underlying sentences, and in general for n conjoined nouns we would have $(n-1)n$ underlying sentences. We will discuss the interpretation of sentences containing the predicate 'be similar' below in the text.

obtain an analogous consequence from (7) and (8):

(11)   The speaker asserts that $\underset{x}{\forall}\,[x \in X \to x$ went to New York]

whereas we will have additional consequences following from (3) due to the fact that the elements of the set X are enumerated: 'The speaker asserts that John went to New York'; 'The speaker asserts that Harry went to New York', which evidently constitutes a necessary condition of the corresponding assertion (11).

The second difference in the interpretation of the four examples above lies in the properties of the two predicates 'to go' and 'be similar', which can be described in the form of implicational statements and thus provide a basis for different consequences. The predicate 'to go' takes two arguments which have different semantic roles and with respect to which it is not symmetric. It is the symmetry of the predicate 'be similar' which is the source of further differences. The predicate 'be similar' takes two arguments with identical semantic roles and thus it is symmetric with respect to these arguments.[14] The property of symmetry, which ordinarily is defined by:

(12) P is symmetric with respect to $x, y \underset{\text{def}}{=} [x\,P\,y \to y\,P\,x]$

will be defined here by:

(13) P is symmetric with respect to
$NP_1, NP_2 \underset{\text{def}}{=} [A: \ NP_1\,P\,NP_2] \to [B: \ NP_2\,P\,NP_1]$

where A stands for 'The speaker asserts that, and B for 'The speaker believes that'. (It is worth noting here that we will define in a similar way the property of being a converse, which holds for many pairs of words, phrases and also for passive constructions.

$\check{P}$ is a converse predicate of
$P \underset{\text{def}}{=} [A: \ NP_1\,P\,NP_2] \to [B: \ NP_2\,\check{P}\,NP_1]).$

Let us first discuss cases in which two arguments of the symmetric predicate 'be similar' are present on the surface. Whenever one of them corresponds to a set, the other to an individual, the consequences will be parallel to the former case (11). From

(14)   John, Harry and Dick are similar to George

(15)   All the 50 or 60 men who I spoke to are similar to George

in either case we will have an assertive consequence corresponding to

(16)   The speaker asserts that $\underset{x}{\forall}\,[x \in X \to x$ is similar to George]

and a belief-consequence due to the property of symmetry defined by (13)

[14] It has been noted in I. Bellert and Z. Saloni, *op. cit.* that if the semantic roles of two arguments of a verb are precisely described and are identical, then the verb can be said to be a symmetric predicate.

(16')   The speaker believes that $\underset{x}{\forall}$ $[x \in X \to$ George is similar to $x]$

As the set X is given by enumeration in utterance (14), we will also have additional assertive consequences of (14) due to (16)

> The speaker asserts that John is similar to George
> The speaker asserts that Harry is similar to George
> The speaker asserts that Dick is similar to George

and additional belief-consequence due to (16')

> The speaker believes that George is similar to John
> The speaker believes that George is similar to Harry
> The speaker believes that George is similar to Dick

Returning now to the examples (9) and (10) we have to notice that the second argument of the symmetric predicate 'be similar' does not occupy its normal position (as in 'x is similar to y'), that is, we may say that it is absent from the surface of these utterances. According to a very general rule concerning symmetric predicates, this is only possible when the first argument corresponds to a set, which may be given either by a description (noun or noun phrase in the plural, possibly with a relative clause) or by enumeration; otherwise a string of words consisting of a symmetric predicate with an argument corresponding to a single 'object' or individual would not satisfy the conditions specified in any of the implications, and could not be interpreted in terms of any consequence (e.g. 'John is similar'). Our examples belong to just that case in which the first argument corresponds to a set. There is a general implication which holds true for all cases of symmetric predicates used with one argument corresponding to a set X

(17) $X \text{ PREDICATE}_{\text{sym}} \to \text{A}:$ $\underset{x,\,y \text{ where } x \neq y}{\forall}$ $[x,\, y \in X \to x \text{ PREDICATE}_{\text{sym}} \, y]$

where A stands for the propositional attitude 'The speaker asserts that . . .'.

The above implication will make it possible to draw the corresponding consequences from utterances (9) and (10), since their structural descriptions will satisfy the conditions indicated in the antecedent. Thus we have an assertive consequence

> The speaker asserts that $\underset{x,\,y \text{ where } x \neq y}{\forall}$ $[x,\, y \in X \to x \text{ BE SIMILAR TO } y]$

Since the set X is given by enumeration in (9), we have additional consequences from (9):

> The speaker asserts that John is similar to Harry
> The speaker asserts that Harry is similar to John

If the set X were given by enumerating n elements, we would then have $(n - 1)n$ consequences.

It could be argued for a certain sense of the term 'be similar' that it has the property of reflexivity. I do not think, however, that in the everyday sense of this term the predicate 'be similar' is reflexive. Thus we will not have consequences of the type: 'John is similar to himself', which would be a case of reflexive predicates.

The proposed interpretation of utterances containing the verb 'be similar' seems also to give a better account of the difference between (10) and (18):

(10)   The 50 or 60 men who I talked to are similar
(18)   The 50 or 60 men who I talked to are erudite

which according to McCawley would consist in the fact that '*Erudite* expresses a property of an individual' (18 asserts that each of the individuals in question has this property). 'Similar expresses a property of a set' (10 asserts that the set described by *the 50 or 60 men I talked to* has that property).[15] According to our interpretation 'be similar' is not treated as expressing a property of an individual either. But neither can it possibly be treated as expressing a property of a set. It is not a property but a binary relation (two-place predicate). However it is not asserted of a set, but of two individuals; in utterances of the type: 'John is similar to Harry', it is asserted just of two individuals, and in others of the type discussed here, it is asserted of any two individuals belonging to a given set. There are of course cases in which a predicate is not understood distributively, and then we can rightly say that it expresses a property of a set. For instance: 'Albanians are not numerous'. However, this is not the case with the utterances in question.

Let us now discuss the problem concerning the number of different propositional attitudes which should be accounted for by a description of a single utterance (if the description is concerned with the semantic interpretation of the utterance). It seems necessary to assume that an adequate deep structure description of any utterance should account for the fact that there is always more than one propositional attitude being expressed. If linguists represent an utterance in terms of a single tree structure, it is because the category of Sentence makes it plausible to conceive of a sentence structure as a single tree; the syntactic dependencies within the description of an utterance can also be represented adequately in the form of a tree. Such a representation, however, no matter how deep it goes and how complex the tree becomes, will not account for the fact that we do interpret utterances, and respond appropriately to them, as if they expressed a set of propositions with

[15] J. McCawley, *The Annotated Respective, op. cit.*

various propositional attitudes that are not dependent on each other, and not just one complex proposition. For instance, the utterance

(19)   Is Berkeley, which I myself have never visited, a big city?

(which is equivalent to: I myself have never visited Berkeley. Is it a big city?) evidently expresses a question and an assertion, and should thus be represented with two performatives in its deep structure. If, however, we take into account propositional attitudes corresponding to assertions, commands or questions, why then should the beliefs or assumptions of the speaker not be taken into account as well, since – as I argue in this paper – we respond appropriately not only to asserted propositions ('This is not true...', 'I deny...', 'You lie...' etc.), or to propositions with the propositional attitude 'The speaker wants the addressee to say (if)...', but we also respond to the purported beliefs or assumptions of the speaker ('Why do you think so'?), 'Do you really believe that...', etc.). The latter must then be part of the meaning of the utterances.

As a matter of fact, we cannot assert anything about nothing, we cannot express our desire to know something about nothing, express our doubts concerning nothing, etc. All assertions, questions, denials, commands, wishes, etc. should thus be represented by at least one predicate with at least one argument[16] which is somehow quantified (in a linguistic sense of the term). And the use of any type of argument implies certain beliefs or assumptions of the speaker (see footnotes 17 and 18). Accordingly, at least two propositional attitudes must be expressed. Let us consider an example.

If someone says

(20)   All the inhabitants of the house at the corner of Baltimore and Chestnut are black

we can just as well answer:

(a) This is not true, Fred who lives there is not black

(b) Do you really believe that there is more than one inhabitant there? Don't you know that this house is inhabited by a single old lady?

(c) Do you believe there is just one house on the corner of Baltimore and Chestnut? I don't know which house you are talking about.

---

[16] See my paper, 'Arguments and Predicates in the Logico-Semantic Structure of Utterances', *Studies in Syntax and Semantics* (ed. by F. Kiefer), D. Reidel Publishing Co., Dordrecht-Holland, 1969. I distinguished three types of arguments. Type 1 is a proper name or a definite description through which we refer to one and only one 'object'. Type 2 is an expression through which we refer to a set of 'objects' that are such and such, and only to those objects (All the girls who are here, The girls whom I talked to in class yesterday, All Chinese people, etc.). An argument of type 3 is an expression with which we refer to a certain number of 'objects' that are such and such (indefinite descriptions).

(d) Do you really believe there is a house at the corner of Baltimore and Chestnut? These streets do not cross each other.

It is hard to deny that each of these answers constitutes a coherent text together with (2). The answer (a) is a response to one of the consequences of (2) with a propositional attitude which is assertive, while (b), (c) and (d) are responses to three different consequences of (20) which express the purported belief of the speaker; the first is a result of the use of the linguistic all operator[17] (all the inhabitants . . .), while (c) and (d) are a result of the use of a linguistic index ('the house at the corner of Baltimore and Chestnut'), defined by analogy to the iota operator[18]. In fact, a most fascinating property of language in its lexical and syntactic aspects is that it has an abundance of means for expressing a set of complex propositions in one short utterance and the semantic structure of an utterance cannot be thus represented adequately by a single tree structure. An interpretative semantic component is therefore indispensable.

Let us now discuss as further examples some utterances which once served as typical instances for demonstrating that a generative transformational grammar is descriptively more adequate than a constituent structure grammar.

[17] I define the use of a linguistic all-operator, which always binds an argument of type 2, by analogy to a general restricted quantifier $\underset{x}{\forall} \varphi(x)$ which is used as an abbreviation for $\underset{x}{\forall} x \in A \to \varphi(x)$. I added, however, propositional attitudes into the implication, and a pseudo-existential condition, which seems to be justified by linguistic evidence. 'There are no girls in this room, and all girls in this room are blond' is not contradictory in the logical sense of a general quantifier, whereas it is contradictory in the sense of our definition of the linguistic all-operator

$$\left.\begin{array}{l}\text{The speaker uses appropriately an}\\ \text{utterance whose structure satisfies}\\ \text{the conditions (All } A\text{)}\,\text{PREDICATE}_{t_i}\end{array}\right\} \to \begin{cases}\text{The speaker believes that there}\\ BE_{t_i} \text{ more than one } x \in A\\ \text{The speaker asserts that}\\ \underset{x}{\forall}\,(x \in A \to x\ \text{PREDICATE}_{t_i})\end{cases}$$

where A is a noun or noun phrase in plural, the name of a set being referred to, and PREDICATE$_{t_i}$ is a predicate in a given tense.

Notice that the first consequent is dependent also on the tense of the predicate.

[18] I define the use of a linguistic index (a proper name, a definite description or a corresponding pronoun) by analogy to a unit function by an iota operator $(\imath x)\varphi(x)$ which must satisfy the condition of existence $\underset{x}{\exists}\,\varphi(x)$ and of uniqueness $\underset{x}{\forall}, _y(\varphi(x) \wedge \varphi(y)) \to (x = y)$

$$\left.\begin{array}{l}\text{The speaker uses appropriately an}\\ \text{utterance whose structure satisfies}\\ \text{the conditions } (\varphi)\,\text{PREDICATE}_{t_i},\\ \text{where } \varphi \text{ is an index}\end{array}\right\} \to \begin{pmatrix}\text{The speaker believes there } BE_{t_i}\\ \text{one and only one } x \text{ which he is}\\ \text{referring to by } \varphi \text{ and which the}\\ \text{addressee may identify}\end{pmatrix}$$

The statements concerning the existence of the x which is referred to by φ (or which belongs to a set, as in the footnote above) are conceived of as pseudo-existential statements, since – as I argue – the interpretation of an isolated utterance, say, 'The king was gay' should be independent of whether the individual being referred to exists in reality, in the context of a novel, a myth or in a reported dream.

(21)   John forced Mary to come
(22)   John promised Mary to come

It was pointed out that in a constituent structure grammar there was no way of indicating in a general manner that *Mary* is the notional subject of *to come* in (21), whereas *John* is the notional subject of *to come* in (22). In a transformational grammar, we can generally account for such (and similar) differences in terms of a deep structure representation, in which in this case the words *John* or *Mary* will occur, respectively, as subjects in the subtrees in which the verb *to come* occurs as the predicate. There are, however, further differences between the interpretation of these two verbs, which would have to be accounted for by a much more complex deep structure tree in a generative semantics description.

In the approach proposed here, those differences would be accounted for by different consequences resulting from certain implications established, respectively, for the two lexical items *to force* and *to promise*. The implications would, roughly, be:

(23) NP_1 FORCE$_{t_i}$ NP_2 $[_S NP_2 VP _S] \rightarrow$

$$\rightarrow \begin{cases} A: & NP_1 \text{ ACT}_{t_i} \text{ at time}_j \text{ WITH THE EFFECT THAT } [NP_2 \text{ VP}_{t_i} \\ & \text{after time}_j] \\ B: & NP_2 \text{ RESIST}_{t_i} \text{ at time}_j \text{ AGAINST } [NP_2 \text{ VP}_{t_i \text{fut}}] \end{cases}$$

where time$_j$ indicates the time of reference, and t_i a tense (excluding progressive; cf. (3))

(24) NP_1 PROMISE$_{t_i}$ NP_2 $[_S NP_1 VP _S]$

$$\rightarrow \begin{cases} A: & NP_1 \text{ INFORM}_{t_i} NP_2 [NP_1 \text{ VP}_{t_i \text{fut}}] \\ A: & NP_1 \text{ BECOME}_{t_i} \text{ RESPONSIBLE FOR } [NP_1 \text{ VP}_{t_i \text{fut}}] \end{cases}$$

where the subscript t_i indicates any tense, and the time of reference is not indicated (in either consequent the time of reference is the same).

If someone says 'John forced Mary to come', we can perfectly well respond by saying 'Did she really resist coming'? Moreover, the utterances

(25)   Mary did not resist coming. I forced her to come

constitute an incoherent discourse, because of the contradiction between the assertion expressed by the first utterance and the belief expressed by the second one.

Similarly, the utterances

(26)   John promised Mary to come on Sunday. He did not inform her whether he would come on Sunday.

do not make up a coherent discourse, because of the implied contradiction.

In the implications (23) and (24) we refer to substrings of the category NP which of course may correspond to different types of arguments. In general a predicate applies to an 'object' or 'objects' referred to by an argument of one or another type. In case of an argument of type 1 (proper name or definite description), the predicate applies to one and only one 'object' referred to; in case of an argument of type 2 (noun phrase in plural preceded by an all-operator), the predicate applies to each 'object' belonging to the set referred to, etc. Implications (23) and (24) are, however, applicable independently of the type of argument a noun phrase corresponds to; similarly, the implications which interpret the use of different types of arguments are also independent of the predicate that occurs with them. There are, however, implications which hold true for a given class of predicates and a given type of argument. Such, for instance, is implication (17), which interprets all symmetric predicates used with only one argument corresponding to a set.

What is not clear and requires more study is the interplay of consequences with different propositional attitudes in complex sentences. If a given predicate does not occur as a main verb, but does occur in an embedded sentence, it appears that consequences with assertive propositional attitudes combine with those that follow from implications concerning the main verb, so that they constitute one assertion. The consequences expressing the beliefs of the speaker do not combine with those concerning the main verb. On the other hand, if the preceding verb is a locutionary verb, the assertions and beliefs of the speaker become the assertions and beliefs of the subject of the locutionary verb. Thus from an utterance

(27)   John said he would wake up the children at seven

we gather that it is John who believed that the children would be sleeping before seven, while from the utterance

(28)   John will wake up the children before seven

we gather it is the speaker's belief that the children will be sleeping before seven.

Consider now some complex utterances and the corresponding consequences due to (23) and (24)

(29)   Dick promised his wife to force Irena to come

A: Dick informed his wife [he would act with the effect that [Irena would come]]

A: Dick became responsible for [he would act with the effect [Irena would come]]

B: Dick believed [Irena would resist against [she would come]]

(30)   Dick forced Danuta to promise John to come

A: Dick acted with the effect that [Danuta informed John [she would come]]

A: Dick acted with the effect that [Danuta became responsible for [she would come]]

B: Danuta resisted against [she would inform John that [she would come]]

B: Danuta resisted against [she would become responsible for [she would come]]

Notice that here we have given only the consequences following from (23) and (24) that are implicational rules which interpret the use of the predicates (*to force* and *to promise*, respectively) without regard to the possible types of arguments.

Now if we wanted to put all the information pertinent to the predicates and the arguments in the deep structure tree, the tree itself and the transformations involved would become inconceivably complex. Moreover, we would in any case have to establish some rules of interpretation for tree structures in order to account for the corresponding interplay of propositional attitudes in complex utterances. Of course, one could argue that the formulation proposed in (23) or (24) is not precise, or that it should be modified somehow. But this is a matter of detail, since the corresponding information has to be accounted for in one way or another.

Suppose now that we have described the lexical items and syntactic relations of a given language, or part of a language, in terms of sets of implications.[19] Generally speaking, the set of all implications established for a given language would make up a component of grammar, which I call the logico-semantic component. The function of this component would be interpretative. Given an utterance with its structural description that satisfies the conditions (specified in formulas F) in a number of implications, we obtain the interpretation of this utterance by deriving, as consequences, all sentences which correspond to the consequents of those implications. The

---

[19] Notice that the interpretation of most syntactic relations has to be included in the implications concerning lexical items. For we cannot describe lexical items in isolation by this method; lexical items can be described only in terms of certain syntactic conditions (specified in formulas F in the antecedents). In fact, nothing can be said to follow from a verb alone or a noun alone, but only from a sentence containing such a noun or verb.

set of pertinent implications would thus interpret an utterance in terms of a set of propositions which should be equivalent to what any speaker that produces that utterance at any time purports to assert, believe, wish, etc., if he uses it appropriately.

It is worth noting that a set of consequences constituting the interpretation of a given utterance will display not only the semantic differences between utterances that contain different lexical items in the same structure (e.g. 'John killed Mary' and 'John kissed Mary'), but would also display the semantic closeness or even sameness of utterances which contain different lexical items or phrases, through a subset of consequences in common. For instance, the utterances

> John killed George
> John murdered George
> John executed George

will have several consequences in common.

For the case in which utterances contain two different, but synonymous, lexical items or phrases, or have synonymous structures (e.g. 'I saw him crossing the street' and 'I saw him when he was crossing the street') the sets of consequences will be the same. In general, the degree of semantic closeness utterances have will correspond to the number of consequences they have in common.

Since selectional restrictions are formulated here by means of implicational rules, the grammar will generate acceptable as well as odd or deviant sentences (those that are not a case of violation of purely syntactic rules[20]). The difference between the interpretation of acceptable and deviant sentences will be only such that in the former case the set of consequences will contain propositions consistent with each other, while in the latter case, the set of consequences will contain propositions which may contradict each other. However, a fact that can hardly be denied is that competent speakers display a capacity of interpreting deviant, odd or awkward utterances. It is precisely this ability that makes it possible to declare them awkward or deviant. Is it not the implied contradictions that are decisive in such cases? Since we are interested in postulating a system of rules that correspond to

---

[20] We propose to describe selectional restrictions in terms of implicational rules, but obviously we do not mean to include Chomsky's rules of strict subcategorization, which belong to the grammar. We assume accordingly that the grammar will generate sentences of the type 'The table was afraid' or 'The moon swallowed the problem', but not sentences of the type 'I eat that the boy came', 'he is black to play'. The former sentences will have an interpretation through their respective sets of consequences – bizarre as it may appear, whereas the latter will have no interpretation.

some aspects of linguistic competence, it seems worth noting here that the postulated explicit rules of implications correspond to the implicit rules of implication which we must make use of in interpreting utterances. Although many problems arise here and require further investigation, such an approach seems to be intuitively close to our linguistic competence. We do interpret utterances and discourses by drawing conclusions which depend on the conditions for using lexical items and syntactic relations. And in the process we do make use of implicit implications. How could we draw any conclusions otherwise?

If it appears too difficult to write all the implications explicitly, this is firstly due to the vagueness of certain linguistic expressions, and secondly because of the fact that language knowledge is intrinsically interconnected with knowledge of the world, and in order to describe a language fully from the semantic point of view, we would have to describe our knowledge of the world in terms of implicational rules. Otherwise we have to make an arbitrary cut which must impoverish our description of language. But this holds true for any possible description of natural language.

University of Montreal, Canada and
University of Warsaw, Poland

MANFRED BIERWISCH

GENERATIVE GRAMMAR AND EUROPEAN LINGUISTICS*

I

The development of the theory of generative grammar during the past fifteen years has led not only to considerable improvements in successive stages, but also to alternative proposals with respect to certain problems of theoretical interest. This concerns in particular the relation between syntax and semantics, where at present at least three different approaches are under lively discussion. None of these alternatives, investigating different possibilities within the general framework of generative transformational grammar, can be taken, however, as representing a separate 'school'. It is also impossible to localize them in any geographical sense. They are simply detailed explorations of alternative hypotheses necessary for an empirically motivated clarification and extension of the theory under discussion. This leads to certain difficulties in the delimitation of the subject matter for the present chapter. Although since the early sixties an increasing number of linguists in Europe have been attracted by the theory of generative grammar, they do not form in any serious sense a particular trend or school or anything of this kind that could be contrasted to corresponding research done elsewhere in the world. Hence the heading *Generative Grammar in Western Europe* does not specify a coherent and selfcontained topic. It would thus be a rather extrinsic approach to the subject of the present paper, if I simply tried to report on some European contributions to research based on the principles of generative grammar. Such a report would be of restricted interest, moreover, since it would have to remain rather incomplete for several reasons. I have therefore chosen to deal with the subject in a fairly different way. In the following sections I will discuss a set of problems that emerge if the principal assumptions of generative grammar are viewed against the background of preceding linguistic theories of European origin. We will see that these problems are in spite of certain similarities, considerably different from those resulting from the corresponding theories developed in the United States.

Such an undertaking seems to me justified for the following reasons. Firstly, the necessity and the validity of the particular claims of a theory

* Reprinted from Thomas A. Sebeok (ed.): *Current Trends in Linguistics*, Vol. **IX**. Copyright by Mouton & Co., The Hague.

F. Kiefer and N. Ruwet (eds.), Generative Grammar in Europe, 69–111. *All Rights Reserved.*
Copyright © *1973 by D. Reidel Publishing Company, Dordrecht-Holland.*

become more distinct and more obvious if they are carefully compared with corresponding claims, achievements and defects of its predecessors. Detailed comparisons of this type have been made with respect to the ideas of American structural linguistics, e.g. in Postal (1964) and Chomsky (1957, 1964). None has yet been made regarding the development of European linguistics since Saussure as summarized most explicitly in the theory of Hjelmslev. (A critical analysis of the theory of Firth and his followers has been given in Langendoen (1964), and hence I will exclude it from the present discussion. The same holds for the views of Martinet, which are analyzed in Postal (1966).) Secondly, a comparison of different theories does not only show the differences among them, the shortcomings of one of them, but also their similarities, the explicit or latent coherence of tradition, and perhaps the unsolved problems transferred from one theory to the other. Finally it may serve to give a certain impression of how the theory of generative grammar fits into the particular European preconditions, continuing and transforming them, which is the only aspect to my mind which has anything in common with European linguistics.

Although I will deal with all problems to be discussed in this paper from the viewpoint of generative grammar, I will not provide an exposition of its conceptual apparatus, but rather take up only particular points where they become relevant in the course of discussion.[1] I shall ignore also, in general, the particular alternatives mentioned above.

In order to shed some additional light on the contrasting features recognizable in the European background, I will first give a brief recapitulation of some problems arising from the American tradition. I would like to stress in advance, however, that several problems which have been widely discussed in connection with the theory of generative transformational grammar are in fact not particular claims of this theory, but rather general assumptions presupposed by any attempt to construct a linguistic description of a particular language and a general theory of language according to which particular descriptions can be made. That a language must be considered as an unlimited range of possible phonetic structures paired in a specific way with an unlimited range of semantic interpretations; that this sound-meaning-correlation cannot be specified by a simple listing of linguistic expressions together with their semantic interpretations because of the unbounded range of this correlation; that the native speaker of a given language knows this sound-meaning-correlation for any arbitrarily chosen expression and that he relies

---

[1] A complete account of the theory of generative transformational grammar, even in a condensed form, would be a large topic on its own. Expositions on different levels of technicality are available, e.g. in Chomsky (1965, 1966a, 1967), Katz (1966), Katz and Postal (1964), Bierwisch (1966).

for this knowledge on effective construction; that nevertheless phonetic and semantic representations cannot be mapped on each other directly in any systematic way, but must be mediated by intervening structures: these are some of the basic, preliminary assumptions to be justified by very general empirical and methodological considerations. Though they seem to be un-controversial and should be acceptable to any linguist, we will see below that some of them have been ignored or even denied by different schools of modern linguistics. Since presuppositions of this type have been formulated explicitly in connection with certain specific tenets of generative transforma-tional grammar, they have often been taken as claims characteristic for a particular school, which they in fact cannot be.

II

The theory of generative transformational grammar, basically formulated by Chomsky (1955) and first published by Chomsky (1957), grew out of the tradition of American structural linguistics. With a few exceptions all the contributions to its further rapid development are due to American scholars. It would nevertheless be wrong to consider it – as has often been done – as a typically American phenomenon. In fact, its essential character has little in common with the behavioristic background of almost all other trends in contemporary American linguistics. Chomsky (1964, 1966, 1968) has made it increasingly clear that the basic tenets of generative grammar can best be understood as an elaboration of quite traditional problems, in particular those that have been at the core of the ideas of philosophical grammar from the 17th until the 19th century, an elaboration, which of course deals with these problems on the level of modern scientific standards, developed in part by the methods of structural linguistics. What Chomsky has in mind when he refers to the tradition of philosophical grammar is a theory of language which attempts not merely to describe or arrange observable linguistic data according to certain systematic criteria, but rather explains such data on the basis of essential principles underlying the cognitive capacity of man as it manifests itself in natural language. These principles are to be explicated formally in terms of formal and substantive linguistic universals. The formal universals consist of a set of linguistic levels on which the different aspects of the structure of linguistic expressions are to be represented and a characteriz-ation of the general form of possible grammars, i.e. of systems of rules, which specify the structural aspects and their interrelations for the expressions of given languages. This in turn involves a formal account of the types of rules occurring in a grammar; of the different components of a grammar and the ways in which they are related to each other; of the principles of rule ordering within these components, and of the manner of rule application. The substantive universals comprise first of all a specification of the basic, primitive elements which might appear in grammars and structural representations of arbitrary languages. These are in particular the universal system of phonetic features, established in universal phonetics, the (as yet little understood) system of basic semantic components, to be established by universal semantics, and the set of universal syntactic categories and features. Since it turned out that a relevant set of the grammatical rules is universal not only with respect to its formal character, but also with respect to the particular regularities which these rules express, they can be extracted from the particular grammars. Thus the substantive universals also comprise a certain substructure of the system of individual rules that function in grammars of individual languages. Obviously this fairly rich system of formal and substantive universals imposes rather strict limitations on the form and the content of particular grammars that can be constructed in accordance with them. It is thus an elaborate hypothesis about the class of all possible natural languages, which explains, if it is right, the highly specific properties of natural languages in terms of these underlying principles.[2]

The linguistic universals in this sense reconstruct the traditional notion of universal grammar as opposed to particular grammars of individual languages. Notice that universal grammar, if construed in this way, is not simply the intersection of possible particular grammars. (Then it would become more and more empty, as more and different languages were taken into account.) It is rather a set of highly specific conditions according to which the necessary information about properties of given particular languages is to be organized in individual grammars, by means of the

---

[2] Thus all natural languages exhibit, e.g. an internal hierarchic organization of their sentences and, moreover, specific relations between sentences – such as active/passive, assertion/question/ imperative – which are determined by highly complex operations based on precisely this hierarchic organization. These facts are explained by the claim that the syntactic component contains phrase structure rules which specify the hierarchic organization of certain basic structures, and transformational rules which are structure-dependent operations on these representations. Further complicated facts are explained by particular conditions on the operation of transformational rules. The transformational rules also account for the possibility of relating a rather abstract level of syntactic deep structure on which the semantic interpretation of a sentence is based to a more superficial syntactic surface structure determining its phonetic shape. They thus explain the observations made above that there is no direct sound-meaning-correlation in natural languages, but that this correlation must rather be mediated by intervening syntactic structures. The linguistic universals embody also implicational claims of the type 'if a language has property A then it has, in general, also property B'. Thus the universal system of phonetic features incorporates, for instance, a formal explanation of the fact that if a language possesses a velar nasal, then it possesses also a dental nasal, but not necessarily vice versa.

linguistic universals.[3] It is in this sense of the notion of universal grammar that the theory of generative grammar is concerned with the principles of cognitive capacity: the universal grammar describes the structure of the general human ability to acquire an arbitrary language, just as a particular grammar describes the particular tacit knowledge resulting from the acquisition of a given language. However, that Chomsky takes up essential ideas of philosophical grammar, does not give us the slightest reason to consider the theory of generative grammar as a continuation and extension of a European tradition. This is unjustified for at least two reasons. First of all, insofar as this tradition was not simply buried during the last century of European linguistics, it does have a character rather different from that which Chomsky refers to. We will discuss this difference briefly in the next section. Secondly, generative grammar simply did not originate in the context of the European tradition, but arose from a critical analysis of contemporary American achievements. Only later did Chomsky and others realize that their ideas were in fact related to a great historical background.

For the purpose of comparison, it is worthwhile to notice briefly the place of the conception of generative grammar in its early stages among the views dominating American linguistics at that time. Besides the important idea of grammatical transformations advanced simultaneously by Harris and Chomsky, though with rather different implications, there is, as far as I can see, only one point where the development of generative grammar shares typical features of contemporary American linguistics. I am referring to the sceptical attitude towards the relevance of meaning in Chomsky's earlier writings. Within the Bloomfield-Harris-tradition, the poor understanding of semantic problems has not been taken as a basic challenge, but rather as an indication that linguistics should be constructed as a science which does not suffer from the chaotic field of meaning. In a similar vein the discussion of the syntax-semantic relationship within the framework of generative grammar was originally focussed on the question how syntactic notions could be

---

[3] Notice that even a very strong set of linguistic universals might not fully determine a unique particular grammar for a given language. Though a given particular grammar uniquely determines a certain language, there may be several or even an infinite number of grammars for one language. As a complement of universal grammar one needs therefore a criterion for evaluating different grammars that are equally compatible with the given language – or more precisely: with the corpus drawn from it. This criterion of evaluation is bound to the linguistic universals in a specific way. It depends on them insofar as it can evaluate only properties provided for by the universals. And it controls the formulation of universals insofar as these must be chosen in such a way that the evaluation procedure based on them leads to an empirically justified decision. For detailed information see, e.g. Chomsky (1965) and Chomsky and Halle (1965). In the rest of this paper I will use the term universal grammar as referring to the set of linguistic universals controlled by the evaluation criterion.

established independently of semantic considerations.[4] The situation changed very soon, however, and at least since Katz and Fodor (1963) attempted to formulate the outline of a semantic theory, problems of meaning became an integrated topic of generative grammar. This does not mean, of course, that since then the understanding of these problems has been radically improved. In fact, a good deal of scepticism with respect to the overwhelming difficulties has rightly been preserved. But the lack of knowledge in semantics in comparison to the achievements in syntax and phonology is now conceived of as a serious gap in the theory, and not as a linguistically irrelevant fact. The focus of attention to the syntactic-semantic relationship is now on the question of how semantic interpretation is determined by syntactic properties.[5]

In all other respects, the theory of generative grammar reflects typical properties of contemporary American linguistics merely in the form of critical discussions. Examples are the analysis of the status of the so-called discovery procedures in Chomsky (1957), the critique of the principles of taxonomic-phonemics in Halle (1959) and Chomsky (1964), the discussion of the limitation of constituent analysis in Postal (1964). The inadequacies that these and many other discussions have revealed in numerous details are consequences of the fact, that all the theories criticized are based essentially on the following assumptions: a language can be described by segmenting given utterances according to certain criteria and classifying the resulting segments in terms of their cooccurrence and distribution; the criteria admitted must be identifiable in terms of external stimuli or external behaviour of native speakers. These assumptions in turn do not follow from empirical considerations, but from methodological prejudices, viz. that the basic notions of a theory – segmentation and distributional classification – should

---

[4] In this early period the task of a grammar was usually formulated as the enumeration or generation of all (and only) the sentences of a given language, where a sentence was taken as a formal syntactic object together with its phonetic interpretation. Only later on was a grammar characterized as a system of rules that specifies the sound-meaning correspondence for the sentences of a language. Though these formulations do not contradict each other, they are indicative of the focus of interest.

[5] As mentioned above there are three views under discussion with respect to this problem: Katz (1967) assumes that syntactic deep structure is the only level relevant for semantic interpretation. Chomsky (forthcoming) claims that semantic interpretation is based on syntactic deep structure, but partially determined also by certain aspects of syntactic surface structure. McCawley (1968) denies the existence of an autonomous level of syntactic deep structure and assumes that the semantic representation must be taken as the proper underlying representation directly related to syntactic surface structure by fairly complex syntactic transformations. (The choice of references here is somewhat arbitrary: there is in fact a fairly large number of papers on this subject.) These three positions represent different empirical claims, different assumptions about formal universals within the common framework of generative transformational grammar.

be as general and simple as possible, and that all criteria should be reducible to objective, i.e. physical data.[6]

These principles sharply contrast with the ideas of universal grammar as mentioned above. Instead of keeping the general claims as empty as possible, universal grammar is looking for the strongest and most detailed universal concepts compatible with the known data. These concepts are not based on arbitrary methodological assumptions – such as the vague notion of simplicity or physical objectivity – but are subject to empirical motivation. And finally universal grammar is not antimentalistic, but takes mental phenomena as its proper subject matter, the physical data being reflexes of this.

Notice that the principles of segmentation and classification, in spite of the antimentalistic character which they are given in the Bloomfield tradition, can and must be interpreted as a claim concerning the cognitive capacity involved in language acquisition. And they are, indeed, closely related to basic assumptions of behaviorist psychology. Viewed in this way, they contribute to a precise explication of a very general conception of language learning, and of learning in general, which assumes that linguistic capacity is based on a few general preconditions such as segmentation, classification, and association of given stimuli. It is in this sense that Chomsky (1968) has recently claimed that the main merit of structural linguistics is that it led to the definite falsification of this theory of language learning: since it has been shown that the principles of segmentation and classification cannot account for certain essential properties of natural languages, any theory of language acquisition based on these principles must be discarded.

These general implications for the theory of cognitive capacity indicate a deep-seated level of contrast between generative grammar and structural linguistics. This contrast, which underlies many of the differences in important details, concerns not only particular claims of generative transformational grammar, but also some of the general presuppositions mentioned in Section I. It receives a somewhat different character, however, if generative grammar is compared with the European variants of structural linguistics, for two reasons: the European schools were scarcely influenced by behavioristic psychology and did not, therefore, share the antimentalistic

---

[6] These two principles, taken as the cornerstone of a misleading methodology, led to awkward consequences. Because of the antimentalistic prejudice only concepts established by means of physical criteria were taken as reflecting properties of the described phenomena, whereas all other, more derived notions (such as, e.g. syntactic construction, subject, predicate, etc.) were considered as arbitrary constructs without any other significance than that of providing for a compact restatement of the given data. Thus the description of a language could be nothing but an arbitrary, though in some undefinable sense convenient, arrangement of data, precisely because of the equally arbitrary principles on which it was based.

axiom; and they retained a little more of the spirit of universal grammar. We will see the consequences below.

III

Turning now to the European scene which the theory of generative grammar entered in the late fifties, I will first concentrate on the theory of Glossematics as summarized by Hjelmslev (1953) and Uldall (1957). This theory gives the most explicit and rigorous formulation of all the ideas that dominated the development of linguistics initiated by de Saussure. Some apparent differences between Glossematics and other concepts, in particular those of the Prague School, will be considered later.

According to Saussure a language is a system of signs organized by two types of relations: syntagmatic relations connect elements within a given sentence (or any other combination of signs); paradigmatic relations[7] contract elements capable of occupying identical syntagmatic positions or functions. A sign in turn is an interdependent combination of a content form and an expression form, which impose a structure on the content substance and the expression substance, respectively. This view is accepted, extended and refined by the theory of Glossematics. The notions involved are reconstructed in a strictly formal and uniform way in terms of a few basic concepts. The resulting system is a very general algebraic structure of a certain type providing the framework for the description of any particular language. This glossematic algebra is understood as a deductive theory which specifies the class of all possible languages[8] and thus has a status very much like the set of formal universals in the theory of generative grammar. Uldall (1957, p. 35), for example, points out that

a deductive theory is no more than a very general and very elaborate hypothesis. Just as the ordinary hypothesis selects and limits the 'facts' to be examined, so does the theory select and limit the terms in which particular descriptions shall be made and thus the laws that can be framed by induction from the sum of particular descriptions.

In spite of this similarity between Glossematics and generative grammar with respect to general premises, there are still certain important differences, discussion of which might bring up some interesting problems. Before turning

[7] The term 'paradigmatic relations' has been replaced by later authors for Saussure's original term 'rapports associatifs' in order to avoid its psychological implications. Notice, however, that this reluctance against psychological terminology has nothing to do with antimentalism. Its rationale is only the precaution to avoid a meaningless and confusing psychologism which suggests pseudo-explanations. The awareness that linguistic facts are essentially mental phenomena underlies all Saussurian tradition.

[8] In fact, it is intended as a specification of the more general class of all semiotic systems and even other social phenomena. We will discuss some implications of this problem below. For the time being we may consider the glossematic theory as concerned with natural language only.

to these questions, we must consider briefly the basic notions of glossematic theory. We may do this by giving a rough and informal sketch.

First of all Saussure's notions of *signifiant* and *signifié* are generalized to expression plane and content plane, extending over signs of arbitrary length and complexity: phrases, clauses, sentences, and even paragraphs and whole texts. The two planes are connected by the sign function. Both consist of two strata, called form and substance, where the form is manifested by the substance. The substance is no longer viewed as an amorphous mass, as in Saussure's view, but as being organized according to independent principles. The primary concern of linguistics, however, is the structure of the form on both planes. In Hjelmslev (1954) the strata of substance are further subdivided into three possible 'niveaus': 'niveau d'appréciations collectives', 'niveau sociobiologique', 'niveau physique', the first of which is the linguistically most relevant one. There are some interesting problems relating to this subdivision. I will ignore it for the most part. Underlying each text is a system according to which the text can be analyzed into parts and functions connecting the parts. Since a text has a content side and an expression side, it is based on a content system and an expression system. The structure of a text is a hierarchy of chains, the structure of a system is a hierarchic arrangement of categories, to which the components of the text belong. A text can be extended without any upper limit. The relation between a (possibly infinite) text and the underlying system is similar, but not identical, to that between a language and its grammar in terms of the theory of generative grammar.[9]

The analysis of a given text is based on a system of functions. It might be illustrated by the following oversimplified example:

(1)   *A* The big green ghost entered slowly

        B The big green ghost   *C* entered slowly

        D The   *E* big green   *F* ghost   *G* entered   *H* slowly

                I big   *J* green   *K* enter   *L* ed   *M* slow   *N* ly

A is a member of the category of all sentences. It is analyzed into the two syntagmatic classes or chains *B* and *C* which in turn are members of the categories of, say, all noun phrases and predicates, respectively. *B* is then analyzed into *D*, *E*, and *F*, members of the categories of the determiners, modifiers, and nouns, respectively. Each step in this procedure analyzes a class into its component, the whole procedure is called a deduction. Such a deduction from the

---

[9] Thus Uldall (1957, p. 33) states: 'if your description of a text (i.e. the postulated underlying system M.B.) is correct, you should be able to deduce from it any number of new texts acceptable to native speakers'. The procedure of deducing a text from a given description has not been formalized, however, within glossematic theory. We will propose a formulation of the relevant concepts below.

chain A based on the underlying paradigmatic system, is in some respect equivalent to what is called in generative grammar a derivation of the string A based on a corresponding phrase structure grammar. Thus the deduction given in (1) can be represented in an obvious way by the following phrase marker, where the node labels correspond to the categories to which the strings A through N belong:

(2)

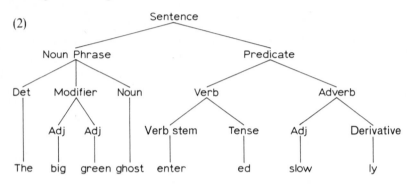

The components into which a chain is analyzed are related to each other by one of three general functions. A function is a connection between two functives. If both functives are necessary in order to establish a member of the category, then the function is called an interdependence. If one is necessary, and the other is optional, then the function is a determination. Two optional functives are contracted by a constellation. Thus B and C, for example, are functives of an interdependence. E and F, or G and H are functives of determinations. I and J are functives of a constellation. A necessary functive is called a constant, an optional functive is a variable. Hence B, C, F and G are constants, H, I and J are variables. Notice that our example (1) gives a deduction on the content plane whose elements are completely abstract entities and must not be confused with their orthographic representations. Even their linear ordering is merely an accidental property of the representation we have chosen, not a constitutive aspect of the content plane, which is organized by the indicated functions only. It is true that each chain or component of the content plane is interdependently connected to some component on the expression plane, which displays a linear ordering, but these components are organized according to their own hierarchy. The deduction of a chain on the expression plane leads to such categories as intonation clause, accent group, syllable, phoneme. It is a central claim of glossematics that the interdependent hierarchies on the content and expression plane are organized according to identical principles, but that they do not conform in detail. Thus whereas *entered* is analyzed on the content plane into the stem 'enter' and the past tense morpheme, these not being phonemic sequences, it would presumably be analyzed on the expression plane into the two syllables *en* and *terd*. This disconformity of content and expression brings up another central claim of glossematics. Because of the autonomous organization of both planes the deduction of a chain must not stop at entities whose content and expression conform, i.e. signs. It must rather proceed to smaller units, called figurae. Thus sign expressions are analyzed into syllables, phonemes and finally simultaneous parts of phonemes. These correspond by and large to distinctive features, though they have a completely different theoretical status.[10] Sign contents are analyzed into grammatical and lexical morphemes – taken in the sense of abstract content forms – and finally components corresponding roughly to syntactic and semantic features.[11] Hence the deduction in our example (1) would have to proceed by analyzing, e.g. *slow* into components such as 'rate of change' and 'low degree', etc. These components are part of the same syntagmatic hierarchy, corresponding somehow to the semantic and syntactic features assigned to syntactic formatives in syntactic deep structures of generative grammar. This then leads to the important claim that a language is not a system of signs, but a system of figurae, these being organized on two planes, where it is the figurae, not the signs which are interdependent. Thus, if we were to substitute, e.g. the content figura 'low degree' in our example by the figura 'high degree', this would entail a simultaneous substitution of *slowly* by *fast* on the expression plane. The ultimate functives emerging in a deduction are called glossemes. Thus glossematics is the algebraic theory of glosseme combinations.

[10] Whereas distinctive – or more precisely phonetic – features as used in generative grammar are based on the linguistic relevance of particular phonetic, i.e. articulatory and auditive, parameters, glossematic elements are motivated exclusively by a systematic partition of expression forms. This is a consequence of the fact that in glossematics the analysis of linguistic form is strictly separated from the analysis of substance. Whether and how the units of form are finally manifested by elements of substance that can be characterized universally, by a universal system of phonetic features for that matter, is a completely different problem. The problems resulting from this separation of form and substance have never been dealt with in any detail in glossematics. (But see footnote 11.) They pose enormous difficulties and are, to my mind, completely meaningless since they are motivated only by a priori assumptions. We return to this question below.

[11] These final content figurae are again purely formal units whose interpretation in terms of cognitive and perceptual parameters and properties is taken as a separate problem. It must be admitted, however, that in the case of syntactic and semantic features this situation is practically the same in generative grammar (and any other attempt): because of the complete lack of insight into a theory of universal semantics, semantic features are motivated exclusively by analyzing and comparing linguistic units. No principled relation to cognitive or perceptual properties has been established so far. (For some vague hints in the case of space perception see Bierwisch (1967).) An attempt in this direction on the basis of glossematic assumptions has been made by Hjelmslev (1935) with respect to case features. Though it raises a lot of interesting and still unexplored problems, it seems to me that the general approach is wrong for several reasons which cannot conveniently be discussed here.

The last point to be taken up here is the assumption that the underlying paradigmatic system is organized according to the same principles that we have illustrated so far. As already noted, each chain is a member of a particular category which is defined by the syntagmatic functions into which its members may enter. Thus a paradigmatic system is a set of categories determining the syntagmatic functions of their members. It is organized again by the three types of functions introduced above. This assumption may be illustrated by the following example. Past and present are interdependent members of the category tense of English since there are no verbs that do not combine with both past and present. Thus both are paradigmatic constants. Imperative and indicative, on the other hand, are connected by a paradigmatic determination, since there are verbs combining with the indicative but not with the imperative (roughly stative verbs like *know*, etc.). Hence imperative is a paradigmatic variable with respect to the indicative, which is paradigmatic constant. And finally particles like *on*, *up*, *out*, etc. are correlated by paradigmatic constellations, since there are always syntagmatic combinations where the one appears, while the other may not. They are thus paradigmatic variables with respect to each other.[12] Similar examples could be given for the expression plane. Finally the general relations between content and expression and form and substance are defined by means of the same primitive notions: The two planes of language are constants in an interdependence, viz. the sign function, form and substance are the constant and the variable in a determination, viz. the function of manifestation. It might be added that even such notions as con-

[12] A more detailed specification of the notions of paradigmatic interdependence, determination, and constellation, and of paradigmatic constant and variable, on which they are based, must rely on the concept of paradigm, from which the notion of category is derived in the following way: Two or more elements or chains form a paradigm if they can alternate in a given syntagmatic connexion. Two or more corresponding paradigms are then said to form a category just as two or more corresponding chains form a paradigm. Two paradigms or chains correspond, if they are defined on the same level of the syntagmatic hierarchy, and have certain components in common. (I need not give here a precise definition of correspondence.) Now a syntagmatic constant is an element which appears in all corresponding chains of a paradigm, a variable is an element which does not. A paradigmatic constant is an element which appears in all corresponding paradigms of a category, a paradigmatic variable is an element which does not. Thus syntagmatic functions are defined via sets of chains and specify relations within these chains. Paradigmatic functions are defined via sets of paradigmatically arranged sets of chains and specify relations within these sets of chains. For details see Uldall (1957). On this basis glossematic theory arrives also at a precise, formal definition of the notion of syntagmatic and paradigmatic relations, the former being both-and functions, the latter either-or functions. Notice, by the way, that two or more categories can be component of a category. Thus the paradigmatic system consists of hierarchies of categories, just as a syntagmatic system consists of hierarchies of chains. For example, the category of all the phonemes of a given language may consist of the two categories of vowels and consonants. The latter in turn may consist of the categories of those that can form a syllable nucleus (roughly liquids) and those that cannot, etc. A hierarchy of categories can again be represented by a labelled tree, corresponding, e.g. to the feature-trees sometimes used in generative grammar to present feature hierarchies.

notative, denotative, and metalanguage are explained in terms of the same underlying concepts. I cannot go into these problems here. For details see Hjelmslev (1953, Chapter 22).

The essential point of glossematic theory can now be summarized as the assumption that all the concepts of the fairly complex algebraic system which is set up to account for the properties of the class of all semiotic systems are based on a small set of primitive terms, viz. class and component, function, necessary and not necessary functive, both-and and either-or function, and certain empirical assumptions, in particular that there are two non-conforming hierarchies, viz. the content and the expression plane, and that each plane consists in turn of two non-conforming hierarchies, viz. form and substance. We might now look at the claims made by this system of formal universals from the point of view of generative grammar.

We notice first of all, that the formal structure of each stratum provided in glossematics is equivalent to a phrase structure grammar and the set of derivations specified by it.[13] It is, more precisely, equivalent to a context sensitive grammar, for the following reason. The syntagmatic functions into which a functive may enter, are either homosyntagmatic or heterosyntagmatic. The former contracts two components of the same chain, the latter contracts a component of one chain to a component of another chain within the same text. Thus there is, e.g. a heterosyntagmatic determination between person and number of the subject noun phrase and person and number of the verb phrase. A case in point on the expression plane is the subordination of secondary to main stress. Heterosyntagmatic determinations and interdependencies must be accounted for by context sensitive rules. A formal proof of the asserted (strong) equivalence between glossematic algebras and a context sensitive phrase structure grammars cannot be given here since it would require too much detail. The concepts on which it could be based are as follows.

P is a paradigmatic system with $\mathbf{C} = \{A_1, \ldots, A_n\}$ as its categories defined by syntagmatic functions and $\mathbf{G} = \{a_1, \ldots, a_m\}$ as its primitive terms, i.e. glossemes.

---

[13] That this structure characterizes not only the formal strata of the content and the expression plane, but also the corresponding strata of substance follows from the glossematic definitions. What such a structure would be in the case of particular phonetic or semantic facts must be left open. There are no glossematic studies showing any details or even examples with respect to this problem. The focus of glossematic investigations has always been on the formal strata, and even there only selected problems have been dealt with. In fact, the lack of any coherent description of at least a fraction of a given language based on and illustrating the glossematic theory is certainly a major flaw in the whole development. Togeby (1951) gives a description of French that is certainly in the spirit of the glossematic theory, but it is by no means a rigorous application of the theory. – For the formal theory of phrase structure grammars, see, e.g. Chomsky (1963).

X is the set of all finite strings over **G**.

If $x = wyz$ for $x \in \mathbf{X}$, then y is a member of $A \in \mathbf{C}$ in x if y exhibits all and only the syntagmatic functions to w and z by which A is defined. (w and z might be empty.) A is a categorial representation of y (in x).

y can be directly deduced from x, symbolically $x \Rightarrow y$, if k is the smallest number such that:

(i) $x = vzw$ and $y = vz_1 \ldots z_k w$ and $z = z_1 \ldots z_k$;

(ii) $z, z_1, \ldots, z_k$ are members of $A, B_1, \ldots, B_k \in \mathbf{C}$ in x respectively.

In this case $x \Rightarrow y$ directly deduces the categorial representation $B_1 \ldots B_k$ for z in x.

y can be deduced from x, symbolically $x \overset{*}{\Rightarrow} y$, if $x = x_1$ and $y = x_n$ and for $1 \leqslant i < n$ holds $x_i \Rightarrow x_{i+1}$.

The set of all categorial representations deduced by $x \overset{*}{\Rightarrow} y$ is called a categorial system of x with respect to y and **C**.

$x \overset{*}{\Rightarrow} y$ is a complete A-deduction of x, iff

(i) x is a member of A;

(ii) $y = y_1 \ldots y_r$ and for no y_i $(1 \leqslant i \leqslant r)$ there is a z such that $y_i \overset{*}{\Rightarrow} z$, i.e. the y_i are either glossemes or strings of glossemes that have no deduced categorial representation with respect to **C**.

The categorial system deduced by a complete A-deduction of x is the complete categorial system $CS(x)$ of x. $CS(x)$ can obviously be represented as a labelled tree with A as its root.

Each direct deduction furthermore imposes a set of syntagmatic functions on the strings deduced by virtue of the functions that define the categories which enter the categorial representation. Let $FS(x)$ be the set of all functions imposed on x by its complete A-deduction.

We might say now that a paradigmatic system **P** admits a chain x over **G** and assigns to x a $CS(x)$ and an $FS(x)$, if there are substrings $x_1 \ldots x_r$, such that $x \overset{*}{\Rightarrow} x_1 \ldots x_r$ is a complete A-deduction of x. $L(\mathbf{P})$ is the set of all x admitted by **P**.[14]

Given now the notion of a phrase structure grammar G generating a string x with the structural description D, where $L(G)$ is the set of all x generated by G. These notions are readily defined in the theory of phrase structure gram-

---

[14] It is claimed in glossematic theory that each deduction starts with a whole text. This would mean that **C** must contain a designated category 'Text' and that A would be this designated category. $L(\mathbf{P})$ would be thus the set of all texts admitted by **P**. In generative grammar on the other hand, the designated initial category is 'Sentence', and $L(G)$ for a given grammar G is the set of generated sentences. For the time being I am not concerned with this distinction. The defined notions $L(\mathbf{P})$ and $L(G)$ correspond sufficiently, even if there were no designated initial category at all. $L(\mathbf{P})$ would then simply contain also the set of all constituents. It might be noted, by the way, that in spite of its theoretical claim, glossematics has scarcely revealed empirical facts bearing on the preference of texts instead of sentences as the scope of linguistic analysis.

mars. Then the equivalence in question can be expressed by the following theorem:

THEOREM: A context sensitive phrase structure grammar G generates a string x over the terminal vocabulary $\mathbf{G}$ with the structural description D if and only if there is a paradigmatic system $\mathbf{P}$ which assigns to x a $CS(x)$ and an $FS(x)$, such that D and $CS(x)$ correspond to each other in an obvious way, and $L(\mathbf{P}) = L(G)$.

We have sketched the framework within which this theorem might be proved. The crucial point of such a proof is to reconstruct in terms of phrase structure grammars the syntagmatic and paradigmatic functions for an arbitrary system $\mathbf{P}$ and the restrictions that these functions impose on the strings and structural descriptions admitted by $\mathbf{P}$.[15] Notice that the existence of heterosyntagmatic determinations and interdependencies require G to contain context sensitive rules. Without these functions the above theorem could be strengthened to context free grammars.

Given the equivalence discussed so far, we can conclude that the theory of glossematics makes empirically inadequate claims with respect to the formal properties of natural languages: it has been demonstrated several times within the literature of generative grammar, most extensively in Postal (1964), that the theory of phrase structure grammar cannot account for the principles according to which the syntactic structure of natural languages is organized. Hence, whatever the general premises and the additional claims of the theory might be, it is inadequate insofar as its basic assumptions are bound to the limitations of (context sensitive) phrase structure grammars.

The second point to be noted with respect to the glossematic theory is its exclusive concern with problems of representations of linguistic structures and the complete absence of the notion of grammatical rules by means of which these representations can be constructed. This flaw, which has far-reaching consequences, is characteristic not only of the theory of glossematics, but of all other trends of structural linguistics in Europe, and also in the United States before the appearance of generative grammar. Just like glossematics, all these schools are concerned with the question of how the

---

[15] The details of this reconstruction are rather clumsy. I can give here only a hint of the lines along which it can be done. Assume that all chains x_i that are members of category B are either of the form $y_{i_1} y_{i_2}$ or simply y_{i_1} with y_{i_1} and y_{i_2} being members of C_1 and C_2, respectively. In this case each chain y_{i_2} is a syntagmatic variable with respect to x_i and hence C_2 a variable category defined by syntagmatic determination. This situation is to be reconstructed within a phrase structure grammar by including the two rules $B \rightarrow C_1 C_2$ and $B \rightarrow C_1$ or simply the rule schema $B \rightarrow C_1$ (C_2), where finally C_1 and C_2 dominate the strings y_{i_1} and y_{i_2}, respectively. In this sense each determination and interdependence between either categories, i.e. sets of strings, or particular terminal strings of the paradigmatic system $\mathbf{P}$ must be rendered by appropriate sets of rules of the equivalent grammar G.

presumed structure of a given utterance might be represented, what types of elements and classes may appear in such representations, and how the inventories of these elements and classes can be represented. This statement might be surprising in view of the fact that I have sketched a fairly plausible way to reconstruct a glossematic algebra in terms of a context sensitive grammar and have asserted, moreover, the strong equivalence of both. And how the rules of a grammar are formulated is, of course, not an essential point, they may very well be given in the form of a set of interrelated categories. But notice that we have modified somewhat the way in which a glossematic algebra is set into operation. The notion of deduction, on which our reconstruction is based, is originally understood as an operation which assigns a structural representation to a given chain on the basis of certain general principles (which are explicitly formulated in glossematic theory[16]), the general form of possible descriptions and the system of categories eventually established in former deductions. This means that the deduction of any new chain may possibly lead to a change in the system of categories established so far, if the new chain must be considered as well-formed for empirical reasons, but cannot be accounted for by the already given categories. Thus the glossematic concept of deduction works in two ways: looking 'backward', on the set of chains already analyzed and those exhibiting the same structure (and this might very well be an infinite set), it corresponds to the notion of generating sentences in terms of generative grammar; looking 'forward' to utterances structurally different from those already encountered, it is a formalization of the process of grammar construction incorporating the claim that the resulting system is always a constituent structure grammar.[17]

[16] These are the principles of analysis, reduction, economy, simplicity, generalization, and exhaustive description. We need not discuss them here in detail, though they contain some interesting general assumptions. Some of them will be taken up below.

[17] This twofold character of the concept of deduction implies, incidentally, the interesting claim that the two psychologically different operations of sentence recognition by the hearer and of language learning are essentially of the same character with the only difference that the former uses those entities and categories that have been already established and used in former processes. In other words, glossematic theory claims that there is no principle difference between models for language users and language acquisition, and moreover, that language use is intimately related to language learning. Viewed in this way, the glossematic concept of deduction implies the weighty assumption that there is, at least with respect to semiotic systems, no basic formal distinction between rule governed and rule changing behavior, a distinction whose importance has been brought to attention by the theory of generative grammar. Though such questions have not been considered explicitly in glossematic writings, this claim deserves some attention, since it is not bound to particular assumptions with respect to the type of grammars involved, and since it is by no means an a priori truth that language use and language acquisition are based on formally different mechanisms. Thus from glossematic theory it would follow, for instance, that language use is governed by the same principles – e.g. simplicity, reduction, generalization – as language acquisition, though these principles would mostly operate without any particular effect in language use. Considerations of this type would have some bearing on

We have picked up the first aspect of the concept of deduction for the above comparison of phrase structure grammars and glossematic systems. This possible interpretation and the fact that glossematic descriptions are meant to account for infinite sets of sentences must not obscure its exclusive interest in representing structures and registrating elements, categories, and functions. The lack of an understanding of the essential role of grammatical rules becomes more obvious if we consider not the formal organization of separate strata, as we have done so far, but the interrelation of several strata.

In order to characterize the structure of an infinite set of utterances (or texts), it is of course not sufficient to specify the representations on the different levels, or strata, but it is also necessary to specify their mapping on each other. No such attempt has ever been made within the glossematic framework.[18] This is, to my mind, a direct consequence of the assumption that the deductive description of a text is nothing but a registration of the elements and functions involved: though it is quite possible to list all the components of the four strata of a given utterance and even the interdependence between components of the content form and the expression form, there is no reasonable way within the glossematic framework to specify constructively these interdependencies for an infinite set of sentences or texts. Certainly the glossematic theory implies a way in which this specification would have to be given. But it leads simply to absurdity.[19] Though glossematic theory displays a reasonable understanding

---

still open questions concerning the nature of the evaluation procedure as conceived in generative grammar, in particular on the claim, challenged in McCawley (1968a), that the postulation of grammars on the basis of collected data and the evaluation of the grammars are separate, successive operations. These problems do not depend on the particular criterion on which the evaluation is based. Notice, incidentally, that the aspect of grammar construction yields a parallel between glossematic deduction and the concept of discovery procedures mentioned in Section II. There is, however, an important difference. Whereas discovery procedures are based on inductive generalization, glossematic deduction is always based on the process of justifying given hypotheses, or functional categories for that matter.

[18] Not even for fragmentary descriptions of particular languages. Where problems of this type have been taken up, e.g. in Bech (1955), considerable changes to the theory have been necessary. Thus Bech introduces certain notions which come near to the concept of transformational rules, and which exceed on principle the power of glossematic algebra.

[19] This way is roughly as follows. The four strata of a given text are considered separate syntagmatic hierarchies, related by the sign function and the function of manifestation, respectively. They are deduced in the first step of the deduction of a given text and must be considered as simultaneous, syntagmatically related hierarchies of chains. Hence the topmost categories of a paradigmatic system are 'Text', 'Text-Content', 'Text-Expression', 'Text-Content-Form', 'Text-Content-Substance', 'Text-Expression-Form', 'Text-Expression-Substance'. A generative grammar would have to reconstruct these assumptions by initial rules roughly like this: Text → TC TE, TC → TCF TCS_i, TE → TEF TES_i, where TCS_i and TES_i are variables over the different possible substances (phonetic, graphic etc.). The further deductions would then be reconstructed in terms of largely context sensitive rules, where the context for the expansion of a given syntactic category is some component of the expression plane, etc. In other words, the expression form

of the abstract character of syntactic and phonemic structures, it is not able to account in a natural way for the systematic interrelation of these structures and for their phonetic and semantic interpretation. This fact results directly from the lack of grammatical rules in general and of transformational rules in particular, because only transformational rules are capable of relating hierarchies to hierarchies in a systematic way.

The third point to be taken up here is the simplicity criterion proposed in glossematic theory. The 'principle of simplicity', which controls the construction of linguistic descriptions, reads as follows:

of two self-consistent and exhaustive descriptions the one that gives the simpler result is preferred. Of two self-consistent and exhaustive descriptions giving equally simple results the one that requires the simpler procedure is preferred (Uldall (1957, p. 25)).

Comments on this principle indicate that by the description giving the simpler result, or, in short, the simpler description, the one is meant which requires the smaller number of unanalyzable, primitive terms. This simplicity criterion is again not a feature peculiar to glossematics, but is shared, at least implicitly, by all schools of structural linguistics. It results from the fact that the main concern of linguistic theory has been considered to provide a formal system for representing the structure of arbitrary utterances and for specifying the items and categories involved. Given this goal, it seems natural to prefer a description which requires, e.g. a smaller number of phonemes, or even distinctive features, than another one. We may call this the principle of minimal inventories. Suggestive as it may be at first sight, it can easily be seen that it leads to absurd results if it is not controlled by some additional considerations: each phonemic system for example can be represented by a set of combinations of only two items (as is done roughly in morse code). Therefore the principle of minimal inventories is in general combined implicitly with what could be called the principle of natural (or simple) interpretation. Thus, e.g. the set of distinctive features would not be reduced if the resulting elements could not be assigned to a natural phonetic interpretation. Even glossematic description must rely tacitly on such considerations. But even with this additional condition the principle of minimal inventories is completely arbitrary and not motivated by any empirical considerations. It could easily

---

must be considered as the contextual condition under which particular categories or elements of the content form can be deduced, and vice versa. (Among these rules there would be many of the form $N \rightarrow$ 'man'/__man, representing roughly the dictionary.) This reconstruction of glossematic assumptions reveals the implicit claim that the phonemic and phonetic form of a given sentence is a context condition of its syntactic and semantic structure, and vice versa. I do not know whether any meaning can be given to this claim. In any case, even if a description of this type were formally possible (I am not sure whether there are unsurmountable obstacles), it seems to be obvious that it leads to absurd artificialities and worthless descriptions.

be shown that strict application of the principle of minimal inventories would force one to incorporate in the description of a language certain important facts in an otherwise unmotivated manner.[20] It is in fact possible to think of many different principles for evaluating given descriptions. One might prefer, e.g. the description that assigns to the generated or admitted sentences structural descriptions with the smallest degree of complexity in some definable sense of this term (call this the principle of minimal complexity); or the description that requires the smallest number of rule applications for the mapping of one level on the adjacent level (call this the principle of simplest mapping, a principle, by the way, that is not applicable in glossematics for the reasons discussed above), and many others. None of these criteria is a priori valid or invalid. The choice depends on theoretical and empirical considerations. I know of no convincing arguments in favour of the principle of minimal inventories. I am sure, moreover, that it must definitely be rejected for strong empirical reasons. Hence the glossematic principle of simplicity is either wrong or at least arbitrary as far as it depends on the principle of minimal inventories. And this is in fact its primary criterion. It is interesting, however, that the glossematic theory realizes the necessity of a further criterion because there may be two or more descriptions equally simple in terms of the minimal inventory criterion. This second criterion refers to the simpler procedure. Procedure is a well defined technical term in the glossematic theory, the most important being that of deduction as discussed above. Hence the simplest procedure is that which requires the smallest possible number of different direct deductions. Thus the glossematic principle of simplicity relies – given the minimal inventories – in the second instance on some aspect of simplicity of grammars or rule systems.[21] It must be noted, however, that this second criterion has no other motivation than the first one has: it is derived from methodological considerations of some sort, not justified empirically.

The last claim of glossematics with respect to formal universals that I will

---

[20] Assume, for instance, that the basic phoneme categories of a given language can be characterized either by the three features [consonantal], [vocalic], and [sonorant] or by the two features [consonantal] and [vocalic]. The principle of minimal inventories would force us to choose the second solution. But there may be some important regularities that could easily be formulated by referring to the feature [sonorant], whereas their description without it would lead to much more complicated statements, involving several feature combinations. Though such a situation could probably not arise in glossematic description for reasons not relevant here, it shows sufficiently clearly that there is no a priori justification for the minimal inventory principle over several other criteria.

[21] What is involved here is, more precisely, that aspect of grammars (or categorial systems, for that matter) that specifies the particular hierarchical structures imposed on generated or admitted strings. It is hence closely connected to what has tentatively been called above the principle of minimal complexity. There is still another aspect of the glossematic simplicity principle that will shortly be taken up in section IV below.

briefly discuss is the number of linguistic levels and their motivation. We have already noted that there are four strata all of which display the same type of organization for which we have asserted equivalence to context sensitive phrase structure grammars. The existence of four particularly interrelated levels is not assumed a priori, but based on very general empirical considerations. Logically there could exist systems with only two or three separate levels.[22] The empirical considerations are of the following kind. Natural languages show an obvious disconformity with respect to their extreme aspects, phonetic and semantic structure. The functives deduced in their analysis have no one-to-one correspondence. Hence two planes must be set up. Within each plane disconformity between two aspects must be realized. Hence the strata of form and substance are postulated. These very gross considerations rely on the a priori principle that it is a necessary and sufficient condition for establishing a new stratum if non conforming hierarchies of components must be deduced from a given chain. This kind of motivation for different levels is obviously completely different from that characteristic in generative grammar where the justification of a linguistic level is based on considerations of roughly the following type. What types of independent representations are necessary and sufficient in order to account for the regularities observed in given languages in terms of most general sets of rules operating on the postulated representations? Thus types of ambiguity, alternations such as *Vater/ Väter, Muter/Mütter*, etc. complicated correspondences such as *Hans ist leicht zu verstehen* vs *Hans ist bereit zu verstehen* may be crucial instances for justification. (For detailed discussion see, e.g. Chomsky (1964).) One of the main sources of this widely differing attitude towards justification of postulated levels is the already mentioned lack of the notion of grammatical rules and constructive characterization of sentences on the part of glossematics. Because of this difference it would be extremely difficult and to a certain extent artificial to compare the levels postulated in generative grammar and in glossematics any further. Despite some superficial similarities, their status within the theory as well as the facts represented on them are too different for a revealing comparison.[23] It might be noted, by the way, that the assumption of four strata

---

[22] The glossematic theory assumes in fact that there are such systems, but that these are not languages. Traffic lights form a simple example of a system that consists of only one stratum of form to which simultaneously a content and an expression substance is related. Systems with no separation of content form and expression form are called symbolic systems, in those cases where they have both an expression and a content substance. Games, on the other hand, comprise in general only two strata, a form and a substance. They are thus strictly monoplanar. Systems of only one stratum are not mentioned at all. They are presumably considered as phenomena of a different type, not belonging to the domain of social and behavioral sciences.

[23] There is on the other hand, another great difference between the glossematic attitude and that of American structural linguistics. Since in the Bloomfield–Harris tradition linguistic levels are

implies a fairly strong claim with respect to the theory of natural language. It presupposes that every human being is able to organize linguistic experience according to four non conforming levels which form, in turn, two interdependent planes with a constant form and a variable substance on each plane. It is an interesting question whether and how certain aspects of this claim are to be reconstructed within the theory of generative grammar.

IV

The previous inspection of particular glossematic claims with respect to formal universals as opposed to those of generative grammar has already shown that they are determined to a large extent by general premises and assumptions. I will return now to some problems connected to these general assumptions.

In an early state of development of his theory, Hjelmslev (1929) considered linguistics explicitly as a particular branch of (cognitive) psychology which has to specify not only the structure of particular given languages underlying the concrete speech behavior, but also the general principles of these structures. He claimed that this specification must be done in a purely immanent fashion, relying only on the internal structure of the considered phenomena. The goal aimed at was a sufficient rich system of formal and substantive universals,[24] i.e. a universal grammar in the sense sketched above. (The tradition meant is explicitly mentioned in the title *Principles de Grammaire Générale*.) Later on the goal was broadened and thus changed in a certain sense. Both Hjelmslev (1953) and Uldall (1957) consider the algebra of functions that they propose as a very general and uniform framework for the

---

the product of inductive generalization – from phone to phoneme, from phoneme sequence to morpheme, etc. – they are supposed to meet such conditions as linear correspondence, phonetic similarity, etc. No such conditions obtain for the deductively established levels in glossematics. Quite to the contrary, Hjelmslev (1953, p. 166) gives the following example from the expression plane: 'In French the formal segment *n* has a variant which is realized on the level of substance as nasality of the preceding segment, if this is a vowel. Thus the sequence *bon* on the level of expression form corresponds to the sequence *bõ* on the expression substance'. This is in an obvious conflict with the conditions on taxonomic phonemics, but rather similar to an analysis in terms of a systematic phonemic and a systematic phonetic level as proposed in generative grammar.

[24] The fact that we have been concerned here only with formal universals, which are of course more basic and more relevant for a comparison of the type undertaken here, must not obscure the interest of glossematics in problems of substantive universals. There is, in fact, a large body of literature on problems of this type, concentrating mostly on morphological categories such as case, number, gender, etc. Thus Hjelmslev (1935) proposes a very elaborate theory of possible case systems and their semantic interpretation. It would be an interesting study in itself to reconsider proposals made in these studies in the light of the theory of syntactic features developed in generative grammar.

description of human (and probably even animal) behavior, social processes, phenomena of history, art, etc. Everything which can be considered as a process based on an underlying system of recurrent components organized in functional categories is taken as an object that can be described in terms of a glossematic algebra. In this respect glossematics is universal in a completely different sense than a theory of universal grammar can ever be. Here the question arises whether such a universality does not reduce the theory to emptiness, in much the same way as any conception based on segmentation and classification only. In fact, how worthwhile is a theory which comprises economics as well as bird song, natural language as well as chess, court ceremonies and eating behavior? One might argue that such a general system specifies the common traits of all systems of behavior and history, just as universal grammar specifies the common features of all natural languages. But notice that there is an important difference here. Whereas universal grammar must be considered as a serious hypothesis about particular facts, viz. the human capacity to learn and use language, a generalization about all types of behavior and history expresses merely a methodological attitude. This might be of some interest, insofar as it provides a uniform frame of reference for social sciences in the broadest sense.[25] But one has to be careful not to exaggerate the relevance of such general systems (as is obviously the case in the present day structuralist movement, in particular, in France), since they do not incorporate, by definition, any empirical insights besides the assumption that there is a general analyzability for a large class of phenomena.

There is, however, a less trivial aspect in the glossematic conception. Human languages are not only subsumed under the class of all semiotic and even non-semiotic systems, they are also distinguished from non-languages by specific properties. They belong, first of all, to the class of systems exhibiting two planes with a diverging form, which is called the class of semiotic systems. By this property natural languages are distinguished not only from simple systems such as traffic lights, but also from probably all systems of animal communication, since these are not organized on two nonconforming levels.[26] Notice that as a direct consequence of their biplanar character semiotic

---

[25] The glossematic theory, as already noted, makes the stronger claim that all phenomena included are ultimately based on systems equivalent to context restricted grammars. This is, however, an a priori claim which ignores, moreover, possible differences: there are certainly not only systems requiring more powerful systems – such as natural languages – but also those which can be accounted for in terms of weaker ones such as context free grammars or finite automata. Such differences might help to characterize at least partially the specific properties of the phenomena involved.

[26] Thus Chomsky (1968, p. 61) assumes that 'Every animal communication system that is known (if we disregard some science fiction about dolphins) uses one of two basic principles: Either it consists of a fixed, finite number of signals, each associated with a specific range of behavior or

systems are systems of figurae. Hence the essential difference between semiotic and other systems is not, that semiotic systems are capable of forming indefinitely many new combinations, while other systems are not. (There may be at the one hand, semiotic systems with only a finite number of possible chains, and on the other hand symbolic or other nonsemiotic systems with indefinitely many possible chains or combinations.) The difference is rather the possibility of forming biplanar signs from monoplanar figurae.

Secondly, human languages are distinguished from other semiotic systems by the fact that their content form can be manifested by all purports, i.e. all possible content substances. In other words, a language is a semiotic system which is able to express everything that can be expressed at all. This characterization is given as a formal definition. Glossematic theory realizes, however, that it is a task of primary importance not only to define this property but to explain it in terms of the specific properties which account for it. In this connection, Hjelmslev (1953, p. 109) writes:

In practice, a language is a semiotic into which all other semiotics may be translated – both all other languages, and all other conceivable semiotic structures. This translatability rests on the fact that languages, and they alone, are in a position to form any purport whatsoever; in a language, and only in a language, we can 'work over the inexpressible until it is expressed' (Kierkegaard). It is this quality that makes a language usable as a language, capable of giving satisfaction in any situation. There is no doubt that it rests on a structural peculiarity, on which we might be able to cast better light if we knew more about the specific structure of nonlinguistic semiotics. It is an all but obvious conclusion that the basis lies in the unlimited possibility of forming signs and the very free rules for forming units of great extension (sentences and the like) which are true of any language . . . in general, a language is independent of any specific purpose.

There is little doubt that Hjelmslev here comes to grips with one of the central topics of what Chomsky has called the tradition of Cartesian Linguistics. Hjelmslev's particular treatment of this topic poses two interesting problems.

The first is that of the specific property itself that distinguishes human language from all other systems. Chomsky (1966) discusses this very problem in terms of the 'creative aspect of language use'. The crucial fact about language is then that it provides the means for this creative use. The aspect of creativity

---

emotional state, as illustrated in the extensive primate studies that have been carried out by Japanese scientists for the past several years; or it makes use of a fixed, finite number of linguistic dimensions, each of which is associated with a particular nonlinguistic dimension in such a way that the selection of a point along the linguistic dimension determines and signals a certain point along the associated nonlinguistic dimension'. 'A communication system of the second type has an indefinitely large number of potential signals, as does human language. The mechanism and principle, however, are entirely different from those employed by human language to express indefinitely many new thoughts, intentions, feelings, and so on'. Obviously, both types of animal communication discussed by Chomsky show typical monoplanar organization and are therefore symbolic systems in the sense mentioned in footnote 22. The difference in mechanism and principle is then, at least partially, that between mono- and bi-planar organization.

is in turn an outcome of the following fact:

in its normal use, human language is free from stimulus control and does not serve a merely communicative function, but is rather an instrument for the free expression of thought and for
appropriate response to new situations (Chomsky, 1966, p. 13).

I have arbitrarily selected one of several formulations that Chomsky gives for
the interrelatedness of the creative aspect of language, its freedom of stimulus
control, and appropriateness to arbitrary situations. (See also note 26.) It
seems to me that the crucial point is the appropriateness to new situations.
The possibility of freedom of stimulus control is certainly necessary for language use, but it obviously holds for other types of human behavior as well.
Painting, singing, or simply the decision whether I go to bed now or later, are
possibly equally free of stimulus control. In this respect, language use is only
one, perhaps the most important type of human activity. (And it is not a priori
clear whether in fact all animal behavior is stimulus bound in a sufficiently
precise sense.) Creativity, on the one hand, can mean that a system with an
indefinite number of constructible entities is involved, and then it reduces to
the fact that this system shows some type of recursiveness. This purely formal
explication of creativity again would apply to many types of behavior that are
not bound to language. Many kinds of games, for example, would show this
type of creativity. Even certain types of bird songs may turn out to be creative
in this sense, viz. bound to finiteness just as language is, only by real time, not
by the underlying system of rules. Therefore the creativity of language that
Chomsky has in mind must be something else, and this, most reasonably, is its
appropriateness to any new situation, the possibility 'to express indefinitely
many new thoughts, intentions, feelings, and so on'. Creativity, and hence
appropriateness, in this sense, however, is precisely equivalent to Hjelmslev's
notion of translatability, or possible manifestation of all purports. This can
easily be seen from the following consideration. Assume that appropriateness
and translatability are not equivalent. Then there must be two languages A
and B such that at least one sentence S of A cannot be translated into a sentence (or a sequence of sentences) of B. But now there must be at least one
situation such that just S is appropriate to it (in a sense which I do not bother
to make precise here). This would mean that B fails not only as to the condition of translatability, but also that of appropriateness. This is contrary to
our assumption. Hence appropriateness implies translatability. The inverse
implication follows from the assumption that for any possible situation whatsoever there is at least one language containing at least one sentence S
appropriate to it. Thus Hjelmslev and Chomsky do not only deal with the
same problem, they make also precisely the same claim, viz. that the essential
property of human language is its possibility to express everything that can

be expressed at all, i.e. that they are in a certain sense complete.[27] It goes without saying that translatability cannot mean that any two languages can express the same things in the same way, i.e. by similar expressions. It might very well be the case that a rather clumsy sequence of sentences in a language B is required to translate a fairly simple sentence of a language A. It is worth noticing, however, that complete translatability implies that the principle of linguistic relativity, i.e. the Whorf-Weisgerber Hypothesis cannot be maintained in its strict sense.

The second problem to be discussed is the way of explication for the property just stated. Chomsky insists on the fact that creativity cannot be accounted for by vague hints at such principles as analogy, grammatical patterns, dispositions, etc., but that an explicit statement of the particular type of structure responsible for the characteristic possibilities of human language must be attempted. A full statement of this type of structure is the universal grammar discussed above. Hjelmslev is looking for an explanation in much the same spirit, if he refers to a structural peculiarity underlying the capability of giving satisfaction in any situation. And he is quite clear in stating the assumption that this peculiarity rests on the particular combinatorial structure of language. He adds, however, a further assumption, viz. that a better knowledge of nonlinguistic semiotics might reveal also insights into the essentials of language. This leads to the non-trivial aspect of the general glossematic conception that I had in mind above. The set of all (possible) languages, delimited by the particular set of linguistic universals and structured moreover by internal correlations such as genetic or typological relatedness, is placed within a hierarchy of semiotic and nonsemiotic systems, organized according to certain general principles, but with essentially different types of complexity. These types of complexity must be formally explained, e.g. in terms of number of levels and types of relations between them. Thus while Chomsky (1968, p. 60) is undoubtedly right when he says that it is of little interest to study language on a level of abstraction that comprises, e.g. systems of animal communication as well, Hjelmslev would argue that a systematic comparison of language with both less and more complex systems (the latter being, e.g. science or poetry) might reveal peculiarities even of language structure. And a systematic study of this type presupposes a certain uniform frame of reference. The difference in attitude is, of course, only one of emphasis, not of principle, if we are careful with respect to the status of such a general framework of comparison. The interesting point at issue, however, is the following. Hjelmslev

---

[27] Katz (personal communication) has observed independently the essential importance of translatability or 'completeness' for which he proposes the term 'effability'. He is not responsible, of course, for the present line of reasoning.

would agree with Chomsky presumably in that the class of natural languages is specified precisely by the set of linguistic universals, both formal and substantive. Hence we are interested in making this set of universals as specific as possible with respect to the collected data. But we are certainly interested also in the question as to what exactly the essential properties explaining the decisive principle of complete translatability are. Thus whereas, e.g. the system of phonetic features is without any doubt an integrated part of the system of linguistic universals, we would certainly not assume that its particular content is decisive for translatability, whereas the principle of its organization might be. The situation may be different with respect to the system of universal semantic components: it could be that not only the principle of its organization, but also its particular content is a necessary condition for translatability. It is premature to go any further here into speculations as to what the essential properties are. I would merely point out that even in this respect the theory of generative grammar is able to formulate more revealing hypotheses than glossematic theory, because of the conception of grammars as systems of rules. In fact, the study of the generative capacity of different systems of rules as exemplified, e.g. in Chomsky (1963) is a first step towards a systematic comparison of the type discussed here, at least with respect to one parameter.

The last point I would like to take up is an aspect of justification of the general theory. Remember first of all that the description of particular facts, say of a given language, can be deduced from – or is determined by – the general theory in the following way: the theory provides a scheme of levels, categories, functions, etc. which the description must fit, and an evaluation measure which selects one particular description, if several possibilities are compatible with the same data. In this respect the role of the general theory in glossematics is completely identical to that assumed in the theory of generative grammar, described, e.g. in Chomsky (1957, pp. 49–56). The selected description has the status of an elaborated hypothesis whose validity is tested by the correctness of the predictions derived from it. Remember furthermore that the general theory is itself an elaborated empirical hypothesis, concerning the general properties of all sets of facts, say all languages, to be accounted for. Its validity is tested by the validity of the particular descriptions derived from it. Hence the evaluation criterion, as discussed above, is an integrated part of the general theory, subject to empirical validation. Now it is a singular feature about glossematics that the general theory is assumed to be evaluated by the same principle of simplicity that we have discussed above with respect to evaluation of particular descriptions. The argument by Uldall (1957, p. 23) goes as follows:

Now it will always be possible to simplify any algebra at the expense of its applicability, and from any algebra thus reduced a limited number of particular descriptions can be deduced which are individually simpler than the corresponding particular descriptions deducible from the more general algebra. In other words, any one material, e.g. any one language, can be described in a very simple way if the descriptive apparatus, the algebra, is adapted to that purpose alone; if it is desired, on the other hand, to give uniform descriptions of more than one material, e.g. of more than one language, then the descriptive apparatus, and hence any particular description, is likely to be less simple. The reason is obvious: particular descriptions differ as to degree of complexity, and the descriptive apparatus must be equipped to deal with the highest degree of complexity that can be foreseen to come within its scope.

The stipulated generality of the descriptive framework is, of course, a necessary condition imposed on the general theory – given the reservations discussed above. Insofar as it relies on simplicity, however, it presupposes an a priori definition of these notions, which deprives them of all empirical content. (Notice that there is no absolute and a priori justification for any one notion of simplicity, not even with respect to such non-empirical things as mathematical theories or axiom systems for logic.) This is the deeper reason for the arbitrary character of the simplicity principle that we have noted above.

In generative grammar the notion of simplicity has a much more specific sense. This is gained, however, at the price of another intuitive and a priori notion, viz. that of revealing insight, or relevant generalization. Notice, that the theory of generative grammar is meant to construct the set of linguistic universals and the corresponding evaluation procedure in such a way that they jointly assign a higher value to that description which embodies the more general statements about the same data. In other words, the descriptive framework must be designed in such a way that the more revealing or more general description is also the simpler one, where simplicity is completely dependent on the proposed descriptive framework. But now the notion of simplicity is based on that of relevant generalization. I do not consider this to be a theoretical flaw, although there may be conflicting cases where it is by no means obvious which generalization is the more important. The glossematic theory, like every other explicit linguistic theory which I know, is free of this heuristic problem. But only because it has relegated the involved questions from any further consideration by subscribing to the arbitrary principle of simplicity quoted above. Thus, far from being a theoretical weakness, the connection between linguistic universals, simplicity, and significant generalization is one of the heuristic stimulations for continuing improvements within the theory of generative grammar.

Let me conclude this discussion of problems of the glossematic theory with the remark that I selected only those general topics that are, in a sense, counterparts to corresponding claims of generative grammar. I tried to show that in spite of enormous differences in particular assumptions, both theories share a certain attitude towards the scope and the status of a linguistic theory. The major flaws of glossematics are that it lacks a precise notion of rule of grammar in general and hence reduces linguistic descriptions to complicated sets of lists of elements and functions, that it lacks, in particular, the notion of transformational rules, and that it underestimates the empirical motivation for both linguistic universals and evaluation criteria.

V

I have discussed at some length particular issues of glossematic theory, because it provides the most explicit formulation of almost all views shared by the other main trend of European structuralism: The Prague School. Except for the fact that the Prague School has not developed its conceptual framework with the same explicitness and theoretical pretensions as glossematics theory, there is one main difference: whereas in glossematics the levels of form and substance on each plane are taken as strictly separate aspects of structure, such that entities of the levels of form must not be established with respect to the units of substance which manifest them, the Prague School has based its functional units always on phonetic and semantic considerations, respectively. Thus in Projet (1931, p. 309) phonology is defined as 'Partie de linguistique traitant des phénomènes phoniques au point de vue de leurs fonctions dans la langue'. Hjelmslev would not admit that the expression form deals with phonetic phenomena. Glossematic theory has been criticized by several authors, e.g. Jakobson and Halle (1956), for this neglect of phonetic substance. What emerges here, however, is an interesting misunderstanding on both sides. First of all, glossematic theory realizes, of course, that the level of form can be approached only by means of its manifestation in a particular substance. The claim it makes is merely that this substance must not enter the functional specification of formal units which are completely abstract. It assumes, furthermore, that a complete description has not only to specify the units of form and its possible combinations, but also its possible manifestations by units of substance. Thus the point at issue is not whether a characterization of units of form without reference to substance is possible, but whether it leads to the appropriate result. If we look at the problem in this way, then the glossematic position shows an essential advantage and a serious defect. As far as it is not bound by its principles to the conditions of linearity, biuniqueness, and phonetic similarity relating expression form and expression substance (i.e. roughly phonemic and phonetic representations), it can achieve important generalizations over and above those of the Prague School theory, which is subject to these conditions. (See footnote 23 for an example of this type.) It is important to remember that the only criterion restricting possible analyses is the principle of simplicity. Since glossematic theory does not provide on the other hand an appropriate system of rules connecting the levels of form and substance, arbitrary solutions for the structure of the level of form are not excluded. The Prague School, however, while necessarily lacking certain important generalizations, cannot run the risk of arbitrariness. From the point of view of generative grammar it is obvious how both shortcomings can be avoided. The abstract representation, foreseen by the glossematic theory, must be supplemented by a system of rules relating it to the phonetic representation, and both the representation *and* the system of rules are to be subject to the evaluation criterion, which must then of course be modified.[28] What has been discussed so far with respect to form and substance of expression, applies – according to the theoretical claims – also to the content plane. And though there has been considerable discussion of these problems by Hjelmslev (1935) and Jakobson (1936), this discussion is rather hard to pursue any further for two reasons: Firstly, because all relevant discussions relate to inflectional categories only, mainly to case categories, which are by no means a typical phenomenon of semantic problems. And secondly, because of the extremely unclear question as to what distinction between linguistic form and linguistic substance would finally turn out to be on the content side.

There are of course, a lot of other ideas originating from the Prague School, which are extremely interesting from the point of view of generative grammar. I need only mention the concept of opposition, further developed into the notion of distinctive features; the concept of marked and unmarked categories; the concept of archiphoneme and neutralization.[29] It is not necessary to deal with them any further here, they have been elaborated and incorporated step by step into the theory of generative grammar with extensive discussion of all related questions, including their origin.

One of the most characteristic features of almost all European structural linguistics before generative grammar is the relatively small interest in syn-

---

[28] Postal (1968) has shown that this criterion can be summarized to what he calls the naturalness condition which claims that the abstract representation is related to the phonetic one by general rules of universal phonetics, unless there are empirically motivated language-particular rules which account for peculiar differences between the two representations.

[29] It is worth mentioning that almost all of them have their formally defined counterpart in the glossematic theory. Glossemes are for example organized into categories where intensic and extensic elements are opposed to each other. These notions are defined with respect to possible manifestation in the pertaining substance, such that the extensic unit under particular conditions may have the same manifestation as the intensic one, but not vice versa. Thus intensic and extensic elements correspond to marked and unmarked ones, respectively. For details see Hjelmslev (1935).

tactic analysis. The bulk of empirical investigations concentrates on problems of phonology and morphology, the latter being understood mainly as semantic interpretation of inflectional categories. With a few exceptions, such as Bech (1955), only the most superficial aspects of syntactic structure have been noted. (This is true, of course, also of American linguistics of that time.) This characteristic gap is not an accidental fact, but rather a necessary consequence of principal theoretical positions, in particular the lack of an explicit notion of grammatical rule, the concentration on problems of representing structures, which in turn reduces grammatical descriptions to lists of inventories or categories and their possible concatenations, resulting essentially in phrase structure representations, as far as syntax is concerned. What is missing can easily be seen from the viewpoint of generative grammar, namely the existence of structure-dependent operations mapping abstract representations on superficial syntactic representations (see footnote 2), in short transformational rules. Without such a theoretical concept syntactic analysis turns out to be unfeasible, or at least unrevealing.

This very limitation applies also to the only true exception to the above remark, the peerless work of Tesnière (1959). But although he realized the central importance of syntax for an understanding of natural language, he too was preoccupied with problems of representing structures, lacking the notion of grammatical rule generating and transforming structures. The system of representation that Tesnière has developed has since been explicated in terms of dependency systems, e.g. by Hays (1964). These in turn have been proven by Gaifman (1965) to correspond in a specific way to context free phrase structure grammars. As these are known to be inadequate to characterize the syntactic mechanism of natural language, the basic principles of Tesnière's system were doomed to failure. He was aware, to a certain extent, of this shortcoming, and tried to escape it by means of certain additional devices, representing phenomena of conjunction, reference identity (mainly the effect of pronominalization), and what he calls 'translation', viz. the further expansion of a single category such as Noun, Adverb, Adjective, by complex syntactic structures. These are, undoubtedly, insightful hints to fairly complex syntactic problems. But they are formulated in terms of graphic schemes for representations only, with no formal basis to provide their theoretical status. What is interesting, however, is the fairly abstract status of Tesnière's syntactic representations. Whenever the syntactic dependencies and the superficial ordering of syntactic constituents conflict, Tesnière decides in favour of the former. Thus, in a sense, his dependency trees are closer to syntactic deep structure than to surface structure in the sense of Chomsky (1965). There is no way, however, to connect them systematically with the set of possible surface structures. In this respect,

Tesnière simply presupposes the intuition of the intelligent reader, instead of explaining it.

I should finally mention that branch of linguistic development that was dominant in the period after World War II mainly in West Germany, viz. the 'inhaltsbezogene Grammatik' as expounded in Weisgerber (1953). I cannot go here through the general assumptions and the particular claims made in this conception. They are of only marginal interest to the present paper, all the more so as this trend is not only devoid of any precise formulation of the notions involved, but refuses any attempt to develop one. I would like to mention only two points. The first is that Weisgerber takes up, besides some of Saussure's concepts, in particular the idea that signs are two-sided entities organizing an amorphous substance of thought and sound, in particular Humboldt's ambiguous notion of inner form. In doing this he revived the Humboldt tradition in present day linguistics long before Chomsky incorporated Humboldt into the tradition of Cartesian Linguistics. The ideas taken from or ascribed to Humboldt are however extremely different in Generative Grammar and the inhaltsbezogene Grammatik. Although both emphasize Humboldt's notion of the creative aspect of language, only generative grammar tries to explicate this vague notion by means of precise theoretical concepts (in particular application of grammatical rules and modification of grammatical rules), while the inhaltsbezogene Grammatik sticks to the original vagueness. And whereas the notion of inner form is explicated in the framework of generative grammar as the abstract, underlying (at least partially universal) structure, the same notion is paraphrased in the inhaltsbezogene Grammatik by such terms as 'Weltbild', 'sprachliche Zwischenwelt', emphasizing the language particular aspect of it and relating it to assumptions corresponding to the Whorf hypothesis. Thus while generative grammar stresses the rationalist tradition continued by Humboldt, the inhaltsbezogene Grammatik is concerned exclusively with the romantic and idealistic traits in Humboldt's iridescent and outstanding work.

The second point is the important place which the notion of 'Wortfeld', developed originally in Trier (1930), occupies in Weisgerber's conception. What lies behind this notion is essentially Saussure's idea that it is only the linguistic form that organizes the amorphous mass of thoughts. Trier hence assumes that only the mutual delimitation of words can lead to articulate concepts, this articulation originating within coherent fields of words. I cannot analyse here the inconsistencies arising from the assumption that on the one hand it is only the mutual delimitation of words imposing a structure on possible thoughts, while on the other hand it must be a field of thoughts given in advance that constitute a particular field. The rationale behind this conception after the elimination of these untenable assumptions is the fact that the semantic analysis of particular words cannot proceed by considering isolated words, but rather appropriate sets of elements exhibiting common and contrasting components in particular interrelations, as I have done, e.g. in Bierwisch (1967). Any detailed effort in this direction shows quite clearly that pure delimitation is by no means a sufficient notion. What is required is rather a detailed conception of different types of interrelations between cognate lexical items. Thus the general notion of 'Wortfeld' as well as the particular facts gathered in this connection call for a critical reanalysis.

I have not given, of course, in the present paper a complete account of the typical problems of European linguistics before the arrival of generative grammar, not even of those that have some bearing on it. But I hope that I have been able to characterize to a certain extent the general scene which it entered in 1960 and the particular facets predetermined by it. Its development since then has shown that none of these preconditions has led to special consequences. The reason for this is, to my mind, that there are no essential problems posed in European structural linguistics which are not or cannot be integrated into the framework of generative grammar. The explicit integration of some of them, however, might still be open.

POSTSCRIPT

Because of some recent results gained in the study of formal properties of grammars, it is possible to characterize two essential points in the theory of glossematics somewhat more precisely than has been done so far. The first point concerns the formal capacity of what has been called glossematic algebras, the second point concerns a decisive difference between content and expression plane with respect to the type of structure they exhibit.

In a paper dealing with problems of the base component of a generative grammar – i.e. the system of rules that specifies the set of underlying structures of a language – McCawley (1968c) considered the following proposal. Assume that a rule of the form $A \rightarrow X_1 \ldots X_n$ is not interpreted in the usual way as a rewriting rule, i.e. an instruction to replace A in a given string of symbols by the sequence $X_1 \ldots X_n$, but rather as a condition applied to a given tree saying that a node labeled A is admissible if it directly dominates the nodes labeled $X_1 \ldots X_n$ and only these. Interpreted in this way a rewriting rule becomes what McCawley calls a node admissibility condition. A system G of such conditions specifies a set of phrase markers $P(G)$ in the following way: A given phrase marker D is said to satisfy G if and only if its terminal nodes are labeled with elements of the terminal vocabulary, each of its nonterminal nodes meets a condition of G, and its root is labeled S. $P(G)$ is the set of all phrase markers which satisfy the system G. A terminal string x is said to be generated by G, if x is the terminal string of a phrase marker D and $D \in P(G)$. The notion of node admissibility conditions can be extended in a natural way to context sensitive rules: A node labeled A meets the condition

(3) $A \rightarrow X_1 \ldots X_1 / Y_1 \ldots Y_m \_\_ Z_1 \ldots Z_n$

if A directly dominates $X_1 \ldots X_1$ and $Y_1 \ldots Y_m$ and $Z_1 \ldots Z_n$ are its left and right environment, respectively. The crucial point now is the following. Whereas in the case of context free rules the interpretation of G as a system of rewriting rules or as a system of node admissibility conditions yields the same set of sentences with the same constituent structure assigned to them,[30] in the case of context sensitive rules there might be a difference between the two interpretations. More precisely, a set of context sensitive rewriting rules may not generate certain strings that are generated by the corresponding node admissibility conditions. (4) gives a simple example of such a system.

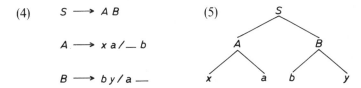

Neither the second nor the third rule of (4) can be applied to the string AB produced by the first rule, if (4) is taken as a rewriting system. Hence (4) does not yield a derivation which ends in the string $xaby$. If on the other hand (4) is taken as a system of node admissibility conditions, it generates the tree (5), since each nonterminal node satisfies a condition of (4). If we designate by $L(G)$ the set of all sentences (i.e. terminal strings of the category S) generated by the rewriting system G, and by $L'(G)$ the set of all terminal strings of the set $P(G)$ specified by the corresponding system G of node admissibility conditions, then we have the following result: There are context sensitive phrase structure grammars G, such that $L'(G)$ properly includes $L(G)$. If on the other

[30] There is one point where this is not strictly the case with respect to the assigned constituent structure. The point at issue is related to rules of the form $A \rightarrow AB$ which do not yield a unique constituent structure tree if interpreted as rewriting rules: they produce consecutive lines of a derivation like $XACY$, $XABCY$, which then give rise to either the structure $XA(BC)Y$ or the structure $X(AB)CY$, if a branching diagram is constructed on the basis of the lines of the derivation. (See Postal (1964) and McCawley (1968c) for further discussion of this point.) Clearly such ambiguities do not arise if the rule in question is interpreted as a node admissibility condition, since such a condition directly applies to a given tree, which is not constructed out of a sequence of strings in a derivation. For the present purpose, we can ignore this divergence between the trees determined by rewriting rules and corresponding node admissibility conditions.

hand G is a context free phrase structure grammar, then $L'(G)$ is identical with $L(G)$. In other words, for context sensitive, but not for context free phrase structure grammars there are systems of rules with $L'(G) \neq L(G)$.

As it is a well known fact – see, e.g. Chomsky (1963) – that the class of all languages generated by context sensitive rewriting systems properly includes the set of all languages generated by context free rewriting systems, the question arises, where the class of all languages specified by context sensitive systems of node admissibility conditions is to be placed within the hierarchy of classes of languages. With respect to this question Peters (1969) proved the following:

THEOREM 1: For every phrase structure grammar G there exists a context free phrase structure grammar G' such that $L(G') = L'(G)$.

In other words, if we interpret an arbitrary (context free or context sensitive) system of phrase structure rules as a system of node admissibility conditions, then the specified language is always generable by a context free grammar. Hence the class of all $L'(G)$ in the sense defined above is equal to the class of context free languages.[31] Thus Peters has shown the class of node admissibility condition systems to be weakly equivalent to the class of context free grammars in the usual sense. This result can be sharpened to strong equivalence in the following way.

First let us say that A_1 through A_n are rule-ancestors of B if there is a set of rules of the following form:

(6) $A_1 \rightarrow \ldots A_2 \ldots / \ldots$
            $A_2 \rightarrow \ldots A_3 \ldots / \ldots$
            $\ldots \ldots$
            $A_{n-1} \rightarrow \ldots A_n \ldots / \ldots$
            $A_n \rightarrow \ldots B \ldots / \ldots$

Let us furthermore designate by $\overline{X}$ the set containing the symbol X and all its rule-ancestors. Obviously $\overline{X}$ is uniquely determined for every X occurring in the rules of a given phrase structure grammar.

Assume now that G_0 is a context sensitive grammar with (3) as one of its context sensitive rules. We construct then a grammar G_1 with 'reduced context sensitivity' in the following four steps.

(i) Replace (3) by the rule (3') where A' is a new and distinct symbol not occurring in G_0.

(3') $A' \rightarrow X_1 \ldots X_1 / Y_2 \ldots Y_m \underline{\quad\quad} Z_1 \ldots Z_n$

(ii) Let $(P_1, P_2, \ldots, P_r)$ be a sequence of rules in G_0 of the type illustrated in

---

[31] Peters' proof of the above theorem is fairly complex and involves the construction of a push-down store automaton that accepts all and only the labeled bracketings corresponding to the trees of $P(G)$.

(6) whose left hand sides are rule-ancestors of A. In the same way let $(R_1, \ldots, R_s)$ be a sequence of ancestor-rules of Y_1. Obviously, there must be some integer i, such that $P_k = R_k$ for $1 \leqslant k \leqslant i$, and furthermore $P_i = R_i$ must be of the form (7):

(7) $W \to \ldots \xi \ldots \alpha \ldots / \ldots$

where $\alpha \in \overline{A}$ and $\xi \in \overline{Y}_1$. Otherwise Y_1 could not be in the left environment of A in any tree specified by G_0 and (3) would be a vacuous rule. Add to G_1 a rule (7'), where α' is not in the vocabulary of G_0, and $\xi' = Y_1$, if $\xi = Y_1$, otherwise ξ' is a new symbol not in the vocabulary of G_0.

(7') $W \to \ldots \xi' \ldots \alpha' \ldots / \ldots$

(iii) Let (8) be the rule P_{i+1} from the sequence $(P_1, \ldots, P_r)$ above with $\beta \in \overline{A}$. Add (8') to G_1.

(8) $\alpha \to \ldots \beta \ldots / \ldots$
(8') $\alpha' \to \ldots \beta' \ldots / \ldots$

As before, β' is a new symbol not in the vocabulary of G_0. The same procedure is applied to P_{i+2} through P_r. It might be, that $P_i = P_r$. In this case α in (7) is A and step (iii) in the construction of G_1 applies vacuously.

(iv) If $R_i \neq R_s$, that is if $\xi \neq Y_1$ in (7), then there is a rule of the form (9) in the new grammar with $\xi, \zeta \in \overline{Y}_1$ in G_0. In this case replace (9) by the rule (9'), where $\zeta' = Y_1$, if $\zeta = Y_1$, and ζ' is a new symbol otherwise.

(9) $\xi \to \ldots \zeta \ldots / \ldots$
(9') $\xi' \to \ldots \zeta' \ldots / \ldots$

The same procedure is applied to all rules of the grammar constructed so far whose left hand side is an element of $\overline{Y}_1$. There might be more than one sequence $(P_1, \ldots, P_r)$ meeting the condition mentioned in (ii). In this case the described procedure is applied to each of these sequences.

Finally all rules whose left-hand side is not a rule ancestor of any terminal symbol, i.e. all rules that have become vacuous with respect to their possible application by the steps (ii) or (iii), are removed from G_1.

By means of this procedure the context sensitivity of the symbol A with respect to Y_1 is 'kicked upstairs' to the rule R_i, where it is changed to a condition expressed without recourse to context. At the same time, the constituent structure specified by G_1 does not differ from that specified by G_0, except for the systematic relabeling introduced in the steps (i) through (iv). If we designate by $\overline{Q}$ that subset of the vocabulary of G_0 for which new symbols have been created in the construction of G_1 and by $\overline{Q}'$ the set of these new symbols, then the following can easily be verified:

LEMMA 1: A phrase marker D satisfies G_0 if and only if there is a unique phrase marker D' which satisfies G_1 and D' is identical with D except that possibly certain nodes labeled by elements of $\overline{Q}$ in D are labeled by the corresponding symbols of $\overline{Q}'$ in D'.

This lemma establishes strong equivalence between G_0 and G_1 in a reasonable way. It is now obvious that the procedure used to eliminate Y_1 from the context of rule (3) in G_0 can be repeated to eliminate Y_2 from the context in rule (3') in G_1. Further repetitions eliminate Y_3 through Y_m and Z_n through Z_1. Thus after $m + n$ applications of the above procedure one arrives at a Grammar G_{m+n} which instead of (3) contains a context free rule with all the context dependencies of the nodes dominated by A pushed upwards and recoded into new, but strictly corresponding symbols. Continuing in the same way with all context sensitive rules of G_0 we finally obtain a context free grammar G' which is still strongly equivalent to G_0 in the sense of lemma 1. This then establishes the following:

THEOREM 2: For every context sensitive system of node admissibility conditions G one can construct a context free system G' of node admissibility conditions such that G and G' are strongly equivalent in the way determined by Lemma 1.[32]

Returning to the glossematic algebras, it can now be shown that they are to be reconstructed in terms of systems of node admissibility conditions rather than in terms of systems of rewriting rules. Hjelmslev's basic operations of analysis and deduction, formally reconstructed by the relations $x \Rightarrow y$ and $x \overset{*}{\Rightarrow} y$ with y being an appropriately categorized segmentation of x, are supposed to provide a structural description for a given object, not to generate it

---

[32] Here is a simple minded example for the construction of G' for a grammar G which specifies the number concord between subject NP and verb by means of context sensitive rules.

G:			G':		
(1)	$S \to NP\,VP$		(1')	$S \to NP'\,VP'$	
(2)	$VP \to V_i$		(1'')	$S \to NP''\,VP''$	
(3)	$VP \to V_t\,NP$		(2')	$VP' \to V_i'$	
(4)	$NP \to NP\#S\#$		(2'')	$VP'' \to V''$	
(5)	$NP \to DetN_{sg}$		(3')	$VP' \to V_t'\,NP'$	
(6)	$NP \to DetN_{pl}$		(3'')	$VP'' \to V_t''\,NP'$	
(7)	$V_i \to s\,V_i/N_{sg}\#S\#\,—$		(3''')	$VP' \to V_t'\,NP''$	
(8)	$V_i \to s\,V_i/N_{sg}\,—$		(3'''')	$VP'' \to V_t''\,NP''$	
(9)	$V_t \to s\,V_t/N_{sg}\#S\#\,—$		(4)	$NP' \to NP'\#S\#$	
(10)	$V_t \to s\,V_t/N_{sg}\,—$		(4')	$NP'' \to NP''\#S\#$	
(11)	$V_i \to \varnothing\,V_i/N_{pl}\#S\#\,—$		(5')	$NP' \to DetN_{sg}$	
(12)	$V_i \to \varnothing\,V_i/N_{pl}\,—$		(6')	$NP'' \to DetN_{pl}$	
(13)	$V_t \to \varnothing\,V_t/N_{pl}\#S\#\,—$		(8')	$V_i' \to s\,V_i$	
(14)	$V_t \to \varnothing\,V_t/N_{pl}\,—$		(10')	$V_t' \to s\,V_t$	
			(12')	$V_i'' \to \varnothing\,V_i$	
			(14')	$V_t'' \to \varnothing\,V_t$	

in the way rewriting systems generate formal objects.[33] More precisely, if y can be directly deduced from x by a Hjelmslevian analysis with $x = vzw$, $y = vz_1 \ldots z_k w$, $z = z_1 \ldots z_k$ and $z, z_1, \ldots, z_k$ are members of the categories $A, B_1, \ldots, B_k$, respectively, then $x \Rightarrow y$ must be based on properties of the underlying paradigmatic system $\mathbf{P}$ that can be reconstructed in terms of node admissibility conditions as follows. Let x be (a part of) the terminal string of a phrase marker D with nodes labeled $B_1, \ldots, B_k$ in D dominating the substrings $z_1, \ldots, z_k$, respectively. Then there is a node labeled A in D meeting the node admissibility condition $A \to B_1 \ldots B_k$. Obviously every direct deduction based on a given paradigmatic system $\mathbf{P}$ can be associated with a corresponding node admissibility condition in this way.[34] If for every z_i of category B_i for which no further deduction is possible, the node admissibility condition $B_i \to z_i$ is added, we obtain a grammar G, which clearly reconstructs $\mathbf{P}$. Moreover, G is of a particularly restricted type, as all its rules – or conditions for that matter – are either of the form $A \to B_1 \ldots B_k$ or of the form $A \to x$ with x being a (string of) terminal symbol(s).

So far we have taken into consideration only homosyntagmatic functions, which are reflected by context free rules. As mentioned above, the class of grammars thus obtained is indifferent with respect to the way we interpret

---

Note that the elimination of N_{sg} from the context of (7) and (8) leads to the same modification of G. After the removal of N_{sg} from (7) this rule might be dropped altogether as now there is already a context free rule (8') with the same right hand side as (7') except for the context restriction. The same is true for (9) through (14). This corresponds to the fact that $\# S \#$ is a sequence that only optionally separates the node in question from its relevant context. D is a phrase marker which satisfies G but not G', D' is the corresponding phrase marker which satisfies G' but not G.

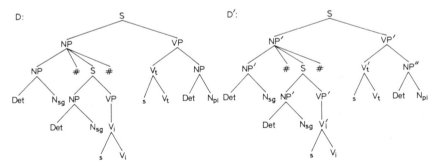

[33] Notice that also the 'inverse' operations of synthesis and induction do not produce formal objects. Rather they are the same procedure looked at from the inverse end. Hjelmslev's deduction and induction correspond roughly to the application of node admissibility conditions from top to bottom and from bottom to top, respectively. See below for further discussion.

[34] See note 15 for the details necessary to account for the homosyntagmatic, i.e. intra-phrasal, functions between the deduced substrings. Heterosyntagmatic, i.e. extra-phrasal functions will be discussed immediately.

the rules. Therefore the heterosyntagmatic functions giving rise to context sensitive rules are crucial for the present problem. A deduction involving a heterosyntagmatic function can be reconstructed along the following lines. Let $x \Rightarrow y$ be a direct deduction as above with the additional condition that v in $y = vz_1 \ldots z_k w$ is a constant in a function that contracts v with some z_i – let us say with z_1. In other words, the occurrence of z_1 as a member of category B_1 always presupposes the occurrence of v as its left neighbor. This condition is incorporated in G by replacing the context free rule $B_1 \rightarrow z_1$ with the context sensitive rule $B_1 \rightarrow z_1/v\underline{\quad}$.[35] In this way all heterosyntagmatic functions involving constants in Hjelmslev's sense can be accounted for by context sensitive rules of a grammar G that reconstructs the paradigmatic system **P** which determines the syntagmatic functions in question. In other words, the system G of phrase structure rules is a way to represent the syntagmatic functions defining the elements and categories of the paradigmatic system **P**. The crucial question now is the following: Does the deductive procedure that relates **P** to the set of structures specified by **P** exhibit the properties that correspond to an interpretation of G as a system of rewriting rules, or to an interpretation of G as a system of node admissibility conditions? Hjelmslev's definition of analysis and deduction is not explicit in this respect. There are, however, several points showing indirectly that only an interpretation of G in terms of node admissibility conditions reconstructs the properties that Hjelmslev requires of an glossematic algebra.

The first point is the existence of heterosyntagmatic interdependence, i.e. functions contracting two constants. The treatment of grammatical agreement in Hjelmslev (1938) is a case in point. Assume for example that in the construction (10a) the occurrence of a always presupposes the occurrence of b, and vice versa. (a and b might be construed as the morphemes to which agreement applies.)

---

[35] For the sake of simplicity I have assumed that z_1 cannot further be analyzed into substrings on the basis of **P**. If this were not the case then by definition of the concept of function there would be an unanalyzable substring of z_1 that is relevant to the supposed function, and the context sensitivity carries over to the rule whose right hand side is just that substring. On the other hand, it is possible that the function in question applies not to z_1 but rather to the category B_1, i.e. the class of all terminal strings that might occur in that position. Clearly, the context sensitivity in this case is to be expressed by the rule $A \rightarrow B_1 \ldots B_k/v\underline{\quad}$. (In this case the fact that B_1 and not just the whole string $B_1 \ldots B_k$ is contracted to v by the function cannot be seen from the rule directly. It rather follows from the fact, that there must be other rules for the expansion of A where the place of B_1 is occupied by some category $C \neq B_1$, and v does not occur as context-restriction in these rules.) Similarly we might consider cases where it is the category V to which v is assigned that is relevant for the function in question. In this case it is the category symbol V rather than the terminal v that appears as the context restriction in the stipulated rules.

(10)   (a)   (b) $A \longrightarrow BC$
                         $B \longrightarrow MN$
                         $C \longrightarrow PQ$
                         $M \longrightarrow x$
                         $N \longrightarrow a/\!\!-P_b$
                         $P \longrightarrow y$
                         $Q \longrightarrow b/aP\!\!-$

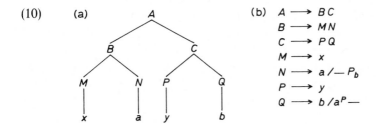

(10b) gives the rules reconstructing the relevant properties of **P**. Clearly, (10a) could not be generated by (10b), if the rules were taken as rewriting rules. Hence, if a string *xayb* with the indicated categorization and with reciprocal determination between *a* and *b* should be deducible on the basis of some paradigmatic system **P**, the deduction based on **P** cannot be reconstructed by a context sensitive rewriting system.

A more general argument follows from Hjelmslev's claim that by a deduction, i.e. a stepwise analysis of a given chain, always an induction is determined, which traverses the deduced hierarchy in the opposite direction. By this induction no new results are gained. (See Hjelmslev, 1953, p. 31.) For a hierarchy like (10a) – given the interdependence between *a* and *b* – this is true only if the deduction is construed as an application of the pertinent node admissibility conditions from top to bottom, and the synthesis as the corresponding application from bottom to top.

Hence every glossematic algebra based on a paradigmatic system **P** is strongly equivalent to some system *G* of node admissibility conditions. More precisely:

THEOREM 3: For every paradigmatic system **P** there is a system *G* of node admissibility conditions such that *D* is element of **P**(*G*) if and only if *x* is the terminal string of *D* and **P** deduces for *x* a categorial system *CS*(*x*) with *CS*(*x*) = *D*.

Hence the class of glossematic algebras is (at least improperly) included in the class of all systems of node admissibility conditions with respect to strong generative capacity. Because of theorem 2 the class of glossematic algebras is included even in the class of context free node admissibility systems.[36] This result then shows that the glossematic theory claims the complexity of the syntactic structure of natural languages not to go beyond the range that can be accounted for by context free phrase structure grammars.

It might be noted that the previous considerations are based on glossematic

[36] The theorem on page 83 is to be interpreted in the light of this result: Generation of a string by a grammar *G* must be taken in the sense in which a string is generated by a system of node admissibility conditions.

algebras with a linear ordering defined over their elements. Though this is a natural condition if a glossematic algebra is interpreted as the formal structure of the expression-plane, it is not necessarily satisfied if the structure of the content plane is considered. In fact, Hjelmslev does not presuppose a linear ordering with respect to the components of the syntagmatic structure of the content plane. This then means that a categorial system $CS(x)$ of a given string x might be considered as the equivalence class of all possible orderings compatible with the relations defined by $CS(x)$. As, however, the components of $CS(x)$ – together with x itself – must finally be mapped somehow on the linearly ordered elements of a structure of the expression plane (this mapping being defined as the interdependence of content and expression), a canonical ordering must be specified to which this mapping applies. It is these canonically ordered representatives of the equivalence classes to which the above statements apply.[37]

The second line to be clarified in this postscript stems from Hjelmslev's assumption that 'the two sides (the planes) of a language have completely analogous categorial structure' (1953, p. 101). This is simply another phrasing of the claim that the theory of glossematic algebras provides precisely the correct framework for the description of both content and expression. This claim, which is at the very heart of glossematic theory, fails in both cases. While a glossematic algebra is too restricted to account for the syntactic organization of natural languages, it is too powerful to express the essential restrictions to be placed on their phonological organization. The detailed specification of the formal character of phonological theory in Chomsky and Halle (1968, pp. 390–9) allows for a fairly precise justification of the latter statement.

As has been pointed out in the main body of the present paper, there is no clear correspondence between the different strata postulated in glossematic theory and the levels of linguistic structure posited in generative grammar. Therefore the point at issue can be demonstrated only indirectly. This will be done in two steps. Consider first the level of underlying systematic phonemic representations. All regularities governing representations on this level, as far as they are not described by the distribution of syntactically functioning formatives and are hence outside the domain of the syntactic component of the grammar, are completely accounted for by a particular kind of phonological rules, which Stanley (1967) has specified as morpheme structure con-

---

[37] This at least implicit ordering makes unfeasable the dubious reconstruction of the content-expression-interdependence in terms of context sensitive rules (as hinted at in note 19). Thus Hjelmslev's claim that the analysis of a text begins with 'the partition into content line and expression line' (1953, p. 98) obscures the character of the internal syntactic organization as opposed to the essentially different sound-meaning-relation.

ditions. The set of strings that can be specified by a system of morpheme structure conditions is always a regular event or finite state language. (See Chomsky, 1963, for an account of these notions.) The details necessary to establish this latter result have been worked out by Johnson (unpublished), and cannot be reproduced here. Intuitively, the essential point is that phonological regularities do not require the consideration of any hierarchical structure but can be expressed by purely linear restrictions. Thus if we consider the following hierarchy of classes of computable sets, systematic phonemic representations are included in the lowest ranking class:

(11)   Recursively enumerable sets
        Recursive sets
        Context sensitive sets
        Context free sets
        Regular sets (= regular events)

As has been shown above, glossematic algebras have the capacity of specifying context free sets. Hence one of the essential features of phonological structure cannot be expressed by a glossematic algebra.

Secondly, it is one of the major insights of generative phonological theory that the regularities of sound structure cannot be stated on a single level of representation, but involve a system of phonological rules mapping underlying phonemic in systematic phonetic representations. By means of a fairly complicated proof, Johnson (unpublished) has shown that the operations performed by the phonological rules lie within the scope of a particularly restricted mapping device, called linear transducer. The essential point is that linear transducers cannot preserve hierarchial structure appearing in the elements of a context free set, this being possible only by the stronger class of push down store transducers. From this it follows that even if we consider the different levels of sound structure, its regularities do not require the capacities connected with a context free phrase structure grammar. Hence, whatever correspondence one chooses to consider between the glossematic notion of expression plane and the sound structure as conceived in generative grammar, the glossematic theory makes inadequate claims with respect to the formal nature of this aspect of language and the descriptive apparatus required to describe it. To conclude these remarks, I repeat that the formal apparatus which Hjelmslev pretends to be derivable on a priori considerations places the structure of both content and expression of natural languages on the same level within the hierarchy of formally characterizable ot jects, viz. on the level of context free sets. Empirically based theoretical investigations have shown this far reaching generalization to be wrong in both directions: It is too weak with respect to sound structure, as this aspect lies within the scope of finite state computation; it is too strong with respect to syntactic (and semantic) structure, as this definitely exceeds the limits of context free grammars.[38] And it lacks any notion of a formal characteristic of the mapping devices necessary to relate different levels of structure to each other.

REFERENCES

Bech, G.: 1955, *Studien über das deutsche Verbum infinitum*, 1. Band, Copenhagen.

Bierwisch, M.: 1966, 'Strukturalismus, Geschichte, Probleme und Methoden', *Kursbuch V*, Frankfurt/Main, pp. 77–152.

Bierwisch, M.: 1967, 'Some Semantic Universals of German Adjectivals', *Foundations of Language* **3**, 1–36.

Chomsky, N.: 1955, *The Logical Structure of Linguistic Theory*, MIT-Library Micro-film.

Chomsky, N.: 1957, *Syntactic Structures*, The Hague.

Chomsky, N.: 1963, 'Formal Properties of Grammars', *Handbook of Mathematical Psychology*, Vol. **2**, pp. 323–418 (ed. by Luce, Bush, and Galanter), New York.

Chomsky, N.: 1964, *Current Issues in Linguistic Theory*, The Hague.

Chomsky, N.: 1965, *Aspects of the Theory of Syntax*, The MIT Press.

Chomsky, N.: 1966a, *Cartesian Linguistics*, New York.

Chomsky, N.: 1966b, 'Topics in the Theory of Generative Grammar', *Current Trends in Linguistics*, Vol. **3**, pp. 1–60 (ed. by Sebeok), The Hague.

Chomsky, N.: 1968, *Language and the Mind*, New York.

Chomsky, N. and Halle, M.: 1965, 'Some Controversial Questions in Phonological Theory', *Journal of Linguistics* **1**, 97–138.

Chomsky, N. and Halle, M.: 1968, *The Sound Pattern of English*, New York.

Chomsky, N.: forthcoming, *Deep Structure, Surface Structure, and Semantic Interpretation*.

Gaifman, C.: 1965, 'Dependency Systems and Phrase-Structure Systems', *Information and Control* **8**, 304–37.

Halle, M.: 1959, *The Sound Pattern of Russian*, The Hague.

Hays, D. G.: 1964, 'Dependency Theory: A Formalism and some Observations', *Language* **40**, 511–25.

Hjelmslev, L.: 1929, *Principes de Grammaire Générale*, Copenhagen.

Hjelmslev, L.: 1935, *La Catégorie des Cas*, Part I, Copenhagen.

Hjelmslev, L.: 1938, 'Essai d'une théorie des morphèmes', *Actes IVe Congrés international de linguistes* 1936, pp. 140–51, Copenhagen.

Hjelmslev, L.: 1953, *Prolegomena to a Theory of Language*, Baltimore.

Hjelmslev, L.: 1954, 'La Stratification du Language', *Word* **10**, pp. 163–188.

Jakobson, R.: 1936, 'Beitrag zur allgemienen Kasuslehre', *Travaux du Cercle Linguistique de Prague* **6**, 240–88.

Johnson, C. D.: unpublished, *Formal Aspects of Phonological Description*, Dissertation, University of California.

---

[38] An adequate specification of the syntactic organization with respect to generative capacity is still pending. Though it is definitely known that the syntactic structure in general exceeds the capacity of context free grammars, certain aspects of it might very well be specifiable in terms of context free grammars. (See Chomsky, 1965, for some discussion.) The overall structure of syntax certainly requires more complicated formal considerations than those of (weak) generative capacity as expressed by the hierarchy (11). It is noteworthy, however, that the glossematic theory fails even with respect to this first approximation.

Katz, J. J.: 1966, *The Philosophy of Language*, New York.

Katz, J. J.: 1967, 'Recent Issues in Semantic Theory', *Foundations of Language* **3**, 124–94.

Katz, J. J. and Fodor, J. A.: 1963, 'The Structure of a Semantic Theory', *Language* **39**, 170–210.

Katz, J. J. and Postal, P. M.: *An Integrated Theory of Linguistic Description*, The MIT Press.

Langendoen, T. D.: 1968, *The London School of Linguistics: A Study of the Linguistic Theories of B. Malinowsky and J. R. Firth*, The MIT Press.

McCawley, J. D.: 1968a, 'The Role of Semantics in a Grammar', *Universals in Linguistic Theory* (ed. by Bach and Harms), New York, pp. 124–69.

McCawley, J. D.: 1968b, 'Can you Count Pluses and Minuses before you can Count?', *Chicago Journal of Linguistics* **2**, 51–56.

McCawley, J. D.: 1968c, 'Concerning the Base Component of a Transformational Grammar', *Foundations of Language* **4**, 243–69.

Peters, S.: 1969, 'The Use of Context-Sensitive Rules in Immediate Constituent Analysis', *International Conference on Computational Linguistics*, Stockholm.

Postal, P. M.: 1964, *Constituent Structure: a Study of Contemporary Models of Syntactic Description*, Bloomington, Ind., and The Hague.

Postal, P. M.: 1966, 'Review Article (André Martinet, *Elements of General Linguistics*)', *Foundations of Language* **2**, 151–86.

Postal, P. M.: 1968, *Aspects of the Theory of Phonology*, New York.

Projet: 1931, 'Projet de Terminologie Phonologique Standardisée', *Travaux du Cercle Linguistique de Prague* **4**, 309–23.

Stanley, R.: 1967, 'Redundancy Rules in Phonology', *Language* **43**, 393–436.

Tesnière, L.: 1959, *Elements de Syntaxe Structurale*, Paris.

Togeby, K.: 1951, *Structure de la Langue Francaise Immanente*, Copenhagen.

Trier, J.: 1931, *Der deutsche Wortschatz im Sinnbezirk des Verstandes*, Heidelberg.

Uldall, H. J.: 1957, *Outline of Glossematics*, Copenhagen.

Weisgerber, L.: 1953, *Vom Weltbild der deutschen Sprache*, Düsseldorf.

HERBERT E. BREKLE

ÜBER DEN BEGRIFF UND DIE BEGRÜNDUNG
EINER ALLGEMEINEN SPRACHLEHRE

EINIGE BEMERKUNGEN ZUM III. ABSCHNITT VON JOHANN
SEVERIN VATERS 'VERSUCH EINER ALLGEMEINEN SPRACHLEHRE'
(1801)*

J. S. Vater (1771–1826) war um die Wende des 18. zum 19. Jahrhundert in Deutschland einer der bedeutenderen Theologen und Philologen. Er war einer der Begründer der deutschen Slawistik; außerdem verfaßte er Grammatiken verschiedener semitischer Sprachen. Für die allgemeine Sprachwissenschaft bedeutsam ist sein Werk *Versuch einer allgemeinen Sprachlehre*, Halle 1801. Aus diesem Werk soll der III. Abschnitt 'Über den Begriff und die Begründung einer allgemeinen Sprachlehre' im folgenden in Ausschnitten kommentierend dargestellt werden. Das Ziel dieser Bemerkungen soll es sein, zu zeigen, daß eine sprachtheoretische Abhandlung aus der Spätphase der deutschen Aufklärung durchaus solche theoretische Überlegungen enthält, die die heutige Grundlagendiskussion in der allgemeinen Sprachwissenschaft befruchten können.

BEMERKUNGEN ZUM III. ABSCHNITT: 'ÜBER DEN BEGRIFF UND
DIE BEGRÜNDUNG EINER ALLGEMEINEN SPRACHLEHRE' (135–162)

Vaters Überlegungen setzen mit der Frage ein, 'ob es überhaupt möglich sey, dem Inhalt der Sprache wirklich allgemeine Ansichten abzugewinnen' (135). Diese Frage wird auch heute noch gestellt und je nach methodologischer Position des betreffenden Sprachwissenschaftlers bejahend oder verneinend beantwortet. Auf der einen Seite stehen die Rationalisten, die eine allgemeine Sprachtheorie fordern; auf der anderen Seite stehen reine Empiriker oder Anhänger der Annahme, daß sich in jeder Sprache eine nur ihr eigene Weltansicht manifestiere. Die Entwicklung bestimmter Strömungen der linguistischen Forschung im letzten Jahrzehnt macht deutlich, daß sich durch die

---

* Dieser Beitrag ist mit geringfügigen Änderungen aus der Einleitung des 3. Bandes der Reihe *Grammatica Universalis* (ed. H. E. Brekle) entnommen: Johann Severin Vater, *Versuch einer allgemeinen Sprachlehre*, Faksimile-Neudruck der Ausgabe Halle 1801 mit einer Einleitung und einem Kommentar von Herbert E. Brekle. 1970 Friedrich Frommann Verlag (Günter Holzboog) Stuttgart-Bad Cannstatt.

F. Kiefer and N. Ruwet (eds.), Generative Grammar in Europe, 112–121. *All Rights Reserved.*
Copyright © 1973 *by D. Reidel Publishing Company, Dordrecht-Holland.*

Einbeziehung eines stärkeren Theoriebewußtseins auch in die vorwiegend empirisch orientierte Forschung, die Waage der Entscheidung zugunsten der Rationalisten zu neigen beginnt.

Vater verneint die Möglichkeit, daß sich 'allgemeine Ansichten . . . aus der Vergleichung, wenn auch noch so vieler einzelner Sprachen' (135) gewinnen lassen. Statt dessen schlägt er vor, aus einer Definition der Sprache nach semiotischen bzw. kommunikationstheoretischen Gesichtspunkten 'allgemeine Ansichten' über formale und substantielle Kategorien der Sprache abzuleiten. 'Sprache ist Inbegriff bedeutender Laute für den Umfang der Gedanken, sie ist Inbegriff der Mittel der Mittheilung; die Handlung des Sprechens ist Mittheilung, ist Bezeichnung und Darstellung' (136). In dieser Definition werden Komponenten eines allgemeinen semiotischen, zeichentheoretischen Rahmens[1] deutlich: die pragmatische Komponente wird bestimmt durch Überlegungen über '(1) den, welcher bezeichnet, (2) den, für welchen man bezeichnet, (3) den Zweck der Bezeichnung, (4) den Erfolg, die Erreichung dieses Zwecks' (137); die morphologisch-syntaktische Komponente ergibt sich aus Betrachtungen über '(5) das Zeichen, das Mittel' (137) und die semantische Komponente aus der Frage nach dem '(6) . . . was bezeichnet wird' (137). Folgerichtig erkennt Vater die Begriffe des Zeichens – genauer der Zeichenform – und des Bezeichneten als wesentliche Ausgangspunkte für eine allgemeine Sprachtheorie an. Er definiert: 'Die Zeichen sind die Laute; das Bezeichnete sind Begriffe, ein einzelner oder mehrere verbundene. Über die Laute selbst, das Materiale der Sprache, läßt sich nichts Allgemeines und Erschöpfendes angeben' (139).

Auf der folgenden Seite spricht unser Autor ausdrücklich von der Relevanz der Semiotik für eine allgemeine Sprachtheorie: '. . . über Zeichen überhaupt stellt die angewandte Logik in einem Abschnitte (der Semiotik, d.i. Zeichenlehre) allgemeine Betrachtungen an, deren Resultate auch für die Laute, insofern sie Zeichen sind, gelten müssen . . .' (140).[2]

Sehr präzise unterscheidet Vater zwischen onomatopoetischen und arbiträren Zeichen: 'Sie [die Zeichenlehre] unterscheidet mit Recht natürliche Zeichen, bei welchen man mehr oder weniger unmittelbar von der Beschaffenheit des Zeichens auf die des Bezeichneten schließen könne, von den willkürlichen, wo kein Bezug jenes auf dieses sichtbar ist; . . .' (140).

Außer semiotischen Voraussetzungen benötigt Vater zur Konstitution der

---

[1] Cf. z.B. Ch. Morris, 'Foundations of the Theory of Signs', 1938 (Vol. 1, 2 der *International Encyclopedia of Unified Science*).

[2] Cf. hierzu J. H. Lambert, 'Neues Organon oder Gedanken über die Erforschung und Bezeichnung des Wahren und dessen Unterscheidung von Irrthum und Schein', 2 Bde, Leipzig, 1764; bes. 2. Band: *Semiotik*, §§ 129 ff. (Nachdruck Hildesheim, 1967).

gegenseitigen Beziehungen zwischen Zeichen und Bezeichneten, die er für eine allgemeine Sprachtheorie für notwendig erachtet, auch die Kategorien der Urteils- und Begriffslogik: 'Wir dürfen als gewiß und anerkannt voraussetzen, daß sich allgemeine Betrachtungen über den Inhalt der Vorstellungen, der Urtheile und der Begriffe, anstellen lassen, wodurch derselbe unmittelbar aus der Art, wie diese Urtheile und Begriffe erfolgen, abgeleitet wird.... Dieser also gefundene Inhalt muß der Inhalt aller Urtheile und Begriffe, also auch derjenigen seyn, von welchen die bedeutenden Laute die Zeichen sind. Denn diese Laute sind nur insofern bedeutend, d.i. Wörter, als sie Begriffen entsprechen; und sie sind die Theile der Sätze, wie Begriffe die der Urtheile' (143/144).

Wenn wir einmal von der grundsätzlichen Insuffizienz des Subjekt-Prädikat-Schemas für die Bestimmung der syntaktischen und semantischen Struktur von Urteilen und Begriffen – wie es von Vater in dem folgenden Zitat postuliert wird – absehen,[3] so ergibt sich doch aus seinen Aussagen eine interessante Diskussion über den strukturellen Zusammenhang zwischen Urteil (Satz) und Begriff (Morphem, Morphemkomplex).

Zunächst erblickt unser Autor bei Urteil und Begriff eine beiden gemeinsame Relation zwischen einem Prädikat und seinem Subjekt: 'Urtheile sowohl als Begriffe bestehen darin, daß man Etwas mit einer Eigenschaft zusammen denkt, die demselben angehöre' (145). Heute würde man sagen, daß diese Relation nicht nur zwischen *einem* Prädikat und *einem* Subjekt anzunehmen ist, sondern – im Falle von relationalen Urteilen – zwischen einem Prädikat und mehreren 'Subjekten' (= Argumenten).[4]

Wir können diese Relation 'Prädikat-Argument-Relation' nennen; im formalen Repräsentationssystem der Prädikatenlogik wird diese Relation z.B. durch ein Klammernpaar um das oder die Argumente eines Prädikatssymbols dargestellt.[5] So kann z.B. der Satz 'Heinrich ist schüchtern' in seiner logischsemantischen Struktur vereinfacht dargestellt werden als

$$f(x_1) \quad \text{wobei 'Heinrich'} = x_1, \text{ 'schüchtern'} = f.$$

Im nächsten Zitat postuliert Vater jedoch 'verschiedene Arten' von Relationen zwischen Subjekt und Prädikat, um die Kategorien 'Urteil' und 'Begriff'

---

[3] Cf. unsere 'Diskussion des Verhältnisses von Subjekt-Prädikat-Aussagen zu Aussagen mit relationaler Struktur', in: *Generative Satzsemantik und transformationelle Syntax im System der englischen Nominalkomposition*, München, 1970, 60 ff.

[4] Cf. hierzu Hans Reichenbach, *Elements of Symbolic Logic*, New York, 1947, § 55, 'Logical Terms in a Syntactical Capacity'.

[5] Cf. Reichenbach, 320: "Although the word 'is' portrays the function-argument relation, it does not denote it. The reason is that, according to the rules of language, the denotation of relations is accomplished in a different way.... The sentence 'Peter is tall' is symbolized by $f(x)$. Here the parentheses play the part of the copula 'is'; they portray the function-argument relation".

voneinander zu unterscheiden. 'Durch die verschiedene Art, wie man Subjekt und Prädikat zusammen denkt, sie im Gemüthe verbindet, unterscheiden sich Urtheile und Begriffe. Wenn ich sage: brauner Tisch, so setze ich dadurch Nichts fest, sondern setze nur voraus, daß das Prädikat: braun, nicht den übrigen Merkmalen widerspreche, welche in dem Worte: Tisch, schon für sich als Merkmale eines Gegenstandes gedacht werden. ... Subjekt und Prädikat [sind] problematisch zusammengedacht. Brauner Tisch ist ebenso gut ein Begriff, als es Tisch für sich allein auch ist' (145).

Wenn man annimmt, daß die zuvor genannte Prädikat-Argument-Relation sowohl in der Struktur von Urteilen wie auch von Begriffen vorkommt – dies nimmt auch Vater an – so muß die kategoriale Differenz zwischen Urteil und Begriff sich aus zusätzlichen Kriterien bestimmen lassen. Aus den Überlegungen Vaters zum Begriff 'brauner Tisch' läßt sich folgern, daß darin die Assertionsrelation – die anschließend noch zu diskutieren ist – nicht enthalten ist. Das 'problematische Zusammendenken' eines 'Subjekts' und eines 'Prädikats' läßt sich auf verschiedene Weise formalisieren: Die erste Möglichkeit, die von Vater nicht notwendig intendiert ist,[6] bietet sich an in dem klassenlogischen Verfahren der Produktbildung zweier Klassen oder Prädikate:

(1) $\{t \cap b\}$.

Es handelt sich hier um das Produkt oder den Durchschnitt zweier Klassen 'Tisch' und 'braun', was die Durchschnittsklasse derjenigen Gegenstände ergibt, für die das Prädikat 'Tisch' und das Prädikat 'braun' zutrifft; formal:

$$(\lambda x) \quad [x \in t \cdot x \in b].$$

Diese Art des 'Zusammendenkens' entspricht jedoch nicht den Erfordernissen einer adäquaten Repräsentation der logischsemantischen Struktur eines sprachlichen Ausdrucks wie *brauner Tisch*, da der Formelausdruck $\{t \cap b\}$ nichts über die Möglichkeit der Einsetzbarkeit in verschiedene strukturelle Kontexte aussagt.

Mit anderen Worten, der Ausdruck $\{t \cap b\}$ ist neutral in bezug auf die beiden möglichen Abstraktionsoperationen, die sich über diesem Ausdruck durchführen lassen: wir können mittels der entsprechenden Abstraktionsoperation einmal zu dem Ausdruck *brauner Tisch* gelangen; formalisiert:

(2) $(\lambda x) \quad [t(x) \cdot b(x)]$

zum anderen aber auch zu dem Ausdruck *das Braun des Tisches*, oder, um ein

---

[6] Cf. jedoch 146: 'Wenn aber das Gemüth die Verbindung selbst, als schon geschehen, voraussetzt, und ohne diese Rücksicht Subjekt und Prädikat neben einander denkt: so ist dies blos ein Begriff; die Merkmale, welche man für sich in dem Begriffe: Tisch, denkt, sind um eins, um die Eigenschaft: braun, vermehrt [sic]'.

morphologisch konziseres Beispiel zu wählen: *Himmelsblau* oder *Himmels-bläue*; formalisiert:

(3) (λf) $[(\exists x)\ H(x) \cdot f(x) \cdot \beta(f)]$[7]

Der Unterschied zwischen (2) und (3) ergibt sich aus der semantischen Ver-schiedensortigkeit der λ-Ausdrücke $(\lambda x)\ldots$ bzw. $(\lambda f)\ldots$, die mit ver-schiedenen Substitutionskontexten gekoppelt ist:

(2) kann als komplexes Prädikat der Ding-Sorte, (3) als komplexes Prädikat der Eigenschaftssorte verwendet werden.[8]

Man kann nun überlegen, ob (2) und (3) durch mit der Abstraktions-operation gekoppelte Topikalisierungsoperationen mit (1) zusammen-hängen.[9] Ein formaler, deduktiver Beweis dafür soll hier nicht geführt werden; jedoch scheint diese Überlegung einige Plausibilität zu haben, da erst durch diese beiden Topikalisierungs- + Abstraktionsoperationen den in dem Ausdruck $\{t \cap b\}$ enthaltenen Prädikaten eine Stufung oder Sor-tierung nach Subjekt und Prädikat zuteil wird: 'blauer Himmel'/'Himmels-blau'.

Nach diesen sehr skizzenhaften Überlegungen – die über die Aussagen Vaters teilweise hinausgehen, im ganzen aber mit seinen Intentionen kom-patibel zu sein scheinen – läßt sich zum Verhältnis der Prädikat-Argument-Relation, die semantische Merkmale relativ ungeformt läßt, zur Begriffs-bzw. Prädikatstruktur folgendes sagen: die Prädikat-Argument-Relation, die, wie Reichenbach 320 f. nachweist, für die formale Organisation logisch-semantischer Strukturen absolut notwendig ist, vermag für sich allein keine als Prädikate fungiblen Ausdrücke zu konstituieren; hinzu kommen muß eine mit der Abstraktionsoperation[10] gekoppelte Topikalisierung einzelner Terme. Erst durch die Verbindung der Prädikats-Argument-Relation mit den genannten Operationen können logisch-semantische Strukturen auf die Ebene des Begriffs bzw. des in seinen jeweiligen Sortenkontexten fungiblen Prädikats gebracht werden.

---

[7] (3) kann nach Reichenbach 1947: §53 noch modifiziert werden, wenn man es für günstig erachtet, ein allgemeines Prädikat, z.B. μ – für alle für H zulässigen Prädikate einzuführen; es ergäbe sich (3)' $(\lambda f)[(\exists x)\ H(x) \cdot f(x) \cdot \mu(f) \cdot \beta(f)]$ wobei $\beta \subset \mu$.
[8] Zum Sortenbegriff in der symbolischen Logik cf. G. Hasenjäger, *Einführung in die Grund-begriffe und Probleme der modernen Logik*, Freiburg/München, 1962, 112 f.
[9] Zum Begriff und Verfahren der Topikalisierung cf. Brekle 1970: 77 ff. und Terence H. Moore, 'The Topic-Comment Function: a Performance Constraint on a Competence Model', Ph. D. Diss., University of California, Los Angeles, 1967.
[10] Cf. Reichenbach 1947: §§55, 56, wo unterschieden wird zwischen 'Logical terms in a syn-tactical capacity' und 'Logical terms in a semantical capacity'; die Prädikat-Argument-Relation fällt unter die zuerst genannte Klasse, insofern sie Substanzen formal und syntaktisch organisiert; Operatoren gehören zur zweiten Klasse: '... operators ... can be conceived as extensions of the operations of conjunction and disjunction ...' (330).

Bei unserem Autor finden wir folgende für die Charakterisierung der Kategorie 'Urteil' relevanten Aussagen: 'Sobald ich aber behauptend sage: der Tisch ist braun: so setze ich fest, daß ein gewisser Tisch, den ich meine, d.i. der nach der Wahrnehmung zu einer gewissen Zeit an einem gewissen Orte stehet, nach der Wahrnehmung wirklich braun sey; und so ist dies ein Urtheil. ... Wenn das Gemüth in der Handlung selbst begriffen ist, auf irgend eine der gedachten Arten die Verbindung des Subjekts und Prädikats zu machen: so fällt es ein Urtheil, und dies wird durch eine bestimmte Erklärung (Assertion) ausgedrückt: der Tisch ist braun' (145/146).

Wie die heutige Logik, so erkennt auch Vater als wesentliche, ein Urteil oder eine behauptete Aussage konstituierende Relation die Beziehung der Assertion an. Ein spatio-temporal verankerter Sachverhalt – z.B. daß einem Tisch zu bestimmter Zeit und an einem gegebenen Ort das Prädikat 'braun' zukommt, wird behauptet. Richtig erkennt auch Vater, daß das 'Gemüth', also ein urteilendes Bewußtsein, das Ich, an jedem Urteilsakte wesentlichen Anteil hat. Dieser Auffassung entspricht Reichenbachs Charakterisierung der Assertionsrelation als einem 'logical term in a pragmatic capacity' (336 ff.).

In der logischen Formelsprache wurde und wird teilweise heute noch zum Ausdruck der Assertion eines Sachverhalts das Symbol '⊢' gebraucht:

$$\vdash f(x_1)$$

kann z.B. die Behauptung, das Urteil repräsentieren, daß ein bestimmter Tisch $(=x_1)$ braun $(=f)$ sei. Reichenbach weist nach, daß das Symbol '⊢' – ebenso wie die Prädikat-Argument-Relation – expressiver Natur ist: "That this sign is expressive, and not denotative, can be seen as follows. The sentence 'I assert 'p' ' may be written in the form

(2)   as $(I, 'p')$

Now, if the assertion sign were denotative, '⊢p' would mean the same as (2), and could be defined by (2). But this is not possible because '⊢p' cannot be negated, whereas (2) can. ... Language cannot dispense with a merely expressive assertion sign" (336 f.).

Der Abstraktionsoperation, mit der Aussagenfunktionen (z.B. $f(x)$) auf die Ebene von Begriffen erhoben werden, entspricht beim Urteil die Assertionsrelation. Dies ist jedoch nur eine formale Analogie, da logische Operatoren (der λ-, $\imath$-, η-Operator etc.) als logische Terme mit semantischer Funktion aufzufassen sind (cf. Reichenbach, §56), während die ein Urteil konstituierende Assertionsrelation als logischer Term in pragmatischer Funktion zu werten ist, da es immer ein Ich ist, das urteilt.

Im wesentlichen trifft Vater dieselbe Feststellung, wenn er sagt: 'Jene Assertion eben ist es, durch welche der Inhalt des Urtheils sich von dem Inhalte des Begriffes unterscheidet' (147).

Im folgenden postuliert Vater eine mögliche Ableitungsbeziehung zwischen einem Urteil und einem Begriff[11]; er verkennt dabei jedoch, daß der Wegfall der Assertionsrelation bei einem Urteil dieses noch nicht automatisch zu einem Begriff macht. Dieser Unterschied in der Auffassung resultiert aus unserer Annahme, daß einem Urteil wie einem Begriff eine gemeinsame aussagenfunktionelle Basis zugrunde liegen kann, daß jedoch erst durch Anwendung von Abstraktionsoperationen aus einer solchen ein Begriff, bzw. durch die Einführung der Assertionsrelation ein Urteil zu gewinnen ist.

Vater erblickt zwischen einem Begriff und einem Urteil folgende Abhängigkeitsbeziehung: 'Eine Verbindung, welche man voraussetzt, muß in dem Gemüthe schon gemacht worden seyn. Jeder Begriff, als Handlung der Seele betrachtet, setzt also eine andre vorhergegangene Handlung derselben, ein Urtheil voraus; und jedes Urtheil, bei welchem man die Assertion aus den Augen verliert, wird ebendadurch ein Begriff' (147).

In pragmatischer Hinsicht kann durchaus 'eine Handlung der Seele' dergestalt angenommen werden, daß Subjekt und Prädikat sozusagen vorläufig in eine in bezug auf Urteils- und Begriffskategorie neutrale Verbindung gebracht werden; dann handelt es sich aber eben nicht um ein Urteil, sondern um eine Aussagenfunktion ('propositional function'), die sowohl einem Begriff wie einem Urteil zugrundeliegen kann.

Wie bei der Konstitution von Begriffen können wir auch bei Urteilen verschiedene Adäquatheitsstufen der Repräsentation logisch-semantischer Strukturen in bezug auf die sprachliche Strukturierung von Aussagen annehmen. Ein Satz wie *Hans schreibt ein Buch* kann einmal als relationales Urteil aufgefaßt werden und in seiner logisch-semantischen Struktur so abgebildet werden:

(1) $(\exists y)[S(x_1, y) \cdot B(y)]$.

Bei dieser Notation ist eine Subjekt-Prädikat-Struktur des Satzes nicht zu erkennen. Wenn wir aussagen wollen, daß *Hans* es ist, der ein Buch schreibt, so muß eine Topikalisierungsoperation angewandt werden, die zu folgendem

---

[11] Cf. E. Bach, 'Nouns and Noun Phrases' in: *Universals in Linguistic Theory* (eds. Bach/Harms) New York, 1968, 121: '. . . I have argued on the basis of many pieces of evidence that it is reasonable to suppose that all nouns come from relative clauses based on the predicate nominal constituent'.

Eines der von Bach gegebenen Beispiele für eine Ableitungsbeziehung zwischen einer Aussage (hier Relativsatz) und einem Begriff (hier Substantiv) ist: 'I never speak to anyone who is a behaviorist' → 'I never speak to a behaviorist'. (31 f.).

Resultat führen kann (im Prinzip ist jeder der denotativen Terme eines Ausdrucks topikalisierbar)

(2) $x_1 \in \overrightarrow{S'y} \cdot (\exists y)B(y)$[12]

(2) läßt sich sprachlich auch wiedergeben als: *Hans ist ein Schreiber eines Buchs.* Wir nehmen an, daß, von stilistischen Differenzen abgesehen, dieser Satz dem Ausdruck *Hans schreibt ein Buch* äquivalent ist und der Annahme gerecht wird, daß 'Hans' als Subjekt bzw. als 'topic' fungiert. Reichenbach handelt über denselben Sachverhalt (ohne den Terminus 'Topikalisierung' zu verwenden), wenn er schreibt: "Consider the sentence, 'a friend of a soldier came'. We would regard the phrase 'a friend of a soldier' as a unit [= 'Subjekt'/'topic'], and the function 'came' as the other unit, which might be called the major function [= 'Prädikat'/'comment']. When we symbolize this sentence, however, we find the following form, with 's' for 'soldier', 'f' for 'friend', and 'c' for 'came':

(1) $(\exists x) \quad (\exists y) \, s(y) \cdot f(x, y) \cdot c(x).$

Here the first unit has disappeared and we find three coordinated functions, among which no major function is distinguishable. . . . If we want to construct a symbolization that corresponds more closely to the pragmatic structure, i.e., the structure as far as emphasis and other psychological intentions are concerned, we may use descriptions . . . .

(2) $c \quad \{(\eta x)f[x, (\eta y) \, s(y)]\}$ (350)".

Aus den beiden Beispielen ist also zu ersehen, daß die symbolische Logik durchaus Mittel bereitstellen kann, um spezifisch sprachliche Strukturen, die pragmatisch oder psychologisch motiviert sind, adäquat abzubilden.

Dieser – wenn auch skizzenhafte – Exkurs in die Problematik der Zusammenhänge zwischen symbollogischen Notationsverfahren und sprachlichen Strukturen sollte einerseits wenigstens andeuten, daß die Sprachwissenschaft in der symbolischen Logik ein Instrumentarium besitzt, das bei der theoretisch konsistenten und formalen Repräsentation sprachlicher Strukturen nützlich sein kann; andererseits sollte gezeigt werden, daß die grundsätzlichen Überlegungen des hier hauptsächlich zu diskutierenden Autors – Johann Severin Vater – zur Begriffs- und Urteilsstruktur tendentiell mit heutigen Fragestellungen innerhalb desselben Bereichs zusammenhängen.

Unser Autor betrachtet es als eine legitime Fragestellung einer 'allgemeinen Sprachlehre' wenn gefragt wird, 'wodurch diese Theile des Urtheils

---

[12] Zum Formalismus cf. *Principia Mathematica* $_*32$, bes. $_*32.18 - _*32.182$.

[viz. Subjekt, Prädikat, Modalitäten etc.] in ihnen [den einzelnen Sprachen] ausgedrückt werden . . .' (152).

Im folgenden Zitat wird deutlich, daß Vater die Problematik der morphosyntaktischen Repräsentation dieser allgemeinen Urteilskategorien richtig einschätzt, insofern diese Kategorien nicht notwendig durch 'ausgezeichnete Formen' repräsentiert zu sein brauchen. 'Es läßt sich durch keine Vernunftgründe erweisen, daß diese, sicher jedem Ausdrucke der Gedanken zugrunde liegenden, Begriffe auch in jeder Sprache irgend eine ausgezeichnete Form der Endung, des Anfangs, der Vokalveränderung im Innern des Wortes, der Stellung des Wortes neben andern Wörtern, oder des Tons der Aussprache, haben müßten' (152).

Trotzdem kann – das ist sicher eine richtige Einsicht Vaters – versucht werden, solche 'ausgezeichneten Formen' durch Vergleichung zu finden und nach ihren syntaktischen und semantischen Funktionen zu fragen.

Vater stellt also fest, 'daß jene Anwendung der allgemeinen Beschaffenheit des Inhalts aller Urtheile zur Begründung einer allgemeinen Sprachlehre führen könne' (155).

Er sieht jedoch auch, daß die 'Fächer', die durch die im Urteil gegebenen logischen Kategorien etabliert werden, einen zu allgemeinen kategorialen Rahmen für eine Sprachtheorie ergeben. Er fordert folgerichtig, daß weitere – eher pragmatisch zu motivierende – semantische Kategorien dazu kommen müssen. Er nimmt an, diese Kategorien seien auf dem Wege der Zergliederung der Arten des Vorkommens des Subjekts oder Prädikats zu finden. 'Es ist an sich wahrscheinlich, daß sich solche Arten unterscheiden lassen, und jeder von uns hat solche Unterschiede aufgefaßt, z.B. zwischen Subjektswörtern (Substantiven) wie: Gold, Vergoldung, Vergolder; levator, levatio, levamentum' (155).

Vater kommt nun zu folgender Definition der Aufgabe der 'allgemeinen Sprachlehre'. Sie ist 'die Zergliederung der Begriffe der wesentlichen Theile des Urtheils, zum Behufe einer allgemeinen Übersicht dessen, was in Sprachen, durch irgend eine Art von charakteristischer Form bezeichnet seyn kann' (157).

Unser Autor konzediert bei der Aufstellung von für die sprachliche Struktur von Urteilen relevanten syntaktischen und semantischen Kategorien eine Art von Toleranzprinzip: 'Auch kann bei Zergliederungen . . . der Eine von andern Rücksichten und Eintheilungsgründen ausgehen, als der Andre, je nachdem er die bequemste Übersicht der Begriffe zu erreichen hofft' (159).

Die heutige Forschungslage im Bereich der allgemeinen Sprachwissenschaft spiegelt dieses Toleranzprinzip wider. Unser Autor schließt den Abschnitt III. *Über den Begriff und die Begründung einer allgemeinen Sprach-*

lehre mit einer Erkenntnis, die grundsätzlich auch in entsprechenden heutigen sprachtheoretischen Aussagen zu finden ist[13] : 'Sie [die allgemeine Sprachlehre] behauptet blos dadurch ihre Allgemeinheit, daß sie das aufstellt, was sich über die möglichen Gegenstände der Bezeichnung im Allgemeinen sagen läßt . . . Keine von diesen möglichen oder nothwendigen Theile des Urtheils muß in den Sprachen bezeichnet seyn. Von der wirklichen Bezeichnung hat also Sprachlehre nichts Allgemeines, also Nichts zu sagen; sondern die Wirklichkeit ist der Sprachgebrauch einzelner Sprachen, welche die Grammatiken derselben schildern. Der Inhalt der allgemeinen Sprachlehre ist demnach nicht weitläuftig; aber groß und umfassend ist der Umfang ihrer Anwendung zur Übersicht aller einzelnen Sprachen' (161/162).

Universität Regensburg

---

[13] Cf. z.B. E. Bach, *loc. cit.* 113: '. . . one could claim that languages all share exactly the same set of substantive elements. . . . this is much better than a hypothesis that languages share no substantive elements. But once again it is too obviously false to merit discussion. The truth must lie somewhere between these two extremes. One frequent claim is that each language makes some undetermined selection from a stock of universal elements'.

J. J. CHRISTIE

SOME UNDERLYING STRUCTURES IN SWAHILI

Recent studies in generative syntax have suggested two interesting hypotheses: that the source of noun phrases should be an embedded sentence, and that auxiliary verbs should be treated as 'full' verbs, or at least as some kind of predicate, on which a subordinate sentence is embedded. (See Bach, 1968; McCawley, 1968; Ross, 1967; Lakoff, to appear, and many unpublished papers by these and others). This article makes similar proposals for Swahili. Its purpose is not to explore these proposals in general, but rather to discuss a relatively limited amount of material and show that both hypotheses can be well motivated, and, further, that they do not result in underlying structures which are 'remote' from surface structures; rather they are, in some cases, 'closer' to surface structure than possible alternatives. The article is in two main parts: the first discusses nominal and pronominal forms; the second, the structure of the verbal group. In both we proceed by presenting Swahili material and traditional accounts of it and then discussing possible alternatives.

I

The problems raised by nominal and pronominal forms can be approached by first considering Example[1]:

(1)   *mtoto alivinunua vitabu*   the child bought the books

This can be given a morphemic segmentation as follows:

(2)   Pref + Stem Pref + Tense + Pref + Radical + Indicat. Pref + Stem
          m + *toto*   *a* + *li* + *vi* + *nunu* +   *a*   *vi* + *tabu*

and might be glossed as: child he + past + them + buy books.

The prefixes on the two nouns illustrate the noun class system in Swahili, and the relationship between the prefixes *m-* and the following *a-*, and between *-vi-* and the following *vi-* illustrate the phenomenon of concord or agreement. A brief account of these can be given as follows.[2] Each noun can be analyzed as consisting of a prefix and a stem, thus *m* + *toto* as shown, and the nouns classified according to the shape of the prefix.

---

[1] Examples are given in standard orthography, unless otherwise indicated.
[2] A fuller account can be found in Ashton (1964), Polomé (1967).

F. Kiefer and N. Ruwet (eds.), Generative Grammar in Europe, 122–140. All Rights Reserved.
Copyright © 1973 by D. Reidel Publishing Company, Dordrecht-Holland.

The following examples will make this clear:

(3) $m + toto$ child
       $wa + toto$ children
       $ki + tabu$ book
       $vi + tabu$ books
       $m + ti$ tree
       $mi + ti$ trees

It can be said then that in the prefix the categories of number and class are cumulated. On the basis of the prefixes a morphological classification of nouns can be established. In this article we shall refer to *mtoto* as being in the M/WA class, rather than speaking of two classes M and WA, or using a numerical classification. The phenomenon of concord can be described simply for our purposes by saying that in the construction N + V the verbal group must have a prefix related to the noun class, and the same holds for other constructions such as N + Adj., N + Demons. etc.

This account however is not fully adequate for syntactic purposes. All nouns in the class M/WA are animate, but not all animate nouns are in this class. Thus *kipofu* 'blind man', *vipofu* 'blind men' have the class KI/VI prefixes but they require the concordial prefixes of the M/WA class. Thus we have:

(4)   *mtoto mkubwa yule anaanguka*   that big child is falling down
       (lit. child big that he + progressive + fall down)
(5)   *kipofu mkubwa yule ananguka*   that big blind man is falling down
(6)   *kiti kikubwa kile kinaanguka*   that big chair is falling down

In (4) there is a sequence of prefixes which can be shown as: *m- m- yu- a-* and in (5) *kipofu* also requires: *m- yu- a-*. To account for this the category of animacy must be added to those of number and class.[3] The prefixes on the three nouns could thus be specified as, respectively: +Animate, +Class M/WA, +Sing., +Animate, +Class KI/VI, +Singular, and −Animate, +Class KI/VI, +Singular. The distinction ±Animate will thus permit the verbal prefix in (5) to be shown as *a-* and not as **ki-*.[4]

The syntactic problem with which we are centrally concerned can now be approached. In example (1) the verbal pronominal can be accounted for in terms of the notion 'control'. That is, it can be said that the noun 'controls' the choice of prefix which is therefore 'in agreement with' the noun. In examples

[3] We assume for convenience that animacy can be regarded as a syntactic category.
[4] We ignore the possibility of pejorative, diminutive and augmentative uses.

(7) and (8) below, this account is not possible:

| (7) | *ananguka* | he is falling down |
| (8) | *tunakusaidia* | we are helping you |

((7) can be segmented as : $a + na + anguka$, he + progressive + fall down; and (8) as: $tu + na + ku + saidia$, we + progressive + you + help). In (7) and (8) we are concerned with deictic pronominals which cannot be accounted for in terms of control. Taken together these examples suggest a rule of the form:

$$(9) \qquad NP \rightarrow \begin{cases} N \\ Pron. \end{cases}$$

with a 'copying' rule which will attach the relevant copy of the noun prefix to the verbal to produce (1).[5] Such an account could make explicit the sense in which some prefixes are 'controlled' by a preceding noun and others are 'uncontrolled'. The problem is however more complex than this. Consider (10) and (11):

| (10) | *mtoto mkubwa ananguka* | the big child is falling down |
| (11) | *mkubwa ananguka* | the big (one) is falling down |

In (10) the prefix on the adjective can be said to be 'controlled' by the noun but this account is not always available for (11). For some instances of (11) we might invoke anaphora and assume that a noun in a preceding sentence has been deleted by a 'rule of discourse', but in other instances it must be accepted as what might be called an 'autonymous adjectival', used with deictic force. It is with the latter cases that we are concerned and, just as there is no case to regard deictic pronominals as derived from an underlying noun, so there is no case to analyze the 'autonymous adjectivals' in this way. This has led some scholars to propose that *mkubwa* in (11) should in fact be analyzed as a nominal and to extend this analysis to *mkubwa* in (10),[6] thus two classes of nominal are established: those like *mtoto* with a very restricted range of prefixes, and those like *-kubwa* with a wide range of prefixes. The difference between *mkubwa* in (10) and (11) is then stated in terms of 'control'.[7] Syntactically this position is untenable. In (10) *mkubwa* must follow the noun, the sequence **mkubwa mtoto* being ungrammatical. The syntactic position is that two classes of item must be distinguished; one class in which the prefixes are not 'controlled' containing both *mtoto* (10) and *mkubwa* (11); and one whose members cannot precede a noun and whose prefixes are 'controlled', containing *mkubwa* (10) but not *mtoto*. If the first class is called

---

[5] See Gregersen (1967) for an account essentially on these lines.
[6] See for example Whiteley (1960).
[7] The terminology used is 'short-series nominals' (nouns) and 'long-series nominals' (adjectives).

'nominal', the distinction between the 'nominals' *mtoto* and *mkubwa* is morphological only: it will be apparent on observation that *mtoto* is restricted in its range of prefixes but this will be of no syntactic significance. The second class might then quite naturally be called 'adjectival'. The issue is not simply a terminological one. If the first class is the class of 'nominals' then *mkubwa* in (11) is a 'nominal'. As a consequence it follows that the lexicon must, for items such as *-kubwa*, contain separate entries such as: *mkubwa*, *kikubwa* etc. and so on for each noun class. In addition it will contain an entry for *-kubwa* as an adjectival. Further the semantic entry for all these items will be identical except for distinction in class prefixes. There are clearly compelling grounds to seek an alternative to the analysis just discussed. It has been considered at some length not only because it has been widely held, but also because it reflects the problems which arise in an approach limited to surface structure analysis. Indeed given such an approach, it seems to be the only account possible.

It has been assumed so far that forms like *mkubwa* are to be treated as syntactically unanalyzed, as *mtoto* might be. Let it now be assumed that they are analyzable. An obvious possibility is that *mkubwa* could be syntactically analyzed as *m + kubwa*. The question which then arises is what the syntactic status of *m-* could be. When examples (7) and (8) were discussed, it was shown that an element Pron. was required for the deictic pronominals. Previous discussion showed that this element must be minimally specified as: ±Animate, +Class, ±Singular. It will be clear that the same specification is required for *mkubwa* as an 'autonomous adjectival'. It is proposed therefore that a structure for such a form be of the type:

(12)

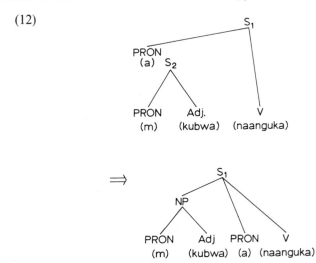

The structure in (12) is of course illustrative only, but it can also be used to indicate the types of operation required to transform (a) to (b). We require adjunction of Pron to Adj in S_2 to form the derived NP (*mkubwa*), and then a raising rule to attach the derived NP to S_1. An identity condition must hold between Pron in S_1 and Pron in S_2 and this in effect captures the notion of 'control', though it will be noticed that it is in fact the verbal pronominal which is 'controlling' since it is the higher node. We return to this point below.

It follows that a structure like (12) will also generate nouns, if we replace the node Adj in S_2 by N, thus producing by Chomsky-adjunction *mtoto*. The proposals embodied in (12) clearly have implications for the status of terms like 'word', 'noun' and 'adjective' in Swahili. These are discussed in Section III, in conjunction with the proposals made in Section II. For the moment, we consider the advantages of a derivation like (12), and its applicability to related structures. It is immediately satisfactory in that it permits us to account for the 'autonomous adjectivals', since their syntactically quasi-nominal status is handled by the derivation from a pronominal; they can be considered as derived adjectival pronominals. There will consequently be no need to list these in the lexicon. In addition, (12) permits a homogeneous account of the prefix system. Firstly there is no need to treat some prefixes as 'merely concordial' or as 'copies' – this, it will be remembered, was the implication of one interpretation of 'control'. Secondly, it simplifies the morphophonological rules. A noun such as *mtoto* can now be entered in the lexicon as -*TOTO* with the relevant feature specification, just as the adjectival stem -*KUBWA* will be entered, but without such features. A common set of rules can then state the realization of feature bundles in accordance with the syntactic environment. Were the nouns not analyzed syntactically as Pron + N, then the familiar problems recur, as they were shown for the adjectivals. Either the nouns must be unanalyzed, a proposal not satisfactory on both morphological and syntactic grounds, or they must be analyzed as two elements. If the first element is not a pronominal, it is difficult to see what its syntactic status could be. If it is not given such status, but treated perhaps as a feature bundle which is 'created' as a segment by transformation, then it must be treated as quite different from the prefix of the 'autonomous adjectival' and from the deictic pronominals, so that no homogeneous account of the prefix system is possible.

The foregoing proposal suggests in essence that both nouns and adjectives have an embedded sentential source. It is therefore pertinent to enquire how relative clauses might be generated. Notice that as well as (10) and (11) (shown again below as (13) and (15)) we may have (14) and (16):

(13)	*mtoto mkubwa anaanguka*	the big child is falling down
(14)	*aliye mtoto mkubwa anaanguka*	the one who is a big child is falling down
(15)	*mkubwa anaanguka*	the big one is falling down
(16)	*aliye mkubwa anaanguka*	the one who is big is falling down

In both (14) and (16) *aliye* can be analyzed as:

(17)   Pron + Cop + Pron + 0

      a   li   yu   o

with a rule $yu + o - ye$. (The segment *-o*, termed by Ashton (*op. cit.*) the 'o of reference' is obligatory in such constructions.) If the pronominals are glossed as 'one' and the 'o of reference' as 'wh', then *aliye mkubwa* in (16) could be glossed as: one be wh-one one-big. In (16) we must thus account for four pronominals, *a-*, *-yu*, *m-*, *a-*. It follows from the structure discussed before that a possible underlying structure for (16) is (18):

(18)

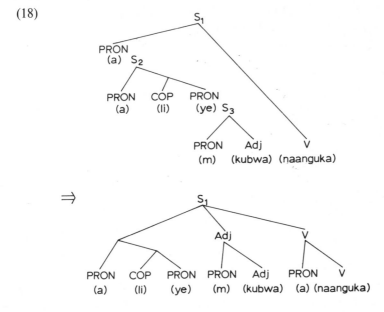

(It is assumed that the 'o of reference' is inserted by a transformation). It seems clear that pairs such as (15) and (16), 'the big one', 'the one who is big' are to be related. It also seems clear that unless the underlying structure of nouns and adjectives is as suggested here then it will be impossible to relate such pairs directly. Further it is now possible to regard (18) as an intermediate stage in the derivation of (12), after which a rule deletes the relative pronominal complex *aliye*.

There are several constructions where the proposal to derive nouns and adjectives sententially offers positive advantages.[8] In current transformational accounts of pronominalization within the sentence, the English 'the boy said that he would go' would be generated from the structure underlying 'the boy said that the boy would go'. The anaphoric 'he' is thus introduced by a transformation and there are two sources for 'he' in the grammar. The proposal made here is simpler to the extent that the second pronominal is already available, since the structure will be of the form 'one who is . . . said that one who is . . .', and need not therefore be transformationally introduced. This account also avoids the difficulty that elements introduced transformationally are only indirectly related to any underlying form. If Pron is introduced transformationally it is related to the Pron generated in the base in form only. Further, the proposal here seems more satisfactory from a psychological point of view: rather than replacing a noun phrase, the speaker, one might say, does not need to repeat it. A further advantage accrues when two definite descriptions are used. In English and in Swahili there are examples like 'John came and he tried to . . .' and 'John came and the fool tried to . . .'. On the proposal here there will be two Pron elements in each sentence and the identity condition can be defined on these alone. Thus in the case of two definite descriptions we shall have the structure: . . . Pron_{S_x} . . . Pron_{S_y}, where $\text{Pron}_1 = \text{Pron}_2$ but where $S_x \neq S_y$. Pronominalization will require that $S_x = S_y$; in the case where this is not so, the notation will capture the identity of reference despite the different descriptions of the referent.

The discussion in this section can be summarized as follows. It was shown that there is compelling evidence to analyze adjectivals in the 'autonymous' cases as consisting of two syntactic elements. The proposal to derive them – and by extension, all adjectives and nouns – from embedded sentences is not in conflict with surface structure evidence, in fact it permits a homogeneous analysis of the prefix system and is in accord with the morphological structure. (Further, there is, as will be discussed later, a traditional analysis in Bantu studies which implicitly supports this view.) The proposal was then shown to be attractive in the generation of other syntactic constructions. The discussion has of course been restricted. No account has been given of demonstratives and quantifiers, nor of the nature of the copula. It is not likely however that these structures will radically affect the basic proposal made here for the pronominals.

---

[8] These brief examples will be familiar from such works as Bach (op. cit.) and others. They are intended only to show that the advantages accrue in Swahili also.

II

In this section a different set of data is examined in order to consider the underlying structure of the verbal group. The discussion is conducted in two parts: the first concerns the occurrence of the infinitive segment *-ku-*; the second, the analysis of tense and aspectual segments.[9]

Consider the following examples:

(19)	*kuimba*	to sing
(20)	*kuja*	to come
(21)	*aliimba*	he sang
(22)	*alikuja*	he came

The first two can be segmented morphemically as:

(23)   Infin. + Radical + Indicative
          ku   imb   a
          ku   j   a

Example (20) can be shown as:

(24)   Pron + Tense + Radical + Indicative
          a   li   imb   a

Example (22) can be segmented in the same way, except for the occurrence of the infinitive segment *-ku-*. Three conditions can be stated for the occurrence of *-ku-*. Firstly, it occurs with a small set of radicals, which, together with the indicative, form a monosyllable: thus *-ja* 'come' above, also *-la* 'eat', *-fa* 'die' and some others. Additionally, it occurs for some speakers with verbs which do not fulfil this condition: *-iba* 'steal', *-oga* 'wash', *-enda* 'go' and others. We shall designate such verbs the set + KU. Secondly, with such verbs *-ku* only occurs when certain tense and aspect segments also occur.[10] Thus we have (25) and (26) but not (27):

(25)	*akaimba*	(and) he sang
(26)	*akala*	(and) he ate
(27)	**akakula*	(and) he ate

We must therefore distinguish a set of tense and aspect segments with which *-ku* may occur, given that the verb belongs to the set +*ku*. This set will include *-li-* 'past' as in (21), but not *-ka-* 'subsecutive' or 'narrative'. This set will again be designated the set + KU. Thirdly, *-ku-* will not occur if an object

[9] I am grateful to P. H. Matthews for comments on an earlier draft of part of this section.
[10] The term 'tense and aspect segment' is loosely used, to cover in addition segments realizing hypotheticals, counter-factuals etc., which occur in the same position.

pronominal does. Thus we have (28) and (29), but not (30):

(28)   *aliziimba*   he sang them
(29)   *alivila*   he ate them
(30)   *alivikula*   he ate them

The occurrence of -*ku*- is usually accounted for in terms of stress, which in Swahili falls regularly on the penultimate syllable of the phonological word. Thus Polomé speaks of -*ku*- as in (22) as 'functioning as a mere stress-bearer in tenses whose marker cannot receive stress' (Polomé, 1967, p. 112); Ashton (1964, p. 35) gives a similar account. Ashton (*op. cit.*), Meinhof (1906) and Steere (1870) identify the -*ku*- with the infinitive -*ku*-, as we have done here, Polomé does not do so directly. On this account the occurrence of *alikuja* (22) but not *alija* is explained by saying that -*li*- cannot 'receive stress', that -*j*- belongs to the set of verbs + KU and that no object pronominal occurs. All the authorities quoted agree in regarding -*ku*- as 'retained' in such cases, and 'dropped' in the others.

There are grounds to question this account of -*ku*- as a 'stress-bearer'. Consider the following examples, the negative versions of (21) and (22):

(31)   *hakuimba*   he did not sing
(32)   *hakuja*   he did not come

These are segmentable as follows:

(33)   Neg. + Pron. +   ?   + Radical + Indicative
           ha   a   ku   imb   a

(where *ha* + *a* − *ha*). The problem here is the analysis of -*ku*- which always occurs in past negative forms. It is customarily regarded as a tense 'marker': Ashton says '*ku* is here the tense-prefix' (*op. cit.*, p. 72) and Polomé makes a similar statement (*op. cit.*, p. 122). The grounds for this can be seen if (33) is compared with (24). Between the Pron. and the Radical in (24) -*li*- 'past' occurs; in (33) this 'slot' is 'filled' by -*ku*-. (This terminology is used by Polomé, *op. cit.*) If it is accepted that there must be a 'slot' specifically for tense and that this must be 'filled', then this account stands. Notice however that -*ku*- in (32) is still the 'stress-bearer', but on this account it is not analyzed as such, though it is in the affirmative (22). An alternative analysis is to treat this -*ku*- also as the infinitive -*ku*-. On this approach the examples can be shown as follows:

(34)   (Neg) + Pron + Tense + Infinitive + Radical + Indicative
(21)   −   a   li   ∅   imb   a
(22)   −   a   li   ku   j   a

| (31) | ha | a | ∅ | ku | imb | a |
| (32) | ha | a | ∅ | ku | j | a |

Apart from its greater simplicity, this proposal has the following advantages. Infinitive in (21) will receive no phonological realization in accordance with the three conditions which were stated above; in the past negative cases, this rule will apply after the rule which gives Tense no realization. This will automatically generate the correct strings. When the stress-assignment rules apply, it will be the case that -*ku*- in (22) and (32) bears the stress, but we need not speak of certain segments as 'unable to receive stress'. The import of this quotation is by no means clear. If it refers to the phonological form of the element then it is incorrect. The phonological sequence -*li*- as a realization of the copula does in fact bear stress (see example (14) in Section I). Notice moreover that verbs like -*iba*, as mentioned above, may occur either with -*ku*- or without it:

| (35) | *aliiba* | he stole |
| (36) | *alikwiba* | he stole |

(*ku* + *i* → *kwi*). The ability of -*li*- to receive stress is here manifestly irrelevant. The proposal embodied in (33) still makes it possible to regard -*ku*- as, in some sense, a 'marker' of tense, not in the sense that it is the tense segment which 'fills' the 'tense slot', but in the more general sense that -*ku*- will in fact occur in past negative forms and that there will be no segmental realization of 'past'. The proposal also makes it possible to make a clear diachronic statement of the sort '-*ku*- dropped when it was unstressed' without invoking the synchronic statement that it is 'retained to bear the stress for elements which cannot receive it'. Finally, it permits a homogeneous treatment of -*ku*- as in each case the infinitive, and this is to be preferred in default of any good evidence to the contrary.

The foregoing discussion raises the question, central to this section, of what the source of the *ku*- segment might be. There seem to be three possibilities. Firstly, it might simply be inserted by transformational rules, subject to the conditions stated above. While this proposal is weakly adequate, it fails to reflect the analysis that *ku*- is, in all these cases, the infinitive *ku*-. It would also fail to reflect the traditional view that the 'stress-bearing' *ku*- is 'retained' rather than 'inserted', this view being based on diachronic evidence. A second proposal might be that -*ku*- is generated as part of the expansion of an Aux. node. Thus there might be a rule of the form:

| (37) | Vbl. → Aux. + V |
| (38) | Aux. → Tense + Infin. |

with subsequent rules for 'dropping -*ku*-'. This would be consistent with the analysis in this paper and appears to be the simplest account. A third possibility also exists: this is to derive the -*ku*- from an embedded sentence. This can be shown to be credible by considering cases where this is arguably the source of the infinitive. In a sentence such as (39):

(39)   *alitaka kuja*   he wanted to come

(lit. he + past + want to + come), we may suggest an underlying structure of the type: S_1 (he want) S_2 (he come). Where the identity condition holds between the two subject pronominals, the embedded sentence is transformed to Infin. + V. A parallel proposal can clearly be made for the cases we have been discussing so far. Thus a possible structure for *anakuja* 'he is coming' might be: S_1 (he Prog.) S_2 (he come) with the same rule operating to produce: He Prog. Infin. + V. In the subsequent discussion we shall consider the merits of the two latter proposals.

The proposal that the infinitive is generated as part of an expansion of Aux. loses much of its simplicity when compound verbal forms are considered. Compare (40) and (41):

(40)   *alikuja*   he came
(41)   *alikuwa anakuja*   he was coming

Example (41) can be shown in two ways. It can be analyzed as: he + Past + BE he + Prog + Infin. + V, which would show the parallel between the first element *alikuwa* and its occurrence in:

(42)   *alikuwa mwalimu*   he was a teacher

(It will be noticed that -*wa* 'be' is in the set + KU.) An alternative is to analyze the whole stretch -*likuwa* in (41), but not (42), as a form of Past. The latter proposal seems unmotivated: not only does it fail to show the obvious parallel, but it also fails to capture the fact that *alikuwa* in (41) and (42) behave identically under negation and relativization:

(43)   *aliyekuwa anakuja*   he who was coming
(44)   *aliyekuwa mwalimu*   he who was a teacher
(45)   *hakuwa anakuja*   he was not coming
(46)   *hakuwa mwalimu*   he was not a teacher

We accept therefore the analysis which involves a form of the copula 'be'. It follows then that on the proposal under discussion we require, for (40) and (41) strings like the following:

(47)   (a) Pron. + Past + Infin. + V
             a   li   ku   ja

         (b) Pron. + Past + Infin. + Cop. Pron. + Prog. + Infin. + V
             a   li   ku   wa   a   na   ku   ja

where (47b) must be derived from two Aux. nodes, the first of which relates to the copula verb, and the second to the main verb. Presumably then the rule (37) must be altered to something like[11]:

(48)   Vbl − Aux. + V
         $Aux._1 + Cop. + Aux._2 + V$

The problem now arises that there are contextual restrictions on what can occur as $Aux._1$ and $Aux._2$. We may have: -li- 'past', -ta- 'future', -me- 'perfect', -na- 'progressive', -a- 'simple', -ka- 'narrative, subsecutive' as $Aux._1$; and -me- 'perfect', -na- 'progressive', -ki- 'continuous' as $Aux._2$. It will be noticed that the sets overlap. The sequences: *. . . me . . . . me, and . . . .*. . . . na . . . . me . . . are however ungrammatical:

(49)   *alikuwa amekuja*   he had come
         (lit. he + Past + be he + Perfect + come)

(50)   **amekuwa amekuja*

(51)   **anakuwa amekuja*

It follows then on this proposal that context-sensitive rules are required to prevent the ungrammatical sequences, or recourse must be made to ad hoc 'interpretive' devices to show the ungrammaticality of (50), (51).

The proposal just outlined, which was initially described as the simpler of the two and the one closest to the surface structure, is thus by no means as simple as it appears at first. Nor is it in fact the closest to the surface structure. It will have been noticed that the compound verbals have the structure of two sentences: see (49), where it is clear that both parts of the verbal can be described as having a subject pronominal, a tense/aspect segment and a verb. Further, either part may be negated. Taken together these facts offer strong support for the third proposal, that embedded sentences are involved in the generation of verbal forms. This evidence is strengthened by the fact that in the compound forms the second part of the verbal is the part which is passivized:

---

[11] See Gregersen (*op. cit.*) for a treatment on these lines.

(52)   *ziliimbwa*   they were sung
(53)   *zilikuwa zinaimbwa*   they were being sung
(54)   Pron. + Past + Radical + Passive + Indicative
        zi   li   imb   w   a

and the structure of the second part of (53) is identical, but for the occurrence of *-na-* 'progressive' in place of *-li-* 'past'. If the sentential source for (53) is accepted, then the passive rule can be formulated for it as it must be for sentences like:

(55)   *alitaka ziimbwe*   he wanted them to be sung

(where *ziimbwe* is a passive subjunctive form). If this approach is not accepted, then the formulation of the passive rule to cover both (52) and (53) will be the more complicated.

As additional evidence for the sentential derivation of the verbals, evidence such as Lakoff has adduced for English can be given. In (56):

(56)   *Juma alikuwa mwalimu mkuu, jambo ambalo halikutokea mpaka baada ya siku nyingi*
        Juma became head teacher, but this did not happen until many days later

it is clear that *jambo* 'this (matter)' replaces something like 'Juma become head teacher' and not 'Juma became head teacher'. On the assumption that only whole constituents can be replaced, it then follows that Past must be outside the sentence 'Juma become head teacher'. If this line of argument is accepted, the problem is then to provide a source for Past. Clearly the sentential analysis proposed here can provide such a source; if *alikuwa* is derived from something like: (he Past) (he become).

The evidence given so far in favour of the sentential derivation has come from the compound verbal forms. We now consider the non-compound forms which also provide a variety of evidence in favour of the proposal.

Consider initially the pair:

(57)   *asiyekuja*   he who does not come
(58)   *asiye mwalimu*   he who is not a teacher

Example (58) can be shown as:

(59)   Pron + Neg + Rel. Pron   N
        a   si   ye   mwalimu
        (lit. he + not + who teacher)

On the sentential analysis proposed, the string *asiye* + *kuja* will be generated after infinitivalization. The derived form *kuja* will be a nominal – notice that this is required in any case for nominalizations such as *kuja kwake* 'his coming' (lit. to + come of + him) – the structure proposed will therefore relate (57) to (58), since both will have a nominal element following the verbal, thus reflecting the clear surface parallel. If a non-sentential analysis of (57) is adopted, then the structural parallel and the uniformity of the nomino-verbal *-kuja* is lost. Compare again the pair:

(60)   *alitaka kuziimba*   he wanted to sing them

(61)   *aliziimba*   he sang them

((60): he + past + want to + them + sing; (61): he + past + them + sing.) On the account proposed here, (61) is at some stage: $a + li + ku + zi + imba$ before *-ku-* is deleted because of the presence of the object pronominal. The parallel between (60) and (61) is thus clear. Further both occurrences of *-kuziimba* are accounted for in the same way, namely as sentential nominalizations. It will also be clear that this analysis will permit the rule which 'places' the pronominal *-zi-* to be specified uniformly for both (60) and (61). A non-sentential analysis of (61) will fail on all these counts.

There is a variety of other evidence which indirectly supports the sentential account. One implication of the latter is that the tense or aspectual segments, for example *-li-* 'past' in (60) and (61), are themselves to be given verbal status, since (61) will have a structure on the lines of (ha + past) (he come). There is both synchronic and diachronic evidence for this proposal. The synchronic state of the verb *-ish-* 'finish' seems to show that what is unquestionably a 'full verb' is also, for some speakers, an 'auxiliary' verb:

(62)   *amekwisha kuimba*   he has finished singing

(63)   *amekwisha imba*   id.

(64)   *ameisha imba*   id.

(65)   *ameshaimba*   id.

((62): he + perfect + infin. + finish infin. + sing). (65) shows an 'allegro' form, me + ish → mesh, and for speakers who have this form there is no distinction to be made between it and the normal perfect:

(66)   *ameimba*   he has sung

The synchronic development of -ish- in fact reflects the diachronic development of the segment -me- 'perfect', which itself has as its origin a verb 'finish'. The diachronic origin of certain other segments supports the 'verbal-source' account. Compare:

(67)	*atakuja*	he will come
(68)	*ataka kuja*	he wants to come
(69)	*atakayekuja*	he who will come
(70)	*atakaye kuja*	he who wants to come

where the verb *-tak-* 'want' is the diachronic source of the *-ta/taka-* 'future' segment. In (71)–(74), the segments *-ja-* and *-je-* occur, respectively the radical and indicative and the radical and subjunctive of *-j-* 'come':

(71)	*hatujafikiri*	we have not yet thought

(lit. neg. + we + perfect + think. Compare the English 'we have not yet come to think . . .')

(72)	*tusije hapa*	lest we should come here
(73)	*tusije tukafikiri*	lest we should (come to) think
(74)	*tusijesoma*	before we read

In (72), *-j-* is a 'full' verb, in (71), (73) and (74) it is, in a loose sense, an aspectual auxiliary. Such diachronic evidence can hardly, of course, be given the same status as the synchronic evidence. Nonetheless, given that the proposal for a sentential analysis was independently motivated on synchronic grounds, then it is reasonable to regard this proposal as all the stronger since it does not contradict, but rather reflects, the diachronic development.

One other implication of the sentential analysis of the simple verbals is that they will at some stage have the structure:

(75)	(Pron Tense) (Infin. V)
	(a li) (ku ja)

rather than simply as a single constituent: (Pron + Tense + Infin. + V), (he + past + to + come). It can be asked therefore whether there is any additional evidence to support the constituent structure in (75). There is in fact both phonological and orthographic evidence in its favour. In (76):

(76)	*alipokwenda*	when he went

(lit. he + past + when + to + go + ; *a + li + po + ku + enda*) the stress falls regularly on the penultimate syllable. There is also a secondary stress on *-li-* (cf. Polomé, *op. cit.* p. 191). If, as proposed, the structure is at some stage: *alipo + kwenda*, then the rule which assigns stress to *kwenda* will also assign it to *alipo*. A subsequent rule can then 'raise' the stress on *kwenda* to form the phonological unit with one major stress. This can also be illustrated by (72) and (74), where *tusije* will in each case receive stress, but in (74), where one phonological unit must be formed, the stress on *-soma* will be 'raised'. If, in fact, this analysis is not adopted, then a separate rule, unrelated to the penultimate stress rule, is required to account for the secondary stress on *-li-* in (76) and on *-si-* in (74). Orthographic evidence supports this constituent division. Although standard spelling requires (76), it could be attested as two orthographic words: *alipo* and *kwenda* (cf. Steere, *op. cit.*). This is still the case with speakers who have little formal education in Swahili.

Further evidence for this particular constituent division can be given from constructions like:

(77)   *walicheza na waliimba*   they played and sang
(78)   *walicheza na kuimba*   they played and sang

Given that the structure of (77) underlies (78) also, then it is clear that the infinitive *ku-* has here replaced *wali-*, and this can be more simply stated if *wali-* is a constituent. (Notice also that on this account, underlying (77) will be: *walikucheza na walikuimba*. The infinitive *ku-* is thus already available and we need not seek yet another source for it.

It will now be useful to summarize the discussion in this section. It has been proposed (a) that a homogeneous and satisfactory analysis of *-ku-* can be given for the constructions discussed, if *-ku-* is in each case treated as the infinitive; (b) that the origin of the infinitive is an embedded sentence. It was shown (c) that the sentential analysis is well-motivated for compound verbals; and (d) that there is also a variety of evidence to support this analysis for simple verbals. Conversely, if the sentential source is not adopted, (a) may still be maintained but there will be no source for the infinitive in the verbals, and the generalizations achieved by (b), (c) and (d) can not be made. The proposal implies that tense and aspectual segments are verbal in source, and that, at one stage of derivation, a verbal like *alikuja* 'he came', will be shown as two constituents, *ali-* and *-kuja*. Synchronic and diachronic evidence was adduced to support both these points.

III

One general line of objection to the analyses proposed might be that they are achieved at the expense of complicating the underlying structures. For example the structure for (79):

(79)   *alikuwa anakuja*   he was coming

will be something like (80):

(80)

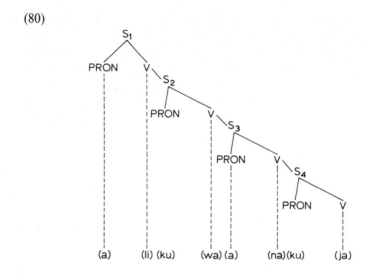

For (79) we require a sentence with three sentences embedded in it. Such objections can be overcome by reiterating the arguments in favour of these structures and repeating that no 'simple' analysis can generate such strings with the same linguistic adequacy. It is perhaps worth adding however that the essential differences between the underlying structure and the surface string consist simply in the deletion of a pronominal and subsequent infinitivalization in S_2 and S_4. There is then, in Swahili, no case for querying such analyses on the grounds of any obvious notion of complexity. Such structures do of course raise many problems, both technical and linguistic, for an overall model of Swahili, but these cannot be explored here.[12]

One final point is worth discussion. A traditional issue in Bantu studies concerns the problem of word division and the applicability of the term 'word'.[13] In Section I, it was proposed that both *mtoto* 'child' and *mkubwa* 'big (one)' would be derived forms and that *anakuja* 'he is coming' would have a double sentential analysis. The question then arises in what sense each of these examples can be termed 'words'. This term is taken to be a term in general syntactic theory, and, following Lyons (1968), a distinction is made

---

[12] For example, notice that in (78), Equi-Pron. Deletion does not operate between S_2 and S_3, and that there will be many restrictions on embedding further S nodes in such a structure. More generally, the outline in (78) implies that there is a complex of superordinate Ss to handle tense and aspect, and that the most deeply embedded S contains the grammatical relationships between major categories. Again, it is clear that NP will be a derived node. It is of general interest that the proposals made in this paper are in accord with the speculations of such scholars as Steere (*op. cit.*) Meinhof (*op. cit.*), Marconnes (1937), Sacleux (1909).

[13] See for example Doke (1935), Guthrie (1948), Gregersen (*op. cit.*).

between phonological and grammatical word 'forms'. For the first two examples there is no difficulty in proposing that the phonological forms which might be shown simply as /mtoto/ and /mkubwa/ satisfy the criterion of penultimate syllable stress. (As an operational definition or discovery procedure, such a criterion is of course circular.) They are analyzed grammatically, however, as consisting of two units, and only the derived form can be taken as satisfying the usual distributional criteria for word status (cf. Robins, 1964). If here we wish to speak of two 'words', then the phonological 'word' will be in conflict with this usage. The verbal form is more complex: grammatically, it is analyzed as four constituents (we continue to ignore the indicative segment -a) from which two are derived (ana + kuja). The finally derived form alone meets the criteria for 'word' status, as does the phonological form /anakuja/. In fact 'word' appears applicable only to derived surface structure forms, unless the criteria mentioned are abandoned. Notice that on this account there is no simple identification possible between 'noun', 'adjective', 'verb' and 'word'. It is again only the derived forms generated from Pron + N which could be considered 'words', not the underlying forms. It follows then that we cannot speak of the 'word' -toto, but might invoke Lyons' term 'lexeme' (Lyons, op. cit. p. 197), using capitals for this by convention. Thus we could speak of the singular form of -TOTO, or -KUBWA. The examples given would then be analyzable as representing three lexemes -TOTO, -KUBWA and -J-, syntactically noun, adjective and verb; as derived grammatical forms Pron + TOTO, Pron + KUBWA and Pron + Prog + Infin + J + Indic; and as phonological forms as shown previously.

It is of interest to see how this analysis compares with the traditional accounts in Bantu studies. In Doke (1935, p. 5–24) the two traditional approaches, the 'disjunctive' and the 'conjunctive' are discussed. He characterizes the former as assuming that 'each entity conveying a complete concept is entitled to be considered a word'. This would lead to 'word' divisions like: m toto a na ku j a (cf. Marconnes, 1931, where Karanga is analyzed on these lines). Doke himself favours the 'conjunctive' approach, essentially on intuitive evidence: 'There is an inherent word-division in all Bantu speech, and Natives are able to divide accurately without fail, as soon as they understand what the investigator is seeking' (p. 14). The formal correlate of this 'natural division' is that in each 'word' there is only one main stress, on the penultimate syllable. Two conflicting notions of 'word' are here in conflict. It is clear that the analyses proposed in this paper take account of both approaches, in that the underlying elements could be regarded as 'disjunctivist' and the derived forms as 'conjunctivist', but it is equally clear that the term 'word' cannot be applied to both types of element. If we prefer the distributional criteria, then the term 'lexeme' is available for what Doke describes as an 'entity conveying a complete concept'.

It may be counted in favour of the analyses suggested in this paper that they can take account of the various approaches which have influenced this debate.

University of Edinburgh, Great Britain

REFERENCES

Ashton, E. O.: 1964, *Swahili Grammar*, Longmans, London.
Bach, E.: 1968, 'Nouns and Noun Phrases', in (Bach and Harms, eds.), *Universals in Linguistic Theory*, Holt, Rinehart and Winston, New York.
Bach, E. and Harms, R.: 1968, *Universals in Linguistic Theory*, Holt, Rinehart and Winston, New York.
Doke, C. M.: 1935, *Bantu Linguistic Terminology*, Longmans, Green and Co., London.
Gregersen, E. A.: 1967, *Prefix and Pronoun in Bantu*, Supplement to *IJAL*. Vol. **33**, No. 3, Memoir 21.
Guthrie, M.: 1948, *Bantu Word Division*, International African Institute Memorandum XXII, OUP, London.
Lakoff, G.: 1971, 'On Generative Semantics', in (Jakobovits and Steinberg, eds.), *Semantics: An Interdisciplinary Reader in Philosophy, Linguistics, Anthropology, and Psychology. C.U.P.*
Lyons, J.: 1968, *Introduction to Theoretical Linguistics*, C.U.P., London and New York.
McCawley, J. D.: 1968, 'The Role of Semantics in a Grammar', in (Bach and Harms, eds.), *Universals in Linguistic Theory*, Holt, Rinehart and Winston, New York.
Marconnes, F.: 1931, *A Grammar of Central Karanga*, Witwatersrand University Press.
Meinhof, C.: 1906, *Grundzüge einer vergleichenden Grammatik der Bantusprachen*, Berlin.
Polomé, E. C.: 1967, *Swahili Language Handbook*, Washington Center for Applied Linguistics.
Ross, J. R.: 1967, Auxiliaries as Main Verbs, (unpublished version), M.I.T.
Sacleux, C.: 1909, *Grammaire des Dialectes Swahilis*, Procure des Pères du Saint Esprit, Paris.
Whiteley, W. H.: 1960, 'Some Problems of the Syntax of Sentences in a Bantu Language', *Lingua*, Vol. **IX**, No. 2.

FRANÇOIS DELL

TWO CASES OF EXCEPTIONAL RULE ORDERING[1]

I

Until very recently, it was generally assumed by linguists working within the framework of generative phonology that grammars must meet the following condition:

(C)   if there exists in a grammar *G* a derivation where a rule *A* applies before a rule *B*, there cannot exist in *G* any derivation where rule *B* applies before rule *A*.[2]

In other words, ordering relations which are defined among the rules of a grammar hold for all derivations within that grammar. In the last few years this principle has been challenged by various writers.[3]

In the present paper we will present two examples which back Bailey's proposal that requirement (C) should be weakened so as to allow individual forms to be marked in the lexicon as undergoing two rules normally applying in the order *A-B*, in the reverse order *B-A*. The first example has to do with vowel nasalization in French, and the second with tonal sandhi in the Chinese dialect spoken in Peking. We will show that in both cases condition (C) cannot be maintained without a loss of generality. This loss of generality can be avoided only by weakening requirement (C) as suggested by Bailey.

II

In French any vowel followed by a nasal consonant itself followed by a consonant or a word boundary becomes nasalized, and the nasal consonant is dropped (Schane, p. 48). Furthermore there are no nasal vowels in the underlying representations, and any nasal vowel is the reflex of an underlying non-nasal vowel which became nasalized through the aforementioned

[1] This article is an enlarged version of Chapter II, Sections 2.3–2.4 of a Doctoral Dissertation written by the author under the guidance of Morris Halle (cf. References). Let him be thanked for his invaluable help. We also wish to thank Richard Kayne for undertaking the arduous task of revising our English writing. We assume that the reader has some degree of familiarity with generative phonology as expounded in Chomsky-Halle (1968).

[2] We leave aside cyclical ordering (cf. Chomsky-Halle, p. 20).

[3] cf. Chafe (1968), Bailey (1968), Carlson (1969), Anderson (1969).

F. Kiefer and N. Ruwet (eds.), Generative Grammar in Europe, 141–153. *All Rights Reserved.*
Copyright © 1973 by D. Reidel Publishing Company, Dordrecht-Holland.

process (Schane, pp. 142–143):

> *bonté* 'kindness' /bɔn + te/ → [bɔ̃te]
> *bon* 'good' /bɔn/ → [bɔ̃]

The grammar of French contains the following rules:

NASAL: $V \rightarrow [+ \text{ nas}] / \underline{} \begin{bmatrix} + \text{ cons} \\ + \text{ nas} \end{bmatrix} \begin{Bmatrix} C \\ \# \end{Bmatrix}$

NAS-DEL: $\begin{bmatrix} + \text{ cons} \\ + \text{ nas} \end{bmatrix} \rightarrow \phi / \begin{bmatrix} - \text{ cons} \\ + \text{ nas} \end{bmatrix} \underline{}$

NAS-DEL must follow NASAL in any derivation, since the presence of a nasal vowel is necessary for the application of NAS-DEL, and the only way a nasal vowel can appear in a derivation is through the application of NASAL. For instance the derivations for *bonté* and *bon vélo* 'good bicycle' are (the final phonetic representations are enclosed in square brackets):

	bɔn + te	bɔn # velò
NASAL	bɔ̃n + te	bɔ̃n # velo
NAS-DEL	bɔ̃ + te	bɔ̃ # velo
	[bɔ̃te]	[bɔ̃velo]

In addition there is a well-known process, called *liaison* ('linking'), which can be described as follows: when in a sequence of two words the first ends in a consonant and the second begins with a vowel, the final consonant of the first becomes the initial consonant of the second, XC # VY → X # CVY. This happens only when the two words are in close syntactic relationship. We need not concern ourselves here with a precise specification of those positions in a sentence where the syntactic relationship is close enough for liaison to occur. Let us assume that such positions are indicated in surface structure by the occurrence of a single word boundary.

LIAIS: $C \# V \rightarrow \# CV$

Any number of consonants remaining at the end of a word are subsequently deleted by a TRUNCation rule:

TRUNC:[4] $[+ \text{ cons}] \rightarrow \phi / \underline{} [+ \text{ cons}]_0 \#$

---

[4] We have grossly oversimplified the facts pertaining to truncation, but the details are irrelevant here. The rule TRUNC is given only for the sake of completeness. Its ordering relationship with NASAL and NAS-DEL poses no particular problem, and we will assume that it always applies after these two rules. For a more detailed discussion of LIAIS and TRUNC, cf. Dell (pp. 54–117).

The functioning of these four rules is exemplified by the following derivations:[5]

	'little friend' *petit ami* pətit # ami #	'little friends' *petits amis* pətitz # amiz #	'good friends' *bons amis* bɔnz # amiz #
NASAL			bɔ̃nz # amiz #
NAS-DEL			bɔ̃z # amiz #
LIAIS	pəti # tami #	pətit # zamiz #	bɔ̃ # zamiz #
TRUNC		pəti # zami #	bɔ̃ # zami #
	[pətitami]	[pətizami]	[bɔ̃zami]

TRUNC must follow LIAIS, for otherwise the derivations of *petit ami* and *petits amis* would both yield *[pətiami], and that of *bons amis* would yield *[bɔ̃ami]. In fact there is no reason to suppose that the application of TRUNC should ever precede that of LIAIS.

We have assumed that in the derivation of *bons amis* LIAIS follows both NASAL and NAS-DEL. But that is not the only possible order. LIAIS could just as well precede both of these rules or apply after NASAL and before NAS-DEL. We would still get the correct output [bɔ̃zami].

Let us now examine some forms which provide crucial evidence for the ordering relations that should hold among LIAIS, NASAL and NAS-DEL, i.e., those forms which contain an underlying sequence /VN # V/.

Consider the parallel behaviour of the last consonant of the personal pronouns *vous* 'you, plur.' and *on* 'one' in the series *A* and *B*:

	context	*A*		*B*	
(1)	____ # #	*voyez-vous?*	[vwayevu]	*voit-on?*	[vwatɔ̃]
		'do you see'?		'does one see'?	
(2)	____ # C	*vous voyez*	[vuvwaye]	*on voit*	[ɔ̃vwa]
		'you see'		'one sees'	
(3)	____ # V	*vous arrivez*	[vuzarive]	*on arrive*	[ɔ̃nariv]
		'you arrive'		'one arrives'	

Column *A* is easily accounted for if one assumes that in surface structure such subject pronouns are separated from the following verb by only one

---

[5] The underlying representation of the phrase *petits amis* is really / # pətit + z # ami + z # /, but we have omitted the initial word boundary and the morpheme boundaries because they play no rôle in the discussion. More generally, the forms that we give as underlying representations differ from the final phonetic output only with respect to features that are relevant to the functioning of the rules under discussion.

word boundary, and that the underlying form of *vous* is /vuz/. In forms 1*A* and 2*A* the final *z* is deleted by TRUNC, while in form 3*A* it undergoes LIAIS. Forms 1*B* and 2*B* pose no problem either. The indefinite pronoun *on* 'one' has the underlying form /ɔn/. *n* triggers the nasalization of the preceding vowel and is then deleted by NAS-DEL. In form 3*B* however it fails to be deleted by NAS-DEL. There is no need to restrict NAS-DEL so as to prevent it from applying in the context ____ # V, for a proper ordering of LIAIS and NAS-DEL does precisely that.[6] Before working out the solution in detail let us give a few more examples of a final *n* being maintained in the context ____ # V:

un ami	'a friend'	[ɛ̃nami]	vs	*un velo*	'a bicycle'	[ɛ̃velo]	
mon ami	'my friend'	[mɔ̃nami]	vs	*mon velo*	'my bicycle'	[mɔ̃velo]	
en auto	'by car'	[ãnoto]	vs	*en velo*	'by bicycle'	[ãvelo][7]	

Similarly consider *bien habillé* 'well-dressed' [byɛ̃nabiye], *rien à faire* 'nothing to do' [ryɛ̃nafɛr], etc.

To account for these forms, let us assume that LIAIS applies after NASAL and before NAS-DEL:

	on arrive
	ɔn # ariv
NASAL	ɔ̃n # ariv
LIAIS	ɔ̃ # nariv
NAS-DEL	
	[ɔ̃nariv]

If NAS-DEL applied before LIAIS it would delete the final *n*, yielding the ungrammatical output *[ɔ̃ariv]. On the other hand if NASAL applied only after LIAIS, it could not apply here, for the application of LIAIS would make the *n* of *on* the initial consonant of *arrive* and an initial nasal consonant does not cause the final vowel of the preceding word to be nasalized (*la nuit* 'the night' is pronounced [lanẅi], not *[lãnẅi]). One would thus get *[ɔnariv].

The ordering NASAL—LIAIS—NAS-DEL is the only one which is compatible with all the facts presented thus far.

---

[6] The forms of column (A) and other similar instances of linking between a personal pronoun and the following verb show that we have good independent reasons to posit a single word boundary between *on* and the following verb.

[7] The fact that there should be only one word boundary between a noun and a preceding article, possessive or preposition, can be seen for instance in *des amis* 'friends' [dezami], *mes amis* 'my friends' [mezami], *sans amis* 'without friends' [sãzami].

III

However, there is a class of cases where as a rule the sequence /XVN # VY/ never yields a nasal vowel. This happens whenever /XVN/ is an adjective which links with the next word:[8] *bon ami* 'good friend' is pronounced [bɔnami] (homophonous with *bonne amie*), not *[bɔ̃nami]. Similarly one says [ləprošɛnavyɔ̃]/ *[ləprošɛ̃navyɔ̃] *le prochain avion* 'the next plane'; [ãplɛnivɛr]/*[ãplɛ̃nivɛr] *en plein hiver* 'in the midst of the winter'. These adjectives are not otherwise exceptions to NAS; one pronounces *bon* as [bɔ̃] in *bons amis* 'good friends', *bon velo* 'good bicycle', *c'est bon* 'it is good', and *plein* as [plɛ̃] in *un plein seau* 'a full bucket', *c'est trop plein* 'it is too full'; similarly when the presence of more than one word boundary prevents linking with the initial vowel of the next word [bɔ̃adir] 'good to say', [plɛ̃akrake] *plein à craquer* 'crowded'. One can thus state the following generalization:

(G)   The only vowels that *can* be exceptions to NASAL are those preceding a nasal consonant which is itself subject to liaison.

IV

Let us now see if we can find any analysis compatible with principle (C) which would account satisfactorily for these facts.

The first idea that comes to mind is to posit the rule R − 1:[9]

R − 1: V → [− rule NASAL]/ _____ [+ nas] # V

[8] cf. Delattre, p. 141. Whatever their phonological make up, adjectives are linked with the following word (i.e., separated from it by a single word boundary) if and only if that word is the noun that they modify, as in the case of *petit ami*, *bons amis* and so on. However the syntactic structure of French prevents most adjectives from ever preceding their head noun, so that there are less than twenty adjectives ending in /VN/ which can link with the next word.

Since the plural forms of adjectives take the ending /-z/, and their feminine forms take the ending /-ə/, the masculine singular forms (naked stems) of adjectives ending in /VN/ are the only ones relevant for our discussion. We will not discuss the behaviour of sequences /XVN # VY/ where /XVN/ is a noun or a verb for the simple reason that such sequences do not exist in French. We can discard plural nouns for they always take the plural ending /-z/. As for singular nouns, they never link with the following word, i.e., they are always followed by at least two word boundaries. Besides, there happen to be no verbal inflexions that end in /VN/. These considerations help us to understand another fact, namely that one cannot find any case of liaison involving nasal consonants other than /n/. There are indeed words ending in /Vm/ or /Vñ/: *parfum* 'perfume' [parfɛ̃] (cf. *parfumer* 'to perfume' [parfüme]); *poing* 'fist' [pwɛ̃] (cf. *poignée* 'handful) [pwañe]), and so on. But these words constitute only a very small minority in the lexicon, and all of them happen to be nouns, or adjectives which are not allowed to precede their noun.

[9] On rules of this type, cf. Chomsky-Halle, pp. 172–175.

The lexical entries for *bon, prochain, plein,* etc. would contain a marking
[+ rule R − 1] while those for *rien, bien, en, on* and the article *un* would be
[− rule R − 1]. Such an analysis merely states the generalization (G)
without relating it to the rest of the grammar. It makes the implicit claim
that there is no more reason for exceptions to NASAL to appear in the context
____[+ nas] # V than in any other context one can think of, say
___[+ nas] # C or # ____.

Another possibility would be to assume that at the point of the derivation
where NASAL should have applied, the sequence *bon ami* behaved as though
it were a single word, with no intervening boundary between *bon* and *ami*
(cf. [bɔnɔ̈r] *bonheur* 'happiness', from /bɔn + ɔ̈r/, where NASAL cannot apply).
Let us therefore postulate the rule R − 2 which deletes a word boundary
immediately after an adjective:

$$R - 2: \quad \# \to \phi \; / \; X]_A \underline{\quad}$$

One can now write derivations like the following:

	bon ami	*on arrive*	*bon velo*
	bɔn # ami	ɔn # ariv	bɔn # velo
R − 2	bɔnami		bɔnvelo
NASAL		ɔ̃n # ariv	bɔ̃nvelo
LIAIS		ɔ̃ # nariv	
NAS-DEL			bɔ̃velo
	[bɔnami]	[ɔ̃nariv]	[bɔ̃velo]

However this analysis has other consequences that make it untenable in its
present form. For it should allow not just *n*'s, but *any* segment appearing
at the end of an adjective, to be treated as though it were word internal. For
instance the behaviour of word final schwas is markedly different from that
of word internal schwas. As shown in Dell (1970), the schwa deletion rules
must be applied after all the rules under discussion here, hence the application
of R − 2 must precede that of the schwa deletion rules.

Consider what would happen to feminine adjectives immediately followed
by their head noun, as in *courte période* 'short period', which has the underlying representation /kurtə # peryɔd/. Schwa drops optionally in the context
CC____#C, while it never drops in the context CC____C. Thus one can
say [kurtəperyɔd] or [kurtperyɔd] for *courte période*, while *lourdement*
'heavily' (/lurdəmã/) always retains its internal schwa: [lurdəmã]/ *[lurdmã].
But once R − 2 has deleted the word boundary in *courte période*, the rules of
schwa deletion can no longer distinguish between the schwa of *courte* and
that of *lourdement*, which is genuinely word internal, and the former should

be treated just as the latter. The grammar would fail to generate the correct form [kurtperyɔd]. Or consider the fact that sequences of the form /VCəCə/ may appear either as [VCCə] or [VCəC] in phonetic representation, while sequences of the form /VCə#Cə/ can only appear as [VCCə]. Contrast for instance *redevenez* 'you become again' [rədvəne] /[rədəvne] (from /rədəvəne/), with *bonne mesure* 'good measure' [bɔnməzür]/ *[bɔnəmzür] (from /bɔnə#məzür/).[10] In this case, a grammar containing the rule R − 2 would generate the ungrammatical representation *[bɔnəmzür]. In order to avoid these ugly consequences, R − 2 would have to be restated so as to delete a word boundary only after the masculine form of adjectives, which is completely ad hoc.

A third solution would be to order LIAIS before NASAL:

	bɔn#ami
LIAIS	bɔ#nami
NASAL	
NAS-DEL	
	[bɔnami]

But then, in order to account for the cases discussed in Section II (type *on arrive* [ɔ̃nariv]), one has to assume that the items *on, en, rien, bien, mon, un,* etc. are marked [− rule LIAIS]. They must furthermore be marked [− rule NAS-DEL] in order to prevent NAS-DEL from deleting the word final *n* which has been spared by LIAIS, for otherwise we would get the ungrammatical output *[ɔ̃ariv].

Notice first that the cases under discussion would be the only exceptions to LIAIS and NAS-DEL, for these rules do not otherwise allow for any exception whatsoever. In other words this analysis forces us to posit exceptions for two rules which otherwise would not have any, and these exceptions must furthermore be distributed in a very peculiar way through the lexicon: an item is an exception to one rule if and only if it is also an exception to the other. This will have to be stated as an ad hoc lexical redundancy rule.

Notice also that from a diachronic point of view, the current situation is not a stable one. Many speakers tend to generalize nasalization to all vowels followed by final *n*'s in liaison. Thus it is not rare to hear people say [ãsyɛ̃nami] for *ancien ami* 'former friend', and speakers who still stick to the more conservative pronunciation [ãsyɛnami] do not pay much attention to this variation, if they notice it at all. On the other hand, pronunciations like [ɔnariv], [anoto] (instead of [ɔ̃nariv] *on arrive*, [ãnoto] *en auto*, cf. Section

---

[10] For a detailed description of these facts and their interpretation, cf. Dell, pp. 1–53.

II) never pass unnoticed and are considered dialectal. This suggests that, contrary to what happens in an analysis where LIAIS always applies before NASAL, it is cases where nasalization fails to apply (as in *bon ami*) rather than those in which it does apply (as in *on arrive*) which should be described as exceptional by an adequate grammar of standard French.

V

All our difficulties disappear as soon as we drop condition (C), for then we can allow NASAL to apply before LIAIS in cases like *on arrive*, and after it in cases like *bon ami*:

	(I)		(II)
	on arrive		*bon ami*
	ɔn # ariv		bɔn # ami
NASAL	ɔ̃n # ariv	LIAIS	bɔ # nami
LIAIS	ɔ̃ # nariv	NASAL	
NAS-DEL			
	[ɔ̃nariv]		[bɔnami]

The difference in rule ordering between derivation (I) and derivation (II) makes a difference only for input strings of the form /XVn # VY/. Other input strings where NASAL and LIAIS interact with each other, i.e., strings of the form /XVnC # VY/,[11] yield the same input under either ordering. One can view the rule NASAL as stating that a nasal consonant nasalizes a vowel that immediately precedes it, *provided that both segments belong to the same syllable at the time the rule is applicable*. If LIAIS applies first, the input string to NASAL has the form /XVn # CVY/; otherwise it has the form /XVnC # VY/, but in both cases *n* belongs to the same syllable as the preceding vowel. This allows us to view the generalization (G) given at the end of Section III not as an arbitrary fact, but as a consequence of the interaction of the rules NASAL and LIAIS, the form of which can be justified quite independently of the facts under discussion in the present paper.

VI

Pekinese has four lexical tones: tone 1 (high flat), tone 2 (rising), tone 3 (low flat) and tone 4 (falling). The digits 1 to 4 stand for certain sets of distinctive features of tone that there is no need to describe in detail.

---

[11] cf. for instance Section II [bɔ̃zami] *bons amis* 'good friends' (from /bɔnz # amiz/).

If two syllables with an underlying low tone occur next to one another inside a phonological phrase, the first shows up with a rising tone in the phonetic representation. This secondary rising tone is completely indistinguishable from a primary one (i.e., one derived from an underlying rising tone). Thus the verbs *mai*³ 'to buy' and *mai*² 'to bury' become homophonous when preceding a syllable with a low tone, so that the phrases *mai*³ *ma*³ 'to buy a horse' and *mai*² *ma*³ 'to bury a horse' are pronounced in the same fashion: [mai² ma³]. This phenomenon of tone sandhi can be represented by the following rule:

$$\text{SAND:} \quad 3 \rightarrow 2 \; / \underline{\hspace{1cm}} \; 3$$

In addition, one must distinguish between stressed and unstressed syllables.[12] Only stressed syllables carry a distinctive tone in the phonetic output. In unstressed syllables, contrasts of lexical tones are neutralized and the melodic curve shrinks into a punctual tone the height of which can be predicted from the tone of the preceding syllable. As a first approximation, one can say that this punctual tone is high (H) when the preceding syllable carries a tone 3, and low (L) otherwise.[13] Contrast for instance the pronunciation of the morpheme *bian*⁴ 'side' in [li³ bian^H] 'inside' (from *li*³ *biàn*⁴) and in [qian² bian^L] 'in front of' (from *qian*² *biàn*⁴).[14] Since the pitch assigned to an unstressed syllable in a particular context is irrelevant to our discussion, it will be sufficient for our purpose to assume that the tone REDuction rule erases the lexical tone of any unstressed syllable and replaces it by a certain 'tone 0':

$$\text{RED:} \quad [-\text{stress}] \rightarrow 0$$

The range of phonetic variants of 0 can be later described by a set of low-level context-sensitive rules that we will not bother to write here.[15] All that is required of the set of features that we are calling tone 0 is that it be distinct from the sets of features defining the lexical tones 1, 2, 3 and 4.

---

[12] Stress assignment in a sentence depends partly on grammatical structure, partly on stress patterns intrinsic to particular lexical items, cf. Cheng, IV-1 and Rygaloff, p. 217 ss.

[13] For a detailed description, cf. Cheng, IV-3.

[14] We write $\dot{x}$ to indicate that the syllable x is unstressed. We shall not use the grave accent in phonetic representations, for a syllable carrying a punctual tone is necessarily unstressed, so that there can be no confusion. Chinese words are spelled according to the *pinyin* system, which is the standard in China nowadays. As we are interested only in suprasegmentals, we have used the *pinyin* spellings, rather than the IPA, even between square brackets indicating phonetic representations.

[15] That these rules apply at a very late stage is shown by the fact that the pitch of an unstressed syllable can always be deduced from the tone appearing in the *phonetic* representation of the preceding syllable, cf. fn. 16 and 17.

Let us now examine the interaction of the processes of tone sandhi and tone reduction.

A low tone undergoes SAND even if the following low tone is itself subject to RED:

(A)   [shou² li⁰] 'in one's hand', from *shou³ li³* [16]
        [xiang² xiang⁰] 'to think a little', from *xiang³ xiàng³*
        [xiao² jie⁰] 'miss', from *xiao³ jiè³*

The derivation of these forms poses no problem if we assume that SAND applies before RED: shou³ li³ → shou² li³ [shou² li⁰]. The rules could not be made to apply in the reverse order for the following reason: RED treats all unstressed syllables alike, regardless of what lexical tone they carry, and once it has applied to a given syllable, there is no way to guess from the output what the tone of that syllable was in the input. If RED applied first, SAND would have to be restated so as to apply not only before low tones, but also before those punctual tones that have taken the place of a low tone, which is impossible to do within the present theory. SAND *must* therefore apply before RED in order to account for forms of type (A).

VII

However, there are a few forms $x^3 y^3$ where the tone of the first syllable does not undergo SAND, mostly lexical items consisting of a reduplicated syllable:

(B)   [nai³ nai⁰] 'granny'[17], from *nai³ nài³*
        [jie³ jie⁰] 'elder sister', from *jie³ jiè³*

Moreover, there are other forms that can be pronounced with sandhi as well as without:

(C)   [da² sao⁰]/[da³ sao⁰] 'to wipe', from *da³ sào³*
        [zao² qi⁰]/[zao³ qi⁰] 'morning', from *zao³ qì³*

All the cases where SAND does not apply (B) or does so only optionally (C) involve morpheme combinations some of whose syntactic or semantic properties cannot be deduced from those of their constituent morphemes, and which should consequently be listed as a whole in the lexicon. The fact

---

[16] Punctual tones are low after a secondary rising tone, as well as after a primary one; compare [shou² liᴸ] and [cheng² liᴸ] 'in town' (from *cheng² li³*).
[17] The punctual tone on the second syllable is a high one: [nai³ naiᴴ]. See also case (C): [da³ saoᴴ] (but [da² saoᴸ] in case the sandhi takes place).

that their second syllable is unstressed is also an idiosyncratic property of these items, and should be represented in their lexical entries.[18] One could account for their irregular behaviour with respect to the rule SAND by assuming that their lexical entries contain the feature [− rule SAND]. One would then have lexical representations like the following:

(B′) $\begin{bmatrix} nai^3 \ nài^3 \\ - \text{rule SAND} \end{bmatrix}$

(C′) $\begin{bmatrix} da^3 \ sào^3 \\ \pm \text{rule SAND} \end{bmatrix}$

But this analysis treats as a mere coincidence the fact that *only those syllables that precede an UNstressed low tone can be exceptions to* SAND; for when in a sequence of two low tones the second low tone is under stress, the first one always undergoes SAND without exception.

Cheng has proposed to handle these facts in the following way: SAND is stated so as to apply to the first syllable of a sequence $x^3 \ y^3$ only if the two syllables are separated by a word boundary.[19] He then explains the difference between forms (A) and (B) by assuming that only the former contain a word boundary. But in most cases the only evidence that allows him to decide whether a given sequence $x^3 \ y^3$ contains a word boundary is precisely its behaviour with respect to SAND, for he gives no independent syntactic or morphological argument.

Furthermore, it seems to us to be a general fact about Chinese dialects that the closer the syntactic relation between two syllables, the more prone

---

[18] Idiosyncratic stress patterns are not restricted to items of types (B) and (C), as opposed to type (A). For instance, the form $xiao^3 \ jiè^3$, which we have listed under type (A), must also be entered as a whole in the lexicon, and the absence of stress on its second syllable cannot be predicted by rule. There are many other such forms in class (A).

[19] But he does not give any convincing justification for this restriction; the argument he gives in favor of his formulation of SAND has to do with the tone pattern of the large class of nouns which end in the (semantically empty) suffix zi^0, nouns like $zhuo^1 \ zi^0$ 'table', $yi^3 \ zi^0$ 'chair', $tu^4 \ zi^0$ 'rabbit'. This suffix is always unstressed (hence it always carries a punctual tone), and it is not separated from the preceding syllable by any word boundary. Cheng assumes that its underlying form must be zi^3, with a tone 3, and he notices that when a syllable preceding zi^0 is itself of tone 3, it does not undergo SAND. For instance the pronunciation of the word meaning 'chair' is [yi^3 zi^0], not *[yi^2 zi^0]. Assuming as he does that the application of SAND always precedes that of RED, the only way to account for this fact is to formulate SAND so that it applies to strings $x^3 \# y^3$ but not to strings $x^3 + y^3$. However we do not agree with Cheng's assumption that zi^0 has a tone 3 in its underlying representation. While it may be true that the suffix zi^0 was once related to the word zi^3 'son', as is suggested by their sharing the same ideogram, we see no semantic or syntactic reason why this should still be the case today. As a matter of fact, we would rather take forms like [yi^3 zi^0] as evidence to the contrary.

they are to undergo rules of tonal sandhi. Cheng's analysis contradicts this generalization, for it sets a threshold above which the relation is *too close* (absence of word boundary) for two syllables to undergo sandhi.

More generally, we believe that it is impossible to find any systematic difference in syntactic or morphological structure between forms of type (A) on the one hand and forms of type (B) or (C) on the other, so that one should give up any hope of stating SAND in such a way that only forms (A) meet its structural description.

VIII

Contrary to what we assumed for forms (A), let us now assume that in the derivation of forms (B), RED applies before SAND. After the application of RED has turned nai^3 $nài^3$ into nai^3 nai^0, SAND can no longer apply, for the form nai^0 does not constitute an adequate context. RED has removed from the string feature specifications which are necessary for the application of SAND. This solution explains why exceptions to SAND appear only before unstressed syllables. Cheng (IV-4) actually took this solution into consideration, but his unquestioning acceptance of principle (C) forced him to reject it. In the framework developed by Chomsky-Halle, cyclic application is the only device which could allow for opposite rule orderings. But Cheng has shown that neither SAND nor RED can be cyclic rules.

Here again we propose that condition (C) should be dropped and that forms of type (B) should be marked in the lexicon as undergoing RED before SAND, contrary to what happens in the normal case. Forms of type (C) will be marked as undergoing the rules in either order.

Massachusetts Institute of Technology

REFERENCES

Anderson, S. R.: 1969, 'West Scandinavian Vowel Systems and the Ordering of Phonological Rules', unpublished Ph.D. dissertation, Massachusetts Institute of Technology, Cambridge, Mass.

Bailey, C.-J.: 1968, 'An Untested Idea on Lexical Exceptions to the Regular Ordering of Phonological Rules of a Language', ERIC/Pegs paper No. 25.

Carlson, B. F.: 1969, 'Unmarked Order and Lexical Exceptions', *University of Hawaii Working Papers in Linguistics* **VI**, 205–212.

Chafe, W. L.: 1968, 'The Ordering of Phonological Rules', *International Journal of American Linguistics* **34-2**, 115–136.

Cheng, Chin-chuan: 1968, 'Mandarin Phonology', unpublished Ph.D. dissertation, University of Illinois, Urbana, Ill.

Chomsky, N. and Halle, M.: 1968, *The Sound Pattern of English*, Harper and Row, New York.

Delattre, P.: 1966, *Studies in French and Comparative Phonetics*, Mouton, The Hague.

Dell, F.: 1970, 'Les règles phonologiques tardives et la morphologie dérivationnelle du français', unpublished Ph.D. dissertation, Massachusetts Institute of Technology, Cambridge, Mass.
Rygaloff, A.: La phonologie du pékinois, *T'oung Pao* **XLIII-3-4**, 183–264
Schane, S. A.: 1968, *French Phonology and Morphology*, The M.I.T. Press, Cambridge, Mass.

MONIKA DOHERTY

'NOCH' AND 'SCHON' AND THEIR PRESUPPOSITIONS

I. ASSERTIONS AND PRESUPPOSITIONS OF 'NOCH' AND 'SCHON'

By comparing sentences with *noch* and *schon* and their negations, a first attempt will be made at the formulation of assertions and presuppositions constituting the meaning of these words.

A question with *noch* will be answered with *noch* in the affirmative, and with *nicht mehr* in the negative.

Compare

Schläft Peter noch?

Ja, Peter schläft noch

Nein, Peter schläft nicht mehr.

A question with *schon* will be answered with *noch nicht* in the negative:

Schläft Peter schon?

Ja, Peter schläft schon

Nein, Peter schläft noch nicht.

The lexicalization of negated *schon* by *noch nicht* points to some interior relationship between *schon* and *noch*. Distinguishing assertions and presuppositions of the meaning of a word by calling presupposition the part of its meaning which remains the same under negation,[1] one can say that the difference between the sentences with *noch* and *schon* is due to a difference in their presuppositions. The part of the meaning of *noch* changed by negation, i.e. its assertion, is exactly the same as the part of *schon* denied under negation: the sleeping of Peter. *Noch* presupposes, however, that the sleeping has been continued, whereas *schon* presupposes that Peter was not asleep before. In other words, *noch* presupposes a preceding phase$_1$ *sleeping*, and asserts a succeeding phase$_2$ *sleeping*; *schon* presupposes a preceding phase$_1$ *not-sleeping*, and asserts a succeeding phase$_2$ *sleeping*.

In general, *noch* and *schon* can be distinguished as follows:

noch	presupposition, P:	phase$_1$(S)[2]
	assertion, A:	phase$_2$(S)
schon	P:	phase$_1$(not-S)
	A:	phase$_2$(S)

[1] For an initial discussion of this problem compare Austin (1962).

[2] S symbolizes the state of affairs described by the meaning of the sentence without *noch* or *schon*.

F. Kiefer and N. Ruwet (eds.), Generative Grammar in Europe, 154–177. *All Rights Reserved.*
Copyright © 1973 *by D. Reidel Publishing Company, Dordrecht-Holland.*

Their negated counterparts deny S for the succeeding phase:

nicht mehr	P:	phase$_1$(S)
	A:	phase$_2$(not-S)
noch nicht	P:	phase$_1$(not-S)
	A:	phase$_2$(not-S).

A number of states cannot be connected with *noch*, e.g. *tot-sein:*

> *Er ist noch tot.

The assumptions above would not suffice for an explication of this phenome-non. Theoretically one could be dead for as many phases as possible. The only thing considered impossible – under normal conditions – is the suc-cession of S, not-S, as given in the assumptions to *nicht mehr*. Hence the deviant character of

> *Er ist nicht mehr tot.

To explain the deviant character of the affirmative sentence and all similar cases, which could be classified under something like *final states:*

> *Peter ist noch alt
> *Elisabeth ist noch groß
> *Es ist noch zu spät,

it is necessary to assume that *noch* presupposes a succeeding phase of not-S. Thus, the presuppositions of *noch* can be said to consist of a sequence: S, not-S. The precise formulation of the interrelation between assertion and presupposition shall be given later.

The presupposition of *nicht mehr* has to be adjusted to the presuppositions of *noch*, in which case not-S will be presupposed and asserted for a succeeding phase.

Schon and *noch nicht* show similar phenomena – as was to be expected:

> *Peter ist schon jung
> *Peter ist noch nicht jung.

This time *initial states* form the class of predicates which cannot be combined with *schon* and its negation. The succession of not-S, S is in these cases deviant, because of their initial position in regard to any time sequence: there could be no other state preceding them, not even not-S.

Analogous to the extension of the *noch* and *nicht mehr* presuppositions, *schon* and *noch nicht* will be modified to: P: not-S, S.

The symmetrical relationship between *noch* and *schon* can be said to be due to the inversion of their respective sequences of the presupposed S and its negation.

II. EQUIVALENCES BETWEEN SENTENCES WITH 'NOCH' AND 'SCHON,' AND THEIR LIMITATIONS

The symmetry proposed for the relationship between *noch* and *schon* is testified to by the equivalence of certain pairs of sentences, although limited by the mere implicative relations of others. To explain the difference, the assumptions concerning *schon* will be extended by a special one belonging to a new semantic level: evaluations.

Their are antonymous pairs of predicates which can be ordered in time, as for example *schlafen* and *wach-sein*. Sentences identical but for these predicates show the equivalence of *noch* and *noch nicht*:

(a)   Peter schläft noch   = Peter ist noch nicht wach
(b)   Peter ist noch wach = Peter schläft noch nicht[3]

The affirmative *noch* is equivalent to the negated *schon*. The opposite distribution:

(c)   Peter schläft schon   → Peter ist nicht mehr wach
(d)   Peter ist schon wach → Peter schläft nicht mehr

shows, however, that the affirmative *schon* can only imply the negated *noch*. Should the sentences under c and d be equivalent, then every second sentence were to be extended by *schon*:

(c′)   Peter schläft schon   = Peter ist schon nicht mehr wach
(d′)   Peter ist schon wach = Peter schläft schon nicht mehr.

There can be no doubt that *schon* has still another meaning other than the one suggested.

If you compare sentences like:

> [??]Er war schon als Greis verheiratet
> Er war als Greis verheiratet
> Er war noch als Greis verheiratet,

---

[3] Not all antonymous pairs of predicates can be ordered in the same way, e.g. *ledig* and *verheiratet* can only be ordered in one direction: ledig, verheiratet, and not vice versa. Therefore we have: er ist noch ledig = er ist noch nicht verheiratet; however, er ist noch verheiratet ≠ er ist noch nicht ledig.

where the first can only be accepted as an 'ironical' statement, *schon* seems to imply some evaluation of the asserted state. It is not an old man's finally being married that would bar the first sentence from appearing in, say, a serious biography, it is the connotation of his being married as early as that, which goes with the sentence. This particular evaluation must be due to *schon*, because it does not belong to the otherwise identical sentence or to the sentence with *noch*. An evaluation is something else than a presupposition or an assertion. The speaker does not claim to express facts by it, he rather gives his opinion on facts. In using *schon* for an event, he indicates that the event is taking place earlier than he would have expected.

Neglecting for the moment the problems of representing an evaluation like 'early' in proper semantic terms, *schon* shall be provisionally extended by it:

> *schon*   Evaluation, E: early of S.

Other cases of evaluation might be sentences with emphatically stressed *noch*, for instance

> Peter schläft noch,

where the stress on *noch* suggests a particularly long duration of the first presupposed phase (stressed *noch* in the context of non-durative verbs excluded):

> *noch*   E: much of phase$_1$ of S.

Because of its position outside the structures of *schon* and *noch* which can be correlated, E will be neglected in the following.

III. STRUCTURAL REPRESENTATION OF 'NOCH'

The variety of constituents modified by *noch* asks for a syntactically motivated form of representation. Assertion and presuppositions will be represented by tree diagrams applicable within the framework of interpretive as well as generative semantics.

Noch is not restricted to states as expressed by durative verbs; it can also modify actions as expressed by non-durative verbs, e.g.

> Peter kauft noch drei Bücher.

The presupposed phase$_1$ does not refer to a preceding phase of buying three books (which would have to be derived from S the way it has been used until now), it does not even necessarily refer to a preceding phase of buying. Spoken without any particular stress[4], the sentence merely presupposes a phase where Peter had been doing something, followed by the assertion that he is doing something else now, namely buying three books.

The presupposed something can consist of various actions, the numbers of them varying from 1 to anything within a man's possibilities. If n symbolizes this amount of presupposed actions, then $n + 1$, will be the order of the asserted action. (1 should not be confused with the number of units involved in the action such as the *three* books of the above sentence.)

A sentence like

> Er wartete noch zwei Stunden

could be analyzed in a similar way presupposing n time sequences and asserting the $n + 1$, namely the two hours. It seems only reasonable to extend this assumption a bit further on those cases of durative predicates which are not accompanied by an explicitly mentioned period of time as in:

> Es lag noch Schnee
> Er war noch verheiratet
> Sie arbeitet noch als Lehrerin
> Es war noch Montag
> Er wartet noch.

All these sentences share a common feature, 'duration', expressing an unspecified number of time units. One can again assume n time sequences, presupposed by *noch*, followed by the $n + 1$, which is more or less identical with the time implicit in the tense of each verb.

Instead of using the undifferentiated *phase of S* one can represent *noch* as an operator forming a series of sets of various elements from which the $n + 1$ is asserted.

Provided the assumptions about the series character of *noch* are correct, they suggest that the mere additive function of it in conjunctions like:

> Da ist eine Schwalbe und da noch eine . . . ,

with *noch* referring to the repeated occurrence of things, i.e. counting things on a very elementary level, lies at the bottom of all the various *nochs*. Since this paper is primarily concerned with the symmetries between *noch* and *schon*, the internal relations between the various functions of *noch* will not

---

[4] The effects of *noch* on contrasted constituents will be discussed in the following chapter.

be further discussed. Only durative predicates provide a clear-cut case for the symmetrical relationship between *noch* and *schon*; a phenomenon which can only be explained after a detailed discussion of both words. The following arguments will therefore concentrate on *noch* with durative predicates.

Since *noch* can modify various constituents of a sentence, there should be a form of representation by which S is differentiated as to the constituents relevant to *noch*. The two semantic models developed within generative grammar, interpretive and generative semantics, are equally well adaptable to the purpose. The following structures could be understood either as output of semantically interpreted deep structures of sentences with *noch* or as input to lexical and other transformations leading to such sentences. For the sake of simplicity, only one way of derivation will be discussed, namely the latter one, and even that beginning at a relatively late stage of development, all problems irrelevant for the presentation of *noch* being neglected. All other constituents of the sentences will be generated according to their particular semantic and syntactic properties, presuppositions and assertions alike. If a pair of presuppositions and assertions meets the requirements stated in the lexical entry to *noch*, it will undergo the relevant lexical transformation. There might be a way to avoid using such labels as Verbal Phrase or Adverbial Phrase in semantic structures, but the effects of *noch* on a sentence are grasped more easily if stated in these highly syntactic terms. The feature 'duration', for example, will be represented as

where the notion TIME UNITS could be specialized by any period of time such as

etc.

The presuppositions of *noch* shall be represented by a conjunction of sentences which are—logically speaking—the argument to a general predicate SERIES ordering states or actions in time:

P:

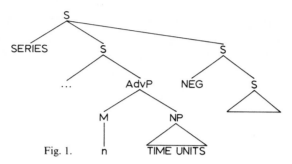

Fig. 1.

The label M classifies sequences of sets.[5]

Only the first sentence implies some period of time relevant to the meaning of *noch*, the second, negated sentence, which is otherwise identical to the first, does not.

The assertion of *noch* reads accordingly:

A:

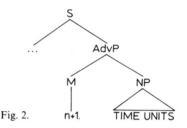

Fig. 2.

Supposing the sentence abbreviated by dots is

      Peter schläft,

the accompanying assertion and presuppositions would mean something like: Having slept n time units, and not being expected to sleep afterwards, Peter is now sleeping the $n + 1$ (set) of time units – in short:

      Peter schläft noch.

Since there is no period of time mentioned in this sentence, TIME UNITS will have to be deleted. In case of a sentence like

      Peter schläft drei Studen

the NP will be preserved together with *drei Studen*. An asserton as given in Figure 2 paired with the presupposition given in Figure 1 will lexicalize the unspecified $n + 1$ as *noch*.

Lexical transformation of *noch*:

[5] The syntactic status of M can only be determined within a comparative study of quantifiers in adverbial phrases, such as: zum drittenmal, and the like. Meanwhile, M can be used syntactically as a place-holder for the series of sets underlying *noch*.

$$\text{X}_-((n+1)_M(\text{TU})_{NP})_{AdvP}/\text{SERIES } \text{X}_-((n)_M(\text{TU})_{NP})_{AdvP} \text{ NEG X}$$

1	2	3		4	5	6		7	8

$$\text{with} \quad 1 = 5 = 8$$

1	noch	0		0	0	0		0	0

(/read: presupposing) TU = TIME UNITS

The resulting structure will be

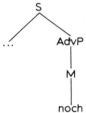

The negation of *noch* is derived accordingly. Given the same presuppositions, the denied assertion will be:

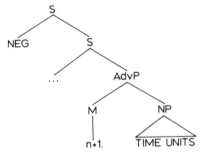

In the context of NEG, $n + 1$ will be lexicalized as *mehr*:

$$\text{NEG X}_-((n+1)_M(\text{TU})_{NP})_{AdvP}/\text{SERIES } \text{X}_-((n)_M(\text{TU})_{NP})_{AdvP} \text{ NEG X}$$

1	2	3	4		5	6		7		8	9

$$\text{with} \quad 2 = 6 = 9$$

0	2	1	mehr	0		0	0		0		0	0

NEG has to be brought to a position before *mehr*.

If the negated sentence contained a quantifier, NEG could be lexicalized as *keine*, e.g.

> Er wartet keine drei Stunden mehr,

with *mehr* permuted to a place after the period mentioned. In a sentence like this, the negation restricts only the amount of units asserted. Also the sentence without negated *noch*:

> Er wartet keine drei Stunden

implies that it will be less than three hours.

Since this particular effect of negation will have to be explained independently of *noch* and *nicht mehr*, it will not be dealt with here.

Owing to the mere restrictive effect of the negation on the numeral, the
presupposed negated state or process expressed by the sentence as a whole
is still to come, in spite of the NEG in the assertion belonging to *keine mehr*;
i.e. in a sentence like

Peter lief keine 20 Meter mehr

a certain distance – although less than 20 metres – still had to be run, before
the presupposed negated phase of the whole process was reached, i.e. before
Peter stopped running.

Before concluding this chapter on representation, a few words should be
said about the generality of the proposed structures and transformations in
regard to *noch* with non-durative predicates. As was pointed out at the beginning of the chapter, sentences involving a certain number of objects, such as

Peter kauft noch drei Bücher

would have to be analyzed in a similar way as sentences involving time units.
In the same way as a specified period of time in the assertion becomes an
unspecified TIME UNITS in the presupposition, the specified action of *buying
three books* becomes an unspecified *n* times DOING SOMETHING:

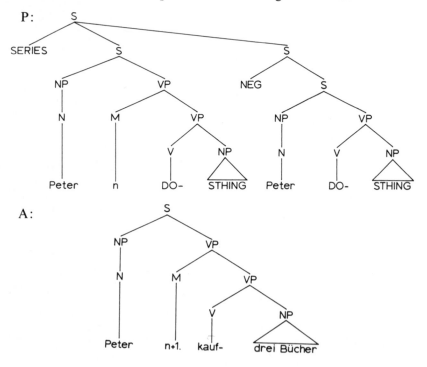

If one neglects the complications arising from this specified-unspecified switch, the lexicalization of $n + 1$ as *noch* or *nicht mehr* will need just a slight modification of the proposed transformations, supplying the structural index with an additional VP as an alternative to AdvP and exchanging TIME UNITS for the more general UNITS of SOMETHING (symbolizing also objects or time periods mentioned explicitly, in which case they will have to be preserved in the transformation). *Noch* will have to be moved to the place before the object. Since this paper concentrates on *noch* and *schon* symmetries, and *schon* does not allow for a comparable generalization, the relevant transformation will not be worked out in detail.

IV. 'NOCH' AND CONTRASTED CONSTITUENTS

The particular effect *noch* has on contrasted constituents will be derived from the preceding assumptions.

Sentences with *noch* and contrasted constituents have an additional implication, asserting and presupposing something else in addition to the fact stated; the sentence

> Die Kínder schlafen noch

for example, implies that someone else is not sleeping any longer.

> In Bérlin liegt noch Schnee

implies that there is no snow left somewhere else.

In contrasting constituents, one generally stresses the fact that it is this and not something else;

> Die Kínder schlafen

says that is is the children who are sleeping and not someone else. Symbolizing the meaning of the contrasted constituent of a sentence S by $\acute{B}$ and the proposition expressed by the sentence with S′, the general rule for contrast might be:

A: $S'(\acute{B})$

Implication, I: not-$S'(C)$,

i.e. the state or process asserted for B is denied for C, with C being an unspecified member of a class which also contains B.

The contrasted constituent in a sentence with *noch* shares its presuppositions, as does any other constituent of the sentence. It differs from these only in that it implies a negated phase about someone else other than the one mentioned, automatically presupposing a preceding phase not only for B but

also for the implied C. The negated state or process implied for C becomes:
nicht mehr S'(C).

Die Kínder schlafen noch

will therefore assert

A:

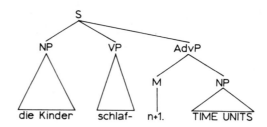

and imply

I:

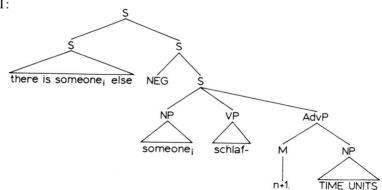

with A presupposing:

P₁:

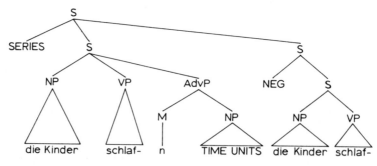

and I presupposing

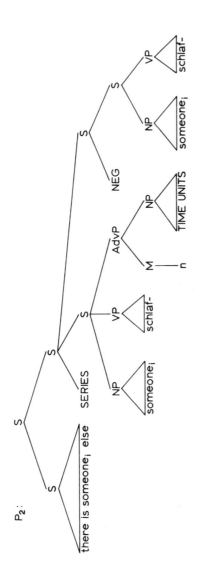

Since *noch* with non-durative verbs does not assert the continuation of a state but the iteration of an action, multiplying its objects accordingly, its effect on contrasted constituents in such sentences is slightly different.

> Peter kauft noch ein Búch

contrasts with something else which Peter *has* bought, and not, as the rule for contrast in the context of *noch* would suggest, with

> *Peter kauft etwas anderes nicht mehr.

Even the acceptable sentence

> Peter kauft nichts anderes mehr

would not be what the contrast implies.

Non-durative verbs have a completely different structure compared with durative verbs. In his analysis of inchoative verbs, Bierwisch distinguishes an initial and a final state presupposed by a change between these particular states.[6]

The presupposed final state being symbolized by Z and the asserted change by B, Z will exclude B for the same time, as B must necessarily have preceded Z. In this sense Z can be said to imply *nicht mehr* B. Peter hat ein Buch$_i$ gekauft implies Peter kauft das Buch$_i$ nicht mehr (with $_i$ symbolizing identical reference), because he has it. In the case of a non-durative Verb Z will be used instead of *nicht mehr* B, presupposing B, however, for the preceding phase. For the sentence

> Peter kauft noch ein Búch

Z would read

> Peter hat etwas anderes gekauft

thus automatically specifying the preceding phase of the presuppositions.

Neglecting for the moment the questions involved in this kind of specification, one can assume a general interdependence of contrast and presupposition, the effects of *noch* on contrasted constituents providing an interesting case thereof.

---

[6] Since some of the inchoative verbs are durative like *dunkeln*, the division into inchoative and non-inchoative verbs is not relevant for *noch*, even in the case of all non-durative verbs being inchoative and therefore representable in terms of inchoative verbs.

V. STRUCTURAL REPRESENTATION OF 'SCHON'

In accordance with the assumption of basically symmetrical relations between *noch* and *schon*, the latter will be represented by an analogous structure and appropriate lexical transformation.

But for the permuted order as to S and not-S, *schon* can be represented in the same terms as *noch*. The lexicalization of the negated *schon* as *noch nicht* asks for a similar treatment of the first sentence within the presupposition by stating an unspecified number of *n* TIME UNITS to be followed by the $n + 1$ of the assertion:

P:

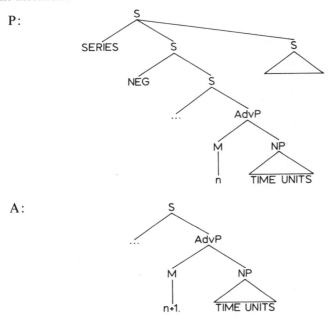

A:

In contrast to *noch* the assertion of *schon* does not mean a continuation of the first phase, but, by its reference to the second, an end of it. The negated *schon* is the one continuing the first phase:

A:

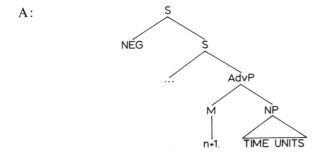

The assertion of *noch nicht* has the same, continuing effect in regard to its presuppositions as the assertion of *noch* in regard to its, the only difference being the value of the phase they continue: *noch* a positive and *noch nicht* a negative.

The rules for the lexicalization of *schon* and *noch nicht* will therefore have the same structural index as those for *noch* and *nicht mehr* but for the permuted order of the presupposed phases.

Transformation of *schon*

$$X_-((n + 1)_M(TU)_{NP})_{AdvP}/\text{SERIES NEG } X((n)_M(TU)_{NP})_{AdvP} \ X$$

1	2	3		4	5	6	7		8
			with $1 = 6 = 8$						
1	schon	0		0	0	0	0		0

The unspecified $n + 1$ is lexicalized as *schon* under the condition of presupposed NEG X . . . X (with X . . . NEG X presupposed, it would be lexicalized as *noch*, cp., p. 161).

In case of a specialized time period as in

Peter wartet schon drei Stunden

drei Stunden will appear in place of TIME UNITS, and will not be deleted in the transformation.

Similarly the transformation for lexicalization of *noch nicht*:

$$\text{NEG X } ((n + 1)_M(TU)_{NP})_{AdvP}/\text{SERIES NEG } X((n)_M(TU)_{NP})_{AdvP} \ X$$

1	2	3	4		5	6	7	8		9
				with $2 = 7 = 9$						
0	2	noch	0	1	0	0	0	0		0

with NEG being brought to a position after *noch*.

As was the case with negated *noch*, negated *schon* can also occur with a specified period of time:

Peter schläft noch keine drei Stunden.

Here too, the particular, restrictive effect of the negation on the number is not produced by the negation of *schon*, since the state mentioned has been going on for a while, only less long than asserted. As the sentence without *noch*

Peter schläft keine drei Stunden

shows the same restrictive effect of the negation, the explication of this phenomenon does not belong to the *noch-schon* analysis.

VI. CONJUNCTIONS OF SENTENCES WITH 'NOCH' AND 'SCHON'

The 'linking effect' of the conjunction of sentences with *noch* and *schon* shows the interdependence of their respective assertions and presuppositions, making an additional assumption about their precise coordination in relation to the time of utterance necessary.

In conjunctions of *schon* and *noch* sentences the *schon* sentence seems to determine the direction of development, making the state connected with *noch* the primary one, and the state connected with *schon* the secondary:

> Hier scheint noch die Sonne und dort regnet es schon,
> Hier scheint schon die Sonne und dort regnet es noch.

In the first sentence the speaker expects the rain to come to his place as well, and in the second the sun to shine in the other place.

Morgan assumes that there is a left-to-right order for the assertion of one sentence becoming the presupposition of the other. There is some syntactic evidence for this. For instance, the sentence asserting the existence of some thing (i.e. making use of the indefinite article) will normally precede the sentence presupposing the existence of this thing (by means of the definite article). Another case would be *auch*, presupposing what has been asserted before for another subject.

On the other hand there are cases like comparative forms of certain adjectives, presupposing for their arguments some unspecified place on their respective dimension:

> Peter ist kleiner als Paul

which can be specified by a following assertion

> ... aber auch groß
> ... und Paul ist nicht groß.

The left-to-right order may cover the majority of the cases, it does not apply, however, to all of them. *Noch* and *schon* specify their presuppositions mutually: if *noch* asserts A then it presupposes not-A for a succeeding phase. B asserted by *schon* specifies not-A as B, its presupposed not-B being specified as A. If *noch*, for instance, asserts sunshine, it presupposes not-sunshine for the following phase. *Schon* asserting rain specifies the presupposed, second phase of *noch*, its own presupposition, being not-rain for the preceding phase, specified similarly by the asserted state of *noch*. Underlining the asserted phases and connecting the presupposed with their respective specifications, one could sketch the linking effect of *noch* and *schon* as:

A, not-A and not-B, B.

In sentences like

Peter ist noch Schüler und Paul ist schon Student

the opposite order would be acceptable only under special conditions:

*Peter ist schon Schüler und Paul ist noch Student,

the deviant character being due to the inversion of the normal sequence, pupil-student; since *schon* specifies the phase following the one asserted by *noch*.

Thus the restriction imposed on the conjunction of predicates through *noch* and *schon* is in accordance with the structural interrelations of these two words. Predicates conjoined in this way should therefore be able to form a sequence in time,[7] and, in the case of a fixed sequence, the one connected with *schon* should never be the preceding element of this sequence.

Some predicates do not allow of mutual specification. In

Er war noch ein kleiner Junge als sie schon eine große
Schauspielerin war

the little boy will not become a great actress, nor even a great actor, and the great actress has never been a little boy. In these cases a general nominator of the two predicates will provide the scale on which the predicate connected with *noch* comes first (probably 'periods of life' in the above sentence).

In each of these conjunctions of predicates through *noch* and *schon*, however general their common features may turn out to be, the predicate connected with *noch* provides the first element, the predicate with *schon* the second of the sequence thus established.

In sentences with explicit time periods the conjunction of *noch* and *schon* produces a somewhat different linking effect. In

?Peter studiert schon drei Jahre und Paul geht noch zwei Jahre in
die Schule

the conjunction induces a slightly awkward feeling concerning the specifica-

---

[7] There are also cases where the sequence produced by *noch* and *schon* is not a sequence in time but a 'sequence' in grades: Das ist noch ein Päckchen und das ist schon ein Paket, where the thing called Päckchen is certainly not going to become a Paket, but is its predecessor on a scale with increasing dimensions. *Das ist schon ein Päckchen und das ist noch ein Paket, is in the same way acceptable only under special conditions as the inversed elements of a temporal sequence are. The preceding or following phase presupposed by *schon* and *noch* with predicates containing a semantic element not-TIME do not simply negate the asserted state for a preceding or following period of time, but limit it to its part on a scale. The predicate connected with *noch* specifies the lower end of the scale, the predicate with *schon* the upper end of it. TIME UNITS would have to be exchanged for something like DEGREES, the internal structures of *noch* and *schon* remaining basically the same.

tion of time. Besides ordering the predicates, the conjunction also forms a sequence of the time periods. However, the sequence of the predicates is just the opposite of the sequence of the time periods. It is obvious that the sentence with *schon* refers to a period before the time of utterance, and the sentence with *noch* refers to a future period, whereas the predicate of the *schon*-sentence refers to a state of affairs still ahead for the subject of the *noch*-sentence and vice versa. The three years of Peter's study are past, the two years of Paul's schooltime are still to come; but Peter's studying or something similarly 'advanced' compared to *going to school*, determines the direction of Paul's development. The double sequence ordering the clauses cross-wise seems to make the conjunction logically muddled. But even when the sequence of predicates is dropped and the same predicate used in both clauses, the logical structure does not become much clearer:

> ?Peter studiert schon drei Jahre und Paul studiert noch zwei Jahre.

Only a conjunction with identical subjects and predicates is really better:

> Peter studiert schon drei Jahre und er studiert noch zwei Jahre.

While the sequence of predicates produced through the conjunction of *noch* and *schon* seems to be relatively loose, the sequence of time periods produced by such a conjunction is apparently much tighter. In this case the mutual specification does not take place between S and not-S, but between first and second phase within S. More precisely, the time period connected with *schon* specifies the phase preceding the time period asserted with *noch*. Time periods connected through *noch* and *schon* form a temporal unit, subdivided into two phases, the first specified by *schon*, the second by *noch*. This tight connection will demand special conditions, when the two phases are to refer to different things. In a sense, this is comparable to the logically confusing task of forming the sum of 2 apples and 2 pears, namely 3 years of Peter's study + 2 years of Paul's, or 3 years of Peter's study + 2 years of Paul's schooltime. That is, a sequence of a first and second phase will appear more natural, if it refers to one and the same situation continued over a certain stretch of time and not to two situations more or less arbitrarily linked together.

As long as there are no particular periods of time mentioned, *schon* specifies the phase following the one asserted by *noch*. Otherwise it specifies the phase preceding the one asserted by *noch*. Whereas the preceding assumptions as to the assertions and presuppositions of *noch* and *schon* do not need any additional specification for the first case, they do so for the second. If the period of time asserted by *schon* lies before the time of utterance, and the period of time asserted by *noch* lies after it, the assertion of the $n + 1$ number of time units in each case, not distinguishing the position of these time units as to the time of utterance, will not completely cover the meaning of *noch* and *schon*. In order to adapt the assumptions about the interdependence of *noch* and *schon* to the requirements arising from their linking effect on time periods, their structural representation must be extended by the respective coordination of time of utterance and TIME UNITS.

The system of the tenses relates the time of the state or process expressed by the verb to the time of utterance. Symbolizing the former by t_i and the latter by t_o, one could represent the various tenses roughly as

$$T_x: \quad \text{present tense} \quad t_i = t_o \ (= \text{expressing close vicinity rather than identity})$$

$$\text{past} \qquad t_i \text{ before } t_o$$

$$\text{future} \qquad t_i \text{ after } t_o{}^8$$

with T_x being the variable for all tenses.

Within the semantic structure of a sentence, tense must be something like an unspecified point of time, comparable to time adverbials like *jetzt*, *demnächst*, *früher*, etc. Its representation should therefore be similar to the representation of an explicitly mentioned point of time. Each particular point of time can be represented as a relation between time of action and time of utterance; neglecting all further details, for instance:

past

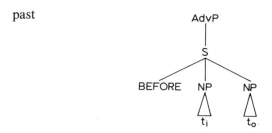

In case of a particular time mentioned, t_i would have to be replaced by it. *Vor drei Stunden*, for instance, would be

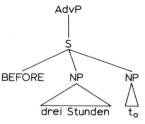

[8] For a very interesting, axiomatic approach to the system of tenses along these lines cf. Wunderlich.

In these terms the period of time asserted by *noch* can be represented as[9]

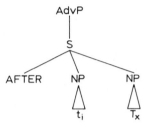

The period of time asserted by *schon* would be accordingly

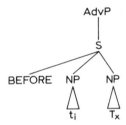

Needless to say, attributing t_i to a certain point of time (through the tenses related to the time of utterance) in the assertions of *noch* and *schon* will automatically relate the presupposed preceding and succeeding phases to this time. With this more precise specification of the notion of time involved, the structures of *noch* and *schon* will read:

noch

P:

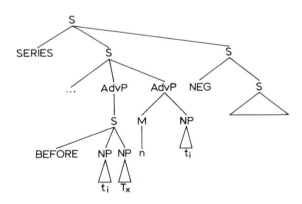

---

[9] A more precise representation would require distinguishing between general AFTER and BEFORE and IMMEDIATELY AFTER and IMMEDIATELY BEFORE, *noch* and *schon* expressing the latter.

A:

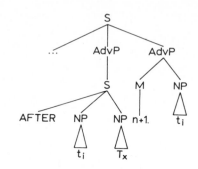

schon

P:

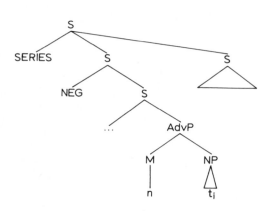

A:

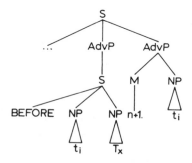

The relation of the time of action to the time of utterance has been neglected wherever it is not relevant to the interrelations of *noch* and *schon*.

In the case of T_x representing the same time, e.g. present, the period of time asserted by *schon* will coincide with the period of time presupposed by *noch* (both of them lying immediately before the time of utterance). With the subject of the *noch*-sentence being identical to the subject of the *schon*-sentence and the predicates being identical in both sentences, the period of time asserted by *schon* can be considered a specification of the period of time presupposed by *noch*.

VII. ASYMMETRICAL RELATIONS BETWEEN 'NOCH' AND 'SCHON'

This chapter will provide an attempt at an explanation of the asymmetrical relations of *noch* and *schon* with predicates expressing non-durative events.

To conclude this study of *noch* and *schon* and their presuppositions, a few words should be said as to the relationship between *noch* and *schon* connected with non-durative verbs. As the preceding chapter pointed out, *noch* continues S after T_x, *schon* asserts its beginning before T_x. Whether S also begins before T_x with *noch*, and whether S is also continued after T_x with *schon*, depends on the notion of time connected with the particular predicate of the sentence, not on the meaning of *noch* or *schon*. Durative predicates differ from non-durative predicates. The state expressed by a durative verb in the present tense, for instance, covers the time of utterance, beginning somewhere before it and ending somewhere after it:

> Peter schläft.

Non-durative verbs, neglecting duration, mostly because of the momentary character of the action expressed by these verbs, are either restricted to the time of utterance or to the time after it:

> Peter kommt

can be said when Peter can be seen coming down the street, or when he has announced his arrival for the following week. Ignoring for the moment the difficulty in the application of the notion *continuation* to non-durative verbs[10] one could say that its implication of an end to S for a time after t_o automatically places the whole action after t_o.

Whereas

> Peter schläft noch

and

> Peter schläft schon

coincide in t_o,

---

[10] The interpretation of the presupposed first phase of processes expressed by non-durative intransitive verbs must be something like: S had been expected for some time, with the second phase finally asserting or denying S. Since this peculiarity does not interfere with the topic under discussion, the common features of *schon* and *noch*, it will not be discussed in detail.

>Peter kommt noch

and

>Peter kommt schon

differ in regard to t_o, with *noch* placing the action after t_o and *schon* placing it at t_o (its initial state having already passed). The symmetrical relation between *noch* and *schon* coinciding in t_o, due to the durative character of some verbs, is distorted by the different placement of *noch* and *schon* due to the non-durative character of other verbs.

Although there is a possibility to interpret a non-durative verb as referring to repeated actions, in that way extending the time of action over and beyond t_o – an effect typical for *noch* with transitive verbs – there is no such effect connected with *schon*.

>Peter kauft noch ein Buch

continues a series of actions unlike

>Peter kauft schon ein Buch

where the action is opposed to a preceding not-yet-doing or not-yet-buying anything.

The superficial symmetry which could be reached in the relation to t_o – the series of actions produced by *noch* covering t_o as the action asserted by *schon* does – is counter-balanced by the number of events involved.

The difference due to *noch* continuing a state of affairs and *schon* merely asserting its beginning is submerged in the durative, i.e. autonomously continuing, character of certain verbs.

It becomes distinct, however, with other verbs which do not supply a continuity through their own meaning. Here, the continuing effect of *noch* shows up, clearly marking it off from the otherwise symmetrical *schon*.

In case of explicitly stated series, *schon* again falls 'into line' with *noch*:

>Peter schreibt schon den dritten Brief

as well as

>Peter hat schon drei Briefe geschrieben

could be the specification of the first phase of

>Peter schreibt noch eine Karte,

analogous to the linking effect of conjoined *noch* and *schon* on time periods or durative predicates.

BIBLIOGRAPHY

Austin, J. L.: 1962, *How to Do Things with Words*, Oxford.
Bierwisch, M.: *Inchoative und Causative Verben*, in preparation.
Morgan, J. L.: 1969, 'On the Treatment of Presupposition in Transformational Grammar',
   Papers from the Fifth Regional Meeting of the Chicago Linguistic Society, Chicago.
Shetter, W. Z.: 1969, 'The Meaning of German noch', *Language* **42**, No. 1.
Wunderlich, D.: 1970, *Tempus und Zeitreferenz*, Berlin, 1969, München, 1970.

FRENCH 'PEU' AND 'UN PEU'. A SEMANTIC STUDY*

In this article I shall be dealing with a specific problem of French grammar. In order to do this adequately, I shall base myself on the well-known concept of linguistic presupposition and shall first summarize the fundamental principles which I shall be using.[1]

When one undertakes to describe the semantic content of an utterance made in a natural language, it is often necessary to distinguish between two different elements: what the utterance presupposes and what it states. In the following sentences for example: *Pierre s'imagine que Jacques viendra* – it is presupposed that Jacques won't come, but it is stated that Pierre believes that Jacques will come. If we consider the different behaviour of the two elements when the utterance is submitted to diverse syntactical transformations, it is clear that this distinction is necessary. The negation: here the presupposition is intact but the statement is altered (*Pierre ne s'imagine pas que Jacques viendra* presupposes also that Jacques will not come). The interrogative: the same thing happens – what is stated is questioned but what is presupposed remains unaltered for when I ask *Est-ce que Pierre s'imagine que Jacques viendra?* I still presuppose that Jacques won't come. We notice furthermore that if a sentence involving presuppositions is coordinated or subordinated to another, the relation established between them only affects what they state – and I shall call this the 'law of concatenation'. If for instance I say *Je suis heureux que Pierre s'imagine que Jacques viendra*, my satisfaction only touches Pierre's belief. The same law of concatenation is apparent in the following: *Pierre est content. Et pourtant il s'imagine que Jacques viendra.*

As far as the semantic interpretation of this distinction is concerned, we find that when the presupposition is an affirmation, it is in fact presented as being self evident – and one behaves accordingly, integrating it so to speak in the universe of discourse in which one intends placing the dialogue. In this way, through the use of presuppositions, some kind of intellectual framework can be imposed on the person to whom one is speaking. That what is presupposed and what is actually stated take on different values in the strategy of speech only reinforces this interpretation. If I refuse to accept what my

---

* This article first appeared in French in *Cahiers de Lexicologie* (1970), pp. 21 – 52.
[1] For a more detailed description, see O. Ducrot (1968a) and (1968b).

F. Kiefer and N. Ruwet (eds.), Generative Grammar in Europe, 178–202. *All Rights Reserved.*
Copyright © 1973 by D. Reidel Publishing Company, Dordrecht-Holland.

interlocutor has stated, this does not mean that I refuse to continue the conversation with him – on the contrary, I keep that possibility open for the polemical aspect remains within the sphere of the discussion. If on the other hand, I attack the presuppositions, i.e. the grounds on which he wanted to base the discussion, then the dialogue itself is put on the rack – my objection becomes an aggression and as a result, the interlocutor is usually held up to ridicule and disqualified as a valid partner.

Presupposing that the reader will behave as if he accepts the assertions I have so forcefully imposed upon him, I shall now enter into my subject: the study of *peu* and *un peu*, study which might prove to be a partial, a posteriori justification of the above mentioned distinction.

When grammarians and lexicologists attempt to describe the opposition between *peu* and *un peu*, they generally hesitate between two rather different explanations; both of which, it would seem, are sanctioned by well-founded facts.

In the first explanation, a purely quantitative distinction is set up: *peu* involving a smaller quantity than *un peu* when both are used in the same context. This is the kind of description given by Jespersen for the equivalent English expressions *little* and *a little*, where each would represent a different degree of magnitude (cf. Jespersen, 1917, p.84). This description is confirmed by such pairs of sentences as *Il a bu peu de vin* and *Il a bu un peu de vin*, and also *Il était peu en retard* and *Il était un peu en retard*.

In certain contexts however, *peu* can hardly be considered to refer to a degree, whatever it may be. This is the case for *Cette situation est peu gênante* and *Cette situation est un peu gênante*. Here the difference is no longer one of degree but of radical opposition: the first sentence is practically a negation and the second an affirmation. Such factors led Littré to consider *un peu* as positive and *peu* as 'practically negative'.

The choice between the two solutions (which I shall call 'quantitative' and 'modal' respectively) seems difficult since the very elements justifying the one are an objection to the other. It is for this reason that I shall put forward a radically different explanation, based on a semantic concept of another nature.

One must be prepared to grant, nevertheless, that a certain number of important facts can be explained within the framework of the quantitative point of view. I shall only deal with one of these, involving the different values of *peu* and *un peu* in a string of sentences. It seems quite reasonable to say, for instance:

(1)   Il semble devenir sobre: il a bu peu de vin hier

and:

(2)   Il semble devenir moins sobre: il a bu un peu de vin hier

Whereas it would hardly seem reasonable to say:

(3)   Il semble devenir sobre: il a bu un peu de vin hier

and

(4)   Il semble devenir moins sobre: il a bu peu de vin hier.

If *peu* implies a minimum quantity and if *un peu* implies a larger quantity, clearly, drinking 'a little wine' could not be taken as evidence of our temperance, whereas in drinking 'little wine' we do in fact prove our moderation.

Such arguments, and many others, might well serve the classical point of view; nevertheless a glance at one factor leads us to doubt its legitimacy. If the distinction between *peu* and *un peu* is only quantitative, then, by attenuating the one and reinforcing the other, one should obtain more or less equivalent expressions. Taking for example *assez peu* and *un tout petit peu*, the distance between these two should then be considerably less than that between *peu* and *un peu*. In fact this is not what happens at all. In the two sentences *Il a bu assez peu de vin* and *Il a bu un tout petit peu de vin*, the distinction is maintained: the first one, in the same way as *Il a bu peu de vin hier*, will confirm the temperance of the person (*Il a bu assez peu de vin hier: il semble donc devenir sobre*); the second one, as *Il a bu un peu de vin*, will have the opposite meaning (*Il a bu un tout petit peu de vin hier: il semble donc devenir moins sobre*) – to remove this meaning one would have to transform it by adding 'ne . . . que' (*Il n'a bu qu'un tout petit peu de vin hier*). It would appear that *peu* and *un peu* belong to entirely different linguistic paradigms, that there is a difference in nature which no quantitative attenuation or reinforcement could remove. This is precisely why the notion of presupposition has been brought in.

Let *a* be a simple sentence, and *A* the same sentence in which the word *peu* has been added as a modifier to a noun, a verb, an adverb or an adjective of *a*, all necessary adjustments to morphological structure having been made.[2] Taking as example of *a* the following:

(5)   Pierre a bu du vin hier

and as example of *A*:

[2] To define a simple sentence is no easy matter. One should say, to be honest, that: simple sentences are those which it would be preferable to consider as simple, given a complete semantic description of French – that is, sentences where the interpretation would not need to be deduced from that of other more elementary sentences they might contain.

(6)   Pierre a bu peu de vin hier,

the semantic modification introduced by *peu* implies, in our theory, that *A* presupposes what *a* has stated, and states that, in the fact here presupposed, the quality, function or object designated by the word qualified by *peu* are small in quantity and weak in intensity. Thus (6) presupposes that Pierre drank some wine yesterday and states that the quantity was small. The sentence containing *peu* states a certain (quantitative) evaluation of an object whose existence is already presupposed. The content stated in (6) could be expressed by the formula: $F(v)$ – where v is the wine drunk yesterday by Pierre, and F is a predicate with a higher order than v – with the approximate meaning: 'is of a small quantity'.

My analysis of *un peu* will be totally different. Let *a* once again be a simple sentence, and *B* the same sentence where *un peu* has been introduced (under the same conditions as above). If we keep the preceding example, we shall obtain for *B*:

(7)   Pierre a bu un peu de vin hier.

The semantic modification introduced by *un peu* entails, in our description, that the utterance *B* states the truth of *a*, assuming that the object (the quality, the action) designated by the word qualified by *un peu* is in small quantity (low degree, weak intensity). Thus (7) states that Pierre has drunk some wine, but restricts the affirmation to a small quantity. Notice that we did not say that '(7) states that Pierre drank a small quantity of wine' which would be equivalent to saying '(7) states the smallness of the quantity' or again '(7) states that little wine was drunk'. What we wish to make clear by this is precisely that *un peu* is never used to state a quantitative evaluation, only to restrict quantitatively a statement. Where *peu* asserts a restriction, *un peu* restricts as assertion. In short, if *a* states the existence of a particular phenomenon, *A* (i.e. *a* + *peu*) presupposes this existence and states that the phenomenon described was of little import; *B* (i.e. *a* + *un peu*) on the contrary states the same thing as *a* but at the same time places it within certain quantitative limits.

Before embarking in possible applications of this, I would like to discuss a first objection which might be put forward. Supposing I say that I have a little money in my pocket, when I happen to have a lot – I will most probably be told that I am lying. What is implied here is that my sentence aimed at a quantitative evaluation of what I had in my pocket. Would it then be legitimate to distinguish between *peu* and *un peu* on the basis that only the first of the two expressions can be used to state a quantitative evaluation?

In order to provide an answer to this objection, it is necessary to distinguish between the levels of 'la langue' and 'la parole'. According to me, the sentence: *J'ai un peu d'argent* does not exclude the possibility, on the 'langue' level, that I have a lot of money. It only states that a certain sum of money is actually in my pocket, without rejecting the possibility – as would be the case for *peu* – of there being a great amount. To assert the presence of a certain amount – which is small – does not imply asserting the smallness of the amount present. Several arguments can be given in favour of this. In the first place, one can quite easily imagine a dialogue of this kind: *Il a un peu d'argent – Il en a même beaucoup*; but if we substituted *peu* where *un peu* was used, the dialogue could hardly be conceivable. Since the word *même* has that invariable semantic feature of only linking two sentences going in the same direction – that is, appearing in the same demonstration – if the expression *un peu* was used to indicate a restriction, i.e. if it set a ceiling, the imagined dialogue would then be impossible. A second argument can be drawn from the behaviour of *un peu* in conditional clauses. Let us take the sentence *Si j'ai un peu de temps libre, je ferai ce voyage*. The length of time given in the condition is evidently not limited – clearly the speaker would *a fortiori* undertake the trip if he had a lot of free time. What he is in fact saying is not that he would need a short holiday, but that a certain holiday period (which he does not require necessarily to be long) would be sufficient to undertake the trip. The emphatic use of *un peu* in familiar French also adds to our argument, in that, on the 'langue' level, *un peu* does not exclude 'much' – cf. "*C'est bien toi qui est Lapointe – Un peu que c'est moi qui est Lapointe*" (G. Duhamel, quoted in the *Robert Dictionary*). Actually, whatever the liberties taken by the so-called 'progressive speech' (slang), these seldom contradict the language itself, rather they exaggerate, through the use of the understatement, the semantic marks outlined in the language. If *un peu* can be stretched to '*beaucoup*', this can only be because the language allows it – whereas it would forbid such an extension for *peu*. In fact familiar language only contradicts, as we shall see, a law of discourse (a law of 'la parole'), setting up against it another law of discourse (i.e. the rhetorical tendency to the understatement).

There remains to be explained why the sentence *J'ai un peu d'argent dans ma poche* is generally interpreted in such a way that 'much' is excluded, although according to our present description such an exclusion is not intrinsic to the meaning given to it in 'la langue'. To do this, we shall resort to a law of discourse which requires that when one wishes to speak on a specific subject, one is expected to say everything one knows about it, wherever it is permitted and in so far as it is supposed to interest the listener. Mental scruples are forbidden – having broken a glass, were I to say only that I spilled it, or again having failed an examination, were I to announce that I didn't get the top mark, people would most likely call me an impostor. We argue that the same thing happens when I say I have a little money: I let it be understood that I really only have a little. The use of *un peu* therefore often has the same effect as *peu*, and enables the listener to conclude that the object referred to is in fact quantitatively small. If this is included in the meaning of *peu*, as given in 'la langue', it is nevertheless only suggested as a secondary effect or implication in the case of *un peu*.[3] We are now in the position to say that *peu*, in 'la langue', states the smallness of a specific quantity whose existence is presupposed, while *un peu* directly states the existence of a specific quantity (which is small as it happens) without declaring anything about a possibly greater quantity.

It can now be demonstrated that our suggested description accounts for everything which classical descriptions explain. Firstly, it evidently enables one to understand the logic of (1) and (2) without difficulty. By virtue of the law of concatenation, the explanatory link (expressed by the symbol ':' in both sentences) involves only what the linked sentences state. *Il a bu peu de vin* can therefore be proof of temperance since it only states the moderation of the quantity drunk and presents the very fact of drinking as a presupposition. It is quite natural on the other hand that the sentence *Il a bu un peu de vin* accentuate the blame that the person has lacked temperance since it states that he has drunk some wine (it being understood that the quantity spoken of was moderate – however, that a little wine does not prevent one from remaining sober is always a possible reply without the dialogue being disrupted). Similarly (3) and (4) can be shown to be illogical, and the reader can check this for himself.

The use of *peu* as an attenuated negation must now be explained within the framework of our description. The question arises why a sentence like *Ce livre est peu intéressant* is employed most of the time to suggest – with much care and moderation – that the book is not interesting. I shall argue that this use results from a shade of meaning originating in 'la parole' and not in 'la langue' (what G. Guillaume terms an "effet de sens"). I shall use the law of understatement to account for this 'effet de sens', and shall formulate it thus: in order to express in an attenuated form the meaning of a sentence *A*, a sentence *B* can be used, that has a weaker stated content than *A*. We found that *peu intéressant* only stated a restriction; it is quite natural that through the effect of the law of understatement, the phrase should stand

---

[3] To my mind there is a distinct difference between the implication, related to 'la parole', and the presupposition, belonging to 'la langue' (cf. Ducrot, 1969).

for the complete negation as stated in *pas intéressant*, but in an attenuated form.

The preceding explanation might seem rather commonplace. To justify it, the formulation I just gave of the law of understatement should be enlarged upon, and the fact that the understatement only affects 'stated' contents should be developed. The latter explains why *un peu* is liable to take on an 'effet de sens' quite opposite to that of *peu*. While *peu* expresses an attenuated negation, *un peu* is more often used to make an affirmation, although in an attenuated fashion. *Ce livre est un peu ennuyeux* is often a polite way of saying that the book is boring. The law of understatement explains this without difficulty. It follows that, in accordance with our description, *un peu ennuyeux* states that a certain quantity of boredom exists (while the fact that some interest might exist is only presupposed by *peu intéressant*). Thus the sentence *Ce livre est un peu ennuyeux* will now with the help of the understatement express a higher degree of boredom, just that degree expressed by the adjective alone in *Ce livre est ennuyeux*. In this manner, the distinction between what is stated and what is presupposed allows for the radical separation between *peu* and *un peu* at the level of 'la langue' already. If one looks closely at what they state, the two expressions clearly belong to quite different semantic categories – *peu* belonging to that of restriction like the

Category of affirmation	Category of restriction
beaucoup de chance (a lot of luck)	*pas de chance du tout* (no luck at all)
de la chance (luck)	*pas de chance* (no luck)
un peu de chance (a little luck)	*peu de chance* (little luck)

other negations, and *un peu* to that of affirmation. In line with this distinction between *peu* and *un peu*, it is understandable that in their actual usage, the two expressions have quite a different fate. Since the law of understatement in the form we gave it only affects the stated contents, it will only have an effect within the preceding categories. Thus, a term will be used to express the same thing as the term one grade higher of the category. It is no longer surprising that *un peu de chance* often creates the same 'effet de sens' as *de la chance*, while *peu de chance* will mean the opposite, i.e. something approaching *pas de chance*.

Clearly, even where the classical description agrees with the facts, the distinction between statement and presupposition leads us, so it seems, to a more natural solution. It allows for a closer relationship between 'la langue' and 'la parole', and in so doing, reduces the so-called freedom of innovation of 'la parole' with respect to 'la langue'. The laws of 'la parole' no longer appear to be a 'Deus ex Machina' which linguists introduce at the last minute to reconcile their obtuse descriptions to the facts. Certain phenomena must now be dealt with that have not been accounted for by traditional interpretations.

I shall begin by analysing a phenomenon somewhat similar to the one with which we have just dealt in that it also involved the 'effets de sens' introduced by *peu* and *un peu*. Let us compare these two sentences:

(8)   Pierre a bu peu de vin blanc

and

(9)   Pierre a bu un peu de vin blanc.

The first one can often imply that Pierre has had something else to drink but white wine – red wine for instance. Such an implication is practically impossible in the second one. How can we explain this difference? Firstly, we shall refer to the general rule defining the use of *peu* and *un peu*; after this we shall study the effect of a law of discourse (a law of 'la parole').

If (8) and (9) are obtained by adding *peu* and *un peu* to the simple sentence *Pierre a bu du vin blanc*, then, according to our general description, (8) must presuppose that 'Pierre has drunk some white wine' and state that 'this quantity of white wine was small'. (9) on the other hand directly states that Pierre has drunk a certain quantity of white wine (the 'certain quantity' being at least small). Given this difference between the two sentences – which we shall place on the 'langue' level – both will be affected by a law of discourse, but the results will be quite different. This law of discourse we shall call the 'law of minimal qualification', requiring that only those modifiers be introduced that contain necessary information for the listener. Although we have called this a law, we are not trying to say that speakers never introduce redundant qualifications, nor that they never introduce qualifications which they know to be redundant. We are only implying that if the listener notices certain redundancies, a tacit law allows him to take advantage of the situation and make fun of the speaker. We therefore concede that this alleged law does not describe an inevitable de facto regularity, but that it is a norm. By its very existence, it cannot however be ignored by linguists of 'la parole'.

What in fact renders a qualification 'informative'? and what can we understand by that? Let A be a sentence including an expression b which is syntactically relatively autonomous (by this we mean that it could be removed from A without the latter becoming incorrect or incomprehensible, after certain small grammatical adjustments have been made). The presence of b in A has an informative value if one of these two conditions is fulfilled:

(a) that the listener cannot infer A from A minus b (i.e. $A - b$)
(b) that the speaker cannot guarantee the truth of $A - b$.

Supposing A is: 'Mushrooms found in fields are never poisonous', and $A - b$ is: 'Mushrooms are never poisonous'. The first condition is not fulfilled here as A can be deduced from $A - b$, but the second one is as the speaker could never be satisfied by $A - b$ – which is not true. In the next example we have the opposite situation: 'Peter gave a lecture in English' = A, 'Peter gave a lecture' = $A - b$. The second condition cannot be fulfilled here since $A - b$ cannot be false if A is true. Generally speaking it is usually the first condition which is fulfilled: with the exception of certain special cases, the listener cannot deduce A (= the lecture was given in English) if he has only been told $A - b$ (= Peter gave a lecture). In one of those special cases (the listener knows that Peter only speaks English for instance), notice that the sentence will most probably be held up to ridicule: 'Of course he couldn't have given it in Chinese!'

Having thus defined what we mean by 'informative value', and assuming that the law of minimal qualification directly influences language in communication, it can then be inferred that all qualifications in a spoken sentence have an informative value – that is, that they fulfill one of the two conditions given above. As we formulated it, to employ A is to imply either that $A - b$ is doubtful or that the speaker cannot deduce all the information in A from $A - b$. Supposing that someone declares to me 'Mushrooms found in fields are never poisonous'; since the truth of this sentence is logically deduced from $A - b$: 'Mushrooms are never poisonous', I am entitled to credit the speaker with the supposition that $A - b$ is false, i.e. that there *are* poisonous mushrooms. Similarly, if I am told that Peter has given a lecture in English, since this implies that Peter *has* given a lecture, $A - b$ is obviously true if A is true; I must therefore infer that A cannot be deduced from $A - b$ – that is, that Peter could have spoken another language but English.[4]

Before we return to *peu* and *un peu*, one last point requires elucidation. The law of minimal qualification, like all laws regulating redundancy in discourse, influences stated contents and in no way affects the presupposed content – on the contrary, repetition of the latter is one of the most permanent requirements of linguistic communication. Thus, the distinction between the stated and the presupposed is once again very essential (as was the case for the law of understatement) if we are to arrive at an accurate definition. We shall then have the following definition: If a sentence A includes an expression b which can be removed from A without altering the structure of the sentence

---

[4] This only applies to where the sentence 'Peter gave a lecture in English' is used alone, i.e. in answer to a question such as: 'What did Peter do?'. When the sentence is integrated in a complex sentence as a subordinate clause, the situation changes (e.g. 'There was a big crowd although Peter had given a lecture in English').

as a whole, then, in normal circumstances, to use A is to imply, either that $A - b$ is doubtful or that the information stated by A cannot be deduced from the information stated by $A - b$.

We can now return to the different implications of:

(8)   Pierre a bu peu de vin blanc

and:

(9)   Pierre a bu un peu de vin blanc

Sentence (9) states that Pierre has drunk a certain amount of white wine. Now this information cannot be deduced from what is stated in *Pierre a bu un peu de vin*, except if the listener knows that Pierre only had white wine in his cellar. The law of minimal qualification has every likelihood of being respected by (9) and, quite in accordance with observations made from the start, no particular implication is expected. The situation is somewhat different for (8); here the stated content is: the amount of white wine drunk was small; but this information can immediately be deduced from what is stated by *Pierre a bu peu de vin*. If sentence (8) is to obey the law, the requirement '$A - b$ is doubtful' must be satisfied. That Pierre has drunk little wine must therefore be doubtful. Sentence (8) will then quite naturally imply that Pierre has drunk a rather large quantity of some other wine (which is not white wine) – and this agrees with our findings at the beginning of this analysis.

The preceding descriptions brought in both the distinction between statement and presupposition and laws of discourse. This is a weakness and a strong point at the same time. It is a strong point in that every explanation of 'effets de sens' created by a sentence (the 'effets de sens' being the only observable data) must at some point bring in such laws. In fact, the best argument one can give to prove that a particular linguistic description is based on 'la langue' and not on 'la parole' is to show that the laws of 'la parole' will only produce the observed 'effets de sens' if they are applied to the semantic description being dealt with. The very fact that we avail ourselves of one semantic description only to explain very different 'effets de sens' which bring in very distinct laws of discourse, renders our demonstration all the more convincing – and this is exactly what I was attempting in the preceding pages. I took two kinds of 'effet de sens' into account: firstly, the use of *peu* to attenuate the negation and that of *un peu* to attenuate the affirmation (effect 1); secondly, the implications introduced by autonomous modifiers in sentences containing *peu* (effect 2). I explained these with the help of two very distinct laws of discourse, the law of understatement and the law of minimal qualification, but in both cases I had to call on the same semantic description of *peu* and *un peu* to account for observed facts – i.e. on the description distinguishing between statement and presupposition. In this way I hope to have demonstrated satisfactorily that I am dealing with a reality pertaining to 'la langue', prior to all psychological pressures placed on 'la parole'.

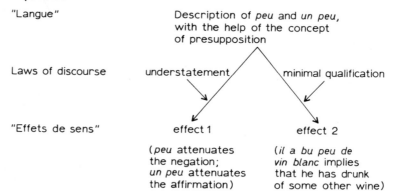

Although nobody could avoid bringing in the laws of discourse, I am well aware that this may also cast a shadow of doubt on the value of my suggested description. Indeed, by simply calling on such laws, cannot all such descriptions be saved? This is why I had mentioned that they may also weaken my analysis, and why it is now essential to introduce certain linguistic facts which can be directly accounted for without referring to the various laws of discourse.

Let us compare these two imperatives:

(10)   Donne-moi peu d'eau

and

(11)   Donne-moi un peu d'eau

The difference in meaning between (10) and (11) is clearly felt, though it is rather difficult to define it, in the difference in use to which each will be put. (11) will be employed when requesting water from someone who has not offered any. (10) will be used when the person is on the point of pouring water in my glass. Furthermore, if that person was not intending to give me any water, he will answer very differently to (10) and to (11). A simple refusal will deal adequately with (11), but to (10), he is likely to answer:

(12)   Mais je n'ai jamais songé à t'en donner (I never intended giving you any).

This sort of reply will always be aggressive – and furthermore, I am likely to become a laughing-stock. The quantitative interpretation of *peu* and *un peu* cannot possibly explain this. If I am asking for less in (10) than in (11), why should the refusal to (10) be more aggressive than to (11)? But in the modal interpretation, (10) represents an attenuated variant of the prohibition: *Ne me donne pas d'eau*. The retort (12) and its latent aggressivity is then easily explained: it seems ridiculous to prohibit something which the person has no intention of doing! (just the same as it seems ridiculous to order someone to do something which he intends doing in any case). Nevertheless, if we apply this law to explain the polemical nature of (12), we have to explain the aggressivity of

(12′)   Mais je n'ai pas l'intention de t'en donner beaucoup

in the same way. But clearly two quite distinct polemical mechanisms are involved here. It is true that in both cases the speaker can be accused of enunciating a prohibition where there was no reason to do so. But, in so far as the absurdity of prohibiting what one does not intend doing is already apparent in (12′), we have to introduce another absurdity for (12) – an absurdity which is difficult to comprehend if we are to base ourselves on the modal interpretation of *peu* and if we are to consider (10) as some sort of interdiction to give water.

My suggested description of *peu* and *un peu* can however provide an easy solution to this problem. As a rule, imperative utterances keep the presuppositions of the corresponding indicative utterance without altering them, and furthermore the command expressed by the former refers to what the latter would have stated. Supposing the imperative:

(a)   'Stop smoking!'

which corresponds to the indicative:

(b)   'You will stop smoking'.

If one analyses (b), one obtains the presupposition 'You used to smoke' and the statement 'You will not smoke'. Clearly the command expressed in (a) does not refer to what (b) presupposes but to what (b) states. Assuming that (a) is derived from:

(a′)   'I am asking you that you stop smoking',

this rule can easily be shown to lead back to the general rule of concatenation. One can in fact predict that what the main clause of (a′) requests will only be what the subordinate clause states (by the law of concatenation).

Now, if we apply this argument to sentence (10), clearly it must include the presupposition of the corresponding indicative sentence:

(10′)   Tu me donneras peu d'eau

and this presupposition must be *Tu me donneras de l'eau*. The command itself, which (10) expresses, can only refer to the content stated in (10′) – i.e. the smallness of the amount of water. In short, (10) should presuppose that the interlocutor will offer some water and should state that the amount given must be small.

We are now in a position to explain the aggressivity of (12): The speaker is rejecting one of the presuppositions of the sentence to which he is replying. We have already seen (page 179) that one cannot reject the presuppositions of an utterance without 'disqualifying' it and without involving a personal criticism. The difference between (12) and (12′) is now apparent. The latter (*Mais je n'ai pas l'intention de t'en donner beaucoup*) does not affect the presuppositions of (10) – its aggressivity consists only in stressing the stupidity of ordering what the person intends doing in any case.

This difference between (10) and (11) – and the fact that my proposed description of *peu* and *un peu* can help to explain it – is still clearer (though in a more indirect manner) when both sentences are qualified by the phrase *par pitié*, giving:

(10′)   Donne-moi peu d'eau, par pitié

and

(11′)   Donne-moi un peu d'eau, par pitié.

It is quite evident here that the pity asked for in (10′) is very different from that in (11′). Once again, the theory of presupposition can account for this satisfactorily. Generally speaking, the rule is that the qualifying phrase *par pitié* can only modify what (10) and (11) command; thus if the command in (10) only involves the restriction placed on the quantity to be given, the pity introduced in (10′) must refer to this restriction (and not to the quantity itself, as is the case for (11′)).

In so far as the distinctions involved in the preceding example are more pragmatic than semantic, the example might be considered inadequate. Basically it deals with the intellectual representations the speaker believes his listener to have, and one could say that it has more to do with the requirements governing the use of such sentences than with the content itself. I have already discussed the possibility of considering presuppositions as requirements for use elsewhere and, on the whole, I do not believe that the distinction between the pragmatic and the semantic is valid when analysing natural languages.[5] Rather than reopening the discussion, let us take examples where the distinction between statement and presupposition accounts for differences which are unmistakably semantic (supposing we are clear on what we mean by this).

Let us take the two contexts:

(a)   Je te demande＿＿＿＿de travail

and

(b)   Je te demande de travailler＿＿＿＿ .

If *un peu* is added in the blank spaces of both, we arrive at the two practically synonymous sentences:

(a1)   Je te demande un peu de travail

and

(b1)   Je te demande de travailler un peu.

But if *peu* is added to (a) and to (b), we then have:

(a2)   Je te demande peu de travail

and

(b2)   Je te demande de travailler peu.

Now, (a2) and (b2) clearly have very different meanings (which is not the case for (a1) and (b1)). The first sentence reminds an unwilling worker that he has not been given too much work to do, whereas the second one advises the over-eager worker not to work too hard. This difference stands out even more clearly when we apply Austin's notion of 'the performative'. Clearly (b2) is a performative utterance, the formulation of which coincides with the act of requesting. (a2), on the contrary, has no performative 'value'; when I say to someone: *Je te demande peu de travail*, I am not requesting, I am only pronouncing a judgement on a request made elsewhere (in the past, in the immediate future, or even in the present providing that the request be made quite independently of (a2) – for instance in writing).

Notice that each of the four utterances (a1), (a2), (b1) and (b2) can be interpreted in two different ways. According to the one, some work is requested from the person spoken to (for convenience we shall call him the 'addressee'); the other involves work which the addressee must make the speaker do (for

[5] cf. Ducrot, O., 1968 (b) and 1971.

instance (a2) can mean: *Je te demande de me donner peu de travail*). However, since the function of *peu* and *un peu* remains the same whichever interpretation is chosen, I have arbitrarily decided to leave aside the second one for the moment, although its very possibility brings up problems to which we shall return at the end of this section).

In order to explain the quasi-synonymity of (a1) and (b1) and also the difference between (a2) and (b2), I shall base myself on the description of *peu* and *un peu* given earlier, on the law of concatenation (already used to explain the reasonings studied on page 178) and finally on a grammatical hypothesis involving the syntactic structure of sentences of type (a) and of type (b). The hypothesis is as follows: type (a) sentences are simple sentences having a subject (*je*), a verb (*demande*) and two objects (the pronoun *te* and the noun *travail*) accompanied by a modifier [*un peu* in the case of (a1) and *peu* in the case of (a2)]. Type (b) sentences are however complex sentences, obtained from the combination of two simple sentences such as *Je te demande quelque chose* and *tu travailles peu* (or *un peu*).

Bearing this hypothesis in mind, it is easy to see the quasi-synonymity of (a1) and (b1). According to my description of *un peu*, (a1) states 'I am requesting some work from you (not necessarily much)'; on the other hand (b1) is obtained from the object clause *Tu travailles un peu* combined with the main clause *Je te demande quelque chose*. Since this object clause states 'You are supplying a certain amount of work (not necessarily much)', the meaning of the whole sentence (which requires that what is stated in the subordinate clause be carried out) must be very close to that of (a1).

The difference between (a2) and (b2) can be analyzed in the same way. According to my description of *peu* and *un peu*, (a2) presupposes 'I am asking you for work' and states 'The amount of work I am asking you for is small'. In other works, the request is included in the presupposition and not in the statement (this could explain the non-performative – or 'constative' – nature of the sentence, but the relation between presupposition and performative function remains to be studied). (b2), as we have seen, is composed of the main clause: *Je te demande quelque chose*, and the subordinate clause: *Tu travailles peu*. Now, according to my description of *peu*, this subordinate clause must presuppose 'You are working' and must state 'The amount of work you are doing is small'. According to the law of concatenation, the request in the main clause can only affect what is stated in the subordinate clause, and not what it presupposes. The complete meaning of (b2) will then be:

Presupposed: 'You are working' (presupposition carried over into the subordinate clause in the complete sentence).

Stated: 'I am asking you that this work be small in quantity'.

Thus, with the help of the general laws of presupposition, very different meanings can be predicted for (b2) and for (a2), whereas very similar meanings were predicted for (a1) and (b1).

One difficulty my explanation of (a1), (a2), (b1) and (b2) meets with, will inevitably strike certain convinced transformationalists. I assumed that sentences of type (a) (i.e. *Je te demande* _____ *travail*) were simple sentences, and I analyzed the word *travail* as an object, in the same way as *Pierre* is the object of *J'ai vu Pierre*, and not as the result of a transformation of nominalization. The objection that (a1) and (a2) are ambiguous can be raised (ambiguity which I mentioned in passing on page 191): *Je te demande peu (un peu) de travail* could involve work I am asking my interlocutor to do, or work I am asking him to make me do. Now it is very easy to account for this ambiguity if the word *travail* is taken as the residue after nominalization of an underlying clause. This clause could in fact be either *Je travaille peu (un peu)*, or else *Tu travailles peu (un peu)*. Sentences type (a) would then have the same deep structure as sentences type (b). The fact that the same ambiguity is present in both cases would be proof that the structure is analogous.

Although this seems at first glance a powerful argument, other facts distinguishing sharply between the ambiguity of type (a) sentences and that of type (b) can be brought up to reduce its import. As an example, let us take (a'1) and (a'2), obtained by adding the phrase *pour Pierre* to (a1) and (a2):

(a'1)   Je te demande un peu de travail pour Pierre

(a'2)   Je te demande peu de travail pour Pierre.

The request made here will relate to work done – or to be done – by Pierre. Thus one only needs to add *pour Pierre* to type (a) sentences to remove the underlying *Je travaille* or *Tu travailles*.

However, when the same is applied to type (b) sentences, the result is surprisingly different. Whatever the interpretation given to:

(b'1)   Je te demande de travailler un peu pour Pierre

and

(b'2)   Je te demande de travailler peu pour Pierre

it can never imply work done or to be done by Pierre, but will always refer to work done or requested by the speaker or the addressee on behalf of Pierre. The very fact that (b1) and (b2) cannot be modified to imply work done by a third person convinces us that the deep structure of these sentences must involve finite tenses such as *Je travaille* or *Tu travailles*. We cannot reasonably apply the same interpretation to (a1) and (a2) where, as we saw, less emphasis is placed on who the person actually doing the work is.

One objection to this could be that (a'1) and (a'2) should not be used to analyze (a1) and (a2), since nothing really proves that (a'1) and (a'2) are really expansions of (a1) and (a2) after *pour Pierre* has been added. It may be that (a1) and (a'1) (or (a2) and (a'2)) have a very different deep structure. We cannot here embark on a discussion to determine whether (a'1) and (a'2) are in fact expansions of (a1) and (a2), but a short cut is available if we can show that in certain cases, and without an object being added, (a1) and (a2) can imply work done by neither the speaker nor the addressee.

Supposing that an employer says (a2) to a foreman who supervises the workers without himself doing the work (the complete sentence could be: *Je vous demande peu de travail, mais un travail soigné* – I am asking you for a little work, but well done work). (a2) only refers to work done by a third person here – the workers. We realize that a rather special situation had to be set up for (a2) in order to deduce this, but what is important is that even in this situation, no type (b) sentence can ever be interpreted in a similar way, however hard we try to do so. The sentence: *Je vous demande de travailler un peu* could never be made to imply work which the foreman must have the workers do (except if one interprets the *vous* in a quite different way to include both foreman and workers). The amgibuity of type (a) sentences is therefore greater than that of type (b) – for in the former, the choice of the person to do the work is almost entirely free.

I believe that this difference is sign of a difference at a deeper level. If certain interpretations of type (b) sentences are impossible, this must surely imply that those which are possible are an essential part of the structure of the sentence and are ascribable to 'la langue'. On the other hand, in type (a) sentences if the addressee is free to give the work to anyone, is it not somewhat arbitrary and with a transformationalist bias to require that all these possible interpretations be already present in the sentence itself? So far, since no other argument has been put forward, it seems much more reasonable to say say that type (a) sentences are not in themselves ambiguous on the 'langue' level.

At this level only a perfectly neutral request for work is expressed – neutral as to who will actually do the work. Of course, each time such sentences are employed both speaker and addressee will have someone specific in mind for the job; but in so far as the choice of the person is not predetermined by the sentence itself – not even in a negative way – there is no reason why the necessity of ascribing this work to a person should be included directly in the sentence. It seems far more natural to turn this necessity into a law which has nothing to do with language and which specifies that one cannot request work to be done without at the same time asking that it be done by someone.

At this point a distributional argument can be brought up to demonstrate the difference in syntax between (a) and (b). It is rather difficult to include *peu* in a phrase governed by the preposition *sans*; one can hardly say – and hardly understand – *Il ne vient jamais sans peu de plaisir*. This also applies where *sans* is followed by an infinitive, itself followed by an object qualified by *peu*; it is hardly acceptable to say: *Il ne vient jamais sans me faire peu de plaisir*. This restriction is however practically removed when the nominal phrase with *peu* is the complement of a second infinitive, itself directly linked to the first one which is governed by *sans*; the following sentence is quite probable, and furthermore understandable: *Il ne vient jamais sans me demander de prendre peu de vacances*. This can be used as a test to help us decide whether *demander du travail* is syntactically analogous to *demander de travailler*. In this case, *peu* can be added to both and each can begin with *Il ne vient jamais sans*. The result of such an operation is however different for each: for *demander de travailler*, the resulting sentence can be understood: *Il ne vient jamais sans me demander de travailler peu*. The other: *Il ne vient jamais sans me demander peu de travail*, is more difficult to interpret. Such facts seem to prove that the difference in the superficial structure corresponds to a difference in deep structure.

If this analysis is correct, there is no reason to ascribe to the deep structure of type (a) sentences a finite tense and grammatical person of the verb *travailler*: in such sentences the work involved is more a thing than an action – a thing which the speaker is asking his listener. On the deep structure level, the idea of work could quite naturally be represented by a noun; in fact, in more precise terms and to use a familiar terminology, this noun would represent a massive quantity (one speaks of *du travail* in the same way as *du fer, de l'eau*). Nothing prevents us now from breaking type (a) sentences down into 'subject + verb + direct object + indirect object' – a very different syntactical structure to that of type (b) sentences. If we remember, this very syntactical difference as well as the general mechanism of presupposition had been introduced to explain the opposition between *peu* and *un peu* in (a) and (b).[6]

When I was explaining the use of *peu* as an attenuated negation, I had provisionally left aside one objection. This objection cannot be neglected completely – and this because it is important and also because by the way certain facts to do with the distribution of *peu* can be accounted for.

According to the rule I gave for the interpretation of *peu*,

---

[6] This result is in agreement with the actual tendency of many transformationalists to limit the field of nominalization (cf. *Chomsky* (1970)).

(13)   Ce livre est peu intéressant

must presuppose the semantic content of the following: *Ce livre est intéressant*. In this case, how is it that (13) can be used as a polite substitute of the negative sentence:

(14)   Ce livre n'est pas intéressant.

Sentence (13) should presuppose exactly the opposite of what sentence (14) states. How shall we explain the fact that they can be interchanged almost indifferently?

This is a very serious objection when one remembers the definition of presupposition given at the outset: that which is presupposed in an utterance is an affirmation included as an independent component in the content of that utterance.

Following our analysis of *peu*, (13) must then affirm, amongst other things, that the book is interesting – which evidently contradicts the negative function usually ascribed to (13). We cannot get rid of this objection simply by answering that in this case, the negative value of:

(14)   Ce livre n'est pas intéressant,

– in which the affirmative proposition

(15)   Ce livre est intéressant

is a component – could not be understood either. Such an answer would reduce the value and the originality of the notion of presupposition. It is true that being a syntactic component of (14), sentence (15) must be 'understood' for (14) to be understood, but this does not mean that (15) will be 'affirmed' when (14) is. But to say that utterance X is presupposed by utterance Y, is equivalent to saying that X is a 'semantic' component of Y, or again that the affirmation of X is latent in the affirmation of Y. Thus if our description of *peu* is correct, it would not be possible to assert (13): *Ce livre est peu intéressant* without asserting in the same breath that the book is interesting – this makes it indeed difficult to account for the real value of (13) in discourse.

To answer this objection we will have to consider a rather peculiar feature in the distribution of *peu*. In speech, most French people will avoid using *peu* in front of certain adjectives having negative overtones. They will hesitate to say *peu ennuyeux* and *peu extraordinaire* for instance. This avoidance will become actual refusal if these adjectives have a negative prefix, and all the more so if the prefix is clearly understood to have a negative meaning; this is the case for phrases as *peu désagréable, peu maladroit, peu inintéressant*, and generally speaking for all adjectives beginning with *in-* (there are exceptions to this rule, for instance one can say: *Cette mesure est peu indispensable*, but here the adjective *indispensable* has no corresponding positive adjective from which it is directly derived).

Now, one can notice that the same adjectives which cannot be preceded by *peu* can easily be preceded by *un peu* (cf. *un peu inutile*). Thus the incompatibility of *peu* and these adjectives cannot be explained by resorting to categorical properties of the adjectives, adding that the latter cannot express degrees of 'categoricalness' – for this would affect both *un peu inutile* and *peu inutile*. The negative meaning of *peu* and the awkwardness of the double negation involved in *peu inutile* is no satisfactory explanation either, since the double negation is quite acceptable in sentences such as *La mesure n'était pas inutile*.

A remark we made earlier may help us find an adequate solution to this problem. We had seen that a negative adjective such as *indispensable* could quite well be preceded by *peu*, and we had noticed that it did not directly correspond to a positive adjective. This observation may be generalized by saying that only those negative adjectives which are directly opposed to a positive adjective (cf. *inutile*, *inintéressant*) cannot be used in conjunction with *peu*. Notice however that this opposition between positive and negative adjectives is not really symmetrical, since the positive ones always have certain properties which their negative equivalents do not have. This asymmetry can be felt for instance in the comparison. Let us consider these two comparative sentences:

(16)   Pierre est plus inutile que Jacques

and

(17)   Pierre est plus utile que Jacques.

Sentence (17) does not imply that Jacques himself is useful (on the contrary). If one wanted to assert that Jacques is also useful, (17) would have to be altered to:

(17′)   Pierre est encore plus utile que Jacques.

On the other hand, a certain uselessness (or lack of usefulness) will more often be attributed to Jacques when interpreting (16) – to which one might very well answer: *Mais Jacques n'est pas du tout inutile*. In other words, the semantic difference between sentence (16) and

(16′)   Pierre est encore plus inutile que Jacques

is less clear cut than that between (17) and (17′). In short: suppose an utterance *X est plus Y que Z*, where *X* and *Z* are things or people and where *Y* is an adjective. If *Y* is a negative adjective of the same kind as *inutile,* and only in this case, the utterance will then imply that object *Z* warrants being qualified by *Y.*

This situation might at first glance seem surprising, for both *X* and *Z* must have quality *Y* if the extent to which the things or people symbolized by *X* and *Z* possess quality *Y* is to be compared. It is therefore difficult to understand why this necessity (which for convenience I shall call the 'requirement of homogeneity') should appear for sentence (16) – which implies that Jacques is useless – and not (or at least it is less apparent) in the case of (17) – which does not specially imply that Jacques is useful.

This can be explained with the help of the phonological concept of marked and unmarked elements. According to phonologists, when a linguistic category includes two opposing elements, one of the two is usually considered to be unmarked – by this they mean that when used in certain contexts, the element can stand for the whole category. Thus the category of explosive dental consonants in German includes these two elements: the voiced /d/ and the unvoiced /t/. /t/ is said to be unmarked because it appears in contexts where there is no longer an opposition between /d/ and /t/ – that is, at the end of words. There it represents the whole category of dental consonants, and no longer only the unvoiced 'pole' of the category. The marked element (/d/ in this case) maintains its 'polar' value throughout. Likewise, one could say that the adjective *utile* in certain contexts (for example in comparisons) generally represents the category or scale of usefulness, whereas in others (when used alone for example) it refers to an aspect or 'pole' of the category – in this case the positive aspect (cf. *Pierre est utile*). But whatever the context, the marked adjective *inutile* will only refer to the negative end of the scale – in exactly the same way as the marked dental consonant /d/ always refers to the voiced 'pole' of the category 'dental consonant' in German.

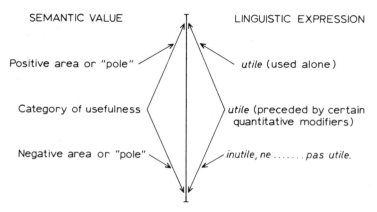

If we adopt this scheme, it is easy to understand why the application of the requirement of homogeneity will give different results for (16) and for (17). When we formulate a comparison using the marked adjective *inutile*, it will be located in the negative area of the category, implying that the two terms compared, Pierre and Jacques here, are both situated in this area. But when the comparison is based on the unmarked adjective *utile*, the whole category of usefulness is involved; the two terms are therefore not required to be localized in one or other of the 'polar' areas. This is exactly what we meant just now when we said that *Pierre est plus utile que Jacques* does not necessarily imply that *Jacques is utile*. As we had formulated it, it was difficult to make this observation agree with the requirement of homogeneity; clearly our problem was due to a sort of homonymy, leading to a misunderstanding. The adjective *utile* is used twice in the sentence before last, but with two different meanings. The first time it is used with *plus* and has a general value, involving all degrees of usefulness; the second time it is used alone and only has its 'polar' value, involving only one of the extremities of our spindle.

We had formulated the requirement of homogeneity in the following way: an utterance type (a), i.e. *X est plus Y que Z* implies utterance (b), i.e. *Z est Y*. To avoid difficulties, (b) should be replaced by (b'): *Z' est Y'*, making it clear at the same time that (b') does not belong to the natural language we are describing but to the metalanguage of the description. Z' and Y' are therefore not words in the natural language, but artificial symbols representing what Z and Y mean in (a) (which is likely to be different to what they mean in (b)). This metalanguage is necessary if Y is an unmarked adjective like *utile* whose value alters according to its use in (a) or in (b).

We shall now be able to deal with the problems of *peu* more easily after this rather long discussion. Let us return to the sentence we had taken as an example:

(13)   Ce livre est peu intéressant.

It can easily be checked that the pair *intéressant–inintéressant* (or *ennuyeux*), just as *utile–inutile*, presents an unmarked element (*intéressant*) and a marked element (*inintéressant*). A modifier accompanies the unmarked adjective in (13) and we shall assume that it represents the category, thereby having a general value. According to our description of *peu* used up to here, (13) should presuppose:

(15)   Ce livre est intéressant,

which, as we saw is incompatible with the use of (13) as an attenuated negation. But this contradiction falls away when we make it clear that *intéressant* in

(15) must be given the interpretation it has in (13) – i.e. that it represents the whole category and not the restricted or 'polar' meaning it has when used alone.

Once more, the whole problem is that we do not as yet have a metalanguage at our disposal, and we have to use the sentences of a natural language to describe the presuppositions of language L. That is why our formulation of the rules of presupposition can never be quite satisfactory. At present, all we can do is partly to modify the description of *peu* with which we started. This will lead us to the following formulation which, although it is more precise, could only be completely clear if we had a semantic metalanguage at our disposal: a simple sentence containing *peu* presupposes what this sentence states when *peu* is removed from it (after necessary grammatical adjustments), leaving aside the modifications to the meaning of the other morphemes occasioned by this removal. Once one is clear on this point, one can see why (13) does not presuppose that the book is interesting (the adjective being taken in its restricted or 'polar' meaning). Similarly, one understands why (13) is used to negate the interest (always with the restricted meaning) of the book since, in what it states, (13) aims at lowering the level of usefulness and is therefore located near the negative pole of the category.

We are now in a position to explain the distributional feature of *peu* we had mentioned: that French people normally avoid associating *peu* to the marked element of an adjectival opposition – for what makes *peu intéressant* feasible, makes *peu inintéressant* difficult to accept. Since it is the marked element of the opposition, the adjective *inintéressant* will be located at the negative pole, even when accompanied by a modifier (exactly what I tried to show in the example with the comparison). Thus:

(18)   Ce livre est peu inintéressant

should presuppose that the book is situated in the negative area of the category (i.e. that it is not interesting) – even after our reformulation for the description of *peu*. This implies that (18) cannot be taken as an understatement; but were it one, what should its 'strong' meaning be? Since (18) states a restriction according to the general description of *peu*, and that the understatement only affects the stated content, *peu inintéressant* should then be the understatement of *pas inintéressant*. But this is in fact incompatible with what (18) presupposes – i.e. that the book is not interesting. The complete explanation of course requires that we show that *peu* followed by an adjective necessarily implies an attenuated negation. We had only pointed to a tendency (page 183) in this direction as we had only brought in a law of discourse (the law of understatement) – and we know that the introduction of such a law cannot be binding evidence. Nevertheless this limitation could only represent a crucial objection if the phenomenon to be explained was in itself absolutely constant – that is, if the phrases *peu inutile* and *peu inintéressant* were strictly speaking impossible, or entirely incomprehensible. But this is not the case as we have only observed a tendency (though very strong) to avoid such phrases; and these can moreover be eventually interpreted. It is perhaps not so unreasonable then to resort to a law of discourse in our explanation, law which in itself can also never determine more than a tendency.

Other distributional features related to the one discussed above can now be accounted for. Phrases as *un peu inutile, un peu inintéressant* can be met with, and generally speaking all phrases made up of *un peu* + marked adjective. It can indeed be predicted that the meaning of

(19)   Cette mesure est un peu inutile

will be located at the frontier of the negative area in the category of usefulness (cf. schema page 198). This meaning coincides more or less with the meaning generally given to (19). Further, one can see why (19) is used to understate politely the affirmation: *Cette mesure est inutile*, for, if the law of understatement applies to (19) – sentence stating the existence of some particular uselessness – it must suggest an even greater uselessness.

Similarly, that phrases such as *un peu utile* are hardly ever met within standard French can be explained. If *utile* represents the category as a whole, *un peu utile* should only state that our object occupies one or other of the levels of the useful. Now this is a tautology, having no informative value. Everything, however useless, must have its place in the scale of the useful. The sentence *Cette mesure est un peu utile* could only carry real information if the predicate *être un peu* + adjective stated a quantitative evaluation, i.e. to what extent the property expressed by the adjective is to be attributed to the object, and therefore only if *un peu* marked off limits above and below. This is however not the function of *un peu* in '*la langue*' as we had pointed it out on pages 185–188 (in a given sentence suppose that *un peu* is replaced by *beaucoup*, the sentence obtained is not necessarily incompatible with the original one). When the sentence *Cette décision est un peu utile* cannot imply neither that the decision is barely useful nor that it is very useful, what exactly is the information I am trying to get across? Our proposed description will enable us to account also for such phrases as *un peu* + unmarked adjective in so-called 'progressive' or familiar French. Here, *un peu* is often employed with a value very similar to *beaucoup* or *très* (cf. *Elle est un peu chouette, cette voiture* and *Il a un peu bu, le camarade*). This emphatic *un peu* remains unaffected by the mechanism which normally excludes the combination *un peu utile* in 'neutral' French. It can easily be checked that wherever this combination is found we are dealing with a near superlative, in other words with the emphatic *un peu*.

École Pratique des Hautes Études, Paris

(Translated by ARIANE ILJON)

BIBLIOGRAPHY

Chomsky, N.: 1970, 'Remarks on Nominalizations', in R. Jacobs and P. S. Rosenbaum, (eds). *Readings in English Transformational Grammar*, Ginn-Blaisdell, Waltham, Mass.

Ducrot, O.: 1968a, 'La description sémantique des énoncés français et la notion de présupposition', *L'Homme* **8**, 37–53.

Ducrot, O.: 1968b, 'La présupposition linguistique, condition d'emploi ou élément du contenu des énoncés?', paper presented at the International Congress of Semiotics at Warsaw, August 1968, to appear in the *Proceedings* of the Congress.

Ducrot, O.: 1969, 'Présupposés et sous-entendus', *Langue Française* **4**, 30–43.

Ducrot, O.: 1971, 'De Saussure à la philosophie du langage', Preface to J. R. Searle, *Speech Acts* (French translation), Hermann, Paris.

Jespersen, O.: 1917, *Negation in English and other Languages*, Copenhagen.

MAURICE GROSS

ON GRAMMATICAL REFERENCE*

Most studies on pronominalization (Bach, 1970; Chomsky, 1965; Dougherty, 1969; Lakoff, 1968; Lees and Klima, 1963; Postal, 1968 and Ross, 1967) postulate that there exists one single operation that applies when two *NP*'s occurring in certain discourses are morphemically identical and coreferential. To the best of our knowledge there are no reasons whatsoever to assume that both *NP*'s should be identical[1] rather than differ in quite a number of possible ways. Moreover, all these studies have isolated certain pronouns (*it, he, she, they, them*), and never deal with the other pronouns, or with demonstrative phrases for example. For us, the decision of singling out certain shapes and excluding others for the purpose of studying reference is entirely unmotivated.

We propose here a description that accounts for many cases of pronominalization, and that relies on quite different assumptions. These assumptions generalize the notion of pronominalization; they will be motivated in various independent ways. We will also attempt to relate the shape of morphemes like pronouns and articles to the meaning of discourses where cross-reference phenomena occur, by means of rules of a transformational nature. In this way, we make explicit the semantic content of pronouns. We will not be concerned with the study of the respective syntactic positions of two coreferential *NP*'s but we will see that our analysis raises new questions about this problem.

The analysis we present here is a direct application of Harris' views on the use of metalinguistic devices (here performatives) in grammatical descriptions.

---

* A preliminary version of this paper was read at the 3rd International Congress for Logic, Methodology, and Philosophy of Science, Amsterdam (August 25–September 2nd, 1967). I am indebted to C. Perdue and S. Schane for many improvements of this paper.

[1] The only 'argument' that we know of consists in replacing by their antecedents the pronouns that occur in a text, and in verifying that the result is on the one hand quasi ungrammatical, and on the other contains repetitions of identical morphemes. A very simple study of these identities shows that they are far from realizing morphemic identity of *NP*'s. In example like:

> The boy with long hair entered the room ... The boy with long hair asked for John

we find two *NP*'s which are coreferential and identical. However, the interpretation of such discourses involves a third *NP* necessarily occurring in the context, and coreferential with each of the present *NP*'s. This third *NP* cannot be identical to the others. Thus, again, one cannot use such examples to justify morphemic identity between *NP*'s.

F. Kiefer and N. Ruwet (eds.), Generative Grammar in Europe, 203–217. All Rights Reserved.
Copyright © 1973 by D. Reidel Publishing Company, Dordrecht-Holland.

I. TYPES OF REFERENCE

The following types of grammatical references can be distinguished.

(i) In the following sentences:

John bought a book. I read it.

the pronoun *it* is understood as the book that has been mentioned in the first sentence (i.e. it is said to be coreferential with *book*). We will say that *it* has *a book* as DISCOURSE REFERENT, (i.e. *it* points to a unit of discourse which is a noun phrase together with its interpretation in terms of the human universe). Discourse reference has been called elsewhere coreference.

(ii) In the sentence

John bought a book. I stole one.

the pronoun *one* is understood as a book that has nothing to do with the one mentioned in the first sentence. We will say that *one* has *book* as LEXICAL REFERENT (i.e. *one* simply points to a lexical item, and avoids repeating it).

(iii) In the sentence

John bought a book. I stole this one.

to the pronoun *one* which is to be understood as in (ii), we have added *this*, whose function is to point to a particular book in the extra-linguistic context of the utterer of the discourse, and not to a book mentioned in the discourse. We will say that *this one* has an EXTERNAL REFERENT.

(iv) In the sentence

(a)   John bought various books. I read one.

the pronoun *one* may be understood as a book which is a member[2] of the set *various books* bought by *John*. Notice that this need not be the case. It would not be true, for example in

John bought various books. I read it.

If *it* refers to a book, which is conceivable in a more extended discourse, then this book may not be a member of the set *various books* bought by *John*.

We could say that *one* provides a new type of reference, say INCLUSION REFERENCE with respect to a set, but the existence of the very precise paraphrase

---

[2] More exactly, a subset of cardinality 1. If we had *some* or *several* instead of *one*, the corresponding interpretation would be 'proper subset of the set {*various books*}'.

(b)   John bought various books, I read one of them.

where *them* has *various books* for discourse referent, allows us, by means of the syntactic operation of deletion:

of them → ∅

to reduce inclusion reference to discourse reference: (b) → (a). The interest of this reduction is the following. When one studies the relative positions in a discourse of a pronoun and its antecedent, one finds that the phenomena are all different according to the various types of reference that we distinguished and to the exact shapes of pronominal elements. Moreover each class of phenomena is complicated, and would need a large number of rules for its description. In reducing inclusion reference to the general case of discourse reference for the pronoun *them*, we save the description of the relative positions of indefinite pronouns (*one*, *some*, etc.) and of their antecedents. The inclusion relation does not raise any special problem, since, as we will see below, the positions between which it holds are fixed within a noun phrase.

There are however certain difficulties in connection with this type of reference. Some have been mentioned by Postal, they have to do with the lack of interpretation of discourses like

Three men arrived, one of *them* asked for a book.
The (other one + four others) did not say a word.[3]

Another problem is found in examples like

I put a book on a table and another one on a shelf. One is red and the other is blue.

The understanding of this discourse is such that the red book and the blue book constitute the same set as the one made of the book on the table and of the book on the shelf, and we do not know where is each book. A natural way to describe this situation is by using the device

of them → ∅,

of them would underly *one* and *the other*, (i.e. *one of them, the other of them*) and *them* would be coreferential with the two books of the first sentence. How to make this coreference relation explicit is not clear, since it has to

---

[3] The + sign is to be understood as a disjunction, and the parentheses as indicating factors with respect to the product: concatenation, *E* will be the unit element (e.g. zero morpheme) for this operation. Terms in italic in an example indicate that they are linked by some reference relation.

do with the correspondence between plurals and conjunctions. At any rate, a device will be necessary that can also be used for the treatment of sentences like

> When John and Mary arrived, they looked tired.

where the pronoun *they* refers to both *John* and *Mary*.

II. COMPONENTS OF REFERENCE

The case of inclusion reference is an example of a complex effect that can be described in terms of two different phenomena (i.e. coreference, and inclusion) of a simpler and more general nature. We will now describe various syntactic devices that play, along the same line, a fundamental role in the description of reference. We will essentially study a basic form from which we can derive (at least for French) the various shapes of definite noun phrases, including most of the pronouns. This form is noted for French

$$\underline{\text{ce Nom}^1 \quad \text{de Nom}^2 \quad \text{Qu S}}$$

Phrases with 'demonstrative pronouns' are very close to this form:

ce lui	des chevaux	qui a gagné
the one	of the horses	that won

Such phrases are analysed in three parts as follows:

– *ce Nom*^{1}, where *Nom*^{1} is realized as a pronoun: *lui* (*one*);
– *de Nom*^{2}, which will be called inclusion complement, and studied in detail below;
– *Qu S*, basic form of the various shapes of relative clauses (*Qu S → qui a gagné* (*that won*), and of sentential complements.

(i) *Inclusion complement*

Nom^2 is always a definite plural noun phrase (i.e. with definite, demonstrative, or possessive determiner, or else a pronoun). Plural can be morphological, as in the example above, or semantic as in

> celui (de la bande + du groupe) qui a gagné.
> *the one (of the gang + of the group) that won.

We also find disjunctions (but not conjunctions) of singular noun phrases as in

> celui (de Pierre ou de Paul) qui a gagné.

The interpretation[4] of phrases or parts of phrases of the general form

$$Nom^1 \text{ de } Nom^2 \qquad (Nom^1 \text{ of } Nom^2)$$

is always the same. Nom^1 and Nom^2 correspond to sets and we have the inclusion relation

$$Nom^1 \subset Nom^2.$$

A consequence of this relation is gender agreement between Nom^1 and Nom^2 when Nom^2 is not a collective noun:

*celle (des chevaux + de Pierre ou de Paul) qui a gagné.

We have been using the component *de Nom²* (*of Nom²*) in order to reduce inclusion reference to discourse reference:

*celui d'eux qui a gagné   (the one of them that won)
→ celui qui a gagné   (the one that won).

(ii) *Deictic relative clauses.*

Definite (non generic) articles may have a referential function, in a sentence like

Une étudiante est entrée dans la bibliothèque. L'étudiante a demandé un livre.
A student entered the library. The student asked for a book.

Both occurrences of *étudiante* (*the student*) are coreferential; but in sentences like

Une étudiante est entrée dans la bibliothèque. La (jolie étudiante + étudiante qui était jolie) a demandé un livre.
A student entered the library. The (pretty student + student who was pretty) asked for a book.

where RESTRICTIVE modifiers are attached to the definite noun phrase, coreference (i.e. discourse reference) disappears.

This fact leads us to relate discourse reference and restrictive relative clauses: these two items occur in complementary distribution. More precisely, if we find, attached to the definite noun phrase, a restrictive modifier

---

[4] It may turn out that this inclusion complement will have to be introduced through relativization since in sentences like:

Il est de ceux qui ont gagné.

the constraints holding between the subject and the *de NP* phrase are very similar to the ones holding between Nom^1 and $Nom.^2$

like: *précédente* (*preceding*[5]), *déjà mentionnée* (*already mentioned*), *dont je viens de parler* (*whom I just talked about*), etc., we still have the possibility of discourse reference.

> Une *étudiante* est entrée dans la bibliothèque. *L'étudiante* que je viens de mentionner a demandé un livre.
> A *student* entered the library. The *student* that I just mentioned asked for a book.

These modifiers have all in common some 'pointing' property which provides a semantic interpretation for the fact that we have just observed. We will then say that part of the discourse reference function is assumed by a zeroable class of modifiers which will be called discourse deictic modifiers, the basic form of which is *Qu S*. The elements of such relative clauses are quite restricted. If we change the subject in the relative clause of the preceding example, then coreference is excluded. The same occurs, if, leaving *je* (*I*) for subject, we change the past tense to future:

> Une étudiante est entrée dans la bibliothèque. L'étudiante que
> (tu viens de mentionner + je mentionnerai) a demandé un livre.
> A student entered the library. The student that (you just mentioned + I will mention) asked for a book.

In fact, these constraints are not absolute, but relative to a performative. In discourses like

> John said that a *student* entered the library. The *student* that John just mentioned asked for a book.

the occurrences of *student* are coreferential, while the subject of the deictic clause is not *I*. If we replaced the second *John* by *I*, then the coreferential interpretation would disappear. In the same way, if *to say* were in the future tense, the tense of the deictic clause would have to be future too.

---

[5] The verbs *to precede* and *to follow* have very special properties in this connection. In the sentence:

> John has the following habit: he drinks.

the adjective *following* has the property of referring *John's drinking* to *habit*. This is not the case for other adjectives:

> *John has the (strange + nice) habit: he drinks.

The nature of the determiner is also involved:
we have:

> John has a (strange + nice) habit: he drinks.

but:

> *John has a following habit: he drinks.

Kuroda (1968) pointed out to us that in sentences like

> The *student* who just entered the library drinks water only when *he* is thirsty.

he and *student* were coreferential, while in the sentence that should be its source, this is not the case:

> *The *student* who just entered the library drinks water only when the *student* that I just mentioned is thirsty.

But M. Bierwisch observed (personal communication) that performative structures like *NP says that* operate quite differently on such sentences and on the conjoined ones that we are using as examples. A detailed study of the occurrence of performatives in complex sentences could perhaps solve this problem and explain why in the sentence

> When the student who just entered the library is thirsty, the student that I just mentioned drinks water.

both occurrences of *student* can be coreferential. This study might also provide the possibility of explaining why in

> He drinks water, when the student who just entered the library is thirsty.

student and *he* may not be coreferential.

In a similar way, it is possible to associate with external reference another set of relative clauses (external deictic modifiers). We have semantic equivalence between the following examples:

> Jean a acheté un livre, et j'ai volé celui-ci.
> John bought a book, and I stole this one.
> Jean a acheté un livre, et j'ai volé celui (que voici + qui est ici).
> John bought a book, and I stole the one which is here.

We are using *ici* (*here*) and not *là* (*there*) because of the difference that these items present when they are used as place adverbials: *ici* (*here*) may only refer to the place where the utterer of the discourse is located, which is precisely the meaning of external reference; *là* (*there*) may refer to an element of the discourse[6]

---

[6] A similar phenomenon can be observed with respect to time: *hier* (*yesterday*) refers to the day that precedes the moment when the utterer produces the discourse, *la veille* (*the day before*) refers to the day that precedes the moment indicated by the tense of the discourse. We find the same difference again between *demain* (*to-morrow*) and *le lendemain* (*the day after*).

J'ai dîné dans un bon *restaurant*. Il y avait *là* beaucoup de monde.
I had dinner in a good *restaurant*. There were a lot of people
there.

The fact that *ci* (*-is*) and *là* (*-at*) correspond to restrictive relative clauses is a
further argument for attributing part of the reference effect to underlying
relative clauses. The morphemes *ci* and *là* do not characterize external
reference since in certain structures *ce* (*ci* + *là*) may refer (discourse reference)
to sentences, and *celui-ci* but not *celui-là* may be synonymous to *il* when it
refers to human nouns.

(iii) *Lexical identity*.

In the examples we gave so far, part of the reference function was assumed
by means of lexical identity: the noun phrase with reference function was
'headed' by a noun (possibly replaced by a pronoun) that was identical with
some other noun of the discourse.

There are however cases of discourse reference without strict lexical
identity. In the sentence

> Une *étudiante* est entrée, cette *étudiante* a demandé un livre.
> A *student* came in. This *student* asked for a book.

the demonstrative noun phrase has for referent the student mentioned in
the first part of the sentence, and we still have lexical identity. But this way of
referring to the discourse is more general. In the sentence

> Une jolie *étudiante* est entrée, cette *jeune fille* a demandé un livre.
> A pretty *student* came in. This *girl* asked for a book.

the demonstrative noun phrase has the *étudiante* (*student*) as discourse referent, although no lexical identity is involved; however some sort of semantic
constraint must hold between the two nouns. Demonstrative noun phrases
(as well as proper names) do not accept restrictive relative clauses. This is
consistent with the properties of deictic relative clauses given in Section
II(ii), and with the fact that demonstrative noun phrases may also be interpreted in terms of external reference. Also such phrases may in French
include the particles *ci* and *là* (*ce N-ci, ce N-là*).

There are also similar cases with definite article instead of demonstrative:

> Un éléphant s'est approché. L'animal avait une profonde
> blessure.
> An elephant approached by. The animal had a deep wound.

where the *animal* and the *elephant* are one and the same animal. We can notice that this identity is harder to obtain in

> Un animal s'est approché. L'éléphant avait une profonde blessure.
> An animal approached. The elephant had a deep wound.

Lexical identity is not limited to nouns but has to be, in certain cases, extended to verbs and modifiers. The following example indicates that the phenomenon is quite general. In order to describe the coreferential relations in the sentence

> The student who first arrived asked for a book, the other one asked for a magazine. The boy who (wanted + had received) the novel looked more serious than the other one.

it is necessary to equate in some sense *student* and *boy*, *book* and *novel*. Here the process involved could be the same as in the previous examples. However, in order to distinguish among the two students, one has to interpret verbs like *to want, to receive*. Notice that if these verbs had a negation, the coreference relations would be permuted. Thus, a rather complicated semantic analysis is necessary to interpret unambiguously this sentence. Still, it is not hard to construct other examples where extra-linguistic knowledge of the universe is necessary in order to state precisely coreferential relations.

At any rate, lexical identity is a property constantly observed, and that may be generalized to some of the above apparent counter-examples. We discuss this condition in the next section.

III. BASIC FORMS AND RULES

We will first describe more precisely the basic form suggested in Section II:

ce N, *ce* basic definite determiner or definite marker (presumably *the* for English) is followed by a noun *N*. This *N* is replaced by a pronoun under certain conditions of lexical identity;

de NP (*of NP*), the inclusion complement described in Section II(i);

Qu S, the source of a relative clause whether deictic or not.

The rule that defines *NP*'s in this way is recursive and does not terminate:

$$NP = ce\ N\ de\ NP\ Qu\ S$$

but there are a number of facts that suggest an extra possibility for the inclusion complement. A sentence like

(c)   J'ai acheté des livres, j'ai lu celui-ci.

can be interpreted according to the set-theoretical formula

$$\{celui\text{-}ci\} \subset \{des\ livres\}.$$

We accounted for this fact by assuming that an inclusion complement *d'eux* (with *eux* coreferential with *livres*) was zeroed.

In the sentence:

(d)   J'ai acheté des livres, j'ai lu celui-ci # de livre.

(these sentences are considered as slightly substandard, # indicates the intonation change characteristic of 'detachment') the pronoun *celui-ci* correspond to a book which is not a member of the set $\{des\ livres\}$. Such examples lead us to assume that the inclusion complement may also have the form *de N*, providing thus the terminal $NP = N$ rule for the recursive rule that defines NP. In this case, we do not have the set inclusion relation but an identity of N's including identity of number (cf. footnote 9). More generally, we will allow in these positions N's that are not identical, but that are related by a classificatory relation of the type

$$N_1 \text{ is } N_2$$
(e.g.: An elephant is an animal).

This possibility will allow us to reduce the cases of coreference without lexical identity to the general case with lexical identity. Examples like the ones we mentioned will have underlying forms of the type

$$ce\ Nom^1\ de\ Nom^2 = ce\ animal\ de\ éléphant$$
(= the animal of elephant)

and the complement de Nom_2 will ultimately be zeroed.

We will consider the following rules. They will be used for deriving the various definite forms and their referential interpretation from the basic form.

When $Qu\ S$ has a deictic content, we can have

$$Qu\ S \rightarrow ci\ (\text{-}is)$$
$$Qu\ S \rightarrow là\ (\text{-}at).$$

The particles that appear in the right member of the preceding rules can be zeroed by the rules $[ci\ z.]$, $[là\ z.]$, in various positions (e.g. *ce livre ci* $\rightarrow$ *ce livre*). The elements *ce*, and *de* are also zeroable, by means of $[ce\ z.]$, $[de\ z.]$.

When a pronoun appears in the inclusion complement (i.e. in the position *de Pronoun*), it is zeroable.

When the N in the position Nom^1 is identical to its antecedent or to the

N of Nom^2, the substitution rule applies:[7]

$$N \rightarrow \text{LUI}$$

(LUI is a basic (abstract) pronoun).

French nouns are represented with two possible marks 'attached' to them: feminine and plural as in

fermier	e	s
N	fem	plur

The rule $N \rightarrow$ LUI operates independently from these marks. The reduction rule LUI $\rightarrow$ LE operates in the same way. Adjustment rules provide the observed forms:

LUI fem = elle; LUI plur = eux; LUI fem plur = elles;
LE fem = la; LE plur = les; LE fem plur = les.

Thus, gender and number agreement between Nom^1 and Nom^2 are consequences of the semantic constraints that hold between them.

We now outline without further justifications[8] examples of derivations using these basic forms and rules.

We will first derive the sequence definite article-noun (*les chevaux*) coreferential with some antecedent. The basic form is

ce cheval plur de cheval plur qui précèdent

lexical substitution $N \rightarrow$ LUI applied to the first occurrence of *cheval* provides:

celui plur de cheval plur qui précèdent[9]

[*ce* z.], [*de* z.] give:

lui plur cheval plur qui précèdent

the reduction rule LUI $\rightarrow$ LE needed for pre-verbal pronouns yields:

le plur cheval plur qui précèdent

---

[7] There might be two different processes of substitution going on correspondingly.
[8] We intend to describe elsewhere the detailed structure of NP's.
[9] From this step, we would derive by detachment (cf. example (d)), the form:

ceux qui précèdent # de chevaux . . .

Notice that we have:

*ceux qui précèdent # de cheval.

namely, number agreement between Nom^1 and $Nom.^2$

and by adjustment:

les chevaux qui précèdent

and we obtain our result by zeroing the deictic relative clause:

les chevaux.[10]

We thus account for the identity of shapes observed for articles and pre-verbal pronouns.[11] Pronouns like *lui, le*, etc. would be derived from the above source by further reduction:

ce LUI plur de cheval plur qui précèdent

→ ce LUI plur de LUI plur qui précèdent

→ ce LUI plur qui précèdent

→ ce LUI plur

[*ce z.*]: → LUI plur = eux by adjustment or by reduction:

→ LE plur.

By adjustment we can obtain *les* or *ils* (or pre-verbal *leur, en*, etc.)

Again, gender and number agreement between article and noun is a consequence of the deep level constraint holding between Nom^1 and $Nom.^2$ The generalization of this agreement process to other parts of speech raises many new questions.

The pronoun *celui-ci* (*this one*) in example (c)[12] above combines inclusion and external reference. We account for its shape and for its meaning by the following derivation:

*ce livre de (ce livres de livres qui précèdent) qui est ici

becomes by substitution under lexical identity (applied 3 times):

*ce lui de (ce eux de eux qui précèdent) qui est ici

---

[10] Thus, it is only at a superficial level that such *NP*'s do not contain a restrictive relative clause. One could perhaps attempt to distinguish generic articles of *NP*'s on this basis. Generic phrases would be the ones that do not contain any restrictive relative clause.

[11] We then consider that articles come from pronouns, while Postal (1966) took the opposite direction: pronouns come from articles. Preverbal pronouns are the ones that occur to the left of corresponding verbs. Some have the same shape as definite articles: *Je (le + la + les) vois, Je (lui + leur) en parle.*

[12] We can notice that phrases beginning by *celui* (*the one*) must be completed by a relative clause. They are coreferential with their antecedent only, if the relative clause is of the deictic type, as in:

A group of *students* came in. I like students, but the *ones* that I just mentioned are too noisy.

Notice that the antecedent cannot be the generic object of *I like*, which is not the case with pronouns like, *he, they*, etc. as in:

A group of students came in. I like *students*, but *they* are too noisy.

and by zeroing of *de eux*:

ce lui de (ce eux qui précèdent) qui est ici.

This form has the desired interpretation. It is further reduced: by zeroing *ce* and the deictic relative clause that indicates coreference:

*ce lui de (eux) qui est ici.

Then, zeroing of *de eux* applies again yielding:

celui qui est ici.

Then, reduction to *ci* of the deictic relative clause that indicates external reference provides the final result:

celui ci.

The treatment of pronominalization that we are proposing has several important properties that distinguish it from other proposals:[13]
– we have generalized considerably the notion of pronominalization, it is now extended to other morphemes that are associated with various types of reference in an integrated way. Most studies dealing with coreference are restricted to the pronouns: *it, he, she, they, him, her, them*, and the possessive adjectives. We consider that this restriction is arbitrary, the same intuitive notion of coreference occurs with phrases of the form:

(the + this + that) (N + one)

---

[13] N. Chomsky and M. Halle pointed out to us that there exists an infinite set of relative clauses that have the same deictic content, thus zeroing rules could not be defined on a particular string of morphemes or words. This observation is quite correct, but there are various ways of coping with this situation. One could consider for example, that we have in the deictic position an abstract element D from which the infinite set of deictic clauses is derived by means of recursive rules. The zeroing rule would be: $D \rightarrow \emptyset$. Or else, more or less equivalently, the infinite set can be organized into a lattice. Actual phrases like *that N just mentioned* would constitute minimal elements of this lattice, and the zeroing rules would be limited to them.

N. Chomsky mentioned to us that the treatment of coreference cannot be distinguished from the general problem of the semantic description of noun phrases. Rules of semantic interpretation are necessary for all noun phrases. Coreference is just a special case among many other types of meanings that NP's can have. Since these interpretation rules will apply to all types of meanings, no special apparatus like our zeroing rules would be needed for the treatment of coreference.

Such a situation might be preferable to what we are proposing here. However, the treatment of meaning by means of interpretation rules has not been so far very successful. Coreference is a category of meaning which is sharply distinguished among others, it is a highly operational notion, presumably because of its morphological and syntactic support (i.e. pronouns). So far, no other semantic notions that could be considered for noun phrases appear to be operational. This situation is sufficient to justify a special treatment of coreference. Chomsky's position could only be well supported if one could exhibit interpretation rules that would apply in the same way, to coreference and to other types of meanings (to be defined), it seems very hard to propose such rules at the moment.

and with pronouns or possessives; thus, any analysis of coreference which does not describe pronouns, possessives and these phrases in a unified way fails in a very serious way;

– we provide a common basic structure for all definite noun phrases;

– we provide a uniform semantic content for the various kinds of pronouns;

– we avoid the so-called 'Bach's paradox', in a different way from Kartunnen's logical approach;

– we propose a new treatment of gender-number agreement, which no longer needs *ad-hoc* context-sensitive rules;

– we use derivations that all have a similar shape. A complex NP that includes a sentence ($Qu\ S$), is progressively reduced to shorter shapes, and after a certain number of steps, to a pronoun (possibly $\emptyset$). It has often been observed that the carriers of reference may belong to any part of speech (article, noun, pronoun, verb, preposition, adjective, etc.). Our solution explains this observation, since we reduce (among other things) a full sentence. Since any part of speech may occur within this sentence, it is quite normal to observe, associated with reference, remainders of a large variety. However, they should not be arbitrary, they have to be components of deictic sentences, which themselves constitute a very restricted subset of sentences;

– we have used several rules applied several times each, within the derivation of a given pronoun. In all previous studies, only one or two rules were proposed to describe pronominalization. Such rules, when studied for ordering with respect to cycle for example, all lead to contradictions. The richer system we have presented leaves much more room for ordering, and should not result in any ordering paradox.

Many new questions are raised, and there are various problems that we have not considered, but we think that this framework will prove adequate and will accommodate many other phenomena, in particular the ones that can be observed in the general description of the determiner system of a language.

University of Paris VIII (Vincennes) and

Laboratoire d'Automatique Documentaire et Linguistique (E.R.A. 247, CNRS)

REFERENCES

Bach, E.: 'Problominalization', *Linguistic Inquiry* **1.1** (1970), 121–122.
Chomsky, N.: *Aspects of the Theory of Syntax* (1965), MIT Press, Cambridge.
Dougherty, R.C.: 'An Interpretive Theory of Pronominal Reference', *Foundations of Language* **4.3** (1969), 488–519.
Harris, Z. S.: 'Elementary Transformations', *TDAP* **54** (1964), University of Pennsylvania.

Harris, Z. S.: *Mathematical Structures of Language* (1968), Wiley, New York.

Karttunen, L.: 'Migs and Pilots', mimeographed (1969), University of Texas at Austin.

Kuroda, S.-Y.: 'English Relativization and Certain Related Problems', *Language* **44** (1968), 244–266.

Lakoff, G.: 'Pronouns and Reference', Harvard mimeo (1968), Available from the Indiana Linguistic Club.

Lees, R. B. and Klima, E. S.: 'Rules for English Pronominalization', *Language* **39** (1963), 17–28.

Postal, P. M.: *Crossover Phenomena* (1968), mimeographed, IBM, Yorktown Heights.

Postal, P. M.: 'On So-Called Pronouns in English', *Georgetown Monographs on Language and Linguistics*, No. 19 (F. P. Dinneen, Ed.), 1966.

Ross, J. R.: 'On the Cyclic Nature of English Pronominalization', *To honor Roman Jakobson*, Vol. III (1967), Mouton and Co., The Hague.

FERENC KIEFER

ON PRESUPPOSITIONS*

1. The question of presuppositions has become a widely discussed topic in linguistic literature (cf. Katz–Postal, 1964; Fillmore, 1970; McCawley, 1968; Chomsky, 1969; Lakoff, 1970; Morgan, 1969; Horn, 1969; and Katz, 1971). The notion of presupposition has been used differently by the various authors. For some of them it means the appropriate use of a sentence, for others it has to do with truth value. Very often it has been relegated to the pragmatic aspects of sentences, in other cases it has been considered as a property of lexical entries. It has also been suggested that selectional restrictions are in fact presuppositions. In the present paper I shall discuss some problems which crop up with respect to the various proposals about the role of presuppositions in linguistic description. I shall put forward the claim that presuppositions play an important role in every part of grammar. In connection with this claim a possible classification of presuppositions will be suggested. I shall make no attempt at a representation of presuppositions in linguistic theory though some hints will be made at along what lines a solution to this problem might be expected.

2. The concept of presupposition is due to Frege, who draws a sharp line between asserted meaning and presuppose meaning. Frege wrote:

If anything is asserted there is always an obvious presupposition that the simple or compound proper names used have reference. If one therefore asserts

(1)   Kepler died in misery,

there is a presupposition that the name 'Kepler' designates something; but it does not follow that the sense of the sentence (1) contains the thought that the name 'Kepler' designates something.
   If this were the case the negation would have to run not

(2)   Kepler did not die in misery

but

(3)   Kepler did not die in misery, or the name 'Kepler' has no reference.

That the name 'Kepler' designates something is just as much a presupposition for the assertion (1) as for the contrary assertion (2) (Frege, *op. cit.*, pp. 69–70).[1]

* This work has been supported by the Bank of Sweden Tercentenary Fund. I have profited much from discussions with a large number of people while lecturing on this topic at various German and Swedish universities. In particular, I wish to thank Manfred Bierwisch and Wayles Browne for valuable criticisms of an earlier draft of this paper. All mistakes are, of course, mine.
[1] The numbering of the sentences and of the references to these numbers are my changes in the text.

F. Kiefer and N. Ruwet (eds.), Generative Grammar in Europe, 218–242. *All Rights Reserved.*
Copyright © 1973 by D. Reidel Publishing Company, Dordrecht-Holland.

We may give Frege's words the following interpretation. The presupposition of (1) is a condition that the name 'Kepler' has a reference, in other words, that Kepler exists. (1) makes an assertion only when this condition is fulfilled. For later reference we shall call such a presupposition an *existential presupposition*.

The next point which Frege makes is that presuppositions remain invariant under negation. Thus, (1) and (2) have exactly the same presuppositions.

Finally, the reason why Frege rejects (3) as a negation of (1) is the following. If (3) were a negation of (1), then (3) must be equivalent to (2), since (2) is also a negation of (1). Under which conditions are the propositions '$\sim p$' and '$\sim p \vee \sim q$' materially equivalent? If and only if '$\sim q$' is a logical falsehood. This is to say that we have to make the absurd claim that the name 'Kepler' never has a reference. (See also Katz for some discussion of this topic.)

Austin (*op. cit.*, pp. 47–52) takes essentially Frege's view on presuppositions. He compares presupposition with entailment and implication. He says:

If p entails q then $\sim q$ entails $\sim p$: if 'the cat is on the mat' entails 'the mat is under the cat' then 'the mat is not under the cat' entails 'the cat is not on the mat'. Here the truth of a proposition entails the truth of a further proposition or the truth of one is inconsistent with the truth of another. Presupposition is, however, unlike entailment: If 'John's children are bald' presupposes that John has children, it is not true that John's having no children presupposes that John's children are not bald. Moreover again, *both* 'John's children are bald' and 'John's children are not bald' alike presuppose that John has children: but it is not the case that both 'the cat is on the mat' and 'the cat is not on the mat' alike entail that the cat is below the mat. . . . What is to be said of the statement that 'John's children are bald' if made when John has no children? It is usual now to say that it is *not* false because it is devoid of reference; reference is necessary for either truth or falsehood.

These considerations lead us to the conclusion that sentences which lack reference (for which the existential presupposition(s) is (are) not fulfilled) are not meaningless. To use Katz's term, the meaning of such sentences is *indeterminate* (Katz, *op. cit.*). Another important point is that the notions 'entailment' and 'presuppositions' should be kept strictly apart from each other.

There is an alternative view to that of Frege's which is represented by Russell. Russell argues that a sentence like

(4)   the present king of France is bald

is false. According to Russell (4) should be understood as a conjunction of three propositions. He derives his argument from the fact that the non-generic (i.e. contextually determined) definite article stands for existence and uniqueness. We may easily express (4) by means of notation of propositional calculus. If we abbreviate the reading of 'present King of France' by K and that of 'bald' by B, then, on Russell's analysis, we get

(5) $(\exists x)(K(x) \wedge (\forall z)(\forall y)(K(z) \wedge K(y) \supset z \equiv y) \wedge B(x))$

The negation of (5) is (6):

(6) $(\forall x)(\sim K(x) \vee \sim(\forall z)(\forall y)(K(z) \wedge K(y) \supset z \equiv y) \vee \sim B(x))$

Sentence (4) is false because its existential claim is false. Without going into details let me summarize some of Katz's views against the Russellian analysis (Katz, *op. cit.*).

(i) Russell assumes, without argument, that the categories of nonsense and statementhood are exhaustive alternatives for the class of declarative sentences. This need not be so, however.[2]

(ii) The propositions expressed by a declarative, its corresponding interrogative, corresponding hortatory, etc. are, respectively, a statement, question, request, wish, etc. by virtue of the satisfaction of the same condition. E.g.

(7)   (i)   The king of France is healthy.
           (ii) Is the king of France healthy?
           (iii) Make the king of France healthy!
           (iv) Oh, were the king of France healthy!

Katz argues, that on the Russellian analysis if there is no king of France at the moment of utterance, the sentence (7)(i) is counted as making a false statement, but the answer to (7)(ii) is not correspondingly 'no' but rather 'cannot be answered either way'. Thus one would have 'to tolerate a wholly unmotivated asymmetry in the treatment of different sentence types'.

(iii) Katz argues, citing Geach, that 'the notion of presupposition has a crucial place in the theory of question'.[3]

---

[2] As Katz puts it: 'the Fregian presuppositional theory . . . says that the three conjuncts isolated in the Russellian analysis of definite descriptions are not on a par with one another but that the first two comprise a condition under which the assertion expressed by the third is true or false. If this condition is not met, if, that is, this conjunction is false, then there is no assertion expressed by the third and the proposition has no truth value. Accordingly, the third category of proposition is the category of propositions which because they are not about anything make no statement. This is like saying that if there is a target then there are hits and misses, but if there is no target then a shot cannot be considered either a hit or a miss but must be assigned to another category, say, the category of wasted shots.' (*op. cit.*)

[3] Geach's argument against Russell reads as follows: "On Russell's view 'the king of France is bald' is a false assertion. This view seems to me to commit the fallacy of 'many questions'. To see how this is so, let us take a typical example of the fallacy: the demand for a 'plain answer – yes or no!' to the question 'Have you been happier since your wife died?' Three questions are involved:

(1)   Have you ever had a wife?
(2)   Is she dead?
(3)   Have you been happier since then?

(iv) There are cases where a distinction must be drawn between assertion and presupposition in order to account for the scope of negation.[4]

On such grounds, it seems to me that the Fregian thesis is preferable to the Russellian one. This conjecture will receive further support from what follows below.

3. We have seen that presuppositions of a sentence were claimed to be conditions which must be fulfilled for that sentence be true or false.[5] The presuppositions we have so far discussed were all of the existential type. We may ask now whether there are only existential presuppositions or also others which do not have to do with existence. Consider sentences (8) and (9):

(8)   John $\left\{ \begin{array}{l} \text{realizes} \\ \text{knows} \\ \text{remembers} \end{array} \right\}$ that Lena loved him.

(9)   John does not $\left\{ \begin{array}{l} \text{realize} \\ \text{know} \\ \text{remember} \end{array} \right\}$ that Lena loved him.

Both (8) and (9) presuppose that 'Lena loved him'. In both cases the truth of the embedded propositions is presupposed. One may stipulate that here, too, we have to do with existential presuppositions. What is presupposed here is the existence of a fact, namely of the fact that 'Lena loved him'. Thus, in contrast to (1) and (4), where the existence of a referent is presupposed, here it is the existence of a fact that is presupposed. For this fact to exist, it must be true.

The act of asking question (2) presupposes an affirmative answer to question (1); if the true answer to (1) is negative, question (2) *does not arise*. The act of asking question (3) presupposes an affirmative answer to question (2); if question (2) does not arise, or if the true answer to it is negative, question (3) *does not arise*. When a question does not arise, the only proper way of answering it is to say so and explain the reason; the 'plain' affirmative or negative answer, though grammatically and logically possible, is *out of place*. This does not go against the laws of contradiction and excluded middle; what these laws tell us is that *if* the question arose 'yes' and 'no' *would be* exclusive alternatives". See for further discussion of this topic Katz, *op. cit.*

[4] What is meant here is that presuppositions are refractory to the operation of negation while assertion is not. The same holds true for the operation of questioning and for some other 'linguistic operations' as well (if an imperative exists for a certain verb, the presuppositions remain unchanged, the same holds for hortatory sentences, etc.).

[5] I shall use the notions 'sentence' and 'proposition' interchangeably in this paper. We must keep in mind, however, that what we want to say about logical properties of a sentence always refers to the logical properties of the proposition expressed by the sentence or by the corresponding declarative sentence (the latter qualification being necessary in order to account for questions, imperatives, etc.).

We can thus say that in cases like (8), too, existence is presupposed. The truth of the embedded proposition is a consequence of the existence of the fact it describes.[6]

In view of the above considerations we might try to define the presuppositions of a sentence as conditions on existence which must be fulfilled for the sentence to be true or false. Apart from problems involving 'negative' presuppositions,[7] there are other cases which seem to indicate that this definition of presuppositions is too narrow. Consider

(10)   (i) Lena agreed to come.
        (ii) Lena did not agree to come.

(11)   (i) Lena refused to come.
        (ii) Lena did not refuse to come.

In (10) and (11) it is presupposed that Lena was asked to come. Suppose that this presupposition were not true. Sentences (10) and (11) could still have a truth value. This explains why sentences (12), though odd, are not meaningless.

(12)   (i) Lena was not asked but she agreed to come.
        (ii) Lena was not asked but she refused to come.

Another type of presupposition is exemplified by (13) and (14).

---

[6] Kiparsky and Kiparsky (1970) have come to similar conclusions. They say that 'there is a syntactic and semantic correspondence between *truth* and *specific reference*. The verbs which presuppose that their sentential object expresses a true proposition also presuppose that their non-sentential object refers to a specific thing' (*op. cit.*, pp. 167–168). It goes without saying that the whole problem of factivity plays an important role in the theory of presuppositions. For details, see Kiparsky and Kiparsky (1970).

[7] The negative presuppositions discussed in Lakoff seem to me somewhat dubious. Apart from the 'unclear' case in connection with the verb *pretend* Lakoff presents as a clear case the counterfactual conditional:

(i)   If Irv were a Martian, I'd be running away from here.
(ii)   It is not the case that if Irv were a Martian, I'd be running away from here.

Lakoff claims that in (i) the negative of both clauses is presupposed. (i) is synonymous with (iii), however:

(iii)   I'd be running away from here, if Irv were a Martian.

The negation of (iii) is (iv):

(iv)   It is not the case that I'd be running away from here, if Irv were a Martian.

which is synonymous with (v):

(v)   I would not be running away from here, if Irv were a Martian.

Thus, the negative of the main clause is not a presupposition.
However, it can be maintained that the if-clause contains a negative presupposition.

(13)   (i) John fears that Lena will come.

        (ii) John does not fear that Lena will come.

(14)   (i) John hopes that Lena will come.

        (ii) John does not hope that Lena will come.

The verb 'fear' presupposes something bad, the verb 'hope', however, something good. What 'John' fears or does not fear appears to him as something unpleasant while what he hopes or does not hope as something pleasant.

In view of examples like (10)–(11) and (13)–(14) we can not claim that presuppositions always have to do with existence. As a working definition we shall adopt the negation test which we have already made ample use of in the above examples.

This definition can be formulated as follows.

(15)   *Let S_1 and S_2 be two sentences. Furthermore, let us assume that S_2 is not asserted by S_1. Then, if S_2 follows from both S_1 and $\sim S_1$, we shall say that S_2 is a presupposition of S_1.*

Notice that the qualification that S_2 is not asserted by S_1 seems to be necessary because if this were the case we would, of course, have an assertion and not a presupposition. In sentence (1), for example, negation not only leaves the existential presupposition intact but also the verb 'olie' (at least on one reading of the sentence) which we, quite naturally, do not want to consider to be a presupposition associated with (1).

I am quite aware of the fact that definition (15) needs further clarification on at least two important points. The first question concerns the exact nature of 'follows' (in what sense do we say that S_2 *follows* from S_1?), the second one the scope of negation. The first question will be left unanswered here and I can make only a few remarks with respect to the second one.

I shall assume that the scope of negation for definition (15) is uniquely determined by the predicate of sentence S_1 if S_1 is a simple sentence and the main clause if S_1 is a complex sentence. This entails considering surface constituent negation (negation of quantifiers, of emphatic constituents, etc.) as deep sentence negation. The principle for determining the scope of negation is essentially that which has been adopted in transformational generative grammar.

4.   We can see that there is some difference in the presuppositional treatment between sentences like (1), (4), (7), on the one hand, and sentences like (8), (10), (11), (13) and (14), on the other. In sentence (1) the existential presupposition is neither the property of 'Kepler', nor that of 'die' or 'misery' but

rather of the whole proposition. Similarly, in (4) the existential presupposition is not part of the meaning of either 'present', or 'king', or 'bald' and not
even of the definite article 'the' but rather of the whole proposition. In contrast to (1), (4) and (7), in (8) the presuppositions are part of the meaning of
the verbs *realize, know, remember*. We do not lose presuppositional information with respect to these verbs if we replace the subject and the object complement in (8) by variables:

$$(16) \quad X \left\{ \begin{array}{l} \text{realizes} \\ \text{knows} \\ \text{remembers} \end{array} \right\} Y$$

The same thing holds for the verbs *fear* and *hope*:

(17)   (i) X fears Y
       (ii) X hopes Y

We shall call the presuppositions which come from lexical entries *lexical presuppositions*. Presuppositions which are not part of the meaning of particular
lexical items but rather arise from the entire proposition will be termed *non-
lexical presuppositions*. It may be observed that existential presuppositions
may be either lexical or non-lexical. Every predicate word may have presuppositions associated with it. The meaning of a lexical item may thus consist of (i) asserted meaning and (ii) presupposed meaning. The same holds
true for the meaning of the whole proposition.

We shall next turn to the question of how presuppositions and selectional
restrictions may be interrelated (**4.1**), then we shall put forward a classification
of lexical presuppositions (**4.2**), finally some scrutiny will be given to the
question of how lexical presuppositions might be represented (**4.3**).

4.1.   It has been suggested that selectional restrictions can be reformulated
as presuppositions (Fillmore, 1970; and McCawley, 1968). Chomsky
(Chomsky, 1965, p. 95) introduces selectional rules by saying that

rules, . . ., which analyze a symbol . . . in terms of syntactic features of the frames in which it
appears, I shall call *selectional rules*. The latter express what are usually called 'selectional
restrictions' or 'restrictions of cooccurrence'.

The features Chomsky makes use of in his selectional rules are such as
[±Abstract], [±Animate], [±Human], [±Common], etc. These features
play an important role in semantics as well. Similar features have been used
by Katz–Fodor and Katz–Postal in their semantic theory for semantic
selection. McCawley points out that selection is completely determined by
semantic processes and suggests that the whole problem of selectional

restrictions should be treated in semantics (*op. cit.*, 264–268). If we want to reformulate selectional restrictions as presuppositions then it is clear that it must be shown that they are entirely a semantic phenomenon (since presuppositions clearly are). Recently some counterexamples have been adduced to this claim (Kuroda, 1969; and Chomsky, 1969; Katz, 1971; and Moravcsik, 1970). It seems to me, however, that all these counterexamples have a rather marginal character and can not affect the claim that selectional restrictions are largely semantic in nature.[8]

The advantage of treating selectional restrictions as presuppositions lies in the fact that we do not need two types of selection, syntactic and semantic, both can be treated as a unified phenomenon.[9] Furthermore, presuppositions need not be kept apart from selectional restrictions and therefore the semantic representation of lexical items will become simpler. It may be noted in passing that the question of syntactic and semantic selection hinges essentially on whether we assume a borderline between syntax and semantics and if so, on where we draw it.

Some examples will give further evidence for the claim that selectional restrictions are presuppositions. Consider

(18)   (i)   he frightens X_1
        (ii) X_2 admires Picasso
        (iii) X_3 is pretty
        (iv) X_4 is a bachelor
        (v) X_5 lasts X_6
        (vi) X_7 elapsed

The negation test shows that X_1 must be [+Animate], X_2 [+Human], X_3 [+Human] and [−Male], X_4 [+Human], [+Male], [+Adult], X_5 [+Event], X_6 [+Time] and X_7 [+Time]. If these presuppositions do not hold then we get anomalous sentences.

---

[8] This can undoubtedly be claimed of the morphological problems of gender agreement in French discussed by Kuroda. Katz's examples are more interesting (*op. cit.*) because they involve semantically synonymous expressions which are distinct only with respect to the features [±Count] or [±Proper], respectively. These features trigger syntactic selection. It is, however, not clear whether the expressions Katz has in mind are really synonymous. Chomsky's examples concern the selection of the head noun of a noun phrase. There are some queer examples where the selection depends on the head noun rather than on the whole noun phrase They require special treatment. Moravcsik argues partly along the same lines as Katz. The second part of his argument seems to be in support of the claim that selection is semantic rather than against it (examples like *I count the mob, the galaxy, the couple). Here again a special feature is needed in order to explain why some nouns which denote 'a set of things' are not 'countable'.

[9] Syntactic selection refers here to selection in terms of partly syntactic features like [±Animate], [±Abstract]. Syntactic subcategorization is a separate problem and does not come under the heading of presuppositions.

Notice that *pretty*, in fact, is not restricted to [+Human], [−Male]. One can say 'What a pretty rock!' or 'What a pretty landscape!', etc. This use of *pretty*, however, seems to be more restricted to the attributive position than the one that presupposes [+Human], [−Male]. Such details need not bother us in the present context, however.

Recall that sentences for which the existential presuppositions do not hold were called indeterminate. Indeterminate sentences are not semantically anomalous. Consequently there must be an essential difference between existential and non-existential presuppositions. The examples of selectional restrictions discussed so far belonged all to the non-existential type of pre-suppositions. Furthermore, since selectional restrictions are defined on lexical items and not on whole sentences, they can only be lexical presuppositions. In view of this one might be tempted to jump to the conclusion that selectional restrictions are non-existential lexical presuppositions. We can take it for granted that all selectional restrictions can be given presuppositional status. The second part of the above claim is, however, more interesting. Those cases of existential lexical presuppositions which we have discussed so far seem to lend support to this claim. I know of one interesting counterexample, how-ever. Consider

(19)   (i) Anybody working in Stockholm pays high taxes.
        (ii) Everybody working in Stockholm pays high taxes.

The cognitive meaning of 'anybody in Stockholm' (at least, for one reading of anybody) and 'everybody in Stockholm' are identical, namely $(\forall x)(S(x))$ where S stands for 'is in Stockholm'. The negation of (19) yields (20):

(20)   (i) Nobody working in Stockholm pays high taxes.
        (ii) Not everybody working in Stockholm pays high taxes.

It would seem that 'anybody' has no presuppositions while 'everybody' has the presupposition 'Somebody working in Stockholm pays high taxes'. The difference between 'any' and 'every' lies in the fact that – as has been pointed out by Vendler[10] – while 'any' is indifferent with respect to existence, 'every' is not; in fact, it presupposes existence. The difference is brought out more drastically in (21):

---

[10] Such a distinction is not a particular feature of English. As Rohrer pointed out the same distinction holds true for the French quantifiers *tout* and *chaque* as well. Consider (i) and (ii):

(i)   Je rendrai la compagnie responsable de tout retard.
(ii)   Je rendrai la compagnie responsable de chaque retard.

(21)   (i)   Any book which appeared was sold.

        (ii)   Any book which might have appeared was sold.

        (iii) Every book which appeared was sold.

        (iv)   *Every book which might have appeared was sold.

While sentences (21)(i) through (iii) are semantically well-formed, (21)(iv) is anomalous because the existential presupposition associated with 'every' is violated.[11]

We may thus conclude that the claim that existential presuppositions can not function as selectional restrictions is false. It might be the case that quantifiers behave exceptionally as they do in many other cases. We must, however, leave this question open here.

It goes without saying that not all existential lexical presuppositions may have a selectional function. Examples like *know, realize, remember* may illustrate this point. It remains to be seen what kind of existential presuppositions other than those associated with some quantifiers have selectional function. On the other hand, it seems to be fairly clear that all non-existential lexical presuppositions can be selectional restrictions. We must add an important qualification here, however. It is plain that selection is a function of predicate words in positions in which they play a predicative role (if they function as predicates, modifiers, quantifiers, etc.). We cannot restrict selection to the predicate position since we have cases like *liquid book, colorless green*, etc. Recall also the examples with *any* and *every*. We might perhaps claim that on some deep syntactic level selection is restricted to predicative position. This question, however, need not concern us here.

In cases they do not function as selectional restrictions the presuppositions constitute part of the conditions which the intended referent must fulfil in order to be appropriate. Consider the function of the presuppositions associated with 'bachelor', 'spinster' and 'father' in the following sentences:

(22)   The *bachelor* next door arrived.

        The old *spinster* has not been here yet.

        My *father* wrote me a letter.

        I saw his *father*.

Therefore, it seems to be more appropriate to speak of the selectional function of presuppositions rather than to put an identity sign between certain types of presuppositions and selectional restrictions.

To summarize, all selectional restrictions can be formulated as presuppo-

---

[11] It was pointed out to me that for some speakers (i) is odd but not impossible while (iv) is clearly ungrammatical.

sitions but not all presuppositions may function as selectional restrictions. Only lexical presuppositions may have this function. They are mostly of the non-existential type.

4.2. Bierwisch argues (Bierwisch, 1970) that presuppositions (what he had in mind were lexical presuppositions) are of two different kinds. In order to illustrate his point let us take some examples.

(23)   (i)   John expects that Lena will come.
         (ii) John hopes that Lena will come.
         (iii) John fears that Lena will come.

All three sentences in (23) have a common presupposition which expresses the selectional restriction to be imposed on the subject. Notice the sentences in (24) violate the same selectional restriction.

(24)   (i)   The rock expects that Lena will come.
         (ii) The rock hopes that Lena will come.
         (iii) The rock fears that Lena will come.

The common presupposition may be expressed in the following way:

(25)   EXPECT(X, Y) presupposes Human(X)

where EXPECT is assumed to be the common reading of *expect*, *hope* and *fear*. The verbs *hope* and *fear* have an additional presupposition with respect to *expect* which has only (25). These are expressed by (26) and (27), respectively.

(26)   hope(X, Y) presupposes FEEL $(X, $ GOOD$(Y))$

(27)   fear$(X; Y)$ presupposes FEEL$(X, $ BAD$(Y))$

where FEEL denotes the relation or attitude of X to Y.

(25) belongs to the *general presuppositions* which need not be stated for each lexical item. They belong rather to the definitions and axioms of the semantics of the lexicon of a given language. In contrast to (25) one should consider (26) and (27) to be *idiosyncratic presuppositions*; they must be part of the lexical representation of the items concerned. Further examples for general and idiosyncratic presuppositions can easily be given.[12] Consider, for example, the adjectives *pretty* and *handsome*. Both are evaluative but they

---

[12] It goes without saying that emotional attitudes form an important subclass of presuppositions. Every language exhibits predicate words with similar 'idiosyncratic' presuppositions as *hope* and *fear*. Bengt Sigurd has collected some such words for Swedish: *drabba* (inflict), *utsätta X för Y* (to expose *X* to *Y*), *tack vare* (thanks to), *chans*, *risk*, etc. Even derivational processes can be triggered by presuppositions. Compare the minimal pairs

differ considerably as to their scopes. *Handsome*, for instance, can be predicated of both males and females while *pretty* is not generally used of adult males. The latter restriction is an idiosyncratic fact about *pretty*. The fact that *mature* refers to human beings while *ripe* to *fruits* etc. is also idiosyncratic about these words. The German adjective *blond* has the idiosyncratic property that it can only be predicated of human hair. This fact has nothing to do with the overall semantic structure of German color words. In English one can say *high building* but not *high man*, although in both cases the same dimension is involved. Very often the difference in meaning between closely related predicate words can be accounted for in terms of idiosyncratic presuppositions. The general presuppositions mark off the classes to which these words belong while the idiosyncratic presuppositions account for what is idiosyncratic about the particular members of this class.

The distinction between general and idiosyncratic presuppositions is, no doubt, justified. I shall be content to make some brief comments on Bierwisch's proposal.

First of all, there seems to be an essential difference between the oddity of sentences (28)(i) and (ii):

(a)	*arbetsfri*	*vapenfri*	*föräldrafri*
	(free of work)	(unarmed)	(free of parental control)
	arbetslös	*vapenlös*	*föräldralös*
	(unemployed)	(unarmed)	(parentless)

The suffix *-fri* has the presupposition that it is good to be free of somebody or something (in short GOOD) and the suffix *-lös* the presupposition that it is bad to be free of somebody or something (in short BAD). No such pairs occur in the following cases:

(b)	*portofri*	*giftfri*	*riskfri*
	*portolös	**giftlös*	**risklös*
(c)	**meningsfri*	**tandfri*	**chansfri*
	meningslös	*tandlös*	*chanslös*

(porto = postage, gift = poison, mening = meaning, tand = tooth). In cases like (a) no presuppositions are associated with the noun stems as to 'goodness' or 'badness'. Therefore, both *-fri* and *-lös* are possible suffixes for these noun stems. In cases like (b) and (c) the following situation holds. We may have a conflict between the noun inherent and the suffix inherent presuppositions (*risk*, *chans*). The derivative *tandfri* would have the presupposition that it is good that one has no teeth, the derivative *meningsfri* the presupposition that it is good that a sentence, for example, has no meaning. These derivatives might appear to be odd but they are not unthinkable. (It would perhaps be more appropriate to put question marks instead of + 's before these derivatives.) It is generally considered to be not good if one has to pay for something. The noun *porto* may but need not have such a presupposition. The derivative *portolös* is anomalous because it cannot be bad to be free of something which is bad. The anomaly of *giftlös* can probably be explained in the same way. It would seem, however, that badness is part of the asserted meaning of *gift* rather than a presupposition. The presuppositions associated with the suffixes *-fri* and *-lös* act as selectional restrictions. Being idiosyncratic they must be part of the lexical characterization. If there is no conflict between the noun stem and the derivational suffix the presupposition of 'goodness' or 'badness' is transferred from the suffix to the noun or, more precisely, to the whole derivative.

(28)   (i) *The rock hopes that Lena will come.

          (ii) *John hopes that Lena will come and he feels that it is bad
               for him if Lena will come.

It goes without saying that in (28)(i) a more fundamental cateogory is violated
than in (28)(ii). The former cannot be understood without creating some
special context. However, the difference between the violation of a general
and an idiosyncratic presupposition is not always as clear as in (28). Take (29),
for example,

(29)   (i) ?John is pretty.

          (ii) *The rock is handsome.

All the sentences in (29) can easily be understood, there seems to be no fundamental difference between (29)(i) and (ii). A non-native speaker of English
with a poor knowledge of the language would probably often make mistakes
like (29). Can we draw the conclusion from this that in (29) no general presuppositions are involved? Unfortunately, the problem is much more complicated. Still there seems to be something more general involved in (28)(ii)
than in (29). This would suggest that we have perhaps a difference in degree
here rather than an absolute difference. Furthermore the distinction made
by Bierwisch links up with the problem of different types of semantic
anomaly. We shall return to this problem briefly in the last section.

Secondly, it is clear that not only the *expect*-type verbs have the presupposition formulated in (25) but many others which seem to be related in some
obscure way to these verbs, e.g. *remember*, *realize*, *know*, as one group,
advance, *put forward*, *suggest*, *propose*, *stipulate* as another group, etc. That
certain characteristically human activities require a human subject comes as
no surprise. Similarly, there are activities that require an animate subject or
activities that require a certain type of object, etc. Such presuppositions are
perhaps semantic primes which must receive a general characterization in the
theory of natural language. Hence they need not be stated in the grammar of a
particular language. It might very well be that we can put an identity sign
between general and universal presuppositions. But this is too speculative at
the present stage of our knowledge of the phenomena involved.

The distinction between general and idiosyncratic presuppositions may be
based, as Bierwisch observed, on the distinction between systematic and
accidental gaps in the lexicon. We cannot think of a new lexical item which
would have the same meaning as, for example, *hope* but would require a
[−Human] subject. On the other hand, it would be quite possible to have a
word which would have the same meaning as *red* but would refer only to

human hair. The idiosyncratic presuppositions can be changed freely, not so the general presuppositions. This seems to be a fairly clear criterion.

4.3. The question of how to represent presuppositions links up with the general problems of semantic representation. Semantic representation hinges very much on the way our grammar is construed as well. This question need not concern us here, however. From what has been said so far it is clear that we cannot define the meaning of a proposition and of a lexical item as

$$M(p) \equiv {}_{def} M_a(p) \wedge Pr(p)$$

$$M(x) \equiv {}_{def} M_a(x) \wedge Pr(x)$$

where p stands for 'proposition', x for a lexical item, M_a for asserted meaning and Pr for presupposition. We can still apply the predicate calculus notation for both the asserted meaning and the presuppositional meaning but these two aspects of meaning cannot be brought under the same formula.

As noted above, the general presuppositions need not be stated for each lexical item. They belong rather to the definitions and axioms of the semantic system of the lexicon. Some of them may turn out to be universal. These are then stated in linguistic theory rather than in the grammar of a particular language. Whatever formalism we develop for the description of presupposition, the notation must express essentially the same as (25) for the *expect*-type verbs. We may, for example, stipulate the following notation:

(30)   Pre: if EXPECT(X, Y) then   HUMAN(X)

where Pre guarantees that (30) does not express entailment. In a generative semantic approach (30) may be part of the base structure. (See, Bierwisch, for an illustrative example.)

It must be made clear that the notation suggested here is *ad hoc* as any other notation proposed for presuppositions until now. From among the presuppositions exemplified so far, the general presuppositions of the factive verbs seem to raise the most difficult problems with respect to their representation. The reason why a notation like (30) would not do for factive verbs lies in the fact that the presuppositions associated with factive verbs seem to underlie some intricate constraints imposed on them by syntactic structure. *Morgan* has pointed out (*op. cit.*, pp. 170–172) that such presuppositions 'flow down the tree'. World creating verbs can, however, block this flow by defining new sets of presuppositions. Factive verbs, on the other hand, are 'transparent to downcoming presuppositions'. The following examples taken from Morgan may illustrate the problem:

(31)   (i)   I dreamed that there was presently a king of France, and that
               Harry dreamed that there was a horse with two heads, and
               that the two-headed horse belonged to the present king of
               France.
        (ii)   I dreamed that Harry dreamed that the two-headed horse
               belonged to the present king of France.
       (iii)   I dreamed that nobody but me knew that Nixon was a
               woman.

where *dream* is a world-creating verb and *know* a factive verb. It would seem
that an adequate account of such phenomena would require a syntax of presuppositions. Several other problems of presuppositions observed by Morgan
and Lakoff seem to lend further support to this conjecture. We refer the
reader to the works by Morgan and Lakoff cited in the bibliography.

   The idiosyncratic presuppositions must be part of the lexical specification
of the various lexical entries irrespective of which approach to grammar we
happen to take. The lexical entry for *bachelor*, for example, would look
something like

   bachelor(x)
   $\cdots$

   $M_a: U(x)$
   Pre: $M(x) \wedge A(x)$

where U = unmarried, M = male, A = adult. We assume here that $H(x)$, where
H = human, is a general presupposition. M_a stands for 'asserted meaning',
Pre for 'presuppositional meaning'.

5. NON-LEXICAL PRESUPPOSITIONS

We have already seen some examples for non-lexical presuppositions. They
were all of the existential type ((1), (4), (7)). Chomsky discusses (Chomsky,
1969) quite a few other types of presuppositions, some of which will be taken
up below. Chomsky argues that some presuppositions involve surface properties. He concludes, therefore, that they can be accounted for by surface structure interpretation rules only.

   Chomsky claims that a sentence such as (32) is taken as presupposing that
John is alive.

(32)   John has lived in Princeton.

(32) can be an answer to the questions 'Who has lived in Princeton?' and
'Where has John lived?'. The presupposition that John is alive holds only if

(32) is considered to be an answer to the former question. In this case *John* is comment of (32). As is well known, comment attracts main stress. It would therefore be more appropriate to focus our attention on the disambiguous sentence (32′) instead of (32):

(32′)   JOHN has lived in Princeton.

where capitalized JOHN means John with main stress or, to put it differently, John is the comment of (32).

Similar considerations hold with respect to (33):

(33)   BILL has eaten up all the food.
BILL has brought me five apples.
BILL has smashed the window.

In (33) it is presupposed that Bill is alive. Notice that this presupposition is not identical to the existential presupposition associated with definite descriptions, i.e. among other things, with proper names.

The existential presupposition is independent of tense. Not so the presupposition of John's or Bill's being alive. It is, however, not the Perfect which is decisive. Consider

(34)   Many people have climbed the hill.

We have here an interesting interplay of person names in subject position and with main stress and the perfect tense which results in the above exemplified presupposition.

Chomsky also claims that the sentence (35) presupposes that John is a Watusi and that the Watusi are generally not tall:

(35)   John is tall for a Watusi.

Consider, however, the negation of (35):

(36)   John is not tall for a Watusi.

It is clear that (35) does not presuppose that the Watusi are generally not tall. It might, however, be claimed that (35) and (36) do presuppose that John is a Watusi. As Chomsky observed the insertion of *even* at various places in (35) leads to some changes in the original presuppositions. (37) seems to indicate that we obtain presuppositions with respect to the standard height of the Watusi:

(37)   John is tall even for a Watusi.
John is not tall even for a Watusi.
Even John is tall for a Watusi.
Even John is not tall for a Watusi.

The presuppositions associated with sentences like (32)–(33) or (35) are idio-syncratic about the English language. Present Perfect or corresponding verbal category cannot be found in every language and even if such a category does occur in some language, it need not lead to the same presupposition as in English. Consider the following examples taken from German and Swedish:

(38)   Karl hat alles aufgegessen.
        Karl hat fünf Bucher gekauft.

(39)   Karl har ätit upp allt.
        Karl har köpt fem böcker.

Notice, however, that both (38) and (39) may have, optionally, the same pre-suppositions as the corresponding English sentences, namely, that *Karl lebt*, *Karl är levande*. This raises a further question about presuppositions to which we shall return presently.

Similar considerations hold for the presuppositions associated with (35). Suffice it to say that the corresponding structure in Swedish would be

(40)   För att vara en Watusi är John lång.

and in Hungarian

(41)   Ahhoz képest hogy Watusi, John magas.

In both cases John's being a Watusi is already asserted and not presupposed.

We conclude that the distinction between idiosyncratic and general pre-suppositions not only holds on the lexical level but also on the syntactic level. We have already discussed one type of non-lexical general presuppositions. These were associated with definite descriptions and were existential. The relation between focus and presupposition discussed by Chomsky (1969) examplifies yet another type of presuppositions. Consider such sentences as (42):

(42)   it is JOHN who writes poetry

Chomsky says:

Under normal intonation (i.e. without emphatic stress, F.K.) the capitalized word receives main stress and serves as the point of maximal inflection of the pitch contour . . . The semantic repre-sentation of (42) must indicate, in some manner, that 'John' is the *focus* of the sentence and that the sentence expresses the *presupposition* that someone writes poetry.

Consider next (43) and (44):

(43)   (i) John writes poetry in his STUDY.
        (ii) John does not write poetry in his STUDY.

(44)   (i) John writes POETRY in his study.
        (ii) John does not write POETRY in his study.

(43) has the presupposition that John writes poetry somewhere and (44) that John writes something in his study. We neglect for our present purpose the more complicated cases and claim that one can obtain the presupposition associated with a focus by replacing that focus by an appropriate pronoun.

The qualification that (42)–(44) should not be uttered with emphatic stress is an important one. Emphatic stress leads to a change in semantic structure which is different from that affected by focus placement. Consider:

(45)   (i)   It is *Bill* who writes poetry
        (ii) It is not *Bill* who writes poetry

where italics means emphatic stress. (45)(i) entails that it is not somebody else who writes poetry but Bill, (45)(ii) entails just the contrary (see for a more detailed discussion Kiefer, 1967).

Let us return to sentences (42)–(44). The presuppositions of these sentences can be reformulated in the following manner:

for (42): there exists someone who writes poetry

for (43): there is a place where John writes poetry

for (44): there is something which John writes in his study.

It is evident that these presuppositions, too, are existential. Furthermore, since focussing is not bound to stress and/or pitch, these presuppositions might be considered to be universal (general).

It should be made clear that the question of how deep structure is defined bears much on the way this type of presupposition is treated. Furthermore, if focussing or topicalization entailed just a difference in presuppositions we might argue that we have to deal here with 'surface presuppositions'. The differences between sentences like (42)–(44) are, however, much more deep-seated. There are good reasons to believe that topicalization is not a surface phenomenon at all. We cannot go into a more detailed discussion of this topic here, however.[13]

Not all non-lexical presuppositions are existential, as we have already seen.

---

[13] That topicalization changes the cognitive meaning of sentences can be shown by means. of examples like:

> Everyone in this room speaks two languages.
> Two languages are spoken by everyone in this room.

> In Sibirien spricht man russisch.
> Russisch spricht man in Sibirien.

Topicalization brings about specific reference and affects the scope of reference. Quite generally, topicalization may lead to different truth conditions hence to a drastic change in cognitive meaning. Furthermore, it may play an important role in the determination of grammatical identity (cf. Schiebe) on a deep semantic level of grammatical description. Finally, it often triggers primary stress placement and is thus related to other structures where primary stress placement has a semantic effect (see Bierwisch, forthcoming, for a detailed discussion of this problem).

Besides (32) and (35) there are quite a few other cases where the non-lexical presuppositions are non-existential and perhaps universal rather than idiosyncratic. This is the case in certain comparative constructions. Compare (46)(a), (b) and (c):

(46)　　(a) John is taller than Bill.
　　　　　　The suitcase is heavier than the handbag.
　　　　　　My problem is more difficult than yours.
　　　　 (b) The Hungarian way of life is more interesting than the Swedish one.
　　　　　　Hungarian cooking is better than Swedish cooking.
　　　　　　Julia is prettier than Lena.
　　　　 (c) Eva is uglier than Brigitta.
　　　　　　Lena is lazier than Julia.
　　　　　　John is more drunken than Bill.

As known, from 'John is taller than Bill' we cannot conclude that Bill is tall, similarly from 'The suitcase is heavier than the handbag' it does not follow that the handbag is heavy and from 'My problem is more difficult than yours' that your problem is difficult. In other words, the comparatives in (a) do not have presuppositions associated with them as to the properties of persons or things compared. Examples (b) differ perhaps from those in (a) in that the comparatives *better*, *more interesting* and *prettier* may but need not have presuppositions as to the second member of the comparative construction. In other words, the Swedish way of life, too, may be interesting and the Swedish cooking, too, may be good. Similarly, 'Julia is prettier than Lena' does not necessarily mean that Lena is pretty but it may have, so to speak optionally, such a presupposition.[14] Examples in (c) seems to be, however, definitely different. 'Eva is uglier than Brigitta' seems to imply that Brigitta, too, is ugly, 'Lena is lazier than Julia' that Julia, too, is lazy and 'John is more drunken than Bill' that Bill, too, is drunken. In contrast to (32) and (35) we have here a more general phenomenon. The presuppositions of type (46)(b) and (c), furthermore, those of type (42)–(44) need not be stated for every language, i.e. in the grammar of a particular language. They are part of the general semantic theory. On the other hand, the presuppositions exemplified in (32)–(37) are language specific and must be accounted for in an adequate grammar of English.[15]

[14] The fact that sentences like (46)(b) may or may not have presuppositions associated with the comparative construction may result in interesting ambiguities which enables us to use such constructions jokingly or in scientific prosa with a particular stylistic effect.
[15] It would seem that measure adjectives belong all to type (46)(a). The corresponding adjectives with negative polarity seem to behave quite similarly:

There seems to be a great number of constructions which do not have non-lexical presuppositions. Consider, for example, (47):

(47)   (i) A beautiful girl is coming to visit me tonight.
        (ii) No beautiful girl is coming to visit me tonight.

In (47)(i) the subject noun phrase has no existential presupposition, the existence of a beautiful girl is neither asserted nor presupposed. In (47)(ii) (i) is simply negated. It would be worthwhile to have a closer look at the NP's which have and those which do not have existential presuppositions. We cannot go into details here, however.[16] I will here content myself with a few remarks with respect to the subject noun phrase. In our previous examples ((1), (4) and (7)) we had (i) a proper name and (ii) the definite article. Some of the non-lexical existential presuppositions seem to be brought about by definite descriptions. This is in accordance with Russell's thesis with the modification that existence is presupposed and not asserted. (47)(i) is an indefinite description, therefore it fails to presuppose existence. The subjects of generic sentences do not presuppose existence either. We cannot agree with Katz's contention, however, that generic sentences are without presuppositions. They may very well have lexical presuppositions. Consider (48):

(48)   (i) Girls usually know that.
        (ii) Girls never refuse to kiss.

Some of the examples discussed in this section seem to suggest that sentences can be classified according to whether they (a) must have, (b) may have and

---

John is shorter than Bill.
The suitcase is lighter than the handbag.
My problem is easier than yours.

The qualifying adjectives seem to work in the following way. Those with positive polarity tend to be of type (46)(b) and those with negative polarity of type (46)(c). A thorough inquiry into this phenomenon is, however, still wanting.

[16] The problem hinges essentially on the description of definite noun phrases. In the case of a sentence like:

John gave Mary the book.

three existential presuppositions are involved, one about *John*, another one about *Mary* and yet another one about *the book*. The definite article cannot be decisive here even if the language under consideration has a definite article. In English the definite article in subject position can denote genericness as well as definiteness. In object position, however, one would normally not use the definite article for genericness, e.g. *I like books*. Similar considerations hold for German: *Ich mag Bücher*. In Hungarian, however, one would use the definite article for the generic case e.g. *Szeretem a könyveket* (like-I book-s-Acc.) and another construction for definiteness, e.g. *Szeretem ezeket (azokat) a könyveket* (I like these/those books).

(c) cannot have certain presuppositions. Non-lexical existential presuppositions must be fulfilled in order to get an appropriate sentence (a proposition with a truth value). Hence sentences (or sentence structures) which have existential presuppositions associated with them belong to type (a). In comparative constructions with qualifying adjectives we have found sentences of type (a), (b) and (c). Sentences with indefinite noun phrase subjects cannot have existential presuppositions. These few remarks may suffice to show that it would be worthwhile to give a more thorough scrutiny to this classification of presuppositions as well.

Let us now return to the formulation of some of the presuppositions discussed in this section.

We may formulate the presuppositions related to definite subjects in the following way:

(49)   Pre: if $P(\imath x)(A(x) \ldots)$ then $(\exists x)(A(x) \ldots)$

The presuppositions which are associated with focus:

(50)   Pre: if $F(p) = x \wedge A(x)$ then $(\exists x)A(x)$

where F stands for focus and p for proposition.

We shall make no attempt here to formulate the idiosyncratic presuppositions associated with sentences (32) and (35). As to the presuppositions of (46)(b) and (46)(c) we can only give a very rough description. Let us denote the qualifying adjectives with positive polarity by

$$[+A, \ldots, +\text{Abs}, +\text{Pol}]$$

and those with negative polarity by

$$[+A, \ldots, +\text{Abs}, -\text{Pol}].$$

For our purpose we shall abbreviate the comparative by Comp. The term to be compared will be referred to as X and the standard of comparison as Y. All other syntactic structure is irrelevant in the present context. We may now stipulate (51) and (52):

(51)   Pre: if X Comp $[+A, \ldots, +\text{Abs}, +\text{Pol}]$ Y then Y be A
          Condition: optional
(52)   Pre: if X Comp $[+A, \ldots, +\text{Abs}, -\text{Pol}]$ Y then Y be A

Notice that for (51) we must add the condition that this presupposition is optional.

The presuppositions (49)–(52) are all general, non-lexical (at least not quite lexical). (49)–(50) are existential presuppositions, (51)–(52) non-existential presuppositions. (49)–(52) are part of semantic theory.

We have left open the question here whether they are presuppositions which are introduced or changed by transformational rules. I could not find any clear case. If there were such presuppositions, however, then we would perhaps have to distinguish between 'deep' and 'surface' presuppositions. We cannot pursue this question any further, however.

6. Some Remarks on Semantic Well-Formedness

We have already made use of Katz's term with respect to sentences which fail to refer, whose existential presuppositions are not fulfilled. We called such sentences indeterminate. The same notion may cover cases where focus presuppositions are not satisfied. We shall have nothing more to say about these sentences. Katz calls propositions which on logical grounds cannot have a satisfied (existential) presuppositions *indeterminable*. Sentences such as (53) are indeterminable:

(53)   (i)   Schwartz visited the female male
          (ii) the female male visited Schwartz

The sentences (53) contain both a contradictory proposition:

(54)   the male is female

The reason why (53) is indeterminable is that the subject or object of the sentences contains a contradictory proposition. Consider next (55) and (56):

(55)   (i)   The married bachelor just arrived.
          (ii) I met the married bachelor.
(56)   (i)   The female bachelor just arrived.
          (ii) The baby bachelor just arrived.
          (iii) The protozoa bachelor just arrived.

It would seem that the subject of (55)(i) and the object of (55)(ii) and the subjects of (56) equally fail to designate. If my analysis of *bachelor* is correct[17]

---

[17] Katz disputes this analysis (*op. cit.*). He thinks that *bachelor* must contain the concept of maleness as a component of the assertion it makes when used predicatively. The sentence:

(i)   All unmarried adult people are bachelors,

is synthetic and false. But if maleness were only presupposed in the application of *bachelor*, we would have to say that (i) is analytic and true. I am willing to agree with Katz that (i) is false but I do not see why maleness must be part of the asserted meaning. We can arrive at false statements in various ways, for example, by violations of general presuppositions, as we have seen.

On the other hand, there are clear examples where *bachelor* asserts only something about the marital status, namely *unmarried*. Consider:

That person is not a bachelor.
John refuses to remain a bachelor all his life.
My uncle is a bachelor.

etc.

then the reason for the indeterminableness of (55) is due to the contradictoriness of

(57)   the bachelor is married

and that of (56) due to the violation of selectional restrictions:

(58)   (i)   the bachelor is female
        (ii) the bachelor is a baby
        (iii) the bachelor is a protozoa

Consequently, indeterminableness can be the result of either (i) contradiction or (ii) violation of selectional restrictions.

Sentences as (12), (28), (29) as well as (58) are not indeterminable, however, The subjects in (58), for example, do not fail to designate. In (58) something is predicated of *bachelor* which cannot meaningfully be predicated of it.

We have already noted the difference between a violation of a fundamental category (general presupposition) and of accidental lexical restrictions (idiosyncratic presuppositions). The former leads to meaningless sentences (cf. (28)(i), (58)(iii)) or we might say that such sentences are necessarily false. But we need not go into this question here.

If idiosyncratic presuppositions are violated, the resulting sentences may be termed odd but not meaningless (cf. (28)(ii), (29)(i), (12), etc.). By violating an idiosyncratic presupposition one commits a lexical error. This seems to yield further support for the distinction between general (universal) and idiosyncratic presuppositions.

7. CONCLUSION

I have perhaps been able to show that presuppositions are closely related to a large number of important linguistic and philosophical problems. I have claimed that presuppositions can be classified first into (i) lexical presuppositions and (ii) non-lexical presuppositions. Another classification is that into (iii) existential and (iv) non-existential presuppositions. We have seen that both lexical and non-lexical presuppositions can be existential and non-existential. Most lexical presuppositions and perhaps all non-existential lexical presuppositions can function as selectional restrictions. A third classification of presuppositions is that into idiosyncratic and general or universal presuppositions. This distinction, too, holds both on the lexical and on the syntactic level. The general presuppositions whether lexical or non-lexical are part of semantic theory. The idiosyncratic presuppositions, however, must be stated separately for each language. The fact that there are so many different types of presuppositions leads us necessarily to the conclusion that they cannot be represented in the same way.[18] It goes without saying that presuppositions are a central issue in semantic theory. An adequate account for them would also solve a number of other important semantic questions such as the role of selectional restrictions and the nature of semantic anomaly.[19]

University of Stockholm and
Hungarian Academy of Sciences, Budapest

REFERENCES

Austin, J. L.: 1962, *How to Do Things with Words*, Clarendon Press, Oxford.

Bierwisch, M.: 1970, 'Selektionsbeschränkungen und Voraussetzungen', *Linguistische Arbeitsberichte* 3, Sektion 'Theoretische und angewandte Sprachwissenschaft an der Karl-Marx-Universität Leipzig', pp. 8–22.

Bierwisch, M.: *Primary Stress Placement and Semantics*, forthcoming.

Chomsky, N.: 1965, *Aspects of the Theory of Syntax*, The M.I.T. Press, Cambridge (Mass.).

Chomsky, N.: 1969, *Deep Structure, Surface Structure, and Semantic Interpretation*, Reproduced by the Indiana University Linguistics Club.

Fillmore, C. J.: 1970, 'Types of Lexical Information', in *Studies in Syntax and Semantics* (F. Kiefer, ed.), D. Reidel Publishing Co., Dordrecht-Holland, pp. 109–137.

Frege, G.: 1966, 'Uber Sinn und Bedeutung', *Funktion, Begriff, Bedeutung, Fünf logische Studien*, Vandenhoeck und Ruprecht, Göttingen, pp. 40–65.

Geach, P. T.: 1964, 'Russell's Theory of Descriptions', in *Philosophy and Analysis* (M. MacDonald, ed.), Philosophical Library, New York, pp. 136–147.

Horn, J. R.: 1969, 'A Presuppositional Analysis of *Only* and *Even*', *Papers from the Fifth Regional Meeting*, Chicago Linguistic Society (R. I. Binnick *et al.*, eds.), Chicago, pp. 98–107.

Katz, J. J.: *Semantic Theory*, in press.

Katz, J. J. and Fodor, J. A.: 1963, 'The Structure of a Semantic Theory', *Language* 39, pp. 170–210.

Katz, J. J. and Postal, P.: 1964, *An Integrated Theory of Linguistic Descriptions*, The M.I.T. Press, Cambridge (Mass.).

Kiefer, F.: 1967, *On Emphasis and Word Order in Hungarian*, Uralic-Altaic Series, Vol. 76, Indiana University, Bloomington (Indiana).

Kiparsky, P. and Kiparsky, C.: 1970, 'Fact', in *Progress in Linguistics* (M. Bierwisch and K. E. Heidolph, eds.), Mouton and Co., The Hague, pp. 143–173.

Kuroda, S.-Y.: 1969, 'Remarks on Selectional Restrictions and Presuppositions', in *Studies in Syntax and Semantics* (F. Kiefer, ed.), D. Reidel Publishing Co., Dordrecht-Holland, pp. 138–167.

Lakoff, G.: 1970, *Linguistics and Natural Logic*, Studies in Generative Semantics, No. 1, The University of Michigan, Ann Arbor.

[18] There are evidently many other ways of classifying presuppositions. I do not claim exhaustiveness here. Another classification, not mentioned in this paper, is due to Lakoff. He observes that since presuppositions are sentences, they, too, may have presuppositions and so forth. In this way we get first, second, . . . order presuppositions. Lakoff makes several interesting remarks on the transitivity of presuppositions. It was quite impossible to take up all these questions here.

[19] (Added in proof.) Katz's book has still not been available to me while correcting the page proofs. Therefore I had to leave out all page references to this work.

McCawley, J. D.: 1968, 'Concerning the Base Component of a Transformational Grammar', *Foundations of Language* **4**, No. 3, pp. 243–269.

Moravcsik, J. M. E.: 1970, 'Subcategorization and Abstract Terms', *Foundations of Language* **6**, No. 4, pp. 473–487.

Morgan, J. L.: 1969, 'On the Treatment of Presupposition in Transformational Grammar', in *Papers from the Fifth Regional Meeting*, Chicago Linguistic Society (R. I. Binnick *et al.*, eds.), University of Chicago, pp. 167–177.

Rohrer, Ch.: 'Contribution à la différence de sens entre *tout* et *chaque* en français', forthcoming.

Russell, B.: 1956, 'On Denoting', in *Logic and Knowledge* (R. C. Marsh, ed.), The Macmillan Company, New York, pp. 49–56.

Schiebe, T.: this volume, p. 503.

Sigurd, B.: 'Ord på gott och ont', forthcoming in Papers published by the Institute of Linguistics, University of Stockholm (PILUS).

Vendler, Z.: 1967, *Linguistics in Philosophy*, Cornell University Press, Ithaca, N.Y.

W. G. KLOOSTER

REDUCTION IN DUTCH MEASURE
PHRASE SENTENCES*

The purpose of this article is to report on some results of preliminary work on certain phenomena exhibited in measure phrase sentences, particularly (but not exclusively) in Dutch. In this article, I will leave the constituents called 'measure phrases' unanalyzed, restricting myself to the problem of accounting for reduction in a certain type of sentences containing them. Most of what I am going to say should be considered tentative. Nonetheless, I believe that the outcome of the considerations in the following strongly suggest that Gruber's proposals concerning the function of the lexicon[1] provide an adequate means for the solution of a set of problems connected with measure phrase sentences.

By 'measure phrases' I mean such expressions as the ones italicized in (1)–(7), below. (The English sentences in quotes are literal translations).

(1)   Jan weegt *80 kilo*.
        'John weighs 80 kilograms'.
(2)   Dat boek kost *12 gulden*.
        'That book costs 12 guilders'.
(3)   De boot steekt *1 vadem*.
        'The boat draws 1 fathom'.
(4)   Het geschut draagt *10 kilometer*.
        'The artillery carries 10 kilometers'.
(5)   Jan is *2 meter* lang.
        'John is 2 meters tall'.
(6)   Ze is *12 jaar* oud.
        'She is 12 years old'.
(7)   Het papier is *0,1 mm*. dik.
        'The paper is 0.1 mm. thick'.

In (1)–(7) the measure phrases ('MP's', for short) occur either as the complements of so-called middle verbs like *wegen* ('weigh') and *kosten* ('cost'), or as the complements of such copula + adjective constructions as *lang zijn*

---

* This is a revised version of an article written in Dutch, entitled 'Reductie in zinnen met "maat-constituenten" ' in *Studia Neerlandica* 5 (1971). I am greatly indebted to Prof. Dr. H. Schultink's criticisms of the earlier version.

[1] Gruber (1965), (1967a, b).

F. Kiefer and N. Ruwet (eds.), Generative Grammar in Europe, 243–283. *All Rights Reserved.*
Copyright © 1973 by *D. Reidel Publishing Company, Dordrecht-Holland.*

('tall be', *be tall*) and *oud zijn* ('old be', *be old*). However, in certain cases they may also occur in combination with just a copula, as is exemplified in (8)–(11).

(8)   Jan is 80 kilo.
        'John is 80 kilograms'.
(9)   Dat boek is 12 gulden.
        'That book is 12 guilders'.
(10)   Jan is 2 meter.
        'John is 2 meters'.
(11)   Ze is 12 jaar.
        'She is 12 years'.

In addition, it can be noted that in a sentence like (6) not only the adjective *oud* (*old*) may be left out, but also the word *jaar* (*years*):

(12)   Ze is 12.
        'She is 12'.

It seems to be appropriate to use the term 'reduction' in connection with sentences like (8)–(12). Sentence (8), then, is a reduction of (1), (9) one of (2), (10) one of (5) and (11) one of (6). Sentence (12) may be considered a reduction of (11) and thus a reduction ultimately derived from (6). Sentences of the type exemplified in (1)–(12) I shall call 'MP sentences' (i.e., simple sentences in which the MP occurs as the complement of such verbs as *wegen* (*weigh*), *kosten* (*cost*), *steken* (*draw*, said of ships), *dragen* (*carry*, said, e.g., of artillery), or as the complement of copula + adjective constructions like *lang zijn* (*be tall, be long*), *oud zijn* (*be old*), etc., as well as the reduced forms).

In this article, an attempt will be made to state the conditions under which such reductions as (8)–(11) may occur. Furthermore, I will argue that the reduced forms (8)–(11) all are derived in a completely uniform way, and that in a formal description it will be necessary to assume that there are deep structural similarities between on the one hand sentences like (1)–(4), which contain verbs like *wegen* and *kosten*, and on the other hand sentences like (5)–(7), which contain combinations like *lang zijn* and *oud zijn*. In the course of my exposition, I shall attempt to show that Gruber's proposals concerning the function of the lexicon have some special advantages.

For ease of reference, and for reasons which will become clear, I shall call such verbs as *wegen* and *kosten*, which have obligatory complements indicating a certain quantity, 'semicopulas'. The class of adjectives that may occur in MP sentences will be referred to as 'measure adjectives'.

All MP's in Dutch contain words referring to units of length, weight, etc.

An exception is formed by sentences in which age of humans is referred to, in which case the 'unit word' may be omitted (cf. (12)). We may call such things as length, monetary value, weight, etc., the 'parameters' relevant to the units in question. The concept of 'parameter' is also relevant to measure adjectives. However, not all measure adjectives take MP's freely.

A number of measure adjectives may occur in combination with an MP only if they are in the comparative form or are preceded by *te* ('too'), as can be seen from the following examples:

(13)   *Het water is 30 graden warm.
        'The water is 30 degrees warm'.
(14)   *Het boek is 12 gulden duur.
        'The book is 12 guilders expensive'.
(15)   Het water is 30 graden warmer/te warm.
        'The water is 30 degrees warmer/too warm'.
(16)   Het boek is 12 gulden duurder/te duur.
        'The book is 12 guilders more expensive/too expensive'.

But, as we saw from (5)–(7), there is no such restriction with respect to such measure adjectives as *lang* (*tall*, *long*) and *oud* (*old*). I will return to this question later.

Another fact deserving attention is that the adjective *lang* used in connection with duration differs from the earlier examples. This can be shown by comparing this particular adjective with other measure adjectives in the following way.

A temperature adjective may not occur as a modifier of the word *temperatuur* (*temperature*). Similarly, adjectives pertaining to height, and those pertaining to monetary value cannot modify the words *hoogte* (*height*) and *prijs* (*price*), respectively, and so on. Expressions like

(17)   *een warme temperatuur
        'a warm temperature'
(18)   *een hoge hoogte
        'a high (tall) height'
(19)   *een lage hoogte
        'a low height'
(20)   *een dure prijs
        'an expensive price'
(21)   *een goedkope prijs
        'a cheap price'

are ungrammatical.[2] On the other hand, (22), below, is perfectly correct:

(22)   een lange duur
         'a long duration'

Furthermore, as a rule measure adjectives cannot be combined with their corresponding semicopulas. Thus we do not have, e.g.,

(23)   *Dat kost duur.
         'That costs expensive'.
(24)   *Dat kost goedkoop.
         'That costs cheap'.
(25)   *Jan weegt zwaar.
         'John weighs heavy'.
(26)   *Jan weegt licht.
         'John weighs light'.

But a sentence like

(27)   De pauze duurde lang.
         'The intermission lasted long'.

is perfectly correct. Although many children, and even a considerable number of adult speakers use expressions like (23), (25) and (26), any native speaker knows they are ungrammatical. The combination *zwaar wegen* ('weigh heavy') may, however, occur in a sentence like

(28)   Dat argument weegt zwaar.
         'That argument weighs heavy'. (carries much weight)

---

[2] In this connection it should be noted that we must distinguish between two uses of the word *hoog*, say, *hoog₁* and *hoog₂*. *Hoog₁* is a measure adjective and carries the meaning 'tall' or 'high' in relation to physical objects. *Hoog₂* expresses extent or degree. Thus we have *een hoge temperatuur* ('a high temperature'), *een hoge prijs* ('a high price'). A similar distinction should be made with respect to *groot₁* and *groot₂*. In general, *groot* may mean 'large', 'big', or 'great'. *Groot₂* occurs with other parameter nouns than *hoog₂* does. We do not have, for instance, **een grote temperatuur* ('a great temperature') or **het wordt verkocht voor een grote prijs* ('it is being sold at a great price'). Rather, it occurs in such expressions as *een grote hoogte* ('a great height'), *een grote afstand* ('a great distance'), etc. The word *gering* may be used as an antonym of *groot₂*, whereas the antonym of *groot₁* is *klein*. The antonym of *hoog* in both senses is *laag* ('low'). *Hoog₂* and its antonym *laag* co-occur with the verbs *stijgen* ('rise') and *dalen* ('drop', 'fall'), respectively; *groot₂* and its antonym *gering* with *toenemen* ('increase') and *afnemen* ('decrease'). Compare, for example,

een hoge/lage prijs	– de prijs stijgt/daalt
'a high/low price'	– the price rises/drops'
een grote/geringe hoogte	– de hoogte neemt toe/neemt af
'a great/small height'	'the height increases/decreases'

But the verb *wegen* clearly is not used in the 'literal' sense here. Or, perhaps more accurately, it is a different verb, not having the meaning of *wegen* used in connection with physical objects, a word with different co-occurrences. Sentence (29), below, is grammatical, but (30) is not.

(29)   Jan weegt veel.
          'John weighs much'.

(30)   *Dat argument weegt veel.
          'That argument weighs much'.

Apparently, the adjective *lang* used in connection with duration is not a 'duration adjective' in the sense in which a word like *warm* is a 'temperature adjective'.

What has been said here concerning *lang* with respect to duration, also goes for the adjective *ver* (*far*) with respect to range, and the adjective *diep* (*deep*) pertaining to draught (cf. *Het geschut draagt ver* ('The artillery carries far') and *Het schip steekt diep* ('The ship draws deep')). I will return to the problem posed by these observations later on.

Much discussion in recent years has been centered around the rôle of semantics in the organization of transformational grammar. According to what has been called by Chomsky the 'standard theory' (as presented in Chomsky (1965)), the base component generates deep structures which are mapped into surface structures by the transformational component. The semantic component assigns semantic representations to the deep structures. This means that synonymy of superficially differing sentences is a necessary condition for their having identical deep structures. But it is not a sufficient condition; we cannot go further than saying that the deep structures of non-synonymous sentences must differ.

Furthermore, the 'standard theory', as presented in Chomsky (1965), states that the lexicon is part of the base component, resulting in the consequence that the terminal strings of deep structure derivations already consist of morphemes. In 1968, Chomsky abandoned the hypothesis that non-synonymous sentences necessarily have different deep structures.[3] His present view is that there are also semantic rules operating upon final derived phrase markers.

---

[3] Chomsky (1968). *See also* Kraak (1967), where it is proposed that we have rules of semantic interpretation which operate on transformationally derived structures, so as to account for meaning differences corresponding to different presuppositions in otherwise identical sentences, such as meaning differences arising from differently placed stresses in negative sentences (as in, e.g., 'Seymour didn't *slice* the salami with a knife' vs 'Seymour didn't slice the salami with a *knife*'. and so on).

A number of linguists, notably James D. McCawley,[4] have challenged the thesis that there is a level of deep structure with the characteristics it is said to have in Chomsky (1965) or in Chomsky's more recent version of transformational theory. They reject the idea that the lexicon is part of the base, and deny that there should be a difference between 'deep structure' and 'semantic representation'. This, of course, still does not mean that synonymy of superficially differing sentences is a condition both necessary and sufficient for identical deep structures. Jeffrey Gruber, one of the first whose views developed in the direction of generative semantics, puts it in the following way:

> The base component generates an underlying language which has immediate semantic as well as syntactic significance. By no means do we imply here, however, that all surface forms that mean the same thing have the same representation in the base tree, i.e., in the semantic language. Certainly it would be unusual in the generation of any language to have an interpretation different from every other such entity. A phrase-structure type grammar of which we propose the base component, will generate an indefinite number of trees that are equivalent in meaning but different in form. (. . .) in addition to the underlying semantic language (. . .) there will still have to be a set of postulates and rules for a calculus by which it can be demonstrated that certain trees of the base language are equivalent in meaning or that they imply or negate each other.[5]

In this article an attempt will be made to show that, in order to account for a number of relationships among MP sentences, it will be necessary to assume that there is an abstract level of representation of a nature which excludes the possibility of monocategorical lexical insertion on the level of base phrase markers, thus supporting Gruber's views on the rôle of the lexicon. I do not intend to argue that the abstract underlying structures to be proposed must be looked upon as semantic representations. Although the idea of a semantic language generated by the rules of the base component seems very plausible to me, I do not think the underlying structures discussed below can be considered structures directly generated by the base rules. I do think, however, that it can be correctly claimed that, e.g., the sentences *Jan en ik wegen evenveel* ('John and I weigh the same amount'), *Jan en ik zijn even zwaar* ('John and I are just as heavy') and *Jan en ik hebben hetzelfde gewicht* ('John and I have the same weight') all derive from the same underlying structure, despite their widely varying surface structures. No calculus in Gruber's sense will be needed to relate them to each other.

Let us return now to the examples (1)–(11). They are given once more below, supplemented with a few others and grouped in a different way:

---

[4] McCawley (1967a), (1968a, b).
[5] Gruber (1967a), p. 48.

Type I

(30a)   Jan WEEGT 80 kilo.
        'John weighs 80 kilograms'.
(30b)   Jan *is* 80 kilo.
        'John is 80 kilograms'.

(31a)   Dat boek KOST 12 gulden.
        'That book costs 12 guilders'.
(31b)   Dat boek *is* 12 gulden.
        'That book is 12 guilders.

(32a)   Jan IS 2 meter LANG.
        'John is 2 meters tall'.
(32b)   Jan *is* 2 meter.
        'John is 2 meters'.

(33a)   Ze IS 12 jaar OUD.
        'She is 12 years old'.
(33b)   Ze *is* 12 jaar.
        'She is 12 years'.

Type II

(34a)   De boot STEEKT 1 vadem.
        'The boat draws 1 fathom'.
(34b)   *De boot *is* 1 vadem.
        'The boat is 1 fathom.

(35a)   Het geschut DRAAGT 10 km.
        'The artillery carries 10 km'.
(35b)   *Het geschut *is* 10 km.
        'The artillery is 10 km'.

(36a)   Het papier IS 0,1 mm DIK.
        'The paper is 0.1 mm thick'.
(36b)   *Het papier is 0,1 mm.
        'The paper is 0.1 mm'.

(37a)   Het bureau IS 10 jaar OUD.
        'The desk is 10 years old'.
(37b)   *Het bureau *is* 10 jaar.
        'The desk is 10 years'.

The examples now are grouped according to whether we have an MP sentence which can be reduced or one which cannot, ignoring the difference between semicopula constructions and copula + adjective constructions.

In order to be able to formulate a rule, or rules, for reduction applying irrespective of whether we have a semicopula sentence or one containing a measure adjective, we shall have to be able to state non-trivial generalizations about the underlying structure of MP sentences. This causes us to look for similarities in the behavior of these sentences, no matter how widely they vary in their surface structures.

The pieces of evidence in favor of the type of underlying structure I am going to propose are the following. In the first place, there appears to exist a significant relation between, on the one hand, the surface verb *hebben* (*have*) and, on the other hand, semicopulas and copula + measure adjective constructions. All MP sentences of the type under discussion have paraphrases containing *hebben*. The relation of semicopulas to *hebben* is, furthermore, borne out by certain phenomena exhibited by *elkaar* (*each other*) sentences, and the fact that *hebben* as well as semicopulas cannot be passivized and are 'stative' verbs. In addition, it will be shown that what can be said of semicopula constructions in these respects is also true of copula + measure adjective constructions.

Secondly, there are a few other facts, not having to do with the relation to *hebben*, which also point in the direction of highly similar underlying structures of MP sentences; in certain cases semicopula sentences have exact paraphrases containing copula + measure adjective constructions. Furthermore, MP's, which are not direct objects in copula + adjective constructions, also do not behave as direct objects of semicopulas.

1. The relation to 'hebben'

All MP sentences have paraphrases containing *hebben*. The following examples are *hebben* paraphrases of sentences given earlier.

(38)   Jan *heeft* een gewicht van 80 kilo. (wegen)
     'John has a weight of 80 kilograms'. (weigh)

(39)   Dat boek *heeft* een prijs van 12 gulden. (kosten)
     'That book has a price of 12 guilders'. (cost)

(40)   Jan *heeft* een lengte van 2 meter. (lang zijn)
     'John has a length of 2 meters'. (be tall)

(41)   Ze *heeft* de leeftijd van 12 jaar. (oud zijn)
     'She has the age of 12 years'. (be old)

(42)   De boot *heeft* een diepgang van 1 vadem. (steken)
     'The boat has a draught of 1 fathom'. (draw)

(43)   Het geschut *heeft* een bereik van 10 km. (dragen)
         'The artillery has a range of 10 kms'. (carry)

(44)   Het papier *heeft* een dikte van 0.1 mm. (dik zijn)
         'The paper has a thickness of 0.1 mm'. (be thick)

(45)   Het bureau *heeft* een ouderdom van 10 jaar. (oud zijn)
         'The desk has an age of 10 years'. (be old)

These paraphrases suggest that the underlying structure of MP sentences in all cases contains an element or elements relatable to the surface verb *hebben*. I will now give a number of reasons for taking this suggestion seriously.

(i) *Semicopulas and 'hebben'*

(a) *'Each other' sentences*. A sentence such as

(46)   Jan zag Wim en Wim zag Jan.
         'John saw Bill and Bill saw John'.

can be paraphrased as

(47)   Jan en Wim zagen elkaar.
         'John and Bill saw each other'.

More pairs like (46) and (47) can be thought up without any difficulty. No doubt there is a regular relationship between *elkaar* (*each other*) sentences and sentences like (46), although it is not entirely clear how this relationship can be made explicit in the form of rules.

One can imagine a situation, for instance, of people playing Monopoly, in which someone observes:

(48)   Eén hotel kost vijf huizen en vijf huizen kosten éen hotel.
         'One hotel costs five houses and five houses cost one hotel'.

We do not have, however, (49):

(49)   *Eén hotel en vijf huizen kosten elkaar.
         'One hotel and five houses cost each other'.

As I will attempt to show, the assumption of an underlying element or string relatable to *hebben* in sentences containing semicopulas is hardly escapable, if we want to determine the source of the ungrammaticality of (49).

With respect to the derivation of reciprocal constructions, in particular of *each other* sentences, various proposals have been put forward in the literature. The 'transformational hypothesis' as Dougherty[6] calls it, implies that

---

[6] The PSR hypothesis is introduced, briefly, in Dougherty (1969). It is presented more fully in Dougherty (1968), from which the rules (II) are quoted here on p. 252.

each other sentences derive from sentence conjunction. In other words, a sentence like (46) is supposed to be representationally significant with regard to the structure of underlying (47). Dougherty's 'Phrase Structure Rule hypothesis' (PSR hypothesis), on the other hand, says that sentence conjunction as well as phrasal conjunction is generated directly by the branching rules of the base component. Thus, the base structure of (47), according to Dougherty, should be something like (I).

(I)

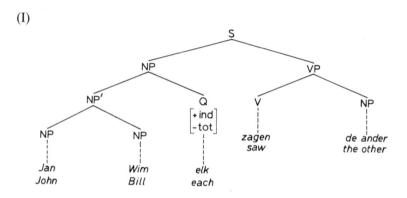

The noun phrase *John and Bill each* is generated by (II), where (b) is a rule schema:

(II)
(a)   NP → NP′ (Q(DADV))
(b)   NP′ → NP (NP)^n

'Q' is a distributive quantifier (*each, all, both, either, respectively*) and 'DADV' is a distributional adverb (*apart, together, mutually, simultaneously, in concert*, etc.). The feature complex

$$\begin{bmatrix} + \text{ individual} \\ - \text{ totality} \end{bmatrix}$$

is manifested in the form of *elk* (*each*) (it presumably may 'fuse' with *de ander* (*the other*) to form the word *elkaar* (*each other*)). *Each* is [+ individual] because it co-occurs with *apart*. It is [− totality] because it does not co-occur with, for instance, *together*.

The transformational hypothesis requires rules which, in a structure like *John saw Bill and Bill saw John,* conjoin the two subjects and convert the 'chiastically' co-referential noun phrases into something realized as *each other*. Deriving *each other* from two noun phrases under 'chiastic' referential identity with the two subject noun phrases is only possible if the former two noun phrases are (in)direct objects or if they are parts of prepositional phrases (where the functions or prepositions associated with them must be the same).

Should we assume that *kosten* is generated directly as the V in the sentence, then it would be impossible to determine from the structure index that the MP (probably some sort of noun phrase) is not a direct object. There is no structural difference between, say (III) and (IV):

(III)

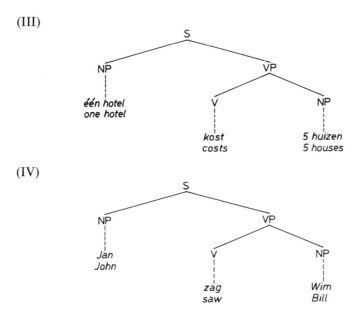

(IV)

Although there is sufficient reason to assume that MP's are not direct objects in MP sentences (see p. 263), we need not call upon this fact in order to explain the ungrammaticality of (49). As we shall see, there is another, more important condition which is not met, namely, that of referential identity.

Suppose that the two sentences *Eén hotel kost 5 huizen* ('One hotel costs 5 houses') and *Eén hotel heeft de waarde van 5 huizen* ('One hotel has the value of 5 houses') have identical underlying structures. In that case we may assume that the *hebben* paraphrase (53) of (48) is representationally significant with regard to the underlying structure of (48):

(53)　　*De waarde* die éen hotel heeft *is 5 huizen* en *de waarde* die 5 huizen hebben *is éen hotel.*
　　　　'*The value* that one hotel has *is 5 houses* and *the value* that 5 houses have *is one hotel.*'

What can be learnt from (53), is that neither the two noun phrases *éen hotel* nor the two noun phrases *5 huizen* can be referentially identical in (48); it is not the case that one hotel is five houses and five houses are one hotel. Rather, the *values* of one hotel and five houses are, respectively, five houses and one hotel. Of each pair of noun phrases in (48) the ones occurring first are the names of phsysical objects that have a certain value, whereas the ones occurring second are the names of the values of physical objects. An object having a certain value cannot be identical to that value. Therefore, the condition of referential identity is not met.

Suppose that the transformational hypothesis is wrong (even if we restrict ourselves to *each other* sentences with only two subjects), and that Dougherty's analysis of *each other* sentences, as illustrated in (I), is essentially correct. In that case the non-occurrence of sentences of the type of (54) must have something to do with the non-occurrence of sentences like (55), which presumably is closer to the base structure:

(54)   *De objecten X en Y kosten elkaar.
        'The objects X and Y cost each other'.
(55)   *De objecten X en Y kosten elk het andere.
        'The objects X and Y each cost the other one'.

The fact that (55) is excluded must be accounted for in the same way as must be the ungrammaticality of (56):

(56)   *Dit object kost het andere.
        'This object costs the other one'.

To be sure, there may be an interpretation of the verb *kosten* giving a grammatical reading of (56). However, in that case we do not have a specification of the value of some object, but a reference to some physical object ('the other one') which will have to be 'sacrificed' in order to obtain the thing mentioned by the subject, as in *This will cost you your front teeth*. But it is not this verb *cost* that I have in mind. The sense intended is that of value specification. Sentence (56) is bad for the same reason as are the sentences (57) and (58):

(57)   *Dit object kost het andere object.
        'This object costs the other object'.
(58)   *Het object X kost het object Y.
        'The object X costs the object Y'.

We know of course that it is nonsense to say that a certain object costs some other object – we do not say, for instance, *This book costs that dollar over there*. But this fact, in itself, does not clarify matters greatly. Consider, however, the *hebben* paraphrases of (58):

(59)   *Het object X heeft een waarde die het object Y is.
      'The object X has a value which is the object Y'.

(60)   *De waarde die het object X heeft is het object Y.
      'The value the object X has is the object Y'.

(61)   *Het object X heeft een bepaalde waarde; die waarde is het object
      Y.
      'The object X has a certain value, that value is the object Y'.

As can be seen from (59)–(61), the ungrammaticality of (54)–(61) must be related to the fact that an object is put on a par with a value. The *hebben* paraphrases of (58) make explicitly clear why sentences like (54) do not occur.

It appears, then, that the ungrammaticality of the *elkaar* sentences considered above can be explained by the fact that the condition of co-reference is not met, irrespective of whether we accept the PSR hypothesis or the transformational hypothesis (in the former case, complex co-reference must be carried by *the other*). The fact that this can be brought out in an explicit way by *hebben* paraphrases lends credence to the claim that the structure underlying MP sentences with semicopulas contain an element (or string) relatable to *hebben*.[7]

(b) *Semicopulas cannot be passivized and are stative.*[8] Both semicopulas and the verb *hebben* cannot be passivized and carry, in Lakoff's terms, the feature [+ stative]. Compare the semicopula sentences below with those containing the verb *hebben*:

passives:

(62)   *Tachtig kilo wordt door Jan gewogen.
      'Eighty kilograms are weighed by John'.

(63)   *Twaalf gulden wordt door het boek gekost.
      'Twelve guilders is cost by the book'.

(64)   *Een fiets wordt door Jan gehad.
      'A bicycle is had by John'.

(65)   *Door Kees wordt geelzucht gehad.
      'By Cornelius jaundice is had'.

---

[7] In Verkuyl (1970) the PSR hypothesis is rejected along with the transformational hypothesis. Instead, it is proposed to derive sentence conjunction transformationally from phrasal conjunction (in the cases where this is semantically possible). But within the framework of Verkuyl's hypothesis analogous arguments can be given.

[8] Lakoff (1966).

stative/non-stative test:

(66)   *Weeg tachtig kilo.
       'Weigh eighty kilograms'.

(67)   *Hij vergat/beloofde tachtig kilo te wegen.
       'He forgot/promised to weigh eighty kilograms'.

(68)   *Jan woog tachtig kilo en Piet deed het ook.
       'John weighed eighty kilograms and Peter did it too'.

(69)   *Heb een fiets. *Heb geelzucht.
       'Have a bicycle'. 'Have jaundice'.

(70)   *Hij vergat/beloofde een fiets/geelzucht te hebben.
       'He forgot/promised to have a bicycle/jaundice.

(71)   *Hij had een fiets/geelzucht en zij deed het ook.
       'He had a bicycle/jaundice and she did it too'.

Stative verbs have the property that they do not occur in command imperatives (or 'true' imperatives), or in the complements of the verbs *vergeten* (*forget*) and *beloven* (*promise*). Verb phrases in which they occur cannot be referred to by *doen* + *het* (*do* + *it*).[9]

There are verbs which can be passivized but nonetheless are stative. Compare, for example, (72)–(75):

(72)   Het geluid werd door iedereen gehoord.
       'The sound was heard by everybody'.

(73)   *Hoor het geluid.
       'Hear the sound'.

(74)   *Hij vergat/beloofde het geluid te horen.
       'He forgot/promised to hear the sound'.

(75)   *Hij hoorde het geluid en zij deed het ook.
       'He heard the sound and she did it too'.

Thus, although the properties of being non-passivizable and being stative do not necessarily go together, they do go together in the case of semicopulas as well as in the case of *hebben*. This again bears out the relation between semicopulas and *hebben*.

(ii) *Copula + measure adjective constructions and 'hebben'.*

Apart from the *hebben* paraphrases (40), (41), (44) and (45), the observations presented above directly or indirectly support the claim that there exists a relation between *hebben* and semicopulas. But in themselves, of course, they

---

[9] *See* Lakoff (1966); Kraak and Klooster (1968), p. 204 ff. and Klooster *et al.* (1969), p. 30 ff., on the properties of 'handelingswerkwoorden' (non-stative verbs).

do not constitute evidence of such a relation between *hebben* and copula + measure adjective constructions. However, all that has been said thus far with respect to semicopulas and *hebben* is also true of *zijn* (*be*) + measure adjective constructions and *hebben*, as I shall now proceed to show.

(a) '*Each other*' *sentences*. Consider the following examples:

    (76)   Het is niet altijd zo dat één dichtregel één vinger lang is en één vinger één dichtregel lang is.
            'It is not always the case that one line of poetry is one finger long and one finger is one line of poetry long'.

    (77)   *Het is niet altijd zo dat één dichtregel en één vinger elkaar lang zijn.
            'It is not always the case that one line of poetry and one finger are each other long'.

The ungrammaticality of (77) cannot be ascribed to the fact that it contains a predicate nominal, for sentences like (78)–(80) are perfectly correct:

    (78)   Jan en Piet zijn elkaar beu.
            'John and Peter are each other tired'. (are fed up with each other)

    (79)   Harry en Estelle zijn elkaar moe.
            'Harry and Estelle are each other tired'. (are tired of each other)

    (80)   Dik en Tom zijn elkaar goedgezind.
            'Dick and Tom are each other kindly-inclined'. (are kindly inclined towards each other)

The explanation of the non-occurrence of (77) is analogous to the one given with respect to (49) *Eén hotel en vijf huizen kosten elkaar* ('One hotel and five houses cost each other'). A certain length cannot be identical with an object which has length. This becomes clear in *hebben* paraphrases:

    (76a)   Het is niet altijd zo dat *de lengte* die één dichtregel heeft *één vinger is* en *de lengte* die één vinger heeft *één dichtregel is*.
            'It is not always the case that *the length* one line of poetry has *is one finger* and *the length* one finger has *is one line of poetry*'.

Sentence (76a) illustrates by explicit formulation that the first occurring phrase *één vinger* (*one finger*) and the last occurring phrase *één dichtregel* (*one line of poetry*) are both specifications of length, not the names of physical objects (*dat de lengte* (...) *één vinger is* ('that the length (...) is one finger'), etc.). The ungrammaticality of (81), below, is related to that of (77) and forms an illustration analogous to the one given earlier with *kosten* (cf. (60)):

(81)   *De lengte die het ene object heeft is het andere object.
        'The length that the one object has is the other object'.

(b) *Measure adjectives are stative.* Sentences containing a copula, of course, cannot be passivized, as is the case with *hebben* sentences and semicopula sentences, and, just as the latter two types, MP sentences containing measure adjectives do not take on a form which is typical of statives. Lakoff (1966) has shown that the distinction 'stative/non-stative' applies not only to verbs but also to adjectives. An example of a non-stative adjective is *voorzichtig* (*careful*):

(82)   Wees voorzichtig alsjeblieft.
        Do be careful.
(83)   Hij vergat voorzichtig te zijn.
        He forgot to be careful.
(84)   Hij beloofde voorzichtig te zijn.
        He promised to be careful.

A difference between verb phrases containing non-stative verbs and those consisting of a copula and a non-stative adjective is that the latter do not occur in *doen* + *het* ('do it') contexts:

(85)   Jan luisterde en Piet deed het ook.
        'John listened and Peter did it too'.
(86)   *Jan was voorzichtig en Piet deed het ook.
        'John was careful and Peter did it too'.

The fact that MP sentences containing a copula do not occur in *doen* + *het* contexts therefore is not significant in this connection. But since the sentences (87)–(89) are also ungrammatical we can still say that what has been said about semicopula sentences above is also true of MP sentences containing a copula.

(87)   *Wees 2 meter lang alsjeblieft.
        *Do be 2 meters tall.
(88)   *Hij vergat 12 jaar oud te zijn.
        *He forgot to be 12 years old.
(89)   *Hij beloofde 2 meter lang te zijn.
        *He promised to be 2 meters tall.

(There is also a sentence in Dutch of the form (88) that is grammatical and means *He forgot that he was twelve years old*, but that of course is not the one intended here).

2. FURTHER EVIDENCE OF THE SIMILARITY OF UNDERLYING STRUCTURES OF SEMI-COPULA SENTENCES AND SENTENCES WITH COPULA + MEASURE ADJECTIVE

(i) *Synonymy of semicopula and 'be' + measure adjective.*

Semicopula sentences questioning an MP and semicopula sentences containing an element of degree (with or without an MP) have paraphrases containing a copula + measure adjective construction. If it is true that the structure underlying MP sentences is removed from surface structure to such an extent that it also underlies the *hebben* paraphrases, then it certainly is plausible that the *a* sentences and the corresponding *b* sentences of the examples below have common underlying structures:

(90a)   Hoeveel weegt ze?
          'How much does she weigh'?
(90b)   Hoe zwaar is ze?
          'How heavy is she'?

(91a)   Hoeveel kost dat boek?
          'How much does that book cost'?
(91b)   Hoe duur is dat boek?
          'How expensive is that book'?

(92a)   Ze woog (2 pond) meer.
          'She weighed (2 pounds) more'.
(92b)   Ze was (2 pond) zwaarder.
          'She was (2 pounds) heavier'.

(93a)   Het boek kost (één gulden) meer.
          'The book costs (one guilder) more.
(93b)   Het boek is (één gulden) duurder.
          'The book is (one guilder) more expensive'.

(94a)   Ze woog (2 pond) teveel.
          'She weighed (2 pounds) too much'.
(94b)   Ze was (2 pond) te zwaar.
          'She was (2 pounds) too heavy'.

(95a)   Jan woog evenveel als Piet.
          'John weighed as much as Peter'.
(95b)   Jan was even zwaar als Piet.
          'John was as heavy as Peter'.
          etc.

The fact that sentences containing the semicopulas *duren* (*last*), *steken* (*draw*) and *dragen* (*carry*) under no circumstances can be paraphrased by a copula + measure adjective construction is related to the fact that the corresponding adjectives (*lang* (*long*), *diep* (*deep*) and *ver* (*far*), respectively) do not pertain to the parameters referred to by the respective semicopulas, as has been remarked earlier (p. 258). I shall return to this matter later on.

(ii) *Irrespective of surface structure, MP's do not occur as direct objects in MP sentences.*

The complements of semicopulas do not have the function of direct object (cf. my remark in connection with diagram (I)), since they do not have a property characteristic of direct objects, as will be demonstrated directly. If it is true that the underlying structures of MP sentences with semicopulas and MP sentences with copula + measure adjective constructions are essentially the same, this is not surprising, since predicate nominal sentences in general do not contain direct objects either. Typically, a direct object becomes part of a *van* (*of*) construction in the case of nominalization, as in the examples below: .

(96a)   Jan raakt het doelwit.
        'John hits the target'.
(96b)   Het raken van het doelwit.
        'The hitting of the target'.

(97a)   Ze eet de pudding.
        'She eats the pudding'.
(97b)   Het eten van de pudding.
        'The eating of the pudding'.

But the *b* examples below are ungrammatical:

(98a)   Jan weegt 80 kilo.
        'John weighs 80 kilograms'.
(98b)   *Het wegen van 80 kilo.
        'The weighing of 80 kilograms'.

(99a)   Mabalêl kostte veel koeien.
        'Mabalêl cost many cows'.
(99b)   *Het kosten van veel koeien.
        'The costing of many cows'.

(100a)   Ze is 12 jaar oud.
          'She is 12 years old'.
(100b) *Het oud zijn van 12 jaar.
          'The being old of 12 years'.

(101a)   Jan is 2 meter lang.
          'John is 2 meters tall'.
(101b) *Het lang zijn van 2 meter.
          'The being tall of 2 meters'.

I will now consider two possible types of underlying structure for MP sentences, and after having rejected them, present arguments in support of a third possibility.

On the basis of the similarities between MP sentences with differing surface structures and their relation to the verb *have*, one might consider assigning an underlying structure to MP sentences which contains the verb *have*, roughly as in (V), below.

(V)

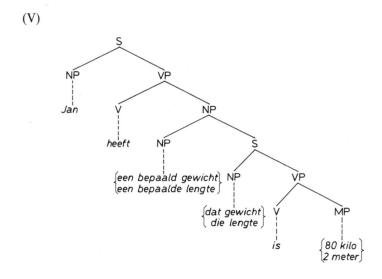

'John has a certain weight/a certain height; that weight/height is 80 kilograms/2 meters'.

An alternative solution, in which no underlying *have* is assumed to be present, could be something like (VI):

(VI)

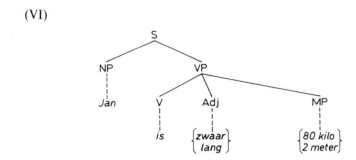

'John is heavy/tall 80 kilograms/2 meters'.

A structure like (VI) would be more in accordance with the following remark made by Ross[10]: "(. . .) there is adequate evidence to support the proposal to relate *be expensive* and *cost*, *be heavy* and *weigh*, etc., in such a way as to derive the verbs from the corresponding adjectives". A difficulty would be that *kosten* and *duur zijn* (*cost* and *be expensive*) or *wegen* and *zwaar zijn* (*weigh* and *be heavy*) differ too much phonologically to be realizations of the same morphological structures. The disadvantages of (V) are similar. If we accept a structure like (V), we must require that *hebben + gewicht* (*have + weight*) may be converted into *wegen* (*weigh*) (and in some cases into *zijn + zwaar* (*be + heavy*), cf. the examples (90a)–(95b)). If we accept (VI), we must require that *zijn + zwaar* (*be + heavy*) may be converted into *wegen* (*weigh*) or *hebben + gewicht* (*have + weight*). (I will not go into the question of the treatment of the determiner in such cases).

No matter which of the two alternatives we choose, the difficulties in either case will be essentially of the same nature: (a) Both solutions necessitate rules that must convert, e.g., *zijn + zwaar* into *hebben + gewicht*, or vice versa, and that must convert either one or the other of these two strings into *wegen*. Such rules, no doubt, are possible, but they would be highly *ad hoc*, that is, suggested by a choice of one of the two types of underlying structure considered above while it is in no way clear that either of them is to be preferred. In either case, the rules required would be just as complex, so even in that respect there is no criterion for a choice. (b) The 'standard theory' requires that the terminal strings of deep structures are strings of morphemes. Consequently, the transformational rules operate on structures with phonologically specified terminal strings. As we noted, the strings that are to be related via transformational rules, differ phonologically to such an extent that such rules, apart from being cumbersome, probably would lead to

[10] Ross (1964).

trivial solutions and would in part take over the task which in standard theory is assigned to the lexicon.

These considerations tend to cause us to look in another direction. Suppose we assign to MP sentences an underlying structure which does not contain morphemes as terminal elements, a structure sufficiently abstract for us to be able to circumvent a choice between an underlying *have* or an underlying adjective for all MP sentences. Such a structure might have the form of (VII):

(VII)

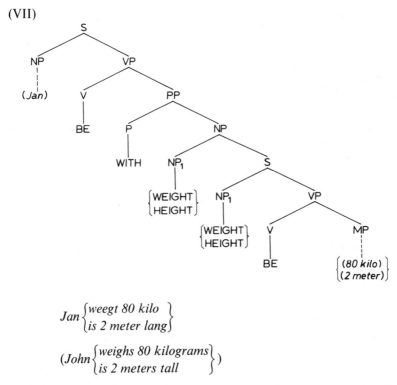

$$Jan \begin{Bmatrix} weegt\ 80\ kilo \\ is\ 2\ meter\ lang \end{Bmatrix}$$

$$(John \begin{Bmatrix} weighs\ 80\ kilograms \\ is\ 2\ meters\ tall \end{Bmatrix})$$

I do not want to imply that a structure like (VII) is a base structure. Quite possibly, a number of structural changes will have to take place before anything like (VII) will result. At present, however, this is of minor importance. Questions concerning the determiner, tense and the structure underlying relative clauses (which possibly are dominated by a determiner) I want to leave out of the present discussion. The words written in capitals in (VII) stand for elements that do not have the status of morphemes, but of semantic categories, and therefore must be considered arbitrary symbols, not 'spellings'. They form part of the vocabulary of the base component, just as the categories NP, VP, V, etc., do. Lexical insertion does not necessarily take place before application of transformational rules.[11] More on the subject of lexical insertion will be said later on. At present, it suffices to say that the categories symbolized as BE and WITH form a string which may become manifest as the word *hebben* (*have*). Strings like WITH + WEIGHT and WITH + HEIGHT may under certain circumstances turn into the adjectives *zwaar* (*heavy*) and *lang* (*tall*), respectively. The latter two words in that case must be taken in their 'neutral' sense.

Measure adjectives occurring in the non-neutral sense have a more complex underlying structure. The WITH string underlying such a non-neutral adjective contains some element of degree or norm. The difference between neutral *lang* (*long*) and non-neutral *lang* (id.) is demonstrated in the following examples:

(102)   Die korte stok is 15 centimeter lang.
         'That short stick is 15 centimeters long'.
(103)   Die stok is lang.
         'That stick is long'.
(104)   *Die korte stok is lang.
         'That short stick is long'.

In (102) *lang* is used in the neutral sense. If we leave out the MP, we obtain (104). Omitting the MP has the effect of turning *lang* into the non-neutral adjective; (103), in which *lang* is non-neutral, is possible, but (104), in which *lang* is non-neutral as well, is odd because *lang* now contradicts *korte* (*short*).

Measure adjectives, then, are analyzed as prepositional phrases, the verb *hebben* as BE + WITH, and semicopulas as BE + WITH + parameter category.

I will now present five arguments supporting the claim that MP sentences have underlying structures of the type of (VII).

(i) The fact that the following *a* examples are synonymous with the corresponding *b* examples is evidence for the relation of *hebben* to *met* (*with*):

(105a)   Een man die een gewicht van 80 kilo *heeft*.
          'A man who has a weight of 80 kilograms'.
(105b)   Een man *met* een gewicht van 80 kilo'.
          'A man with a weight of 80 kilograms'.
(106a)   Een stoel die vier poten *heeft*.
          'A chair that has four legs'.
(106b)   Een stoel *met* vier poten.
          'A chair with four legs'.

[11] McCawley (1968b) suggests the possibility that lexical attachment takes place after application of the transformational cycle but before the post-cyclical rules.

Examples like (105a, b) are possible with all kinds of MP's. Pairs like (106a, b) to which can be added an unlimited number of similar ones, illustrate, moreover, that the relation to *met* is not restricted to MP sentences.

(ii) Apart from the synonymy between the *a* and *b* examples above, the possibility of generalizing the rule of Relative Clause Reduction also constitutes an argument in favor of an underlying structure containing the category WITH in constructions like (105a)–(106b). If we analyze *hebben* as BE WITH, the relation between the relative clauses in (105a) and (106a) and the prepositional phrases in (105b) and (106b) can be described in the same manner as the relation between the relative clause in (107a) and the prepositional phrase in (107b):

(107a) Een patient die onder behandeling is.
'A patient who is under treatment'.
(107b) Een patient onder behandeling.
'A patient under treatment'.

In (107b) as well as in (105b) and (106b) deletion of an underlying 'be' can be assumed, in accordance with Relative Clause Reduction, which within the framework of the 'standard theory' has been formulated as follows:

Relative Clause Reduction

$$\text{S. D.: } X - \left[NP - \left[\left[\begin{matrix} NP \\ NP \end{matrix} {}_S + Wh \right] \left\{ \begin{matrix} Aux & be \\ [X & be] \\ Aux\ Aux \end{matrix} \right\} - X \right] \right] - X \overset{OPT}{\Rightarrow}$$

$$\qquad\qquad\qquad\qquad\qquad\qquad SNP$$

	1	2	3	4	5
S.C.:	1	2	0	4	5

(iii) The analysis of *be* + adjective and *have* + noun as BE followed by a WITH string provides the opportunity to state a generalization with respect to different languages. In the following examples the *a* and *b* sentences are exact translations of each other:

(108a) Ik *heb honger.*
(108b) I *am hungry.*

(109a) J'*ai soif.*
(109b) I *am thirsty.*

(110a) Ze is *zwanger.*
(110b) She is *with child.*

(111a) Quel *âge as*-tu?
(111b) How *old are* you?

(112a) Ich *bin schläfrig*.
(112b) Ik *heb slaap*.

(113a) Ik *ben bang*.
(113b) J'*ai peur*.

A close approximation of the Estonian sentence (114a), below, is given, by Ilse Lehiste,[12] in the form of (114b), that of the synonymous sentence (115a) in the form of (115b). In Estonian, there is no surface verb 'have'. The word *on* is the third person singular of '*be*' in the present tense. *Noormees* ('the young man') is the singular form of the nominative and *uhke hoiakuga* ('proud bearing') is the singular form of the comitative. *Noormehel* in (115b) is in the adessive case and *uhke hoiak* is in the nominative case.

(114a) Noormees on *uhke hoiakuga*.
(114b) 'The young man is *with a proud bearing*'.

(115a) *Noormehel on* uhke hoiak.
(115b) '*The young man has* a proud bearing'.

Apparently, the closest approximation of the comitative case ending is the preposition *with*. The verb *have* presumably expresses adequately the relation of 'possession' (Ilse Lehiste's characterization) given with the adessive case. The comitative case ending may correspond to the abstract relational category symbolized above as WITH. It may be that underlying the structure of the form $NP_1 + BE + WITH + NP_2$ there is still more fundamental structure of the form $NP_2 + BE + TO + NP_1$ (cf. *c'est à moi, mihi est*). TO then would correspond to what in Fillmore's terminology would be Dative[13], under which the Estonian adessive would have to be subsumed.

(iv) If we reject *ad hoc* transformational rules mapping phonological strings onto totally unrelated ones, and accept in principle structures of the kind of (VII) not containing a base category 'Adj'. we will be able to state a generalization otherwise missed. If we were to assume a base category 'Adj' for MP sentences, we would not be able to account for the fact that *Type I* sentences like (30b) *Jan is 80 kilo* and (32b) *Jan is 2 meter* are both instances of *optional* reduction. It cannot be maintained that in the former sentence obligatory deletion has taken place of an underlying adjective *zwaar* (the

---

[12] Ilse Lehiste (1969), p. 336.
[13] *See* Fillmore (1968a, b), especially the latter.

non-occurrence of *Jan is 80 kilo zwaar notwithstanding), whereas in the latter sentence the adjective *lang* has been optionally deleted.

(v) Without the generalization made possible by the assumption of an underlying WITH string, it would be difficult to explain the ungrammaticality of the *Type II* sentences (34b) *De boot is 1 vadem ('The boat is 1 fathom') and (35b) *Het geschut is 10 km. ('The artillery is 10 kms'.), for, provided we do not consider the possibility of an underlying verb 'have' (which would lead to trivial solutions anyway), we would be stuck with an impossible choice between two remaining explanations, numbered (1) and (2) below.

(1) We could point to the fact that neutral parameter adjectives pertaining to draught and range do not exist (*diep* (*deep*) and *ver* (*far*) do not pertain to draught and range but to depth and distance, respectively), while their occurrence in the absence of a semicopula in the sentence would be required because otherwise the message would lack necessary information.

There is no decisive argument for or against such an explanation. On the one hand it is true that no neutral 'draught' or 'range' adjective exists and that in the case of draught or range explicit mention in one way or another of the parameter we are talking about cannot be dispensed with. But on the other hand, even if the adjectives in question existed (and according to this explanation, they would just be non-deletable), we would like to take into account a rule which apparently in one form or another operates upon the structure of MP sentences, and which has the effect that in such sentences the occurrence of a neutral parameter adjective is delimited by the existence in the lexicon of the appropriate semicopula (e.g., not *Jan is 80 kilo zwaar because there exists a semicopula *wegen*). In order to account for this regularity we could consider the alternative explanation (2).

(2) The alternative explanation would have to be based on the hypothesis that in *Type I* sentences as well as in *Type II* sentences the underlying measure adjective is prohibited from becoming manifest as a word if an appropriate semicopula occurs in the lexicon. Suppose we accept this hypothesis. We could then claim that there are rules which somehow exclude *b*-type sentences if there is an appropriate semicopula or there is the necessity of explicitly stating, by means of a measure adjective, what parameter we are talking about.

However, such a claim cannot be substantiated because it presupposes the existence of underlying adjectives in *Type II* sentences like (34a) and (35a) (with *steken* (*draw*) and *dragen* (*carry*), respectively), which under no circumstances become manifest as words (whereas, in the case of *Type I*, we can at least point to the existence of the words *zwaar* (*heavy*) and *duur* (*expensive*) in connection with the semicopulas *wegen* and *kosten*). Hence, it would be rather arbitrary to prefer (2) over (1).

Thus, should we abandon the idea of an underlying WITH string, a choice would be forced upon us between two possible explanations neither of which is really satisfactory. On the other hand, if we should substitute in 2 'underlying WITH string' for 'underlying measure adjective', the latter explanation would no longer be based on an arbitrary claim, since, as we saw, there is evidence supporting the assumption of such a string.

I shall now devote a few paragraphs to the question of how polycategorial attachment of lexical material is supposed to take place in the case of underlying structures of the type of (VII).

Following Gruber, I shall assume that the lexicon contains lexical entries which take on the form of tree diagrams and which are associated with phonologically specified strings. The lexical entry for *wegen* thus might look like (VIII):

(VIII)

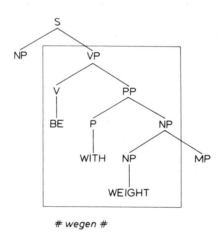

 # wegen #

The boxed-in configuration represents the 'simultaneous environment'. The rest of the entry is the 'peripheral environment'. The simultaneous environment represents the part of a generated structure where actual attachment takes place. The peripheral environment acts as a contextual restriction on the occurrence of a word.

The lexical entry for *zwaar* (in the neutral sense) may have roughly the form of (IX):

(IX)

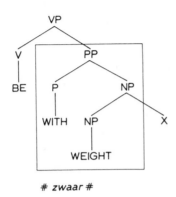

zwaar

In (IX), the symbol 'X' stands for some element of degree or norm, as *zwaar* may only occur in sentences containing such an element, if it is used in the neutral sense.

The 'rule' mentioned above to the effect that the occurrence of a neutral measure adjective is subject to restrictions determined by whether or not there exists an appropriate semicopula, can be considered an instance of a very general principle governing the processes of lexical insertion, called, by Gruber, 'disjunctive ordering'. This principle is, roughly, that, of two entries (one of which also occurs as part of the other) the greater one takes precedence over the smaller one, and that if the greater entry may apply, the smaller one may not. More precisely, the entry in which the simultaneous environment contains one or more categories which are outside (and generally to the left of) the simultaneous environment of an otherwise identical entry, takes precedence over the latter. Insofar as there is no absolute precedence, this is due to conditions statable in terms of the peripheral environment and the cyclical application of lexical rules. (Cf. Gruber, (1967a), pp. 94ff).

As can be seen from (X), in which one entry is superimposed over another, the simultaneous environment of *wegen* contains a category which is outside and to the left of the simultaneous environment of *zwaar*. *Wegen* is disjunctively ordered before *zwaar* in non-comparative MP sentences. The entries in (X) are modified versions of the ones given before. Instead of the label 'MP' at the rightmost node, we may have some element Y which may or may not dominate an MP and which, in the case of *zwaar*, dominates at least an element of degree or norm. If, in the case of *wegen*, Y does not dominate an MP, it must dominate an element which underlies *veel* (*much*) and probably is the same as the aforementioned element of degree.

(X)

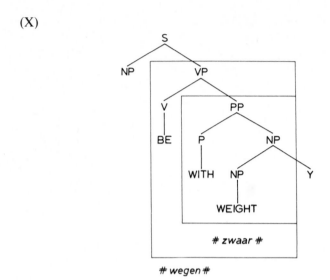

Before a lexical element is attached, some structural changes of the subtree are necessary. These structural changes appear to be always of the same nature, so that possibly they can be viewed as governed by conventions.

The first step in restructuring, say, the subtree identical with the simultaneous environment of *wegen*, consists in an operation known as 'Chomsky adjunction'.

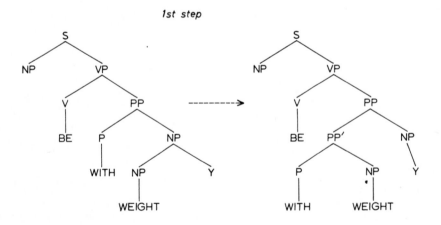

Next, we have once more Chomsky adjunction:

2nd step

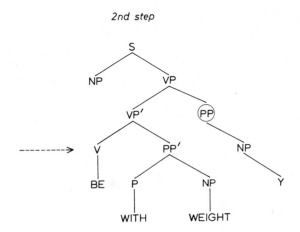

The encircled label has now become irrelevant and the corresponding node is pruned. (A category is irrelevant if it does no longer dominate its left-branching head). Next, the order of the terminal nodes is reversed in two steps, after which lexical attachment takes place.

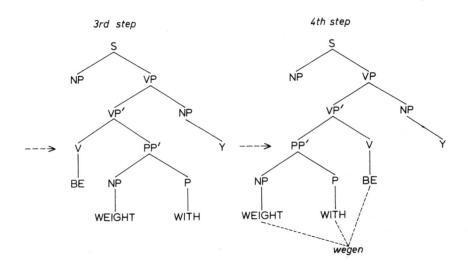

The order reversal principle is supported by a number of observations presented by Gruber (1965) and (1967a) (see, in the latter, pp. 131ff.). Gruber has observed that polymorphemic words corresponding with expressions consisting of more than one word show, as a rule, a morpheme order which is the exact reverse of that in the corresponding many-word expressions.

(*homeward* – *toward home, John's* – *of John, enter/exit* – *go in/go out, traverse* – *go across, painted* (past) – *did paint, redden* – *become red, re-do* – *do again, overturn* – *turn over, body-snatch* – *snatch bodies,* etc.), and has hypothesized that this morphemic order distinction is universal.

Let us now return to the question of reduction, and ask, first, under what conditions it may occur. It appears that reduction is possible at least:

(i) in sentences with a human subject, if the parameter is that of age, height or weight,

(ii) in sentences with a non-human subject, if the parameter is that of area, volume, weight or price.

There are a number of cases which do not meet (ii) but are nonetheless not entirely ungrammatical. Thus, the following two sentences are not completely unnatural:

(116)   Die toren is 100 meter.
         'That tower is 100 meters'.

(117)   Deze lat is 2 meter.
         'This lath is 2 meters'.

It appears, however, that most Dutch native speakers prefer (118) and (119), respectively:

(118)   Die toren is 100 meter hoog.
         'That tower is 100 meters tall'.

(119)   Deze lat is 2 meter lang.
         'This lath is 2 meters long'.

To a greater extent than is the case with 'height' and 'length' sentences, contextual and/or situational conditions have to be met for (120)–(122) to sound natural. Given in isolation, they sound odd:

(120)   ?Dit stuk karton is 0.5 millimeter. ('thickness')
         'This piece of cardboard is 0.5 millimeter'.

(121)   ?Mijn schrijfbureau is 2 meter. ('width')
         'My desk is 2 meters'.

(122)   ?Deze put is 10 meter. ('depth')
         'This well is 10 meters'.

A general rule with respect to one-dimensional spatial parameters seems to be that it is more acceptable to omit explicit mention if they are associated with the greatest axis of a physical object and if we view this axis as 'height' or 'length'. 'Thickness' is not related to a greatest axis. 'Breadth' in a number of cases is, but reduction in 'breadth' sentences always is unnatural. Reduction in 'depth' sentences is even more unnatural. As far as I can ascertain, reduction in the case of other parameters is wholly excluded. I shall not go any further into the matter of possible reduction under special circumstances. As far as reduction in *van* ('of') + MP constructions (in which *van* means 'which is') is concerned, suffice it to say that in such constructions reduction is not subject to as many restrictions as it is in simple MP sentences, as can be seen from the following examples:

(123)   Een toren van 100 meter (hoog/hoogte).
         'A tower of 100 meters (high/height)'.
(124)   Een bureau van 2 meter (breed/breedte).
         'A desk of 2 meters (wide/width)'.
(125)   *Een put van 10 meter.
         'A well of 10 meters'.
(125a)   Een put van 10 meter diep/diepte.
         'A well of 10 meters deep/depth'.

We may consider a rule for reduction in MP sentences which has roughly the form of (XI). This rule may be followed by a permutation rule having the form of (XII):

(XI)   S.D.: $[X\,Pm_1]$ — BE — WITH$[Pm_1]$ — MP $\overset{\text{OPT}}{\Rightarrow}$
              NP   NP   NP   NP

         S.C.:   1   2   3   4
                  1   2   0   4

(XII)   S.D.: $[X\,Pm_1]$ — BE — WITH$[Pm]$ — $[Y\,Pm_2]$ $\overset{\text{OBL}}{\Rightarrow}$
              NP   NP   NP   NP MP   MP

         S.C.:   1   2   3   4
                  1   2   4   3

'X' and 'Y' are possible categories dominated by NP and MP, respectively. 'Pm' stands for 'parameter category'. Here, it is assumed that the subject NP dominates, among other things, a parameter category which may or may not be identical to the one dominated by the NP in the WITH string and/or the one which is assumed to be part of the MP. In the case of identity the Pm's are marked with the same integer. The symbol '*Pm*', in italics, is not just a parameter category, but a category pertaining to one of the 'main parameters' associated with the subject (in the case of physical objects: weight or price, etc.

The WITH string is moved obligarorily by (XII) if the main parameter category is not identical to the Pm dominated by MP. That is to say, in the case of, e.g., 'height' the WITH string is moved to the right of the MP, in accordance with the fact that the adjectives *hoog* and *lang* (which may both mean 'tall') in the surface structure stand to the right of the measure phrase. Thus (XII) exclusively causes the strings underlying measure adjectives to occur to the right of MP's. However, (XII) has a serious shortcoming: in the case of cubic measures the MP parameter category probably will be identical to the one dominated by the subject NP. But the WITH string related to cubic measures underlies an adjective (*groot*, 'big'). However, it will not be moved, because of the identity just mentioned. There is no solution to this problem, unless we abandon the idea of a pre-lexical permutation transformation. As we shall see, it is possible to set up a post-lexical transformation serving the same purpose for which (XII) was intended. It probably is feasible to replace (XI) by lexical rules. However, I will not elaborate on that possibility in this article.

In the following paragraphs I will briefly inquire into the possibility of treating copula + measure adjective combinations as compound words, after which I will consider a post-lexical permutation transformation of the kind indicated in the preceding paragraph.

Suppose we consider such combinations in Dutch as *diep zijn* (*be deep*, lit. 'deep be'), *lang zijn* ('long/tall be'), *hoog zijn* ('tall/high be'), etc., as single words, contrary to orthographic convention. We could then explain why the infinitive forms of these 'verbs' show the order adjective – copula, instead of copula – adjective. The explanation could be given in terms of the order reversal principle, which should also govern the behaviour of separable compound verbs.

Gruber (1967a) proposes to characterize a word as a string of morphemes separated by no more than one boundary symbol '#' (*op. cit.*, p. 122). It may very well be that, as Gruber contends, the criteria for spelling as a single word differ from language to language. If I interpret him correctly, he furthermore suggests that, in the case of German, the strings which are written as single words may be defined as the set of morphemes which are all attached at once. This would mean that *lang sein* ('long be') is not attached at once. However, let us suppose that Gruber's criterion for spelling as a single word in German and Dutch is not correct, but that the characterization of a word as a string of morphemes separated by no more than one '#' symbol is right. In addition, let us suppose that the linguistic notion 'word' is such that *lang zijn* and, e.g., *opeten* (*eat up*, lit. 'upeat') must be equally considered 'words'. The schematized post-order reversal trees below may give the reader an idea of how productive affixation can be treated:

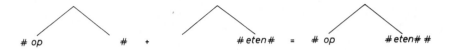

The combination *lang zijn* then can be treated in the same fashion:

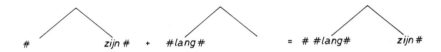

If two forms are separated by more than one '#' symbol, they are separated by a word boundary. Therefore # # *lang* # *zijn* # and # *op* # *eten* # # are single words if they occur in strings in which the former is followed by an item starting with at least one boundary symbol, and in which the latter is preceded by an item ending in at least one boundary symbol.

One difference between *lang* and *op* in *lang zijn* and *opeten*, as they occur with their noun phrase complements, is demonstrated in the following examples (with preserved word order in the literal translations):

(126a) Jan *is* 2 meter *lang*.
'John *is* 2 meters *tall*'.

(126b) Twee meter *lang* kan Jan niet *zijn*.
'Two meters *tall* can John not *be*'. (Two meters tall John can't be).

(127a) Jan *eet* de koek *op*.
'John *eats* the cookie *up*'.

(127b) *De koek *op* kan Jan niet *eten*.
'The cookie *up* can John not *eat*'.

The status of *lang* differs from that of *op* in that with the former a noun phrase is associated whereas with the latter this is not the case (instead, *opeten*, or perhaps *eten* is associated with *de koek*). This difference is reflected in the fact that *op* is an affix and *lang* is not. In *lang zijn*, *zijn* in this view should be looked upon as the affix. *Zijn* thus can be seen as the element which makes *lang zijn* a verb, much like *-en* with respect to the verb *loensen* (*be slightly cross-eyed = loens zijn*).

The entries of a pair like *lang zijn* and *lang* (the one superimposed over the other in (XIII) below) now could be analogous to the ones for the pair *wegen* and *zwaar* (cf. diagram (X), above):

(XIII)

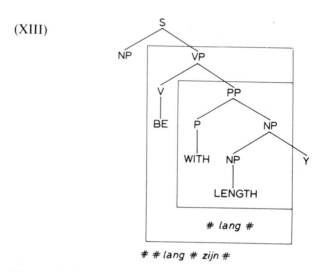

The entry for *zijn* now should indicate that it occurs as part of a 'word':

(XIV)

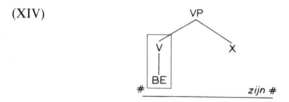

The subtree which is the simultaneous environment for *lang zijn* now is restructured in the same way as the one for, e.g., *wegen*:

(XV)

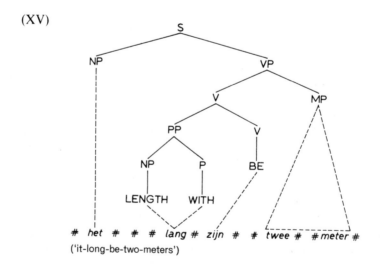

('it-long-be-two-meters')

We can now replace (XII) by an obligatory post-lexical transformation which converts a structure like (XV) into a structure like (XVI):

(XVI)

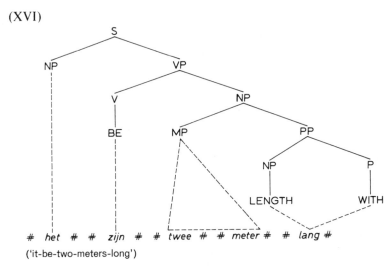

('it-be-two-meters-long')

This measure adjective movement transformation may be tentatively formulated as (XVII):

$$(XVII)\quad S.\,D.: \quad \#\,X\,\#\,\#\,-\,\#\,Y\,\#\,-\,zijn\,\#\,-\,\#\,MP\,\#\overset{OBL}{\Longrightarrow}$$

$$S.\,C.: \quad \begin{matrix} 1 & 2 & 3 & 4 \\ 1 & 3 & 4 & 2 \end{matrix}$$

Further discussion about the advantages or disadvantages of this possible treatment of copula + measure adjective constructions is outside the scope of this article. See, however, the remarks on p.   , below.

Finally, I would like to raise two problems and discuss them briefly. These are (1) the question of how to account for the fact that certain MP sentences (e.g., temperature MP sentences) can only have the form NP + Copula + MP or the periphrastic form with *hebben* + parameter noun, and (2) the question in what way sentences with the semicopula *duren* (*last*), *dragen* (*carry*) and *steken* (*draw*) are related to the corresponding measure adjectives.

With respect to the first problem I would like to observe that the sentence

(128)   Het water is 50 graden.
         'The water is 50 degrees'.

is not a reduction in the sense in which, e.g., *Jan is 2 meter* is one. The point

is, rather, that the Dutch lexicon happens to lack an entry for a phonologically non-null neutral temperature adjective. This means that we may
have a pair of lexical entries having the form of (XVIII):

(XVIII)

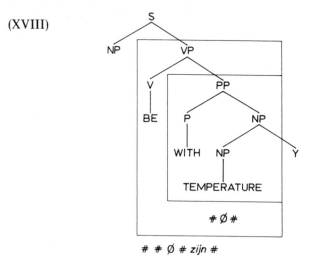

Clearly there is an infinite number of concepts which can be circumscribed
but for which single words do not exist. There is, for example, no word for
the concept circumscribed in (129), and there certainly never will be:

(129)   Intermittently hurting upper left premolar of ambidextrous
          bipeds inhabiting the southern hemispheres of Mars, Earth and
          Ganymede.

Obviously, it would be nonsense to include an entry in the lexicon for a
phonologically zero word expressing (129), since the non-existence of such
a word does not really constitute an irregularity. There is no tendency in
the lexicon on the basis of which we could call the non-existence of the word
in question an unexpected fact: it does not constitute a 'gap' in the lexicon
in any reasonable sense. The fact that there is no neutral temperature adjective, on the other hand, does seem to be an irregularity. The alternative
course we could take in dealing with temperature MP sentences and a few
others of the same type would be to set up an obligatory transformation
deleting the underlying WITH string just in case a neutral parameter adjective
is lacking. However, the conditions to which the application of this rule
would be subject would, as far as I can see, do no more than list a number
of special cases. This would amount to essentially the same (but in the wrong
component) as what in fact the lexicon is supposed to do. Therefore, I think
it is justified to prefer a solution within the lexicon.

In general, there are no neutral adjectives or semicopulas for parameters of recent origin, such as voltage, luminosity and electrical resistance. There are, however, exceptions (such as horsepower, for which the neutral adjective *sterk* ('strong') is available), and, furthermore, it should be noted that only in a restricted number of these cases the MP sentence takes on the form NP + Copula + MP. In the remaining cases, only the periphrastic form with *hebben* is used. The fact that there is no temperature semicopula nor a neutral temperature adjective may nonetheless have something to do with the historically relatively recent invention of devices capable of giving an objective measure of temperature.

The second problem, finally, concerns the status of, in particular, the italicized adjectives in the sentences (130)–(132):

(130)   De wedstrijd duurde *lang*.
         'The match lasted long'.
(131)   Het geschut draagt *ver*.
         'The artillery carries far'.
(132)   De boot steekt *diep*.
         'The boat draws deep'.

Obviously, sentences like *De wedstrijd duurde 10 minuten* ('The match lasted 10 minutes'), (34a) *De boot steekt 1 vadem* ('The boat draws 1 fathom') and (35a) *Het geschut draagt 10 km* ('The artillery carries 10 km'.) are not instances of 'normal' reduction.

The following six pairs of examples can be accounted for if we accept the hypothesis that the structure underlying *duren* sentences, at least in certain cases, does not contain one but two WITH strings, namely, WITH DURATION + WITH LENGTH.

(133)   De pauze duurde *lang*.   – Jan weegt *veel*.
         'The intermission lasted long'.   'John weighs much'.
(134)   De pauze duurde *langer*.   – Jan weegt *meer*.
         'The interm. lasted longer'.   'John weighs more'.
(135)   De pauze duurde 10 minuten *langer*.   – J. weegt 2 kilo *meer*.
         'The interm. lasted 10 minutes longer'.   'J. weighs 2 k.'s more'.
(136)   *De pauze duurde *veel*.   –*Jan is *veel*.
         'The interm. lasted much'.   'John is much'.
(137)   *De pauze duurde *meer*.   –*Jan is *meer*.
         'The interm. lasted more'.   'John is more'.
(138)   *De pauze duurde 10 minuten *meer*.   –*J. is 2 kilo *meer*.
         'The interm. lasted 10 minutes more'.   'J. is 2 k.'s more'.

The structure underlying the sentence *Jan weegt veel* ('John weighs much'), which is a paraphrase of *Jan is zwaar* ('John is heavy'), must be something like 'John is with much weight'. Similarly, *lang*, in the case of *duren*, may be analyzed as something like 'with much length'. From this viewpoint, the structures underlying (133) must be roughly 'the intermission was with duration with much length' and 'John is with much weight'. The underlying structures of (135) then would be 'the intermission was with duration with 10 minutes more length' and 'John is with 2 kilograms more weight'. The paraphrases of the *wegen* examples of (134) and (135) are *Jan is zwaarder* ('John is heavier') and *Jan is 2 kilo zwaarder* ('John is 2 kilograms heavier'), with adjectives in the comparative form, as in the *duren* examples. The ungrammaticality of (136)–(138) now can be explained by saying that, in sentences with an underlying 'much' or 'more', the WITH string directly associated with either of these elements may not be deleted. Apparently, this restriction holds irrespective of whether or not we have a structure that otherwise may undergo reduction (cf. the *wegen* example of (138), which is ungrammatical although *Jan weegt 80 kilo* (without the *meer*) may undergo reduction). In (136)–(138), then, WITH LENGTH and WITH WEIGHT have been deleted in violation of this restriction. (We note, in passing, that the restriction in question does not hold if the sentence contains a *dan* (*than*) phrase or clause).

Possibly, we must have two different lexical items *duren*, (XIXa) and (b).

(XIXa)

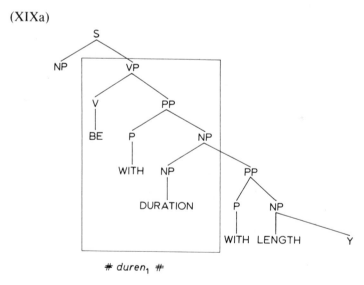

duren₁

(where *Y* must dominate at least an element of degree).

(XIXb)

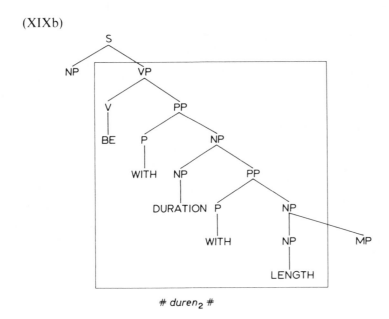

duren₂

The peripheral environment in (XIXb) contains an MP and causes *duren₂* to occur only in MP sentences (not containing an element of degree). In addition, *duren₂* is disjunctively ordered before *lang* in the case of simple MP sentences. That is, we do not have *duren₁* + *lang* in such sentences, but *duren₂*, which incorporates *lang*. (Not *De pauze duurde₁ 10 minuten lang* ('The intermission lasted 10 minutes long'), but *De pauze duurde₂ 10 minuten* ('The intermission lasted 10 minutes'.).

The analysis of *duren₁* and *duren₂*, especially in connection with the transformational relation between *gedurende* (*for the duration of*) phrases and *duren* sentences, is elaborated upon in W. G. Klooster and H. J. Verkuyl, (to appear).

The morphemic order in the infinitive construction *lang duren* probably is not evidence for its being a single 'word'. Compare, in this connection, the places of stress in *láng zijn* and *ópeten* with those in *lang dúren* and *hard wérken* (*work hard*). In both pairs, the stress may be moved, but *lang zijn* and *opéten* as well as *láng duren* and *hárd werken* are not 'neutral' but contain contrastive stress. However, these observations about stress do not constitute conclusive evidence in favor of the one word/many word distinction to be made between *lang zijn* and *lang duren*, for otherwise we would be compelled to assume without inquiring any further into the matter, that such forms as *een bóek lezen* (*to read a bóok*) and *de páp opeten* (*to eat up the pórridge*) are also single words, which may or may not be true. It may be of interest, in this connection, to note that, apparently, as Gruber (1967a) remarks, in Japanese there are some pieces of evidence (stress, phonological rules and subsequent application of transformations) "that post-positions, quantifiers and other things which manifest left-branching (. . .) actually form one word". He then goes on to say,

> But while the order between the verb and its object is also left-branching (object followed by verb) there is no similar evidence that we have formed one word here. It would be reasonable to claim that Japanese is a language which likes to preform its constituents in the lexicon before attaching to the derived tree. Suppose left-branching is normal for morphemes being attached to the derived tree as one lexical item (. . .) We could then explain the word order between the object and the verb in Japanese if we claimed they were attached at once by a lexical entry (. . .) But these are treated as separate words by transformations and phonological rules, and hence we see that the rule holds that the two # boundaries make two words. It appears that the entry must be doubly incomplete here, because both the verb and the object are open word classes. Articles and postpositions form a closed class, however, so that they can be listed as a small set of productive affixes. Also they never appear except with nouns, whereas NP may appear elsewhere than as the object of the verb; thus, while articles and postpositions can be treated as affixes, the object of a verb cannot be productively treated so (p. 124).

However this may be, suppose the analysis presented above of [*lang*] *duren* is essentially correct. We could then explain analogous facts about the behavior of [*ver*] *dragen* ('carry [far]') and [*diep*] *steken* ('draw [deep]') by assigning to the semicopulas of range and draught entries containing double WITH strings similar to the one proposed for *duren*$_2$ in the case of simple MP sentences and single ones in the remaining cases. Thus, we may analyze [*ver*] *dragen* as BE WITH RANGE [WITH DISTANCE] and [*diep*] *steken* as BE WITH DRAUGHT [WITH DEPTH].

As a final remark, I would like to remind the reader that the proposals presented above are highly tentative. Thus, for instance the analysis of measure adjectives and semicopulas will probably have to be refined in order to arrive at still more general statements. The parameter categories given as LENGTH, WIDTH, DEPTH, etc., may have to be analyzed further in terms of more fundamental categories.[14] Nevertheless, it is hoped that the suggestions that have been put forward will eventually lead to an adequate and satisfactory account of the regularities underlying the seemingly chaotic behaviour of measure phrase sentences.

University of Amsterdam

---

[14] *See* for an interesting analysis of measure adjectives Bierwisch (1967).

BIBLIOGRAPHY

Bierwisch, M.: 1967, 'Some Semantic Universals of German Adjectivals', *Foundations of Language* **3**, 1–36.

Chomsky, N.: 1965, *Aspects of the Theory of Syntax*, Cambridge, Mass.

Chomsky, N.: 1968, 'Deep Structure, Surface Structure and Semantic Interpretation', mimeographed (M.I.T.), to appear in *Semantics: An Interdisciplinary Reader in Philosophy, Linguistics, Anthropology and Psychology* (L. A. Jakobovits and P. P. Steinberg, eds.).

Dougherty, R.: 1968, 'Coordinate Conjunction', mimeographed (M.I.T.).

Dougherty, R.: 1969, Review of S. C. Dik, 'Coordination', *Language* **45**, 624–36.

Fillmore, C. J.: 1968a, 'The Case for Case', *Universals in Linguistic Theory* (Emmon Bach and Robert T. Harms, eds.), New York.

Fillmore, C. J.: 1968b, 'Lexical Entries for Verbs', *Foundations of Language* **4**, 373–93.

Gruber, J. S.: 1965, *Studies in Lexical Relations*, M.I.T. Doctoral Dissertation, mimeographed.

Gruber, J. S.: 1967a, *Functions of the Lexicon in Formal Descriptive Grammars*, Technical Memorandum 3770/000/00, System Development Corporation, Santa Monica.

Gruber, J. S.: 1967b, 'Disjunctive Ordering among Lexical Insertion Rules', mimeographed (M.I.T.).

Klooster, W. G., Verkuyl, H. J., and Luif, J. H. J.: 1969, *Inleiding tot de Syntaxis*, Culemborg/Keulen.

Klooster, W. G. and Verkuyl, H. J.: 'Measuring Duration in Dutch', *Foundations of Language*, to appear.

Kraak, A.: 1967, 'Presuppositions and the Analysis of Adverbs', mimeographed (M.I.T.), to appear in *Nederlandse Transformationele Studies* (W. G. Klooster and H. J. Verkuyl, eds.).

Kraak, A. and Klooster, W. G.: 1968, *Syntaxis*, Culemborg/Keulen.

Lakoff, G.: 1966, 'Stative Adjectives and Verbs in English', *NSF Report* **17**, Cambridge, Mass.

Lehiste, I.: 1969, ' "Being" and "Having" in Estonian', *Foundations of Language* **5**, 324–41.

McCawley, J. D.: 1967a, 'The Respective Downfalls of Deep Structure and Autonomous Syntax', *42nd Annual Meeting*, LSA, Chicago, Ill.

McCawley, J. D.: 1967b, 'Meaning and the Description of Languages', *Kotoba No Ucho* **2**, Nos. 9–11.

McCawley, J. D.: 1968a, 'The Role of Semantics in a Grammar', *Universals in Linguistic Theory* (Emmon Bach and Robert T. Harms, eds.), New York.

McCawley, J. D.: 1968b, 'Lexical Insertion in a Transformational Grammar without Deep Structure', *Fourth Regional Meeting*, Chicago Linguistic Society, Chicago, Ill.

Ross, J. R.: 1964, 'The Grammar of Measure Phrases in English', read at the December meeting of the LSA, mimeographed (M.I.T.).

Verkuyl, H. J.: 'Kwantificering, Conjunctie en Pluralisvorming in Zinnen met Frekwentie', unpublished paper (University of Amsterdam, Instituut voor Neerlandistiek).

EWALD LANG

ÜBER EINIGE SCHWIERIGKEITEN BEIM
POSTULIEREN EINER 'TEXTGRAMMATIK'

Es gibt derzeit eine gewisse Euphorie in 'Textlinguistik'. Innerhalb und
ausserhalb der Linguistik ist in den letzten Jahren zunehmend die Forderung
nach einer 'Texttheorie', die linguistisch fundiert sein müsse, erhoben
worden. Zweifellos reflektiert dieses Interesse auch einige sich objektiv
abzeichnende Tendenzen in der linguistischen Theoriebildung. Gleichzeitig
aber zeigt das Bemühen um 'Textlinguistik' viele Symptome einer Modeer-
scheinung. Es fehlt noch die präzise Gegenstandsbestimmung, Abgrenzung
und Verbindung zur sog. Satzgrammatik sind unbestimmt, die Argumentation beruht auf recht heterogenen Details oder weitausladenden Globalent-
würfen. Dies, zusammen mit der inzwischen angesammelten Fülle em-
pirischer Daten über Textstruktur, gibt Anlass, eine methodologische
Zwischenbilanz zu versuchen, mit dem Ziel, wenigstens in einigen Punkten
deutlicher herauszustellen, *wie* so etwas wie 'Text' zum linguistischen
Explicandum werden könnte. Die Diskussion kann sich, ihrer Absicht
gemäss, durchaus auf die Betrachtung einer Auswahl von Problemen und
theoretischen Ansätzen beschränken.

I. QUELLEN DER 'TEXTLINGUISTIK'

Die Forderung, eine 'Texttheorie' zu entwickeln oder linguistische
Analyse- oder Bewertungsverfahren auf empirisches Textmaterial zu appli-
zieren (beides figuriert unter 'Textlinguistik'), hat zunächst zwei unterscheid-
bare Quellen. Zum einen sind es bestimmte Problemstellungen, die von Dis-
ziplinen ausserhalb der Linguistik (etwa Pädagogik, Ästhetik, Literatur-
theorie; Information/Dokumentation; Wissenschaftstheorie u.a.) als
mögliche interdisziplinär zu bearbeitende Themen formuliert werden und
für die die Linguistik als Grundlagenwissenschaft oder als Fakten- und
Aspektzuträger fungiert. Zum anderen sind es Motive, die sich aus dem
Entwicklungsgang der Linguistik im weiteren Sinne selbst ergeben. Unterscheiden wir, der Einfachheit halber, externe und interne Ursachen für das
Postulieren einer 'Texttheorie'.

Zu den externen Anstössen will ich hier nur bemerken, dass sie, vorausgesetzt die entsprechenden Problemstellungen sind bereits theoretisierbar
formuliert, inbezug auf die Konstitution einer 'Texttheorie' als Orientierung

F. *Kiefer and N. Ruwet* (eds.), *Generative Grammar in Europe*, 284–314. *All Rights Reserved.*
Copyright © 1973 *by D. Reidel Publishing Company, Dordrecht-Holland.*

und/oder als heuristisches Mittel dienen können. Sie sind orientierend insofern, als sie einen zu theoretisierenden Untersuchungsbereich eröffnen, Konzentration bewirken und damit in die spontane, disziplininterne Theoriebildung günstig oder ungünstig, auf jeden Fall regulierend, eingreifen. Darin liegt ein Teil der heuristischen Funktion von Problemstellungen, die von seiten der Praxispartner der theoretischen Linguistik kommen. Ein anderer Teil mag darin bestehen, dass mit einer ausserlinguistischen Problemformulierung – im günstigsten Falle – auch Anlass gegeben ist, das der Problemformulierung zugrunde gelegte Inventar an Konzepten und die Verfahren zur Modellierung der das Problem bildenden Zusammenhänge, linguistisch zu interpretieren bzw. zu übernehmen. Allgemein aber gilt, dass externe Anstösse erst über eine komplizierte Prozedur von Vermittlungen konstitutiv werden können für eine linguistische 'Texttheorie'. Die tatsächliche Fruchtbarkeit interdisziplinärer Querverbindungen zum Thema 'Text' aber wird – dies zum Stichwort Euphorie – entscheidend von den nächsten Schritten zur Ausarbeitung einer eigenständigen linguistischen Konzeption zur Erfassung derjenigen Aspekte, die unter dem Namen 'Texteigenschaften' u.ä. vorläufig einsortiert sind, abhängen.

Die internen Ursachen für die Postulierung einer 'Texttheorie' bzw. einer 'Textgrammatik' lassen sich in zwei Gruppen teilen, die ich, wiederum vereinfachend, als Blickrichtung (1) 'Vom Satz zum Text' und als Blickrichtung (2) 'Vom Text zum Satz', bezeichnen will. Dahinter verbergen sich zweierlei methodische Zugänge, die weit verschiedener sind, als die Oberflächenähnlichkeit dieser Bezeichnungen glauben macht.

II. METHODOLOGISCHE VORBEMERKUNGEN

In der folgenden Diskussion werden verschiedene linguistische Motivationen für die Konstruktion einer 'Textgrammatik', die ja, in offensichtlicher Analogie zum Begriff 'Satzgrammatik', Kernstück einer linguistischen 'Texttheorie' werden soll, betrachtet, mit dem Ziel, die unterschiedlichen Prämissen herauszustellen, die in den diskutierten Vorstellungen meist nur implizit enthalten sind.

Ein solches Vorgehen scheint mir deshalb nötig, weil in der Literatur zur 'Textgrammatik' häufig angesichts unbestreitbarer Fakten gerade deren theorieaffizierende Interpretation methodologisch unabgesichert bleibt. Es geht also vornehmlich um die Interpretation von Fakten, genauer: um die Ausgrenzung derjenigen Aspekte an beobachteten Faktengruppen, die in einem von der Explikationsdomäne 'Satz' verschiedenen theoretischen Rahmen untergebracht werden müssen.

Ein linguistischer Text-Begriff kann natürlich nur ein theoriegebundenes Konstrukt sein, basierend auf einigen Grundannahmen, die das Fundament der theoretischen Linguistik überhaupt ausmachen. Von einem Textbegriff, der auch nur einige der zahlreichen, zweifellos signifikanten, intuitiven Urteile über das, was ein sprachliches Gebilde zum 'Text' macht, theoretisch befriedigend rekonstruiert, sind wir, so glaube ich, noch weit entfernt. Es kann nur darum gehen, Aspekte des zu beschreibenden Gegenstandes zusammenzutragen, die – durch empirische Analysen gedeckt – von ihm abgehoben werden können, und zu versuchen, diese Aspekte in einen auf das Beschreibungsziel – Struktur und Funktionieren des Sprachsystems – bezogenen Zusammenhang zu bringen. Dabei wird nach wie vor der Einheit 'Satz' eine zentrale Stellung zukommen, vorallem deshalb, weil sich mit dem durch eine generative Grammatik spezifizierten Begriff 'Satz', eben diesem theorie-gebundenen Konstrukt, die Reichweite des Kombinationsspielraums der sprachlichen Grundeinheiten im Format lexikalischer und syntaktischer Kategorien erfassen lässt. Der 'Satz' stellt *die* Domäne für die Distributions- und Kombinationregeln der Einheiten des Sprachsystems dar. Der Satz hat seine Entsprechung im kognitiven Elementarvorgang des Prädizierens, dessen Manifestation eben sprachlich als (minimaler) 'Satz' erscheint. Die Logik hat davon die Grundeinheit 'Proposition' abstrahiert. Und in klarer Übereinstimmung damit, dass der 'Satz' diejenige Einheit ist, mithilfe der sich die Konstitution und Verbalisierung von Sachverhalten zuträgt (Prädikation!), spielt die Struktureinheit 'Satz' im Prozess der Spracherlernung die primäre Rolle. Davon haben wir auszugehen bei der Suche nach einem tragfähigen Text-Begriff.

Vor der Diskussion der Aspekte, die eine 'Textgrammatik' begründen könnten, will ich noch zwei Festlegungen voranschicken, die die Kontinuität der Grundannahmen bei der Gewinnung theoretischen Neulands sichern sollen: (1) Eine Grammatik ist ein Mechanismus der wechselseitigen Zuordnung von Laut- und Bedeutungstrukturen. (2) Eine Grammatik ist die formale Rekonstruktion der Kompetenz des Sprecher/Hörers qua 'interiorisierte Grammatik'. Damit ist die Frage, was eine 'Textgrammatik' spezifizieren soll, deutlicher eingegrenzt, zumindest für den ersten Schritt. Inwiefern Aspekte der Sprachverwendung hierauf bezogen werden können, wird in Abschnitt 4.1 diskutiert. Eine Texttheorie auf Performanz festzulegen hat ebensowenig Sinn wie eine eigensinnige Beschränkung auf Kompetenz. Aber erst durch die strenge methodische Scheidung wird eine Zuordnung von Aspekten beider Provenienzen in einer elaborierten Texttheorie möglich und sinnvoll.

III

3.1. *Blickrichtung 1: 'vom Satz zum Text'*

Die Blickrichtung vom Satz zum 'Text' (sie kommt in vielen Publikationen explicite so zum Ausdruck) ist derzeit vorherrschend. Sie geht fast ausschliesslich darauf zurück, dass durch den Gebrauch eines bestimmten Analyseverfahrens neue linguistische Fakten ans Licht kamen, die im ursprünglich angenommenen Grammatikfragment nicht zu beschreiben und schon gar nicht zu erklären waren, aber das ist bei einer gesunden linguistischen Forschung der Regelfall, der, ebenso normal, zur Folge hat, dass das Modell so modifiziert wird, dass die neu entdeckten Fakten integriert und als Klasse von Erscheinungen prädiziert werden können. Innerhalb der fortwährend in der Theorieentwicklung geschehenden Revisionen gibt es nun eine bestimmte Menge von Modifizierungsvorstellungen, die in der Forderung kulminieren, die "Domäne der Grammatik zu erweitern" und eine "Textgrammatik" zu konstruieren als höhere und adäquatere Stufe einer 'Satzgrammatik'. Methodologisch betrachtet heisst das, es wird vorausgesetzt:

(1)   Es gibt eine verlässliche Differenzierung von 'Satz' und 'Text'.

(2)   Dieser Unterschied ist dergestalt, dass 'Text' diejenige linguistische Einheit ist, die die 'über die Satzgrenze hinausweisenden Strukturzusammenhänge' trägt.

(3)   Der Begriff 'Text' ist auf eine signifikante Weise dem Begriff 'Satz' so vorgeordnet, dass eine befriedigende Beschreibung und Explikation von 'Satz' nur via 'Text' erfolgen kann.

Unter diesen drei Voraussetzungen könnte dann eine 'Textgrammatik' als Modell einer höheren Adäquatheitsstufe postuliert werden.

Von diesen drei Voraussetzungen macht (1), obwohl grundlegend, die grössten Schwierigkeiten, was ich im folgenden noch zeigen will. Dafür dass (2) zutrifft, gibt es eine Reihe von Argumenten, dafür dass (3) gilt, kann man ebenfalls Gründe anführen, nur sind diese, wie mir scheint, zumindest zum Teil, aus einer anderen Blickrichtung gewählt, so dass insgesamt weder diese drei Voraussetzungen gesichert noch ihr Abhängigkeitszusammenhang geklärt sind.

Nun ist aber mit der vorläufigen Ungesichertheit der Voraussetzungen der Weg zu einer sinnvollen Theoriebildung noch nicht verbaut, vielmehr soll ja die Elaborierung des Modells zugleich eine schrittweise Explikation der gemachten Voraussetzungen liefern. Wenn wir das methodologisch weiterverfolgen, so bedeutet dies: Wer eine 'Textgrammatik' postuliert und sich

an ihre Konstruktion macht (unter der meist stillschweigenden Voraussetzung (1)–(3)), muss sich fragen bzw. die Frage gefallen lassen, *was* an den
neu entdecken Fakten neue Qualitäten im Beschreibungsmodell erforderlich
macht, und ferner, *was* die neuen Qualitäten des neuen Modells sind, die
ja, gemäss dem theoriegebundenen Begriff von Adäquatheit, Eigenschaften
sein müssen, die das alte Modell aus *prinzipiellen* Gründen nicht haben
kann.[1] Anders gefragt: Wer unter der Blickrichtung 'vom Satz zum Text'
eine 'Textgrammatik' postuliert, muss zeigen können:

(4)   Was sind modellsprengende Fakten? (Durch Demonstration
        eines für eine Klasse von Phänomenen stehenden Beispiels)

(5)   Was sind qualitative Veränderungen in einem Beschreibungs-
        modell? (Im Gegensatz zu, sagen wir, additiven Veränderungen
        oder/und Veränderungen im Arrangement der Komponenten)

(6)   Wie sind die gerechtfertigten Fälle von (4) auf die gerecht-
        fertigten Fälle von (5) zu beziehen, damit die postulierte Ad-
        äquatheitsstufe erreicht wird?

Erst wenn die Voraussetzungen (4)–(6) und im Zusammenhang damit
auch (1)–(3) durch Demonstration wenigstens plausibel erfüllt sind,
besteht ausreichend Grund, im Übergang von einer 'Satzgrammatik' zu
einer 'Textgrammatik' mehr zu sehen als eine terminologische Umbenennung. Die Gefahr, durch Umbenennung eine scheinbare Erweiterung der
Domäne erreicht zu haben, besteht vor allem dann, wenn aufgrund bestimmter Fakten in komplexeren Gebilden (etwa in Folgen von Sätzen) eine
zentrale linguistische Einheit 'Text' postuliert wird, die in ähnlicher Weise
in der Hierarchie der linguistischen Einheiten über 'Satz' rangiert wie dieser
über 'Wort' oder 'Syntagma', je nach Zerlegungsschema. Ein auf diese
Weise, d.h. 'Text' dominierend eine Folge von Sätzen, eingeführter Text-
begriff entnimmt aus dem intuitiv zweifellos vorhandenen Verständnis von
Text das recht vage nur angebbare Moment, dass als 'Text' erst ein kom-
plexeres Gebilde anzusehen ist, das sich aus 'Sätzen' zusammensetzt. So
wird 'Text' häufig (schon bei Harris' *Discourse Analysis*) bestimmt als
"alles von der Folge aus zwei Sätzen bis zur Grössenordnung Roman,
Abhandlung, Gesetzeswerk usw.". Interessant ist, dass Grenzangaben nach
oben hin hierbei immer in funktional bestimmten literarischen Kategorien
vorgenommen werden, während die untere Grenzangabe in neutralen, wenn

---

[1] 'Prinzipiell' etwa im Sinne der Adäquatheitsbewertungen, die den grundsätzlichen Unterschied
zwischen PSG-Grammatiken und Transformationsgrammatiken hinsichtlich ihrer empirischen
Angemessenheit ausdrücken. Die Analogie soll nicht hinsichtlich der Sache, sondern nur in
Bezug auf das theoretische Gewicht von 'prinzipiellen' Argumenten gelten.

man will, 'grammatischen' Kategorien wie 'Satz', 'Satzfolge', 'Satzkette' etc. erfolgt, jedenfalls aber mit dem Begriff 'Satz' als Komplexitätsmass. Die Heterogenität dieser Grenzangaben macht schon einiges von der Schwierigkeit deutlich, 'Text' und 'Satz' irgendwie quantitativ zu definieren. Auch die in der generativen Literatur zum 'Text' häufig anzutreffende Gleichsetzung " 'Texte', d.h. Satzfolgen" oder umgekehrt "Satzfolgen, also Texte" (so bei Isenberg (1968a, b), Steinitz (1968), Thümmel (1970), Heidolph (1966, 1971) u.a.), die eine obere Grenze noch offen lässt, hilft nicht weiter. Es ist keineswegs klar, weder intuitiv, noch in der theoretischen Rekonstruktion, bis zu welchem Komplexitätsgrad eine zusammenhängende sprachliche Struktur noch ein 'Satz' ist und ab wann sie schon ein 'Text' ist. Auch die Differenzierung von Satzkomplexionen und Satzketten (Satzfolgen) hilft nicht weiter, weil eben diese beiden Strukturtypen vielfach als Paraphrasen voneinander auftreten und daher transformationell aufeinander zu beziehen sind, wie Thümmel (1970) gezeigt hat. Hierzwischen die Grenze von 'Satz' zu 'Text' zu legen hat kaum einen Sinn, ebenso wie die mit der einfachen Dominanz 'Text'-über-Satzfolge verbundene Aufstockung der herkömmlichen 'Satz'-Grammatik zur 'Textgrammatik' füglich als problematisch bezeichnet werden darf.

Als Faktenbasis für solche Ausweitung wird z.B. die Topologie der Konjunktsätze bei zusammengesetzten Sätzen betrachtet (Thümmel (1970)), wobei ein oberster Knoten TEXT die Operationsdomäne für Permutationen von Tochter-P-Markern begrenzt, also ein technisches Moment, was hier zur 'Textgrammatik' führt; Regularitäten der Distribution text- und/oder situationsdeiktischer Elemente; Koreferenzphänomene; Kontextabhängigkeiten 'über die Satzgrenze hinweg'. Die beiden letztgenannten Faktengruppen werden unten in Abschnitt 3.2 exemplarisch diskutiert nach Massgabe von (1)–(6), mit dem Ziel, zu zeigen, dass die angeführten Faktengruppen weder einzeln genommen noch zusammengezählt ausreichen, um für die Grammatik eine von 'Satz' verschiedene erweiterte Domäne 'Text' zu fordern, wiewohl die genannten Fakten in unterschiedlicher Weise zu Modifikationen im bisherigen Beschreibungsapparat nötigen. Andererseits sind mit der Aufdeckung solcher Fakten – Wünschelruteneffekt der 'Textgrammatik'! – Zusammenhänge ins Blickfeld gerückt, die auf jeden Fall in der linguistischen Beschreibung untergebracht werden müssen, wenngleich sie – meiner Ansicht nach – noch diesseits der Entscheidung liegen, ob nun 'Satz' oder 'Text' die eigentliche Domäne der Grammatik sei. Und in der Fortsetzung dieser Linie scheint mir das für die nächste Zeit lohnende Feld für die Untersuchung von Textaspekten zu liegen. Sie werden im Abschnitt 3.3 diskutiert.

3.2. *Diskussion einiger Faktengruppen*

3.2.1. Die am häufigsten als Argument für die Notwendigkeit einer 'Textgrammatik' ins Feld geführten Fakten stammen aus dem Bereich des Determinationssystems oder – allgemeiner noch – aus dem Bereich der Referenzbeziehungen. Die mit einer 'Satzgrammatik' als nicht zu Ende analysierbar ausgegebenen Effekte solcher Referenzverhältnisse auf die semantische Interpretation von Sätzen und auf die Organisation ihrer Oberflächenstruktur sind das Motiv, eine 'erweiterte Domäne' zu postulieren. (Vgl. Annear (1968); Dressler (1971); Heidolph (1966); Isenberg (1968a, b); Petöfi (1971); Stempel (1971); van Dijk (1971); u.v.a.) Zweifellos werden durch die Betrachtung solcher Beziehungen und der von ihnen systematisch regulierten Variationen in der semantischen Interpretation und/oder in der Oberflächencharakteristik von Sätzen Regularitäten sichtbar, über die der kompetente Sprecher/Hörer verfügen muss. Und sofern die Linguistik die Kompetenz zum Gegenstand hat, sind solche Referenzbeziehungen, genauer: zumindest die davon abhängenden Effekte im Laut-Bedeutungs-zuordnungsmechanismus, ihr Untersuchungs- und Explikationsobjekt. Die Einschränkung ist nötig, weil bisher keineswegs klar ist, ob die mit der Setzung oder Rekonstruktion einer Referenzbeziehung verbundenen kognitiven Operationen selbst zur Sprachkompetenz gehören oder zur – sagen wir – kognitiven Kompetenz im allgemeinen.

Die unzähligen Arbeiten auf diesem Gebiet haben sich daher auch nur mit der Spezifikation der komplizierten Bedingungen beschäftigt, denen gemäss zwei sprachliche Einheiten innerhalb einer zusammenhängenden grösseren Struktur koreferieren, d.h. dasselbe Denotat haben, oder nicht koreferieren, d.h. unterschiedliche Denotate haben. Gegenstand der linguistischen Untersuchung ist somit nicht das Referieren an sich (also das Verhältnis Zeichen-Denotat), sondern die verschiedenen Weisen von Koreferenz und Referenzdistinktion in ihrer sprachlichen Manifestation. Das Vorhandensein einer kognitiven Operation des Referierens (Herstellung der Beziehung Zeichen – Denotat) ist somit vorausgesetzt, ebenso wie die um eine logische Stufe höher liegende Beziehung der Referenzgleichheit bzw. – distinktion. Inwieweit das hier Vorausgesetzte zur Sprachkompetenz gehört, oder zur Kognition überhaupt, ist, wie gesagt, noch offen.

Aus der Tatsache, dass wir es nur mit den Regularitäten der *sprachlichen Manifestation*[2] von Koreferenz oder Referenzdistinktion zu tun haben, lässt sich zweierlei folgern:

---

[2] Dieses Konzept wird anhand von McCawley's Vorschlägen zur Behandlung von Referenz-Problemen ausführlicher diskutiert in Lang (1969).

(1) Die sprachliche Manifestation, d.h. der sprachliche Reflex, von/ Koreferenz und Referenzdistinktion, lässt sich erfassen als Menge von über den gesamten Mechanismus der Laut-Bedeutungszuordnung (= Grammatik) verteilten Einschränkungen.

(2) Da bisher verschiedene Modellierungen dieses Mechanismus (= Grammatik) existieren, fällt der Account für den genannten Reflex entsprechend verschieden aus.

Dass Folgerung (2) vernünftig ist, bezeugen die mindestens in fünf Typen einzuteilenden Beschreibungsfragmente z.b. zur Pronominalisierung, die im grossen und ganzen ein und dieselbe Faktenmenge erfassen.[3] Eine Revue dieser Modelle im Adäquatheitswettbewerb hat noch nicht stattgefunden. Mindestens vier davon (Lakoff, Gross, Jackendoff und klassische Varianten) machen keinen Rekurs auf 'Text'.

Die Folgerung (1) ist gerechtfertigt, wenn man folgendes akzeptiert als Definition von 'sprachlich manifestiert':

(7)   Eine (nicht-sprachliche) Beziehung R zwischen den Objekten x und y ist dann sprachlich manifestiert, wenn sich R in systematischer Weise auf Beziehungen zwischen den sprachlichen Repräsentanten von x und y abbilden lässt.

Für die Manifestation von Koreferenz und Referenzdistinktion heisst das: Jede Instanz von Koreferenz wird konstituiert durch eine konditionierte Paarbildung aus sprachlichen Einheiten E_i, E_j. Die Paarbildung wird bestimmt hinsichtlich ihrer Koreferenzfähigkeit (entsprechend komplementär: ihrer Referenzdistinktion) durch eine konjunktiv aufgezählte Auswahlmenge von Relationen, an denen E_i und E_j als Argumente beteiligt sind. Dabei verstehen sich E_i, E_j als Variable über der Menge der referenzfähigen NP-Belegungen ('referentials'). Die Menge der Relationen zwischen E_i und E_j, die hinreichend oder notwendig sind für die Koreferenz, ist über sämtliche Komponenten der Grammatik verteilt, d.h. Koreferenz zwischen E_i und E_j ergibt sich aus dem Zusammenwirkungen struktureller Zusammenhänge auf verschiedenen Repräsentationsebenen der Grammatik. Die Menge der linguistisch fixierbaren Beziehungen zwischen E_i, E_j, aus der mit Und/Oder-Verknüpfung ausgewählt wird, umfasst u.a.:

---

[3] Es sei hier nur grob klassifiziert: (1) 'Klassische' Variante: Transformationelle Ersetzung von vollspezifizierten NP. (2) Derivation mit durch '+PRO' geblockter Lexikoneinsetzung und abgebrochener Subkategorisierung. (3) Pronomina in der Tiefenstruktur. (4) Einführung durch Relativ-Sätze. (5) Referenzstellen als Variablen in der Tiefenstruktur, die 'aufgefüllt' werden. (6) Surface Interpretation.

(8)   – Lautidentität
             – semantische Identität
             – semantischer Spezifikationsgrad (z.B. das weiter zu zerlegende
               Verhältnis von Promina zur 'vollen' NP hinsichtlich der kon-
               gruenzbestimmenden Merkmale, vgl. Steinitz (1968)).
             – Definitisierung (das, was z.B. *ein* und *der* verbindet)
             – Spezifizierung (das, was die Objekte in *Peter wollte schon im-*
               mer ein Auto haben, plötzlich erbte er eins/ein Auto) verbindet
             – Dominanz
             – Command
             – Akzentparallele (vgl. Bierwisch (1969)).
             – parallele pitch-contour (vgl. Cantrall, 1970).

Auswahlen aus dieser Liste spezifizieren die möglichen Paarbildungen E_i,
E_j für Koreferenz und ordnen zugleich die Paare nach der Charakteristik
VORGÄNGER (E_i, E_j) bzw. NACHFOLGER (E_i, E_j).

Jede referenzfähige NP ist potentieller Teilhaber an einer Koreferenz-
beziehung. Durch die in (8) aufgezählten Beziehungen wird für jede vorkommende referenzfähige NP bestimmt, ob sie ein möglicher Vorgänger
oder ein möglicher Nachfolger ist und wie ein möglicher Gegenpart kon-
ditioniert ist zur Konstituierung der Koreferenz.

Der in Folgerung (1) genannte linguistische Account für die Manifestation der Koreferenz ist nur der sich über die gesamte Grammatik er-
streckende Mechanismus, der vermittels der in (8) aufgezählten linguistisch
explizierten Relationen die Paarbildungen E_i, E_j spezifiziert. Damit ist
eine allgemeine Forderung genannt, der jedes Grammatikmodell in der
einen oder anderen Weise (möglicherweise im Form globaler Derivations-
beschränkungen im Sinn von Lakoff) gerecht werden muss, sofern es sich
um Beschreibung und Explikation der Kompetenz bemüht.[4]

3.2.2. Wieso kommen nun verschiedene Autoren angesichts der mit der
Manifestation der Koreferenz verbundenen Regularitäten auf 'die Erweiterung der Domäne der Grammatik vom Satz zum Text'? Ganz einfach
dadurch, dass sich diese Autoren bemühen, für bestimmte in isolierten
Sätzen auftretende NP, die gemäß der Beziehungen in (8) als Nachfolger

---

[4] Es geht hier im Moment nicht um Aspekte des aktuellen Textverständnisses aus der Sicht des
Hörers oder um die Strategie der Textentwicklung aus der Sicht des Sprechers. Letzteres wird
bisweilen als das für eine 'Textgrammatik' in Bezug auf Referenzverhältnisse zu beschreibende
Problem genannt (z.B. Kummer (1971). Mir aber scheint, dass der aktuellen Textentwicklung
ler Fundus der in (8) genannten Bedingungen für die Paarbildung zugrundeliegt und die Verfügung über diesen Fundus zur Kompetenz gehört und von daher Strategien aufgebaut werden.

charakterisiert sind, den entsprechenden Gegenpart zu rekonstruktruieren, um die Charakteristik 'Nachfolger' damit systematisch zu explizieren, d.h. jede als 'Nachfolger' ausgewiesene NP als Teilhaber an einer Koreferenz-Beziehung zu beschreiben. Und dies geschah in verschiedenen Versionen dadurch, dass man aus technischen Gründen zum P-Marker des betreffenden Satzes 'Kontext-Sätze' in Form von P-Markern hinzukonstruierte und mit ihm verkettete, so dass entsprechende Referenzregeln operieren können. Die Bewertung 'technisch' ist gerechtfertigt, weil der Grund für *diese Form* der Analyse der Manifestation der Koreferenz tatsächlich in den damaligen Vorstellungen über die Arbeitsweise und den Aufbau des Regelsystems der Grammatik liegt. Man hat damals, ausgehend von einem Konzept der syntaktischen Tiefenstruktur nach Chomskys 'Aspects', die determinierenden Faktoren für die Organisation der Oberflächenstruktur ziemlich undifferenziert der transformationellen Manipulation aufgebürdet. Die einzelnen Varianten werden ausführlicher diskutiert in Lang (in Vorbereitung). Die damaligen Vorstellungen über den Beschreibungsapparat haben auch die Frage nach dem, *was* zur Charakterisierung einer NP linguistisch von Belang ist, verstellt: Die betreffende NP ist zu charakterisieren *als ob* sie Vorgänger oder Nachfolger in einem koreferenzkonstituierenden Paar ist, gleichgültig, ob der betreffende Gegenpart explizit verbalisiert auftritt oder nicht.

Die Tatsache, dass Paare E_i, E_j als Vorgänger und Nachfolger explizit auch verteilt über eine Folge von Sätzen auftreten können und dabei genau den in (8) genannten konditionierenden Beziehungen genügen müssen, hat dazu verführt, einen einzelnen Satz mit einer Nachfolger-NP als isoliert genommen semi-grammatischen Sonderfall zu betrachten und ihn deshalb nur als eingebettet in einen angenommenen 'Kontext' zu analysieren. Daher die Vorstellung, daß die "Erweiterung der Beschreibungsdomäne" durch Hinzusetzen von 'Kontexten' ein Spezialfall der sich auf Satzfolgen (= 'Texte') beziehenden Beschreibung und somit eine 'Textgrammatik' der angemessene Rahmen für eine 'Satzgrammatik' sei.

Nun scheint mir aber die Bewertung eines isolierten Satzes wie *Er kommt heute* oder *Der andere Kerl grinst bloss* als semi-grammatisch nicht den Kern der Sache zu treffen, vor allem aber sind die genannten Konklusionen nicht zwingend. Als Satz, d.h. als Ergebnis der Anwendung bestimmter Kombinations- und Distributionsregeln der Einheiten des Sprachsystems innerhalb fixierter Spielräume (vgl. Abschnitt 2 oben), ist *Er kommt heute* gewiss vollgrammatisch, d.h. in voller Übereinstimmung mit den Regeln des Sprachsystems. Was ihm die Bewertung 'semi-grammatisch' eingebracht haben könnte ist wohl eher dies, dass eine einleitungslos hervorgebrachte

Äusserung *Er kommt heute* möglicherweise unakzeptabel ist, wenn der Referent von *er* im situativen Kontext nicht auffindbar ist, und somit die Konstituierung eines Referenten beim Hörer gestört ist, da ja auch die andere Variante, nämlich über ein verbal eingeführtes Vorgänger- Pendant zu *er* einen Referenten zu konstituieren, ausscheidet. 'Unakzeptabel' bedeutet aber hier, dass man mit einem solchen Satz als Gesprächseinleitung gegen die guten Sitten der Kommunikation verstösst, indem man beim Kommunikationspartner (a) Kenntnisse unterstellt, die er nicht hat und sich nicht auf normale Weise verschaffen kann, (b) ihn des Nutzens der Mitteilung beraubt usw. Es bedeutet dies, die Kommunikation ist zweckentfremdet, insofern, als sie in diesem Falle nicht mehr – zumindest vom Hörer – planvoll in Zusammenhänge des praktischen Verhaltens eingeordnet werden kann. Zweifellos versteht der Hörer den Satz, mühelos kann er dessen semantische Lesung interpretieren, wobei *er* für ihn soviel Informationsgehalt hat wie *jemand*. Aber anfangen kann er nichts mit dem Satz. Und gerade das ist der eigentliche mit 'unakzeptabel' bewertete Mangel, der nicht dem Satz als grammatisch determiniertes Gebilde anhaftet, sondern seiner Verwendung unter diesen Bedingungen. Chomsky (1965) hat 'Grammatikalität' und 'Akzeptabilität' streng geschieden und letztere in den Bereich einer Performanz-Theorie verwiesen, während die Spezifizierung der Grammatikalität in die kompetenzreflektierende Grammatik gehört. Dem letztgenannten ist voll zuzustimmen, aber man sollte sich hüten, einer Äquivokation zu verfallen und etwa auch die soeben diskutierte Akzeptabilitätsbewertung kurzerhand in eine Performanztheorie abzuschieben. Die von Chomsky aufgezählten Faktoren der Akzeptabilitätsbewertung grammatischer Sätze sind nämlich anderer Art "having to do . . . with memory limitations, intonational and stylistic factors, 'iconic' elements of discourse" (Chomsky (1965: 11–12)).

Die Akzeptabilität, mit der wir es hier zu tun haben, wird aber bestimmt durch funktionale Aspekte der Kommunikation. Dafür ist der richtige theoretische Ort erst noch zu suchen.

3.2.3. Ich will nun die Konzeption der "Erweiterung der Beschreibungsdomäne von Satz zu Text" vor dem Hintergrund der oben formulierten Voraussetzungen (1)–(3) und der zu erfüllenden Postulate (4)–(6) an einem exemplarischen Fall durchsprechen – an Isenbergs Fundierung einer 'Textgrammatik' aufgrund seiner Analyse der Distribution von *a* vor direkten Objekten im Spanischen (*Studia Grammatica* **IX**). Hier ist ein solches Konzept von 'Texteigenschaften' meines Wissens am ausgiebigsten dargestellt. Vorweg noch dies: Ich bin weder willens noch in der Lage, die von Isenberg angeführten Fakten zu bestreiten oder einen alternativen Apparat zu ihrer Beschreibung vorzuschlagen, mein Einwand betrifft lediglich die modellaffizierende Interpretation der Fakten und der verwendeten Beschreibungsmittel. Isenberg kommt nach einer sehr subtilen Analyse der lexikalisch-semantischen Bedingungen für die Setzung bzw. Nicht-Setzung der Präposition *a* bei direkten Objekten im Spanischen zu dem Schluss, dass eben diese Bedingungen nicht ausreichen, um die Verteilung der Präposition und die verschiedenen Grade von Verletzungen durch Fehlbesetzung zu erfassen und zu erklären. Einen solchen nicht abgedeckten Faktenbereich stellt er von Abschnitt 2.5. an vor, wo er zeigt, dass die Präpositionalität eines direkten Objekts auch von dessen Vorkommensstelle in einer Serie von Objekten abhängt. Isenberg beginnt mit einer Serie in Form einer Satzfolge, der er isolierte Sätze gegenüberstellt:

(9)   (a) (1) Pedro vio una silla
             (2) *Pedro vio a una silla
             (3) Pedro vio una niña
             (4) Pedro vio a una niña

      (b) (1) Pedro vio a una niña. Pedro vio a una mujer.
                Pedro vio *a* una silla.
             (2) *Pedro vio a una niña. Pedro vio a una mujer.
                Pedro vio una silla.
             (3) Pedro vio una niña. Pedro vio una mujer.
                Pedro vio (*a) una silla.
             (4) *Pedro vio a una silla. Pedro vio (a) una niña.
                Pedro vio (a) una mujer.

Das Prinzip ist klar: Wenn das erste Objekt einer solchen Serie korrekterweise (vgl. (a)(2) und (b)(4)!) die Präposition *a* hat, dann bekommen alle folgenden ebenfalls *a*, auch wenn sie es in isolierten Sätzen nicht haben dürften (vgl. (a)(2) und (b)(1)), und wenn das erste Objekt einer solchen Serie korrekterweise die Präposition *a* nicht hat, dann bleibt sie auch bei allen folgenden Objekten weg, auch wenn diese sie haben könnten. *Ergo*: Die Position in einer Serie mit bestimmten Akzentmuster (vgl. Isenbergs Anm. 42) relativiert zu einem Teil die inhärenten lexikalischen Bedingungen. Isenberg nennt solche Satzfolgen 'zusammenhängende Texte' und schreibt die sich abzeichnenden Regularitäten der Präpositionalität den 'Texteigenschaften' einer solchen Folge zu und postuliert für ihre Beschreibung eine Grammatik, die auf 'Kontextsätze' rekurrieren kann, also eine 'Textgrammatik'. (p. 62ff.) Der Rekurs auf – in diesem Falle – Vorgängersätze und die Zuhilfenahme von Begriffsbildungen wie Vorerwähntheit von Konstituenten (im Anschluss an Heidolph (1966)) veranlassen Isenberg, diese Phänomene der Präpositionsverteilung in eine auf Referenzbeziehungen sich gründende 'Texttheorie' einzugliedern. Er schreibt:

> Die Argumente, auf denen diese Annahme beruht, sind nicht deshalb zwingend, weil sie die Darstellung von Textregularitäten als solche demonstrieren, sondern weil sie zeigen, dass die innere Struktur einzelner Sätze von der Struktur des jeweiligen Textes abhängig ist, in dem sie auftreten. (p. 243–44).

Dieses Zitat scheint die oben genannten Voraussetzungen (1)–(3) als erfüllt zu beinhalten, ich will nun zeigen, dass das zumindest für die in (9) exemplifizierten Fakten nicht der Fall ist.

Zunächst darf man bezweifeln, ob Satzfolgen wie die in (9)(b) tatsächlich dem intuitiven Verständnis von 'zusammenhängendem Text' entsprechen. So betrachtet sind die Serien als Text stilistisch spröde und praktisch rar.

Aber dies ist noch kein Argument, für linguistische Demonstrationszwecke kann man das schon hinnehmen. Die Sprödigkeit solcher 'Texte' erklärt sich aus dem zweiten, nun wirklich triftigen Einwand gegen Isenbergs Interpretation dieser Phänomene: Sie sind nicht primär eine Konsequenz aus bestimmten Textzusammenhängen, sondern ein Effekt des all diesen Erscheinungen zugrunde liegenden Prinzips der Koordination. Dieser Parallelisierungseffekt[5] der Koordination trifft auf Konjunktserien innerhalb der Satzgrenze ebenso zu wie auf Serien koordinierter Sätze, gleichviel, ob sie asyndetisch oder konjunktional verknüpft sind. Die Sprödigkeit der 'Texte' in (9)(b) erklärt sich nun daher, dass diese Satzfolgen mit dem bekannten stilistischen Makel nicht-reduzierter Konjunktsätze versehen ist. Zunächst aber will ich meine Behauptung, dass die genannten 'Textregularitäten' de facto eine Koordinationserscheinung sind, abstützen. Die Beispiele dafür sind Isenbergs Arbeit entnommen. Nach Konstituierung einer 'Texttheorie' aufgrund der Beobachtungen an Satzfolgen wie (9)(b) bringt er in Abschnitt 2.5.5. weitere Typen grammatischer Strukturen, an denen dieselben Regularitäten ablesbar sind:

---

[5] Es scheint, dass mit der Koordination als Strukturprinzip eine ganze Hierarchie von Parallelisierungseffekten verbunden ist, die sich auf die inhärente Semantik der Konjunkte beziehen, oder auch die Determinierung einer Interpretation bei Serien gleichermassen ambiger Sätze: In

(i)   Peter hasst Verwandtenbesuche. Susi schätzt sie

kann beide Male entweder nur 'besuchen' oder beide Male nur 'besucht werden' gemeint sein. Oder die Rekonstruktion des Verbs in

(ii)   Eine Gedichtrezitation oder ein Liederabend machen mir immer Spass

kann entweder nur beide Male 'produzieren' oder beide Male 'konsumieren' sein, aber nicht gemischt. Weitere Beispiele für Kongruenzangleichung und andere Oberflächenerscheinungen in Lang (in Vorbereitung).

Elliptische Sätze:

(10)　　Pedro vio a una niña. *A* una bicicleta. *A* una banca. (vgl. *Pedro
　　　　vio *a* una banca)

unreduzierte koordinierte Sätze:

(11)　　Pedro vio a una niña y Pedro vio *a* una banca.

reduzierte koordinierte Sätze:

(12)　　Pedro vio a una niña y a una banca.
　　　　Pedro vio una banca y una niña.
　　　　*Pedro vio una banca y *a* una niña.

Isenberg selbst bemerkt, dass 'Texte' wie (12) nur aus einem Satz bestehen.
Das widerspricht nicht seinen Annahmen, in denen er ausdrücklich den
Ein-Satz-Text als Sonderfall von 'Text' erwähnt. Seine Annahmen werden
aber in ihrer Aussagekraft wesentlich vermindert, wenn sich herausstellt,
dass bezogen auf einen isolierten Satzes mit gleicher Deutlichkeit dieselben
Regularitäten gelten wie bezogen auf eine Satzfolge;dadurch fällt innerhalb
dieses Faktenbereichs die Spezifik der 'Textzusammenhänge' weg und
damit das konstitutive Moment für die Postulierung einer Texttheorie.
Nun könnte man einwenden, dass dieser Parallelisierungseffekt bei der
Präpositionsverteilung durchaus eine notwendige Begleiterscheinung koordinierter Strukturen sein mag, dass aber eben dann nur ein gemeinsamer
Name für diese Erscheinungen gefunden wäre, die nach wie vor als 'Textregularitäten' zu beschreiben wären. Ein solcher Einwand ist zur Hälfte
richtig, er besagt, dass Isenberg den heuristischen Fehler gemacht hat, seine
Faktenbeispiele ungünstig zu ordnen, statt 'von innen nach aussen' vor-
zugehen, d.h. die Expandierung koordinierter Strukturen zu verfolgen, ist
er 'von aussen nach innen' herangegangen, indem er zunächst expandierte
Beispiele (9)(b) diskutiert, darauf seine Theorie aufbaut und die anderen
Fälle (10)–(12) mehr à propos erwähnt. Die zweite Hälfte des Einwandes
ist aber nicht stichhaltig, denn die Grammatikalitätsbedingungen für
koordinierte Strukturen sind unter diesem Aspekt der Präpositionalität
innerhalb eines Satzes und bezogen auf eine Satzfolge dieselben. Anders
gesagt, die Koordination ist gerade das Strukturprinzip, das für die Differenzierung von 'Satz' und 'Text' nichts hergibt, das demzufolge die Erfüllung
der Voraussetzungen (1)–(3), die ja auch im Zitat von Isenberg anklingen,
nicht in sinnvoller Weise gestattet. Nach (3) können wir resümieren, dass
hier 'Text' dem Begriff 'Satz' nicht in der Weise vorgeordnet ist, dass eine
befriedigende Explikation und Beschreibung von 'Satz' nur via 'Text'
möglich wäre.

Die von Isenberg sorgfältig beobachten Regularitäten scheinen mir im
Rahmen einer umfassenden Beschreibung koordinierter Strukturen besser
untergebracht zu sein. Und dass diese – jedenfalls in Bezug auf Präpositionali-
tätsprobleme – nicht notwendig auf Kontextzusammenhänge jenseits der
Satzgrenze rekurrieren, lässt sich zeigen an Isenbergs Beispielen (p. 96f).

(13)   Pedro vio a una niña y a una banca
(14)   Pedro vio a una niña y una banca

die im Falle von (13) als 'non-joint' (zwei Ereignisse oder Sachverhalte
bezeichnend), im Falle von (14) aber als 'joint' (beide Objekte gehören zu
ein und demselben Vorgang) interpretiert werden. Isenberg sieht demzufolge auch zweierlei Ableitungen vor, für (13) die der Konjunktsatz-
Reduktion, für (14) die durch Basis-NP-Koordination. Das Interessante
an (14) ist nun, dass hier die aufgrund der Hypothese von der 'Kontext'-
Abhängigkeit eigentlich zu erwartende Setzung von *a* vor das zweite Objekt
nicht stattfindet wie etwa bei (9)(b)(1) oder (10)–(12). Wenn dasselbe nun
auch gilt für Sätze mit Verben, die ein 'joint'-Objekt haben müssen, wie
etwa bei

(15)   El curo casó a un hombre y (*a) una mujer
(16)   Pedro juntó a un hombre y (*a) una cabra

wo, wenn es wirklich um den Kontexteinfluss innerhalb einer Serie von
Sätzen oder Satzgliedern ginge, die Setzung von *a* prädiziert würde, dann
scheint damit ein Argument gegeben, dass die genannten Regularitäten
tatsächlich eher eine Koordinationsangelegenheit sind. Sie gelten für isolierte
Sätze, wo 'joint'-Objekte, obwohl sie eine Serie von Objekten umfassen
können, als *eine* syntaktische Einheit auftreten, ebenso wie für syndetisch
oder asyndetisch koordinierte Satzfolgen. Auch die von Isenberg angeführten
Typen von syntaktischen Konstruktionen, bei denen eben dieser Parallelisierungseffekt auftritt (Frage-Antwort-Korrespondenz, Korrektursätze,
Echo-Fragen) lassen sich durchaus als Koordinationssymptome interpretieren.

Ich bin mit Isenberg einer Meinung, dass die Setzung oder Vermeidung
der Präposition *a* in den einschlägigen Fällen ein morphologischer Ober-
flächenreflex systematisierbarer Bedingungen der spanischen Tiefengram-
matik ist. Ich bezweifle aber, dass es sich hierbei um den Reflex von 'Texteigenschaften' in irgendeinem spezifischen Sinne des Wortes handelt. Als
vergleichbare Phänomene würde ich etwa den nur bei koordinierten Objekten möglichen Wegfall des definiten Artikels im Deutschen anführen.
vgl. (17), und die in Anm. 5 genannten Beispiele.

(17)　　(1)　Peter hat sich am Kopf und an den Schultern verletzt
　　　　　(2)　*Peter hat sich an Kopf verletzt
　　　　　(3)　*Peter hat sich an Schultern verletzt
　　　　　(4)　Peter hat sich an Kopf und Schultern verletzt

Da also die diskutierten Fakten über Präpositionalität sich auf isolierte Sätze wie auf Satzfolgen, für die Isenberg den Begriff 'Text' postuliert, gleichermassen verteilen, scheint mir eine darauf sich gründende 'Textgrammatik', wenn man ihre Postulierung an den in Abschnitt 3.1 an den Anfang gestellten Voraussetzungen (1)–(3) misst, nicht hinreichend gerechtfertigt zu sein. Soweit ich die Fakten interpretieren kann: Für eine Modellierung bedingen sie keine signifikante 'Erweiterung der Domäne der Grammatik'.

3.2.4.　Ähnlich ist es mit den linguistischen Fakten, die Isenberg für die Oberflächenrealisierungen ko-referenter Terme im Zusammenhang mit der Präpositionalität bietet. (vgl. die Kap. 6–8). Isenberg bringt wiederum eine Fülle subtiler Beobachtungen und einen sehr weit elaborierten Subkategorisierungsmechanismus, die 'speziellen Referenzmerkmale', die unter den NP-Vorkommen listifiziert werden, wobei es 'Listen für Kombinationsbeschränkungen' für die Komplexbildung aus solchen Merkmalen gibt, die die zulässigen Kombinationen spezifizieren und damit auch die Bedingungen für die Anwendung von 'Textregeln' bzw. die Arten von 'Textverletzungen hinsichtlich der betreffenden Regeln' definieren. Damit ist ein Teil der oben dargelegten 'Manifestation der Koreferenz' systematisch beschrieben, es bleibt aber die Frage offen, ob diese Bedingungen, die ja auch wieder satzintern und satzgrenzenüberschreitend parallel vorliegen (Reflexivierung, lexikalisch-, aber nicht referenz-identische Subjekt- und Objekt-Belegung usw.) tatsächlich Reflex von Texteigenschaften sind, oder ob nicht vielmehr gilt, dass Referenzbeziehungen sich über sprachliche Strukturen aller Komplexitätsgrade erstrecken, dass sie demzufolge auch satzintern und auf Satzfolgen bezogen korrekt oder inkorrekt manifestiert werden können, wobei nicht etwa durch die Bezugsdomäne bedingt grundsätzlich verschiedene Verletzungen definiert werden müssten. Die unterschiedlichen Verletzungsgrade sind auch bei Isenberg vornehmlich danach definiert, ob es sich um Verletzungen der inhärenten lexikalisch-semantischen Merkmale oder um Verletzungen der Parallelität oder der Koreferenzmanifestation handelt. Für das Verhältnis von Referenzbeziehungen und Textkonstitution kann man vorläufig nur folgendes gesichert formulieren: Korrekte Koreferenzmanifestation über eine Folge von Sätzen hinweg ist weder ein hinreichendes noch ein notwendiges Kriterium dafür, dass diese Folge ein intuitiv befriedigender 'Text' ist, wohl aber sind Verletzungen dieser Manifestation ausreichend dafür, eine Folge als abweichend zu disqualifizieren in dem Sinne, dass dadurch die Integration der einzelnen Satzbedeutungen zu einem 'Textganzen' gestört sein kann – und nur in diesem Sinne sind abweichende Realisierungen intendierter Koreferenz 'Textverletzungen'.

Wenn man dies akzeptiert, ist es einleuchtend, dass eine Texttheorie einen Account für die Referenzbeziehungen enthalten muss, aber es ist umgekehrt nicht notwendig, dass von der Analyse der Referenzbeziehungen aus eine Textgrammatik postuliert werden muss. Soviel zur Interpretation der Fakten.

3.2.5. Nun soll der von Isenberg vorgeschlagene Beschreibungsapparat noch kurz vor dem Hintergrund der Postulate (4)–(6) betrachtet werden, also unter dem Gesichtspunkt der Veränderungen im Aufbau der Grammatik.

Isenbergs Grammatik erzeugt 'Basis-Textmarker', die die herkömmlichen P-Marker als Substrukturen enthalten, gemäss seiner Initialregel (p. 73):

(18) $\text{TEXT} \rightarrow (\# S \#)^n$ $(1 \leqslant n < \infty)$

Einem 'Text' aus drei Sätzen würde folglich die Struktur (19) zugewiesen:

(19)

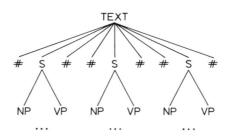

Mit (18) ist zugleich die formale Entsprechung der 'Erweiterung der Domäne der Grammatik' gegeben, deren Funktion es ist, durch Erweiterung der Strukturbäume eine erweiterte Domäne für Regelanwendungen zu liefern. Der technische Sinn der Aufstockung ist, dass durch TEXT und $\# S \#$ Zyklengrenzen für Regelanwendungen gegeben werden. Neben den herkömmlichen Transformationsregeln, die zyklisch operieren in der Domäne, die durch $\# S \#$ begrenzt ist, gibt es in Isenbergs Modell sog. Text-Regeln transformationellen Charakters, die post-zyklisch operieren und aus einer Folge von $\# S \#$ – Symbolen nach weitausgreifenden Bedingungen bestimmte # S # – Ableitungen eliminieren. Die Schwierigkeit aber besteht darin, für die durch (18) bestimmte Superstruktur über # S # eine theoretisch signifikante Interpretation zu finden. Alle drei eine Baumstruktur definierenden Beziehungen bleiben für diese Superstruktur linguistisch uninterpretiert:

(1) Was besagt die Relation [# S #, TEXT]? (Dominanz)
(2) Welche Beziehung besteht zwischen zwei # S # unter TEXT? (Verkettung)
(3) Gibt es eine lineare Ordnung der # S # unter TEXT und was besagt sie und wie wird sie mit den Text-Regeln abgestimmt?

Die Fragen (1) und (2), nämlich die der sachgerechten Interpretation der P-Marker konstituierenden 'ist-ein'-Relation und der Relation zwischen Geschwisterknoten, sind für die Koordinationsbeschreibung ebensowenig gelöst wie hier, wo sie unter anderem Namen auftreten. So gesehen werden auch hier ungelöste Fragen weitergeschleppt und diese Art von 'Textgrammatik' ist weder im Bestand ihrer Komponenten, noch im Hinblick auf ihre Regeln und Repräsentationsebenen qualitativ verschieden von einem herkömmlichen Satzgrammatik-Modell.

Ich will nun einige Gegenvorschläge unterbreiten, die in der Blickrichtung 'vom Satz zum Text' liegen und meines Erachtens hinsichtlich ihrer Konsequenzen für das Beschreibungsmodell den anfangs aufgestellten Voraussetzungen (1)–(6) eher entsprechen als die bisher diskutierten, wenngleich es Fakten sind, die auch wiederum nur einige Aspekte von 'Text' ausmachen.

3.3. *'Text' als Integrationsergebnis von Satzbedeutungen*

3.3.1. Es gibt eine Reihe von Regularitäten zur Kohärenz sprachlicher Gebilde, deren Wirkungsbereich insofern über die Satzgrenze hinausgeht, als dabei kognitive Operationen involviert sind, die über Satzbedeutungen ausgeführt werden. Der 'Textaspekt' der Kohärenz ist der folgende: Während die Kohärenz eines Satzes (wie komplex er auch sei) den Regeln folgt, nach denen seine syntaktisch kategorisierten und lexikalisch belegten Konstituenten zu einer Satzbedeutung amalgamiert werden, wird die Kohärenz eines 'Textes' bestimmt durch die Integration von Satzbedeutungen zu übergreifenden Einheiten. Satzbedeutungen repräsentieren – vereinfacht gesprochen – Sachverhalte, ihre sprachliche Manifestation unterliegt zumindest partiell einzelsprachlichen Regeln. Die Integration von Satzbedeutungen zu text-konstituierenden Komplexen repräsentiert Zusammenhänge zwischen Sachverhalten. Die dabei in Regeln zu fassenden Operationen sind allgemein kognitiver Natur, also universell. Hierzu zwei Beispiele, die für weite Untersuchungsfelder zu 'Text'-Aspekten stehen.

3.3.2. *Gemeinsame Einordnungsinstanz.* Den Integrationsmechanismus kann man z.b. bei der Interpretation koordinierter Sätze studieren. Dabei würde ich den Konjunktionen den Status von Satzoperatoren zuschreiben, die den 'Umgang' mit den Satzbedeutungen der Konjunktsätze steuern. Der durch die Koordination fundierte Zusammenhang wird ausgehend von der Satzbedeutung der Konjunktsätze durch Operationen wie: Auffinden von Strukturparallelen, Deduktionen aus Komponenten von Satzbedeutungen, Supplierung von Voraussetzungen[6] hergestellt und bildet sozusagen eine semantische Superstruktur. Diese Superstruktur kann, aber muss nicht, explizit in einem Kontextsatz auftreten, in dem der den Zusammenhang reflektierende Gesichtspunkt verbalisiert wird. Die jeweils konstituierte Superstruktur nenne ich 'gemeinsame Einordnungsinstanz'. Man vergleiche die folgenden Satzreihen, wo trotz jeweils gleicher erster Konjunktsätze jeweils verschiedene Zusammenhänge deduziert werden, letztere werden der Illustration halber in einem durch '/' abgetrennten Kontextsatz verbalisiert.

(20)   Peter lernt Französisch und Susi besucht einen Stenokurs./ Die QUALIFIZIERUNGSLEHRGÄNGE sind angelaufen.

(21)   Peter lernt Französisch, Susi verehrt Balzac und Rudi ist Romanist. /Die ganze Familie ist FRANCOPHIL.

(22)   Peter lernt Französisch, Susi wäscht ab und Rudi sitzt vorm Fernseher. /Die Kinder sind IM MOMENT BESCHÄFTIGT.

Die hervorgehobenen Teile der Kontextsätze sind eine der möglichen Manifestationen des aus den Konjunktsatzbedeutungen deduzierten übergeordneten Gesichtspunktes. Trotz gewisser Varianz stellen sie jedoch das notwendige Integrationsmoment dar. Die Kontextsätze könnten unter den Folgen (20)–(23) nicht ausgetauscht werden, ohne das nicht-akzeptable 'Texte' entstünden. Die Nicht-Akzeptabilität beruhte dann auf Inkongruenz von deduzierter Superstruktur und explizit verbalisierter. Aus der zugrunde liegenden, isoliert 'neutralen' Satzbedeutung von *Peter lernt Französisch* (die natürlich bei (20) und (21) das Merkmal 'habituell', bei

---

[6] Auf die gesamte Präsuppositionsproblematik will ich hier nicht eingehen. Zweifellos muss sie auch in Untersuchungen zu 'Text'-Aspekten aufgenommen werden. Bei den hier angedeuteten Voraussetzungen handelt es sich nicht um die von lexikalischen Einheiten, sondern um z.B. bestimmte Annahmen über die normale Welterfahrung oder über Konventionen der Dialogführung u.ä., um Dinge also, die nur am Saume noch linguistisch systematisierbar sind.

(22) aber 'aktuell' haben muss; der Satz wird also kontextbedingt disambiguiert) werden in Abhängigkeit von der Bedeutungsstruktur der übrigen Konjunktsätze, jeweils andere semantische Portionen ausgegliedert, die als Bausteine für den Integrationsgesichtspunkt in die 'Text'-Konstitution eingehen. Die ganze Grammatik der Koordination, und damit eines der wichtigsten Mittel der 'Text'-Komposition, hat es mit diesen Bedingungen der Deduktion semantischer Gemeinsamkeiten zu tun, aus denen heraus unter Einschaltung vieler Vermittlungsinstanzen ein in Sach-, Situations- und Modellzusammenhänge eingebetteter 'Text'-Sinn gewonnen wird. Gerade darauf beruht übrigens auch die tatsächlich 'Satz' und 'Text' differenzierende Möglichkeit der Reduktion oder Verdichtung. Bei Sätzen erfolgt diese nach syntaktisch determinierten Regeln, bei 'Texten' nach Prinzipien der eben skizzierten Integration von Satzbedeutungen. Dass die letzteren aber auch für die Satzsyntax, die 'traditionelle', beachtet werden müssen, ergibt sich aus der Tatsache, dass die Grenzen der semantischen Portionen aus den Satzbedeutungen, die für die Einordnungsinstanz tragend werden, auch syntaktisch reflektiert werden. So ist es zu erklären, weshalb

(23)   Die Sonne scheint und die Vöglein singen

eine akzeptable Folge ist; es werden *zwei* Sachverhalte eingeordnet, weshalb aber andererseits die mutmasslich transformationelle Ableitung von (23) in der Form[7]

(24)   Die Sonne und die Vöglein scheinen bzw. singen

kaum akzeptabel ist: Hier wird *ein* Sachverhalt suggeriert, die semantischen Gemeinsamkeiten abzuleiten ist einmal auf die NP-Domäne und einmal auf die Verb-Domäne eingegrenzt, sinnvolle übergeordnete Gesichtspunkte sind offenbar nicht deduzierbar. Hier wird wieder deutlich, was in Abschnitt 2. über die zentrale Rolle des Satzes als Konstitutivum für die Aufteilung der Welt in Sachverhalte gesagt wurde.

3.3.3.   *Nicht-rekonstruierbare Tilgungen.* Die Gesamtbedeutung der synonymen Folgen (25) und (26) kann als ziemlich 'direkt', d.h. als explizit verbalisierte, Kausalrelation interpretiert werden.

(25)   Es hat Frost gegeben und die Blumen sind erfroren

(26)   Die Blumen sind erfroren, denn es hat Frost gegeben

---

[7] Das Problem hat McCawley (Vortrag in Berlin, 1969) formuliert, jedoch ohne 'idea, what's going on here'.

Anders ist es bei

(27)   Es hat Frost gegeben, denn die Blumen sind erfroren

wo eine diagnostische Interpretation vorliegt, deren semantische Repräsentation es erfordert, dass man das fehlende Zwischenglied mitrepräsentiert.
Sätze nach *denn* haben die Voraussetzung 'faktiv' (im Sinne der Kiparskys),
der erste Konjunktsatz in (27) aber bezeichnet einen reduktiv erschlossenen
Sachverhalt. Explizit: "Die Blumen sind erfroren. Daraus schliesse ich,
dass es Frost gegeben haben muss". Die Tatsache, dass hier induktiv er-
schlossen und nicht deduktiv abgeleitet wird wie in (25) und (26), muss
beschrieben werden. Ähnlich bei sog. epistemischen Modalverben. Ein
anderer Faktenbereich, wo 'Vermittlersätze' repräsentiert werden müssen,
um den Integrationszusammenhang zu erfassen, sind Verknüpfungen
verschiedener Satztypen:

(28)   Wann ist Peter weggegangen oder hast du nicht auf die Uhr
           geschaut?
(29)   Verschwinde jetzt, denn ich bin müde!

Die hier fehlenden Zwischenglieder sind von grundsätzlich anderer Art
als an der Oberfläche fehlende aus der Basissyntax rekonstruierbare Satz-
glieder, wie sie bisher in der Grammatik behandelt wurden.

3.3.4.   Der für die skizzierten Koordinationsprobleme wie für die Tilgungen
gemeinsame Beschreibungsgegenstand, der eben, wie ich glaube, eine
notwendige Zwischenstufe zu einer 'Textgrammatik' darstellt, ist der, dass
die semantische Repräsentation solcher Satzkomplexe ihre Interpretation
als Sachverhaltszusammenhänge wiedergeben muss als Integration von
Satzbedeutungen. Dies sind in gewissem Sinne modellsprengende Fakten
und ihre Bewältigung erfordert die Hinzunahme neuer Beschreibungsmittel: Die Eingliederung von Regeln, die logische Deduktionen aus Satzbedeutungen und verschiedene andere Operationen mit semantischem
Material (Bezugnahme auf Kenntnisse, Situationstypen usw.) als Kom-
petenzleistungen darzustellen gestatten. Auf diesem Wege vollzieht sich
eine mögliche Annäherung 'vom Satz zum Text'.

IV. BLICKRICHTUNG 2 'VOM TEXT ZUM SATZ'

4.1.   Dieser Zugang zur Aufstellung einer 'Texttheorie' ist viel seltener
explizit anzutreffen. Er ist keineswegs die einfache Umkehrung von Blickrichtung 1 oder etwa deduktiv, während jene induktiv zu verstehen wäre,

oder dieser analytisch und jene synthetisch, obgleich solche Momente schon zuzuordnen wären. Aber da beide Zugänge noch im semi-theoretischen Stadium stecken, sind solche Unterscheidungen verfrüht.

Diskutieren wir diesen Zugang anhand der von Isenberg (1970: 3) aufgestellten Forderung, dass eine linguistische Texttheorie von den Faktoren auszugehen hätte, die "die globale Strukturierung von Texten determinieren". Isenbergs anschliessender Argumentationsgang umfasst – obwohl von ihm vermischt – zwei zu unterscheidende Faktengruppen, deren theoriebezogene Implikationen ich mit Blickrichtung 2a und 2b benennen und getrennt diskutieren will.

4.2. *Blickrichtung 2a*

Diese Blickrichtung geht von der Annahme aus, dass 'Text' die eigentliche Seinsweise aller Äusserungsformen in der sprachlichen Kommunikation ist. Das heisst, 'Text' ist der Generalnenner für Äusserungen. Äusserungen sind gemäss dieser Auffassung kommunikative Gebilde, denen Sätze zugrunde liegen (nach Art des Type-Token-Verhältnisses), was ihre interne 'grammatische', d.h. durch die Regeln des Sprachsystems vorgeschriebene Struktur betrifft. Äusserungen werden aber darüber hinaus durch weitere Determinanten der Kommunikation wie Zweck der Mitteilung, Verhältnis der Kommunikationspartner, Modus der Kommunikation, Anlass und Gegenstand der Kommunikation (im weiteren Sinne als 'Thema' oder 'topic' zu verstehen, also als etwas nicht notwendig explizit Genanntes) charakterisiert, kurzum durch eine Reihe von Faktoren, die man vorläufig als 'pragmatisch' eingeordnet hat.

Nimmt man nun einen solchen Faktor oder mehrere zusammen in verschiedener Kombination als Kriterien, so lassen sich damit verschiedene Äusserungstypen bilden (z.B. 'Nachricht', 'Appell', 'Kundgabe' usw.), die sämtlich irgendwie unterschiedbare kommunikative Gesten oder Grundhaltungen kennzeichnen.[8] Entsprechend bilden Äusserungen dann einen 'Kundgabetext', einen 'Nachrichtentext' usw. . . . . 'Text' an sich kommt gar nicht vor, sondern geht als undefinierter Term in das Hilfsvokabular der Theorie ein, weil er nur Bestandteil der eigentlich zu explizierenden Begriffsbildungen wie "Kundgabetext" usw. ist. Wir sehen, dass der hier verwendete Textbegriff mit dem in Blickrichtung 1 intuitiv angenommenen Textbegriff wenig zu tun hat. Zur Abgrenzung von Blickrichtung 1 gilt ferner: Da Äusserungen unter dem Aspekt der kommunikativen Gesten im obengenannten Sinne hinsichtlich ihrer Länge und Komplexität nur nach der

---

[8] Nicht zufällig sind die genannten Grundhaltungen identisch mit den drei Funktionen der Sprache in Bühlers Modell.

Seite des Minimums (das nicht 'Satz' ist) abgegrenzt sind, andererseits aber beliebig viele Sätze in beliebiger Komplexität umfassen können, und dennoch als Ganzes der Charakterisierung 'Nachricht' oder 'Appell' usw. genügen können, kann diese Theorie für die für Blickrichtung 1 relevante Differenzierung Satz vs. Text nichts beitragen, es ist auch nicht ihre Aufgabe. Insgesamt hat Blickrichtung 2a also primär andere Fakten und Zusammenhänge zum Gegenstand als Blickrichtung 1. Eine Verbindung zwischen beiden kann über die folgende Hypothese hergestellt werden:

(30)   Kommunikative Charakterisierungen wie 'Nachricht', 'Appell' usw. sind zu interpretieren als Projektionen auf die in den Äusserungen enthaltenen Satzbedeutungen mit der Massgabe, dass zwischen dem Typ der kommunikativen Charakteristik (Gestus) und der Verbalisierung von Satzbedeutungen zu Äusserungen eine Auswahlfunktion wechselseitig etabliert werden kann.

Um diese Hypothese zu verifizieren und um dann eine zusammenhängende Theorie zu konstruieren, die Fakten und Zusammenhänge aus beiden Blickrichtungen integriert, ist folgendes notwendig zu beachten: Die Voraussetzungen von Blickrichtung 2a müssen zutreffen, nämlich:

(1)   Jedes sprachliche Gebilde kann mit einer solchen kommunikativen Charakteristik versehen werden.

(2)   Es gibt Relationen der in (30) beschriebenen Art.

und es muss gezeigt werden, was zwischen den in (30) genannten Ebenen vermittelt. Um dies zu können, braucht man zumindest die folgenden theoretischen Mittel:

(31)   (a) Eine Grammatik, die das, was mit Blickrichtung 1 intendiert ist, adäquat leistet, u.a. also eine umfassende Beschreibung der Integrationsmöglichkeiten von Satzbedeutungen liefert.

(b) Eine Spezifizierung der kommunikativen Charakteristiken in einer eigenständigen Theorie.

(c) Eine Bestimmung der Zuordnung von Elementen aus (b) auf abgrenzbare Teilmechanismen aus der Grammatik von (a).

(d) Einen Formalismus, der (b) über (c) auf (a) bezieht und dadurch die Konstruktion einer zusammenhängenden Theorie gestattet.

Dies scheint mir als methodisches Vorgehen nötig zu sein, um die genannten

Faktoren der 'globalen Textstruktur' mit den Explicanda aus den Abschnitten in einen Beschreibungszusammenhang zu bringen.

Betrachten wir nun einen weiteren Aspekt, der aus der Blickrichtung
'vom Text zum Satz' für die 'globale Strukturierung von Texten' angeführt
wird.

4.3. *Blickrichtung 2b*

4.3.1. Isenberg (1970: 12) bringt als Beispiel für globale Strukturiertheit
eines 'Mehr-Satz-Textes' vom Typ 'Erzählung' in Anlehnung an Labov/
Waletzky (1967) eine Aufzählung der kompositorischen Rollen, die einzelne Abschnitte des Text-Ganzen charakterisieren. So besteht ein Erzähltext aus folgenden kompositorischen Elementen: (1) Orientierung; (2)
Komplizierung; (3) Bewertung; (4) Lösung; (5) Coda. Diese Anatomie ist
für die Analyse der Belege und Analyseabsicht der Autoren vollkommen
überzeugend. Aber ihr Gegenstand und ihre Fragestellung haben mit den
in Blickrichtung 1 und dem von Isenberg (1970 bis Seite 12) (= Blickrichtung 2a) gemeinten bestenfalls einen schmalen Durchschnitt. Labov/
Waletzky setzen ein literarisches Gebilde 'Erzählung' anderen literarischen
Gebilden wie 'Sage', 'Märchen', 'Epos', 'Anekdote' usw. gegenüber, fragen
nach Unterschieden in der Komposition und Performation solcher Gebilde
und konzentrieren sich auf die Spezifik mündlich vorgetragener Geschichten
als Verbalisierungen persönlicher Erfahrungen der Erzähler und zugleich
als Mittel der Selbstdarstellung im sozialen Kontext. Obwohl die Autoren
von der Globalcharakterisierung 'Erzählung' über die Zerlegung in Abschnitte daraus mit den genannten Rollen 'zum Satz' kommen, in dem sie
für die Erfüllung der jeweiligen Rolle möglicherweise typische Kennzeichen
der Satzverknüpfung, Pausensetzung, Emphaseelementen usw. heraus-
zufinden suchen, so ist damit weder eine Verbindung von Satz zu 'Text' im
Sinne von Blickrichtung 1 noch eine unmittelbare Einwirkung von 'globaler
Strukturierung' auf die Satzstrukturierung im Sinne von Blickrichtung 2a
intendiert. Man kann 2a und 2b nicht kollabieren, denn die Autoren der
Untersuchung zur Komposition einer 'Erzählung' interpretieren die auf der
Ebene der (Oberflächen-) Satzstruktur gefundenen Kennzeichen z.T. als
Symptome der Zugehörigkeit zu einer bestimmten sozialen Gruppe, andere
als Niederschlag von Imponierhaltungen, wieder andere als Grenzmarken
für Abschnitte der Erzählstrategie. Solche Bewertungen bilden, der Unter-
suchungsabsicht der Autoren gemäss, auch den Kriterienrahmen für die
von ihnen vorgeschlagene Rollenzuordnung für die Abschnitte eines
Kompositionsschemas für 'Erzählung'. Somit stehen weder 'Erzähltext'
aus 2b mit 'Nachrichtentext' oder 'Kundgabetext' aus 2a auf einer theore-

tischen Ebene, noch gilt, dass kompositorische Rollenkonzepte wie 'Komplizierung', 'Bewertung', 'Coda' aus 2b in der gleichen Weise die Struktur
von Äusserungen organisieren wie kommunikative Grundhaltungen der
Art 'Nachricht', 'Appell' aus 2a. Wir sehen, wieder ist der primäre Unter-
suchungsgegenstand ein anderer und demgemäss sind die Begriffsbildungen
spezifisch.

4.3.2.　Fragen wir nun, wie sieht eine aus Blickrichtung 2b hervorgehende
Theorie aus und wie ist diese mit 1 und 2a zu verbinden. Eine Theorie aus
2b hat folgende hypothetisch formulierten Zusammenhänge im Blick:

(32)　　　(a) Eine Teilmenge möglicher – in der Regel komplexer –
　　　　　　　sprachlicher Gebilde ist einem bestimmten (unabhängig
　　　　　　　entwickelten) Kriteriensatz nach in Kompositionstypen zu
　　　　　　　klassifizieren ('Erzählung', 'Epos', 'Märchen', 'Witz' usw.).

　　　　　(b) Zur Explikation von (a) werden ausgewählte sprachliche
　　　　　　　Gebilde in Abschnitte segmentiert gemäss einem wiederum
　　　　　　　unabhängigen Kriteriensatz. Die Segmentierung in Ab-
　　　　　　　schnitte erfolgt aufgrund ihrer Distinktion mithilfe dieser
　　　　　　　Kriterien, die damit jedem Segment zugleich eine 'dramatur-
　　　　　　　gische Rolle' zuweisen, dergestalt, dass eine kombinatorisch
　　　　　　　eingeschränkte Serie solcher Rollen das Kompositions-
　　　　　　　schema einer Äusserung im Hinblick auf einen Komposi-
　　　　　　　tionstyp bildet, diesen also definiert.

Die grösste Schwierigkeit liegt hier natürlich im Herausfinden eines angemessenen Kriteriensatzes für (b), der ja in der Zielstellung den tradierten
Kriteriensatz von (a) ersetzen bzw. explizieren soll. Aber der Theorie-
konstrukteur für 2b ist zunächst ganz unabhängig, nur ein Teil der ihn
interessierenden Kriterien hängt mit den nach Blickrichtung 1 und 2a zu
beschreibenden Fakten zusammen, diese bilden auch die Brücke für eine
Integration der Theorie 2b in die eigentliche Domäne der Grammatik. Sie
erfordert die Beantwortung folgender Frage:

(33)　　　In welcher Weise determiniert ein Kompositionstyp der ge-
　　　　　nannten Art, repräsentiert durch ein Rollenschema, die Verbali-
　　　　　sierungsvarianten der den Äusserungen zugrundeliegenden
　　　　　Satzbedeutungen?

Dies umfasst zumindest folgende Teilfragen:

(34)　　　(a) In welcher Weise interrelieren die Abschnitte eines Rollen-
　　　　　　　schemas mit den in 4.1 diskutierten kommunikativen

Charakteristiken? (Da ja jede Äusserung einer solchen
zuzuordnen ist, können die in einen Kompositionsabschnitt
vorkommenden Äusserungen ja auch entsprechend determiniert werden)

(b) In welcher Weise gibt es eine Zuordnung von Rollen und
Verbalisierungsvariation von Satzbedeutungen – mit oder
ohne intermittierende kommunikative Charakteristiken?

(c) Was sind die Vermittlungsinstanzen dieser Zuordnung und
wie sind sie formal zu explizieren?

(d) Was sind die 'Umrechnungsmoduli', die die Theorie (34)
(a)–(c) mit Theorie (31)(b)–(d) und/oder der Theorie von
Blickrichtung 1 zu verbinden gestatten?

Die mögliche Theorie zu 2b ist spezifischer als die aus Blickrichtung 1 und
2a, sie setzt sie in einem bestimmten Sinne sogar·voraus, z.B. was jenen
Anteil am Kriteriensatz aus (32)(b) angeht, der sich auf Oberflächenstrukturen bezieht.

4.3.3.   Der schmale Durchschnitt der beiden Ansätze, kurz 'Integrations-
aspekt' und 'Pragmatik' genannt (Blickrichtung 1 und 2a) mit einer 'Texttheorie' des 'Narrativen', was wir hier am Beispiel der Analyse von Labov/
Waletzky exemplifizieren, besteht in folgenden gemeinsamen Explicanda:

(1)   Kohärenz einer Menge aufeinanderfolgender Äusserungen durch
ein Abbildungsverhältnis zwischen zeitlicher Abfolge der erzählten Ereignisse und zeitlicher Abfolge (Anordnung) des Erzählens der Ereignisse. Die
Autoren nennen das 'referential function' einer Erzählung. Solche Zusammenhänge sind Gegenstand einer Texttheorie in jedem Sinne, insofern
als sie ein Strukturmoment hinreichend komplexer Äusserungen (oder
Satzkomplexionen) darstellen.

(2)   Angenommen, der Inhalt einer komplexen Äusserung vom Typ
'Erzählung' besteht darin, dass eine Menge von einzelnen Sachverhalten
(oder Ereignissen) dargestellt und miteinander in Zusammenhang gebracht
werden soll. Dann kann man sich vorstellen, dass es hierfür eine abstrakte,
neutrale, logisch-semantische Repräsentation gibt, für die eine Menge von
Verbalisierungsvarianten existieren, die untereinander nun nach verschiedenen Kriterien verglichen werden können. Eine Teilmenge daraus ist
semantisch äquivalent und paarweise durch Transformationen im herkömmlichen Sinne aufeinander zu beziehen, eine andere Teilmenge ist
ebenfalls semantisch äquivalent, aber ihre paarweise Zuordnung erfordert
prälexikalische Transformationen, Deduktionen und möglicherweise andere,
auf logischer Äquivalenz basierende Operationen. Über diese allen Varian-

ten bis zu dieser Stufe gemeinsamen semantischen Interpretation hinaus gibt es nun aber Differenzierungen in den Verbalisierungsvarianten, die sich in der Oberflächenstrukturiertheit niederschlagen. Diese Differenzierungen sind zurückzuführen auf kommunikative Beigaben unterschiedlichster Art zu der 'neutralen' semantischen Interpretation, die allen Varianten gemeinsam ist.

V. SCHLUSSBEMERKUNGEN

Zusammenfassend will ich noch einmal graphisch verdeutlichen, wie ich den mit den drei diskutierten Zugängen zum Phänomen 'Text' verbundenen faktischen und theoriebezogenen Zusammenhang sehe. Die Integration der drei Theorien, die alle jeweils legitim wesentliche Aspekte von 'Text' erfassen, geschieht nicht durch irgendwie geartete Zusammenballung oder durch einseitige 'Erweiterung der Domäne', sondern sie wird möglich in dem Masse, wie zwischen den von einzelnen Theorien jeweils erfassten Fakten Zusammenhänge hergestellt werden können. Die Interpenetration der Theorien ist symbolisiert durch Konturüberschneidungen. Die mit den jeweiligen Blickrichtungen verbundenen Ausgangsbeobachtungen erscheinen als geometrische Figur, das gestrichelte Pendant steht für die Gesamtheit der theoretischen Aussagen über diese Beobachtungsdaten.

(35)

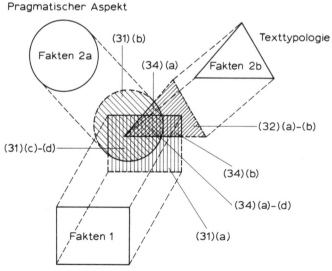

Wenn man annimmt, dass jede Theorie ihren eigenen Formalismus aus-
gebildet hat, dann kann man durch die Anzahl der Schraffurüberkreuzungen
die Anzahl der zur Vermittlung zwischen den Formalismen notwendigen
Zuordnungsfunktionen darstellen, also das, was in (31)(c)–(d) und (34)
(c)–(d) postuliert wurde.

Die in (35) graphisch veranschaulichten Zusammenhänge von separaten
Teiltheorien bei der Konstituierung einer integrativen Gesamttheorie sind
auch in allgemeiner Form gültig und können definitorisch formuliert
werden. Die Definition für 'theoretisch explizierbarer Zusammenhang' entspricht den Prinzipien, die Ruben und Wolter (1969) unabhängig von unseren
Überlegungen für die Definition des Modellbegriffs vorgeschlagen haben.
Ein Unterschied ist: Wir befinden uns bei der Konstruktion einer Gesamttheorie aus Teiltheorien auf der nächstfolgenden Stufe der Modellbildung.
Eine mögliche Fassung der relevanten Definition lautet dann:

(36)   Es seien A und B Fakten oder Faktenbereiche, die in Aussagen-
         form im Kenntnisvorrat adäquat repräsentiert sind. A und B
         stehen dann in einem *theoretisch explizierbaren Zusammenhang*,
         wenn es eine Theorie $\mathfrak{A}$ über A und eine Theorie $\mathfrak{B}$ über B gibt,
         die in der Weise aufeinander bezogen sind, dass gilt:
         (1) Ausgehend von A gelangt man in Termen von $\mathfrak{A}$ zu einer
             Aussage P_i über A aus der Menge $P_1, \ldots, P_n$ aus $\mathfrak{A}$.
         (2) Ausgehend von B gelangt man in Termen von $\mathfrak{B}$ zu einer
             Aussage Q_j über B aus der Menge $Q_1, \ldots, Q_m$ aus $\mathfrak{B}$.
         (3) P_i bezüglich A wird in $\mathfrak{A}$ wahr gdw. Q_j über B in $\mathfrak{B}$ wahr
             wird.

Als einfaches Illustrationsbeispiel nehmen wir an, A sei das Phänomen der
Gezeiten, B sei der Erscheinung des Mondumlaufs um die Erde. Nehmen
wir weiter an, die Theorie über die Gezeiten enthielte als Aussage P_i:

(i)   Zum Zeitpunkt t_k tritt im Gebiet der geographischen Koordi-
         naten $(L; B)$ Flut auf.

Und die Theorie über den Mondumlauf enthielte als Q_j die Aussage:

(ii)   Zum Zeitpunkt t_1 steht der Mond in einem Einfallswinkel α
         zum Gebiet $(L; B)$.

Wenn nun (i) wahr ist gdw. (ii) wahr ist – was empirisch leicht überprüfbar
ist – dann ist mit dieser Äquivalenz der Grundstock für eine Theorie gelegt,

die einen Zusammenhang von Gezeiten und Mondumlauf theoretisch
fixiert hat und zu einer erklärenden Theorie dieses Zusammenhangs ausgebaut werden kann. Dass historisch gesehen die Theoriebildung über die
Ursache der Gezeiten wahrscheinlich anders verlaufen ist als hier in unserer
Rekonstruktion gibt für das Beispiel keinen Ausschlag. Andere Beispiele,
die nun auch historisch 'stimmen', liessen sich zeigen für formalisierte
Theorien, etwa wenn P_i aus $\mathfrak{A}$ eine Aussage aus der Theorie des Prädikaten-
kalküls ist und Q_j aus $\mathfrak{B}$ eine Aussage aus der Mengentheorie, und wenn
beide werteverlaufsgleich, also äquivalent, sind.

Ich will nun aber (36) für den Fall einer integrativen Texttheorie illustrativ
belegen. Dazu wollen wir annehmen, dass das allgemein bekannte Phänomen
'Nachrichtensendung' einmal als A erscheint, nämlich als Gegenstand einer
Theorie 2b 'Texttypologie', und einmal als B, nämlich als Gegenstand
einer Theorie 1 'Text als Integrationsergebnis'. Dass A und B hier in einund-
demselben empirischen Phänomen gründen ändert nichts daran, dass A und
B als Gegenstände einer jeweils nur bestimmte Aspekte und Merkmale des
empirischen Gegenstands erfassenden Theorie so verschieden sind wie
Gezeiten und Mondumlauf (vgl. auch in diesem Zusammenhang Ruben
und Wolter (1969: p. 1232 ff.)).

Nun sei P_i eine Aussage über Nachrichtensendung in Termen der Theorie 2b (Texttypologie):

(iii)   Ein Kompositionsschema ORIENTIERUNG (Subtyp: Ankündi-
          gung der Mitteilungsabsicht) – MITTEILUNG₁ – ... – MITTEIL-
          UNG$_n$ – CODA (Subtyp: explizite Abkündigung) konstituiert den
          Texttyp 'Nachrichtensendung'.

Dabei seien ORIENTIERUNG, MITTEILUNG, CODA kompositorische Rollenkonzepte wie die unter 4.2 oben diskutierten. Das Spezifische dieses Schemas
gegenüber den entsprechenden Schemata für 'Erzählung' oder 'Witz' mag
darin bestehen, dass ein dramaturgisch wenig strukturierter Mittelteil
(MITTEILUNG₁ – ... – MITTEILUNG$_n$) durch token-reflexive An- und Abkündi-
gung begrenzt wird. Dass die Abfolge der Mitteilungen in einer Nachrichtensendung nach einer zusätzlichen Dimension 'propagandistische
Wichtigkeit' geordnet wird, so dass die Hierarchie der Wichtigkeit der
mitzuteilenden Sachverhalte auf die Erwähnungsfolge ihrer Mitteilung abgebildet wird, ist ein Aspekt, der wiederum gesondert zu betrachten ist und
in einem Grenzbereich zwischen Theorie 2a 'Pragmatik' und einer Theorie
der Konnotationen liegt. Für die Theorie 2b ist die Charakterisierung in
(iii) zunächst hinreichend. Sodann sei Q_j eine Aussage über Nachrichtensendung in Termen der Theorie 1 ('Text als Integrationsergebnis'):

(iv)   Ein Eröffnungssatz bzw. ein Abschlusssatz wie *Sie hören Nach-richten* (bzw. *Das waren die Nachrichten*) stellt die explizite Einordnungsinstanz dar für die Integration der nachfolgend (bzw. voraufgehend) asyndetisch aneinandergereihten Sätze zu einem kohärenten Text des Typs 'Nachrichtensendung'.

Die Vertextung dieser Satzmenge, die inhaltlich völlig unzusammenhängende Mitteilungen umfasst, geschieht nicht durch lineare Ordnungsbeziehungen oder semantische Abhängigkeiten, sondern dadurch, dass jeder der asynde-tisch koordinierten Ein- oder Mehrsatz-Abschnitte als Spezifikation der allem gemeinsamen Einordnungsinstanz 'Nachrichten' interpretiert wird.

Nun können wir sagen, dass bezüglich des Phänomens 'Nachrichten-sendung' als texttheoretischen Untersuchungsobjekt die Aussage (iii) in Theorie 2b gerechtfertigt ist gdw. (iv) in Theorie 1 gerechtfertig ist. Dabei ist 'gerechtfertigt' zu verstehen im Sinne von 'Wahrheitsgehalt hypothetischer Aussagen', wie sie bei empirisch kontrollierter Theoriebildung beständig vorkommen. Mit dieser Beziehung zwischen (iii) und (iv) ist die Basis gegeben für eine *Theoretisierung des Zusammenhangs* der in (iii) und (iv) analysierten Aspekte des Phänomens 'Nachrichtensendung'. So zum Beispiel, dass man nun Zuordnungen herstellen kann zwischen theoretischen Einheiten wie 'Orientierung' in (iii) und Einheiten wie 'Einordnungsinstanz: 'Nach-richten'' in (iv) bzw. Zuordnungen zwischen der dramaturgisch wenig strukturierten Folge von MITTEILUNGEN in (iii) und der asyndetischen Anreihung in (iv). Solche Zuordnungen wurden in (33) und (34)(a–d) oben postuliert. Diese Zuordnungen leisten nun die Integration der Blickrichtung 'vom Satz zum Text' (vertreten durch (iv)) mit der Blickrichtung 'vom Text zum Satz' (vertreten durch (iii)) in einer Gesamttheorie. Die Zuordnungen zwischen den Einheiten der Analyse aus (iii) und (iv) jeweils ermöglichen bei entsprechender Elaboriertheit die Etablierung einer Überführungsfunktion, die es gestattet, Aussagen aus der Theorie 2b in der Theorie 1 zu inter-pretieren. Verallgemeinernd kann man daher im Anschluss an (36) formu-lieren:

(37)   Die Menge der durch Äquivalenz gebildeten Paare von Aussagen über A aus $\mathfrak{A}$ und Aussagen über B aus $\mathfrak{B}$ bildet die Grundlage für eine Theorie $\mathfrak{T}$, die die Zusammenhänge von A und B zu fixieren und zu erklären gestattet.

(38)   Die Theorie $\mathfrak{T}$ verfügt über eine Überführungsfunktion zwischen Aussagen aus $\mathfrak{A}$ und Aussagen aus $\mathfrak{B}$, auf der auch die Her-leitung der Äquivalenz von P_i aus $\mathfrak{A}$ mit Q_j aus $\mathfrak{B}$ beruht.*

Deutsche Akademie der Wissenschaften, Berlin

* Manfred Bierwisch, Karl Erich Heidolph, Horst Isenberg und Renate Steinitz habe ich für hilfreiche Kritiken zu danken.

LITERATUR

Annear, S.: 1968, *Relative Clauses and Conjunctions*, Pola 2, Ohio.

Bierwisch, M.: 1969, 'Semantics and Primary Stress Placement', unpubl. ms., Berlin.

Cantrall, W.: 1969, 'Pitch, Stress and Grammatical Relations', *Papers from the 5th Regional Meeting of the CLS*, Chicago.

Chomsky, N.: 1965, *Aspects of the Theory of Syntax*, Cambridge, Mass.: MIT Press.

Dressler, W.: 1971, 'Towards a Discourse Grammar', *Papers from the 7th Regional Meeting of CLS 1971*, Chicago.

Heidolph, K. E.: 1966, 'Kontextbeziehungen zwischen Sätzen in einer generativen Grammatik *Kybernetika* **2**, 274–81; auch in: H. Steger (ed.): *Vorschläge für eine Strukturale Grammatik des Deutschen*, Darmstadt: Wiss. Buchgemeinschaft, 1970.

Heidolph, K. E.: 1971, 'Zur grammatischen Struktur von Texten'. Beitrag zu der Kollektivarbeit: B. Goretzki, B. Haftka, K. E. Heidolph, H. Isenberg, E. Agricola: *Aspekte der Linguistischen Behandlung von Texten*; Erscheint in *Textlinguistik* **2**, Dresden.

Isenberg, H.: 1968a, *Das Direkte Objekt im Spanischen* (= *Studia Grammatica IX*), Berlin: Akademie-Verlag.

Isenberg, H.: 1968b, 'Überlegungen zur Texttheorie'. *ASG-Bericht* Nr. 2, 1–18, Berlin: DAW; auch in: J. Ihwe (ed.), *Literaturwissenschaft und Linguistik: Ergebnisse und Perspektiven*, Bd. 1, Bad Homburg v.d. H.: Athenäum, 1971.

Isenberg, H.: 1970, 'Der Begriff "Text" in der Sprachtheorie', *ASG-Bericht* Nr. 8, 1–21, Berlin: DAW.

Kiparsky, P. & C.: 1970, 'Fact', in M. Bierwisch and K. E. Heidolph (eds.). *Progress in Linguistics*, The Hague: Mouton.

Kummer, W.: 1971, 'Referenz, Pragmatik und zwei mögliche Textmodelle', in: D. Wunderlich (ed.), *Probleme und Fortschritte der Transformationsgrammatik*, München: Hueber.

Lakoff, G.: 1969, *Pronouns and Reference, I*, unpubl. paper, Indiana Linguistics Club.

Lakoff, G.: 1970, *Global Rules or the Inherent Limitations of Transformational Grammars*, unpubl. paper.

Lang, E.: 1969, Review of J. D. McCawley: 'On the Role of Semantics in a Grammar', *ASG-Bericht* Nr. 4, 1–35, Berlin: DAW.

Lang, E. (in Vorbereitung): *Koordination und Textstruktur*.

Petöfi, J.: 1971, 'Transformationsgrammatiken und die grammatische Beschreibung von Texten', *Linguistische Berichte* **14**, 17–33.

Ruben, P. und H. Wolter: 1969, 'Modell, Modellmethode und Wirklichkeit', *Deut. Z. Philos.* **17**, 1225–39.

Steinitz, R.: 1968, 'Nominale Pro-Formen'. *ASG-Bericht* Nr. 2, II, 1–21, Berlin: DAW.

Stempel, W. D.: 1971 (ed.), *Beiträge zur Textlinguistik*, München: Fink.

Thümmel, W.: 1970, *Vorüberlegungen zu einer Textgrammatik. Koordination und Subordination in der generativen Transformationsgrammatik*, Habil. Schrift, Stuttgart.

I. A. MEL'ČUK

ON THE POSSESSIVE FORMS OF THE
HUNGARIAN NOUN

The morphological interpretation of the possessive forms of the noun, that is, the 'possessive endings' themselves, is one of the controversial questions of Hungarian grammar. There is no doubt as to what constitutes the set of these endings; the rules for their use are also well known. The problem lies in breaking down these possessive endings into morphs and in relating these morphs to particular morphemes. Several different points of view on this matter are presented and compared in L. Antal's works [3]–[5]. We are going to develop here a new approach, and we will try to keep it as free as possible from the deficiencies of the descriptions now in existence.[1]

A very simple instance will be treated first – the possessive forms of nouns of the type *ház* 'house' (mutatis mutandis, nouns of the type *könyv* 'book'). The point of view suggested is formulated and explained above all with reference to this type (other types of possessive forms are brought in only where they are necessary for purposes of comparison, etc.). Only after the fundamental idea of the author's propositions is sufficiently clear will an attempt be made to show just how all the other cases (nouns with a vowel stem of the type *szoba* 'room', *kefe* 'brush', or of the type *ajtó* 'door', *erő* 'strength'; the noun types *gomb* 'button', *kert* 'garden', etc.) are accommodated within the framework of the proposed interpretation.

More detailed information of a descriptive nature and all necessary explanatory remarks can be found in [1], [8], [11], [13], and [16]–[18].

1. We will begin by examining the following forms: *ház* 'house'; *házak* 'houses'; *házam* 'my house'; *házaim* 'my houses'.

Theoretically, a great many different descriptions of the above forms are possible. There are different ways of determining the boundary between the stem and the ending: either *ház*, *háza-m* (with variation in the stem), or *ház*, *ház-am*; so that the stems of the singular and plural forms be the same or different: either *ház-am*/*ház-aim* vs. *háza-m*/*háza-im*, or *háza-m*/*ház-aim* (Zs. Simonyi [16]) vs. *ház-am*/*háza-im*. For a fixed ending it is possible to adopt:

---

[1] Certain inaccuracies in an earlier work of the author on the same subject [14] have been corrected in the present article. All discrepancies between [14] and this essay are to be interpreted in favor of the latter.

F. Kiefer and N. Ruwet (eds.), Generative Grammar in Europe, 315–332. *All Rights Reserved.*
Copyright © *1973 by D. Reidel Publishing Company, Dordrecht-Holland.*

(1) a single-morph interpretation – that is, to consider all possessive endings morphologically simple (see the list in Table I);

(2) a double-morph interpretation – to separate the markers of person and number for the possessor and the marker of number for the possessed, e.g., *ház-am/ház-ai-m* (J. Lotz [11], p. 68ff.) or *ház-am/ház-a-i-m*, where *-a . . . m* is a single discontinuous morph with the infixed plural marker *-i-* (L. Antal [3]–[5]);

(3) a triple-morph interpretation – to mark off the person/number marker of the possessor, the number marker of the possessed, and an 'empty' morph, an 'auxiliary, or connective, vowel'[2]: *ház-a-i-m* (R. Hall [8], A. Sauvageot [15]). We shall not treat all the possible and/or actually suggested approaches in detail, but will limit ourselves to indicating those qualities which make it impossible to accept any one of them and which force us to seek a new description; these indications will in fact prove to be conditions imposed on the sought-after description.

TABLE I

Possessive endings of the Hungarian noun

Possessor number	Possessed / person	One	Many
One	1	-am, -om, -em, -öm, -m	-aim, -jaim, -eim, -jeim, -im
	2	-ad, -od, -ed, -öd, -d	-aid, -jaid, -eid, -jeid, -id,
	3	-a, -ja, -e, -je	-ai, -jai, -ei, -jei, -i
Many	1	-unk, -ünk, -nk	-aink, -jaink, -eink, -jeink, -ink
	2	-atok, -otok, -etek, -ötök, -tok, -tek,-tök	-aitok, -jaitok, -eitek, -jeitek, -itok, -itek
	3	-uk, -juk, -ük, -jük	-aik, -jaik, -eik, -jeik, -ik

1.   The single-morph interpretation does not show some obvious relations between many possessive endings: cf. the element *-i-* (in the right-hand column of Table I), which is obviously connected with the plurality of the possessed object; or the elements *-m*, *-d*, *-nk*, which are connected with the person and number of the possessor – 'my', 'thy', 'our', respectively. We want the description to prevent a 'multiplication of entities' and to take into

[2] A better term would be 'connective element' (CE), cf. *gomb-ja-i-m* (*-ja-* = CE).

account the unquestionable fact that the possessive endings are complex formations and consist of smaller components.

2. If a connective element is understood as a separate ('empty') morph, one of two unacceptable situations arise:

(a) Either the connective element is postulated throughout the whole paradigm:

(1) ház-a-m   (4) ház-u-nk
(2) ház-a-d   (5) ház-a-tok
(3) ház-a-ϕ (6) ház-u-k

in which case it turns out, first, that the obvious difference in meaning between the non-possessive form *ház* 'house' and the possessive form *háza* 'his (her) house'[3] must be related not to -*a*, but to a zero suffix, which will have to be postulated in the form *háza* – -*a*, after all, is an empty morph and cannot communicate differences in meaning. We, however, think that the zero marker should not be introduced if any other obvious physical difference is present. We do not, therefore, want to consider -*a* in *háza* an empty morph. Secondly, if -*u*- in *házuk* 'their house' is an empty morph and -*a*- in *házak* 'houses' is also an empty morph (this latter assumption is intuitively quite natural and agrees with some widely held opinions), then it is impossible to understand what the difference in meaning between the two forms should be correlated with. For this reason we cannot consider -*u*- in *házuk* to be an empty morph, either.

(b) Or the connective element is introduced only into a part of the paradigm, e.g.:

(1) ház-a-m   (4) ház-u-nk
(2) ház-a-d   (5) ház-a-tok
but
(3) ház-a   (6) ház-uk

where -*a* and -*uk* are not empty morphs, but person/number markers of the possessor ('his (her)' and 'their') in the same series with the other person markers: -*m*, -*d*, -*nk*, -*tok* (Zs. Simonyi [17]). In the plural possessive forms, -*a*- is treated either as a connective element or as a part of the plural suffix:

ház-a-im   ház-ai-m
ház-a-id or ház-ai-d
ház-a-i   ház-ai

This point of view is intuitively more convincing than the former one. The

---

[3] Translating the form *háza* as 'his (her) house' is inexact; see below, p. 318.

absence of the connective element in forms (3) and (6) is in particular explained very naturally by a 'vowel' suffix. Even here, however, there are two important deficiencies. First, the 3sg possessor marker always coincides with the connective element in the plural forms of the possessed (with the same stem): if the 3sg marker for *ház* is *-a*, then the connective element in the plural will also be *-a-* (that is, if we have *ház-a*, then we also have *ház-a-i-m*, *ház-a-i-d*, *ház-a-i* . . .); if the 3sg marker for *kalap* 'hat' is *-ja*, then the connective element in the plural will also be *-ja-* (*kalap-ja* – *kalap-ja-i-m*, *kalap-ja-i-d*, *kalap-ja-i* . . .). The material identity (the same *signans*) which accompanies the similarity in distribution forces one to lean towards an interpretation in which *-a* and *-ja* in *háza and kalapja* are considered fully identical with *-a*, *-ja* in *házaim, házaid, házai* . . . and *kalapjaim, kalapjaid, kalapjai* . . . In other words, we want to have one morph *-a* and one morph *-ja* rather than two homonymous *-a* (and two homonymous *-ja*): (1) *-a*(*-ja*) – the 3sg possessor marker; (2) *-a-*(*-ja-*) – the connective element (before *-i-* in the plural). Secondly, the 3sg possessor marker *-a* is semantically non-parallel to the markers for the 1st and 2nd persons: *házam, házad* mean 'my house' and 'your/thy house', but *háza*, generally speaking, does not mean 'his (her) house'. Cf., for example, *barát háza* 'friend's house', *diákok háza* 'students' house', etc. It must be stressed that the form *háza* is also used in possessive constructions with a noun where the possessor is in the *plural*, that is, where one 'should' use the form *házuk*: after all, if the form *háza* by itself meant 'his (her) house', its use with a plural possessor would contradict the meaning of the construction (the form 'their house' would be necessary). Cf. also *munkások[1] száma[2]* 'number[2] of workers[1]' (lit. 'workers number-his (?)'), *Horváthék[1] lánya[2]* 'Horvaths'[1] daughter[2]', etc. This is yet another argument in favor of the opinion which states that *háza* by itself does not designate 'his (her) house' – in contrast to *házam* 'my house', *házad* 'thy house', . . . *házuk* 'their house'. The form *háza* means (and is translated) 'his (her) house' *only* when it is not preceded by a noun in the absolute form (or with the suffix *-nak/-nek* in preposition or postposition). Thus, the meaning 'his (her)' comes not only from the ending *-a*, but from this ending plus a zero marker – the absence of another noun in the indicated form and position. When such a noun is present the ending *-a* has a somewhat different meaning – it simply shows that this other noun depends on the given one. For this reason, we feel that the ending *-a* in *háza* should not be treated on the meaning level in the same way as the endings *-m*, *-d*, etc.

3.   If the discontinuous morphs (*-a* . . . *m*, *-a* . . . *d*, *-a* . . . *nk* etc. in *-aim*, *-aid*, *-aink*) are allowed, the intuitive notion of Hungarian as a language in which

the morphs are distributed particularly linearly without discontinuities or penetrations is upset. The infixation of *-i-* in the suffixes *-am*, *-ad*, etc. remains an absolutely isolated fact[4]: other instances of infixation and discontinuous morphs are unknown in Hungarian. It is only natural to demand, therefore, that discontinuous morphs and infixes alien to Hungarian not be introduced into a description of possessive endings.

Moreover, with regard to its meaning the suffix *-a* in *háza* occurs in the same series as the suffixes *-m*, *-d*, *-nk*, *-tok*, *-am*, *-ad*, *-unk*, *-a . . . m*, *-a . . . d*, *-a . . . nk*, *-a . . . tok*, *-a . . . k*, which, as was indicated above, is undesirable.

Finally, Antal's discontinuous morphs differ from the corresponding continuant morphs in their distribution: these latter have (in each series) two variants – in *-o-* and *-a-* (*pont-om*, *ház-am*; accordingly *tükr-öm*, *könyv-em*), and the discontinuous morphs also have two variants, but entirely different ones – yotized and non-yotized, i.e., such as the 3sg possessor suffix (cf. *pont-ja-i-m*, not **pont-o-i-m*; *tükr-e-i-m*, not **tükr-ö-i-m*, etc.). In other words, the vowel element in Antal's discontinuous suffixes corresponds to the 3sg suffix (if a given stem takes the 3sg yotized suffix, then there will be yotization in the discontinuous suffixes, and vice versa), but does not correspond to the vowel element of the appropriate continuant suffix (if a given stem takes suffixes in *-o-*, cf· *pont-ok*, *pont-ot*, *pont-om . . .*, then the vowel element in the discontinuous suffixes will all the same be not *-o-* but *-a-* or *-ja-*, depending on the 3sg suffix for the possessed in the singular). The above fact is yet another argument against the introduction of discontinuous morphs, which requires us to equalize suffixes such as *-om = -a . . . m = -ja . . . m* (i.e., *-o- ∼ -a- ∼ -ja-*), and at the same time is an argument in favor of identifying the 3sg suffix (*-a*, *-ja*) and the vowel element of the possessive suffixes for all persons when the possessed is in the plural (always *-a-* or *-ja-*).

It should be emphasized, however, that the perceptible connection between the element *-a-* in *házai-* and the elements *-m*, *-d*, *-nk*, *-tok* is shown consistently in this approach (L. Antal); this is an indubitable merit of such an approach. And although we do not want to adopt Antal's viewpoint as a whole, we consider it necessary to develop this particular part of it: our description should in any event reflect the connection between *-a-* on the one hand, and *-m*, *-d*, *-nk*, *-tok* on the other.

4. In all approaches where *-a-* in *háza*, *házaim*, *házaid*, etc. (accordingly,

---

[4] In general, infixation in the affixes instead of in the stems is an extremely rare phenomenon (if it occurs at all) in natural language. Some authors would, however, claim that such processes occur in a few Indonesian languages. (Incidentally, infixation plays an important role in these languages, cf. Gy. Szépe's remark in [13], p. 78.)

-ja- in *pontja, pontjaim, pontjaid* . . . from *pont* 'point') are taken to be the connective element, the following deficiency is apparent. In the noun forms an unquestionable connective element is found – with the 'consonant' suffixes *-k* 'plural', and *-t* 'accusative'. This connective element has four variants: *-a-, -o-, -e-, -ö-*, the choice of which is completely determined by the stem (*ház-ak, ház-at; dolog* 'thing' – *dolg-ok, dolg-ot; könyv* 'book' – *könyv-ek, könyv-et; tükör* 'mirror' – *tükr-ök, tükr-öt*).

Accordingly, the roots can be divided into four classes: R_a (*ház*; having the connective element *-a-*), R_o(*dolog*), R_e(*könyv*), $R_ö$(*tükör*). It turns out that the element *-a-(-ja-)* in the 3sg of the possessor and in the plural of the possessed does not, in general, conform to the root class: *dolg-ok* (class R_o), but *dolga, dolgaim, dolgaid; tükr-ök* (class $R_ö$), but *tükre, tükreim, tükreid*, not to mention the fact that element *-ja- (-je-)* is not at all an 'unquestionable' connective element. This fact once again argues against considering the *-a-* in *háza, dolga* (*házaim, dolgaim* . . .) and *-ja* in *pontja* (*pontjaim* . . .) a connective element (as R. Hall does [8]). We feel that when describing possessive endings, only that component of an ending which coincides with an 'unquestionable' connective element characteristic of a given root should be considered a connective element (*-o-* in *ablakom* 'my window' can be considered a connective element, since there are the forms *ablakot* – acc. of 'window' and *ablakok* – the plural; the last *-a-* in *ablaka, ablakaim* . . . , however, cannot be considered a connective element).

5. An 'unquestionable' connective element in a certain sense is drawn to the suffix, not the stem; as Antal correctly shows ([5], p. 51), "an auxiliary vowel cannot be part of the stem, since it often occurs not only between the root and the suffix, but also between the plural suffix and the following case suffix": cf. *házakat, házakon, dolgokon* (*dolgokat, könyveket, könyveken, tükröket, tükrökön*). Moreover, one more argument can be added to Antal's: *-a-, -e-*, which undoubtedly belong to the stem, that is, are its terminus, are always lengthened before the suffixes *-k-, -t, -m, -d*, etc., cf. *szoba* 'room' – *szobák, szobát, szobával, szobáig* (*kefe* 'brush' – *kefék, kefét, kefém, kefével, keféig*), but the connective elements *-a-, -e-* are never lengthened before these endings (*ház-a-k, kez-e-k*), i.e., they behave exactly opposite the terminal elements of the stems. For this reason it is inconvenient to consider them individual (empty) morphs – in such a case *-a, -e* would also have to be lengthened before the following suffixes. On the basis of what has been shown here we reject the most traditional interpretation – *háza-m, ablako-m, keze-m, tükrö-m*, etc., for *ház, ablak* . . . (that is, the so-called *hangtoldó tövek*, Zs. Simonyi [17], J. Szinnyei [18], and others), and also the point of view which considers the

connective element an independent morph, and require that the connective element belong to the suffix (see below pp. 322 and 327).

Let us sum up our requirements: (1) a possessive ending should not as a rule be considered monomorphic; (2) -a (-ja) in *háza* (*pontja*) and -u (-ju) in *házuk* (*pontjuk*) should not be considered empty morphs (connective elements); (3) -a in *háza* and -a- in *házaim*, *házaid* . . . should be considered identical (analogically, -ja in *pontja* and -ja- in *pontjaim*, *pontjaid* . . .); (4) the element -a (-ja) in *háza* (*pontja*) should not have a meaning which is exactly parallel to the meaning of the elements -m 'my', -d 'thy', etc.: -a (-ja) is not simply 'his (her)'; (5) the intuitively perceptible relation between the element -a- (-ja-) in *házaim* and the personal suffixes should be reflected; (6) there should be no discontinuous morphs; (7) a component which is determined to be a connective element in a possessive ending should coincide with the connective element in the (non-possessive) plural and accusative forms; (8) connective elements should not be considered as part of the stem.

It is important to fully understand that all of these requirements (stating deficiencies in the descriptions proposed earlier) cannot be rigorously substantiated. We cannot *prove* (in the exact meaning of the word) that a monomorphic interpretation of the possessive suffixes is unsuitable, that the -a- in *háza* should not be an empty morph, etc. These requirements are axioms which can be neither proved nor disproved in theory. Their acceptability is determined above all by their greater or lesser naturalness from the point of view of linguistic intuition. The principal argument in favour of the proposed axioms, however, is the expediency of the conclusions that can be derived from them, that is, of the interpretation of possessive endings which they stipulate. This expediency is in turn evaluated by what possibility we obtain of constructing (on the basis of the developed interpretation) an adequately simple and natural system of rules which generate possessive forms for Hungarian nouns. In other words, we feel that the morphological description should not be orientated towards the 'ready-made' word-forms as they are found in a text, but rather towards the process through which they are built by some logical device. It is just such a generative approach, that is, a dynamic, rather than a static view of things, which makes it possible to propose a new description of the possessive endings.

2.   All of the opinions on Hungarian possessive endings known to the author have one general feature: the meaning of these endings is broken down into three elementary meanings – 'number of the possessed', 'person of the possessor', 'number of the possessor', e.g., -*aim* 'pl.' + 'my (= '1p.' + 'pl.')', -*aink* 'pl.' + 'our (= '1p.' + 'pl.')', etc. In other words, independently of

their reduction into morphs, the possessive endings are always considered to be trisememic. Our most important step consists in refuting precisely this viewpoint. In meanings such as 'my' or 'our' the meaning 'belong' is postulated: 'my' = 'belong' + 'I' (= '1p.' + 'sg.'), 'our' = 'belong' + 'we' (= '1p.' + 'pl.'). The meanings of 'thy', 'his', 'her', 'your', and 'their' are broken down in exactly same way. Thus, a quatrisememic interpretation of the possessive endings is proposed: 'number (possessed)' + 'belong' + 'person (possessor)' + 'number (possessor)'.

Can we prove that the meaning 'belong' separate from the meanings of 'I', 'thou', 'we', etc. is 'in fact' hidden in the possessive endings? No, but we can show that if we accept this assumption we will be able to obtain a description of the possessive endings that satisfies all of the demands formulated above.

Hence, we shall assume that four units of meaning (sememes) correspond to the possessive endings on the semantic level, and that on the morphological level they consist of three morphemes: 'number' + 'belong'[5] + 'person/number' (of the possessor).[6] This allows us, in a completely different way than previously to arrange the segments of the possessive endings with regard to their morphemes. Namely, the -a- in *háza* and *házaim, házaid* . . . (exactly like -u- in *házuk*, -ja- in *pontja* and *pontjaim, pontjaid* . . ., -ju- in *pontjuk*) is the 'belonging' marker, which does not specify to just whom the object designated by the stem belongs; this is shown by the elements -m, -d, -nk, -tok, which pertain to other (than -a-, -ja-) morphs.

Thus, both the relative independence of the elements -a-, -ja- and the elements -m, -d, -nk, -tok (a morphological boundary passes between them), and their close relationship is shown in the description (purely semantically, the elements -a-, -ja- are names of the predicate 'belong', and the elements -m, -d, -nk, -tok are names of one of the arguments of this predicate: 'belong → to me', 'belong → to thee', etc.). It is easy to show that all the rest of our requirements are satisfied in such a description.

K. Bergsland [6] has come the closest to the interpretation we have proposed in his brief mention of the possibility of distinguishing 'possessive' and 'non-possessive' stems (*dolga-* on the one hand, and *dolog ∼ dolgo-* on the other), and K. Ebeling (*Linguistic Units*, 1960, 124) points out that the

---

[5] The term 'belong(ingness)' is used here in an especially conditional manner: it would be more precise to speak of a 'bond (relation) of a general nature', cf. *olvasásom* 'my reading' or *szeretetünk* 'our love'. J. Lotz [12] emphasizes that the meaning of a possessive ending 'is not at all limited to belonging...' but is connected with the most varying semantic relations, as, for instance, *az apám¹ képe²* 'a portrait² of my father¹', *Stockholm¹ városa²* 'the city² of Stockholm¹', *március¹ tizedike²* 'the tenth² of March¹', *az anyák¹ legjobbika²* 'the best² of mothers¹', etc.

[6] For the inclusion of two sememes – person and number of the possessor – to the same morpheme, see note 1.

form *dolguk* can be broken down into three parts ('morphemes'): *dolog* + *u* + *k* 'plural possessor's thing'; unfortunately, Ebeling did not develop his profound casual remark.

Within the framework of the proposed interpretation, the form *háza*, taken out of context, does not mean (and should not be translated) 'his (her) house'. It means 'the house belonging to . . .' – it has, so to say, an open valence, or an unfilled place in the predicate 'belong'. This 'incompleteness' of the predicate is marked by the zero personal ending (*háza* ϕ), which opposes this form to the possessive forms with 'filled-in' places (*házam, házad, házaim, házaid*). As for the forms *ház* and *háza*, they are contrasted with regard to the presence/absence of a meaningful and physically expressed morph – the marker of belonging (and not the zero marker, as in R. Hall [8]; see above, p. 322).

The open semantic valence of forms such as *háza* is always satiated in the context:

(a) either by a noun (in a definite form and position) – *a barát[1] háza[2]* 'the friend's[1] house[2]', *győzelemnek[2] a napja[2]* 'day[2] of victory[1]', *pattogása[1] hangos[2] ostoroknak[3]* 'rustling[1] of loud[2] whips[3]', *olcsó[1] husnak[2] híg[3] a leve[4]* 'the broth[4] of cheap[1] meat[2] is thin[3]', *a diákok[1] könyve[2]* 'the students'[2] book[1]';

(b) or by the substitutes *he, she, it, they*,[7] which in Hungarian usually, if there is no semantic emphasis involved, have a zero expression in a given construction, but not through the help of zero suffixes: the pronoun-substitute is marked by the absence of the replaced noun in the necessary position (a 'zero complement' or 'zero attributive'). Cf. *A háza[1] szép[2]* 'His (her) house[1] is beautiful[2]' or *Érdekes[1] a könyve[2]* 'His (her) book[2] is interesting[1]', where 'his (her)' is marked, first of all, by the presence of an open valence for the words *háza* and *könyve* (marker of belonging), and secondly – (NB!) – by the absence of a noun which could satiate this valence.

It is important to note that the pronoun-substitute in Hungarian is usually expressed by the absence of something: a 'zero subject' with finite verbs, a 'zero complement' with verbs in the objective conjugation. Cf. *Bejött[1] a tanító[2]. Elővette[3] az osztálynaplót[4]*. 'The teacher[2] entered[1]. He took out[3] the (class) register[4]', *Nem[1] adom[2] vissza[2] ezt[3] a könyvet[4]. Még[5] olvasom[6]* '(I) will not[1] return[2] this[3] book[4]. (I) am still[5] reading[6] it'. In these sentences, the pronouns *he* and *it* appear in the translation because there are no nouns capable of closing the subject valence of the verb *elővette* ('. . . took out') and the object valence of the verb *olvasom* ('I am reading . . .'). It is no coin-

---

[7] That is, real pronouns, in contrast to the personal nouns *I, thou, we, you*, which do not replace nouns.

cidence that it has become necessary to introduce special rules into the algorithm of machine translation from Hungarian into Russian [2] which establish the absence of (1) a noun in the Nom. or Dat. with a noun in the 3sg (pp. 243–244), (2) a noun in the Nom. with a verb in the 3p. and (3) a noun in the Acc. with a verb in the objective form (p. 248); if such nouns are absent, the rules indicated introduce into the text pronouns-substitutes, providing them (usually from the left) with a suitable antecedent and matching them in gender and number with this antecedent. In other words, a pronoun-substitute in Hungarian which functions as a dependent member is usually (if there is no emphasis) expressed with zero, that is, by the absence of a noun capable of satiating an open valence, with the noun as well as the verb. This is yet another argument in favor of the proposed interpretation: it takes this important feature of Hungarian into account.

Hence, the morphological structure of forms of the type *házaim* is in our opinion the following:

$$
\begin{array}{cccc}
\textit{ház} & \textit{-a} & \textit{-i} & \textit{-m} \\
\text{'house'} & \text{'belonging'} & \text{'plural'} & \text{'1p.' + 'sg.' = 'I'} \left.\rule{0pt}{2.2em}\right\} \text{'my houses'} \\
 & \text{(possessed)} & \text{(possessor)} &
\end{array}
$$

3.   Now let us turn to some more difficult cases. Let us take, for example, a form of the type *pontom* 'my point'. Where is the belonging marker here? After all, it is most natural to regard *-o-* as a connective element, cf. *pontok* 'points', *pontot* 'point (acc.)', *ponton* 'on the point'. All the more so as the belonging marker for *pont* is different: *pontja, pontjaim, pontjaid* ... The matter seems to be even worse when we come to vowel stems: *kapu* 'gate(s) – kapum, kapud, kapui, kapuim, kapuid* ... or *fésű* 'comb' – *fésűm, fésűd, fésűi, fésűim, fésűid* (with the 3sg forms – *kapuja, fésűje*, where *-ja* and *-je* are clearly markers of belonging). It is impossible to find belonging markers in such forms. Will it really be necessary to propose a different morpheme structure for different forms of the same paradigm?

Before we answer this question, we will formulate a general premise, and in proceeding from it we will try to solve the problem. The following conviction is widespread in modern linguistics: describing the morphological structure of a word-form means taking the word-form *in the form in which it is spoken* (in phonetic, or perhaps phonemic, transcription), breaking it down into consecutive segments (morphs) and showing the interrelationship of these segments with meaning (relate the morphs to morphemes). In doing this, one usually attempts to obtain an identical morphological structure for the forms occurring in the same paradigmatic series. It is for this reason that cause trouble instances such as the Spanish [keřé] (Fut. lsg from [ker-] 'to love'), where the Fut. lsg forms such as [trabax-a-ré], [dorm-i-ré], [kom-e-ré] etc. are clearly reducible, or the English [spræŋ] (past tense of [spriŋ]), when the past tense forms like [tɔːk-t], [áːnsə-d], [kɔːl -d], [pǽ t-I d] are easily broken down into morphs. The above approach proceeds from a tacit assumption about the agglutinative nature of language (i.e., Language in general). In fact, in order for any word-form to be able to be easily reduced to segments corresponding to elementary meanings (which make up the meaning of this word-form), it is necessary that these 'semantic' segments (morphs) always be arranged like a child's building blocks – in such a way that their individuality and the morphological boundaries between them are preserved.

The author, however, is of another opinion. Language, generally speaking, is far from always agglutinative. Morphological and phonological processes which erase morphological boundaries and upset the clarity of the morphological structure of textual word-forms are operative in all languages. It is necessary, therefore, to speak of morphological structure not in reference to finished (ready-made) word-forms as they are found in speech, but with regard to their generation process, i.e., their formation out of elementary 'semantic' segments – morphs. Describing the morphological structure of a word-form in such an approach involves indicating the process through which it can be obtained, or, in other words, showing the history of its generation (see above, p.324). (This viewpoint lies at the heart of the theory of generative grammars – N. Chomsky, M. Halle and others; cf. the description of the syntactic structure of a sentence through showing its generation history – its 'derivation'.) If we accept the above point of view it is not necessary to look for the belonging marker in 'finished' forms of the type *kapui* or *dolgom*; it is sufficient to give the rules which, proceeding from the following morpheme structure:

$$
\begin{aligned}
\{\text{'kapu'}\} &+ \left\{\begin{array}{l}\text{'marker of}\\\text{belonging'}\end{array}\right\} + \left\{\begin{array}{l}\text{'plural'}\\\text{(possessed)}\end{array}\right\}\\
\text{or}&\\
\{\text{'dolog'}\} &+ \left\{\begin{array}{l}\text{'marker of}\\\text{belonging'}\end{array}\right\} + \left\{\begin{array}{l}\text{'singular'}\\\text{(possessed)}\end{array}\right\} + \left\{\begin{array}{l}\text{'1 sg'}\\\text{(possessor)}\end{array}\right\}
\end{aligned}
$$

will result in the construction of the indicated forms. The possessive form construction rules are included in their full extension into the Hungarian noun-form generation system (and are described elsewhere). Here we will indicate only two rules for processing the belonging marker. First, Rule IIC (1)1 – 'Truncation of the BM (belonging marker) immediately before the possessor person-number suffix, with the exception of the 3pl suffix', which carries out the following transformation:

$$\text{IIC(1)1}$$
$$pont + ja + m \rightarrow pont + m$$

$$\text{IIC(1)1}$$
$$pont + ja + nk \rightarrow pont + nk$$

(but: $pont + ja + i + m \rightarrow pontjaim$, since -ja- does not stand *immediately* before -m).

Together with this rule there are rules which govern the vocalism of 'consonant' suffixes [IIC(2)1–4], and also Rule IIC(1)2 – 'Truncation of the BM between a vowel (not *i*) and the suffix -*i*-', cf. $kapu + ja + i \underrightarrow{\text{IIC(1)2}}$ *kapui* ($kapu + ja \rightarrow kapuja$: 3sg) or $fésű + je + i + nk \underrightarrow{\text{IIC(1)2}}$ *fésűink* (but: $fésű + je + ig \rightarrow fésűjeig \rightarrow fésűjéig$, or $kocsi + ja + i \rightarrow kocsijai$, since Rule IIC(1)2 is inapplicable here).

Thus, on the morphological level (morphemes, then morphs) forms such as *pontom, házam, kapum, pontjaim, házaim, kapuim* are assumed to have an *absolutely identical* structure:

$$\{\text{'stem'}\} + \{\text{'BM'}\} + \left\{ \begin{array}{l} \text{'number'} \\ \text{(possessed)} \end{array} \right\} + \left\{ \begin{array}{l} \text{'person/number'} \\ \text{(possessor)} \end{array} \right\}$$

When we switch over to the phonological level, however, these morphemes are subjected to *different* morphonological transformations:

$$\text{IIC(1)1} \qquad \text{IIC(2)4}$$
$$pont + ja + m \rightarrow pont + m \rightarrow pontom$$

$$\text{IIC(1)1}$$
but: $kapu + ja + m \rightarrow kapu + m \rightarrow kapum$
$pont + ja + i + m \rightarrow pontjaim$

$$\text{IIC(1)2}$$
but: $kapu + ja + i + m \rightarrow kapu + i + m \rightarrow kapuim$

As a result the 'finished' forms can turn out to be directly non-comparable.

Now we should dwell on a very important, albeit peripherical, case which can be regarded as an argument against the proposed interpretation (the author himself in [14], p. 273, treated this instance in just such a way). Namely, the final -*a*, -*e* in the roots is lengthened before the suffix -*i*- (pl. possessed): *szoba/szobái, kefe/keféi*; thus, it would seem that this -*i*- should be regarded as a 'lengthening' suffix (in contrast, for example, to -*kor*, -*ként*, *képpen*: *óra/órakor, anya/anyaként*). At the same time, -*a*, -*e* at the end of the belonging marker which we have isolated is not lengthened before -*i*-: *ház-a-i, pont-ja-i*, although these -*a*, -*e*'s are usually lengthened before other 'lengthening' suffixes: *ház-á-ban, pont-já-val*, etc. It is necessary, therefore, either to make an essentially inexplicable reservation concerning the reason why these *-a, -e*'s before *-i-* are not lengthened, or we must assume that the segments *-ai-, -jai-, -ei-, -jei-* are morphologically indivisible, and that the elements *-a-, -ja-, -e-* and *-je-* function as 'vocalizations' of the suffix *-i-* (as is done in [17] and [18]).

Another explanation, however, seems to be more convincing. The suffix *-i-* should be considered non-lengthening in the same way as its homonym, adjectivizing *-i-* (*fizika* 'physics' – *fizikai* 'physical' or *zene* 'music' – *zenei* 'musical'). The lengthening of *-a, -e* in cases such as *szobái, keféi* (in contrast to *szobai* 'room-', *kefei* 'brush-') can be attributed to the influence of the always lengthening suffix *-ja, -je*, i.e., the belonging marker which, having caused lengthening, is dropped in conformity with Rule IIC(1)2. Thus, the generation process for forms of the type *szobái, keféi* is described as follows: *szoba + ja + i → szobá + ja + i* (like *szoba + ja → szobája*) → *szobái* (like *ágyú* 'cannon' *+ ja + i → ágyúi*). We must emphasize that this explanation makes it possible to take care of cases of the type *szobái, keféi* (for all their specificity) within the framework of the general rules introduced for all cases ('lengthening of *-a, -e* at the end of all morphs before lengthening suffixes' and 'truncation of the belonging marker between the vowel ending of the stem (not *i*) and the suffix *-i-*') without any reservation or ad hoc additions. The above cases thereby prove to be yet another argument in favor of the proposed interpretation.

So that the reader does not get the false impression that absolutely all is well, we will mention the following instance, which poorly conforms to the proposed interpretation of possessive endings. There are a number of nouns in Hungarian which show some fluctuation between yotized and non-yotized endings in the singular of the possessed: *oszlop – oszlopa/oszlopja, tanár – tanára/tanárja, sziget – szigete/szigetje, bélyeg – bélyege/bélyegje*, etc. In the plural of the possessed, however, only the non-yotized endings for the same words are possible: *oszlopai, tanárai, szigetei, bélyegei*, etc. ([10], 65). This fact would seem to lean towards a different interpretation of *-a* and *-a-(i), -e* and *-e-(i)*, etc. (e.g., *-a, -e, -ja*, and *-je* are possessive suffixes, and *-a(i), -e(i), -ja(i), -je(i)* are vocalisms of the suffix *-i-* as is suggested in [17] and [18]). However, this is not obligatory: it is possible to assume that the belonging markers for such nouns have two optional variants in the singular of the possessed and only one variant in the plural of the possessor.

It is probably impossible to produce an ideal description free from difficulties and nowhere contradicting intuitive notions. If we prefer the above interpretation, it is because we feel that it involves the fewest 'rough spots' and runs counter to intuition as little as possible (the intuition of the author, at any rate).

4. In conclusion, some remarks of a typological nature. It is known that nouns with possessive forms are widespread in the languages of the world. Of course, it would not make sense to treat all of these possessive forms in the manner proposed for Hungarian, that is, to single out a belonging marker (BM) as a separate morph distinct from the person/number possessor marker. For this to be expedient, two general conditions are evidently required (it seems that these conditions are necessary; it is possible that they are also sufficient).

(1) In all, or at least in the majority, of possessive forms, a common element which one might 'suspect' of being the BM should be present; in those forms where there is no 'suspected' BM, its absence should be explained by simple and intuitively acceptable rules. This condition is not fulfilled, for example, in languages such as:

Indonesian (Bahasa Indonesia)

rumah-ku	'my house'	(no form)	
rumah-kau	'thy house'	*rumah-mu*	'your house'
rumah-nja	'his, her house'	*rumah-nja*	'their house'

Arabic

bajt-ī	'my house'	(no form)	
bajtu-ka/kī	'thy (masc./fem.) house'	*bajtu-kumā*	'your (of two persons) house'
bajtu-hu/hā	'his/her house'	*bajtu-humā*	'their (of two persons) house'

bajtu-nā	'our house'
bajtu-kum/kunna	'your (masc./fem.) house'
bajtu-hum/hunna	'their (masc./fem.) house'

Abkhazian

s-ω°nə 'my house'   *ha-ω°nə* 'our house'
u-ω°nə 'thy (man, thing, nature) house' ⎤
bə-ω°nə 'thy (woman) house'   ⎦ *š°-ω°nə* 'your house'
i-ω°nə 'his (man) house'   ⎤
l-ω°nə 'her (woman) house'   ⎬ *r-ω°nə* 'their house'
a-ω°nə 'its (thing, nature) house'   ⎦

(2) If the first condition is fulfilled, the 'suspected' BM should be able to be used independently in at least one form, without the subsequent person/number possessor marker. This second condition is not fulfilled, for example, in Tajik:

xona-am	'my house'	*xona-amon*	'our house'
xona-at	'thy house'	*xona-aton*	'your house'
xona-aš	'his, her house'	*xona-ašon*	'their house',

where the initial element of the possessive ending (-a-) does not occur without the subsequent person-number suffix – neither in possessive forms of the noun taken separately, nor in the possessive constructions consisting of two nouns: there is no construction in Tajik of the type **korgar xona-a* or of the type **xona-a korgar* 'the worker's house' (this construction is formed in the literary language as *xonai korgar*, and in the colloquial Tadjik also as *korgar xonaaš*, 'the workers' house' being *korgaron xonaašon*).

This condition is, however, met in Hausa: together with the possessive paradigm

gida-na	*uwa-ta*
gida-nka/nki	*uwa-rka/rki*
gida-nsa/nta	*uwa-rsa/rta*
gida-mmu (<nmu)	*uwa-rmu*
gida-nku	*uwa-rku*
gida-nsu	*uwa-rsu*
(*gida* 'house')	(*uwa* 'mother')

Hausa has the possessive constructions *gida-n Dauda* 'Daud's house', *gida-n masoya* 'the friends' house', *uwa-r Dauda* 'Daud's mother', *uwa-r sarakuna* 'the chiefs' mother', i.e., the elements -n- and -r- also occur without the person-number suffixes (in traditional Hausa grammar these elements are regarded as possessive particles or suffixes – as pure relationship markers).

The Alaskan Tlingit offers an analogous situation: in the possessive paradigm

Ax-hît-î	*ha-hît-î*
i-hît-î	*yi-hît-î*
du-hît-î	*hʌs du-hît-î*

(*hît* 'house')

the suffixial element -î- (with the variants -yî after a vowel and -wo, -wu following u or o) also occurs separately, without the pronominal prefixes:

Axic hît-î	'my father's house'
łingitq! hît-î	'(many) people's house'

î is thereby a pure BM. Both of the conditions mentioned are also fulfilled in many (perhaps in all?) Turkish languages, which in respect to possessive endings are the closest to Hungarian, Cf., for example:

Uzbek		Tatar		Khakass	
ujim	*ujimiz*	*öjem*	*öjebez*	*ibĭm*	*ibĭbĭz*
ujing	*ujingiz*	*öjeng*	*öjegez*	*ibĭng*	*ibĭngar*
uji	*ujlari*	*öje*	*öjləre*	*ibĭ*	*ibleri*
(*uj* 'house')		(*öj* 'house')		(*ib* 'house')	

The Uzbek element *-i*, the Tatar *-y/e* and Khakass *-i/ĭ* mark the possessive construction and are connected to the name of the possessed independently of the number of the possessor:

Uzbek
{ *iščining uji*   'the worker's house'
{ *iščlinarning uji*   'the workers' house'

Tatar
{ *ukytučynyng öje*   'the teacher's house'
{ *ukytučylarnyng öje*   'the teachers' house'

Khakass
{ *ügretčinĭng ibĭ*   'the teacher's house'
{ *ügretčilerning ibĭ*   'the teachers' house'

From this it follows that it is also possible to distinguish a special BM in Turkish languages, all the more so as forms such as Uzbek *uji*, Tatar *öje*, etc. mean not 'his (her) house', but 'the house belonging to ...' with an open valence, similar to Hungarian *háza*.

The material we have examined here makes it possible to make a proposition concerning the following language universal (not included in J. Greenberg's list [7]).

If there are possessive endings (or prefixes) in a language and they have the form

$$xA_{1sg} \quad xA_{1pl}$$
$$xA_{2sg} \quad xA_{2pl}$$
$$x \quad\quad x(A_{3pl})$$

the left index for A indicates person, the right index – number, i.e., A_{1sg} = 1st person sing. possessor (I) marker, etc.,

where the order of the elements x and A is not important, a possessive (genitive) construction of two nouns in this language must be formed by element x, which most likely is connected to the name of the possessed:

$\overset{\frown}{A\ \ Bx}$, or $\overset{\frown}{A\ \ xB}$, or $\overset{\frown}{Bx\ \ A}$ (the form of the element x does not depend on A!).

These are the most likely types of possessive constructions.

The inverse statement can also be true. If there are possessive constructions in the language formed with an element x which is independent of the possessor (of the types indicated above), and if this language also has possessive endings, these endings will have the form xA_{1sg}, xA_{2sg}, x; xA_{1pl}, xA_{2pl}, xA_{3pl}.

This universal is based on the elementary argument to the effect that if a special element which is a pure belonging marker (more precisely, the marker of the 'genitive' relationship) can be clearly distinguished either in the sphere of possessive (pronomial) endings or in the sphere of possessive constructions with a noun, it is natural that this same element also be used in the other sphere. This is, of course, probable rather than obligatory (Tajik is in particular a contradictory example), so that the given universal, like all others, is a probable, rather than an absolute, regularity. It would be interesting to check the validity of this interrelationship for a large number of languages of various families.

ACKNOWLEDGEMENTS

The author is sincerely grateful to A. A. Zaliznjak, L. N. Iordanskaja, L. S. Levickaja and K. E. Majtinskaja, who read the manuscript and offered a number of valuable comments, and also to F. Papp and D. Varga for their helpful discussions. Written in 1966; published in Russian in *Проблемы структурной лингвистики*, 1967; *Москва*, 1968, pp. 326 – 343.

REFERENCES

[1] Майтинская, К. Е.: 1955, *Венгерский Язык*, Часть I, Москва.
[2] Мельчук, И. А.: 1958, *О Машинном Переводе с Венгерского Языка на Русский – Проблемы Кибернетики*, Вып. 1, 222–264.
[3] Antal, L.: 1959, 'Gondolatok a Magyar Főnév Birtokos Ragozásáról', *Magyar Nyelv* **55**, 351–357.
[4] Antal, L.: 1961, 'On the Possessive Form of the Hungarian Noun', *General Linguistics* **5**, 39–46.
[5] Antal, L.: 1963, 'The Possessive Form of the Hungarian Noun', *Linguistics*, No. 3, 50–61.
[6] Bergsland, K.: *Review of: R. A. Hall, Hungarian Grammar*, Suppl. to *Language* **20**, No. 4 (*Language Monograph*, No. 21); Baltimore, 1944; *Lingua* **4**, 1954, No. 1, 107–109.
[7] Greenberg, J.: 1963, 'Some Universals of Grammar with Particular Reference to the Order of Meaningful Elements', *Universals of Language*, 58–90, Cambridge (Mass.).
[8] Hall, R. A., Jr.: 1944, *Hungarian Grammar* (Supplement to *Language*, Vol. 20, No. 4.), Baltimore.

[9] Hall, R. A., Jr.: 1956, 'Remarks on Bergsland's Review of Hall, Hungarian Grammar', *Lingua* 5, 298–301.

[10] Hámori, Antonia: 1959, 'A 3. személyű birtokosra vonatkozó személyrag-változatok használata mássalhangzós tövű szavainkban', *Magyar nyelv* 55, 55–67.

[11] Lotz, J.: 1939, *Das ungarische Sprachsystem*, Stockholm.

[12] Lotz, J.: 1949, 'The Semantic Analysis of the Nominal Bases in Hungarian', *Travaux de Cercle Linguistique de Copenhague* 5, Recherches structurales, 185–197.

[13] 'A magyar főnév birtokos ragozásáról. Hozzászólások Antal László cikkéhez', I (Berrár J.), II (Szépe Gy.), III (Tompa J.), *Magyar Nyelv* 56, 1960, 43–51.

[14] Mel'čuk, I.: 1965, 'A magyar főnév birtokos személyragjainak morfológiai felépítéséről', *Magyar nyelv* 61, 264–275.

[15] Sauvageot, A.: 1961, Compte-rendu de *Magyar Nyelv*, 1959–1960, *BSL* 56, f. 2, 333–335; 57, 1962, f. 2, 241.

[16] Simonyi, Zs.: 1880, *Magyar nyelvtan tanodai s magánhasználatra*, Budapest.

[17] Simonyi, Zs.: 1895, *Tüzetes magyar nyelvtan*, Budapest.

[18] Szinnyei, J.: 1912, *Ungarische Sprachlehre*, Berlin und Leipzig.

J. MILLER

A GENERATIVE ACCOUNT OF THE
'CATEGORY OF STATE' IN RUSSIAN*

In this paper I wish to examine those phenomena in Russian which have led Soviet linguists (with very few exceptions) to set up a new part of speech, to which has been given the label 'category of state'. The approach I adopt is that of generative grammar, a theory which is either regarded with suspicion or rejected outright by many European, not to say American, linguists. The objections levelled against generative grammar usually concern the 'psychological' validity of the generative-transformational model, the use of a calculus in grammars of natural languages and the nature of that calculus, the nature of the deep structure categories and the more bizarre aspects of derived constituent structure. It can be maintained, although there is not space in this paper to argue the position in detail, that these objections bear upon those areas which are being debated by generative linguists themselves and which might be expected to change in any case, and that these deficiencies do not seriously detract from the merits of Chomsky's hypothesis. In the discussion of the Russian data I will try to show that the generative model, with its essential distinction between deep structure and surface structure enables one to achieve certain insights into the 'category of state' problem and to make positive statements which cannot be made within other frameworks, traditional or modern.

The crux of the 'category of state' is that in Russian there are some words whose syntactic function is obvious, although they cannot be assigned to any of the traditional morphological classes. These words came to the notice of nineteenth-century scholars, but the problem was first stated in detail by Ščerba (1928), who devised the term 'category of state'. In spite of the fact that Ščerba proposed this new 'category of state' with some hesitation, his suggestions were accepted expanded by Soviet linguists such as Vinogradov (1938) and Meščaninov (1945). The 'category of state' was first called in question by Šapiro (1955) and Travniček (1956), and defended by Pospelov (1955). Although the objections of Šapiro and Travniček have not been given any satisfactory answer, and although linguists such as Galkina-Fedoruk (1957) remind their readers that the question of a 'category of state' is not yet settled, in practice many Soviet linguists accept the 'category of

* I wish to thank Dennis Ward for commenting on an earlier version of this paper.

F. Kiefer and N. Ruwet (eds.), Generative Grammar in Europe, 333–359. *All Rights Reserved.*
Copyright © 1973 *by D. Reidel Publishing Company, Dordrecht-Holland.*

state', and one of the most recent studies, that by Tixonov (1960), presents an extremely detailed list of words which are to be assigned to that category.

What I propose to do in this paper is take the sub-classes of words given by Tixonov and the constructions in which they occur and suggest a generative account of these constructions. No claims are made in advance that all the examples cited by Tixonov can be satisfactorily handled. This paper purposes only to demonstrate that some of the core examples which have been analyzed by Soviet linguists from Ščerba to Tixonov, can be handled so neatly and economically as to leave no doubts about the advantages to be gained by adopting generative grammar.

The constructions which will be discussed in this paper are exemplified in the following sentences:

(1)   *V gorode bylo teplo, syro i dušno* – 'In-town-was-warm-damp-and-stuffy'

(2)   *Mne bylo bol'no* – 'To me-was-painful'

(3)   *Ivanu bylo gor'ko i dosadno* – 'To Ivan-was-bitter-and-annoyed'

(4a)   *Jasno, čto 'Volga' – xorošaja mašina* – 'Clear-that-'Volga'-good-car'

(4b)   *Sram tak xalatno rabotat'* – 'Shame-so-carelessly-to work'

(5)   *Nme nužno exat' v Moskvu* – 'To me-necessary-to go-to-Moscow'

I wish to begin by considering (1)–(3). The 'category of state' words in these sentences are *teplo, syro, dušno* in (1), *bol'no* in (2), *gor'ko* and *dosadno* in (3). *Bylo* is the third person singular, past tense, neuter form of *byt'* ('to be'). In (1) *V* is a preposition, translated into English as 'in', and *gorode* is the prepositional singular case form of *gorod* ('town'). In (2) *mne* is the dative singular case form of *ja* ('I'), and in (3) *Ivanu* is the dative singular case form of *Ivan*.

At first sight there seem to be two morphological classes to which the 'category of state' words might be assigned. (1) They might be classed as adverbs, since in Russian adverbs formed from adjectives end in *o*: e.g. *gor'kij* ('bitter'), *gor'ko* ('bitterly'), *šumnyj* ('noisy'), *šumno* ('noisily'). (2) They might be classed as adjectives, since the singular neuter short form of adjectives ends in -*o*. (The term 'short form' needs a word of explanation. In Russian adjectives occur in the attributive and predicative positions. In the attributive position adjectives agree in number, gender and case with the nouns they modify, e.g. (nominative case forms) *krasivyj dom* ('beautiful house' – masculine gender), *krasivaja devuška* ('beautiful girl' – feminine gender), *krasivoe pal'to* ('beautiful coat' – neuter gender). In the predicative position adjectives are usually in the nominative case, with certain exceptions which are not relevant to the present discussion, and may occur either in their long form or in their short form, e.g. *Mal' čik krasivyj* or *Mal' čik krasiv* ('The boy is handsome'), *Devuška krasivaja* or *Devuška krasiva* ('The girl is beautiful'), *Pal'to krasivoe* or *Pal'to krasivo* ('The coat is beautiful').

Two points must be mentioned with respect to these examples. Firstly, there are in some instances clear semantic differences between the long and the short forms of adjectives, but in many cases there appears to be little or no semantic difference. Where the latter is the case, there is a tendency in Modern Russian to replace the short form by the long form. (For a discussion *see* Ward, 1963, pp. 190–203.). Secondly, in the above sentences containing adjectives in predicative position there is no morph in the Russian which would correspond with *is* in the English. If, however, the above sentences were put into the past or future tenses, they would contain the appropriate past or future tense form of the copula *byt'* ('to be'): e.g. *Mal' čik byl/budet krasivyj/krasiv* ('The boy was/will be handsome'). *Devuška byla/ budet krasivaja/krasiva* ('The girl was/will be beautiful'), *Pal'to bylo/budet krasivoe/krasivo* ('The coat was/will be beautiful')).

The standard Soviet account of sentences (1)–(3) excludes these possibilities. Sentences like (2), *Mne bylo bol' no* ('To me-was-painful'), are described as 'impersonal sentences' (bezličnye predloženija), by which is meant that they have no subject (cf. Rudnev, 1963, pp. 55–56). From a syntactic point of view, *bol' no, teplo, gor'ko*, etc., are predicative words, but cannot be classed either as verbs or as adjectives. Verbs differ from such predicative words in that to verb stems are added inflexional endings which express present or past tense, number and person (in the present tense) or gender (in the past tense), whereas with predicative words like *teplo* tense is expressed 'analytically', by means of an auxiliary verb – *byt'* ('to be'). (With verbs, adjectives, and 'category of state' words, future tense is expressed by means of the appropriate future tense form of *byt'*: e.g. *Ja budu pisat'* ('I will write'), *Ivan budet bolen* ('Ivan will be ill'), *Petru budet xolodno* ('To Peter-will be-cold'). Šapiro, however, points out that this feature does not really reduce the gap between verbs on the one hand and adjectives and 'category of state' words on the other, because the latter do not express voice, whereas the former do: e.g. *Ivan budet pisat'* ('Ivan will write' – active voice) – *Pis'mo budet napisano* ('The letter will be written' – passive voice).

It is clear from the preceding paragraph that, quite apart from the semantic differences, verbs and 'category of state' words have rather different formal properties. But there are not such obvious differences between adjectives and 'category of state' words. With both, tense is expressed by means of the verb *'byt'*, and 'category of state' words and the singular neuter short form

of adjectives have the same suffix, – o. Why not, then, regard *teplo*, etc. as
adjectives? The standard Soviet objection to this suggestion is that the
essential function of adjectives is to modify nouns; in sentences (1)–(3) there
are no words which might be said to be modified by *teplo, bol' no, dosadno*,
etc., therefore these words cannot be classified as adjectives. A similar argument is used to show that it is undesirable to classify these words as adverbs.
Adverbs describe the properties of actions but *teplo*, etc., describe states.
Adverbs modify verbs; *teplo*, etc., do not modify anything.

These arguments have not led all Soviet grammarians to the same conclusion. Many have supposed that it was necessary to set up another part of
speech, the 'category of state'. Šapiro's conclusion is that there are 'orphan'
words which cannot be included in any of the existing morphological classes,
and that one should not set up extra classes but should simply accept the
fact that no all-inclusive classificatory system can be devised for any language.

The traditional Soviet account is not very satisfactory, since one either
has to accept a new part of speech or some loose ends in one's taxonomy.
The question which now has to be answered is whether generative grammar
offers any new insights into sentences (1)–(3). It will be assumed in this paper
that verbs and adjectives are surface-structure categories which derive from
a single deep-structure category which will be called Predicator. Arguments
in favour of this hypothesis can be found in Lyons (1966) and Lakoff (1965).
Arguments based on Russian material are to be found in Miller (1970a).

To a linguist whose goal is to write as economical a set of rules as possible
for generating sentences like (1)–(3), certain features are important.
(a) They can all contain prepositional phrases with *ot* (literally 'from'),
which refer to the cause of a particular state.

(4) (a) *V komnate xolodno ot moroza/ot vetra* – 'In-room-cold-
         from-frost/from-wind'
     (b) *Mal' čiku xolodno ot moroza/ot vetra* – 'To boy-cold-from-
         frost/from-wind'
     (c) *Petru bylo dosadno ot etix slov* – 'To Peter-was-annoyed-
         from-these-words'

(5) (a) *V gorode neprijatno ot doždja/ot žary* – 'In-town-unpleasant-
         from-rain/from-heat'
     (b) *Pioneram neprijatno ot doždja/ot žary* – 'To pioneers-
         unpleasant-from-rain/from-heat'
     (c) *Mne žutko ot etoj povesti* – 'To me-terrified-from-this-tale'

(b) They can all contain durative and habitual time adverbs.

(6) (a) *V kvartire vsegda bylo temno* – 'In-flat-always-was-dark'
     (b) *Mne vsegda bylo tošno* – 'To me-always-was-sick'
     (c) *Petru vsegda bylo obidno* – 'To Peter-always-was-offended'

(7) (a) *V škole ves' den' bylo šumno* – 'In-school-all-day-was-noisy'
     (b) *Emu ves' den' bylo durno* – 'To him-all-day-was-bad', i.e.
          'He felt unwell all day'
     (c) *Ivanu ves' den' bylo gor'ko* – 'To Ivan-all-day-was-bitter'

(c) They cannot contain adverbs of manner such as *bystro* ('quickly'), *lovko* ('skilfully'), *nebrežno* ('carelessly'); nor with adverbs referring to instruments, e.g. *nožom* ('with a knife').

(8) (a) **V komnate bystro/lovko/nebrežno bylo xolodno* – 'In-room-quickly/skilfully/carelessly-was-cold'
     (b) **Mal' čiku bystro/lovko/nebrežno bylo xolodno* – 'To boy-quickly/skilfully/carelessly-was-cold'
     (c) **Petru bystro/lovko/nebrežno bylo obidno* – 'To Peter-quickly/skilfully/carelessly-was-offended'

(9) (a) **V gorode bylo teplo solncem* – 'In-town-was-warm-by sun'
     (b) **Ej bylo teplo solncem/plamenem* – 'To her-was-warm-by sun/by flame'
     (c) **Petru bylo žutko povest' ju* – 'To Peter-was-terrified-by tale'

In technical terms, the (a), (b) and (c) sentences above share the same selectional restrictions. Using the technique developed by Lakoff in his paper on instrumental adverbs (Lakoff, 1968), one can argue thus. A very economical grammar for the above sentences would be one in which the selectional restrictions had to be stated only once. This would be possible if the (a), (b) and (c) sentences all derived from the same underlying structure. Therefore, one should try to postulate a deep structure from which all three types of sentence can be derived. This task looks quite easy with respect to the (b) and (c) sentences, since they differ only in that the 'category of state' words in the (b) sentences refer to physical feelings, whereas the 'category of state' words in the (c) sentences refer to psychological feelings, this difference not being reflected in any formal distinction between the (b) and (c) sentences. The (a) sentences, however, contrast with the (b) and (c) sentences in that they contain a prepositional phrase consisting of the preposition *v* ('in') followed by a noun in the prepositional case, where the latter contain a noun in the dative case.

My contention is that the distinction between dative, genitive and prepositional case forms is a surface structure phenomenon, and that the different superficial case forms are simply different realizations of underlying locatives. (It will be assumed that these underlying locatives may be realized as a noun + case ending, or as a preposition + noun + case ending, or, if one is dealing with a language like English, as a preposition + noun). In this connection the following sentences are very instructive:

(10)   (a)   *Teorija Ivanu ponjatna* – 'Theory-to Ivan-understandable'
        (b)   *U Ivana ponimanie teorii* – 'At-Ivan-understanding-of theory'

(11)   (a)   *Ivanu veritsja, čto* . . . – 'To Ivan-believes-that . . .'
        (b)   *U Ivana vera, čto* . . . – 'At-Ivan-belief-that . . .'

(12)   (a)   *Ivanu prinadležit dača* – 'To Ivan-belongs-dacha'
        (b)   *U Ivana dača* – 'At-Ivan-dacha'

The essential difference between the (a) and (b) sentences is that where the (a) sentences have a verb or an adjective, *ponjatna*, *veritsja*, *prinadležit*, the (b) sentences have a nominalization, *ponimanie* and *vera*. The exception is (12b), which has neither a nominalization nor a verb or adjective. This difference is accompanied by two other distinctions. All the sentences contain two nouns, one animate, the other inanimate. In the (a) sentences the animate noun is in the dative case and the inanimate noun is in the nominative case but in the (b) sentences the animate noun is in the genitive case and is preceded by the preposition *u* ('at') and the inanimate noun is also in the genitive case in (10b). Whether the animate noun in these sentences is in the dative case or in the genitive case depends on whether the sentence contains a verb/adjective or a nominalization. In other words, the contrast between the dative case and the genitive case is not important, the two being in complementary distribution.

The crucial feature of the (b) sentences is that the animate noun in the genitive case preceded by *u* is identical in form with constructions which do denote the location of people or objects, e.g.:

(13)   (a)   *U okna kreslo* – 'At-window-armchair'
        (b)   *U dveri zerkalo* – 'At-door-mirror'
        (c)   *Petr stojal u vxoda* – 'Peter-stood-at-entrance'
        (d)   *U Gali dom* – 'At-Galja-house'
        (e)   *U reki stoit dom* – 'At-river-stands-house'

Not only are (13d) and (13e) identical in form, they also share the following selectional restrictions:

(a) they can both contain durative and habitual time adverbs;

(b) they cannot contain adverbs of manner such as *bystro* ('quickly'), *sentuziazmom* ('enthusiastically'), *lovko* ('skilfully');

(c) they cannot occur with instrumental adverbs.

Moreover, it makes sense semantically to interpret possession in terms of location: *X* has *Y*/*Y* is at *X*. Basing my proposal on these three criteria – formal identity, shared selectional restrictions, semantic similarity – I suggest that *U Gali* in (13d) and *U reki* in (13e) both derive from underlying locatives. Since (10a, b), (11a, b), (12a, b) share the selectional restrictions which apply to (13d) and (13e), and since it has been shown that the dative case forms in (10d), (11a) and (12a) are in complementary distribution with the *U* + noun stem + genitive case form construction in (10b), (11b) and (12b), I suggest that the nouns in the dative case form derive from underlying locatives, and that the nouns in the dative case form in (4b), (5b), (6b), (7b), (8b) and (9b) also derive from underlying locatives. The sentences (4a)–(9a) present no problem as they contain overt locative constructions.

The deep structures of *V komnate xolodno* ('In-room-cold') and *Ivanu xolodno* ('To Ivan-cold') are shown in Figures 1 and 2.

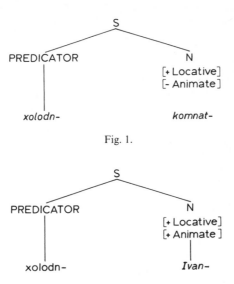

Fig. 1.

It is assumed here that the feature [+ Locative] is realised as a superficial dative case ending (e.g. *Ivanu*) or as a preposition and a prepositional case ending (e.g. *v komnate*), the choice depending, interalia, on whether the N has the feature [+ Animate] or [− Animate]. The structure shown in Figure

2 also underlies sentences like *Ivanu dosadno* ('To Ivan-annoyed'). The deep structure of sentences such as (10a), *Teorija Ivanu ponjatna* ('Theory-to Ivan-understandable') is approximately that shown in Figure 3.

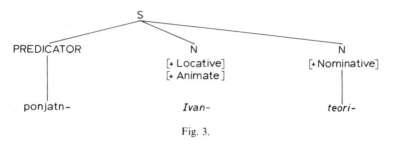

Fig. 3.

In the above argument it was assumed that sentences such as (2) *Mne bylo bol' no* ('To me-was-painful'), derive from the same underlying structure as sentences like (10a), *Teorija Ivanu ponjatna* ('Theory-to Ivan-understandable'). Prima facie, this assumption seems very plausible – both sentences contain an animate noun in the dative case form, both contain an adjective (this statement will be defended later), in both types present tense is not expressed by any overt morph and past and future tense are expressed by means of the appropriate form of *byt'*. In addition, both types of sentence are subject to the selectional restrictions mentioned in earlier paragraphs. The only difference is that in sentences such as (2) there is only one noun, whereas in sentences like (10a) there are two nouns, the additional one being a noun in the nominative case with which the adjective agrees in gender, case, and number.

There is one further piece of evidence in support of this assumption. Consider the following pair of sentences:

(14)   (a)   *Teorija studentu ponjatna* – 'Theory-to student-understand-
              able'
       (b)   *Student ponimaet teoriju* – 'Student-understands-theory'

(14a) and (14b) describe the same situation, although they differ syntactically. In (14a) the animate noun *studentu* is in the dative case, but in (14b) it is in the nominative case. In (14a) the inanimate noun, *teorija*, is in the nominative case, but in (14b) it is in the accusative case. In (14a) the adjective *ponjatna* agrees with the inanimate noun in gender and case (there are no gender distinctions in the plural forms of adjectives) but in (14b) the verb agrees with the animate noun in person and number. In Miller (1970b) the case is argued for deriving both (14a) and (14b) from the deep structure underlying (14a), and a process of topicalization is invoked to account for the nominative case form of the animate noun in (14b). If the animate noun is made the topic of the sentence it is realized in the appropriate nominative case form; otherwise it is realized in the appropriate dative case form. It is worthwhile mentioning here that the notion of topicalization brings in its train a more subtle problem, that of deciding whether this syntactic process is governed by recategorization. In other words, do any/some/all native speakers of Russian interpret the student as playing a more active role in the situation as described in (14b) than in the situation as described by (14a)? I have no comments to offer at the moment but I will return to the problem later (cf. also Lyons, 1968, pp. 350–351).

Exactly the same notion of topicalization is needed to account for the paraphrase relations holding between the following pairs of sentences.

(15)   (a) *Ivanu skučno ot bezdel'ja* – 'To Ivan-bored-from-idleness'
        (b) *Ivan skučaet ot bezdel'ja* – 'Ivan-is bored-from-idleness'

(16)   (a) *Studentu žalko poterjannogo vremeni* – 'To student-sorry-lost-time'
        (b) *Student žaleet poterjannogo vremeni* – 'Student-is sorry-lost-time'

(17)   (a) *Petru stydno druzej* – 'To Peter-shameful-of friends'
        (b) *Petr styditsja druzej* – 'Peter-is ashamed-of friends'

The (a) and (b) sentences describe the same situation. The (a) sentences all contain words which have been assigned to the 'category of state' by Soviet linguists – *skučno, žalko, stydno*. To the left of these words is an animate noun in the dative case, *Ivanu, studentu, Petru*, while to the right of these words is a noun in the genitive case, *bezdel'ja, vremeni, druzej*. (15a) differs from (16a) and (17a) in that the noun in the genitive case is preceded by the preposition *ot* ('from'). Following Fillmore (1968), who argues that underlying cases may be realized as case endings or as prepositions and case endings, I will assume that the presence of *ot* in (15a) is an accidental feature of the surface structure and that what is essential is the presence of genitive forms in all three sentences.

Where the (a) sentences have 'category of state' words, the (b) sentences have verbs from the same root; and where the (a) sentences have an animate noun in the dative case, the (b) sentences have an animate noun in the nominative case. The noun in the genitive case remains unchanged. The arguments put forward in Miller (1970b) for deriving (14b) from the structure underlying (14a) also apply to (15a, b), (16a, b) and (17a, b). In other words, (15b), (16b) and (17b) are to be derived from the structures underlying (15a), (16a) and (17a) respectively. In the case of both (14a, b) and e.g., (15a, b) the actual process of topicalization is almost identical, the underlying Predicator being realized as an adjective in the (a) sentences and as a verb in the (b) sentences, and the animate noun which turns up in the dative case in the (a) sentences turning up in the nominative case in the (b) sentences. The only difference is that in (15a), (16a) and (17a) the noun in the genitive case, referring to whatever has given rise to the feelings of boredom, etc., plays a different role from a noun in the nominative case in (14a) and is not affected by the process of topicalization.

(Other examples are: *Petru bojazno* ('To Peter-fearful') – *Petr boitsja* ('Peter-fears'); *Ivanu obidno* ('To Ivan – offended') – *Ivan obidelsja* ('Ivan-has taken offence'); *Igorju dosadno* ('To Igor'-annoyed') – *Igor' dosaduet* ('Igor'-is annoyed'); *Boitsja, obidelsja, dosaduet* are verbs).

Finally, I wish to defend my earlier description of *bol'no* (and, by implication, all the other 'category of state' words) as adjectives. Firstly, and this is a negative reason, the same process of topicalization applies to *Teorija emu ponjatna* ('Theory-to him-understandable') as to *Emu stydno druzej* ('To him-ashamed-of friends'). In both cases the Predicator is realized as a verb if topicalization takes place, this being ensured by marking the Predicator [+ Verb] instead of the feature it had originally. Now the statement of feature change is going to be complicated if this original feature may be [+ Adjective] or [+ Category of State]. In other words, considerations of simplicity (even if in a rather trivial sense) persuade one that the creation of a new category is to be avoided if possible.

Secondly, and more importantly, one can attack the main argument for not recognizing *stydno*, etc., as adjectives, which turns on the fact that there is no noun in sentences like *Emu stydno druzej* which *stydno* might be said to modify and with which it might be said to agree in gender and case. How valid is the reasoning which concludes that an adjective can only be an adjective when there is a noun for it to modify? Interpreted in terms of locatives, the sentences *Mne xolodno* and *Mne stydno* mean 'At me is cold' and 'At me is shameful' respectively. *Xolodno* seems to refer to a physical feeling and *stydno* to a psychological feeling, but it is difficult to specify exactly what it is that is cold. It is because of this that there is no noun which *xolodno* might be said to modify. But in this respect there are sentences just like the two above. For example, the sentence *Dver' otkrylas'* ('Door-opened'), there is no noun referring to the person who opened the door. No one, however, would dream of saying that *otkrylas'* is not a verb just because the speaker could not or would not specify who performed the opening of the door.

There are other sentences which are closer to the *Mne stydno* type, e.g. *Tepleet* ('Is getting warm'), *K oseni xolodaet* ('Towards-autumn-grows cold'). There is no noun with which the third person singular verbs *tepleet* and *xolodaet* agree in person and number and about which they might convey information, because it is difficult to say just what it is that grows warm or cold. Yet no linguist has suggested that *tepleet* and *xolodaet* are not verbs. Another interesting class of sentences includes constructions such as *Molniej ubilo soldata* ('With lightning-killed-soldier'). *Molniej* is the instrumental singular form of the noun *molnija*, *ubilo* is the perfective aspect, third person singular past tense *neuter* form of *ubit'*, and *soldata* is the accusative singular form of *soldat*. The noun *molnija* cannot be regarded as denoting an agent, but it is impossible in this case to specify the agent, and the verb is therefore assigned the neuter form. In other words, there is no noun referring to an agent of which the phrase *molniej ubilo soldata* can be said to be predicated, in contrast with the sentence *Ivan ubil soldata nožom* ('Ivan-killed-soldier-with knife'), where *nožom* is the instrumental singular form of *nož*, and where *ubil soldata nožom* is predicated of *Ivan*. With respect to such sentences it has not been suggested that *ubil* be classed as a verb but that *ubilo* be classed as something else.

Lastly, it must be pointed out that there are a number of noun + adjective constructions, such as *Ivan rad* ('Ivan-glad'), *Petr sčastliv* ('Peter-happy'), *Student otčajannyj* ('Student-desperate'), which from a semantic point of view have to be analyzed in the same way as *Ivanu dosadno* ('To Ivan-annoyed') but which seem to be syntactically parallel to constructions like *Moroženoe xolodnoe* ('Ice-cream-cold') and *Komnata nevzračnaja* ('Room ugly'). There is, however, some indirect evidence which indicates that *Ivan rad* and *Petr sčastliv* should be derived from underlying structures which can be glossed as *Ivanu rado* ('To Ivan-glad') and *Petru sčastlivo* ('To Peter-happy'), although there are no superficial Russian constructions *Ivanu rado* and *Petru sčastlivo*. The evidence is this: From *rad* is formed a noun *radost'* ('joy'); and from the root *sčast*-of *sčastlivy* is formed *sčast' e* ('happiness'). These nouns occur in sentences such as *Ivanu byla/budet radost'* ('To Ivan-was/will be-joy'), *Petru bylo budet sčast'e* ('To Peter-was/will be-happiness'). These two sentences could be most easily generated, and their connection with the sentences *Ivan byl/budet rad* ('Ivan-was/will be-glad') and *Petr byl/budet sčastliv* ('Peter-was/will be-happy') most clearly brought out if they were derived via nominalization from underlying structures which can be glossed as *Ivanu bylo/budet rado* ('To Ivan-was/will be-glad') and *Petru bylo/budet sčastlivo* ('To Peter-was/will be-happy'). The structure *Petru bylo sčastlivo*, it may be argued, is transformed into the structure

underlying *Petr byl sčastliv* ('Peter-was-happy') by means of the topicalization which is needed to explain the phenomena discussed earlier.

(It has been drawn to my attention that many of the 'category of state'
words are related to adjectives which mean 'causing such-and-such a
feeling'. E.g., *dosadno* in *Ivanu dosadno* ('To Ivan-annoyed') is related to
dosadnyj ('annoying'), and the sentence *Ivan dosadnyj* (if indeed it is a possible
sentence of Russian) means ('Ivan is an annoying person'). Similarly
skučno in *Petru skučno* ('To Peter-bored') is related to *skučnyj* ('boring'),
which occurs in sentences like *Eto skučnyj gorod* ('This-(is)-boring-town').
Rad, however, always means 'full of joy', never 'causing a person to be full
of joy'. That is to say, if there were a superficial Russian sentence **Ivanu
rado* ('To Ivan-glad') it would be parallel semantically and syntactically to
Ivanu skučno ('To Ivan-bored'), and one would expect *Ivan rad* ('Ivan-glad')
to be semantically and syntactically parallel to *Ivan skučnyj* (*čelovek*)
('Ivan-boring-person'). In fact, only the latter expectation is met, but the
gap is filled by the adjective *radostnyj* which means, not 'experiencing joy',
but 'expressing joy' – as in *radostnoe lico* ('joyful face'), ('full of joy') – as in
radostnoe nastroenie ('joyous mood'), or 'causing joy' – as in *radostnoe
sobytie* ('joyful event'). It may still be argued, I think, that the non-
occurrence of *Ivanu rado is simply an accident of the surface structure of
Russian.)

The point of the above paragraph is simple. Given the sentence *Petr
sčastliv* ('Peter-happy'), Soviet linguists would classify *sčastliv* as an adjective. If the deep structure which is postulated as underlying this sentence
were actually realized in Russian as *Petru sčastlivo*, the same Soviet linguists
would classify *sčastlivo* as a 'category of state' word. That is, it is impossible
to find semantic criteria which clearly separate 'category of state' words
from adjectives. Of those adjectives which describe psychological states
some occur in the *Mne dosadno* ('To me-annoyed') type of construction,
while others occur in the normal type of noun + adjective construction. The
boundary between adjectives and 'category of state' words becomes even
more suspect in the light of the proposed deep structure of *Petr sčastliv*
('Peter-happy'). Since all the 'category of state' words which might turn up
in sentences like (1), (2) and (3) are identical in form with the neuter singular
short form of adjectives, and since they differ from adjectives only in that
there is no noun which they modify, it seems sensible, bearing in mind the
above discussion of *molniej ubilo soldata* ('With lightning-killed-soldier'), to
conclude that these 'category of state' words can be regarded as adjectives.

I wish now to consider the type of construction exemplified in (5) and in
the following sentences.

(18)   (a) (5) *Professoru nužno exat' v Moskvu* – 'To professor-necessary-to go-to-Moscow'

(b)   *Ivanu nado polučit' propusk* – 'To Ivan-necessary-to receive-pass'

(c)   *Nam nevozmožno dostat' etu knigu* – 'To us-impossible-to obtain-this-book'

(d)   *Vam neľ zja mešat' načaľ niku* – 'To you-not necessary-to disturb-boss', i.e. 'You mustn't disturb the boss'

(e)   *Možno otkryt' okno* – '(To you)-possible-to open-window', i.e. 'You may open the window'

(f)   *Generalu neobxodimo ovladet' krepost'ju* – 'To general-necessary-to capture-fortress'

These sentences contain an animate noun in the dative case, e.g. *professoru* in (18a) (the exception is (18e) which does not actually contain an animate noun although one is 'understood'), a 'category of state' word, *nužno, nado, nevozmožno, neľzja, možno, neobxodimo,* and an infinitive phrase. The infinitive phrase consists of the infinitive form of a verb, e.g. *exat'* in (18a), *polučit'* in (18b), followed by a noun whose case form is determined by the infinitive. *Knigu* in (18c), *propusk* in (18b) and *okno* in (18e) are in the accusative case. (This is how the latter two nouns would be described in the standard grammars of Russian. In fact, the nominative and accusative case forms of the lexeme PROPUSK are both *propusk*, of the lexeme OKNO – *okno*). *Načaľniku* in (18d) is the dative singular case form of *načaľnik, mešat'* being a verb which takes the dative case, and *krepost'ju* in (18f) is the instrumental singular case form of *krepost', ovladet'* being a verb which takes the instrumental case. In (18a) the infinitive, *exat',* is followed by a prepositional phrase consisting of *v* ('to') and *Moskvu,* the accusative case form of *Moskva.*

Three of the above 'category of state' words, *nužno* in (18a), *nevozmožno* in (18c) and *neobxodimo* in (18f), are identical in form with the neuter singular short form of the adjectives *nužnyj, nevozmožnyj* and *neobxodimyj,* respectively. These adjectives occur in sentences such as

Ja dostal vse nužnye dokumenty – ('I-have obtained-all-necessary-documents')

Eto posobie – neobxodimoe – ('This-handbook-essential')

Po-moemu, eto nevozmožnoe rešenie – ('In-my opinion-that-impossible-solution').

As with the so-called 'category of state' words such as *dosadno, skučno,* etc., it seems that the main reason why Soviet linguists refuse to classify *nužno* in (18a), *nevozmožno* in (18c) and *neobxodimo* in (18f) as adjectives is that there is no noun which they modify and no object of which they might be said to denote a property.

This reasoning turns out to be invalid as soon as one begins to search for possible deep structure sources for infinitives, because this search soon directs one's attention to the parallel syntactic behaviour of nouns and infinitive phrases. (In what follows the influence of Rosenbaum's work will be obvious).

(A) Both nouns and infinitive phrases occur as the objects of verbs.

(19)   (a) *Petr ljubit stixotvorenija Puškina* – ('Peter-loves-poems-of Puskin')

       (b) *Petr ljubit igrat' v šaxmaty* – ('Peter-loves-to play-at-chess')

(20)   (a) *Pavel predpočitaet romany Tolstogo* – ('Pavel-prefers-novels-of Tolstoy')

       (b) *Pavel predpočitaet ostat'sja v Moskve* – ('Pavel-prefers-to stay-in-Moscow')

(21)   (a) *Vse xotjat mira* – ('Everyone-wants-peace')

       (b) *Vse xotjat ezdit' na Kavkaz* – ('Everyone-wants-to go-to-Caucasus')

(22)   (a) *Ja poobeščal emu novoe pal' to* – ('I-promised-to him-new-coat')

       (b) *Ja poobeščal emu prijti v 7 časov* – ('I-promised-to him-to come-at-7 o'clock')

(B) Both nouns and infinitive phrases can be referred to by *čto* (what).

(23)   *Čto vam nužno?* – ('What-to you-necessary?')

       (a) *Mne nužna novaja avtoručka* – ('To me-necessary-new-pen')

       (b) *Mne nužno kupit' pal' to* – ('To me-necessary-to buy-coat')

(24)   *Čto vam nravitsja?* – ('What-to you-pleases?')

       (a) *Mne nravitsja rabota etogo studenta* – ('To me-pleases-work-of this-student')

       (b) *Mne nravitsja smotret' futbol* – ('To me-pleases-to watch-football')

(25)   *Čto bespolezno?* – ('What-useless?')

       (a) *Ego teorija bespolezna* – ('His-theory-useless')

       (b) *Pomogat' emu bespolezno* – ('To help-to him-useless') i.e. 'It's useless helping him')

One can account for this parallel syntactic behaviour of nouns and infinitive phrases by postulating that infinitive phrases derive from nouns in the deep structure. More explicitly, I suggest that (20b), for example, derives from the structure shown in Figure 4 (Features on nouns have been omitted for the sake of clarity).

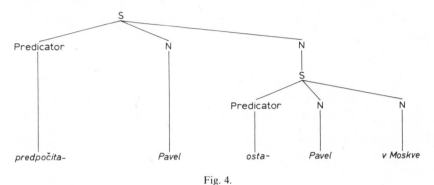

Fig. 4.

(24b) derives from the structure shown in Figure 5.

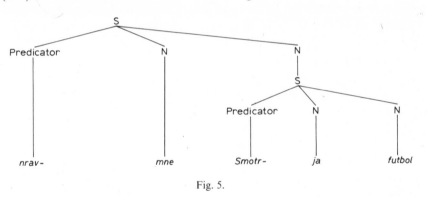

Fig. 5.

It is clear that infinitives are not exactly like ordinary nouns since they do not have inflexions expressing case, number and gender and are never accompanied by adjectives in attributive position. Nevertheless, certain advantages are offered by the hypothesis that infinitives are a special type of noun. Firstly, it enables one to say that in sentences (18a), (18c), and (18f) the words *nužno*, *nevozmožno* and *neobxodimo* are adjectives which modify respectively the infinitive phrases *exat' v Moskvu*, *dostat' etu knigu* and *ovladet' krepost'ju*. Secondly, it enables one to provide a plausible explanation for *nado* in (18b). Soviet linguists have hesitated to call *nado* an adjective not just because they thought there was no noun for it to modify in such sentences, but because there are no forms *nad, *nada which could be the masculine and feminine short forms of an adjective *nadyj. Within the framework of the above hypothesis, however, one can point to the parallelism between nado and nužno, both of which can modify infinitive phrases, e.g.

(26)   Mne nado/nužno sdat' ekzamen – ('To me-necessary-to sit-exam')

In addition to nužno there are forms nužen and nužna, masculine and feminine short forms respectively, and nužno itself also occurs with ordinary nouns, e.g.

(27)   (a)   Etot karandaš mne nužen – ('This-pencil-to me-necessary')
         (b)   Vaša kniga mne nužna – ('Your-book-to me-necessary')
         (c)   Eto pal'to mne nužno – ('This-coat-to me-necessary')

Keeping in mind the structures shown in Figures 4 and 5, one can say that a Predicator accompanied by an N dominating an S may be realized as nužno or nado, but that a Predicator accompanied by an N not dominating an S may be realized only as the appropriate form of nužnyj. That is, one can treat nado as an adjective.

Two other points must be mentioned with respect to nado and infinitives. The first has to do with the realization of underlying sentences as infinitives. The structure like that shown in Figure 6 may be realized as two different types of surface structure.

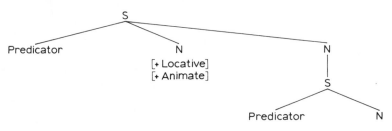

Fig. 6.

This structure may be realized as Jasno, čto Ivan uexal ('Clear-that-Ivan-has gone away') or as Mne nado uexat' ('To me-necessary-to go away'). In the first sentence there is no animate noun in the dative case accompanying jasno, but in many sentences with jasno there is such a noun and in this particular case one can argue that such a noun is 'understood'. This intuition is captured by having in the underlying structure a noun with the features [+ Locative] and [+ Animate]. In the case of the second sentence this noun is actually realized in the surface structure as mne. In the first sentence the S dominated by N is realized as a sentence preceded by čto, which indicates that the sentence is fulfilling the syntactic role of a noun. (In traditional terms, the sentence is realized as a noun clause). In the second sentence the S dominated by N is realized as an infinitive phrase, and the N in that S is deleted because it refers to the same person as the N [+ Locative], [+ Animate] dominated by the topmost S. Because there is no noun left with which the Predicator could agree in person and number, the Predicator is subjected to a nominalizing transformation which yields a surface structure infinitive (cf. Kiparsky, 1967). (These remarks serve to dispose of the 'category of state' word *jasno* ('clear') in (4a). *Jasno* derives from an underlying Predicator which modifies an N, and this N dominates the S which is realized as the *čto* clause. Granted the validity of the structure in Figure 6, it may be argued that the *čto* clause, like infinitives, is a special type of nominal, and that in a surface structure classification *jasno* may be treated as an adjective. (4b) can be accounted for even more simply if it is regarded as consisting of two nominals, the first one *sram* ('shame') being an 'ordinary' noun, and the second one being the infinitive phrase *tak xalatno rabotat'* ('so-carelessly-to work'). Some Soviet linguists worry about the fact that in a sentence such as *Sram bylo tak xalatno rabotat'* the word *bylo* ('was'), the neuter form, does not agree in gender with *sram*, which is a masculine noun. Using the generative approach, however, and treating the infinitive phrase as a nominal, one can see that the sentence *Sram bylo tak xalatno rabotat'* is parallel in structure to *Eto byl Ivan* ('That-was-Ivan') and *Eto byla Marija* ('That-was-Marija'). In each of the latter sentences the past tense form of *byt'* agrees in gender not with *eto* but with *Ivan* and *Marija*. In *Sram bylo tak xalatno rabotat'* *bylo* does not agree in gender with *sram* but with the infinitive phrase. Since such a nominal cannot be either masculine or feminine in gender, it is regarded as neuter. This argument can be extended to sentences like *Žal' bylo prodavat dom* ('Pity-was-to sell-house'), *žal'* being a masculine or feminine noun but *bylo* being a neuter form. Although *žal'* occurs only in such sentences and only in this form, sentences with *srambylo* and sentences with *žal' bylo* are parallel in structure, and since *sram* does occur elsewhere as a noun the parallelism makes it possible to treat *žal'* as a noun.

The second point concerns the proposed account of *nado*, against which counter examples may be advanced, namely sentences like *Mne nado knigu* ('To me-necessary-book'). In this sentence *nado* does occur with an ordinary noun, but the strange thing is that this noun is not a neuter noun with which *nado* might be regarded as agreeing in gender but is the accusative case form of the feminine noun *kniga*. Now, since nouns usually turn up in the accusative case when they are the object of a verb, it is tempting to suppose that the sentence *Mne nado knigu* derives from an underlying structure which can be glossed as *Mne nado dostat' knigu* ('To me-necessary-to obtain-book'). This solution may turn out to be the most suitable one for *nado*, but there are similar sentences which cannot be handled so easily. Among the stative sentences discussed in Miller (1970a) there are the following:-

(28)   (a)   *Ivanu slyšna muzyka* – ('To Ivan-audible-music')
          (b)   *Petru viden gorod* – ('To Peter-visible-town')

Slyšna and *viden* are adjectives which agree in gender with the noun in the nominative case. The process of topicalization which converts the structure underlying *Petru ponjatna teorija* ('To Peter-understandable-theory') into the structure underlying *Petr ponimaet teoriju* ('Peter-understands-theory') converts the structures underlying (28a, b) into the structures underlying (29a, b).

(29)   (a)   *Ivan slyšit muzyku* – ('Ivan-hears-music')
          (b)   *Petr vidit gorod* – ('Peter-sees-town')

Slyšit and *vidit* are verbs.

From the discussion in Miller (1970a) there emerges a pattern of plausible and satisfying deep structures and a regular, general process of topicalization. Tikhonov, however, quotes a number of examples which do not fit into this picture (Tikhonov, (1960 pp. 18–26)).

(30)   (a)   *Zvezdy vidno* – ('Stars-visible')
          (b)   *Saxar nužno* – ('Sugar-necessary')
          (c)   *slyšno krik* – ('Audible-cry')

In these sentences the words *slyšno*, *nužno* and *vidno* seem to be neuter singular short forms of adjectives, but none of the nouns is neuter. *Zvezdy* in (30a) is the nominative plural form of *zvezda*, which is a feminine noun, and *saxar* in (30b) and *krik* in (30c) are both masculine nouns. A sentence like *Mne vsju kartinu vidno* ('To me-all-picture-visible') complicates matters even more, because *kartinu* is the accusative case form of *kartina* ('picture'). Since nouns which are the objects of verbs are normally in the accusative case, it looks as if sentences like (30a–c) are being affected by sentences like (29a, b), which do contain verbs. In other words, these sentences are, as it were, half-way between sentences like *Petru slyšna muzyka* ('To Peter-audible-music') and *Petr slyšit muzyku* ('Peter-hears-music'), and this can be accounted for by saying that one of the rules in the process of topicalization, that which changes the feature of the Predicator from [+ Adjective] to [+ Verb], has failed to apply.

It should be noted that the analysis presented above does not have to be abandoned because of sentences (30a–c). Firstly, these sentences seem to be a peripheral phenomenon in the sense that they result from, in surface structure terms, a contamination of one sentence by another. That is, they represent a departure from the large number of regularities which the analysis does account for. Secondly, it is not clear from Tixonov's account (Tixonov, 1960, p. 18) whether he means that words like *vidno*, *nužno* usually govern nouns in the accusative case or whether he means simply that in constructions such as those in (30a–c) the 'category of state' word is usually *vidno*, *nužno*, *slyšno*, *možno*, *žal*, *nado* and a few others. One would like to know whether such constructions belong to the colloquial rather than the literary language, and one would like to have much more information about the variety of Russian spoken by those people who use sentences like (30a–c). Thirdly, even if it turned out that *slyšno*, etc., had to be treated as functioning as verbs, although they shared none of the latter's morphological characteristics, one would not be justified in creating another part of speech for perhaps a dozen words out of the total vocabulary of Russian.

Of the so-called 'category of state' words in (18a–f), *nel'zja* and *možno* have still to be dealt with. From a generative point of view, *nel'zja* has to be regarded as the superficial realization of an underlying Predicator. The rules of the grammar can be formulated so that Predicators in the deep structure are assigned no feature at all or are marked [+ Verb] or [+ Adjective], and *nel'zja* can be derived from a Predicator without any feature. The advantages of this analysis are that it shows explicitly the syntactic role of *nel'zja* while avoiding the problems of finding a suitable niche for it in a taxonomy of surface elements.

In the final section of this paper I wish to discuss *možno*, a word which offers the possibility of a rather interesting analysis of a large set of Russian sentences. First of all it must be decided how *možno* is to be classified if it is not to be treated as a 'category of state' word. The solution is clear from a comparison of (18a), *Professoru nužno exat' v Moskvu* ('To professor-necessary-to go-to-Moscow') and (18e), *Možno otkryt' okno* ('Possible-to open-window'). *Otkryt' okno* derives from an underlying sentence dominated by N, and *možno* derives from a Predicator marked [+ Adjective]. In surface structure terms, *možno* is an adjective modifying the nominal *otkryt' okno*.

The obvious objection to this statement is that, although *možno* looks like the neuter singular short form of an adjective, there are no masculine and feminine singular short forms, *možen* and *možna*, no plural short form, *možny*, and no adjective *možnyj*, which might occur in attributive position.

Consider, however, the pair of sentences below.

(31)　(a)　*Možno dostat' etu knigu v Moskve* – ('Possible-to obtain-this-book-in-Moscow')

　　　(b)　*Vozmožno dostat' etu knigu v Moskve* – ('Possible-to obtain-this-book-in-Moscow')

(31a) is identical with (31b) except that the latter has *vozmožno* where the former has *možno*. What is interesting is that related to *vozmožno* are the type of short and long forms which *možno* lacks.

(32)　(a)　*Takoj isxod vozmožen* – ('Such-outcome-possible')
　　　(b)　*Ego teorija vozmožna* – ('His-theory-possible')
　　　(c)　*Ja predvidel vozmožnyj isxod dela* – ('I-foresaw-possible-outcome-of affair')

Since *vozmožno* is distinguished from *možno* only by the prefix *voz-*, it seems plausible to assume that the Predicator from which they derive may be realized as *možno* or *vozmožno* if it is accompanied by an N dominating an S which is realized as an infinitive. Otherwise the Predicator is realized as a *voz-* form. Not only does this account rest on a very plausible assumption, it is also a very economical solution. But the analysis cannot stop here, because the inclusion of forms like *vozmožno* leads to another set of sentences, those containing various forms of *moč'* ('to be able').

(It must be mentioned that this treatment ignores all morphophonemic problems. The form *mož*, which is the root in *možno* and *vozmožno*, occurs in the second person singular present tense forms of *moč'*, *možeš'* and *možet*, and in the first and second person plural present tense forms, *možem* and *možete*. But the first person singular form is *mogu* and the third person plural form is *mogut*. If one were doing a morphophonemic analysis of Russian one would postulate an underlying form *mog-*).

The first point to be noticed, then, is that the root *mož-* occurs in *možno* and *vozmožno*, which are adjective forms, and in *možeš'*, *možet*, etc., which are verb forms. The second point is that the adjective and verb forms are connected semantically, as is shown by the following sentences, which are paraphrases of each other.

(33)　*On možet prijti zavtra* – ('He-may-come-tomorrow')
(34)　*Vozmožno, čto on pridet zavtra* – ('Possible-that-he-will come-tomorrow')

There are other paraphrases for (33) which must be taken into consideration.

(35)   *Emu razrešili prijti zavtra* – ('To him-they have allowed-to come-
         tomorrow')

(36)   *On sposoben prijti zavtra* – ('He-capable-to come-tomorrow')

Sposoben in (36) can mean either 'physically capable of doing something'
i.e. lifting a boulder, or 'capable, e.g., of making the most outrageous
remarks'.

(36) is to be interpreted as meaning e.g. 'He is quite capable of turning up
tomorrow although he has not been invited'. The paraphrase sentence (35)
is interesting in that not only can (33) be understood in the same way as (35)
but there is an important syntactic constraint shared by sentences containing
forms of *moč* ('be able') and sentences containing forms of *razrešat'* ('allow').
This constraint is exemplified in the examples below.

(37)   (a)   *Petr ne možet otvetit' na etot vopros* – ('Peter-not-can-
                 reply-to-this-question')

         (b)   *Petr možet ne otvetit' na etot vopros* – ('Peter-can-not-
                 reply-to-this-question')

         (c)   *Petr možet ne otvečat' na etot vopros* – ('Peter-can-not-
                 reply-to-this-question')

(38)   (a)   *Ivan ne možet prijti* – ('Ivan-not-can-come')

         (b)   *Ivan možet ne prijti* – ('Ivan-can-not-come')

         (c)   *Ivan možet ne prixodit'* – ('Ivan-can-not-come')

The (a) sentences contain the sequence negative – *možet* – infinitive, the
infinitive being in the perfective aspect, and may be interpreted in two ways,
either as 'Ivan cannot come (because he is ill)', or Ivan is not allowed to
come'. The (b) and (c) sentences differ from the (a) sentences in that they
contain the sequence *možet* – negative – infinitive. In the (b) sentences the
infinitives are in the perfective aspect, *otvetit'* and *prijti*, whereas in the (c)
sentences the infinitives are in the imperfective aspect. Corresponding to this
difference in form is a semantic distinction. The (b) sentences can be interpreted as meaning only 'It is possible that . . .', the (c) sentences as meaning
only 'Peter/Ivan is allowed not to . . .'. That is, (37b) can be paraphrased as
Vozmožno, čto Petr ne otvetit na etot vopros ('Possible-that-Peter-not-will
reply-to-this-question'), and (37c) can be paraphrased as *Petru razrešili ne
otvečat' na etot vopros* ('To Peter-they-have allowed-not-to reply-to-this-
question').

   When *možet* means 'is allowed', the infinitive in the sequence *možet* – *ne* –
infinitive is always in the imperfective aspect, and when *razrešili* is followed

by *ne* and an infinitive, that infinitive too is always in the imperfective aspect. Cf. the unacceptability of the following examples.

(39)   (a) **Petr možet ne projti kurs po algebre* – ('Peter-may-not-to take-course-in-algebra')

         (b) **Petru razrešili ne projti kurs po algebre* – ('To Peter-they-have allowed-not-to take-course-in algebra')

(40)   (a) **Ivan možet ne prijti na lekciju* – ('Ivan-may-not-to come-to-lecture')

         (b) **Ivanu razrešili ne prijti na lekciju* – ('To Ivan-they have allowed-not-to come-to-lecture')

What are the important facts which an account of sentences (33)–(38) must explain?

(1) In none of these sentences can the forms of *moč'* be said to refer to an action. *Moč'* refers rather to a state.

(2) Common to all the sentences is a semantic component which may be glossed as 'possible', the possibility being contingent upon a person's physical or mental abilities, or upon permission being given or upon other favourable circumstances.

(3) Any account must explain why *On možet ne prijti* ('He-can-not-come') can be paraphrased by *Vozmožno, čto on ne pridet* ('Possible-that-he-not-will come'). It must also explain why the root *mož* occurs both in *vozmožno* and in *možet*. (In both cases deriving from an underlying *mog*.)

(4) *Možno* itself can mean 'is possible' or 'is allowed', e.g. *Možno pročest' etu knigu v dva časa* ('Possible-to read-this-book-in-two-hours') and *Možno otkryt' okno* ('Possible-to open-window') i.e., 'It is allowed to open the window'. *Možno* never has the meaning 'capable'.

(5) Sentences containing a form of *moč'* ('be able') can be paraphrased by sentences containing forms of *sposobnyj* ('capable') or forms of *razrešat'* ('allow') or *vozmožno* ('possible').

As a first step towards an analysis I am going to assume that *sposobnyj* and *razrešat'* are superficial elements only which are created by 'lexical realization' rules (cf. Anderson, 1968) operating on underlying structures containing the root *mož*. Secondly, I am going to assume that the superficial verbal forms *mogu, možeš'*, etc., do not derive from terminal elements in the base phrase marker but arise as the result of a topicalization transformation. Thirdly, I suggest that sentences (31)–(38) all have in their derivational history a base phrase marker which, apart from some slight differences, is identical with the phrase marker shown in Figures 3 and 5. That is, the structure underlying sentences like (31a) is:

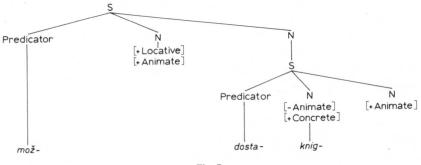

Fig. 7.

Neither of the animate nouns is realized in the superficial sentence *Možno dostat' knigu* ('Possible-obtain-book'), but the animate noun dominated by S might have been realized as a lexical item. The phrase-marker in Figure 7 is not detailed enough. Following the suggestions in Miller (1970b), I propose to mark the Predicator dominated by S as [+ Stative], stative Predicators being those which are accompanied by one noun or two nouns, one of which is [+ Animate] and [+ Locative]. This Predicator is also marked [+ Adjective], which indicates that it is to be realized as a superficial adjective. I wish to propose, furthermore, that Predicators be marked [± Modal] and that Predicators which are [+ Modal] be marked as, say, [+ Possibility] or [+ Necessity] in order to show what type of modality is involved. Thus the phrase marker in Figure 7 has to be replaced by the phrase marker in Figure 8.

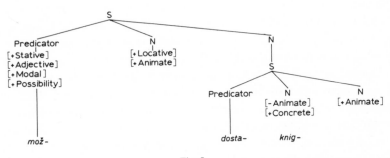

Fig. 8.

(The above structure would be considerably more complex if the study of aspect in Miller (1970a) were taken into consideration. Where the aspect of a Predicator marked [+ Verb] has to be indicated, the feature [± Perfective] will be used. This feature is simply a shorthand representation of a more complex structure.)

The Predicator dominated by S in Figure 8 has to be assigned one more feature to show what type of possibility is involved. This feature is one of three, $[+P_1]$, $[+P_2]$, $[+P_3]$. I deliberately use the symbols P_1, P_2, and P_3, in order to avoid labels which might give rise to disagreement among other linguists. $[+P_1]$ indicates that something is possible because permission has been given; $[+P_2]$ indicates that something is possible because of a person's physical and/or mental capacities; and $[+P_3]$ indicates that something is possible because of other favourable circumstances. The Predicator dominated by S in Figure 8 must have the feature $[+P_3]$.

It was mentioned above that *možno* never has the interpretation 'capable'. In fact, only the verb forms *mogu*, *možeš'*, etc., can have this interpretation. I am going to postulate a transformation which applies obligatorily whenever a Predicator is marked $[+P_2]$. This transformation is the same one which was invoked earlier in the discussion of *ponjatnyj* ('understandable') and *ponimat'* ('to understand'), *stydno* ('shameful') and *stydit'sja* ('to be ashamed'). This transformation changes [+ Adjective] to [+ Verb] on the Predicator in the topmost S and changes to [+ Agentive] the feature [+ Locative] on the noun immediately to the right of that Predicator. On page 341 I mentioned the problem of trying to decide whether the person referred to by the animate noun *Petr* in *Petr ponimaet teoriju* ('Peter-understands-theory') is interpreted by Russians as playing a more active role than the person referred to by the animate noun *Ivanu* in the sentence *Ivanu ponjatna teorija* ('To Ivan-understandable-theory'). In the case of *ponjatna* and *ponimaet* this problem is extremely difficult to decide, but the different criteria connected with the distinction between *možno* and the related verb forms enables one to be more definite since only the verbal forms can have the interpretation 'capable'. I wish to suggest that a person for whom something is possible because of his physical or mental abilities is regarded as playing a more active role in the situation than a person for whom something is possible because someone else has given permission or because the weather is fine. In the absence of experimental evidence from psychologists, this statement, of course, can be considered no more than an extremely plausible conjecture, on semantic grounds, but it does have the added merit of permitting the formulation of a very general hypothesis.

The operation of this topicalization transformation can be well illustrated by the sentences *Možno (vam) idti domoj* ('Possible-(to you)-to go-home') and *Vy možete idti domoj* ('You-can-go-home'). These two sentences derive from the structure shown in Figure 9:

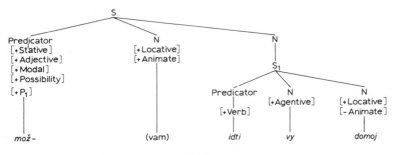

Fig. 9.

If the N immediately to the right of the Predicator in S is not made the topic, the feature [+ Adjective] on the Predicator is realized as the adjective suffix -*n*-. The N [+ Locative], [+ Animate] in S may or may not be realized as *vam*. Whether or not the latter is realized, the N [+ Agentive] in S_1 is deleted because it refers to the same person as the animate noun in S. When this happens, as was said earlier, the Predicator [+ Verb] is operated on by a nominalizing transformation which converts it into an infinitive. If the topicalization transformation does take place, the resulting structure is that in Figure 10:

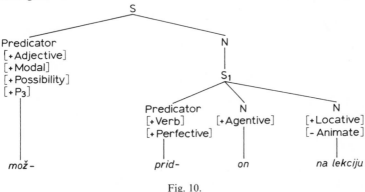

Fig. 10.

(N.B. The lexical items below each phrase marker are put in only to help the reader interpret the diagrams. The animate noun in S would not be realized as *vam*, which form would then be changed to *vy* if topicalization took place. Rather, no substitution of lexical items is carried out until the topicalization rules have been applied or passed over).

The sentences *On možet prijti na lekciju* ('He-can-come-to-lecture') and one of its paraphrase sentences, *Vozmožno, čto on pridet na lekciju* ('Possible-that-he-come-to-lecture') derive from the structure illustrated in Figure 11:

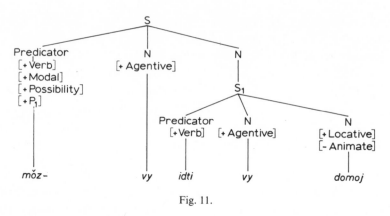

Fig. 11.

This structure differs from the other structures discussed above in that S dominates only one N, which is not [+ Locative], [+ Animate]. This structure reflects the fact that the sentence *Vozmožno, čto on pridet na lekciju* does not mean that it is possible for the person concerned (though this is undoubtedly the case) but that his coming to the lecture is, in general, possible. I suggest that the structure in Figure 11, which is realised as *Vozmožno, čto . . .* by the addition of the prefix *voz-* and the insertion of *čto* ('that'), is converted into the structure underlying *On možet prijti na lekciju* by a transformation called 'subject-raising' which in this particular case detaches from S_1 the branch which ends in N, [+ Agentive] and attaches it to S. A second transformation would change [+ Adjective] to [+ Verb] on the Predicator in S. The Predicator in S_1 is realized as an infinitive because there is now no noun in S_1 with which it can agree in person and number. (This subject-raising transformation is the one which in English converts the structure underlying *It is likely that he will go* into the structure underlying *He is likely to go*).

This discussion of *možno* demonstrates how, using the generative approach, one can reveal a large number of relationships between sentences, and in doing so discover that a lexical item like *možno*, which appeared to have broken away from the major parts of speech, is so closely bound to them by formal and transformational ties that the notion of a new part of speech comes to seem totally unnecessary. What emerges from this paper is not a new part of speech but the traditional category of adjective playing a role in a special type of construction. This paper has done no more than sketch out the various types of surface structures and show how they can all be viewed as deriving from one type of deep structure. A detailed study of these constructions, with lists of fully explicit rules, would have to address itself to technical problems for which there is no space here – the ordering of rules, the point in the generative process at which the substitution of lexical items takes place, the process by which features are realized as superficial morphs, the process by which underlying structures are realized as single superficial lexical items (for instance, the verb *razrešat'* ('to allow') may derive from a structure which can be glossed as 'cause X to be in a state such that to X is possible ('to do such-and-such'). In conclusion, I suggest that the data and theoretical proposals presented here reinforce the remarks in Miller (1970b) to the effect that it might be desirable to have a generative model in which the Predicator was the governing nuclear constituent, and that it might be fruitful to devise a model which did not have one monolithic set of base rules but rather different systems of rules for different types of sentences. These suggestions about a Predicator/verb- dependency grammar and systems of rules, neither of which is new in the European linguistic tradition, will, I think, become of increasing interest to the practitioners of generative grammar.

University of Edinburgh

REFERENCES

Anderson, J. M.: 1968, 'On the Status of "Lexical Formatives"', *Foundations of Language* **4**, 308–18.

Galkina-Fedoruk, Je.M., Gorškova, K. V. and Šanskyj, N. M.: 1957, *Sovremennyj Russkij Jazyk*, Moscow.

Kiparsky, C. and Kiparsky, P.: 1967, 'Fact', unpublished paper, M.I.T. To appear in Bierwisch, M. and Heidolph, K. E. (eds.), *Recent Developments in Linguistics*, The Hague.

Lakoff, G.: 1965, *On the Nature of Syntactic Irregularity* (Report No. NSF-16, Mathematical Linguistics and Automatic Translation), Cambridge, Mass.

Lakoff, G.: 1968, 'Instrumental Adverbs', *Foundations of Language* **4**, 4–29.

Lyons, J.: 1966, 'Towards a "Notional" Theory of the Parts of Speech', *Journal of Linguistics* **2**, 209–36.

Lyons, J.: 1968, *Introduction to Theoretical Linguistics*, Cambridge.

Meščaninov, I. I.: 1945, *Členy Predloženija i Časti Reči*, Moscow-Leningrad.

Miller, J.: 1970a, *Tense and Aspect in Russian*, Ph.D. Thesis, University of Edinburgh.

Miller, J.: 1970b, 'Stative Verbs in Russian', *Foundations of Language* **6**, 488–504.

Pospelov, N. S.: 1955, 'V Zaščitu Kategorii Sostojanija', *Voprosy Jazykoznanija* **(2)**, 55–65.

Rosenbaum, P. S.: 1967, *The Grammar of English Predicate Complement Constructions*, Cambridge, Mass.

Rudnev, A. G.: 1963, *Sintaksis Sovremennogo Russkogo Jazyka, Moscow*.

Šapiro, A. B.: 1955, 'Est' li v Russkom Jazyke Kategorija Sostojanija kak Čast' Reči?', *Voprosy Jazykoznanija* **(2)**, 42–54.

Ščerba, L. V.: 1928, 'O Častjax Reči v Russkom Jazyke', Russkaja Reč', Novaja Serija, Moscow. Reprinted in Ščerba, L. V., 1957, *Izbrannye Raboty po Russkomu Jazyku*, Moscow.

Tixonov, A. N.: 1960, *Kategorija Sostòjanija v Sovremennom Russkom Jazyke*, Samarkand.

Travniček, Fr.: 1956, 'Zametki o "Kategorii Sostojanija"', *Voprosy Jazykoznanija* **(3)**, 46–53.

Vinogradov, V. V.: 1938, *Sovremennyj Russkij Jazyk*, Vypuski 1 and 2, Moscow.

Ward, D.: 1965, *The Russian Language Today*, London.

HALDUR ÕIM

ON THE SEMANTIC TREATMENT
OF PREDICATIVE EXPRESSIONS

0. General

In this paper I want to discuss some problems of semantics which, as it seems
to me, are crucial with respect to many topics under discussion in present-day
semantics but which have so far remained almost unnoticed. I presuppose as
the general frame of discussion the theory of generative grammar in the form
which has become known under the name of generative semantics.

1. Sentences, speakers and hearers

No linguist will deny the special status of sentences in language. And hardly
in any other theory of language has the category of sentence had such an
important role as in the theory of generative grammar. The whole description
of a language is defined here as description of all the sentences possible in this
language. In this respect the theory of generative semantics does not differ at
all from the traditional conception of generative grammar. But – surprisingly
enough – it does not become clear from this treatment of sentences what a
sentence is from the semantic point of view: what are these semantic properties
that give sentences their special status in language? Why do we always speak
by means of sentences, and not by means of noun phrases or verb phrases,
for instance?

It has been generally accepted that the special feature of a sentence is its
predicativity. A sentence is a predicative structure in which (or by means of
which) something is asserted or questioned about or in which someone is
ordered to do something, in contrast to noun phrases, for instance, where
such uses are not possible. One may think, therefore, that one has at least
partially explained what a sentence is and where it derives its specific status
from when one has explained what predicativity is from the semantic point
of view.

But what is predicativity? Although in present-day semantic theory such
concepts as predicate, presupposition, assertion, etc. are very often used, these
by themselves do not give any explanation of predicativity in the sense we are
interested in, i.e., predicativity as the phenomenon which underlies the special
role of sentences in communication. These notions do not reveal why the
sentence is just the unit by means of which people communicate.

F. Kiefer and N. Ruwet (eds.), Generative Grammar in Europe, 360–386. All Rights Reserved.
Copyright © 1973 by D. Reidel Publishing Company, Dordrecht-Holland.

Communication is something that always takes place between a speaker and a hearer. Every sentence by means of which something is communicated is formed by a speaker and received and decoded by a hearer. If we are interested in what a sentence is – or, more narrowly, what predicativity is – then we shall have to find out, apparently, what sentences are for the speaker and what they are for the hearer. The first point that I want to emphasize here is that from the point of view of semantics these two aspects – the aspect of the speaker and the aspect of the hearer – are wholly different. In the semantic sense a sentence is for the speaker something quite different from what it is for the hearer. If the function of a sentence in communication is – as it is usually said – to tell something new about something previously known, it is clear that this opposition of new and known information has sense only from the hearer's point of view: the speaker should know previously everything that is contained in the sentence he tells to the hearer. Therefore, there is little hope of solving the problem of the semantic nature of predicativity as long as we look at sentences from a position that is neutral with respect to the speaker and the hearer. From this position sentences are only 'abstract objects' of a certain type that have nothing to do with communication. Only when we accept the position of the speaker or of the hearer do we have the possibility of examining what communication amounts to for one or the other of them, and, correspondingly, why communication occurs in the form of predicative structures.

Although theoretically the position of generative grammar is declared to be neutral with respect to speaker and hearer, in generative semantics, as it seems to me, there is a tendency to accept the position of speaker as the position departing from which the facts of language, among them also the facts connected with predicativity, are treated. For instance, the notions of assertion and presupposition are treated, as a rule, in the contexts 'the speaker asserts that' and 'the speaker presupposes that'. Also, the so-called reference indices are treated as something that 'corresponds to items in the speaker's mental picture of universe' (McCawley, 1968, p. 140). Maybe it is the generative approach itself that suggests the speaker's point of view. In any case, very little has been done to solve the problem of what these notions – in particular, those of assertion and presupposition – constitute when looked at from the position of the hearer. Nevertheless, the claim that I want to make here is just that it is the aspect of the hearer that is most significant when one wants to solve the problem of predication.

In a certain sense, language as a whole exists for hearers and because of hearers (because there are hearers). In this sense, the structure that an expression of language has exists, first of all, for the hearer. When the speaker gives a sentence a certain structure, he does this with the intention that the hearer be able to decode the message he wants to tell him. Accordingly, it is only from the hearer's point of view that one can decide for certain what a certain structure actually amounts to.

In particular, as I have already said, the predicative organization of sentences makes sense only from the point of view of the hearer. If we agree that in some – however vague – sense the basis of predicativity consists of notions such as 'known information', 'new information', 'adding of new information to the known one', etc., then we have to admit also that predicativity is a phenomenon that is wholly oriented towards the hearer; and so is language as a whole, in so far as it can be said that language consists of sentences.

Accordingly, if one wants to discover the true nature of predication one has to look at this phenomenon from the position of the hearer. One has to find out what the hearer does with the sentences he receives; only then can one understand why speakers always speak by means of sentences.

I want to emphasize that I am not proposing here any theory of linguistic performance. When I speak of 'what the hearer does' I have in view only the facts and regularities that can be established by purely linguistic means. I do not want to describe the real psychological processes which are going on in the head of the hearer. It is just one of the goals of this paper to show that it really is possible to establish the corresponding facts by linguistic means only.

2. PREDICATION – WHAT IT IS FROM THE POINT OF VIEW OF THE HEARER

What does it mean for the hearer, to understand a sentence, a message? Does it mean merely 'relating' the sentence to its semantic representation, as it is described in present-day semantic theory? Hardly.

The fundamental property of natural language is that by means of it, it is not only possible to 'tell something to someone' but it is also possible to communicate on quite definite themes. Communication is, as a rule, ABOUT something – about definite 'objects' (persons, things, places, events, etc.) which the hearer should be able to identify when he receives a message. And communication amounts (for the hearer) to receiving some new information about these objects. In order to identify the objects in question the hearer should have some previous knowledge about these objects. He should have certain 'descriptions' of these objects in his memory. And when receiving new information about these objects he has to change the descriptions of these objects in his memory. Here we come to the central idea of this paper: for the hearer, the meaning of a sentence – of a predicative structure – is not any stable structure representing some fact or state of affairs in an abstract form. The meaning of a sentence can be explained only through the change it causes in the knowledge of the hearer (= the descriptions) of the objects which the sentence is about. To put it differently, predicative structures should be treated as instructions for the hearer to modify his knowledge of the world in definite points and in definite ways. From this point of view, the task of the semantic description of sentences is to bring out explicitly what these modifications consist in.

Formally, semantic descriptions of sentences should not be given as static structures which merely show hierarchical orderings of predicates. Instead, sentences should be treated as representing certain rules for transforming argument-structures of one form into argument-structures of another form. The 'result' of a sentence in this sense should constitute a definite list of argument-structures which represent new descriptions of the 'objects' the sentence was about.

It should be noted that such a treatment of the meaning of sentences is generally accepted in computational linguistics (*see*, for instance, such works as Quillian, 1969, or Schwarcz, 1969, among others). But in this context the treatment is practice-oriented rather than theory-oriented. The criteria in accordance with which the analysis of concrete sentences is claimed acceptable acceptable are resolved on the basis of practical considerations and, in addition, the set of sentences which are analyzable is usually quite restricted. A principal treatment on the ground of which any sentence could be given a theoretically acceptable interpretation – and which could serve as the basis of practical approaches – is possible only in the frames of linguistics. Almost the only work in this direction that I have met here is D. T. Langendoen's paper 'On Selection, Projection, Meaning and Semantic Content' (1967), where it has been explicitly suggested that the semantic content of verbs (predicates) should be treated as 'purely projective', i.e. that in the process of semantic interpretation of sentences this content should be entirely projected onto corresponding NP's (arguments). I myself have treated the problem in Õim, 1970b.[1]

The foregoing general discussion should have already made it clear that the semantic description of a sentence should explicitly bring out at least the following points: (a) what 'objects' – in the most general sense – the sentence is about? (b) what constitutes the hearer's previous knowledge of these objects? (c) what new information does the hearer receive about these objects

---

[1] It may be noted also that such a treatment of sentences can be taken as an explication of the well-known viewpoint of Saussure according to which sentences belong to 'parole' and not to 'langue'.

from the given sentence? (d) what are the modifications in the descriptions
of these objects that are caused by the new information and, accordingly,
what constitute the new descriptions of the objects that remain in the hearer's
memory after he has distributed the new information?

It should be quite obvious that no definite answers to questions (a)–(d)
can be seen in the usual semantic representations of generative semantics.
For instance, let us take the following sentence:

(1)   John persuaded Mary that Tartu is a greater town than Tallinn.

Its semantic representation would be something like (1a) (*see*, for instance,
Lakoff, 1970, p. 59).

(1a)

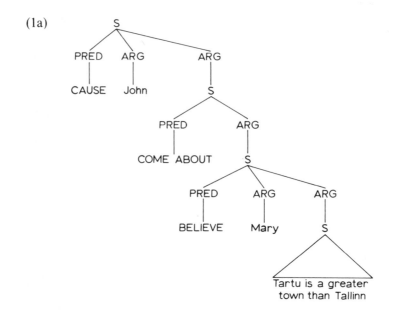

We would say that the sentence (1) is about John as well as about Mary, in
the sense that the hearer does receive definite new knowledge about both of
them. But the structure (1a) does not reveal this in any explicit way, neither
does it reveal what the descriptions – the knowledge of the hearer – of these
individuals are, before the new information contained in the sentence is
asserted about them, and what modifications occur in these descriptions,
i.e., what it is that the hearer comes to know about these persons after he has
received the sentence. But, as we can easily see, the hearer should at least
know about Mary that she formerly did not believe that Tartu is a greater
town than Tallinn, that she now believes this and (maybe) that it was John

who made her believe this; and about John he should know that John has made Mary believe the mentioned fact. It means, the 'result' of the sentence (1) should consist of the descriptions of the individuals named John and Mary that contain just the given information. (Note also that the sentence (1) cannot be treated as being – in the same sense – about the towns Tartu and Tallinn, although their names occur in the sentence, since the hearer does not directly obtain any new knowledge of these towns; the towns are involved only through the descriptions of John and Mary.)

There is no need to dwell upon the details of the given sentence. The fact is that the structure (1a), taken by itself, does not answer the questions (a)–(d). From this representation it cannot be seen at all that the sentence (1) should change something in certain descriptions (resp. in someone's knowledge of something). But this means that it cannot be seen that this structure is a predicative one, either. Such representations by themselves are unable to explain what predicativity is.

But how do we nevertheless understand intuitively what holds about Mary and about John as the 'result' of the sentence (1)? For instance, how do we realize that after the sentence (1) is asserted it will hold about Mary that she believes that Tartu is a greater town than Tallinn? Of course, it is because we know the meaning of the predicate *persuade* that we can infer this fact from the sentence (1). Since the structure (1a) shows this knowledge is reduced to knowledge of the meanings of the predicates CAUSE, COME ABOUT and BELIEVE. Apparently, just these predicates are the units that determine what will hold and what will not hold about the corresponding persons after the sentence (1) is asserted. And this is wholly natural. Only predicates that are contained in a sentence, and nothing else, can ultimately determine what the 'result' of the corresponding sentence will be when it is asserted. There should be definite rules connected with every single predicate that determine the modifications this predicate will cause when it is asserted. To know the meaning of a predicate is to know just these rules. Only by the fact that there are such rules connected with every predicate and that we know these rules is it possible to explain how we are always able to decide what the hearer will know after our certain sentence about one or another individual which is mentioned in the sentence. The ability to decide this is undoubtedly one of the most natural components of our linguistic competence.

The task of semantics from the hearer's point of view can be formulated in the following way: first, to determine, in the case of every predicate, what rules belong to it – i.e., what modifications its assertion will cause in its arguments; and second, to describe the interaction of the rules connected with individual predicates in actual sentences. In the following, my attention will

first be directed towards the concretization of the general framework that is
required by such treatment of predication and then towards the problem of
how the rules of modification – transformations – connected with it are
established in the case of a single predicate, and how the corresponding modifications are described. I can make only some general remarks about the
treatment of actual sentences.

Now, an important question remains, namely, at which point in the generation of a sentence the described 'processing' should occur. The previous
example has already made it clear that this processing is ultimately determined
by the elementary predicates that are contained in the corresponding sentence, and by their organization. Consequently, the processing should start
from the structures where the elementary predicates and their organization
are explicitly given, i.e. in fact from the structures of type (1a). But instead of
transforming these structures into surface structure representations the rules
under consideration here should process them in the opposite direction – towards the final representations in the hearer's memory.

But before exploring all these problems in detail, I want to present some
concrete facts that are relevant to the described approach.

3. SOME RELEVANT FACTS

3.1.   In the treatment of 'possible lexical items' the following principle has
been formulated, among others: 'lexical items can replace only a constituent
which is not labelled S'. (Morgan, 1968). This means that no single word can
have the same meaning as the whole sentence. But why is this so? If we treat
sentences as static structures, alongside NP's and VP's and the like, we can
really only state the given fact – it cannot be derived from any general principle. But if sentences are treated semantically as unstable structures that
represent transitions from static (argument) structures of one form to static
structures of another form, this fact receives quite a natural explanation.

3.2.   One can speak of analytic and synthetic sentences, but it apparently
does not make sense to speak of analytic or synthetic noun phrases. The
distinction between analyticity and nonanalyticity makes sense only in the
case of sentences where something is asserted about something. But again,
why is this so? Why does it make sense to say that the sentence *a thing has a
shape* is an analytic structure, but does not make sense to say about the noun
phrase either *the shape of a thing* or that it is analytic or that it is nonanalytic,
although both structures are built from the same basic items, *thing* and *shape*?
The reason for this will not be difficult to find if we treat sentences along the
lines suggested above.

In addition to analyticity there are also other semantic properties that are connected with sentences but not (at least not in the same sense) with other linguistic structures. For instance, contradictoriness (*The boy who is tall is not tall*) and redundancy (*The tall boy is tall*). It is not at all surprising that the true nature of predicativity appears most clearly in its 'abnormal' types.

3.3. But the facts that most clearly point to the need for a new treatment of predicativity in semantics are connected with pronominalization.

It is generally accepted that the pronominalization transformation, which replaces a NP by a pronoun, can occur only if there is a coreferent NP present in this sentence, to which the pronoun can be said to refer back and if certain formal conditions with respect to relative positions of the two NP's are met (*see* Ross, 1967; Langacker, 1969; Karttunen, 1968, 1969 – to mention only a few). The apparent semantic reason for such a treatment of pronominalization lies in the fact that in this way it is possible to explain how hearers are able to discover, in the case of such sentences, what exactly the information identified by a pronoun in a given case is. But from the semantic point of view this means that the NP replaced by the pronoun and the antecedent NP should be not merely coreferential but also semantically identical – they should identify precisely the same information.

In most cases the formal treatment of pronouns conforms to their semantic function, i.e. the formal antecedent of the pronoun does indeed identify the same information as we intuitively find to be identified by the pronoun. But it appears that this is not always the case. First, let us take the following piece of discourse.

(2)   Mary received a new book. It is about semantics.

In such a case, as has already been pointed out by some authors (e.g. Bellert, 1967), the pronoun *it* does not refer merely to 'a new book' as it would be expected on the ground of formal treatment but, rather, to 'the new book which Mary received'. This means that the pronoun *it* identifies the corresponding object (the book) taken with the information which has already been asserted about it in the previous sentence.

Strictly speaking, the given example is beyond the scope of generative grammar since we have here two independent sentences. But it is not difficult to combine such sentences into one sentence by means of the appropriate conjunctions, so that the observed phenomenon will be preserved. Moreover, if we consider such complex sentences more closely we shall find two clear types among them that differ just in that in the case of one type the information identified by the pronoun is the same as the information identified by its

formal antecedent, while in the case of the other type the information identified by the pronoun already contains the new information asserted about its
antecedent in the corresponding clause. The sentences (3a) and (3b) are of the
first type, the sentences (4a)–(4c) of the second type.

(3a)   John closed the door since the wind was blowing through it.

(3b)   John closed the door although the wind didn't blow through it.

(4a)   John closed the door $\genfrac{}{}{0pt}{}{\text{and}}{\text{so that}}$ the wind did not blow through it
any more.

(4b)   John closed the door $\genfrac{}{}{0pt}{}{\text{and}}{\text{so that}}$ nobody was able to open it.

(4c)   John closed the door but the wind continued to blow through it.

In case of (3a) and (3b), as it can easily be seen, the doors referred to by the
pronoun *it* in the corresponding second clauses should be open. And the same
should hold about the corresponding doors when these are referred to by the
NP's *the door* in the first clauses: this is clearly a presupposition that should
hold about the corresponding doors in order that the clauses were meaningful.
As we see, in both cases the pronoun *it* and its antecedent identify precisely
the same information.

On the other hand, in the case of (4a)–(4c) it is equally easy for us to see
that the doors each time referred to by the pronoun *it* should be closed, while
the doors refered to by the corresponding antecedent NP's should be open.
Precisely as in the case of the example (2) the pronoun *it* identifies here the
corresponding object (the door) as taken with the information which is
asserted about this object in the clause where the formal antecedent of the
pronoun occurs. What is particularly important here is the fact that we are
intuitively able to distinguish clearly between these two cases – where the
information asserted about the antecedent is already added to the description
of the object referred to by the pronoun, and where it is not. This means that
these two cases should also receive different treatment in the theory of pronominalization.

From the semantic point of view in sentences (4a)–(4c) the antecedents of *it*
cannot be merely the NP-structures underlying the corresponding phrases
the door in the first clauses of these sentences, since in the semantic representations of these clauses these NP's should identify the corresponding doors as
open. The antecedents of the pronouns should be NP-structures that
explicitly describe the identified doors as closed. Such NP-structures are not
overtly present in these sentences. These structures have to be created in each
case, before *it* can be introduced into the corresponding second clauses. And

it should be clear that they can be created only as results of processing the first clauses, in the course of which the new information carried by these clauses – that the corresponding doors become closed – will be added to the corresponding NP-structures. Sentences (3) and (4) differ just in the way in which the processing of the first clause and the introducing of *it* into the second clause are ordered with respect to each other: in the case of the sentences (4) this processing of the first clause precedes *it*-introduction, in the case of the sentences (3) the order is reversed. It is apparent that this ordering is formally determined by the conjunction which connects the two clauses. But essentially it depends on the order of the events expressed by the corresponding clauses; in most simple cases this is merely a temporal ordering (as in the case of the conjunction *and* in (4a) and (4b)) but in more complicated cases some more general relation is involved.[2] It is not possible here to analyze these facts in detail. These examples are important for us because they reveal with particular clarity what the application of semantic treatment of predicativity requires. Such examples prove that actual speech – and its understanding – is really built up by transforming argument-structures of one form into argument-structures of another form.

Finally, let me present some more examples in addition to sentences (4a)–(4c) (mostly of types well known from literature, but discussed there in other connections).

(5)   Yesterday Sam found a new girl and kissed her.

her = the new girl Sam found yesterday.

(6)   Before Mary realized that someone had broken into her room, he had stolen her jewels and fled.

he = the one who had broken into Mary's room.

(7)   Whenever you put former servicemen in a room, they start discussing their problems.

they = former servicemen who are put (are?) in a room.

(8)   Mary realized that the boy wanted to take away her bag and she began to scream, so that he hastily ran away.

she = Mary, who realized that . . .
he = the boy who wanted to . . .

---

[2] I have treated the types of examples discussed in a little more detail in Õim (1970c); there I have made the claim that this relation is, in fact, the relation of presupposition.

(9)   Mary believed that the boy wanted to take away her bag and she
        began to scream, so that he hastily run away.

she = Mary, who believed that . . .
he = the boy of whom Mary believed that . . .

4. PRESUPPOSITIONS AND IDENTIFYING STRUCTURES

Treatment of predicativity along the lines described above – as modifying
definite argument-structures that present (the hearer's) known information,
under the influence of new, asserted information – requires, first of all, that
it be possible to differentiate explicitly the known information and the new
information which shall be added to the known one in the semantic representation of every single predicative structure. In the present section I will
consider the question of determining, in the case of a certain predicative
expression, the known information connected with this expression and
presenting this information formally.

In fact, the concept we are interested in here – as the whole differentiation
under discussion – already exists in semantic theory. This is the concept of
presupposed information, or presuppositions, which is contrasted with
asserted information. The question lies merely in how the concept of presuppositions should be treated in the present context, i.e. in what sense presuppositions can be considered 'known information'.

First, it should be noted that although the concept of presuppositions has
become one of the most popular concepts in semantics, the theoretical function of this concept is not very clear. This vagueness reveals itself most clearly
in the fact that the twin-concept of presuppositions – that of new, asserted
information – has received almost no attention. Nevertheless, only a little
reflection is needed in order to realize that these concepts are only two sides
of one and the same phenomenon and that it is just the concept of asserted
information which is primary: something can be presupposed only in so far
as something will be done on the basis of this presupposition – in this case,
some new information will be given to the hearer. It follows that in order to
understand the role of presuppositions in the functioning of language we
should treat them just in the context of predication.

So far the relation of presupposition has been considered mostly as a relation between whole sentences; and beyond this it has been considered almost
exclusively from the point of view of the speaker (*see*, for instance, Fillmore,
1970, p. 59; Lakoff, 1970, Ch. V). There is no doubt, of course, that the one
who 'does the presupposing' is always the speaker. But, as I have already
pointed out, the real meaning of the phenomena connected with predicativity

will become evident only when we look at what they mean for the hearer.

But what does it mean from the hearer's point of view that certain information is presupposed in the case of a certain sentence, in particular, when contrasted with the new information immediately carried by the sentence? According to our viewpoint, understanding of new information means that this information is added in a definite way – in a way determined by the message itself – to the argument-structures which the message is about. But from this point of view the fact that certain information is presupposed can mean only that this information should already be contained in the corresponding argument-structures, before the new information carried by the message will be added to them. The assertion made in a message should operate upon argument-structures that already contain the presupposed information. In this sense, it can be said that to presuppose certain information means, in fact, to presuppose its existence in the hearer's memory.

But it is important to explain in what sense precisely, 'previous existence in memory' is meant here. It does not mean that not a single sentence can be communicated to a hearer before all the facts identified by the presuppositions of the corresponding sentence are really known to him. But it means that in the case of every individual sentence the hearer should be able to discover all presuppositions connected with this sentence, and when he has discovered them he should first process them – if he did not know them before – and only then can he begin to process the real assertion made by this sentence. Taken by themselves, even presuppositions are nothing but certain messages; but they are messages that precede – or have preceded – the proper assertion of the sentence. And they precede this in the sense that they should be (or should have been) processed and stored by the hearer before the proper assertion. It is only from the point of view of this proper assertion that they are presupposed.[3]

Let me present some simple examples that illustrate my treatment of presuppositions as discussed above. Take a sentence of the well-known type.

(10)   The door opened.

As is generally admitted, one of the presuppositions of this sentence about the door in question is that it was closed; and the sentence asserts that it became open. If we describe these facts from the point of view of the hearer, it will become obvious that no matter whether the hearer really did or did not know, before receiving this sentence, that the door was closed, he could not

---

[3] In the case of such a treatment, it appears also as quite a natural fact that "for any assertion, it may be the case, then, that all previous assertions in the utterance or discourse act as presuppositions". (Camelot, 1968, p. 17).

understand this sentence appropriately, unless he understood that the door was closed and then became open. He could not change the 'description' of the door under consideration in his memory into the description of an 'opened door', as is required by the given sentence, if he had not understood the description of this door as a closed door. And just this is pointed out by the fact that it is presupposed that the door was closed.

Or let us take an example of a somewhat different kind that still more clearly will demonstrate the nature of presuppositions as 'previous knowledge'.

(11)   John is the youngest son of Jones.

Let it be said as an answer to the question 'Who is John?' to someone who already knows who Jones is. In this case, the list of presuppositions of this sentence includes, at least, the following ones.

(11a)   Jones has children.
(11b)   There are some sons among the Jones' children.
(11c)   Among the sons of Jones there are at least three who are of different ages.
(11d)   John is one of these sons of Jones.

And the proper assertion made by the sentence (11) is, then:

(11e)   John is the youngest of Jones' sons.

Again, it is not important whether or not the hearer actually knows some of the facts (11a)–(11d) before he receives sentence (11). All of them may appear new to him. The crucial point is that logically (11a)–(11d) are prior to (11e): it is possible for the hearer to know (11a)–(11d) without knowing (11e), but he cannot know (11e) without knowing (11a)–(11d). And, apparently, the facts (11a)–(11d) in their turn are ordered as they are given above: knowledge of (11d) presupposes knowledge of (11a)–(11c), knowledge of (11c) presupposes knowledge of (11a)–(11b), and so on. From this point of view the hearer's processing of the sentence (11) should be represented as processing the messages (11a)–(11e) one after another in just the order given. The sentence (11) carries immediately only the message (11e). But in order to understand this immediate message the hearer has to take some steps 'backwards', to discover and process the messages (11a)–(11d), and only then can he process the proper assertion of (11).

Now we come to the question of in what form – assuming the general frame of formal representations of generative semantics – presuppositions should be given in semantic descriptions of predicative expressions. Of course, I am aware of the complexity of this problem. But I am trying to solve it only in (and for) the context fixed here; and even in this context the solution should be taken as a tentative one.

The most important fact to be remembered from the foregoing discussion is that according to my treatment, presuppositions are always connected with definite arguments; they present material that is contained in arguments. It may be said that every presupposition is a presupposition about a certain 'object' namely, about one of the objects about which the corresponding sentence (or, more concretely, the corresponding predicate) asserts its new information. And, apparently, the converse also holds: with every argument about which the given predicate asserts something definite presuppositions should be connected which form the identifying description of the 'object' referred to by the corresponding argument. All this suggests for the general form of argument-structures the representation which is illustrated by the structure (12).

(12)

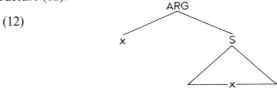

Here x is a referential index (representant of the corresponding individual) and S is the sentence (or conjunction of sentences) which presents the pre-supposition(s) about x (or, more generally, the information which the hearer knows about x and of which the information presupposed about x in case of some concrete assertion forms, in general, only a definite part). The given structure can be thought of as the general form in which descriptions of 'objects' in the hearer's memory are represented – i.e. as the general form of identifying knowledge. For instance, if in the case of the sentence (10), as we pointed out above, the presupposition about the door in question is that it was closed, then the corresponding argument-structure should have, roughly, the following form (if we ignore the question of ordering, or hierarchy, among the presuppositions themselves):

(13)

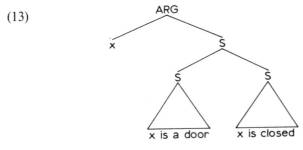

I am unable to present here any conclusive argument for choosing just this form of representation. But nevertheless, many facts can be found that clearly point in this direction. First of all, it should be stressed that since presuppositions have such an important role in the functioning of language, it has to be supposed that language itself has worked out certain standard means for presenting this information. I think there exist facts that indicate that the structure (12) is just the basic form of such representations.

(1) The most typical identifying structures (on the level of surface structure) are undoubtedly noun phrases. Usual types of noun phrases, as we know, are such as adjective + head noun, noun (in genitive) + head noun, head noun + preposition phrase, head noun + relative clause. A question arises as to whether it is possible to find among these types one definite type which can be considered the primary one – in the sense that other types can be derived (in formal as well as in semantical sense) from this type, but this itself cannot be derived from any other type. According to the treatment so far given to noun phrases in generative grammar, such a primary type is head noun + relative clause, i.e. the type which formally matches the structure (12).

Still more, it can be said that from the semantic point of view every single noun is an example of identifying structure; apparently, the form in which semantic material is organized in nouns should very closely reflect the organization of this material in our memory. But, according to the treatment of Bach (1968), as is well known, every noun should be semantically represented by a structure that has just the form of the structure (12).

(2) On the one hand, it is a known fact that relative clauses are always presupposed; i.e. the information they represent is always presupposed about the individual referred to by the head noun. On the other hand, every time we find a certain implicit presupposition to be connected with an identifying expression in a sentence, it is possible to express this presupposed information explicitly in the form of a relative clause without making the whole sentence unmarked. For instance:

(14a)   The door of my room opened.
(14b)   The door of my room, which was closed, opened.
(15a)   My brother regrets now that he did not go to the movie.
(15b)   My brother, who did not go to the movies, regrets now that he did not go to the movies.

In (14b) and (15b) the presupposed information – about the door and my brother, respectively – which is implicit in the corresponding sentences (14a) and (15a) is expressed explicitly by relative clauses. As we see, this transformation does not make these sentences unmarked, although it makes them somewhat redundant; but this is quite natural, since the added relative clauses express information which in both cases is already apparent without them.

It can be inferred that a clear correspondence exists between presupposed information, on the one hand, and information that can be expressed by relative clauses, on the other. This justifies the choice of relative clauses as the primary form for representing presuppositions.

(3) The form chosen here for representing identifying information matches also, it seems to me, the general form of argument-structures as established by Bellert (1969a, 1969b). Bellert distinguishes between three types of arguments, according to three types of operators with which the arguments can be prefixed and which Bellert calls the iota operator, the all operator and the indefinite operator, respectively. As the general forms of the first two types of arguments Bellert offers the following (the third type I. Bellert does not present formally):

(16) $(\iota x)\varphi(x)$
        'the x which is φ'

(17) $(\text{All } x)\varphi(x)$
        'all the x's which are φ'

In the present paper we are not interested in the differences between arguments which are connected with the use of different operators. In other respects, however, as can be seen, the structure (12) matches completely the structures (16) and (17).

5. PREDICATION AS CHANGING THE IDENTIFYING STRUCTURES

Here I shall try to show, by means of an illustrative example, how I think the modifications of identifying structures take place. I will treat this problem here on the basis of semantic analysis of a concrete predicate word. The problems which are involved in describing actual sentences I will touch upon in the following section.

As the concrete predicate for analysis I have chosen the verb *to understand*, in the meaning which is illustrated by the following sentences.

(18)   The boy understood that he wouldn't escape from the punishment.

(19)   I understood that I had chosen the wrong way.

(20)   From the gloomy expression on John's face I understood that he had failed the examination.

As we saw above (Section 2), the modifications caused by a concrete predicate in its arguments depend on the elementary predicates into which the meaning of the corresponding word can be analyzed. For instance, in the case of *persuade* we found that the modifications determined by this word depend on the elementary predicates CAUSE, COME ABOUT and BELIEVE. With every elementary predicate individual rules of modification should be connected which the users of the corresponding language know and from which they derive modifications that correspond to concrete (i.e. nonelementary) predicative structures. Consequently, first we have to describe the meaning of *understand* in terms of elementary predicates.

In the situation which the word *understand* (in the given meaning) represents we have quite clearly to do with a fact of acquiring definite knowledge. Each of the sentences (18)–(20) presents a situation where the person mentioned comes to know a definite fact. That the concept of knowledge is really involved in interpreting the verb *understand* can also be seen from the possibility of such sentences as (21).

(21)   I had understood long ago that I had chosen the wrong way but it was very difficult for me to get used to this knowledge.

The main question is how this knowledge is acquired. Understanding something is not identical with acquiring information from direct messages. For instance, we do not generally understand the sentence (19) in the sense that someone directly told me that I had chosen the wrong way. On the other hand, we speak of understanding in the case of such types of indirect information as hints, metaphors etc.

This suggests that understanding in the given sense is in fact analogous to making inferences from definite (previously known) facts, from direct messages, etc. Notice also that, as the sentence (20) shows, in the case of *understand*, just as in the case of *infer*, an expounder can occur that identifies the source from (or on the ground of) which something is understood.

Nevertheless, the situations described by *understand* and by *infer* are not identical, as is intuitively clear to us. If we look more closely, we find that the whole difference in the meanings of these words lies in the fact that *infer* is an active verb, it denotes an activity that is intentionally carried out by the corresponding person, but *understand* does not denote such an activity. We can speak of someone as trying intentionally to understand something, but understanding itself is something that 'happens' and cannot be carried out on intention. This is shown also by the possibility of such expressions as *suddenly he understood that . . , at last he understood that . . .* (*suddenly he inferred that . . . , *at last he inferred that . . .*). But what the verbs *to understand* and *to infer* have in common is that in both cases the acquired knowledge

comes from other definite knowledge that the corresponding person already
has in his possession.

In brief, we have found the following: the verb *to understand* in the given
sense describes a situation in which a certain person acquires—passively—
knowledge of a definite fact (a knowledge which he did not consciously
possess previously), and this knowledge is derived from definite other
knowledge of the same person. So we may say that *understand* as a predicate
is about the corresponding person; it asserts that this person—let us denote
him as x—gets to know a definite fact, y; and it presupposes, apparently,
two main things about x: that x does not previously know fact y and that he
knows a definite other fact, z, from which his knowledge of y is derived.
The identifying structure which describes the hearer's knowledge of x
before the predicate *to understand* is asserted, should have, then, the following
form (we ignore again the question of possible hierarchy among the given
presuppositions):

(23)

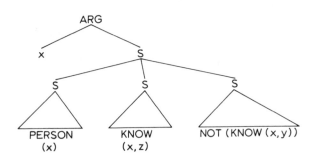

We should ask now what elementary predicate should represent the assertion
of *understand*. This is an important question, since it should be a predicate
that inherently, but at some more general level, represents the modification
that is called for by the predicate *understand*, when asserted. As I have
pointed out, what the assertion of *understand* consists in is that x, who does
not possess the knowledge of y, comes to possess this knowledge. This idea
of 'coming to possess', I think, is just the idea that is carried, at the most
general level, by the verb *to get* in its central meaning (= *to obtain, to receive*).
Apparently, it is not a casual fact that *to get* in this sense has basically the
same argument frame as the verb *to understand* (who – what – from where/
what). The whole structure corresponding to the predicate *to understand*
is the following:

(24)

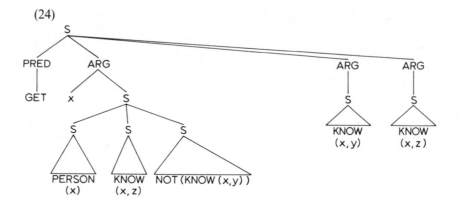

'x, who is a person, who knows z and who does not know y, gets the know-ledge of y from his knowledge of z'.

The structure (24) is a predicative structure. The 'outcome' of this structure, as it is clear from the previous discussion, should be an identifying structure that describes x as having the knowledge of y, i.e. the structure

(25)

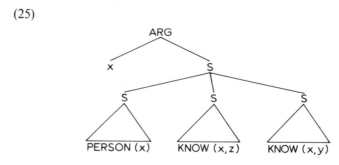

If, in describing semantically the predicate *to understand*, we confine ourselves to giving merely the structure (24), then such an 'outcome' can not directly be read out from this structure. But the structure (24) is to be treated only as an 'instruction' for carrying out definite modifications in the corresponding identifying structures, not as a static structure. The unit which determines the required modifications here is the elementary predicate GET. From this point of view the predicate GET is nothing but a unit which embodies a definite rule for modifying the argument-structures with respect to which it occurs as a predicate, i.e. about which it is asserted. As the comparison of the structures (23) and (25) reveals, the modification in the given case lies in that the structure under the second argument (KNOW (x, y)) is introduced into the first argument, into the description of x, where it replaces the structure NOT (KNOW (x, y)). This basic operation is accompanied by definite other operations which the realization of this basic operation calls for in a natural way: the predicate GET is deleted (since it has done its job); the same thing occurs to the symbol S dominating the whole structure (and indicating that it is a predicative structure); and, lastly, in the given case, the third argument apparently also gets deleted.[4] In this way, from the predicative structure (24) we get the identifying structure (25) which represents the modified description of the person x.

The important point here is that the basic modification described above – the insertion of the structure under the second argument into the description of the individual x – is wholly determined by the predicate GET. This modification always takes place when GET occurs as a predicate. The main requirements that the predicate GET itself imposes on its arguments are apparently the following: the first argument should denote an individual; the structure under the second argument can denote anything that one can 'come to possess', and the third argument identifies a 'place' or 'source' in a very abstract sense. The additional function of *understand* is to determine more concretely the content of these arguments: in particular, that the contents of the second and the third argument represent definite knowledge. In this sense, the situation defined by the predicate *understand* can be considered as a concretization of a more 'primitive' situation represented by the predicate GET.

There are still many other words that can be considered definite concretizations of the same underlying situation. In fact, the use of the surface verb *to get* itself – as, for instance, in sentences (26)–(27) – can also be taken as one such concretization.

(26)   The boy got a new book from his friend.

(27)   The soldier got a letter from his home.

The received objects in both cases are material things and the 'source' is represented by a person (26) or by a concrete place (27). There is yet one more difference between this use of *get* and the described use of *understand* in that here we would say of the corresponding thing (which has been received) that the person x will HAVE it; i.e. that the expression denoting the corresponding thing should in x's description stand in the object-position of some such predicate as HAVE. This fact suggests that perhaps knowledge should also be regarded as something that people have, just as they have things;

---

[4] I am not very sure of the position of this third argument. If it is merely deleted, the question may arise, why this argument is needed at all in the given representation. Apparently, in a more profound treatment, a definite semantic relation should be stated between y and z (e.g. that y were deducible from z). But it is not very clear to me how this should be done in the present context.

i.e. that there should be an additional predicate, HAVE, which has the structures KNOW (x, y) and KNOW (x, z) as its objects in the argument-structures representing x's descriptions in the structures (23)–(25) above, and the function of GET is to bring the content of the second argument – whatever it would be – into the object-position of this predicate HAVE. In fact, it does not contradict our intuition at all to treat the predicate *to know* itself as a concretization of the predicate *to have*. But I am not going to discuss this possibility more thoroughly here.

The complex rule which is embodied by the predicate GET can formally be treated as a transformation in the usual sense of the term and represented as follows:

$$
(28) \quad
\underbrace{\underset{S}{(} \; \underset{}{GET} \; \underset{ARG}{(} \; \underset{}{x}}_{1} \; \underbrace{\underset{S}{(} \; \underset{}{Y} \; \underset{S}{)} \; \underset{}{)}}_{2} \; \underbrace{\underset{S}{(} \; \underset{ARG}{Y} \; \underset{ARG}{)}}_{3} \; \underbrace{\underset{ARG}{(} \; \underset{}{Z} \; \underset{ARG}{)}}_{4\;5} \; \underbrace{\underset{ARG}{(} \; \underset{ARG}{W} \; \underset{S}{)} \; \underset{}{)}}_{6}
$$

$$1\;2\;3\;4\;5\;6 \Longrightarrow 2\;5\;3$$

Many more verbs can be found that can be considered concretizations of the same 'GET-situation' and that are relatively similar to the verb *understand*. Take, for instance, a verb such as *to remember* (in its inchoative meaning). The meaning of this verb does not differ from that of *understand* in anything else than in an additional presupposition about x to the effect that x at some previous time has known the corresponding fact.[5] On the other hand, we may take the predicate structure *to become convinced* which differs from the analyzed verb to understand by the feature that instead of the predicate KNOW the predicate BELIEVE occurs everywhere. But the modification which these predicates – *get, remember, become convinced* – cause in their arguments can be described in precisely the same way. This is the modification which is determined by the elementary predicate GET. And it is just for this reason that we can consider all these predicates variants of the 'GET-situation'. What these facts show is that the treatment of predication as described above offers, in addition to other possibilities, a definite basis for analyzing certain semantical groupings of words. It is possible to find it out and describe, in quite formal terms, what in the case of a concrete group of words the semantic basis which connects these words is and in what respects the meaning of the concrete words in this group differ from this basic situation and from one another.

The other important fact to note in connection with the proposed treatment of predication is that such a treatment gives us a quite strong instrument

[5] It is interesting to note that in Estonian there is a verb *mõistma* and in Finnish there is a verb *muistaa*; they are, undoubtedly, of common historical origin, but the first of them means 'to understand' while the other means 'to remember'.

for deciding how adequate one or another combination of elementary predicates is for describing the meaning of a definite word. If definite rules which determine the modifications to be carried out in the corresponding arguments, are connected with every elementary predicate in describing the meaning of a concrete word, we have to choose a combination of elementary predicates such that the final modifications caused by this combination in the corresponding arguments will be just the modifications which the given word itself determines.

It has to be admitted, lastly, that the treatment given in this section is incomplete in several respects. In order to give more profound treatment of the problems involved here far more extensive analysis of empirical material would be needed. My purpose here was to show in general terms how I imagine the modifications in identifying structures take place and how descriptions of these modifications could be included into general descriptions of predicative expressions.

6. ON THE TREATMENT OF ACTUAL SENTENCES

We have seen how in the case of a single predicate word – a single predicative structure – the idea of predication as changing identifying structures can be realized. In the case of actual sentences the problem is far more complicated. Sentences contain much more semantic material – first of all, they usually consist of several words, and as we know, every word has to be treated as a predicate in the semantic description of a sentence – so that in every concrete case a question arises as to how this material is organized in the sense we are interested in: what part of this material constitutes the new information, what part the identifying information? In a certain sense this is the old and well-known problem of topic – comment analysis of sentences. But, as it seems to me, a great deal of traditional topic-comment problematics turns out to be irrelevant from the point of view of the present approach. In the case of a concrete sentence the question here is not how it could be more naturally divided into topic and comment. We are more interested in analysing messages than sentences. Because of this, in the case of a concrete sentence all possible ways of using this as a message in some concrete situation should be described, and not merely the most 'natural' or 'typical' use of it should be accounted for. For instance, if we have a typical Subject-Verb-Object sentence, such as (29)

(29)   The boy hit the ball.

it is relatively unimportant for us to decide what is more correct to treat here as presenting the new information: is it the Object, or Verb + Object, or only the Verb, or something else? Instead, we have to establish all the different possibilities of distributing new (asserted) and presupposed information in this sentence, and every possibility should be described separately, since it presents a different message. That there are several such possibilities will become clear if we begin to paraphrase the given sentence in the following way:

(29a)   What the boy hit was the ball.
(29b)   The one who hit the ball was the boy.
(29c)   What the boy did to the ball was to hit it.

etc.

It should be clear that (29a)–(29c) are all quite different messages. And it should also be clear that depending on the concrete situation, the sentence (29) can be used to carry any of these messages.

The following important point is that once we have chosen to describe one of these interpretations, our choice automatically determines a definite ordering of the material contained in the sentence. In fact, to every predicate contained in the given sentence there corresponds its own 'sentence' (message). One of these is always the last, or the highest one; and, choosing a definite interpretation of a sentence means just determining this last message made by the corresponding sentence. But once this last message has been determined, the possible hierarchical ordering(s) of the other ones is also determined, whereas every message which stands lower in this hierarchy can function as a presupposition with respect to the higher ones. For instance, if we choose the interpretation (29a) of (29) we shall get, roughly, the following hierarchy of the material contained in this sentence:

(30)

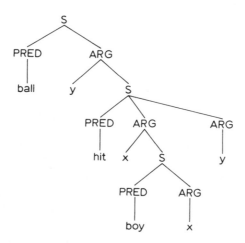

There was a boy; the boy hit something; what the boy hit was the ball.

If we choose the interpretation (29b), the hierarchy will be the following:

(31)

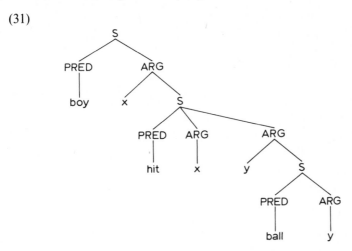

There was a ball; someone hit the ball; the one who hit the ball was the boy.

And only the interpretation (33c) corresponds, more or less, to the analysis which is usually given to sentences of the type (29):

(32)

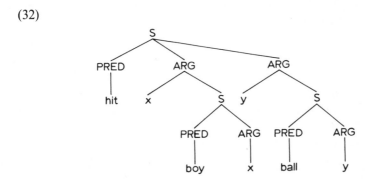

There was a boy; there was a ball; the boy did something to the ball; what the boy did to the ball was that he hit the ball.

As the interpretations (30)–(32) show, the usual sentences (as, for instance, (29)) should be treated, from the point of view of semantics, as certain logically ordered discourses rather than single acts of asserting (as is supposed by topic-comment analysis). Through such an approach, I think, it is possible to connect the treatment of single predicates (as demonstrated earlier) with the treatment of actual sentences. In the case of such an ordered treatment of sentences we always have only one predicate to process at a time. And the material that has resulted from the processing of earlier predicates belongs already to the corresponding arguments and can function as 'previous knowledge' about the objects identified by these arguments when the next higher predicate will be processed.

It is important to note that such an ordered analysis of sentences is by no means a speculatively established procedure but is rather the typical way of interpreting sentences in actual communication (i.e. in the context of a concrete situation where the corresponding sentence is uttered). This claim can also be supported by purely linguistic means, by showing that linguistic context itself often establishes a definite ordering of material in a given sentence. A well known phenomenon in this respect is, of course, emphasis. Emphatic stress always brings out the 'last' message of the corresponding sentence and, thus, also orders the rest of the material contained in the sentence in a definite way. Still other examples can be found where the linguistic context fixes a definite order among the messages in a sentence or clause. We may use here an R. Lakoff's (1968) type of example (used here according to Hakulinen (1970).

(33)   John was not happy although many of us thought so.
(34)*   John was unhappy although many of us thought so.

These sentences show that in the case of (33) but not of (34) the 'last' predicate in the first clause is the negation predicate (negated is the sentence *John was happy*.). The second clause functions in these sentences as an 'order-establishing' context with respect to the corresponding first clause. Since in (34) the order which the second clause requires is impossible in the first clause on implicit grounds, the sentence as a whole becomes unmarked. It may also be pointed out that in the case of (33), normally only the word *not* (and not *happy* or *John*) can be emphatically stressed in the first clause; this demonstrates, in turn, that the 'order of asserting' in this clause is already fixed.

7. CONCLUDING REMARKS

In the above sections I have tried to present the treatment of predicative expressions as instructions (for the hearer) to change in a definite way the identifying structures which the corresponding message is about. As I have said, such an approach is not new in principle. This is well known e.g. in general communication theory or in computational linguistics; but not in linguistics proper. I tried to show that this approach is also wholly in reach of linguistic semantics. It may be shown that every sentence determines, in a certain sense, its own 'domain of discourse' or 'data base', i.e. the objects about which it gives some new information, and the modifications it causes in the hearer's knowledge of these objects. Apparently, only such a linguistic treatment can offer the final required theoretical basis for carrying this approach through consistently in the corresponding practical fields.

The above treatment is, of course, incomplete in many of its details. In particular, I have analysed only the assertive use of language; but it should be clear that there are in principle no obstacles to treating other uses of language along the same lines also (see, for instance, Schwarcz, 1969). My attention was mainly directed towards exploring the general framework in which the idea under discussion could be realized in linguistics and, in particular, in generative semantics. With this intention I have also specially chosen for the above analysis a verb which inherently has a change-of-state meaning. In the case of such verbs what assertion of a predicate amounts to most clearly comes to light. But the important fact is that principally the same types of modifications occur in the assertion of any predicate. They occur also in the case of such predications as, for instance, *John is walking*. Since the general presupposition is always that the hearer does not previously know the fact that is asserted by the corresponding sentence, interpretations of such sentences should also be something like the following: 'I say to you about John, of whom you don't know that he is walking, that he is walking'.

REFERENCES

Bach, E.: 1968, 'Nouns and Noun Phrases', in E. Bach and R. T. Harms, eds., *Universals in Linguistic Theory*, Holt, Rinehart and Winston, New York, pp. 90–122.

Bellert, I.: (in press), 'On the Semantic Interpretation of Subject-Predicate Relations in Sentences of Particular Reference', to appear in M. Bierwisch and K. E. Heidolph, eds., *Progress in Linguistics*, Mouton et Co., The Hague.

Bellert, I.: 1969a, 'Arguments and Predicates in the Logico-Semantic Structure of Utterances', in F. Kiefer, ed., *Studies in Syntax and Semantics*, D. Reidel Publ. Co., Dordrecht-Holland, pp. 34–54.

Bellert, I.: 1969b, 'On the Use of Linguistic Quantifying Operators in the Logico-Semantic Structure Representation of Utterances', International Conference on Computational Linguistics, Stockholm, Preprint No. 28.

Fillmore, C. J.: 1970, 'Subjects, Speakers, and Roles', *Working Papers in Linguistics* No. 4, The Ohio State University, Columbus, Ohio, pp. 31–62.

Hakulinen, A.: 1970, 'Negaatiosta ja lauseiden välisistä suhteista', *Transformaatioita*, Publications of the Phonetics Department of the University of Turku No. 7, pp 22–40.

Karttunen, L.: 1968, 'Coreference and Discourse', Presented at the 43rd Annual Meeting of the Linguistic Society of America.

Karttunen, L.: 1969, *Problems of Reference in Syntax*, mimeo, University of Texas.

Lakoff, G.: 1970, *Linguistics and Natural Logic*, Studies in Generative Semantics No. 1, Phonetics Laboratory, The University of Michigan.

Lakoff, R.: 1968, *Abstract Syntax and Latin Complementation*, MIT Research Monograph No. 49.

Langendoen, T. D.: 1967, 'On Selection, Projection, Meaning, and Semantic Content', *Working Papers in Linguistics* No. 1, The Ohio State University, Columbus, Ohio, pp. 100–109.

McCawley, J. D.: 1968, 'The Role of Semantics in a Grammar', in E. Bach and R. T. Harms, eds., *Universals in Linguistic Theory*, Holt, Rinehart and Winston, New York, pp. 124–169.

Morgan, J. A.: 1968, 'On the Notion "Possible Lexical Item" ', Presented at the 43rd Annual Meeting of the Linguistic Society of America.

Quillian, M. R.: 1969, 'The Teachable Language Comprehender: A Simulation Program and Theory of Language', *Communications of the ACM*, Vol. 12, No. 8, pp. 459–476.

Ross, J. R.: 1967, 'On the Cyclic Nature of English Pronominalization', in *To Honor Roman Jakobson*, Vol. III, Mouton & Co., The Hague, pp. 1669–1682.

Schwarcz, R. M.: 1969, 'Towards a Computational Formalization of Natural Language Semantics', International Conference on Computational Linguistics, Stockholm, Preprint No. 29.

Õim, H.: 1970a, 'On the Relation between Semantic and Syntactic Representations', *Soviet Fenno-Ugric Studies*, Vol. 6, No. 1, pp. 25–36.

Õim, H.: 1970b, *Isiku mõistega seotud sõnarühmade semantiline struktuur eesti keeles*, Väitekiri filoloogiakandidaadi kraadi taotlemiseks, Tartu Riiklik Ülikool, Eesti keele kateeder.

Õim, H.: 1970c, 'On Pronominalization and Semantic Treatment of Sentences', *Abstracts of the Annual Meeting of the Research Group for Generative Grammar*, Tartu State University, Department of Estonian Language, Tartu, pp. 58–63.

H. RÄTSEP

GOVERNMENT STRUCTURE TYPES OF THE VERBS
OF SAYING AND ACTION SITUATIONS

1. The following analysis represents a part of a more extensive work treating the government structure types of Estonian simple verbs. The government structure type joins all the government structures which are possible in the case of a certain fixed meaning of a certain verb into one unity. To consider all secondary classes (the element forming the subject included) that can occur with the verb and the possibility and/or the form of occurrence of which are fully dependent on the given verb, on its meaning, as the elements of the government structure. These secondary classes may be either obligatory or optional (the latter will be given in parentheses) members of the government structure type. For details about these classes and the ways in which they are presented in the description of the government structure type *see* Rätsep (1969).

An analysis of the government structure types of Estonian verbs reveals that a different government structure type corresponds to each different meaning of the verb. It becomes evident that even small modifications in the meaning of the verb are connected with a change in the government structure type. The above is also valid for the verbs of saying analyzed below.

The government structure types looked upon in such a way are surface structure phenomena. Their form depends on the structure of the respective language, its morphology. In Estonian certain groups of verbs may have rather complicated government structure types. Undoubtedly one reason lies in the fact that the morphology of the Estonian language is rather complicated and rich in elements (14 cases and parallel to them almost a hundred postpositions, some prepositions, five-six infinitives).

In the deep structure the base of the government structure types is formed by semantic structures and their generalizations, types of semantic structures. In the present paper, situation descriptions are used to present the qualities of such semantic structures. The Estonian verbs of saying and structure types corresponding to them constitute the concrete material.

2. If we consider common simple sentences concentrated around one verb, we can see that the base of each such sentence is formed by a certain situation which is in some way marked by the sentence and with respect to which the speaker presents his attitude. Usually the verb or its equivalent

F. Kiefer and N. Ruwet (eds.), Generative Grammar in Europe, 387–406. *All Rights Reserved.*
Copyright © *1973 by D. Reidel Publishing Company, Dordrecht-Holland.*

expresses action (in the broad sense of the word) which organizes the situation. The situation elements participating in the action become evident as various secondary parts of a sentence in the surface structure.

As the situation forming the base for the sentence is characterized by a certain action (or more exactly action, state, situation, etc.) we may call these situations *action situations*. We make a distinction between action situations and *communicative situations*. A situation where the speaker uses a certain sentence is called a communicative situation. In the present paper some action situations are analyzed. Concerning communicative situations *see* Rätsep (1971).

These elements of the action situation that must or may be expressed as members of the government structure of the verb in the surface structure are called relevant elements of the action situation. In an action situation there may be one or more relevant elements. A corresponding action joins them all into one whole. Similar actions have similar action situations. A concrete sentence describes a situation in its concrete form. Proceeding from the government structure type we get an action situation in a general form. The number of general action situations is very big but it is still possible to join even them into groups where a certain general action situation prevails. The other action situations belonging here may be considered as variants of the general action situation.

Not every verb has its own specific action situation. Usually several verbs share the same action situation. In such a case their difference becomes evident in the surface structure only, if at all. Although in general relevant situation elements in the surface structure are marked by the secondary parts of a sentence belonging to the verb, some situation elements may in certain cases be expressed not only as independent units in the surface structure but also in the stem of the verb. We should mention that we consider a sentence acceptable if it can occur free of context. Context-restricted sentences will be omitted from the fixation of government rules, since quite different rules operate in their formation. For details about situation analysis *see* Rätsep (1970).

3. We consider speaking situations to be variants of informing situations. Besides speaking situations singing and several signalling situations belong here.

In a general informing situation we distinguish the following relevant elements:

INFORMING {INFORMER, RECEIVER, TEXT, INFORMATION, OBJECT, CODE, INSTRUMENT, LOCATION, STARTING POINT, DESTINATION}

Let us treat these situation elements in more detail. INFORMER is the person from whom the information proceeds, who informs. RECEIVER is the person to whom the information is directed. TEXT is the information itself, either in a concrete (e.g. *George informed (us) that his father had been ill. George announced: 'My father was ill'.*) or general form (e.g. *George informed the monitor about the data*). INFORMATION OBJECT is the object or phenomenon the information refers to. CODE is the system of signs (natural languages included) by which TEXT is rendered. INSTRUMENT – the instrument for the rendering of the text (voice, technical device, letter, etc.). LOCATION is the place where both INFORMER and RECEIVER are located (e.g. *George informed Peter about the letter only in Tallinn*). If there is a distance in space between INFORMER and RECEIVER the notion LOCATION is more general. STARTING POINT is the place where INFORMER is located and DESTINATION the place where RECEIVER is located.

Such general INFORMING is expressed in Estonian by the verb *teatama I* 'inform'. The verb *teatama* has some other, narrower meanings in Estonian and therefore we have to number them. *teada andma* 'let know' has the same meaning and situation.

The elements of the informing situation in the case of these verbs are expressed in Estonian as follows:

$$\text{INFORMER} \to \text{N} + \text{nom.}; \quad \text{RECEIVER} \to \text{N} + \text{all.}; \quad \text{TEXT} \to \text{N} + \text{ngp.}$$
$$\sim \text{KL} = \text{OK}; \quad \text{INFORMATION OBJECT} \to \text{N} + \text{el.}; \quad \text{CODE} \to \text{Ll}; \quad \text{INSTRUMENT} \to \text{N} + \text{kom.} \sim \text{N} + \text{nom.}; \quad \text{LOCATION} \to \text{Loc}; \quad \text{STARTING POINT} \to \text{De}; \quad \text{DESTINATION} \to \text{Di.}$$

Some notes on the symbols: N = (noun) substantive, nom. = nominative, all. = allative, ngp. = nominative $\sim$ genitive $\sim$ partitive (the choice of the case depends on other circumstances), el. = elative, kom. = comitative, Ll = a local substitution class of forms marking the language, De = extra-local substitution class referring to the direction, Di = intra-local substitution class referring to the direction, KL = subordinate clause, OK = direct speech.

Usually N + nom. denoting INFORMER is the subject in the surface structure but a form designating INSTRUMENT may also function as such in which case it likewise stands in the nominative (N + nom.).

If we take into account the obligatoriness – optionality of the elements of the government structure type and their mutual limitations, the government structure type of the verb *teatama I* in Estonian is as follows:

$$\text{N}' + \text{nom. V}\{\text{N}^2 + \text{ngp.} \sim \text{N}^3 + \text{el.} \sim \text{KL} = \text{OK}\}\,(\text{N}^4 + \text{all.})$$
$$(\text{N}^5 + \text{kom.})\,(\text{Loc})\,(\text{De})\,(\text{Di})\,(\text{Ll})$$

$$N^5 + \text{nom. V} + 3.p.\{N^2 + \text{ngp.} \sim N^3 + \text{el.} \sim \text{KL} = \text{OK}\}$$
$$(N^4 + \text{all.})(\text{Loc})(\text{De})(\text{Di})(\text{Ll})$$

As can be seen the surface structure manifestations of TEXT and INFORMATION OBJECT in Estonian are in the relation of substitution. In the case of the given verb one of them must be represented but together they cannot be represented in the same sentence. *3.p.* after the symbol of the verb *V* in the second line refers to the fact that the verb may be in the third person only. Some examples of this government structure type follow.

> *Isa teatas oma telefoninumbri.* 'Father gave (us) his telephone number.'

> *Isa teatas oma saabumisest.* 'Father informed (us) about his arrival.'

> *Isa teatas, et ta tuleb esmaspäeval.* 'Father informed (us) that he would come on Monday.'

> *Isa teatas: 'Tulen esmaspäeval.'* 'Father announced: 'I shall come on Monday'.'

> *Isa teatas pojale oma telefoninumbri.* 'Father gave his telephone number to (his) son.'

> *Isa teatas telegrammiga oma telefoninumbri.* 'Father reported his telephone number in a telegram.'

> *Isa teatas pojale Tallinnas oma telefoninumbri.* 'Father gave his telephone number to (his) son in Tallinn.'

> *Isa teatas Tallinnast pojale oma telefoninumbri.* 'Father reported his telephone number to (his) son from Tallinn.'

> *Isa teatas Tartusse oma telefoninumbri.* 'Father reported his telephone number to Tartu.'

> *Isa teatas oma saabumisest eesti keeles.* 'Father informed (us) about his arrival in Estonian.'

> *Telegramm teatas isa telefoninumbri.* 'The telegram reported father's telephone number,' etc.

4. As we have already mentioned, speaking situations where the action is expressed by means of the so-called verbs of saying form a kind of informing situation. All the verbs denoting the human activity of speaking in its various aspects are regarded as verbs of saying. The Latin term *verba dicendi* has also been used to refer to these verbs in grammar-books. A whole doctoral dissertation has been dedicated to a comparative semantic analysis of the verbs of saying in the Balto-Finnic languages (Siro, 1949).

We shall now consider some special cases of speaking situations and their representations in the surface structure of Estonian.

The verbs of saying and the situations corresponding to them may be divided into two groups: primary verbs of saying and speaking situations and secondary verbs of saying and speaking situations.

It is speaking (or saying) as informing that is predominant in the meaning of the primary verbs of saying and the corresponding situations. This can be seen, for instance, in the following Estonian sentences:

> *Peeter kõneles Jürile oma uuest plaanist.* 'Peter spoke about his new plan to George.'

> *Jüri jutustas Peetrile oma reisist.* 'George told Peter about his trip.'

> *Peeter ütles Jürile, et ta läheb koju.* 'Peter told George that he would go home.'

> *Jüri ei lausunud Peetrile ühtki sõna.* 'George did not say a single word to Peter.'

Secondary verbs of saying denote actions which are carried out by means of speaking but where the speaking is not primary. The aim of speaking, that of the speaker himself, is primary. This can be seen in the following Estonian sentences, e.g.:

> *Peeter noomis Jürit hilinemise pärast.* 'Peter rebuked George for his being late.'

> *Jüri kaebas Peetrile oma õnnetust.* 'George complained about his misfortune to Peter.'

> *Peeter riidles Jüriga koera pärast.* 'Peter scolded George because of the dog.'

> *Jüri kiitis Peetrile oma uut koera.* 'George praised his new dog to Peter.'

In the present article we can only treat primary verbs of saying in more detail.

5.0. The situation defined by the following elements forms the base for the most common informing by speech:

SPEAKING {SPEAKER (= INFORMER), LISTENER (= RECEIVER), TEXT, OBJECT OF SPEAKING (= INFORMATION OBJECT), LANGUAGE (= CODE), INSTRUMENT, LOCATION, STARTING POINT, DESTINATION, HINDRANCE}

The brackets contain the corresponding elements in the general informing situation. One element, HINDRANCE, has been added. It points to the obstacle in the way of speech through or over which speaking occurs. It is absent from the general informing situation. This most common speaking situation is represented in the surface structure of Estonian by means of the following elements:

SPEAKER – N + nom.; LISTENER – N + all.; TEXT – N + ngp. ∼ KL = OK; OBJECT OF SPEAKING – N + el. ∼ N + gen. kohta; LANGUAGE – Ll; INSTRUMENT – N + ad. ∼ N + kom. ∼ N + nom.; LOCATION – Loc; STARTING POINT – De; DESTINATION – Di; HINDRANCE – Dt_2.

Some explanations of the new symbols: N + gen. kohta – (noun) substantive in the genitive with the postposition *kohta;* ad. – adessive; Dt_2 – translocal substitution class whose members refer to the object through or over which a certain action occurs.

Several government structure types, the differences between which are mainly expressed in the obligatority – optionality and mutual conditionality of the elements, are based on this speaking situation in Estonian.

5.1.

$$N' + \text{nom. } V(\{\{N^2 + \text{ngp. } \sim KL = OK \text{ v } N^3 + \text{el.}\}$$
$$= \{\{N^2 + \text{ngp. } \sim KL = OK\} (N^3 + \text{gen. kohta})$$
$$(N^4 + \text{all.}) (\text{De})) (N^5 + \text{ad. } \sim N^6 + \text{kom.}) (\text{Loc})$$
$$(\text{Di}) (Dt_2) (Ll)$$

$$N^{5 \sim 6} + \text{nom. } V + 3.\text{p.} (\{\{N^2 + \text{ngp. } \sim KL = OK \text{ v } N^3 + \text{el.}\}$$
$$= \{\{N^2 + \text{ngp. } \sim KL = OK\} (N^3 + \text{gen.}$$
$$\text{kohta})\}\} (N^4 + \text{all.}) (\text{De})) (\text{Loc}) (\text{Di}) (Dt_2) (Ll)$$

Such a government structure type is characteristic first and foremost of the verbs *kõnelema 3* ('speak, tell') and *rääkima 3* ('speak, tell'). Examples:

(1)   *Sepp kõneles.* 'The smith was speaking.'

(2)   *Sepp kõneles pika loo.* 'The smith told a long story.'

(3)   *Sepp kõneles oma lapsepõlvest.* 'The smith spoke about his childhood.'

(4)   *Sepp kõneles pojapojale oma lapsepõlve kohta pika loo.* 'The smith told a long story about his childhood to his grandson.'

(5)   *Sepp kõneles aias.* 'The smith was speaking in the garden.'

(6)   *Sepp kõneles voodist.* 'The smith was speaking from (his) bed.'

(7)   *Sepp kõneles poisi kõrva sisse.* 'The smith was speaking into the boy's ear.'

(8)   *Sepp kõneles eesti keeles.* 'The smith was speaking in Estonian.'

(9)   *Sepp kõneles tasase häälega.* 'The smith was speaking in a low voice.'

(10)   *Tasane hääl kõneles eesti keeles.* 'A low voice was speaking in Estonian.'

(11)   *Tasane hääl kõneles ukse tagant.* 'A low voice was speaking from behind the door.'

Kõnelema ja *rääkima* are dialectal variants in literary Estonian.

Some explanatory notes on the above statements. The double representation of OBJECT OF SPEAKING $N + el.$ and $N + gen.$ *kohta* deserves special mention here. There are differences in the possibilities of occurence of these two elements. Namely $N + gen.$ *kohta* can occur only when an element denoting TEXT is present in the sentence, while $N + el.$ may occur even when the latter, i.e. TEXT is absent. Cf. sentences (3) and (4). **Sepp kõneles oma lapsepõlve kohta.* 'The smith was speaking about his childhood' is not acceptable.

Differences in the possibilities of occurrence of the elements $N + ad.$ and $N + kom.$ denoting INSTRUMENT are due to the contents of the members of class N. In the case of some (noun) substantives these elements are equivalent (*Ta rääkis valjul häälel = Ta rääkis valju häälega.* 'He was speaking in a loud voice.'), in some other cases only $N + kom.$ is possible (*Ta kõneles kõlava baritoniga.* 'He was speaking in a resonant baritone.'). When the element denoting INSTRUMENT occupies the place of the subject in the sentence, it occurs in the form $N + nom.$ Cf. sentences (10) and (11).

The possibilities of occurrence of $N + all.$ representing LISTENER are more limited than those of other elements of this type. $N + all.$ can occur only when either TEXT or OBJECT OF SPEAKING is realized. In the opposite case the sentence is not acceptable in the context-free form. Cf. sentence (4) and

Sepp kõneles pojapojale. 'The smith was speaking to his grandson' which is not acceptable.

Here we should mention that the substantive in the allative case which denotes the owner of some inalienable property in the sentence and is equivalent to the substantive in the genitive, has usually been omitted from the government structures. For example, *Sepp kõneles poisile kõrva sisse* 'The smith was speaking into the boy's ear' which is equivalent to sentence (7).

In the case of more complicated government structure types that have more elements we can observe a general phenomenon in Estonian. Namely, the more different government structure elements we include in one sentence, the more difficult it is to form an acceptable sentence. The word order becomes more and more fixed. In the end the sentence loses its clarity, its links become loose and the sentence inacceptable. It is obvious that in cases of the verbs of saying, the so-called maximum sentences, i.e. sentences where all situation elements are simultaneously realized, are not acceptable either.

Let us compare the acceptability of the following sentences:

(12)   *Sepp kõneles aias pojapojale oma lapsepõlvest pika loo.* 'In the garden the smith told (his) grandson a long story about his childhood.'

(13)   *Sepp kõneles aias tugitoolist pojapojale oma lapsepõlvest pika loo.* 'The smith told (his) grandson a long story about his childhood from the armchair in the garden.'

(14)   *Sepp kõneles aias tugitoolist pojapojale kõrva sisse oma lapsepõlvest pika loo.* 'The smith told (his) grandson, into the ear, a long story about his childhood from the armchair in the garden.'

(15)   *Sepp kõneles aias tugitoolist pojapojale kõrva sisse eesti keeles oma lapsepõlvest pika loo.* 'The smith told (his) grandson, into the ear, a long story in Estonian about his childhood from the armchair in the garden.'

(16)   *Sepp kõneles aias tugitoolist pojapojale läbi suud katva marli kõrva sisse eesti keeles oma lapsepõlvest pika loo.* 'The smith told (his) grandson, through the gauze covering his mouth (and) into the ear, a long story in Estonian about his childhood from the armchair in the garden.'

It seems that if more than six different situation elements are represented in a sentence, it loses the compactness of links, becomes obscure and unacceptable (cf. sentences (14), (15), (16)). The transition to unacceptability seems to be gradual.

5.2.

$$
\left.
\begin{array}{l}
N' + \text{nom. V } N^2 + \text{ngp.}(N^3 + \text{el.} = N^3 \\
+ \text{gen. kohta}) (N^4 + \text{ad.} \sim N^5 + \text{kom.}) \\[6pt]
N' + \text{nom. V}\{KL = OK\} (N^3 + \text{gen.} \\
\text{kohta}) (N^4 + \text{ad.} \sim N^5 + \text{kom.}) \\[6pt]
N^{4\sim5} + \text{nom. V} + 3.\text{p. } N^2 + \text{ngp.}(N^3 \\
+ \text{el.} = N^3 + \text{gen. kohta}) \\[6pt]
N^{4\sim5} + \text{nom. V} + 3.\text{p.}\{KL = OK\} \\
(N^3 + \text{gen. kohta})
\end{array}
\right\}
\begin{array}{l}
(N^6 + \text{all.}) (\text{Loc}) (\text{De}) \\
(\text{Di}) (\text{Dt}_2) (\text{Ll})
\end{array}
$$

The verbs *ütlema I* 'say' and *lausuma I* 'utter' have such a government structure type. The base for the type is formed by the same situation which was present in the previous type. Differences occur in the obligatority-optionality and limitations of the elements. Examples:

(1)   *Sepp ütles ainult ühe sõna.* 'The smith said only one word.'

(2)   *Sepp ütles oma lapsepõlvest ainult ühe lause.* 'The smith said only one sentence about his childhood.'

(3)   *Sepp ütles oma lapsepõlve kohta ainult ühe lause.* 'The smith said only one sentence about his childhood.'

(4)   *Sepp ütles pojapojale ainult ühe sõna.* 'The smith said only one word to (his) grandson.'

(5)   *Sepp ütles valjul häälel ainult ühe sõna.* 'In a loud voice the smith said only one word.'

(6)   *Sepp ütles aias ainult ühe sõna.* 'The smith said only one word in the garden.'

(7)   *Sepp ütles toa nurgast ainult ühe sõna.* 'The smith said only one word from the corner of the room.'

(8)   *Sepp ütles pojapoja kõrva sisse ainult ühe sõna.* 'The smith said only one word into his grandson's ear.'

(9)   *Sepp ütles läbi trellide ainult ühe sõna.* 'The smith said only one word through the bars.'

(10)   *Sepp ütles eesti keeles ainult ühe sõna.* 'The smith said only one word in Estonian.'

(11)   *Sepp ütles asja kohta, et ta ei tea midagi.* 'The smith said he knew nothing about the matter.'

(12)   *"Ma ei tea midagi," ütles sepp selle asja kohta.* ' "I know nothing," the smith said about this matter.'

As compared with the action denoted by the previous verbs, we can see that the verbs *ütlema I* 'say' and *lausuma I* 'utter' do not express continuous actions as is the case with the verbs *kõnelema 3* 'speak, tell' and *rääkima 3* 'speak, tell.' Therefore TEXT of the first mentioned verbs cannot be a long unit but must be limited, short one (word, sentence), if it is represented at all. It is impossible to say: *Sepp ütles pojapojale pika loo oma lapsepõlvest.* 'The smith told a long story about his childhood to (his) grandson.'

The main difference between this and the previous government structure type arises here: the representation of the situation element TEXT in a context-free sentence is obligatory. Thus *N + ngp., KL* or *OK* must be represented in the sentence. The sentence *Sepp ütles* 'The smith said' is not acceptable.

In addition there are differences in the representation of OBJECT OF SPEAK-ING: element *N + el.* cannot occur when TEXT is denoted by the elements *KL* or *OK*. Consequently, the sentence* *"Ma ei tea midagi," ütles sepp sellest asjast.* ' "I know nothing," the smith said on this matter.' is not acceptable in Estonian and the other representative of OBJECT OF SPEAKING in the surface structure, element *N + gen. kohta* must be used in the given sentence.

The verbs *ütlema I* 'say' and *lausuma I* are full synonyms. What is valid for *ütlema I* is also valid for *lausuma I*.

5.3.

$$N' + \text{nom. } V\{KL = OK\} (N^2 + \text{all.}) (N^3 + \text{ad.} \sim N^4 + \text{kom.})$$
$$(\text{Loc}) (\text{De}) (\text{Di}) (\text{Dt}_2) (\text{Ll})$$

$$N^{3 \sim 4} + \text{nom. } V + 3.\text{p.}\{KL = OK\} (N^2 + \text{all.}) (\text{Loc}) (\text{De})$$
$$(\text{Di}) (\text{Dt}_2) (\text{Ll})$$

The verb *sõnama* 'say' has such a government structure type. It is conspicuous that the element OBJECT OF SPEAKING is absent in the situation forming the base, i.e. we regard as unacceptable such sentences as:

> *Peeter sõnas uksehoidjale võtme kohta: "Ma ei tea sellest midagi."* 'Peter said to the doorkeeper about the key, "I know nothing about it." '

> *Peeter sõnas uksehoidjale võtmest: "Ma ei tea sellest midagi."* 'Peter said to the doorkeeper about the key, "I know nothing about it." '

On the other hand, the following sentence is quite acceptable:

Peeter sõnas uksehoidjale: "Ma ei tea sellest midagi." 'Peter said to the doorkeeper, "I know nothing about it." '

Unlike the previous elements, TEXT is realized in the surface structure here. Only the subordinate clause (KL) or direct speech (OK) are possible, while the substantive in the nominative, genitive or partitive (N + ngp.) cannot occur. Therefore the following sentence is not acceptable:

*Peeter sõnas uksehoidjale ainult ühe sõna. 'Peter said only one word to the doorkeeper.'

5.4.

$N' + $ nom. $V(\{\{N^2 + $ ngp. $\sim OK$ v $N + $ el.$\} = \{N^2 + $ ngp. $\sim OK(N^3 + $ gen. kohta)$\}$ v $N^4 + $ ad. $\sim N^5 + $ kom. v Loc v Ll$\}(N^6 + $ all.) (De) (Di) (Dt$_2$))

$N' + $ nom. $V(\{N^4 + $ ad. $\sim N^5 + $ kom. v Loc v Ll v KL$\}$ (N^6 + all.) (De) (Di) (Dt$_2$))

$N^{4\sim5} + $ nom. $V + $ 3.p.$(\{\{N^2 + $ ngp. $\sim OK$ v $N^3 + $ el.$\}$ $ = \{N^3 + $ ngp. $\sim OK(N^3 + $ gen. kohta)$\}$ v Loc v Ll$\}(N^6 + $ all.) (De) (Di) (Dt$_2$))

$N^{4\sim5} + $ nom. $V + $ 3.p.$(\{$Loc v Ll v KL$\}(N^6 + $ all.) (De) (Di) (Dt$_2$))

The verbs *jutustama 2* 'tell', *pajatama 1* 'tell' have such a rather complicated government structure type. The same action situation as in the case of the verb *kõnelema 3* 'speak' (**5.1**) forms the base here. Even the correspondences of the situation elements in the surface structure are exactly the same. Differences occur in the mutual limitations of the surface structure elements. These verbs denote the oral rendering of longer information. Examples:

Sepp jutustas. 'The smith was telling (a story).'

Sepp jutustas pika loo. 'The smith told a long story.'

Sepp jutustas oma lapsepõlvest. 'The smith was telling about (his) childhood.'

Sepp jutustas oma lapsepõlve kohta pika loo. 'The smith told a long story about his childhood.'

Sepp jutustas aias. 'The smith was telling (a story) in the garden.'

Sepp jutustas eesti keeles. 'The smith was telling (a story) in Estonian.'

Sepp jutustas tasase häälega. 'The smith was telling (a story) in a low voice.'

Sepp jutustas pojapojale pika loo. 'The smith told a long story to (his) grandson.'

Sepp jutustas tugitoolist pojapojale muinasjutu. 'The smith told a fairy-tale to (his) grandson from the armchair.'

Sepp jutustas pojapojale kõrva sisse toreda loo. 'The smith told a nice story to (his) grandson *into the ear.*'

Sepp jutustas sõpradele läbi võre, kuidas tal läks. 'The smith told (his) friends through the bars (about) how he had fared.'

Tasane hääl jutustas, kuidas madrus päästeti. 'A low voice told (about) how the sailor had been saved.'

The main specific feature of the government structures of these verbs is the fact that the elements of this government structure type fall into two groups: the elements belonging to one group may alone, together with the verb, form a complete context-free sentence; those belonging to the other group always require the presence of some of the elements of the first group. Thus the sentences **Sepp jutustas tugitoolist* 'The smith was telling (a story) from the armchair.' **Sepp jutustas kõrva sisse.* 'The smith was telling (a story) into the ear.' **Sepp jutustas läbi võre.* 'The smith was telling (a story) through the bars.' are unacceptable.

Moreover, OBJECT OF SPEAKING cannot be represented as a separate surface structure element in the sentence when TEXT is represented by a subordinate clause (KL). This limitation refers to the fact that OBJECT OF SPEAKING and TEXT are as if joined together. Therefore the sentences **Sepp jutustas lapsepõlvest, kuidas ta kalu püüdis.* 'The smith told (us) how he had gone fishing in his childhood.' *Sepp jutustas lapsepõlve kohta, kuidas ta kalu püüdis.* 'The smith told (us) how he had gone fishing in his childhood.' are not acceptable.

6. So far we have treated speaking situation types where the information has been conveyed in one direction: the speaker imparts some information to the listener. But speaking, rendering the information, may also occur in two directions. We would call such a speaking situation TALKING. In this situation some situation elements have been altered. If we consider the basic situation presented above, the following alternations take place. The elements SPEAKER-LISTENER 1 and SPEAKER-LISTENER 2 have been substituted for SPEAKER and LISTENER, i.e. there are two elements in the situation, both in the functions of both INFORMER and RECEIVER. The reciprocity of the information is stressed by a separate RECIPROCAL ELEMENT. TEXT cannot occur in this situation as it requires the reference to the source. In the present situation there are two speakers-listeners and it is impossible to ascertain the author of the text. The elements STARTING POINT and DESTINATION are not possible in this situation, either as they denote the location of SPEAKER and LISTENER separately. On the other hand, the element LOCATION is present and refers to the common location of both SPEAKER-LISTENER. The situation elements are the following:

TALKING {SPEAKER-LISTENER 1, SPEAKER-LISTENER 2, OBJECT OF SPEAKING, RECIPROCAL ELEMENT, INSTRUMENT, LANGUAGE, LOCATION, HINDRANCE}

These situation elements are expressed in the surface structure of Estonian as follows:

SPEAKER-LISTENER $1 - N' + $ nom.; SPEAKER-LISTENER $2 - N^2 + $ kom. $\sim N^2 + $ nom.; OBJECT OF SPEAKING $- N^3 + $ el. $\sim N^3 + $ gen. üle $\sim [N^3 + $ gen. $\sim A + $ ad.$] N^4 + $ ad.;   RECIPROCAL ELEMENT $-$ substitution class R; INSTRUMENT $- N^5 + $ ad. $\sim N^6 + $ kom.; LANGUAGE $-$ substitution class Ll; LOCATION $-$ substitution class Loc; HINDRANCE $-$ substitution class De$_2$.

The government structure type pointing to the limitations and relations of the surface structure is the following:

$$\begin{cases} N' + \text{nom. V } N^2 + \text{kom.} \\ N' + \text{nom. ja } N^2 + \text{nom. V (R)} \\ N + \text{nom.} + \text{pl. V (R)} \end{cases} \begin{cases} (N^3 + \text{el.} = N^3 + \text{gen. üle} \\ \sim [\{N^3 + \text{gen.} \sim A + \text{ad.}\} \\ N^4 + \text{ad.}])(N^5 + \text{ad.} \sim N^6 \\ + \text{kom.}) (\text{Loc}) (\text{Dt}_2) (\text{Ll}) \end{cases}$$

This government structure type is characteristic of the reciprocal verbs *jutlema* 'talk', *kõnelema 13* 'speak', *rääkima 13* 'speak', *vestlema* 'talk'. Some explanations and examples of this type follow.

SPEAKER-LISTENER 1 and SPEAKER-LISTENER 2 may be represented in the surface structure of Estonian in three ways.

(a) SPEAKER-LISTENER $1 - N' + nom.$, SPEAKER-LISTENER $2 - N^2 + kom.$ In such a case one feels that the role of SPEAKER of the first element and the role of LISTENER of the second element are more active. For example, *Jaan kõneles Jüriga* 'John was speaking to George.' *Jaan vestles Jüriga* 'John was talking to George.'

(b) SPEAKER-LISTENER 1 – N' + *nom.*, SPEAKER-LISTENER 2 – N^2 + *nom.*, i.e. both substantives are in the nominative. In this case both sides are equally active in their roles of SPEAKER and LISTENER. For example, *Jaan ja Jüri kõnelesid.* 'John and George were speaking.' *Jaan ja Jüri vestlesid.* 'John and George were talking.'

(c) Both situation elements are joined into one plural element in the surface structure – N + *nom.* + *pl.* Here one need not distinguish between the elements and we can speak of them in a general form as there is no need to differentiate their activity. For example, *Noormehed kõnelesid.* 'The young men were speaking.' *Noormehed vestlesid.* 'The young men were talking.'

In the last two cases the reciprocity may be stressed by means of words of pronominal character such as *üksteisega* 'with one another,' *teineteisega* 'with each other,' *omavahel* 'between themselves,' *isekeskis* 'among themselves,' which we have joined into the substitution class R. For example: *Jaan ja Jüri kõnelesid teineteisega.* 'John and George were speaking with each other.' *Jaan ja Jüri vestlesid omavahel.* 'John and George were talking between themselves.' *Jaan ja Jüri kõnelesid isekeskis.* 'John and George were talking among themselves.' *Noormehed konelesid üksteisega.* 'The young men were speaking with one another.' *Noormehed kõnelesid teineteisega.* 'The young men were talking with each other.' *Noormehed kõnelesid omavahel.* 'The young men were speaking between themselves.'

In literary Estonian there is a rule which says that *teineteisega* 'with each other' refers to only two SPEAKERS-LISTENERS, *üksteisega* 'with one another' more than two SPEAKERS-LISTENERS. In colloquial speech the rule is not always followed. The substitution class R cannot occur in case (a) as the reciprocity is not complete and equal here as was observable in the above example.

OBJECT OF SPEAKING in this type may occur in very many forms. Between the elements N + *el.* and N + *gen. üle* there are the relations of equality. Cf. *Jaan kõneles Jüriga lastekasvatamisest.* 'John was speaking to George on the education of children.' *Jaan kõneles Jüriga lastekasvatamise üle.* 'John was speaking to George about the education of children.'

The third complex representation of OBJECT OF SPEAKING presupposes the obligatory attribute N + *gen.* or A + *ad.* and is rather special, since the number of substantives belonging to N^4 is very limited. For example,

> *Jaan ja Jüri kõnelesid huvitaval teemal.* 'John and George were speaking on an interesting subject.'

> *Noormehed vestlesid muusika teemadel.* 'The young men were talking on the subject of music.'

7.   There exists one more kind of reciprocal speaking where the emphasis is not so much on reciprocity as on the transmission of information for the purpose of achieving something. Let us compare the following sentences with the previous ones from this point of view.

> *Peeter kõneles direktoriga autobussi pärast.* 'Peter was speaking to the director on account of the bus.'

> *Peeter kõneles direktoriga autobussi üle.* 'Peter was speaking to the director about the bus.'

> *Tuttav hääl kõneles esikus direktoriga autobussi pärast.* 'A familiar voice was speaking to the director on account of the bus in the vestibule.'

Even here we have two SPEAKERS-LISTENERS, but one of them is the main SPEAKER, the active SPEAKER. Therefore it is impossible to stress the reciprocity of the action by a specific element in this situation. Otherwise the situation elements are the same as in the previous type.

As regards the representation of the situation elements in the surface structure and as compared with the previous type, the difference lies in the fact that SPEAKER-LISTENER 2 is expressed by N + *nom.* only, i.e. possibilities (b) and (c) are excluded. OBJECT OF SPEAKING is rendered by the elements N + *gen. pärast* ~ N + *gen. üle*. The representation of INSTRUMENT may be the subject of the sentence. In the previous type it was impossible because of the action.

The government structure type occurring in the surface structure is as follows:

$$N' + \text{nom. V } N^2 + \text{kom.}(N^3 + \text{ad. } \sim N^4 + \text{kom.})(N^5 +$$
$$\text{gen. pärast} = N^5 + \text{gen. üle}) (\text{Loc}) (\text{De}) (\text{Dt}_2)$$
$$(\text{Ll})$$
$$N^{3\sim4} + \text{nom. V} + 3.\text{p. } N^2 + \text{kom.}(N^5 + \text{gen. pärast} = N^5$$
$$\text{gen. üle})(\text{Loc}) (\text{De}) (\text{Dt}_2) (\text{Ll})$$

The verbs *kõnelema* 14 'speak, tell' and *rääkima* 14 'speak, tell.'

8.   Addressing somebody with a speech represents a special situation. In this situation the elements DESTINATION and HINDRANCE are absent. The situation elements are the following:

> {SPEAKER, LISTENER, TEXT, OBJECT OF SPEAKING, LANGUAGE, LOCATION, STARTING POINT}

Several government structure types in the surface structure correspond to this situation.

8.1.

$$N' + \text{nom. V } N^2 + \text{ngp.}\{N^3 + \text{el.} = N^3 \text{gen. kohta}\}(N^4 +$$
$$\text{all.} = N^4 + \text{gen. ees})(N^5 + \text{ad.} \sim N^6 + \text{kom.})$$
$$(\text{Loc}) (\text{De}) (\text{Di}) (\text{Dt}_2) (\text{Ll})$$

$$N^{5\sim6} + \text{nom. V} + 3.\text{p. } N^2 + \text{ngp.}\{N^3 + \text{el.} = N^3 + \text{gen.}$$
$$\text{kohta}\}(N^4 + \text{all.} = N^4 + \text{gen. ees}) (\text{Loc})$$
$$(\text{De}) (\text{Di}) (\text{Dt}_2) (\text{Ll})$$

As can be seen, two equivalent elements $N + all.$, $N + gen. ees$ in the surface structure correspond to LISTENER in this type.

Such a structure is characteristic of the verb *pidama* 2 'make, have.' Examples:

> *Professor peab loengu.* 'The professor will give a lecture.'

> *Professor peab üliõpilastele loengu.* The professor will give a lecture for the students.'

> *Professor peab kõne poliitikast.* 'The professor will make a speech on politics.'

> *Professor peab üliõpilaste ees kõne.* 'The professor will make a speech before the students.'

> *Professor peab ettekande oma avastuse kohta.* 'The professor will make a report on his discovery.'

> *Professor peab aulas ettekande.* 'The professor will make a report in the assembly hall.'

> *Pastor peab kantslist eesti keeles jutluse.* 'The pastor will give a sermon in Estonian from the pulpit.'

In the present type we have considered the surface structure equivalents of OBJECT OF SPEAKING the secondary part of the sentence belonging to the verb and not that of substantive denoting TEXT. The verb itself is a little different in this type as it does not refer (i.e. its stem) to the speaking action anyway. It acquires its full contents only in connection with the verb expressing TEXT. Therefore the presence of TEXT in the sentence is obligatory.

8.2.

N + nom. V (N + all. = N + gen. ees) (N + kom. (N + el.))
(Loc) (De) (Ll)

This government type is characteristic of the verb *esinema 2* 'appear, address, make.' Examples:

> *Professor esines.* 'The professor appeared (before the audience).'
>
> *Professor esines üliõpilastele.* 'The professor addressed the students.'
>
> *Professor esines kõnega.* 'The professor made a speech.'
>
> *Professor esines üliõpilastele kõnega.* 'The professor made a speech to the students.'
>
> *Professor esines oma avastusest loenguga.* 'The professor lectured on his discovery.'
>
> *Professor esines aulas.* 'The professor appeared (before the audience) in the assembly hall.'
>
> *Professor esines kõnetoolist.* 'The professor addressed (the audience) from the rostrum.'

The characteristic feature of this type is that the verb *esinema* is sufficiently independent to be able to form a sentence without the representation of TEXT. TEXT is represented by the substantive in the comitative (N + kom.) and OBJECT OF SPEAKING by the surface structure element *N + el.* which can occur only in a case where the representative of TEXT is present in the sentence.

8.3.

N + nom. V (N + el.)(N + all.)(Loc)(De)(Ll)

The verbs of this government structure type are *kõnelema* 10 'speak, tell' and *rääkima* 10 'speak, tell.' For example,

> *Prorektor kõneleb.* 'The assistant rector is speaking.'
>
> *Prorektor kõneleb ülikoolist.* 'The assistant rector is speaking about the university.'
>
> *Prorektor kõneleb külalistele.* 'The assistant rector is speaking to the guests.'

Prorektor kõneleb aulas. 'The assistant rector is speaking in the assembly hall.'

Prorektor kõneleb kõnetoolist. 'The assistant rector is speaking from the rostrum.'

Prorektor kõneleb inglise keeles. 'The assistant rector is speaking in English.'

Prorektor kõneleb külalistele aulas ülikoolist. 'The assistant rector is speaking about the university to the guests in the assembly hall.'

At first it may seem that in the case of the given verb TEXT is absent from the situation elements. In reality this is not so. Even in the present situation TEXT is one situation element, but this element is represented differently here. We come across another possibility of representing the situation element in the surface structure: embedding into the verb stem, i.e. the equivalents of the situation element TEXT in the surface structure are the verb stems *kõne-, rääki-.* In Estonian such embedding of situation elements into the verb is a rather common phenomenon.

In this type OBJECT OF SPEAKING is rendered by the element $N + el.$ only. $N + gen.$ *kohta* as the representation of OBJECT OF SPEAKING cannot occur as it usually presupposes the presence of TEXT as a separate secondary part of a sentence. Therefore the sentence **Prorektor kõneles külalistele ülikooli kohta* 'The assistant rector was speaking about the university to the guests' is not acceptable.

8.4. The compound verb *üles astuma* 2 'appear' denoting 'making a speech' presupposes a still more limited number of situation elements. Even STARTING POINT is absent here, in addition to the previous ones. The government structure type is the following:

$$N + nom. \ V \ [N + kom. \ (N + el.)] \ (N + gen. \ ees) \ (Loc) \ (Ll)$$

According to this structure type, OBJECT OF SPEAKING is expressed in the surface structure only as an attribute of $N + kom.$ denoting TEXT. LISTENER is represented by the element $N + gen.$ *ees.* For example,

Prorektor astus üliõpilaste ees üles kõnega õppimise viisidest. 'The assistant rector addressed the students (with a speech) on the ways of studying.'

9. In conclusion some words on the simplest verbs of saying. Undoubtedly the situation which refers to the presence of speaking ability only is the simplest speaking situation. In comparison with the previous ones this is a rather abstract situation. Here we have only two situation elements: OWNER and SPEECH. These elements are represented in the surface structure so that OWNER – *N* + *nom.*, while SPEECH is embedded into the verb stem. So we get the government structure type

N + nom. V,

which in the case of the given situation is characteristic of the verbs *kõnelema I* 'speak, tell,' *rääkima I* 'speak, tell.' For example,

Peetri poeg kõneleb juba. 'Peter's son can talk already.'

10. A separate situation also denotes the speaking of a certain language, the ability to do so. The government structure type is

N + nom. V Lp,

where *N* + *nom.* denotes SPEAKER and *Lp* is a substitution class of partitive character and denotes LANGUAGE. For example,

Professor kõneleb mustlaskeelt. 'The professor can speak the Gypsy language.'

Professor valdab jiidišit. 'The professor can speak Yiddish.'

Professor rääkis sanskritti. 'The professor could speak Sanskrit.'

Such a government structure type is characteristic of the verbs *kõnelema 7* 'speak, tell,' *rääkima 7* 'speak, tell,' *valdama 3* 'master, be able to (speak).'

11. A situation where two men are speaking in a certain language has yet to be added. Here the situation is more concrete and its elements are

{SPEAKER-LISTENER 1, SPEAKER-LISTENER 2, LANGUAGE, RECIPROCAL ELEMENT, LOCATION}

As can be seen, TEXT and OBJECT OF SPEAKING are absent in the situation because the whole action is concentrated on the element LANGUAGE. The government structure type is accordingly

$$\left\{ \begin{array}{l} N' + nom.\ V\ N^2 + kom. \\ N' + nom.\ ja\ N^2 + nom.\ V\ (R) \\ N\ + nom.\ + pl.\ V\ (R) \end{array} \right\} Lp\ (Loc)$$

This type is characteristic of the verbs *kõnelema 12* 'speak, tell' and *rääkima 12* 'speak, tell.' For example,

Professor rääkis külalisega saksa keelt. 'The professor spoke German with the guest.'

Professor ja külaline rääkisid saksa keelt. 'The professor and the guest spoke German.'

Külalised rääkisid omavahel saksa keelt. 'The guests were speaking German among themselves.'

If we compare the present situation with the TALKING situation presented under point **6**, we can detect one difference in the representation of LANGUAGE: here LANGUAGE is expressed partitively in the surface structure, while in the TALKING situation it was expressed locally, or more exactly inessively. Let us compare the following TALKING sentences with the previous ones:

Professor rääkis külalisega saksa keeles. 'The professor spoke (in) German with the guests.'

Professor ja külaline rääkisid saksa keeles. 'The professor and the guest spoke (in) German.'

Külalised rääkisid omavahel saksa keeles. 'The guests spoke (in) German among themselves.'

12. The verbs of saying analyzed above present primary speaking situations in Estonian. The verbs of saying of onomatopoeic character and secondary verbs of saying have been omitted from the present paper. The government structure types of the verbs of saying are more complicated than those of any other kind of verb and it is probably for this reason that elucidation of the corresponding action situations is especially necessary.

REFERENCES

Rätsep, H.: 1969, 'On the Form of Government Structure Types of Estonian Simple Verbs', Annual Meeting of the Research Group for Generative Grammar, Tartu, pp. 20–28.
Rätsep, H.: 1970, 'Government Structure Types of the Verb and Situation Analysis', Annual Meeting of the Research Group for Generative Grammar, Tartu, pp. 28–34.
Rätsep, H.: 1971, 'Kas kaudne kõneviis on kõneviis? Verbivormide situatsioonianalüüsi', *Keel ja Struktuur* **5**, Tartu, pp. 43–69.
Siro, P.: 1949, 'Puhumista merkitsevät verbit itämerensuomalaisissa kielissä', *Mémoirs de la Société Finno-Ougrienne* **XCIII,** Helsinki.

C. ROHRER

SOME PROBLEMS CONNECTED WITH THE TRANSLATION OF RELATIVE CLAUSES INTO PREDICATE CALCULUS

Traditionally the distinction between restrictive and non-restrictive relative clauses has been defined as follows: A restrictive relative clause restricts the extension of the concept, expressed by the NP, to which the restrictive relative clause is attached. A non-restrictive relative clause leaves the extension of the respective concept unmodified.

Within the framework of TG, relative clauses constitute one of the major problems. In most grammars it is assumed that restrictive relative clauses come from a sentence which is embedded in a noun-phrase. There exist two variants of this analysis: the Art-S-analysis and the NP-S-analysis. Both analyses lead to insurmountable difficulties. Non-restrictive relative clauses are usually derived from a conjunction of sentences. The sentence which yields the relative clause is attached to the highest S and inserted at the appropriate place by post-cyclical rule. The various approaches have been summarized in the UCLA grammar together with the arguments to support them. I therefore see no need to go through them again. Instead I want to propose my own attempt at a solution.[1]

In this attempt the base component looks like a predicate calculus. It contains the usual inventory of logical connectives, predicates, individual variables and constants, as well as quantifiers; moreover there are formation rules, rules of derivation and axioms. It would of course also be possible to present such a logical analysis under the title of transformational analysis. Because what is a transformational analysis?

As Ch. Fillmore put it, 'the ordinary working grammarian is confused about what it takes for something to be a generative grammar'.[2] In this general confusion I could claim to be still a generative grammarian.

In a logical analysis a sentence like

(1)   John knows the woman who slapped the chancellor.

---

[1] There is one approach in which both types of relative clauses are derived from a conjunction. cf. S. Annear Thompson, 'The Deep Structure of Relative Clauses', *Working Papers in Linguistics* No. 6, Sept. 70, Ohio State University, Columbus. More exactly, the author claims that at the level of deep structure, there is no significant difference between restrictive and non-restrictive clauses. For this author the difference between the two types is a function of the presuppositions which the speaker has about the hearer's knowledge.

[2] Ch. Fillmore, 'On Generativity', *Working Papers in Linguistics,* No. 6, September 1970, The Ohio State University, Columbus Ohio, pp. 1–20.

F. Kiefer and N. Ruwet (eds.), Generative Grammar in Europe, 407–418. All Rights Reserved.
Copyright © 1973 by D. Reidel Publishing Company, Dordrecht-Holland.

is presented as follows:

> Knows [John, ($1x$) [woman (x). slapped (x, ($1y$) chancellor (y))]]

The difference between a restrictive and a non-restrictive relative clause can be represented by different scopes of the iota-operator. Sentence (1) allows a restrictive and a non-restrictive interpretation.

(2)   The apartment which Mary rented is small.

To the restrictive version corresponds formula (   )

(3)   Small [($1x$)(apartment (x). rented (Mary, x))]

In the non-restrictive version, the iota-operator has a smaller scope.

(4)   Small ($1x$) apartment (x). rented [Mary, ($1x$) apartment (x)]

Formula (4) can also be paraphrased as:

(5)   The apartment is small and Mary rented it.

This paraphrase shows the close relation which exists between non-restrictive relative clauses and a conjunction of sentences, a relation which has been commented upon by many grammarians and logicians.[3]

Relative clauses which modify a definite NP in the plural are derived from if-then sentences. The classical example

(6)   Les femmes qui sont belles ne sont pas fidèles.

receives thus the following representation

(7)   (x) [Femme (x) $\wedge$ Belle (x) $\rightarrow$ $\overline{\text{Fidèle } (x)}$]

If sentence (6) is interpreted non-restrictively, which is equivalent to the sentence 'all women are beautiful and all women are unfaithful', then we obtain a conjunction of if-then sentences.

(8)   (x) [Femme (x) $\rightarrow$ Belle (x)] $\wedge$ (x) [Femme (x) $\rightarrow$ Belle (x)]

I. ADVANTAGES OF A LOGICAL ANALYSIS

Such an analysis allows us to avoid some of the difficulties and paradoxes of the NP-S-derivation.

---

[3] cf. for instance the following quotation 'and we may pass over unrestrictive clauses, for they are only stylistic variants of coordinate sentences', W. O. Quine, *Word and Object*, Cambridge Mass., 1960, p. 110.

It can be shown that in order to derive sentence (9) with the rule NP →
NP (S)

(9)   La municipalité détruira les belles vieilles maisons blanches que
l'on voit là-bas,

one needs 15 sentences in the deep structure. If the sentence contained 10
(reduced) restrictive relative clauses, the number of sentences in deep structure would already be greater than 1000.[4]

(10) (x) [Maison (x) ∧ Belle (x) ∧ Vieille (x) ∧ Blanche (x) ∧ Voir
(j_1, x) → Détruire (z_1, x)]

The famous Bach-Peters paradox also finds a simple solution in a logical
analysis. Whereas the sentence

(11)   Les linguistes qui ne trouvent pas les exemples qu'ils cherchent
les fabriquent.

presupposes an infinite deep-structure in the NP-S-analysis, it receives a very
simple representation in a logical analysis

(12) (x) (y) [Linguiste (x) ∧ Exemple (y) ∧ Chercher (x, y) ∧
$\overline{\text{Trouver } (x, y)}$ → Fabriquer (x, y)]

A logical analysis can also help to bring out certain ambiguities that have
gone unnoticed so far. Thus L. Karttunen[5] has been able to show that sentence (13) has two readings, which can be paraphrased by (13a) and (13b)
respectively.

(13)   The pilot who shot at it hit the Mig that chased him.
(13a)   The pilot who shot at the Mig that chased him hit it.
(13b)   The Mig that chased the pilot who shot at it was hit by him.

Karttunen represents the two readings by formulas (14a) and (14b).

(14a) $(\exists x)$ $(\exists y)$ (hit (x, y). $x = (1z)$ [pilot (z). shot at $(z, (1w)$ [Mig (w).
chased (w, z)]. $y = (1v)$ [Mig (v). chased (v, x)]])

(14b) $(\exists x)$ $(\exists y)$ (hit (x, y). $x = (1z)$ [pilot (z). shot at (z, y)]. $y = (1w)$
[Mig (w). chased $(w, (1v)$ [pilot (v). shot at (v, w)]]])

Formula (14a) represents the meaning of sentence (13a) and formula (14b)
the meaning of sentence (13b).

---

[4] C. Rohrer, *Funktionelle Sprachwissenschaft und Transformationelle Grammatik*, München
1971, S. 215 SS.
[5] L. Karttunen, *Migs and Pilots*, mimeographed, University of Texas, Austin, 1969.

In addition to the readings (a) and (b) there exists even a third one. This third reading is difficult to paraphrase and even more difficult to notice in actual performance. In logical terms the reading looks as follows:

(14c) $(\exists x)\,(\exists y)\,(\text{hit}\,(x, y).\ x = (1z)[\text{pilot}\,(z).\ \text{Mig}\,(w).\ \text{shot at}\,(z, w)]$
$.\ y = (1w)[\text{Mig}\,(w).\ \text{pilot}\,(z).\ \text{chased}\,(w, z)]$

The formulas (14a–c) are very far from the surface realization (13). I therefore tried to find a symbolic representation which is closer to the surface form. We are inclined to interpret sentence (13) as a relation between a pilot and a Mig, so that these two terms should occupy analogous positions in the symbolic formulation.

In *Funktionelle Sprachwissenschaft und Transformationelle Grammatik*,[6] I proposed a notation, which, if applied to reading (13a), yields formula (15).

(15) $(1x)[\text{pilot}\,(x).\ x\ \text{shot at}\,(1y)\,(\text{Mig}\,(y).\ y\ \text{chased}\,x)]\ \text{hit}$
$(1y)[\text{Mig}\,(y).\ (1x)\,(\text{pilot}\,(x).\ y\ \text{chased}\,x)\ \text{shot at}\,y]$

When I proposed this formula, I assumed that the iota-term in the first part of the formula $(1y)\,[\text{Mig}\,(y)\ldots]$ was codesignative with the iota-term in the second part $(1y)\,[\text{Mig}\,(y)\ldots]$. It turned out that the two iota-terms are indeed codesignative in all data-bases that Karttunen describes in his paper.[7] However, consider the following new data-base.

(16)

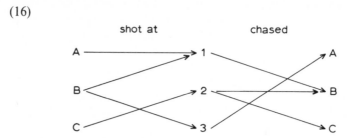

In the above chart, the numbers 1–3 represent Migs, the letters A–C represent pilots and an arrow between a number and a letter signifies that the relation '*chased*' or '*shot at*' holds between the items in question. The noun-phrase '*the pilot who shot at the Mig that chased him*' designates pilot C. Pilot C is the only pilot to whom the description

(17) $(1x)\,[\text{pilot}\,(x).\ \text{shot at}\,(x, (1y)\,(\text{Mig}\,(y).\ \text{chased}\,(y, x))]$

[6] C. Rohrer, *Funktionelle Sprachwissenschaft und Transformationelle Grammatik*, München 1971, p. 229.
[7] L. Karttunen, *Migs and Pilots*.

is applicable. It does not apply to pilot A, because he was not chased by the Mig he shot at. Pilot B is also ruled out because he was chased by several Migs.

The Mig, which pilot C shot at, is Mig 2. Thus the iota-term in (18)

(18) $(1y)$ (Mig (y). chased (y, x))

denotes Mig 2. But if we try to interpret the term

(19) $(1y)$ [Mig (y). shot at $((1x)$ [pilot (x). chased (y, x)], $y)$]

it turns out that this term is not interpretable in data-base (16). The term $(1x)$ [pilot (x). chased (y, x)] in (19) presupposes, that there is a y (i.e. a Mig) which chases only one pilot. However, this cannot be Mig 2, because Mig 2 chased more than one pilot. Mig 1 and Mig 2 chased only one pilot, but they are not shot at by the pilot they chase. Therefore the iota-term (19) cannot be interpreted in this data-base. Furthermore this example shows that the iota-terms beginning with $(1y)$ in formula (15) are not co-designative.

If the relation *'chased'* were a one-one-relation, then the two terms would designate the same objects. Our notation would thus be correct for a sentence like:[8]

(20)   the girl who loves the man she married buys him a whisky.

A logical analysis can also *explain* certain restrictions in the distribution of relative clauses which were inexplicable in earlier transformational analyses. Consider for instance the behavior of relative clauses under negation. In her paper 'Determiners and Relative Clauses', C. Smith remarks correctly that the following sentences are ungrammatical, if the relative clause is interpreted non-restrictively.[9]

(21)   *He didn't write a novel, which was published by McCraw Hill.

(22)   *No antique dealer, who had any sense, wanted to buy the table.

However she cannot explain why these sentences are ungrammatical. The ungrammaticality of (21) is closely connected with that of the following sentence.

---

[8] The discussion of examples (14 a–c) shows furthermore that there is no one-one correspondence between pronouns and variables. The difference between pronouns in natural language and variables in predicate calculus manifests itself most clearly in the use of definite (or indefinite) descriptions in Bach-paradoxical sentences. If one tries to replace the existential quantifiers in the following sentence by indefinite descriptions (cf. H. Reichenbach, *Elements of Symbolic Logic*, New York, 1947, S. 265), we run into the same difficulties as we did with the iota-operator.

(24)   A pilot who shot at a Mig that chased him hit it.

[9] C. Smith, 'Determiners and Relative Clauses', *Language* **40** (1964) p. 68.

(23) *He didn't write a novel and $\left\{ \begin{array}{c} \text{this novel} \\ \text{it} \end{array} \right\}$ was published by McCraw Hill.

From a logical point of view it is obvious why (21) is ungrammatical. This sentence affirms in its first part that there exists a novel and in its second part it negates the existence of this very same novel. This is a contradiction. The speaker of (21) affirms p and $\bar{p}$. cf. formula (25).

(25) $(\exists x)$ [Write (y_1, x) ∧ Novel (x) ∧ Write (y_1, x) ∧ Novel (x) ∧ Publish (z_1, x)]

At the same time we can explain why the following sentences, which C. Smith considers as ungrammatical, are grammatically and logically correct.

(26) He didn't eat the mango, which was overripe.
(27) He didn't use the air mattress, which belongs to the Halls.

In our deep structure sentence (26) is represented as follows:

(28) $(\exists x)$ [Mango (x) ∧ (y) (Mango $(y) \leftrightarrow y = x)$ ∧ $\overline{\text{Eat } (z_1, x)}$ ∧ Overripe (x)]

This formula shows, that it is not the existence of the mango which is negated, but the fact that it was eaten. Sentence (26) therefore does not contain a contradiction.

A further advantage of a logical analysis lies in the fact that it explains why relative clauses, modifying a NP with an indefinite article, show no distinction between a restrictive and a non-restrictive reading. Consider sentence (29):

(29) The bank bought a house which cost $20.000.

In a logical representation, there is only one possible formula, namely

(30a) $(\exists x)$ [bought $((1y)$ bank $(y), x)$. house (x). cost $20.000 (x)$]

Let's assume, contrary to what we stated above, that sentence (29) has a second reading which can be represented as (30b).

(30b) $(\exists x)$ [bought $((1y)$ bank $(y), x)$. House $(x))$. $(\exists x)$ [house (x). cost $20.000 (x)$]

If, as we are forced to assume, the two conjuncts in (30b) denote the same individual, then (30a) and (30b) are logically equivalent. If they do not denote the same individual, then we cannot transform (30b) into a relative clause, but it has to be translated as (31).

(31)   The bank bought a house and another house cost $20.000.

I therefore conclude that relative clauses modifying an indefinite NP can be interpreted semantically in one way only.

There are two types of apparent counterexamples. The first type consists of generic sentences like (32).

(32)   A dog which barks does not bite.

The indefinite article in this sentence has to be translated by means of the universal quantifier and we therefore can disregard it in this section which deals only with the existential quantifier.

(33) $(x) [\text{Dog } (x). \text{ Bark } (x) \rightarrow \overline{\text{Bite } (x)})]$

An instance of the second type of examples is sentence (34).

(34a)   Jean cherche une secrétaire qui $\left\{ \begin{array}{l} \text{sait} \\ \text{sache} \end{array} \right\}$ le russe.
(34b)

Version (a) means that John has a particular person in mind. I therefore could replace the NP '*une secrétaire qui sait le russe*' by a proper noun. In version (b) John is not looking for a specific person. He may not even be sure whether a person with the qualifications required in the relative clause does exist. The former version is called [+ specific] or *de re*, the second version is called [− specific] or *de dicto*.

I want to claim that the distinction between the specific and the non-specific reading of sentence (34) has nothing to do with the distinction between restrictive and non-restrictive relative clauses. I can prove this claim by showing that the distinction between the versions (34a) and (34b) can occur in a *restrictive* clause modifying a definite NP. Consider sentence (35).

(35)   John is looking for the man who invented the snowmobile.

I assume that the relative clause is restrictive. Even in the restrictive reading the NP '*the man who invented the snowmobile*' can be interpreted in two ways. It may mean that John is looking for a particular person, let's call him Mr. Smith, and that John refers to him as 'the man who invented the snowmobile'. (This interpretation corresponds to the [+ specific] reading of sentence (34)). It may also mean that John does not know who invented the snowmobile and that he is looking for this man, whoever he may be. (This reading corresponds to the [− specific] version of sentence (34)).

This example shows that the distinction [± specific] is independent of the distinction between restrictive and non-restrictive relative clauses, because it occurs even if only one type of relative clause is present.

If my claim is correct that relative clauses modifying a nounphrase with an existential quantifier are unambiguous, then all transformational analyses, which have been presented so far, are incorrect because they assign two different deep structures to these sentences.

II. UNSOLVED PROBLEMS

Besides its advantages the logical analysis presented so far has also several severe drawbacks. It is based on a system of logic like Russell's *Principia Mathematica*. This system has been criticized for several decades for its inability to do full justice to natural language. This criticism comes mainly from the analytical philosophers. I want to discuss those alleged inadequacies which are relevant for the description of relative clauses.

III. UNIVERSAL QUANTIFIER

I have derived sentences like (6) from an *if-then* sentence.

(6)   Les femmes qui sont belles ne sont pas fidèles.
$$(x)\,[F(x) \wedge B(x) \rightarrow \overline{F(x)}]$$

This derivation is justified for some sentences containing a universal quantifier but certainly not for all sentences. Consider the following two examples

(36a)   Les étudiants, auxquels Marie a parlé hier, veulent changer d'université.

(36b)   Si Marie a parlé hier à un étudiant, il veut changer d'université.

In (a) the speaker of the sentence presupposes that *Marie* spoke to some students. If she didn't speak to any, then the speaker either wants to deceive his audience or the sentence is non-sensical. In contrast, (b) still makes sense even if Mary didn't speak to anyone.

An adequate representation of all-statements like (a) has to capture the fact that the speaker presupposes the existence of the objects denoted by the respective NP. Or, to quote I. Bellert, 'A speaker uses appropriately an all-statement, only if his purported belief is that there is more than one 'object' which is φ, and his purported claim is that any 'object' which is φ is φ.[10]

---

[10] I. Bellert, *On the Use of Quantifying Operators in the Logico-Semantic Structure Representation of Utterances,* Coling, Sept. 1969, Stockholm.

IV. IOTA-OPERATOR AND EXISTENTIAL QUANTIFIER

In discussing the sentence

(37)   John is looking for the man who invented the snowmobile

I mentioned two functions of the definite NP. These two functions have been called respectively [+ specific], referential, *de re* and [− specific], attributive, *de dicto*. K. Donnellan characterizes them as follows:[11]

> A speaker who uses a definite description *attributively* in an assertion states something about whoever or whatever is the so – and – so. A speaker who uses a definite description referentially in an assertion, on the other hand, uses the description to enable his audience to pick out whom or what he is talking about and states something about that person or thing. In the first case the definite description might be said to occur essentially, for the speaker wishes to assert something about whatever or whoever fits that description; but in the referential use the definite description is merely one tool for doing a certain job – calling attention to a person or thing – and in general any other device for doing the same job, another description of a name, would do as well. In the attributive uses the attribute of being the so – and – so is all important, which it is not in the referential use.

The difference between the two functions can be illustrated by a Graf Bobby joke.

(38)   Graf Bobby goes to an athletics event for the first time. The sprinters are just getting ready for the 100m race. Graf Bobby's friend explains to him the basic principles of the race and ends his explanations with 'The one who arrives first will get the prize', to which Graf Bobby replies: 'But then why do the others run?'

Graf Bobby interpreted 'the one who arrives first' referentially, whereas his friend used the term attributively.

It has been claimed that it is impossible to capture this ambiguity by means of symbolic logic.[12] This is correct if one equates symbolic logic and first order predicate calculus. However, as soon as modal concepts are used, the difference between an attributive NP and a referential NP can be accounted for satisfactorily.

One representation is proposed by J. Hintikka. He works with the sentence

(39)   *A* believes that the next Governor of California will be a Democrat.

He comments on the two meanings of sentence (39).

---

[11] K. S. Donnellan, 'Reference and Descriptions', *Philosophical Review* **75** (1966) S. 285.
[12] cf. B. Drubig, *Untersuchungen zur Syntax und Semantik der Relativsätze im Englischen*, Diss. Stuttgart, 1970.

[. . .] someone may have a belief concerning the next Governor of California, whoever he is or may be, say that he will be a Democrat. This is different from believing something about the individual who, so far unbeknownst to all of us, in fact is the next Governor in California.[13]

He then illustrates the distinction, in formal terms, by the pair of statements.

(40a) B_a (g is a Democrat)
(40b) $(\exists x)\,((x = g).\, B_a\,(x$ is a Democrat$))$

(40a) represents the attributive or, to use Hintikka's terminology, *de dicto* reading and (40b) the referential or *de re* reading.[14]

The distinction between the two readings of indefinite NP's (cf. sentence (34)) can be handled in a similar manner. The ambiguity in question occurs only in modal contexts.

In addition to the referential or attributive reading of a definite description there exists still another source of ambiguity. When people talk about a particular object, they can refer to it by different descriptions. For instance, one can refer to a particular person as Mr. Smith, the professor, the guy you met in the subway last night, the idiot, etc. These different ways of referring to an object are a source of ambiguity in *oratio obliqua*.

Let us examine sentence (41).

(41)   Mary believes that the mayor of Stuttgart is a communist.

The description '*The mayor of Stuttgart*' may be Mary's way of referring to the person in question or it may be the speaker's. In some cases it is clear who furnishes the description. In sentence (42)

(42)   Columbus believed that Castro's island was China.

there is no doubt that it is the speaker who refers to Cuba as Castro's island, because Columbus could not possibly have known that Castro was to rule over Cuba in the 20th century. The source of the description is also obvious in the next sentence.

(43)   Maria möchte einen Heiratsschwindler heiraten.
        'Mary wants to marry a marriage impostor'.

The speaker uses the description '*Heiratsschwindler*'. If Mary knew that the person in question is a *Heiratsschwindler*, then she probably would not want to marry him any more.

---

[13] J. Hintikka, 'Semantics for Propositional Attitudes', in J. Hintikka, *Models of Modalities*, Dordrecht-Holland, 1969, S. 103.
[14] In order to understand how these formulas are to be interpreted, *see* J. Hintikka, 'Modality and Quantification', and 'Existential and Uniqueness Presuppositions', which are both contained in *Models for Modalities*.

I now want to argue that this ambiguity can only arise if the definite (or indefinite) description is used referentially. If it is used attributively the speaker must use the same description as the subject of the clause which dominates the *oratio obliqua*.

Let us go back to sentence (43). If the description '*ein Heiratsschwindler*' is used attributively, then it cannot be the case that the speaker uses a description which does not coincide with Mary's. In the referential reading the speaker could use any description which refers to the person in question like '*a Swede*', '*a swinger*', '*an anthropologist*', etc., without changing the truth value of the sentence. In the attributive reading the substitution of the description 'a Swede' for 'ein Heiratsschwindler' changes the truth value, because then Mary wants something else.

In French, the speaker can mark overtly that he is only reporting the description used by the subject of the main clause.

(44a)   Jean a promis d'apporter un livre qui contient un article de Sartre.

(44b)   Jean a promis d'apporter un livre qui contiendrait un article de Sartre.

The description '*un livre qui contient un article de Sartre*' can be due to the speaker or to *Jean*. The description in (44b) however can only come from the speaker, because the verb *contenir* is in the conditional mood.

Example (44b) raises an interesting question. If a description consists of several predicates, say F, P and Q, is it then possible that F and P come from the subject of the main clause and Q from the speaker? It looks as if in (44b) the predicate '*livre*' were due to the speaker and '*qui contiendrait un article de Sartre*' due to *Jean*. Unfortunately I do not have any good arguments to justify this intuition.

V. SUMMARY

It has been shown that a translation of relative clauses into predicate calculus solves some of the problems and paradoxes of previous transformational analyses. Moreover it helps to uncover and to represent certain ambiguities that have gone unnoticed so far. It explains co-occurrence restrictions between some quantifiers and a certain type of relative clause. Finally this translation shows us why relative clauses which modify a NP containing an existential quantifier are unambiguous, in other words, why they cannot be interpreted restrictively and non-restrictively.

If a modal predicate calculus is used, then the distinction between specific and non-specific NP's can also be represented in a satisfactory way. A major problem that remains without a solution arises in *oratio obliqua*. The speaker of a sentence in *oratio obliqua* may refer to an object in a different way than the subject of the verb which dominates the *oratio obliqua*. A notation has to be developed which indicates whether the reference is made by the speaker or by the subject of the main clause.

University of Stuttgart

NICOLAS RUWET

HOW TO DEAL WITH SYNTACTIC IRREGULARITIES: CONDITIONS ON TRANSFORMATIONS OR PERCEPTUAL STRATEGIES?*

0. Since the beginnings of generative grammar, one of the preoccupations of linguists has been the problem raised by a large number of transformational rules, which have considerable generality, yet which are inapplicable under certain specific conditions. This is particularly true of the various movement transformations which apply amongst other things in the formation of relatives, interrogatives, cleft-sentences and clitic pronouns by moving noun phrases, prepositional phrases, pronouns, etc. One example of restrictions on these transformations is the following. In French, a prepositional phrase of the form *de NP* can regularly be taken from its position in deep structure and either relativized, questioned, clefted or cliticized, whether its position and function in the deep structure be that of indirect object, adverbial, or noun complement. We have:

(1) (a) je parle *de ce livre*
     (b) le livre *dont* je parle
     (c) *de quel livre* parles-tu?
     (d) c'est *de ce livre* que je parle
     (e) j'*en* parle

(2) (a) je viens *de Paris*
     (b) l'endroit *d'où* je viens
     (c) *de quelle ville* viens-tu?
     (d) c'est *de Paris* que je viens
     (e) j'*en* viens

(3) (a) j'ai lu la préface *de ce livre*
     (b) le livre *dont* j'ai lu la préface
     (c) *de quel livre* as-tu lu la préface?
     (d) c'est *de ce livre* que j'ai lu la préface
     (e) j'*en* ai lu la préface

* I am deeply grateful to Jacques Mehler who first drew my attention to the type of problems dealt with here, and thanks to whom I was able to read Klima's text (1970) before it was distributed; I have had with him many talks directly relevant to the subject of this article. I am also very grateful to Richie Kayne, who read an earlier version of this paper, and who made many helpful suggestions. I alone am responsible for all errors left.

F. Kiefer and N. Ruwet (eds.), Generative Grammar in Europe, 419–444. All Rights Reserved.
Copyright © 1973 by D. Reidel Publishing Company, Dordrecht-Holland.

In certain circumstances, however, the movement of *de NP* is impossible;
thus from (4)(a), none of the operations mentioned above results in a grammatical sentence, cf. (4)(b)–(4)(e):

(4)   (a)   je pense à la préface *de ce livre*

          (b)   *le livre *dont* je pense à la préface

          (c)   **de quel livre* penses-tu à la préface?

          (d)   *c'est *de ce livre* que je pense à la préface

          (e)   *j'*en* pense à la préface

It is important to note that (4) is not an exception through any accidental,
lexical reason; the exception is systematic, and it is possible to formulate it in
general terms: that any movement of a prepositional phrase of the type *de NP*
is blocked if it is embedded in another prepositional phrase. In this case, *de ce
livre* is embedded in *à la préface* . . . There are other examples:

(5)   (a)   j'habite *dans* la banlieue *de Paris*

          (b)   *j'*en* habite *dans* la banlieue

(6)   (a)   je compte *sur* la préface *de* ce livre

          (b)   *j'*en* compte *sur* la préface

(in (5), (6), the only example given is that of clitic-placement; it is however
easy to verify that the other types of movements mentioned are also blocked).

     Whatever systematicity this exception has, it is nonetheless the case that it
constitutes a 'serious gap in the generality of the rule' (Klima, 1970). Although
it is often, but not always, possible to account for these exceptions by means
of conditions on the application of specific movement rules, it is obvious that
a mere condition on a rule will never have any explicative value. If our aim is
to construct a convincing model of language learning – in this case to account
for the fact that a French child, after a few years learning his language, rejects
(4)(b)–(4)(e), (5)(b), (6)(b), etc., while having no hesitation in accepting all
the examples in (1)–(3) – it will be necessary to discover the general principles
which account for these differences in grammaticality.

     Linguists have therefore attempted to discover universal constraints, very
abstract in character, which would apply for example to movement transformations. Thus it was that Chomsky (1964, 1968) proposed the 'A-over-A'
principle, which, by the way, as R. S. Kayne (1969) has shown, can be used to
explain the example we have chosen, the irregular behavior of (4)–(6). In
many cases, however, the formulation of universal constraints has come up
against serious difficulties. It is widely known, for example, that the universal
validity of the 'A-over-A' principle has been questioned by Ross (1967), who
proposed replacing this one principle by several independent constraints,

whose explanatory power is unfortunately relatively weak precisely because they are too specific. Indeed, in some cases even Ross's specific constraints seem to be inadequate,[1] one fact amongst others which has prompted some linguists, Lakoff for example, to propose making the theory more powerful by introducing global derivational constraints (*see* Lakoff, 1970a) or even transderivational constraints (*see* Lakoff, 1970b). These constraints are so powerful that it is legitimate to wonder whether a theory which includes them retains any interest at all (*see* Chomsky, 1970b).

With these problems in mind, and also with the purpose of trying to explain why such constraints as Ross's, in the cases where they seem to work, are required, E. S. Klima (1970) recently proposed a completely new way of dealing with restrictions on transformations; I think that Klima's proposal, even though it is still in its first stages of formulation, deserves serious attention, and I propose to illustrate it here with examples taken from French.

1. Factitive constructions

The syntax of French factitive constructions presents a large number of peculiarities. Its problems have been explored in detail in a recent study by R. S. Kayne (1969). To account for the facts presented in (7)–(10), Kayne proposes giving French factitive constructions the deep structure (11), upon which operate the three transformations (12)–(14)[2]:

(7)   (a)   je laisserai Jean partir
        (b)   je laisserai partir Jean

(8)   (a) *je ferai Jean partir
        (b)   je ferai partir Jean

(9)   (a) *je ferai Jean parler à Pierre
        (b)   je ferai parler Jean à Pierre

(10)   (a) *je ferai Jean lire ce livre
      (b) *je ferai lire Jean ce livre
      (c) *je ferai lire ce livre Jean
      (d)   je ferai lire ce livre à Jean

---

[1] For French, several cases of this type are discussed in Marie-Louise Moreau's (1970) thesis on cleft and pseudo-cleft sentences.

[2] I am simplifying here. Firstly, to account for (7)(b), term 2 of the structural analysis of transformations (12)–(14) should mention, not simply *faire*, but a small class of verbs including *faire*, *laisser*, *regarder*, etc. . . . , and it should be specified that (12) is obligatory for *faire* and optional for the others. Furthermore R. S. Kayne (personal communication) has pointed out to me that to account for other facts, it is probably necessary to reformulate (12)–(14) differently. These problems do not affect what interests us here.

(11) $NP - \begin{Bmatrix} laisser \\ faire \end{Bmatrix} - [_S NP - VP]$

(12) $T_1 : X - faire - NP - V - Y$
$$1 \quad 2 \quad 3 \quad 4 \quad 5 \Rightarrow 1 - 2 - 4 - 3 - 5$$

(13) $T_2 : X - faire - V - NP - NP - Y$
$$1 \quad 2 \quad 3 \quad 4 \quad 5 \quad 6 \Rightarrow 1 - 2 - 3 - à + 4 - 5 - 6$$

(14) $T_3 : X - faire - V - à NP - NP - Y$
$$1 \quad 2 \quad 3 \quad 4 \quad 5 \quad 6 \Rightarrow 1 - 2 - 3 - 5 - 4 - 6$$

Notice that (11)–(14) account not only for the facts given in (7)–(14), but also predict that from the deep structure of (15)(a), it is possible to generate (15)(b), which is acceptable at least for certain speakers, and indeed (15)(c), which is not grammatical ((15)(d) is not grammatical either, but would not be generated directly by (11)–(14)):

(15)   (a)   je ferai [_S Jean porter ce message à Pierre]
          (b)   ?je ferai porter à Jean ce message à Pierre
          (c)   *je ferai porter ce message à Jean à Pierre
          (d)   *je ferai porter ce message à Pierre à Jean

We shall leave aside the problem raised by the non-grammaticality of (15)(c) (and of (15)(d)), which is perhaps explainable in terms of an independent constraint excluding all occurrences of two prepositional phrases of the form *à NP* immediately dominated by the same *VP* node, and where, perhaps, the two *NP*'s are marked [+ human] (notice that sentences such as *je ferai prendre conscience de ceci à Jean, je ferai répondre ceci à Jean pour Pierre* – with *Jean* subject – are grammatical) since in any case something like (15)(b), (15)(c) or (15)(d) must be envisaged as an intermediate stage in derivations including certain movement transformations which give (16)(a)–(16)(d):

(16)   (a)   Jean, à qui j'ai fait porter ce message à Pierre, . . .
          (b)   à qui as-tu fait porter ce message à Pierre?
          (c)   c'est à Jean que j'ai fait porter ce message à Pierre
          (d)   à Jean, j'ai fait porter ce message à Pierre

The interesting problem here is this: while all sentences in (16) are grammatical, none of those in (17) is, apparently (given of course that (17) is derived from (15)(a); (17) would be grammatical if derived from *je ferai* [_S *Pierre porter ce message à Jean*]):

(17)   (a) *Pierre, à qui j'ai fait porter ce message à Jean, ...
        (b) *à qui as-tu fait porter ce message à Jean?
        (c) *c'est à Pierre que j'ai fait porter ce message à Jean
        (d) *à Pierre, j'ai fait porter ce message à Jean.

In other words, given a structure such as (15)(b), which is the result of the application of the two transformations T_1 and T_2 above, and in which occur two prepositional phrases in *à NP*, only the one corresponding to the deep subject (*Jean*) of the embedded sentence can be moved by a movement transformation, while any movement of the deep structure indirect object (*Pierre*) is prohibited.

None of the universal constraints on transformations which have been proposed until now accounts for the exclusion of the examples in (17), and these examples are all the more surprising in that they do not reflect any general constraint on the movement of the indirect object. The indirect object can perfectly well be moved under other conditions; an example would be these same factitive constructions where the deep structure subject appears in surface structure accompanied by the preposition *par* instead of *à*, see (18)[3]:

(18)   (a) Pierre, à qui j'ai fait porter ce message par Jean
        (b) à qui as-tu fait porter ce message par Jean?
        (c) c'est à Pierre que j'ai fait porter ce message par Jean
        (d) à Pierre, j'ai fait porter ce message par Jean

In the absence of a universal constraint which would automatically exclude (17), one would be forced within the framework of 'classical' transformational theory to introduce an ad hoc condition which would block the transformations in cases corresponding to (17). If the general formulation for leftward movement rules is (19) (*see* Klima, 1970):

(19) $$W - X - \begin{Bmatrix} NP \\ PP \end{Bmatrix} - Y$$

        1   2   3 $4 \Rightarrow 1 \quad 3+2 \quad \emptyset \quad 4$

then the condition could be something like (20):

---

[3] For an analysis of constructions of this type, *see* Kayne (1969), who proposes deriving them from a deep structure in which the sentence embedded under *faire* has undergone the passive transformation (more precisely, the Agent-Postposing transformation in the sense of Chomsky (1970a)).

(20)   Condition: (19) is blocked if (i) term 3 of the structural index =
          $\grave{a} + NP$, and (ii) if term 2 of the structural index = Z faire V à NP
          $(NP)^4$ (this supposing that movement transformations operate
          on a sequence of the type (15)(b)).

It is obvious that this condition is completely *ad hoc*, it explains nothing. But
this is not all. Condition (20) is in fact too strong. As it stands, it would exclude
for example (21)(b), which can be derived by embedding (21)(a) in a factitive
construction which in turn is clefted. (21)(b), however, is much better than
(17):

(21)   (a)   Jean a porté ce colis à la prison
          (b)   c'est à la prison que j'ai fait porter ce colis à Jean

Given this new difficulty, we can legitimately ask whether it is at all possible
to formulate a condition for (19) which would effectively exclude (17) without
excluding (21)(b), and which would conform to the pattern of conditions
normally accepted in transformational grammar. I shall not however pursue
this question any further since I propose now to consider the same facts from
a completely different viewpoint, that suggested by Klima (1970) to account
for facts of English having a certain similarity with those presented here.

We shall leave aside for the moment the traditional problem of generative
grammar, that of deriving well-formed surface structures from deep structures,
by means of transformations which are ordered and subject to certain constraints. We shall turn to another question, which has until now been considered quite distinct from the first. Whereas the first has to do with competence, this has to do with performance, and more particularly with the model
of recognition, or comprehension, the model of the hearer. How does a native
speaker come to understand the meaning of a sentence he hears? Specifically,
how does a native speaker recover from what he hears, i.e. surface structure,
the deep structure grammatical relations which determine the semantic
interpretation of the sentence?[5]

A natural way of answering this question would be to postulate that native

---

[4] The brackets round *NP* are there to account for sentences like *c'est à Paul que j'ai fait répondre
à Pierre*, which require us to postulate an intermediary structure *NP faire V à NP à NP*, with
no direct object. Notice that the presence or absence of a direct object do not influence the grammaticality or ungrammaticality of such sentences. Notice also that sentences such as *c'est à Jean
que j'ai fait parler de Pierre* and *c'est de Pierre que j'ai fait parler à Jean* are both grammatical
and ambiguous. The blocking of the indirect object movement thus depends only on the occurrence in the string of two *à NP* phrases.

[5] I am admitting here, with the interpretative theory (cf. Chomsky, 1970b) that if certain aspects
of surface structure contribute in determining the meaning of a sentence, when it is a question
of the semantic function of grammatical relations, only the deep structure grammatical relations
are relevant.

speakers make use of certain heuristic techniques, 'a set of well-organized strategies' (Klima) and that these techniques allow them to recover the deep structure relations from clues given in the surface structure. Such strategies, which would enable the speaker to recognize the main clause, the subject of a sentence, the object of the verb, etc. have been proposed and studied in the recent work of Bever, Fodor, Mehler, etc. These researches are summarized in Bever (1970).

Let us assume that there exist one or several strategies for recovering the deep structure subject, object and indirect object of a sentence from what is heard. These strategies will take into account various data, such as the position of a phrase with respect to the verb in the surface structure, certain morphological marks, the lexical content of the items, and so on. We may now return to the examples under discussion (16)–(18). We can see that (18) is straightforward from the point of view of comprehension strategies; each deep structure function, subject (*S*), direct object (*D.O.*) and indirect object (*I.O.*) is marked unequivocally in surface structure; there is no confusion possible between the three, since *D.O.* is placed immediately after the verb with no preposition in between, *I.O.* has the form *à NP* and *S* has the form *par NP*.[6] Furthermore, it is possible that in (15)(b) the relative order of the two *à NP* phrases, one before, one after the *D.O.*, is used to differentiate them as being respectively *S* and *I.O.* In each case, over and above the lexical-semantic and contextual information which may be given, surface structure provides structural clues, either syntactic or morphological, which make it possible to recover deep structure. But this is not the case for (16) and (17). Given that in (22) *à Paul* can just as naturally be interpreted as deep subject or deep indirect object,

(22)   j'ai fait porter ce message à Paul,

we see that in (16)(c) and (17)(c), for example, the structural difference between *S* and *I.O.* has disappeared from surface structure. This is a case of what Klima calls *absolute structural ambiguity*, and his thesis is that natural language cannot tolerate this type of ambiguity,[7] while tolerating lexical ambiguity (lexical homonymy, that of *voler*, 'to steal' or 'to fly in the air', or of *bank* 'of a river' vs 'for savings'), or that due to the fact that two

---

[6] It goes without saying that as well as structural or morphological clues, there are lexical considerations which operate in allowing us to distinguish, for example (18)(d) from *je lui ai fait porter ce message par pneumatique*, or *j'ai fait porter ce message à Jean par Pierre* from *j'ai fait partir cet homme à Bruxelles par le train*.

[7] In fact, (22) also represents a case of absolute structural ambiguity; and (22) is however acceptable in both its interpretations (see also (31) below). As the following quotation indicates, Klima sees a difference between the multiple occurrence of a category, and the case where a category occurs only once; in this later case it appears that absolute ambiguity is allowed.

or more constructions have different surface structures while being represented by the same sequence of morphemes (structural homonymy, cf. *j'ai
tué l'homme a la carabine, flying planes can be dangerous*, etc.). Klima puts
forwards the following hypothesis:

> When there are multiple occurrences of the same category in one construction, without lexical
> or morphological differentiation, then a simple algorithm exists for distinguishing their function
> and no transformation will have such an effect on a string as to interfere with the effectiveness of
> the algorithm.

There is a way here of accounting for the facts while dispensing with condition (20). Provisionally, one could suggest replacing condition (20) by the
following strategy (or heuristic) which is the first approximation to Klima's
type of algorithm:[8]

(23)   STRATEGY I: All else being equal, and in the absence of particular
         morphological marks or lexical-semantic distinctions, if two
         prepositional phrases of the form *à NP* are present in a surface
         structure which corresponds to a factitive construction, then the
         position/ $V (NP)$___is that of the deep indirect object.

This strategy would operate like a filter. There would be no constraint on
transformations like (19); and (17), as well as (16) and (18) would be deemed
transformationally well-formed. The resultant surface structures would however subsequently undergo (23), which would exclude (17) while allowing (16)
and (18). It can be seen that the all-important innovation here is to give to
perceptual strategies – that is, to something traditionally considered to belong
to performance – a function traditionally given either to conditions on specific
rules (part of the grammar of a specific language) or to universal constraints
(part of the general theory, involving language universals, the innate 'faculty
of language'). This obviously leads us to ask whether it isn't necessary to
revise the traditional distinction between competence and performance. I
shall return briefly to this question in the conclusion.

Quite apart from the difficulties to be encountered in formulating non-ad
hoc constraints on transformations which account for the facts, there are
other arguments in favour of choosing a perceptual strategy rather than a

---

[8] R. Kayne asked me how such a strategy could differentiate (16)(c) from, for example, (i) *j'ai dit
à Jean que j'ai fait porter ce message à Pierre* (where *à Jean* is the *I.O.* of the higher verb *dire*,
the embedded sentence being ambiguous: *Pierre = S* or *I.O.*). The crucial point here is that we
must see the hearer when he applies perceptual strategies as processing the string from left to
right. In the case of (i), *à Jean* will immediately be recognized as being the *I.O.* of *dire*, and will
play no role when the processing will come to *à Pierre*. On the other hand, when processing
(16)(c), at the point when the hearer reaches *à Jean*, he will have to disambiguate it between an *S*
and an *I.O.* interpretation. He will have to keep track of it and it is only when he reaches *à Pierre*
that strategy (23) will intervene and retrospectively interpret *à Jean* as being *S*.

constraint on transformations. Transformations, like constraints on transformations, have a typically all-or-none character; if the structural index of a
transformation is met by any given sequence, the transformation may be, and
if it is obligatory it must be, applied, and if specific conditions which block its
application are met, the transformation cannot apply. If on the other hand a
perceptual strategy is applied to a sequence, some variation is to be expected,
given that other factors (other strategies) can be relevant.

Indeed, if the examples are examined more closely than I have done it up
to now, it can be seen that they are not as unequivocal as they appear from
my presentation of them, in which for example (17) is completely disallowed
and (21)(b) is completely acceptable. I have in fact simplified. Firstly, certain
speakers of French consider (16) and (17) to be ambiguous; for them, there
is simply a distinct hierarchy of possible interpretations: the interpretation of
an *à NP* phrase in the context / *V NP* ____ as a *I.O.* is very natural, whereas
its interpretation as a *S* is very difficult to get. Furthermore, sentences such
as (21)(b) are probably not entirely natural. One might have thought that
there is a structural difference between indirect objects (*à Pierre*) and directional abverbials (*à la prison*) and that the constraint (20) applies only to the
indirect objects. But I know of no good reason for having such a structural
difference between indirect objects and directionals (both being introduced
by the rule *VP → V (NP) (PP)*, where *PP* can be expanded as *à NP*, among
other things); the fact is that (21)(b) is not completely acceptable, and, moreover, there are other borderline cases, such as (24), whose degree of acceptability seems to lie somewhere between that of (21)(b) and that of (17):[9]

(24)   c'est à la bibliothèque de Harvard que j'ai fait emprunter ce livre
         à Pierre

Facts of this type – and I do not see how they could be accounted for by classical type constraints on transformations – can be naturally treated by allowing
several different (perceptual) strategies to operate as filters. Some of these
strategies, like (23), would use structural information, others morphological
aspects, others semantic or selectional information – the exact way for these
strategies to interact is of course still to be determined (would they operate

---

[9] Notice that (26)(a) (*see* below) is ambiguous, *à la bibliothèque de Harvard* being interpretable
either as a directional phrase or as a locational phrase. However, this ambiguity is carried over to
(24) and thus has no bearing on our point. Another example (pointed out to me by R. Kayne) is:

(i)   c'est à mon pantalon rose que j'ai fait donner un coup de fer à Marie

from:

(ii)   j'ai fait [$_S$ Marie donner un coup de fer à mon pantalon rose]

whose acceptability status is also somewhere between that of (21)(b) and that of (17).

simultaneously, would they be ordered etc.?) – If for example, in (21)(b), *Jean* can be rather naturally interpreted as *S*, this is because (21)(a) appears natural and because (25) appears unnatural:

(25)   *la prison a porté ce colis à Jean;

a lexical-semantic strategy, which would take into account the fact that the verb *porter* usually takes an animate subject, would therefore operate here as well as (23). If (24) is less natural than (21)(b), while being more natural than (17), this is doubtless because (26)(b), while being less natural than (26)(a), is nevertheless perfectly conceivable – because it is more difficult in this case for a semantic strategy alone to differentiate *S* from *I.O.*

(26)   (a)   Pierre a emprunté ce livre à la bibliothèque de Harvard
        (b)   la bibliothèque de Harvard a emprunté ce livre à Pierre

Thirdly, if (17) is almost impossible, this is because (27)(a) and (27)(b) are both perfectly natural and because a purely semantic strategy is inoperable here; the weight of the interpretation of (27) rests therefore entirely with (23).

(27)   (a)   Jean a porté un message à Pierre
        (b)   Pierre a porté un message à Jean

This being said, a strategy such as (23), even though it avoids placing ad hoc constraints on movement transformations and corresponds to the type of facts we have, is nonetheless itself fairly ad hoc. There is something arbitrary in the formulation of (23) (why, for example, is it the indirect object which is preferred in the position / $V NP$____?); we cannot claim that this dissymmetry between the treatment of subject and indirect object has been explained. It is not difficult, fortunately, to subsume (23) under a more general hypothesis. Before formulating this, I would however prefer to move on to other sets of facts, which appear to be of a totally different nature, but which, as we shall see, give rise to problems eminently comparable to those set by factitive constructions. It will then be possible to propose more convincingly a general hypothesis on the nature of certain strategies which use structural information and of which (23) is merely one particular case.[10]

2. NOUNPHRASE COMPLEMENTS

There is known to exist a very general correspondence between 'possessive

[10] I have completely excluded from the discussion a type of sentence which at first sight depends on the same sort of considerations; these are factitive sentences in which either the subject or the indirect object of the embedded sentence has undergone CLITIC-PLACEMENT; at first blush, the facts are exactly parallel to those in (16)–(18), cf.:

adjectives' and nounphrase complements in *de NP*, whatever the range of semantic relation may be between these elements and the head noun of the *NP* to which they belong:

(28)   (a)   le livre *de Jean*
        (b)   *son* livre

(29)   (a)   l'arrivée *de Jean*
        (b)   *son* arrivée

(30)   (a)   l'histoire *de la France*
        (b)   *son* histoire

It is also known that the relationship between the nounphrase complement

---

(i)   (a)   je lui ai fait porter ce message à Pierre
           (b)   *je lui ai fait porter ce message à Jean
           (c)   je lui ai fait porter ce message par Jean

(where the deep structures are the same as those postulated for (16)–(18)).

However there are differences between sentences of type (i) and sentences of type (16)–(18). Firstly whereas we saw that the difference between (16) and (17) is in fact a difference of relative acceptability, it is clear that (i)(b) with indirect object *lui* and subject *Jean* is completely impossible. Secondly – and this is more important – whereas the examples in (ii) are completely normal, (iii)(a) is doubtful and (iii)(b) completely impossible.

(ii)   (a)   c'est à Marie que je ferai répondre Jean
           (b)   voilà la fille à qui j'ai fait répondre Jean

(iii)   (a)   ?je lui ferai répondre Jean
           (b)   *je me ferai répondre Jean

Sentences (ii)–(iii) differ from the preceding ones by an absence of direct object; out of the three rules (cf. 12–14) which operate in the derivation of factitive constructions, they have therefore only undergone the first, T_1. The result is that they do not feature a case of absolute structural ambiguity and, as expected, the examples in (ii) are acceptable. But this means also that the strategy (23) is not sufficient in itself to exclude (iii) (notice that *je lui ferai répondre par Jean* is correct). R. S. Kayne, who has closely examined these facts (cf. Kayne, 1969), tries to account for them by a difference in the derived structures, obtained after application of (12)–(14), depending on whether the prepositional phrase *à NP* was derived from deep subject or deep indirect object. But aside that certain of the facts he bases his argument on seem rather doubtful to me, this allows him to account neither for the difference between (ii) and (iii) nor for the difference in grammaticality between (iii)(a) and (iii)(b) (between ordinary and reflexive clitic pronouns). Given the doubtful nature of these facts and the complexity of the phenomena considered, I think it is preferable deliberately to leave aside these clitic constructions; thus the problems they raise still need a solution.

Let me point out another type of fact I have no explanation for at present, but which is perhaps linked to these considerations. While (iv) is completely normal (with the interpretation where *Pierre* is subject and *Marie* is indirect object), (v)(a) is fairly difficult for me to accept and (v)(c) is impossible; now the only difference between (iv) and (v) is that in (v) a phrase – but this time the direct object – has been replaced by a clitic pronoun in (v)(a) and a reflexive clitic pronoun in (v)(b):

(iv)   c'est à Pierre que je ferai présenter Paul à Marie

(v)   (a)   ?c'est à Pierre que je le ferai présenter à Marie
           (b)   *c'est à Pierre que je me ferai présenter à Marie.

and the head noun is often ambiguous, and that this ambiguity can be found equally well in the relation between the 'possessive adjective' and the head noun. Thus in (31)(a), *Jean* can be the painter of the portrait, the person featured in the portrait or the owner of the portrait; and these interpretations are also true of (31)(b):

(31)   (a)   le portrait de Jean
         (b)   son portrait

From now on, I shall use the following symbols to indicate the nature of the relation between the *de NP*, or 'possessive' adjective, and the head noun: *S* indicates a relation comparable to that holding between subject and verb, *O* a relation comparable to that holding between verb and object, and *POSS* is used when *le N de NP* can be paraphrased as *le N que NP a*, ('the N that NP has'); this does not of course preclude the possibility of other interpretations.

It has been generally agreed by transformational grammarians that 'possessive adjectives' are not generated as such in deep structure, that (28)(b), (29)(b), (30)(b), (31)(b) should be derived from structures similar to those in (28)(a), (29)(a), (30)(a), (31)(a), in which the *NP* of the complement is a pronoun; in the derivation of the phrases (28)(b)–(31)(b), there occurs therefore a movement transformation formally similar to those subsumed under (19). For the sake of clarity, I shall represent this transformation in (32).[11]

$$(32) \quad X - \begin{bmatrix} \text{Art} \\ +\text{DEF} \end{bmatrix} - Y - N - Z - de - \begin{bmatrix} \text{NP} \\ +\text{PRO} \end{bmatrix} - W$$

1	2	3	4	5	6	7	8 $\Rightarrow$
1	2͡7	3	4	5	$\varnothing$	$\varnothing$	8

(Condition: 1–8 is dominated by *NP*, and 4 is the head noun of 1–8.)

---

[11] The sign ⌃ is used here in an ad hoc way to indicate that (7) is incorporated in (2). The truth is that rule (32) simplifies things too much. Firstly, it should be broken down into several stages. Secondly, there are arguments (cf. Kayne, 1969) for saying that underlying the 'possessive adjectives' we do not have *de NP* but rather *à NP* (cf. for instance *un ami à moi* compared with *mon ami*); phrases such as (28)–(31) would therefore be represented at a certain level by *le livre à Jean, le livre à lui*, etc., and in (32) term 6 would be *à* and not *de* (a further transformation would then convert *à* into *de* under certain conditions in the context *N ____ NP*). In fact this is not important for the point that concerns us here. If the restrictions I am about to discuss should be dealt with in terms of constraints on transformations, those constraints (condition (41)) should apply to whichever of the transformations that are being applied ((32) is therefore a résumé of these transformations) moves the pronoun (term 7 of (32)) over the head noun of the phrase, and (41) should undergo only trivial modifications. If on the other hand these restrictions must be treated in terms of perceptual strategies, the details of the transformational derivation are not important, the only thing which counts being the correspondence between the surface structures (a) and (b) of examples (28)–(31).

Furthermore, complements in *de NP* are subject to the normal movement transformations in the same way as were the *à NP* phrases in factitive constructions; cf. (3) above.

I shall be concerned here with *NP*'s presenting multiple occurrences of the sequence *de NP*, on which these different movement transformations and, in particular, (32), may operate. We saw that (31) was ambiguous, *Jean* being interpretable either as *S*, *O*, or *POSS* in relation to *portrait*. There are constructions where for example *S* and *O* are simultaneously present. *S* and *O* are often morphologically differentiated by the use of different prepositions; thus in (33)(a) and (34)(a), *O* is indicated by *de* and *S* by *par*, whereas in (35)(a) *O* is indicated by *pour* and *S* by *de*. On the other hand, in (33)(b)–(35)(b) both *S* and *O* are indicated by *de*:[12]

(33)　(a)　le portrait d'Aristote par Rembrandt
　　　(b)　le portrait d'Aristote de Rembrandt

(34)　(a)　la critique de Harris par Chomsky
　　　(b)　la critique de Harris de Chomsky

(35)　(a)　la haine des Nazis pour les Juifs
　　　(b)　la haine des Juifs des Nazis.

The following results are obtained if movement transformations, (32) in this case, operate on phrases in *de NP* within constructions like (33)–(35).

(36)　(a)　son portrait par Rembrandt　(*son = d'Aristote*)
　　　(b)　*son portrait de Rembrandt　(*son = d'Aristote*)
　　　(c)　son portrait d'Aristote　(*son = de Rembrandt*)

(37)　(a)　sa critique par Chomsky　(*sa = de Harris*)
　　　(b)　*sa critique de Chomsky　(*sa = de Harris*)
　　　(c)　sa critique de Harris　(*sa = de Chomsky*)

(38)　(a)　leur haine pour les Juifs　(*leur = des Nazis*)
　　　(b)　*leur haine des Nazis　(*leur = des Juifs*)
　　　(c)　leur haine des Juifs　(*leur = des Nazis*)

The following facts can be noticed: *de NP* phrases can be moved by (32) and converted into 'possessive adjectives' in all cases except where the *de NP* cor-

---

[12] I shall not concern myself here with the question of what exactly is the deep structure of the phrases (33)–(35). In my opinion (but *see* note (9) above) this deep structure should not be vastly different from the surface structure, and in any case I imagine that everyone would agree that in (33) or (34), (*d'*)*Aristote* et (*de*) *Harris* are indeed deep objects of *portrait* and *critique* respectively (we shall see below that this is the essential point). For a study of this type of construction in English, some of whose conclusions seem to me to be valid for French, *see* Chomsky, 1970a.

responding to O is followed by another *de NP* corresponding to S. For the other movement transformations (question, relative, clefts) the facts are less straightforward due to the influence of further restrictions[13] but the restriction under discussion can also be noticed; for example:

(39)   (a)   de qui as-tu vu le portrait par Rembrandt?
        (b)   *de qui as-tu vu le portrait de Rembrandt?
        (c)   de qui as-tu vu le portrait d'Aristote?

(40)   (a)   Aristote, dont j'ai vu le portrait par Rembrandt
        (b)   *Aristote, dont j'ai vu le portrait de Rembrandt
        (c)   Rembrandt, dont j'ai vu le portrait d'Aristote

[13] Thus it is that for some speakers of French (39)(a), although undeniably better than (39)(b), is still fairly doubtful. Moreover, certain French speakers seem to distinguish between (i) and (ii):

   (i)   ?c'est d'Aristote que j'ai vu le portrait par Rembrandt
   (ii)   c'est Aristote dont j'ai vu le portrait par Rembrandt

Furthermore, the following sentences, corresponding to (33) and (35), are completely impossible:

   (iii)   *par qui as-tu vu le (un) portrait d'Aristote?
   (iv)   *c'est par Rembrandt que j'ai vu le (un) portrait d'Aristote
   (v)   *Rembrandt, par qui j'ai vu le (un) portrait d'Aristote
   (vi)   *pour qui méprises-tu la haine des Nazis?
   (vii)   *c'est pour les Juifs que je méprise la haine des Nazis
   (viii)   *les Juifs, pour qui je méprise le haine des Nazis

If we also take into account the impossibility of deriving (ix) from (x):

   (ix)   *c'est aux ennemis que César a décrit la reddition de la ville
   (x)   César a décrit [$_{NP}$ la reddition de la ville aux ennemis],

we are forced to think that there exists a constraint preventing leftward movement of a prepositional phrase embedded in a *NP*, if the preposition is not *de* (and there would be restrictions even for *de*).

   This is not the place to try to explain those new constraints. However it seems to me that, here too, one would be led to look for an explanation in terms of perceptual strategies, an explanation which would also require the intervention of a certain notion of hierarchy in syntactic functions. Example (ix) is illuminating here; (ix) is quite acceptable if it corresponds not to (x), but to (xi):

   (xi)   César a décrit aux ennemis la reddition de la ville.

Similarly (vii) is acceptable if it is understood as an approximate paraphrase of (xii):

   (xii)   par égard pour les Juifs, je méprise la haine des Nazis

In other words, when the *à NP* and the *pour NP* are verbal or sentential complements, they can perfectly well be moved. This suggests that a certain hierarchy of functions of prepositional phrases exists, depending whether they are verbal (or sentential) complements or noun complements. The chief function of a phrase in *à NP*, in *par NP* or in *pour NP* is to be a verbal or sentential complement, it is only secondarily a noun complement. When a phrase of this type appears, for example in the context *c'est ____ que*, a recognition strategy would give priority to its interpretation as a verbal or sentential complement. On the other hand, it is clear that the function of phrases in *de NP* as noun complements is as important as their function as verbal or sentential complements (it has often been said that *de NP* is the unmarked form of the noun complement) and it is this which would explain their different behaviour.

Thus we find ourselves with a situation very similar to the one we had when dealing with factitive constructions. The absence of any universal constraint like the 'A-over-A' principle or Ross' constraints means that with the normal transformational framework we can only exclude (36)(b)–(40)(b) by imposing an ad hoc and bizarre constraint on the movement transformations. In other words, it is necessary to add yet another condition on (19) (the same thing obviously applies to (32)):

(41)   Condition: (19) is blocked (i) if term 3 of the structural index = *de* + *NP* and (ii) if term 4 of the structural index = *de NP U*; both sequences *de NP* being dominated by the same *NP*.

Apart from the fact that the formulation of this condition (41) is still in fact inadequate,[14] (22), it is evidently completely ad hoc and unilluminative, and nothing more than a different formulation of the observable facts. Without wasting any more time over the formulation of (41), let us therefore turn the problem round and ask in what way a model of comprehension could recover the base relations (*S* and *O*) from the surface facts. One can imagine here as well that French speakers call on partial heuristic techniques, getting information from observable facts such as word-order, morphological distinctions, etc. . . . It can be seen that, in (33)(a) and (34)(a), the subject is unequivocally marked by the preposition *par* (as in the factitive constructions) while in (35)(a) it is on the contrary the object which is unequivocally marked by the preposition *pour*. But in (33)(b)–(35)(b), such morphological information being absent, and *S* and *O* having the form *de NP*, it seems that it is the order (i) *O* (ii) *S* which allows us to differentiate them – notice at once to this end that, although in (35)(a) the order *S – O* is the opposite of that in (33)(a), (35)(b) and (33)(b) have the same order of complements.

In (36)(a)–(40)(a), the morphological information provided by the prepositions makes it always possible to determine unequivocally whether a complement is an *S* or an *O* (depending on the preposition) whereas this information has disappeared in cases (b) and (c) which are in fact cases of absolute structural ambiguity in Klima's sense of the term. I propose therefore suppressing condition (41) on (19) (and the corresponding condition on (32)) and replacing it with the strategy (42).

[14] As the second *de NP* is not explicitly mentioned in the transformation, it is inadequate to the extent that the last part of the restriction ('both *de NP* sequences being dominated by the same *NP*') is impossible to state. One would have to introduce a fair number of further complications, and even perhaps the functional notions of subject and object, in formulating transformations and constraints, for the formulation to be correct.

(42)   STRATEGY II: All else being equal, and in the absence of particular
         morphological marks, if in a surface structure two *de NP* pre-
         positional phrases (or one such *de NP* phrase and one equivalent
         pronoun such as *son* or *dont*) are both possible complements of
         the same noun, the position / N____is that of the deep object.[15]

This strategy accounts for all the facts in (33)–(40), in particular both for the
non-acceptability of (36)(b)–(40)(b) and for the order inversion of the complements *S* and *O* from (35)(a) to (35)(b).

An important argument in favour of adopting the strategy (23) rather than
a condition on the transformations in the case of factitive constructions was
that movement of the *I.O.* was in fact possible even if an *S* of the same form
à NP was present, provided that certain semantic conditions were met (cf.
(21)(b) and (24)), and this seemed to indicate that the disallowed examples
were not disallowed for strictly grammatical reasons. We could attempt to
find a similar argument for noun complements.

Notice firstly the contrast in acceptability between the following examples
(in which *Rembrandt*, *Aristote*, *les Juifs*, *les Nazis* keep the same functions
as above):

(43)   ? le portrait de Rembrandt d'Aristote
                            S   O

(44)   ?*la haine des Nazis des Juifs
                         S   O

While (43) is almost completely acceptable, I find it very difficult to understand (44) other than in the interpretation where the Jews hate the Nazis.
There is a fairly natural explanation for this, but it is not based on grammatical
considerations (nor even on strictly semantic considerations, depending as it
does on extra-linguistic knowledge); almost everybody knows that Rembrandt was a famous painter and that Aristotle was not; and everybody knows
as well that the Jews had as many reasons at least for hating the Nazis as did
the Nazis for hating them. When information of this type is not present, I
think that (leaving aside the case of *POSS*) no French speaker will hesitate
for (45)–(46) in interpreting *Pierre* as *O* and *Paul* as *S*:

---

[15] I have left aside the cases where one of the phrases in *de NP* can be interpreted as possessive
(and the cases where the three functions *O*, *S* and *POSS* are present, as in *le portrait d'Aristote de
Rembrandt de ce collectionneur célèbre*; in these cases only the *de NP* corresponding to *POSS*
can be moved, cf. *son portrait d'Aristote de Rembrandt* compared with **son portrait (d'Aristote)
de ce collectionneur célèbre* or **son portrait (de Rembrandt) de ce collectionneur célèbre*. There is
therefore a hierarchy between *POSS*, *S* and *O*. Notice that if, instead of a human *POSS*, we
have a nonhuman locative, as in *le portrait d'Aristote de Rembrandt du Louvre*, subject movement
is possible, cf. *son portrait d'Aristote du Louvre*.

(45)   le portrait de Pierre de Paul
(46)   la haine de Pierre de Paul

Secondly, consider the case in which S and O are differentiated in terms of the feature [±human], as in (47):

(47)   (a) j'ai lu la description du cataclysme par Pline
        (b) j'ai lu la description du cataclysme de Pline

Clearly there exist here, independently of the structural information, lexical-semantic clues for recovering the deep subject and object from the surface structure. Thus not only does the permutation of the two *de NP* become possible, as in (48):

(48)   ? j'ai lu la description de Pline du cataclysme

but certain movement transformations can apparently be applied to the *de NP* functioning as O:

(49)   (a) ?(ce cataclysme) j'*en* ai lu la description de Pline
        (b) ?le cataclysme *dont* j'ai lu la description de Pline

(Contrast (49)(b) with *l'*écrivain dont j'ai lu la description de P̲l̲ine*.)

As in the case of factitive constructions, it is difficult to see how it would be possible to account for these differences in terms of constraints on transformations, whereas they can be accounted for in terms of the combined effect of different strategies which would apply to different aspects of the surface structure (while taking into consideration the semantic information provided by the lexical items). Admittedly, the problem of the exact way in which these different strategies would interact remains to be solved, in particular whether they are in any hierarchy. For example, the fact that there is no difference in acceptability between (36)(b) and (38)(b) (compared with (43)–(44)) would seem to indicate that the strategy using purely structural considerations has preference over lexical-semantic strategies.

3. INTERROGATIVE SENTENCES

The syntax of French interrogative sentences raises extremely complicated questions which I do not pretend to be able to answer here. I should nevertheless like to point out that at least some of these questions seem to be of the same type, and should be treated in the same way, as the questions we have just been looking at.

As is well known, the derivation of interrogative sentences uses a special case of (19) called WH-FRONTING, which moves the interrogative phrase to the front of the sentence. It is this rule which accounts for the position of *où* in (50)(b):

(50)   (a)   Pierre travaille à Vincennes
         (b)   je voudrais savoir *où* Pierre travaille

This rule applies vacuously for the case where the interrogative phrase is subject of the sentence, cf.

(51)   je voudrais savoir *qui* travaille à Vincennes
(52)   *qui* est venu hier?

There is a rule which may apply after WH-FRONTING, which inverts subject and verb and which, following Kayne (1969) I shall call STYLISTIC INVERSION;[16] I shall formulate it in the following simplified way:

(53)   STYLISTIC INVERSION: X *wh* NP V Y
                                1   2   3   4 5 $\Rightarrow$ 1 2 4 3 5
                                (where *wh* represents an interrogative
                                phrase)

Simplifying a lot, the derivation of sentence (54) can be represented as in (55):

(54)   où travaille Pierre?
(55)   BASE: Q Pierre travaille où →(WH-FRONTING) →
              où Pierre travaille →(STYL-INV) →
              où travaille Pierre?

Rule (53) has considerable generality.[17] It can apply in particular if the interrogative word fronted by WH-FRONTING is a direct object. Given a simple transitive sentence like (56)(a): to obtain the corresponding question in which the questioned word is the subject ((56)(b)), WH-FRONTING is applied vacuously, and to obtain that in which the questioned word is the object ((56)(c)), WH-FRONTING and STYL-INV are applied.

(56)   (a)   Pierre a mangé une pomme.
         (b)   *qui* a mangé une pomme?
         (c)   *qu'*a mangé Pierre.

The problem which interests us here is illustrated by the following sentences

---

[16] Recall (*see* Kayne, 1969) that this rule is completely different from that (called 'subject clitic inversion' by Kayne) which applies in *Pierre est-il venu*? I shall not concern myself at all with this type of interrogative sentences here.
[17] It applies elsewhere and not only in questions, cf. *l'homme qu'a rencontré Pierre*, etc. It is also subject to certain further restrictions which do not concern us here.

(57), apparently strictly parallel to (56), the only difference being that, in (56) the object is [−human], whereas it is [+human] in (57):

(57) (a) Pierre a rencontré Paul.
      (b) *qui* a rencontré Paul?
      (c) **qui* a rencontré Pierre?

It becomes immediately clear that the reasons why (57)(c) is unacceptable are not based on any impossibility of having *qui* as a fronted direct object – *see* (58), which is the result of a further transformation permuting the subject pronoun and auxiliary (cf. n. 13) – nor on any restriction on STYL-INV involving a [+human] object, *see* (59):

(58) qui Pierre a-t-il rencontré?
(59) l'homme qu'a rencontré Pierre . . .

It is fairly evident, intuitively, that the impossibility of having (57)(c) is linked with the impossibility of finding in surface structure any indication at all, be it structural, morphological or otherwise which would allow us to distinguish subject from object. In other words, (57)(c) is a case of absolute structural ambiguity.[18] We are therefore forced yet again either to attach an ad hoc condition, similar to (20) or (41), to rule (53), or to turn to a strategy similar to (23) or (42). I shall not stop to formulate here a condition on (53) (it will soon become clear that this is in fact impossible) but propose straight away this strategy:

(60) STRATEGY III: Given an interrogative sentence of the form *wh V NP X* (where *wh* corresponds to an *NP*), and in the absence of any structural, morphological or semantic criterion differentiating subject from object, the position /V____is that of the object.

In the case of questions, indications that it is preferable to resort to strategy III (60) rather than use a condition on transformation (53) are much more clear than they were in the case of noun complements and even in the case of factitive constructions. I should say that at present I have no explanation to offer for these differences.

Notice first of all that, with impressive unanimity, traditional grammarians give the risk of ambiguity as the explanation for the non-grammaticality of sentences of the type (57)(c) (*see* Martinon, 242, n.2, Grevisse, 130, Wagner-

---

[18] Compare (57)(c) to (59), which contrasts with *l'homme qui a rencontré Pierre*. In relative clauses, the contrast between subject and direct object relative pronouns is morphologically marked: *qui* vs *que*.

Pinchon, 535, Chevalier *et al.*, 93). In fact, as we noticed with the factitive construction, sentences (57)(b)–(c) do seem to be recognized as being ambiguous by a lot of French speakers, although with an overwhelming preference for the reading where *qui* is subject. Secondly, morphological differences give greater acceptability to sentences which in other respects have exactly the same derivation as (57)(c), cf. the singular/plural contrast in (62) as opposed to (61), or (64) as opposed to (63):

(61)   (a)   cet imbécile critiquera Pierre
         (b)   *qui critiquer*a* cet imbécile?

(62)   (a)   ces imbéciles critiqueront Pierre
         (b)   qui critiquer*ont* ces imbéciles?

(63)   (a)   ce conférencier cit*e* cet auteur
         (b)   *quel auteur cit*e* ce conférencier?

(64)   (a)   ce conférencier *a* cité divers auteurs
         (b)   quels auteurs *a* cité ce conférencier?

It is even likely that differences of acceptability can be felt between written and spoken language, due to the presence of morphological distinctions in written language which are not phonetically marked in spoken language; the following sentences are examples which seem fairly natural to me when written and which would be extremely doubtful if spoken:

(65)   (a)   quels auteurs cite ce conférencier?
         (b)   quel animal mangent ces poissons?
         (c)   qui frappent ces flics?

Thirdly, the sentences under review can be made more acceptable thanks to selectional restrictions or to semantic information which resolve the ambiguity of the construction. Thus the French verb *concerner* requires an abstract subject and can have a human object, cf. (66)(a)–(b); (66)(c) is therefore unambiguous and acceptable for a lot of French speakers:[19]

---

[19] Although other speakers of French find it difficult to accept. I shall return in the conclusion to this variation of intuition. We have the same problems with a sentence like *qui amuse cette histoire*, which, although unambiguous, is accepted by some and not by others. Lastly let me point out that those sentences:

(i)   qui a réuni l'entraîneur? (R: il a réuni Pierre, Paul et Jacques)
(ii)   qui commandent ces officiers? (R: ils commandent ces fantassins)

seem more difficult for me to accept than (67)(c) or (68)(c); this is doubtless due to the fact that in the latter, where only the determiner (*quel*) is questioned, the presence of a lexically full noun makes immediately explicit the semantic relation with the verb, which is not the case with (i) and (ii) (*réunir* for example requires a [−semantically singular] object, and *quelle équipe* evidently has this feature, whereas *qui* is not specified for it).

(66)   (a)   cette décision concerne Pierre

(b)   *Pierre concerne $\begin{cases} \text{Paul} \\ \text{cette décision} \end{cases}$

(c)   qui concerne cette décision?

Similarly, *réunir* requires an object specified [– semantically singular] – cf. (67)(a)–(b); (67)(c) is therefore acceptable:

(67)   (a)   l'entraîneur a réuni l'équipe de rugby

(b)   *l'équipe de rugby a réuni l'entraîneur

(c)   quelle équipe a réuni l'entraîneur?

The factors allowing the ambiguity of a question of this type to be resolved, and which at the same time make it more acceptable, can depend in the last resort on the knowledge of the world which speakers have. Take for example the verb *commander*; in a normal world where 'law and order' are upheld, sentence (68)(a) is very natural and sentence (68)(b) very strange:

(68)   (a)   ces officiers commandent ces soldats

(b)   ces soldats commandent ces officiers

(c)   quels soldats commandent ces officiers?

(68)(c) is theoretically ambiguous; it is a question corresponding either to (68)(a) or to (68)(b); however, in this 'normal' world it does seem to me that the most natural interpretation will be that in which (68)(c) corresponds to (68(a) – in other words, the order of preference for readings is the opposite of that we had, for example, for (57)(c). It is however not difficult to imagine a situation – that prevailing in revolutionary Russia in 1917 for instance – where (68)(b) would have become 'normal'; it would be in no way surprising if the conditions for interpreting (68)(c) were modified under such circumstances. Similarly a sentence like (63)(b) seems fairly acceptable to me personally, doubtless because it seems more natural to me that a lecturer quotes an author rather than the opposite. And so on.

4.   At the end of Section 1, I remarked on the ad hoc aspect which strategy (23) still had. It should be clear, as from now, that strategies (23), (42) and (60) have distinct similarities; we should be able to generalize so that they can be presented as special cases of one general strategy.

Each of these strategies' function is to determine from an absolutely ambiguous surface structure which element corresponds to deep subject and which element corresponds to deep object (whether direct or indirect depending on the case). Let us recapitulate the main point of each strategy:

(23)   ... the position / V (NP)＿＿ is that of *I.O.*

(42)   ... the position / N＿＿is that of *O.*

(60)   ... the position / V＿＿is that of *O.*

It is not difficult to notice that each strategy interprets as an object the phrase which in surface structure has the position corresponding to that where an object is generated in deep structure. This fact leads us to replace strategies (23), (42), (60) which apply to particular cases, by a more general strategy (I shall restrict myself here to instances of structural ambiguity caused by two occurrences of one and the same category).

(69)   STRATEGY IV: All else being equal, in the absence of particular morphological marks or lexical-semantic information, each time a sentence has absolute structural ambiguity in surface structure because one and the same category occurs twice, this sentence is only acceptable in the (this sentence is acceptable with the preferred) reading for which at least one of these two occurrences keeps the position it had in deep structure.

Notice that this strategy also predicts that sentences where there are two occurrences of identical categories and where both have been moved from their deep structure position are less acceptable for both their possible readings; and this does seem to be the case:

(70)   (a) l'homme à qui c'est $\left\{ \begin{array}{c} \text{*à} \\ \text{chez} \end{array} \right\}$ Pierre que j'ai fait porter ce message

       (b) Rembrandt, dont c'est $\left\{ \begin{array}{l} \left\{ \begin{array}{l} \text{*Aristote dont} \\ \text{*d'Aristote que} \end{array} \right\} \text{j'ai vu le portrait} \\ \text{à Aristote que j'ai donné le portrait} \end{array} \right\}$

       (c) la femme dont j'ai vu $\left\{ \begin{array}{c} \text{?*son} \\ \text{ce} \end{array} \right\}$ portrait est très belle

       (where *son* = *de Rembrandt*)

Obviously, it would be necessary to try to apply this strategy to other cases, to see if it has real generality. I cannot undertake an exhaustive study of this problem within the framework of this article, but I shall point out just one more case where this strategy seems to me to be applicable. This concerns sentences like (71)(a)–(72)(a), to which a transformation permuting the object and the predicate complement can be applied in certain circumstances, cf. (71)(b), (72)(b):

(71)   (a)   on a nommé ce pauvre type président
         (b)   on a nommé président ce pauvre type

(72)   (a)   je trouve tous ces bonshommes ridicules
         (b)   je trouve ridicules tous ces bonshommes

In these sentences, object and predicate complement are differentiated either because they belong to different categories (*NP* and adjective in (72)), or by their internal structures (no determiner in the predicative noun in (71)). But this is not always the case, cf.:

(73)   (a)   ils ont surnommé le barbu le vieux sourd
         (b)   ils ont surnommé le vieux sourd le barbu

The fact is that it is extremely difficult to accept (73)(b) as being synonymous with (73)(a); while the natural interpretation for (73)(a) is that where a bearded man has the nickname *le vieux sourd*, the natural interpretation for (73)(b) is that where an old deaf man has the nickname *le barbu*; these facts follow directly on from (69) if we allow the deep structure *verb–object–predicate complement*.

However, although the example in (73) offer confirmation of the hypothesis of (69), other related sentences give what seem to be counter-examples:

(74)   (a)   ils l'ont surnommé le barbu
         (b)   c'est le vieux sourd qu'ils ont surnommé le barbu

One of the two *NP*'s which follow the verb in the deep structure of (a) and (b) has been moved by CLITIC PLACEMENT or by CLEFTING. At first sight, (69) would predict that the *NP* remaining to the right of the verb, *le barbu*, corresponds to the deep object – in other words, these sentences should have an interpretation related to that of (73)(a). But the opposite is true; both examples of (74) mean that an old deaf man has been nicknamed *le barbu*.

In point of fact, these seeming counter-examples can be explained by the existence of independent constraints on the movement of predicate complements in this construction. Thus although (75)(b) is grammatical, (76)(b) (corresponding to (71)) is not grammatical:

(75)   (a)   ce pauvre type est président
         (b)   ce pauvre type l'est (président)

(76)   (a)   on l'a nommé président
         (b)   *on l'a nommé ce pauvre type

The facts are less clear for cleft-sentences than they are for clitic pronouns. However, I find that, firstly, (77) is not natural and is only just possible with an extra constrative accent on *président*; secondly, (74)(b), provided there is a constrative accent on *le vieux sourd*, can also be interpreted like (73)(a):

(77)   ?c'est président qu'on a élu ce pauvre type

In other words, independent reasons can be given for saying that, in normal cases of sentences like (71)–(73), only the direct object can be moved to the left; thus there is no problem having to avoid absolute structural ambiguity in sentences like (74).

5.   I shall not discuss at length here the theoretical implications of the approach I have followed. The essential thing is that this approach redistributes, so to speak, the roles played by the theory of competence and the theory of performance: types of facts which up till now have been described in (grammatical) terms of transformations or of constraints on transformations (or on derivations as in Lakoff 1970a, 1970b) are described now in terms of behavioural constraints. For a full theoretical discussion of this new approach, *see* Klima (1970) and Bever (1970). I shall however deal here with one or two aspects of it which merit special attention.

Firstly, if strategy (69) proves to be efficient, this would tend to give a certain psychological reality to a concept of deep structure which is similar to that of Chomsky (1965), being not too remote from the surface structure and not identifiable with semantic structure; as we have seen, ideas like that of deep subject, deep direct or indirect object, are crucial to the present formulation. At the same time this analysis would help throw doubt on the validity of other hypotheses which have been made about the order (or the absence of order) of the elements in the underlying structure of sentences; *see* for instance Fillmore (1968) and McCawley (1968).

Secondly, it is evidently important to indicate in what way the proposed strategies differ from the transderivational constraints proposed by Lakoff (1970b). It would be possible at first sight to think that the difference lay purely between two notational variants. This is however absolutely not the case, and for two reasons. One, transderivational constraints, despite their enormous power, have no explanatory character. Consider the examples given by Lakoff, and one notices that these constraints merely provide a means of giving the facts a precise formulation, no more; perceptual strategies represent on the contrary the application to the particular case of language of psychological mechanisms which are both specific and have a field of application larger than language. We may therefore hope that a linguistic theory drawing partly on grammatical mechanisms whose power remains limited, partly on perceptual mechanisms which are also specific may delimit the characteristics of human language much more clearly than would a theory allowing mechanisms as powerful as derivational and transderivational constraints.

Two, and this is more important, transderivational constraints, like transformations and constraints on transformations, characteristically allow all or nothing; they can block, or not block a derivation at a certain stage, by comparison with another derivation, and this is all. But as we saw in the case of factitive constructions, and even more clearly in the case of questions, the facts considered are completely different in character; it was not merely a question of blocking certain constructions (for a particular interpretation) because these constructions were structurally ambiguous; this blocking of a transformation is somehow only a limiting case. Even if a transderivational constraint is capable of blocking (57)(b) – *Qui a rencontré Pierre* – from *Q Pierre a rencontré wh + PRO* by reference to the possible, allowable derivation of the same sentence from *Q wh + PRO a rencontré Pierre*, not only does it explain nothing, but furthermore it is not capable of accounting for the fact that the difference between the two possible readings of (57)(c) is not one of grammatical versus non-grammatical, but rather one which establishes a hierarchy between these two readings. Indeed it is not capable of accounting for the fact that, for a lot of French speakers, sentences like (66)(c) *qui concerne cette décision*, or indeed (cf. n.10) *qui amuse cette histoire*, while being better than (57)(c) are nevertheless rather doubtful. It is clear that all these facts are linked, and to resort to different strategies, operating on the different aspects of syntax, morphology and semantics seems the only way of accounting both for what they have in common and for what is different.

This leads me to a final remark. One of the things that struck me most, and something for which this article provides no solution, was the considerable variations of linguistic intuition from one French speaker to the next, and this was particularly true in the case of questions. For some of my informants, for example, as soon as it was possible to resolve the ambiguity for some reason or another, all interrogative sentences showing STYLISTIC-INVERSION became acceptable – only sentences of the type (57)(c) were not allowed (or rather considered to be less good); for other informants, all sentences of the type (61)–(68) are doubtful to unacceptable, and furthermore one finds intermediary dialects (there are even French speakers for whom all sentences having the form *qui V NP* are fairly doubtful, even if *qui* is interpreted as subject). I can't pretend to give the explanation for these differences, but I feel that an analysis which was content to distinguish different dialects and to describe each one in terms of different grammatical rules and constraints, would be superficial. On the contrary, one can begin to see how an analysis done in terms of the interaction of grammatical rules and various strategies could help throw light on these facts. Klima and Bever have given much weight to the fact that the different systems (systems of grammatical rules, perceptual strategies etc. . . . .) which determine the way adult language functions, are all learned at the same time, and that they mutually interact: in particular 'the way we use a language as we learn it can determine the manifest structure of language once we know it' (Bever, 1970). It is perfectly possible that the interaction between these systems during the period of learning leaves a certain freedom, that it can happen in different ways, and this would account for differences in linguistic intuition between speakers of a language, without our having to postulate mechanisms, let alone grammars, which would be fundamentally different from one speaker to another. This is obviously very speculative; and long and varied psycholinguistic research will certainly be necessary before we can be anything more than speculative.

University of Paris VIII (Vincennes)   *Translated by* CLIVE PERDUE

REFERENCES

Bever, T. G.: 1970, 'The Cognitive Basis for Linguistic Structures' in J. R. Hayes, ed., *Cognition and the Development of Language*, Wiley, New York, pp. 279–352.
Chevalier, J.-Cl., *et al.*: 1964, *Grammaire Larousse du Français contemporain*, Larousse, Paris.
Chomsky, Noam: 1964, *Current Issues in Linguistic Theory*, Mouton, The Hague.
Chomsky, Noam: 1965, *Aspects of the Theory of Syntax*, MIT Press, Cambridge, Mass.
Chomsky, Noam: 1968, *Language and Mind*, Harcourt, Brace and World, New York.
Chomsky, Noam: 1970a, 'Remarks on Nominalizations', in R. Jacobs and P. S. Rosenbaum, eds., *Readings in English Transformational Grammar*, Ginn-Blaisdell, Waltham, Mass.
Chomsky, Noam: 1970b, 'Some Empirical Issues in the Theory of Transformational Grammar', mimeographed, MIT.
Fillmore, C. J.: 1968, 'The Case for Case' in Emmon Bach and R. T. Harms, eds., *Universals in Linguistic Theory*, Holt, Rinehart and Winston, New York, pp. 1–88.
Grevisse, M.: 1955, *Le Bon Usage*,[6] Duculot, Gembloux.
Kayne, R. S.: 1969, *The Transformational Cycle in French Syntax*, Ph.D. Diss., MIT, unpublished (to appear, MIT Press).
Klima, E. S.: 1970, 'Regulatory Devices against Functional Ambiguity', *IRIA Conference on Formalisation in Phonology, Syntax, and Semantics*, ed. by M. Gross, to appear, The University of Texas Press, Austin.
Lakoff, George: 1970a, 'Global Rules', *Language* **46.3**, 627–639.
Lakoff, George: 1970b, 'Some Thoughts on Transderivational Constraints', mimeographed, University of Michigan.
Martinon, Philippe: 1927, *Comment on parle en français*, Larousse, Paris.
McCawley, J. D.: 1968, 'English as a VSO Language', mimeographed, University of Chicago.
Moreau, Marie-Louise: 1970, *Trois aspects de la syntaxe de C'EST*, Thèse de doctorat, Université de Liège, unpublished.
Ross, J. R.: 1967, *Constraints on Variables in Syntax*, Ph.D. Diss., MIT, unpublished.
Wagner, R.-L. and Pinchon, J.: 1962, *Grammaire du français classique et moderne*, Hachette, Paris.

RUDOLF RŮŽIČKA

REFLEXIVE VERSUS NONREFLEXIVE
PRONOMINALIZATION IN MODERN RUSSIAN AND
OTHER SLAVIC LANGUAGES

A Conflict between Domains of Rule Application

0. In this paper I am discussing some striking phenomena of anaphoric (forward) pronominalization in modern Standard Russian and, in a rough survey, in modern Standard Polish, Slovakian, Czech, Upper Sorabian, Serbo-Croatian and Slovenian.

The facts I am going to describe might throw some light on very topical problems of pronominalization, in special reflexive pronominalization in underlying complex sentences of Slavic and other languages. Furthermore, there will be some demonstration in our discussion of an interplay of semantics and syntax. I shall assume throughout familiarity with the main concepts of generative transformational grammar.

1.1. The pronominalizations under discussion occur under clearly definable syntactic (1) and semantic (2) conditions:

(1) They take place in sentences in which there is a verbal phrase 'VP' directly dominating – besides the verb – a noun phrase functioning as a (dative or accusative) object and a following second noun phrase dominating in its turn an infinitive construction (*infinitival*), in other words, a *subjectless infinitive complement*, originating from an embedded sentence. The underlying subject noun phrase of this sentence must not be referentially identical[1]

---

[1] The concept of identity used in the rules for pronominalization and/or deletion of noun phrases is not quite clear. Lexical identity is required to be accompanied by referential identity. Referential identity or – as James D. McCawley argues in his article 'The Role of Semantics in a Grammar' (pp. 136–142) in *Universals* . . . mentioned below – identity of the 'intended referent', if not paired with lexical identity, would include periphrases of preceding noun phrases having the same (intended) referent. In such a case pronominalization, clearly, could not apply, because periphrases, that is, the variation of possible anaphorical repetition of reference is an alternative to pronominalization (cf. the study of E. V. Padučeva, 'Anaphoric Relations and their Representation in the Deep structure of a Text', printed in: M. Bierwisch, Karl-Erich Heidolph, eds., *Progress in Linguistics*, The Hague-Paris, 1970, pp. 224–232). The condition of identical reference alone is not sufficient for reasons pointed out by E. Bach in his paper 'Nouns and Noun Phrases', published in *Universals in Linguistic Theory*, ed. by E. Bach and Robert T. Harms, New York, 1968 (pp. 108–112). I adopt the understanding of identity expressed by Bach in the cited article (p. 110): "I would like to claim that in every transformation including a condition NP = NP, what is meant is *only* the identity of the referential index (or here variable)". In the same

F. Kiefer and N. Ruwet (eds.), Generative Grammar in Europe, 445–481. All Rights Reserved.
Copyright © 1973 by D. Reidel Publishing Company, Dordrecht-Holland.

with the subject of the embedding sentence. This is, of course, a preliminary sketch of the structures involved.

(2) All verbs which may occur in the verbal phrase shortly characterized under (1) have some general semantic property in common which might be specified by a feature like 'behavioral steering' or, perhaps better, 'metaactivity' or 'metaactive'. I shall use [± metaactive] in the following considerations. Some further relevant semantic features involved may be provisionally and incompletely represented in 'chains' of implications, that is lexical redundancy rules:

(a) [+ metaactive] → [± verbal communication]

EXAMPLES:

$$
\begin{bmatrix} \text{приказ(ыв)ать;} \\ \text{(по)просить; велеть;} \\ \text{предлагать/предложить} \end{bmatrix} : \begin{bmatrix} \text{заставлять/заставить;} \\ \text{при вы-нуждать/при} \\ \text{вынудить; приучать/} \\ \text{приучить; помогать/} \\ \text{помочь; убеждать/убедить} \end{bmatrix}
$$

(b) [+ verbal communication] → [± appeal]

EXAMPLES:

$$
\begin{bmatrix} \text{приказ(ыв)ать; (по)про-} \\ \text{сить; запрещать/запре-} \\ \text{тить; уговаривать/} \\ \text{уговорить; предложить/} \\ \text{предлагать} \end{bmatrix} : \begin{bmatrix} \text{советовать; (от)реко-} \\ \text{мендовать; разрешать/} \\ \text{разрешить} \end{bmatrix}
$$

(c) [− appeal] → $\begin{bmatrix} \left\{ \begin{matrix} [± \text{ consent}] \\ \vdots \\ \vdots \end{matrix} \right\} \end{bmatrix}$

EXAMPLES:

[разрешать/разрешить] : [(по)обещать)]

---

paper (p. 111) Bach, using a formulation suggested to him by Paul Postal, points out that "... the analysis of pronominalization which depends on the condition NP = NP leads to the contradiction that an NP is identical with a proper part of itself". I am fully aware of 'Bach's paradox' (cf. Ray C. Dougherty, 'An Interpretive Theory of Pronominal Reference', in: *Foundations of Language*, Vol. 5, No. 4, S. 491) but I do not think it could invalidate, or be detrimental to, the following arguments, statements and rules.

See further the very illuminating paper of Lauri Kartunnen 'Pronouns and Variables', printed in 'Papers from the Fifth Regional Meeting of the Chicago Linguistic Society', April 18-19, 1969, pp. 108–116.

(d)
$$\begin{bmatrix} [+\text{appeal}] \\ [+\text{consent}] \\ \cdot \\ \cdot \\ \cdot \end{bmatrix} \begin{bmatrix} \pm\text{ conventional and/or} \\ \text{official pattern} \end{bmatrix}$$

EXAMPLES:

$$\begin{bmatrix} \text{приказ(ыв)ать;} \\ \text{(по)просить;} \\ \text{разрешать/разрешить} \end{bmatrix} \begin{bmatrix} \text{умолять/умолить; уговари-} \\ \text{вать/уговорить; приз(ы)} \\ \text{вать; да(ва)ть; позволять/} \\ \text{позволить} \end{bmatrix}$$

(e)
$$\begin{bmatrix} +\text{ conventional and/or} \\ \text{official pattern} \end{bmatrix} \rightarrow [\pm\text{ categorical}]$$

EXAMPLES:

$$\begin{bmatrix} \text{приказ(ыв)ать;} \\ \text{запрещать/запретить} \end{bmatrix} \quad [\text{(по)просить}]^2$$

(f) $[\text{categorical}] \rightarrow [\pm\text{ enforceable}]$

The feature $[\pm\text{ enforceable}]$ is introduced, because – according to Ю. Д. Апресян[3] – it is characteristic for the meaning of приказ(ыв)ать that the fulfilment of the order can be enforced or the refusal to obey it lead to punishment.

There is no full symmetry between (1) and (2). For example, the verb предупреждать/предупредить, though specifiable by the features $[+\textit{meta-active}]$, $[+\textit{verbal communication}]$ and $[+\textit{appeal}]$ will not turn up in our discussion, because, quite idiosyncratically, it cannot be followed by an infinitive construction. Further, the verb (по)обещать, for example, can be characterized by the feature values $[+\text{metaactive}]$, $[+\text{verbal communication}]$, $[-\text{appeal}]$ and $[-\text{consent}]$. The negative values of the last two features may be considered to account for the possibility that the subject of the embedding sentence, *he who promises*, is identical with the underlying subject of the infinitival.

---

[2] (a) through (f) is, of course, a tentative and provisional scheme which will need modification. Some open questions are e.g. whether '$[\pm\text{ categorical}]$' presupposes $[+\text{conventional and/or}$ official pattern]. Further, the conjunction of the features $[+\text{metaactive}]$ and $[+\text{verbal communication}]$ is, certainly, not exhaustively specified by the disjunction '$[+\text{appeal}]$ or $[\pm\text{con-}$ sent]'. A specifiable part of the verbs concerned are 'causative'. I am not sure about appropriate feature specifications for помогагъ/помочъ and some other verbs.

[3] cf. Ю. Д. Апресян, О языке для описания значений слов, Известия Академии Наук СССР, Серия литературы и языка 1963, выпуск 5, том XXVIII, сентябрь-октябрь, pp. 415–428; "Для приказа же существенно не право повелевать, а возможность добиваться выполнения повеления под угрозой наказания" (421).

(1)   Борис обещал мне возвратить нам все книги

Verbs specified by [+ verbal communication] and either [+ appeal] or
[+ consent] are incompatible with the identity of subjects just mentioned.
Разрешать and позволять, if used in conventional idioms like (2) and
(3) could not be characterized by [+ verbal communication]:

(2)   я позволю себе обратиться к вам
(3)   я разрешаю себе пригласить вас на вечер . . .

(По)обещать either disallows the identity of noun phrases which is a
prerequisite to the type of pronominalization under discussion, that is the
identity of the underlying subject of the embedded infinitival and of the
(dative or accusative) noun phrase of the embedding sentence, or disallows
the underlying embedded sentence to be transformed to an infinitival:

(4)   он обещал мне, что работа будет сдана через день

That is why (по)обещать will not appear in our considerations. The
verbs given in (a) through (e) seem to be the bulk of, or representative of,
all that can occur in the constructions to be discussed.

1.2.   I am not going to examine more closely the semantic properties of
the verbs concerned. However, I think it would be difficult to dispense
with the above mentioned features or some modification of them in a semantic description of those verbs. Moreover, it is very likely that the most
appropriate formal arrangement in which these (modified) features and
others should be accommodated are expressions in the predicate calculus.
The features given in (a) through (e) may serve as part of the characterization
of the relation (many place predicate) which is to represent the meaning of
the respective verb. The meaning of 'metaactive' verbs suggests the general
form of a representation by many place predicates, one argument of such
a predicate constituting a proposition. In special, the representation of the
'action' on behalf of which somebody appeals to somebody will have to be
represented by a proposition serving as one argument of the predicate
which represents the meaning of a 'metaactive' verb, e.g. приказ(ыв)ать.

1.3.   In terms of the 'classical' theory of N. Chomsky's *Aspects of the
Theory of Syntax*, 'strict' syntactic subcategorization of the verbs listed in
(a) through (f) and further verbs which might be added would have to record
two noun phrases: [+___ NP NP]. The first of them is a (dative or accusative) noun phrase which is generally presupposed on the strength of
the meaning of the verb to denote human beings. The second noun phrase

immediately dominates a sentence symbol. According to idiosyncratic specifications of the main verb, the embedded underlying sentence will end up in surface structure as an infinitival or as a clause introduced by the conjunction (complementizer) 'чтобы', for example *приказ(ыв)ать*, *(по)просить*. Some verbs of our list, e.g. *заставлять/заставить* and *да(ва)ть* are restricted to infinitival complements. We are concerned here solely with the latter ones. Thus, the special (reflexive) pronominalization to be discussed here will be definable so far on (1) membership in a certain semantic class of the verb of the embedding sentence; (2) on structures resulting from the optional or obligatory (*заставлять*, *давать*) application of infinitive complement transformations, which are rules governed by lexical items or classes, and (3) on referential indices for certain noun phrases.

2.1. Let me introduce now some first examples of the constructions I am dealing with

(5)   командир $\begin{Bmatrix} \text{приказал} \\ \text{велел} \end{Bmatrix}$ $\begin{Bmatrix} \text{Борису} \\ \text{дежурному} \\ \text{мне} \\ \text{часовому} \\ \text{адъютанту} \\ \text{ему} \end{Bmatrix}$ разбудить

себя ровно через два часа

(6)   командир $\begin{Bmatrix} \text{приказал} \\ \text{велел} \end{Bmatrix}$ $\begin{Bmatrix} \text{Борису} \\ \text{дежурному} \\ \text{мне} \\ \text{часовому} \\ \text{адъютанту} \\ \text{ему} \end{Bmatrix}$ разбудить

его ровно через два часа

(7)   я приказал разбудить *себя* ровно через два часа

(8)   я приказал разбудить *меня* ровно через два часа

(9)   командир приказал $\begin{Bmatrix} \text{разбудить} \\ \text{отвести туда} \end{Bmatrix}$ себя и его

(Example (9) from В. П. Недялков).

Both (5) and (6) are meant to compress twelve analogous sentences. Some representation similar to (f) may be fairly correctly assumed to appear at a more or less early stage in the derivation of (5) or (6). I shall not be concerned here with the problem of finding an appropriate 'deepest' or initial linguistic representation of e.g. (5).

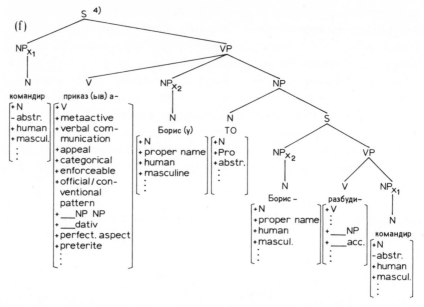

Phrase-markers for (7) and (8) would be quite similar to (g) [cf. footnote (4)] or (f) differing from them in that 'NP$_{x_2}$' dominates a Pro-Noun specifiable by '[− definite], [+ human], [+ anonymous]'. Such a pronoun is, generally, subject to deletion in modern Russian (cf. 3.2.).

2.2.   Let us turn now to the crucial facts which gave rise to our discussion. The embedded sentence in the first example of (5) and (f) contains an object noun phrase (командир-) that is subject to pronominalization, obviously on the basis of its referential identity with the subject noun phrase of the embedding sentence. The identity is expressed in (f) by an identical index assigned to both noun phrases. Now, if (5) and (6) as well as (7) and (8) are synonymous, and that is what they are, we must conclude that we have a choice here of two possible pronominalizations in an identical phrase marker. We can choose between the nonreflexive pronominalization and the reflexive pronominalization of one and the same noun phrase at whatever point in the derivation the pronominalization will be required to apply. In other words, let us assume that we have two classes A and B of structural descriptions defining the applicability of the nonreflexive (a) and the reflexive (b) pronominalization respectively. There will be, then, an intersection of

⁴ See page 451.

[4] Diagram (f) is simplified and shortened considerably. I have paid little attention to matters having no bearing on the problems discussed. Feature matrices, which are rather defective, are arranged in the traditional way under lexical elements. Aspect features like the ones given have morphological status and are introduced transformationally, being theoretically predictable from other features or categories in the sentence. A 'deeper' representation of (5), which is in some accordance with more recent versions of generative semantics as proposed by James D. McCawley, P. Postal, G. Lakoff, И. А. Мельчук, Ю.Д. Апресян, А. К. Жолковский and others, would be similar to (g). The features of (a)–(f) appear as predicates.

(g)

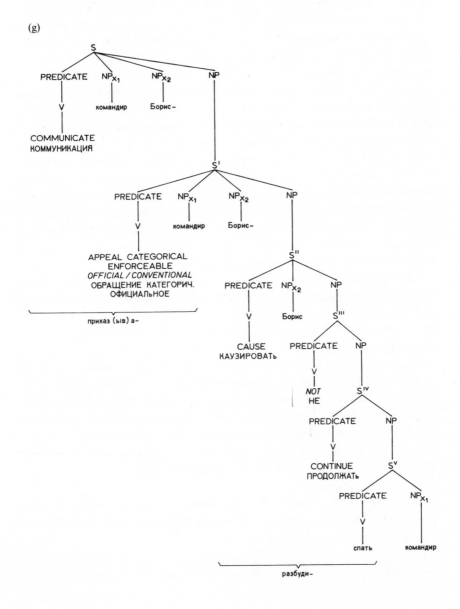

the two classes A and B of structural descriptions in which either pronominal-ization can apply, the reflexive one or the nonreflexive one. Of course, the set of sentences (6), not sentence (8), has two more semantic interpretations: (a) его may still refer to a noun phrase occurring in one of the preceding sentences, most likely in the preceding one (anaphorical reference); (b) его may be used in a deictic sense or reference. Thus in sentences like (6), not (8), there is a threefold ambiguity of его. However, this possible polysemy of его (and их) cannot be made use of in conjunctions of these pronouns resulting from the conjunction of embedded infinitivals of the type under discussion. Let us take (9) for an example of this restriction. The trans-formations resulting in the conjunction of the pronouns себя and его should operate either on the conjunction of infinitivals (I) отвезти туда/разбудить его₁и отвезти туда/разбудить его₂ or on (II) отвезти туда/разбудить себя и отвезти туда/разбудить его₂ where его₁ and себя are coreferential, referring to командир, while его₂ is anaphorical or deictic. This is in accordance with the rules valid for single embedded infinitivals. If we have (I), the conjunction of the pronouns его₁ and его₂ involves the obligatory substitution of the reflexive pronoun себя for его₁. Of course, a *general restriction* seems to exclude the conjunction of identical pronouns carrying different reference, if they are not used in a deictic situation. Identical reference of identical pronouns, on the other hand, seems to be restricted to extraordinary cases of emphatic repetition.

The embedded object noun phrase in (5) through (8) undergoes one of the two pronominalizations just mentioned by virtue of its referential identity with the subject noun phrase not of the same underlying simplex sentence, but of the embedding sentence. As to the underlying subject noun phrase of the embedded sentence (NP_{x_2}, Борис- in (f)), it is deleted according to the very general rule of identical noun phrase deletion, be it identical with the subject, as in (1) through (3), or with the object, as in (5) through (8), of the embedding sentence. Identity with the subject – be it 'later' deleted or not – of the same simplex sentence has been generally considered a necessary condition of reflexive pronominalization. The rule, however, which is required to account for себя in (5) and (7) should be at variance with Klima's and Lees' rules for pronominalization in English:[5]

"(A) Reflexive Rule:

$X - \text{Nom} - Y - \text{Nom}' - Z \rightarrow X - \text{Nom} - Y - \text{Nom}' + \text{self} - Z$ where Nom = Nom' = a nominal, and where Nom and Nom' are within the same simplex sentence.

[5] R. B. Lees and E. S. Klima, 'Rules for English Pronominalization', in: *Language*, Journal of the Linguistic Society of America, Vol. 39, No. 1, January–March 1963, p. 23.

(B) Pronoun Rule:

$X - \text{Nom} - Y - \text{Nom}' - Z \rightarrow X - \text{Nom} - Y - \text{Nom}' + \text{Pron} - Z$
where Nom = Nom', and where Nom is in a matrix sentence while Nom' is in a constituent sentence embedded within that matrix sentence. The rules are to be applied in the order given. Later morphophonemic rules will then yield the appropriate pronoun form '*me, myself, yourself,* . . .', *themselves*; etc".

3.1. Before discussing some different and more specified rules let us look more closely at the examples (5) through (8). One might be tempted to look for an explanation of the reflexive pronominalizations illustrated there in the fact that the embedded verb 'разбудить' is semantically irreflexive – nobody could normally wake himself. So, one might conclude, in case referential identity of себя with the subject of the same simplex sentence is excluded on semantic grounds, the reflexive pronoun might be allowed to refer to the subject noun phrase of the embedding sentence. Examples (5) through (13) are sentences in which even both verbs occurring there are semantically irreflexive. If in such a sentence a reflexive pronoun (себя, себе) occurs, it could not be referentially identical with the subject of the underlying sentence as the object of which it functions, that is себя etc., can only be referred to the subject of the simplex sentence in which it is not an object. Now, the case that an object себя etc., occurring in the embedding sentence, could refer to the subject of an embedded sentence through backward (kataphoric) pronominalization seems to be excluded. The other case, however, is quite normal as (5) and (7) and the following examples show.

(10)   Борис (по)просил меня разбудить себя ровно через час
(11)   Борис (по)просил Ивана разбудить себя ровно через час
(12)   Я (по)просил дежурного разбудить себя ровно через час
(13)   Борис (по)просил его разбудить себя ровно через час
(14)   Борис (по)просил друга разбудить себя ровно через час

'себя' is coreferent with 'Борис' or 'меня' (12). Identity with 'меня' or any of the other four noun phrases of (11) to (14), which, in their turn, are identical with the underlying subject of the embedded sentence, is ruled out on semantic grounds. However, explanations of the reflexive pronominalization in (5), (7) and (10) to (14), based on the semantic irreflexiveness of the infinitival verb, would fail immediately on simple empirical grounds. Semantic irreflexiveness of the verb is no necessary condition for reflexive pronominalization of this type as is shown by the following examples.

(15)   командир приказал адъютанту соединить себя с медсанбатом
(16)   командир приказал адъютанту соединить его с медсанбатом
(17)   он попросил ее вскипятить себе чашку чая
(18)   он попросил ее вскипятить ему чашку чая
(19)   командир приказал дежурному принести себе койку
(20)   командир приказал дежурному принести ему койку

(21)   он разрешал нам именовать себя $\left\{ \begin{array}{c} \text{нашим} \\ \text{своим} \end{array} \right\}$ шефом

(22)   он разрешал нам именовать его шефом
(23)   он разрешал Борису назвать себя археологом
(24)   он разрешал Борису назвать его археологом

(25)   они попросили нас $\left\{ \begin{array}{c} \text{вычеркнуть} \\ \text{исключить} \end{array} \right\}$ себя из списка участвующих

(26)   они попросили нас $\left\{ \begin{array}{c} \text{вычеркнуть} \\ \text{исключить} \end{array} \right\}$ их из списка участвующих

The verbs соединять/соединить, вскипятить, приносить/принести, наз(ы)ватъ, именовать, вычеркивать/вычеркнуть and исключать/исключить are not irreflexive. Those sentences of (15) through (26) in which a reflexive pronoun себя/себе occurs are subject to two interpretations, one in which себя/себе is referentially identical with the underlying subject noun phrase of the embedded infinitival (I), e.g. with 'адъютанту' in (15), and one in which it is interpreted as referentially identical with the subject of the embedding sentence, e.g. with 'командир' (II). The meaning of the main (metaactive) verb may suggest or further interpretation (I):

(27)   он предложил ей вскипятить себе (-ей) чашку чая

[cf. (17), (18)]

If we substitute for any себя/себе in (15) through (26) его, ему or их, the resulting sentences, (16), (18), (20), (22), (24) and (26) will have interpretation (II) or the above mentioned anaphoric or deictic interpretation. There might be a certain preference for nonreflexive pronominalization in sentences like (15) through (26) in case interpretation (II) is intended, but I can say nothing definite about this (*see* 4.5.). In any case, sentences like (15), (17), (19), (21), (23) and (25) are correct and acceptable in interpretation (II).

3.2.1.   Some special attention must be paid to sentences perfectly analogous to the previous ones but not containing superficially a noun phrase functioning as a (dative or accusative) object. The most important property of this type of sentence is that the syntactic and semantic alternative (I) or (II) discussed in the preceding section does not hold. They are open to interpretation (II) only (cf. 3.2.2.). Besides (7), (8) and (9) containing irreflexive verbs I present the following examples:

(28)   командир приказал соединить себя с медсанбатом

(29)   командир приказал соединить его с медсанбатом

(30)   директор попросил соединить себя с заведующим отделом

(31)   директор попросил соединить его с заведующим отделом

(32)   он разрешал именовать себя заместителем директора

(33)   он разрешал именовать его заместителем директора

(34)   они попросили исключить себя из списка участвующих

(35)   они попросили исключить их из списка участвующих

(36)   зачем – такой молодец, а позволил себя ранить?

(Симонов)

(37)   он велел запереть себя в поезде

(38)   он велел себя убить

(39)   она сразу же велит отвести себя в его комнату

(40)   он не позволял $\left\{ \begin{array}{l} \text{говорить о себе худое} \\ \text{себе что-либо запретить} \\ \text{навязать себе что-либо} \end{array} \right\}$

To account for such sentences I propose to posit a hypothetical object noun phrase in the embedding sentence and, correspondingly, an identical subject noun phrase in the embedded sentence. Both noun phrases are specified by a set of syntactic and semantic features containing [+ human], [+ anonymous] [− definite], but they never get a phonological feature matrix, that is they are not manifested lexically. They are coreferential. The subject noun phrase (category symbol and features) is deleted according to the general rule of identical noun phrase deletion applying in embedded infinitivals. We simply proceed in the same way as we do in sentences having a surface (dative or accusative) object. The embedded underlying subject to be deleted is recoverable on behalf of its identity with the preceding object noun phrase, which is subject to deletion in its turn. The following phrase-marker shows an intermediate stage in the derivation of (28) or (29). It is simplified and shortened considerably, much syntactic and semantic information is neglected.

(h)

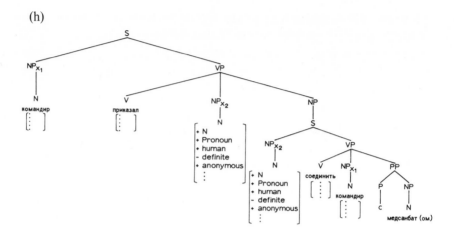

The representation of the noun phrases NP_{x_2} is, apart from an idiosyncratic plural specification, the same that could be used in an abstract representation of so called 'indefinite personal' sentences like говорят, говорили, несут. Note that both noun phrases NP_{x_2} are deleted without having received a phonological representation. As already mentioned, in generating (28), the first occurrence of NP_{x_2} in (h) rendering theoretically possible the deletion of the second (embedded) one is deleted in its turn; in other words, the recoverability of the second NP_{x_2} is a purely formal assumption: In maintaining that the embedded NP_{x_2} can be deleted, because it is recoverable by virtue of the existence of the preceding NP_{x_2}, we simply put off the justification of the deletion of the first NP_{x_2}, that is of a noun phrase whose recoverability is not based on an identical noun phrase remaining in the surface structure.

The structure (h) I am assuming for sentences like (7), (28) implies the claim that superficial nonoccurrence of certain types of noun phrases may allow their double recovery. It would be rather an empty objection to say that too much structure is lost as a result of the two deletions for the two noun phrases to be recoverable. The problem rather is this: what kind of syntactic information and semantic presuppositions, which clues to the full explicit structure of such utterances are available to account for the recoverability of objects characterizable by the features [+ human], [− definite], [+ anonymous] and others. I think one might try to explain these facts (1) by looking for relations subsisting between the syntactic and semantic feature structure of noun phrases and their 'omissibility', and (2) by examining whether certain semantic classes of verbs might have a special force of 'radiating' their contextual structure. Let us illustrate (2) by the following example

(41)   Туманан . . . позвонил по телефону, вызвал 'двойку',
         потребовал какого Ильина и, узнав, что тот спит,
         приказал разбудить

(Симонов)

In the context of . . . приказал . . . an indefinite personal object noun (phrase) has to be recovered and the same noun (phrase) must be reproduced as the subject of the infinitival разбудить.

These are deletions of the type we are just discussing. The omission of a noun phrase as the object of разбудить is of quite a different character. Here we are concerned with a noun phrase, referentially identical with *Ильин* which is present in surface structure.

3.2.2.   Sentences like (28) having structural properties roughly similar to those assumed in (h) are noteworthy in a discussion of reflexive pronominalization in an important respect: they rule out interpretation (I) (cf. 3.2.1.).

A subject noun phrase of the type just analyzed, which ends up without getting a phonological representation, may be resumed as an object noun phrase in the same simplex sentence and, consequently, be subject to reflexive pronominalization. However, it seems that such a pronominalization must result in the affix -ся. Себя is reduced to -ся and the word boundary separating it from the preceding verb is deleted. It would appear that себя cannot be preserved, because the conditions for using себя and not the corresponding shorter form -ся, may be incompatible with the character and the phonetical 'zero' appearance of the noun phrase under discussion. So, if себя appears, it could only be a coreferent of the surface subject. W. Sperber pointed out to me the following examples:

(42)   Он велел встать и умыться
         он велел запереться в комнате   (cf.(37))

In case there are no synonymous pairs #себя : -ся, reflexive pronominalization on behalf of referential identity with the subject of the embedded sentence seems to be excluded in the presence of noun phrases with the feature values [− definite], [+ human], [+ anonymous], *see* example (38).

3.3.   Before trying to formulate some rules accounting for these striking phenomena of reflexive and nonreflexive pronominalization I shall offer some more examples.

(43)   командир приказал (дежурному) позвонить себе в
                                              десять часов

(44)   командир приказал (дежурному) позвонить ему в
                                              десять часов

(45)   отец $\begin{Bmatrix} \text{запретил} \\ \text{разрешит} \end{Bmatrix}$ (мне) позвонить себе поздно ночью

(46)   отец $\begin{Bmatrix} \text{запретил} \\ \text{разрешил} \end{Bmatrix}$ (мне) позвонить ему поздно ночью

(47)   брат $\begin{Bmatrix} \text{советовал} \\ \text{рекомекдовал} \end{Bmatrix}$ (мне) разбудить себя в шесть
                                                       часов утра

(48)   брат $\begin{Bmatrix} \text{советовал} \\ \text{рекомендовал} \end{Bmatrix}$ (мне) разбудить его в шесть
                                                       часов утра

(49)   она просила (меня) подождать себя
(50)   она просила (меня) подождать ее
(51)   она попросила себя подождать
(52)   она попросила ее подождать
(53)   она уговорила Бориса позвонить себе
(54)   она уговорила Бориса позвонить ей

I have been using again parentheses and braces to economize the list of examples. By exchanging the verbs put in braces we get a new but perfectly analogous sentence. Leaving out the noun phrase put in parentheses gives a similar sentence lacking a superficial object as discussed under 3.2.

4.1. Suppose we accept the rules of Klima and Lees quoted above slightly modifying them in the following way:

(A')
SD: $X - NP_{x_i} - Y - NP'_{x_i} - Z$

$$\longrightarrow$$

$$X - NP_{x_i} - Y - \begin{bmatrix} N \\ \begin{bmatrix} + \text{Pronoun} \\ + \text{reflexive} \end{bmatrix} \\ \vdots \end{bmatrix} NP'_{x_i} - Z$$

(B′)

SD: $X - NP_{x_j} - Y - NP'_{x_j} - Z$

$$\longrightarrow$$

$$X - NP_{x_j} - Y - \left[\begin{array}{c} N \\ \left[\begin{array}{c} + \text{Pronoun} \\ - \text{reflexive} \end{array} \right] \\ \vdots \\ \vdots \end{array} \right] NP'_{x_j} - Z$$

Reinterpreting the conditions of the application of (B) for (B′) in terms of a newer version of transformational grammar we would say that the noun phrase to be pronominalized (NP'_{x_j}) is required to recur in a sentence embedded by the sentence in which the antecedent 'NP_{x_j}' occurs. There must be at least one intermediate symbol 'S' separating the two noun phrases which are referentially identical. In these cases nonreflexive pronominalization takes place. Although, generally speaking the regularities of pronominalization connected with complexity and embedding of sentences as well as with textual structure are still not very well known, the facts motivating the conditions for rules like (A′) and (B′) are fairly clear. It will be remembered, however, that the rules are ordered, (A′) preceding (B′), and that (A′) is not allowed to apply after (B′) has applied. Thus sentences like

(55)   I have no money about me

instead of

(56)   *I have no money about myself

are accounted for by ordering (A′) and (B′), (A′) not being allowed to operate on a phrase marker representing (55) to change it into a phrase marker for (56) although the structural description for (55), after a hypothetical relative clause is reduced, would meet the conditions for the application of (A′). In other words, cyclical relations in the operation of (A′) and (B′) were not taken into consideration in the paper mentioned.[6] While a special case like (55) and analogous English sentences could be accounted for without assuming cyclical rules, there are other cases in English as well as Russian which cannot be explained without them. It appears to me that a different explanation for (55) and (56) must be found in view of the fact

[6] Comp. the following statement of J. R. Ross: "Only if Pronominalization is formulated as a cyclic rule, obligatory in most environments . . . can the unnecessary conditions be avoided which would be required if it were considered to be either pre-cyclic or post-cyclic". ('On the Cyclic Nature of English Pronominalization', in: *To Honour Roman Jakobson* (Den Haag–Paris, 1967, p. 1682)).

that exclusive application of (A') and (B') (by disjunctive ordering) as postulated by Klima and Lees is not tenable. Let us take first an English example, and discuss it in an informal way:

(57)   John believed that John is an expert →
        John believed that he is an expert

In the first cycle nonreflexive pronominalization (B') takes place changing the second occurrence of *John* into the pronoun *he*. If the optional transformation of complement subject raising is applied we shall get (58):

(58)   *John$_{x_1}$ believed *him*$_{x_1}$ to be an expert

The phrase-marker underlying (58) is subject to transformation (A') in the second cycle, (A') obligatorily applying after (B') has applied. A perfectly analogous situation arises in Russian:

(59)   Борис$_{x_1}$ считал, что Борис$_{x_1}$ крупный специалист
        $\longrightarrow$
        Борих$_{x_1}$ считал, что он$_{x_1}$ крупный специалист

according to (B'). After COMPLEMENT SUBJECT RAISING we shall get:

(60)   *Борис$_{x_1}$ считал его$_{x_1}$ крупным специалистом

which must undergo (A') to result in the correct sentence

(61)   Борис$_{x_1}$ считал себя$_{x_1}$ крупным специалистом

A further example:

(62)   они$_{x_1}$ считали, что они$_{x_1}$ вправе требовать . . .
        *они$_{x_1}$ считали их$_{x_1}$ вправе требовать . . .
        они$_{x_1}$ считали себя$_{x_1}$ вправе требовать . . .

A slightly more complicated case of complement subject raising with obligatory operation of (A') in the second cycle is illustrated by

(63)   я вижу в нем преемника себе

It seems perfectly clear that cyclical operation of (A') in relation to (B') is necessary to derive sentence types like those mentioned above.

4.2.   Let us turn now to the constructions under discussion from the viewpoint of cyclical rule application. The structural descriptions for any of our examples containing as main verb one of the verbs listed in (a) through (f) and a semantically irreflexive verb in the embedded infinitival do not meet the structural index of (A') in the first cycle of derivation. Referential non-identity of subject and object must be provided for by a semantic feature assigned to the respective verb. In case embedded non-irreflexive verbs occur (examples (15) through (26)) the conditions of (A') are met, if the subject noun phrase and the object noun phrase of the embedded sentence are referentially identical [vid. discussion in 3.1. of interpretation (I)]. In this case rule (A') will apply in the first cycle of the derivations of e.g. (15), (17), (19), (21), (23), (25). Let us take for further discussion sentence (15). In the course of the derivation of (15) some transformation will yield the infinitive complement, where the underlying subject noun phrase may be assigned features characterizing the dative and after that be deleted.[7]

Finally, the embedded 'S' is deleted and a phrase marker arises which again meets the conditions for (A') because of the coreference of the dative object 'адъютанту' and 'себя', which is the object of 'соединить'. (A') would operate vacuously now leaving *себя*.

Rule (A') does not apply in the first cycle, if the embedded object noun phrase is not referentially identical with the subject of the embedded sentence but with the subject of the embedding one. As mentioned above this is the only type of referential identity possible with embedded irreflexive verbs. In this case, following the rules so far at our disposal, (B') will apply giving sentences like (6), (8), (16), (18), (20), (22), (24), (26), (29), (31), (33), (35), (44), (46), (48), (50), (52), (54). (8) has the original pronoun 'меня'.

Now it has been discussed in detail and demonstrated above that exactly in such cases of referential identity as are presented in the examples just enumerated *reflexive* pronouns may be used as easily and normally as the nonreflexive ones, comp. the parallel examples e.g. (5), (7), (10) through (14), (15), (17), (19), (21), (23), (25), (28), (30), (32), (34), (36), (37), (38), (39), (43), (45), (47), (49), (51), (53).

How can we account for this type of reflexive pronominalization? At first glance it would appear that we could simply let (A') apply in the second cycle to phrase-markers underlying sentences like those enumerated in the former list ranging from (6) to (54), that is to the output of rule (B'). But this would, of course, be perfectly wrong, because (A') is an obligatory rule leaving none of those sentences unchanged; that is, our grammar would not generate the set of correct sentences which is exemplified by the former list (6)–(54), if we are not prepared to make (A') an optional rule, when it applies in the second cycle, which would appear to be quite unnatural. Of course, we might do the opposite, namely, let (A') operate obligatorily in the

---

[7] Comp. Bernard Sterling Comrie, 'Nominalizations in Russian', (Manuscript pp. 18, 19), Clare College Cambridge, 1969; Lew, R. Micklesen, 'Impersonal Sentences in Russian', American Contributions to the Sixth International Congress of Slavists, Prague, 1968, August 7–13. Volume I *Linguistic Contributions*, ed. by Henry Kučera, p. 15.

second cycle changing его or их into себя, and construct some rule operating optionally on the output of (A') to reestablish его, их or меня etc.

However, this again appears to be quite unnatural and out of the question. So, it would appear, the parallel examples of the latter list (5)–(53) must be generated in a different way. We have to do something to the contrary first, namely prevent (A') from being applied to the output of (B'), that is to phrase-markers underlying sentences like those illustrated in the list (6)–(54). Thus, a special constraint has to be put on (A') by specifying a structural description which, while being a special case of the structural description for (A'), will block its application. Such a description fully coincides with the structural index required for an optional rule of reflexivization which will change phrase markers underlying sentences like those given in the former list ((6) . . . (54)) into phrase markers underlying sentences exemplified in the latter one ((5) . . . (53)), those we want to explain.

Let us call the optional rule to be set up rule '(C)'. Then, the constraint we must put on rule (A') can be expressed as a condition for the application of (A') which has the simple form: *Condition*: $SD\ (A') \neq SD$ (C). Since a special optional rule is indispensable to account for reflexivization of the type discussed, the exceptional restriction to be put on (A') can be described quite conveniently. At the same time the idiosyncratic character of the reflexivization under discussion is reflected by the identity of structural description pairing an exception to a very general obligatory rule with a very special optional one.

(C)   SD: $X - NP_{x_i} - Y - V - Z - \text{infinitive} + V - U -$
            1   2   3   4   5   6   7

$$\left[NP_{x_i} \begin{bmatrix} N \\ +\,\text{Pronoun} \\ -\,\text{reflexive} \\ \vdots \end{bmatrix} \right] NP_{x_i} \quad - W$$

                        8   9

SC: $8 \rightarrow \left[NP_{x_i} \begin{bmatrix} N \\ +\,\text{Pronoun} \\ +\,\text{reflexive} \\ \vdots \end{bmatrix} \right] NP_{x_i}$

4.3. Let us take a look at the following sentence:

(64)   Борис обещал нам исключить себя из списка участвующих

The structure index for (C) is not met by a derived phrase marker for (64), because the pronoun would be characterized '[+ reflexive]' being the result of the operation of (A'), which has applied in the first cycle on behalf of the referential identity of the object noun phrase occurring in the embedded infinitival with the underlying subject noun phrase 'Борис' of the same clause. Let us call this the 'inner subject'. 'Себя' in (64) is, at the same time, co-referential with the subject noun phrase of the embedding sentence. We shall call this the 'outer subject'. A second – vacuous – operation of (A') will take place in the second cycle.

(По)обещать is a 'metaactive' verb, but verbs like '(по)обещать' cannot precede infinitival complements in structures satisfying (C). Further, there is no danger of sentences like the following coming under the structural description of (C).

(65)   Борис вчера хотел застрелить $\left\{ \begin{array}{l} \text{себя} \\ \text{его} \end{array} \right\}$

Either 'себя' occurs, which is '[+ reflexive]' and coreferential with the 'inner' and 'outer' subject 'Борис', or 'его', which can only refer to a person not mentioned in the given sentence. In the first case a second – vacuous – operation of (A') will take place.

4.4.   It is clear that in sentences like (64) or (65) rule (C) will not operate on 'себя', because it requires a non-reflexive pronoun arising from the previous application of (B'). On the other hand, (B') does not operate in the second cycle on the pronominal result 'себя' of (A') in (64) or (65), because there will be no embedded 'constituent' sentence after the appearance of the infinitival effected by transformations including the deletion of the underlying identical subject and of the symbol 'S'. However, a more general constraint seems to be valid here, excluding any change of a reflexive pronoun by further pronominalizations. Let us take the following example:

(66)   Борис$_i$ обещал, что он$_i$ исключит себя$_i$ из списка участвующих

'Борис', 'он' and 'себя' are coreferents. Rule (A'), applying first, will pro-nominalize the third occurrence of underlying 'Борис' changing it into 'себя', while (B'), applying after (A'), pronominalizes the second occurrence of 'Борис' generating 'он'. A second operation of (B') in the course of the derivation of (66), namely on 'себя' on the basis of its identity with the 'outer' subject 'Борис', which would change 'себя' into 'он', could be ruled out by introducing the general constraint just mentioned or, provisionally, by providing (B') with the feature [– reflexive], which is to be added to the noun phrase undergoing pronominalization.

4.5. Let us shortly return to those sentences which are ambiguous, because their reflexive pronoun following a non-irreflexive verb may be identical with the 'outer' or with the 'inner' subject. I repeat two examples:

(67)   командир приказал ⎰ соединить себя (его) с штабом ⎱
        дежурному   ⎱ принести себе (ему) койку   ⎰

(68)   мы попросили его исключить себя (нас) из списка
        участвующих

Recall (3.2.2.) that ambiguity is lost in cases like (69):

(69)   он велел себя убить

If the nonreflexive pronoun is preferred to the reflexive one to avoid the ambiguity mentioned above, in case of coreference with the 'outer' subject, e.g. in sentences like (67), (68), I propose to reflect this situation by making use of characterizations of *markedness*. If optional transformational rules, in special (C), are allowed to be characterized by symbols for '*m*arked' and '*un*marked', the following conventions for their interpretation could be introduced here:

(i) $m(C) \rightarrow +(C)/X -$ infinitive $+ V \qquad - Y$

$$\begin{bmatrix} + V \\ \vdots \\ + NP \\ - \cdot \\ \vdots \\ \pm \text{ reflexive} \\ \vdots \end{bmatrix}$$

(j) $u(C) \rightarrow +(C)/X -$ infinitive $+ V \qquad - Y$

$$\begin{bmatrix} + V \\ \vdots \\ + NP \\ - \cdot \\ \vdots \\ - \text{ reflexive} \end{bmatrix}$$

where [± reflexive] ('not-irreflexive') and [− reflexive] ('irreflexive') represent semantic properties characterizing the verb of the infinitival appearing in the structural description of (C). Thus, the specification of the context in (i) and (j) must be included in the structural index of (C). According to a general convention (i) implies 'u (C) $\rightarrow$ $-$ (C)/ . . .' and (j) implies 'm (C) $\rightarrow$ $-$ (C)/ . . .'.[8]

Dealing in this way with optional rules we might be in a position to specify the global concept of optionality of transformational rules and to distinguish domains of their application which are subject to restrictions and conditions from those which are not.

5.1.   Let us turn now to a series of analogous constructions in which the antecedent 'metaactive' verb is not a verb of 'verbal communication'. These verbs are mentioned in our list (1.1.). I shall divide them into two groups (5.2.; 5.3.). In the first group we shall be concerned with заставлять/ заставить; да(ва)ть; принуждать/принудить ; вынуждать/вынудить.   In the second group we shall deal with помогать/помочь and приучать/ приучить. Constructions with any of these verbs in the main (embedding) sentence satisfy the structural index of (C). The verbs of the first group, excepting да(ва)ть are not irreflexive.

5.2.1.   What is peculiar about the derivation of sentences containing заставлять/заставить and да(ва)ть is that transformation (C), which has been qualified as optional, changes into an obligatory one.

(70)   Борис заставил себя $_i$ ждать

---

[8] It was pointed out to me by O. Kade that the mentioned preference of the non-reflexive pronoun in sentence-types like (67), (68) containing a semantically not irreflexive verb, possibly, reaches the limit of exclusive use of the non-reflexive pronoun in case the subject of the main sentence is a first or second person personal pronoun :

(67′)   я$_i$ приказал дежурному соединить меня$_i$ с штабом
(67″)   *я$_i$ приказал дежурному соединить себя$_i$ с штабом

(68) would possibly be wrong, too, in its first variant containing себя.
    The reason for this can be looked for in the fact that меня тебя, нас, вас etc. are perfectly unambiguous, while third person non-reflexive pronouns like *его*, if 'preferred' in cases of coreference with the 'outer subject' in sentences like (67), still are referentially ambiguous in the sense discussed under 3.1. Thus, it might be supposed that the possibility to use the reflexive pronoun, that is to apply rule (C) even when the verb of the infinitival is semantically not irreflexive, is preserved by the unavoidable referential ambiguity of его, e.g. in (67). Such reasoning is quite in accord with our general discussion of the referential ambiguity of pronouns which gave rise to the conflict between reflexive and non-reflexive pronominalization (cf. page 474). If it turns out that reflexive pronominalization is indeed impossible in case the object of the infinitival is coreferential with the 'outer' subject manifested by a first or second person pronoun and the verb in the infinitive is semantically not irreflexive, a further condition must be imposed upon (C). Application of (C) would have to be ruled out if the main subject is specified as first and second person, respectively, and the verb of the infinitival is not irreflexive. A corresponding specification or condition would have to be added to the structure index for (C).

and not

(71)   *Борис$_i$ заставил его$_i$ ждать
          *он$_i$ уважать его$_i$ заставил

where '*себя*' and 'его' are direct objects of ждать in the underlying embedded sentence. 'себя' (70) and 'его' (71) are referentially identical with 'Борис', which is indicated by the subscript '*i*'. Analogical coreference is presupposed in the following examples:

(72)   Борис заставил друзей себя ждать
(73)   Борис заставил друзей ждать себя
(74) $^{(*)}$Борис заставил друзей его ждать
(75) $^{(*)}$Борис заставил друзей ждать его
(76)   Борис заставил себя уважать
(77)   Борис заставил уважать себя
(78)   Он уважать себя заставил (Пушкин)
(79)   Борис заставил друзей уважать себя
(80) $^{(*)}$Борис заставил друзей уважать его
(81)   Борис заставил друзей себя уважать
(82) $^{(*)}$Борис заставил друзей его уважать
(83)   я . . . два раза летать к себе не заставлю (Симонов)
(84) $^{(*)}$я два раза летать ко мне не заставлю
(85)   . . . и в неполных шестнадцать лет заставил взять
          себя в солдаты . . . (Симонов)
(86)   он заставлял себя долго упрашивать
(87)   он заставил себе сказать, что . . .
(88)   Борис дал себя уговорить
(89)   *Борис дал его уговорить
(90)   *Борис дал уговорить его
(91)   Борис не дал друзьям уговорить себя
(92)   Борис не дал друзьям себя уговорить
(93) $^{(*)}$Борис не дал друзьям его уговорить
(94) $^{(*)}$Борис не дал друзьям уговорить его
(95)   Борис не дал о себе знать
(96)   Борис не дал знать о себе
(97)   *Борис не дал о нем знать
(98)   *Борис не дал знать о нем
(99)   Борис не дал родственникам знать о себе
(100) $^{(*)}$Борис не дал родственником знать о нем
(101)   За ту храбрость, с которой
          никому не давал себе помогать и

никогда ни на что не жаловался   (Симонов)

(102)   Он не дал моим слезам растрогать себя

(103)   она не давала себя $\left\{\begin{array}{l}\text{задержать}\\ \text{удержать}\\ \text{спугнуть}\\ \text{обмануть}\\ \text{одурачить}\\ \text{совратить}\end{array}\right\}$

Note that *ждать* is an irreflexive verb and *уважать* a non-irreflexive one. It would be semantically normal, then, if *себя*, functioning as the direct object of *уважать*, be referentially identical with the underlying subject noun phrase of this verb, that is with the 'inner' subject.

However, this possibility is clearly ruled out on syntactic grounds in sentences like (76) or (77). There are two conceivable underlying noun phrases which might function as an 'inner' subject in (76) and (77). One is the hypothetical noun phrase we have posited in Section 3.2. above as a representation for an indefinite human anonymous subject. *Себя* in (76) and (77) however, can not be identical with a noun phrase of this type on the basis of the syntactic restrictions valid for the pronominalization of such noun phrases (cf. 3.2.2.). The character of the noun phrase, then, disallows referential identity here. The second – and last – possibility of positing an underlying noun phrase functioning as the 'inner' subject of the infinitival in (76) or (77) would repose on the noun phrase *Борис*, no other noun phrase turning up at all. But in this case *Борис* would be, at the same time, the underlying object of the embedding sentence, that is of *заставить*. This would be, however, at variance with restrictions on noun phrase deletion. Object noun phrases identical with the subject noun phrase of the same simplex sentence, that is, the embedding sentence in our example, are not deletable, they are not 'implied' by 'zero'. So, the possibility of *Борис* functioning as the underlying subject of the embedded infinitival is ruled out. The 'inner' subject, then, of the infinitival in (76) and (77) can be nothing else but the noun phrase posited for personal anonymous subjects, which is obligatorily deleted. Such a noun phrase, however, as mentioned above, cannot be referred to by the reflexive pronoun 'себя' in constructions of the type exemplified by (76) and (77) and other examples given in Section 3.2.

So, leaving aside a point to be discussed immediately, there is no ambiguity at all concerning the referential identity of 'себя' in these sentences. A different syntactic structure may be assigned to (70) in which себя resulting from the application of (A′) is the object noun phrase of the embedding sentence. This is possible, because *заставлять/заставить* is not irreflexive. An analogous interpretation seems hardly possible for (76), (77), because an object noun phrase is not deletable after *уважать*, whereas it is deletable after ждать. So, sentence (76) is correct, only if 'себя' is the object of уважать. But this is a special case which is not my concern here. We are not faced with a full syntactic ambiguity in (70). This sentence, if interpreted according to the former variant, has a phonological phrase boundary separating . . . заставил and себя . . . Presence or absence of a phonological phrase boundary manifesting itself as a slight pause is a superficial reflex of a fundamental difference in syntactic structure. This reflex can appear, in case the object of the embedded sentence is placed before the embedded verb (infinitive). The permutation is feasible, only if no object of the verb of the embedding sentence is present in surface structure, that is, if it is an 'anonymous' human object.

Sentences (70) through (103) show different degrees of grammaticality or, to put it more cautiously, meet with different degrees of willingness on the part of native speakers to accept them as normal or correct. Sentences with underlying anonymous human object in the embedding sentence and, consequently, a corresponding subject in the underlying embedded sentence are correct only, if the pronoun object of the infinitival which is coreferential with the subject of the embedding sentence is a reflexive one, comp. (70) with (71); (88) with (89) and (90); (95), (96) with (97), (98). If the embedding sentence has an object expressed in superficial structure and, consequently, an identical underlying subject in the embedded sentence, a nonreflexive pronoun seems to be acceptable in place of the reflexive one, comp. (80), (82), (84), (93), (94). Apparently, however, in such sentences reflexive pronominalization is preferable, too.

The claim that exclusiveness or preference of reflexive pronominalization obtaining in the examples containing заставлять/заставить and да(ва)ть is not quite independent of a touch of idiomaticity could be substantiated by provisions in our rules:

(1) The normally optional rule (C) must be made obligatory in these cases, that is, in structures containing the antecedent verb заставлять/заставить or да(ва)ть and a hypothetical underlying noun phrase of the type described, which is subject to deletion. (C) will be obligatory, then, if in its structural description 'V' will be one of those both verbs and 'Z' in (C) contains a noun phrase NP characterized by the known features causing its deletion.

(2) To account for the preference of constructions like e.g. (72), (73), (79) over (74), (75), (82) a convention (k) analogous to (i) and (j) modified by the special context mentioned above, might be introduced.

(k) $m\,(C) \rightarrow\, -\,(C)\Big/\,\begin{matrix}4 = \\ 5 \neq\end{matrix}\begin{Bmatrix}\text{заставлять/заставить}\\ \text{да(ва)ть}\end{Bmatrix}$

$$\begin{bmatrix}\\ {}_{NP}\begin{bmatrix}\quad\quad N\\ {}_{} \begin{bmatrix}-\text{ pronoun}\\ +\text{ indefinite}\\ +\text{ anonymous}\\ \vdots\\ \vdots\end{bmatrix}\end{bmatrix}{}_{NP}\\ {}\end{bmatrix}$$

The numbers refer to rule (C). (k) implies '$u\,(C) \rightarrow\, +\,(C)/$ . . .'.

5.2.2. The other two verbs of this group seem to behave differently. Referential identity of себя and его respectively with the initial noun phrase 'Борис' is again presupposed.

(104)   Борис вынудил нас ждать себя

(105)   Борис вынудил нас ждать его

(106)   *Борис вынудил себя ждать

(107)   *Борис вынудил его ждать

(108)   *Борис принудил себя ждать

(106) through (108) appear to be correct sentences only if they are understood in a way which would correspond to a deep structure in which *себя* or *его* are noun phrases functioning as objects of вы-, принудить. An underlying object noun phrase of these verbs which is deleted on behalf of the known characteristics '[− definite], [+ human], [anonymous]' does not seem to be 'evoked' in sentences like (106) through (108). This is, clearly, a consequence of semantic properties of the given verb, which does not allow for deleted (personal, anonymous) objects in the way other metaactive verbs like приказ(ыв)ать, заставить do. If, however, an explicit surface object of the two verbs occurs, both pronominalizations for the embedded object noun phrase (of ждать) seem to be equally possible, viz (104) and (105).

5.3. Let us look now at the second group of verbs mentioned under 5.1. Помогать/помочь is mostly followed by embedded infinitivals although there is a possible variety of prepositional phrases. Sentences in which помогать/помочь occurs as the main verb may satisfy the structure index for (C). Помогать/помочь is irreflexive in its basic meaning.

(108')   я$_i$ помог брату$_j$ перевязать себя$_{i,j}$

(109)   я$_i$ помог брату перевязать меня$_i$

(110)   солдат$_i$ помогал перевязать себя$_i$

(111)   солдат$_i$ помогал перевязать его$_i$

(112)   солдат$_i$ помог санитарке$_i$ перевязать себя$_{i,j}$

(113)   солдат$_i$ помог санитарке перевязать его$_i$

Перевяз(ыв)ать is not irreflexive. Consequently, (108') is ambiguous, one interpretation coinciding with the only interpretation of (109), the other identifying 'себя' and 'брат', (*see* footnote 8). If interpreted in the latter way, (108') is the result of the application of (A'), if interpreted in the former way it must have undergone (C), – if this is possible (*see* footnote 8) – reflexivizing a first person pronoun in this case. (110) is not ambiguous, it must have been arrived at by the application of (B') and (C). The application of (A') in the sentence underlying the infinitival, which involves a second interpretation, is excluded on grounds discussed in 3.2. (111) has been subjected to transformation (B'), it has not undergone the optional operation of (C). A second and third interpretation of (111) are possible, in which 'его' refers anaphorically to a noun phrase or is used deictically. (112), finally, is apparently disambiguated semantically, because a 'санитарка' does not usually dress her own wounds and that with the help of a soldier. But, of course, such an interpretation is not excluded on principle. So, in the derivation of (112) (A') may have been involved. Normally, (112) will be the result of applying (B') and (C), which are contingent on the referential identity of the embedded object noun phrase with *солдат*. If (C) is not applied, the result will be (113). But (113) may have the anaphoric or deictic interpretation mentioned above. помогать/помочь, differs from other meta-active verbs in involving the participation of its subject in the action, which, consequently, is a joint action of the subjects of the main clause and the infinitival.

5.4.   Let us call the reflexivization resulting from (A) 'inner' reflexivization and the one resulting from (C) 'outer' reflexivization. Then, the reduction of the reflexive pronoun себя to . . . + ся seems to be possible only in cases of 'inner' reflexivization.

(114)   сильные и крепке моряки . . . помогали спасаться
            товарищам

The interpretation must be that the 'товарищи' save themselves with the help of the sailors (моряки) and not that the comrades (товарищи) save the sailors with the help of the sailors themselves.

5.5.   The verb приучать/приучить has a syntactic context similar to that

of помогать/помочь, differing from it in the case of the object noun phrase.
It is not irreflexive, however.

(115)   хвалю тебя за то, что ты приучил себя диктовать
          (Чернышевский):[9]

(116)   Борис приучил других ждать себя

(117)   Борис приучил ждать себя

(118)   Борис приучил ждать его

(119)   Борис приучил себя ждать

ждать being irreflexive, the interpretation is perfectly clear and there is
no ambiguity in sentences (116) through (119). In all of them rule (B′) has
applied. Besides that rule (C) has applied in (116), (117) and (119). If in
(119) a phonological phrase boundary passes between *приучил* and *себя*,
the derivation of the sentence must have included the application of (B′)
and (C). If not, rule (A′) has applied in the embedding simplex sentence,
that is, себя is referentially identical with Борис, as it is in the former interpretation, but it functions as the object of приучать/приучить. In the first
case 'outer' reflexivization has taken place; in the second 'inner' reflexivization. Apart from the assumed phonological phrase boundary separating
приучил and 'себя', full syntactic polysemy obtains in (119). A similar
twofold interpretation is excluded in (115) because of semantic restrictions
on the objects of *диктовать*.

6.1.   It seems clear that the rules and regularities discussed above will not,
or not fully, apply to more or less idiomaticized constructions like e.g.
владеть собой, вести себя, брать с собой, жалеть себя. For a verb like
лишить себя чего-н a special context must be construed for 'outer' reflexivization, but even then the sentence is doubtful.

(120)   *онц$_i$ не могли не просить его лишить себя$_i$ некоторых
         привилегий

More generally, it appears that a subclassification of the second verb
(position 6) in rule (C) is necessary, that is, not all verbs can be subjected to
this type of optional reflexivization:

(121)   *Борис$_i$ попросил отца послать себя$_i$ на фронт

6.2.   Self-embedding of structures satisfying (C) poses at least two more
questions.

[9] The example is taken from **Словарь современного русского литературного языка,
Москва.**

(122′)   *Борис позволил себя уговорить заставить себя долго упрашивать

(122″)   Борис попросил командира приказать адъютанту разбудить себя через два часа

The first question is whether 'outer' reflexivization in (122″) is based on the referential identity of the noun phrase underlying *себя* with the noun phrase *Борис* or with the noun phrase командира, or whether coreference of either noun phrase and себя is possible, so that (122″) would be ambiguous on behalf of its ambiguous reflexive pronominalization. In other words, is 'outer' reflexivization contingent upon the coreferential antecedent functioning as a surface subject (implying coreference with Борис), or does the syntactic function of the coreferential antecedent play no role, so that coreference of командир(а) and себя in (122″) would meet the structural index of outer reflexivization as well as it meets it in (5)? If syntactic function is relevant, (C) must be reformulated by assigning case features to NP_{x_i}. This, indeed, does appear to be the case. NP_{x_i}, then, should be provided with features determining the nominative. The only interpretation possible for (122″) seems to be the one that involves coreference of себя and Борис. It is not clear, whether case features can account adequately for the coreferential restriction under discussion. The second question illustrated by (122′) concerns cyclical repetition of outer reflexivization. In (122′) outer reflexivization has taken place two times, rule (C) changing first the right-most occurrence of Борис into себя and then, in the next cycle changing the next surface occurrence of Борис to the left into себя. The direct object of both позволил and заставить is a noun phrase subject to deletion on account of the features [+ indefinite], [+ anonymous] as discussed above. The question is, whether the application of (C) changing the right-most Борис is based on the coreference of this occurrence of Борис and its next occurrence to the left, a question which, as mentioned above, may have to be answered in the negative. The correctness of this answer would be borne out by the observation that double 'outer' reflexivization does not seem to be possible at all: Provided that 'outer' reflexivization is contingent on the antecedent noun phrase functioning as the surface subject, repeated applications of (C) would have to be based on the coreference of the items to be reflexivized with the surface *subject*. However, cyclical processes of 'outer' reflexivization of several coreferential and identical underlying noun phrases should not, normally, be expected to 'look back' to the first and uppermost occurrence of this noun phrase, skipping nearer occurrences of it in higher sentences of the cycle. (122′) was rejected by virtually every informant.

7. SOME CONCLUSIONS

7.1. Erasure of the node labelled 'S' (by tree-pruning rule) dominating the sentence underlying the infinitive complement is a necessary condition for 'outer' reflexivization in the framework of rules (A′), (B′) and (C). Further, it does not seem questionable after the preceding discussion that semantic reflexiveness and irreflexiveness of the verb in the embedded infinitival and semantic properties (metaactive, causative a.o.) of the antecedent main verb, under which the infinitival is embedded, as well as selectional restrictions imposed on both verbs, have a certain influence on the possibility and/or grammaticality of 'outer' reflexivization. Perhaps, superficially quite similar sentence types having 'inner' reflexivization like

(123)   Борис обещал мне соединить себя с секретарем

have contributed to the development of 'outer' reflexivization.

The crucial structural difference between 'inner' (A′) and 'outer' (C) reflexivization lies in the fact that in (A′) the noun phrase to be pronominalized is an immediate constituent of a verbal phrase, which need not be separated from the subject, its antecedent, by a further verbal phrase into which it is embedded, while in (C) there must be an intermediate verbal phrase containing a metaactive verb. That is why (A′) 'takes exception' to the structural index (C). We are facing a conflict between two domains of rule application, namely the application of the rule for reflexive pronominalization. The conflict goes on about the inclusion of structures as described by (C) into the process of reflexivization. One would like to find some more substantial explanatory aspects for the intricate state of reflexivization described above. It seems reasonably speculative to assume that we are faced with an unstable partial system of pronominalization in Russian grammar, vacillating between two decisions, one avoiding the Scylla of ambiguity of 'inner' and 'outer' reflexive pronominalization, and the other avoiding the Charybdis of a threefold ambiguity including anaphoric and deictic pronominalization. The unstability, syntactic variation, or as I called it, field of intersection of two classes of pronominalization, can be explained by the following facts:

There are at least four types of pronominalization:

(1) reflexive pronominalization, (2) nonreflexive inner sentence pronominalization, (3) pronominalization beyond sentence boundaries and (4)

deictic pronominalization. But there are only two classes of pronouns available for those four types: reflexive (себя, себе . . .), and nonreflexive ones, that is anaphoric (kataphoric) or personal ones (его, я, ты).[10] (cf. further paragraph 9).

7.2. Russian grammar does not manifest here a strongly marked idiomaticity. This will be shown now by looking shortly at other Slavic languages in their standard forms, namely Polish, Slovakian, Czech, Upper Sorabian, Serbo-Croatian and Slovenian.

Investigating the constructions under discussion in different languages we must take into account constraints imposed on embedded infinitivals, which are considerable in Modern Czech and Sorabian, reaching the limit of nonexistence in Bulgarian. Thus, the possibility to meet the structure index of rule (C) is severely restricted in some Slavic languages. In Modern Standard Russian, Polish and Slovakian 'outer' reflexivization in sentences with embedded infinitivals has had the chance to advance more than in other Slavic languages on account of the strong development of embedded infinitivals in those languages. However, once infinitivals of the type defined in (C) do occur, their proliferation is of secondary importance for the existence of 'outer' reflexivization.

8.1. POLISH

(124)   Komendant$_i$ rozkazał adiutantowi obudzić siebie$_i$ za dwie godziny

(124) is perfectly analogous to 'outer' reflexivization in Russian (*see* example (5)). There have been some objections to the acceptability of (124), especially from representatives of the older generation: '. . . bo to źle po polsku'. But acceptance was unanimous in most cases and nobody rejected the sentence.

(125)   Komendant$_{(i)}$ rozkazał adiutantowi obudzić się$_{(i)}$ za dwie godziny

---

[10] I must mention here that, perhaps, referential ambiguity is only or predominantly present on paper, that is, there may be perceptible (audible) 'identity tags' signalling coreference of noun phrases. I am referring to a paper of William R. Cantrall ('Pitch, Stress, and Grammatical Relations', in: Papers from the Fifth Regional Meeting of the Chicago Linguistic Society, April 18–19, 1969, Chicago 1969, pp. 12–13) in which he ". . . found that coreference is accompanied by a sort of 'pitch concord' . . . If pitch concord were as simple as it sounds it would have been remarked upon long since. Still, it is as simple and systematic as it can be, given the variety of structures it must reflect . . . The important consideration is that each referent possess a unique pitch".

It would be very interesting to investigate, how this hypothesis, for which good evidence has been found by Cantrall for English, Italian, Spanish, Greek, German, Finnish and Chinese would work in Russian and other Slavic languages.

(125) is ambiguous, one interpretation – which is preferable – coinciding with that of (124), the second being determined by *obudzić się* being a reflexive verb. A Russian parallel to this verb would be 'разбудиться', which, however, is *prostorečie*, corresponding to Standard Russian пробудиться. The second interpretation is felt to be semantically awkward in view of the semantic relation between 'order' and 'wake up'.

(126)   Komendant rozkazał adiutantowi obudzić go za dwie godziny.

There is no full analogy to Russian here. The interpretation identifying go_i and $komendant_i$ meets with some reserve. Some speakers '... odczuwają to jako niepoprawne'. More usually, in (126) *go* is interpreted as referentially identical with a third person mentioned before or a person present in the deictic context.

(127)   Komendant$_i$ rozkazał obudzić siebie$_i$ za dwie godziny.

The interpretation of (127) fully corresponds to that of (124).

(128)   Komendant$_i$ rozkazał obudzić się$_i$ za dwie godziny.

The interpretation given by the indices is preferable. There is a second one in which an unspecified personal noun is the underlying subject of the *reflexive* verb infinitival. The semantic difficulties mentioned above (125) are similar here.

(129)   Komendant rozkazał obudzić go za dwie godziny

It seems clear that for (129) the interpretation of *go* as referring to a third person, that is, neither to *komendant* nor to the unspecified addressee of *rozkazał*, seems preferable. The interpretation identifying *go* with *komendant* meets with objections more lively than those raised against the analogous interpretation of (126).

(130)   Komendant$_i$ rozkazał (adiutantowi) przynieść sobie$_i$ mleko

In view of the semantics of *przynieść* there seems to be only one interpretation of (130) where *sobie* and *komendant* are referentially identical.

(131)   Minister pozwalał mi nazywać siebie szefem
(132)   Minister$_i$ pozwalał nam nazywać siebie$_i$ szefem

Plural *nam* and singular *szefem* are incompatible. That is why (132) is disambiguated and left with the single interpretation given by the indices. (131) is ambiguous with *siebie* being referentially identical either with *minister* or with *mi*. The latter would lead to the application of rule (A') which provides for the feature [+ reflexive], undeletable in the further course of derivation. The former would involve rule (B') being applied first with rule (C) operating optionally afterwards.

(133)   Minister$_i$ pozwalał nazywać siebie$_i$ szefem.

There is only one interpretation possible in accordance with the general constraint discussed above (3.2.).

(134)   Minister pozwalał nam zwracać się do siebie i per szefie

Besides the interpretation referring *siebie$_i$* to ministr$_i$, there is a second one in which *do siebie* involves a reciprocal meaning in relation to *nam*. (134) provides good evidence for the clear distinction to be made between 'reflexive verbs' and reflexive pronominalization.

(135)   Borys kazał przyjaciołom czekać na siebie

The double interpretation is analogous to that of (134).

(136)   Ojciec pozwolił mi $\begin{Bmatrix} \text{dzwonić} \\ \text{przyjść} \end{Bmatrix}$ do siebie wieczorem

(136) is ambiguous again. Outer reflexivization [rule (C)] as well as inner 'clause mate' (P. Postal) reflexivization [rule (A')] may result in surface structure (136).

(137)   Ona$_i$ radiła mi recenzować siebie$_i$
          (*example from K. Pisarkowa*)

This is a clear case of 'outer' reflexivization with the embedded clause containing a semantically irreflexive verb.

(138)   Komendant$_i$ rozkazał (adiutantowi) połączyć siebie$_i$ ze sztabem.

This example is similar to the Russian ones (15), (28); the enclitic form of the pronoun, however, seems to bring the sentence much closer to the reflexive verb interpretation:

(139)   Komendant rozkazał (adiutantowi) połączyć się ze sztabem.

The following are clear cases of idiomatic sentences.

(140)   Borys$_i$ dał się$_i$ przekonać
(141)   *Borys$_i$ dał go$_i$ przekonać
(142)   Borys$_i$ dał sobie$_i$ wytłumaczyć
(143)   Borys$_i$ nie dał braciom znać o sobie$_i$

Exactly as in Russian, conjunctions introducing the infinitival, change the picture considerably. The presence of some particle like *чтобы.*, *żeby, aby* will have to be disallowed in the structural index of (C).

(144)   Komendant$_i$ rozkazał adiutantowi żeby go$_i$ obudzić za dwie godziny.

It seems that there are no deep-seated differences between Modern Standard Polish and Modern Standard Russian concerning 'outer reflexivization'. At least the evidence presented here does not appear to suggest that there are. However, the necessity for a more detailed study of this subject in Polish is quite obvious.

8.2.   SLOVAKIAN

In Modern Standard Slovakian 'outer' reflexivization is well established in a way which is similar to Modern Russian and Modern Polish. The situation in Slovakian is quite distinct from that in Modern Czech in this respect. Embedded infinitivals are much more common in Standard Slovakian than they are in Standard Czech. A certain more or less rigorous constraint imposed upon the surface structure position of 'sa' may be supposed to serve as a superficial signal indicating coreference with the directly preceding subject noun phrase. In the following examples we use the form 'sa'; 'seba' implies a contrastive or emphatic sense. The coreferent noun phrases have subscribed indices.

(145)   *Dôstojník$_i$ sa$_i$ rozkázal (pobočníkovi) zobudit' o dve hodiny*
(146)   *Dôstojník$_i$ rozkázal (svojmu pobočníkovi) zobudit' ho$_i$ o dve hodiny*

Sentences like (146) are ambiguous in the sense discussed under 2.2.

(147)   *Dôstojník$_i$ rozkázal svojmu pobočníkovi aby ho$_i$ zobudil o dve hodiny*

'ho' again implies two more interpretations referring this pronoun to a person in the (deictic) context.

(148)   *Otec sa$_i$ rozkázal (synovi) zavolat' do úradu*
(149)   *Ministr$_i$ sa$_i$ dovolil (úradníkom) nazývat' šéfom*
(150)   *Ministr$_i$ dovolil úradníkom nazývat' ho$_i$ šéfom*
(151)   *[ja]$_i$ Pomohol som sa$_i$ bratovi obviazat'*
(152)   *Vojak$_i$ pomohol sa$_i$ sestričke obviazat*
(153)   *Vojak pomohol sestričke$_i$ obviazat' ju$_i$*

The new complication of referential relations as shown by the identity of *sestričke_i* and *ju_i* may, perhaps, be ascribed to the special sense of joint common activity inherent in the semantics of *pomôct'*. In other words, *vojak* in (153) may be taken as the second or only underlying subject of the infinitival (*see* (170)).

(154)   *Priateľ* prinútil nás na seba_i čakat'

The verbs 'dat' and 'nechat' have 'outer' reflexivization in perfect regularity.

(155)   [ja]_i Nenechám nikoho dva razy k *sebe_i* chodit'
(156)   [ja]_i Nedám nikomu dva razy k *sebe_i* chodit'
(157)   *Boris_i sa_i* dal prehovorit' (presvedčit')
(158)   *Boris_i* nedal o *sebe_i* nič (rodičom) vediet'
(159)   *Boris_i si_i* nedal $\left\{ \begin{matrix} \text{nikomu} \\ \text{od nikoho} \end{matrix} \right\}$ pomôct'

The situation in Slovakian seems to corroborate our assumptions concerning the regularities and relevant factors for 'outer' reflexivization. Excepting surface differences we find a striking similarity with the situations in Standard Russian and Standard Polish.

8.3. CZECH

The constraints imposed on infinitive complements are rather severe here. (160) is the only equivalent to (5).

(160)   Dustojník rozkázal svému pobočníkovi, aby ho probudil za dvě hodiny.

Again 'outer' reflexivization obligatorily occurs quite currently in all constructions with the main verbs *nechat* and *dá(va)t*.

(161)   Nechal_i na sebe_i čekat.
(162)   Boris_i se_i nechal $\left\{ \begin{matrix} \text{přesvědčit} \\ \text{přemluvit} \end{matrix} \right\}$
(163)   Boris_i nenechal si_i od nikoho pomoci
(164)   Nenechám_i nikoho dvakrát k sobě_i chodit
(165)   Nedal_i o sobě_i nič (rodičům) vědět.

'Outer' reflexivization occurs with verbs like *přinutil* and *pomoci* exactly as in Slovakian.

(166)   Přinutili nás na sebe čekat
(167)   (ja)_i Pomohl jsem bratrovi sebe_i obvázat

(168)   Pomohl jsem bratrovi$_i$ ho$_i$ obvázat
(169)   Voják$_i$ pomohl sestřičce sebe$_i$ obvázat
(170)   Voják pomohl sestřičce$_i$ ji$_i$ obvázat

It seems clear, that Czech grammar notwithstanding the constraints upon infinitivals generally is open to outer reflexivization.

8.4. UPPER SORABIAN

(171)   Komandant$_i$ přikaza (adjutantej) wubudźić jeho$_i$ za dwě hodźinje.

(171) is an acceptable sentence but synonymous sentences like (172), (173) in place of (171) are claimed to be much 'better'.

(172)   Komandant$_i$ přikaza adjutantej, zo by jeho$_i$ . . . wubudził
(173)   Komandant$_i$ přikaza, zo bychu jeho$_i$ wubudzili

In any case, 'outer' reflexivization in sentences containing embedded infinitivals like (171) is absolutely impossible. It is ruled out in Upper Sorabian in constructions which correspond to those in which it occurs normally in Russian, Polish and Slovakian. The following reflexive construction is of the 'reflexive verb' type:

(174)   Komandant přikaza adjutantej, wubudźić so za dwě hodźinje.

That is, the aide-de-camp is allowed to rest for two hours.

(175)   Minister$_i$ dowoli nam, jeho$_i$ 'šef' mjenować

'better': . . . . zo bychmy jeho$_i$ 'šef' mjenowali

(176)   Minister dovoli nam$_i$, zo bychmy so$_i$ 'šefojo' mjenowali.
(177)   Minister dovoli nam$_i$, so$_i$ 'šefojo' mjenować.

'Outer' reflexivization appears to be possible only after the verb *dać* in its special idiomaticized meaning.

(178)   Wón$_i$ da so$_i$ přerěćeć
(179)   Wón njeda sej wujasnić
(180)   Wón daše na so čakać
(181)   Wón da so česćić

8.5 SLOVENIAN

(182)   Komandant$_i$ je ukazal prebuditi sebe$_i$ ob šestik

(183)   Komandant$_i$ se$_i$ je ukazal prebuditi ob šestik
(184)   Vojak$_i$ je pomagal sestri obvezovati sebe$_i$ samega
(185)   Minister$_i$ se$_i$ jim je dal imenovati šef
(186)   Dal je na se čakati
(187)   Dal se je prepričati
(188)   Dal si je pojasniti

The few examples demonstrate that 'outer' reflexivization in infinitivals is not unknown in Modern Slovenian. Of course, a deeper and more comprehensive study of these phenomena and their restrictions in Slovenian is quite indispensable.

8.6. SERBO-CROATIAN

(189)   Ministar$_i$ je dozvoljavao zvati sebe$_i$ šefom
(190)   Ministar$_i$ je sebe$_i$ dozvoljavao zvati šefom
(191)   Dao sam sebi objasniti
(192)   Davao se pozivati
(193)   Ministar$_i$ se$_i$ davao moliti

9. Excepting Bulgarian, in which there are no infinitivals, the evidence seems perfectly conclusive. The Slavic Languages in which infinitivals occur have developed the principle of outer reflexivization. It is embedded infinitivals which are concerned because of the obligatory deletion of their underlying subject. We cannot draw on the usual cyclical rule of reflexivization to do the job of providing for the reflexive pronoun, as 'outer' reflexivization is not obligatory. It generally alternates with nonreflexive pronominalization. The two pronominalizations competing in infinitivals may be supposed to represent an intermediate, perhaps transitory complication or variation of the system of pronominalization rules. We are facing a conflict between the autonomy in (cyclical) rule application of embedded sentences on the one hand and their annexation to the main sentence, after they have been turned into infinitivals, on the other.

ACKNOWLEDGEMENTS

I express my warm gratitude to my colleagues and friends K. V. Archangel'skaja (Moscow), G. Nedjalkova (Leningrad), V. P. Nedjalkov (Leningrad), K. Pisarkowa (Kraków), Z. Topolińska (Warsaw), C. Piernikarski (Warsaw), F. Michałk (Budyšin), L. Heine (Leipzig), J. Abichtova (Leipzig), J. Oravec (Bratislava), a d J. Toporišič (Ljubljana), who were kind enough to 'lend' me their linguistic intuition as native speakers. Of course, the responsibility for any judgements on grammaticality or acceptability passed in this paper is fully mine.

Karl Marx University of Leipzig, D.D.R.

ZUM PROBLEM DER GRAMMATISCH
RELEVANTEN IDENTITÄT

0. Einleitung

Bekanntlich treten in vielen grammatischen Regeln Identitätsbedingungen auf. Dies gilt vor allem von Tilgungstransformationen verschiedener Art. So lassen sich ja beispielsweise die Zusammenhänge zwischen den (a)- und (b)-Sätzen in (1)–(6) mit Hilfe von Transformationen erklären, die in der Ableitung des (b)-Satzes aus einer dem (a)- und dem (b)-Satz gemeinsam zugrunde liegenden Struktur gewisse Elemente auf Grund ihrer Identität mit anderen Elementen in der Struktur tilgen.

(1)   (a) Karl hat mit ihm über sie gesprochen, und auch Martin hat mit ihm über sie gesprochen

         (b) Karl hat mit ihm über sie gesprochen, und auch Martin

(2)   (a) Er hat mit jemandem über sie gesprochen, und zwar hat er mit Martin über sie gesprochen

         (b) Er hat mit jemandem über sie gesprochen, und zwar mit Martin

(3)   (a) Er hat ebenso oft mit ihm über sie gesprochen, wie ich mit ihr über ihn gesprochen habe

         (b) Er hat ebenso oft mit ihm über sie gesprochen wie ich mit ihr über ihn

(4)   (a) Er ist mit jemandem unzufrieden, aber ich weiss nicht, mit wem er unzufrieden ist

         (b) Er ist mit jemandem unzufrieden, aber ich weiss nicht mit wem

(5)   (a) Ich hoffe, dass ich um fünf Uhr fertig bin

         (b) Ich hoffe, um fünf Uhr fertig zu sein

(6)   (a) Nimm du den braunen Koffer, dann nehme ich den schwarzen Koffer

         (b) Nimm du den braunen Koffer, dann nehme ich den schwarzen

Auch viele der Regeln, die das Auftreten von Pronomen bestimmen, müssen

F. Kiefer and N. Ruwet (eds.), Generative Grammar in Europe, 482–527. All Rights Reserved.
Copyright © 1973 by D. Reidel Publishing Company, Dordrecht-Holland.

bekanntlich von gewissen Identitätsbedingungen Gebrauch machen, wie die Beispiele (7)–(9) andeutend zeigen.

(7)   (a) Karl weiss, dass Peter krank ist, was $\left\{\begin{array}{l}\text{Hans}\\ \text{*ich}\end{array}\right\}$ dagegen nicht weiss

  (b) Karl weiss, dass Peter krank ist; $\left\{\begin{array}{l}\text{Hans}\\ \text{*ich}\end{array}\right\}$ weiss dagegen nicht, dass Peter krank ist

(8)   Er hat ebenso oft mit ihr gesprochen, wie Karl es getan hat = Er hat ebenso oft mit ihr gesprochen, wie Karl mit ihr gesprochen hat

(9)   Wer ist mit sich unzufrieden? $\neq$ Wer ist mit wem unzufrieden?

Schliesslich sei hier an die Regularitäten erinnert, die für nebengeordnete Strukturen kennzeichnend sind. Welcher Art die diesbezüglichen Regeln auch sein mögen, so benötigen sie doch wahrscheinlich ebenfalls Identitätsbedingungen, um Zusammenhänge wie die in (10) angedeuteten zu erfassen.

(10)   (a) Man feierte $\left\{\begin{array}{l}\text{ihn}\\ \text{uns}\end{array}\right\}$

  (b) Man beglückwünschte $\left\{\begin{array}{l}\text{ihn}\\ \text{uns}\end{array}\right\}$

  (c) Man gratulierte $\left\{\begin{array}{l}\text{ihm}\\ \text{uns}\end{array}\right\}$

  (d) Man beglückwünschte und feierte $\left\{\begin{array}{l}\text{ihn}\\ \text{uns}\end{array}\right\}$

  (e) *Man gratulierte und feierte $\left\{\begin{array}{l}\text{ihn}\\ \text{ihm}\\ \text{ihm bzw. ihn}\\ \text{uns}\\ \text{uns bzw. uns}\end{array}\right\}$

Allerdings scheinen die Verhältnisse bei nebengeordneten Strukturen noch so wenig geklärt zu sein, dass wir diese Konstruktionen in der folgenden Diskussion weitgehend ausklammern müssen.

  Die Klärung der Frage, welcher Art die von syntaktischen Regeln geforderte Identität ist, stellt naturgemäss eine wichtige Aufgabe für die Sprachwissenschaft dar. Es gilt, aus den einzelnen Regelbedingungen möglichst allgemeine Prinzipien dafür abzuleiten, auf welche Weise verschiedene Aspekte sprachlicher Struktur für diese grammatisch relevante Identität von Bedeutung sein können. Einigen Teilfragen dieses Problemkomplexes wollen wir im folgenden nachgehen.

1. GRAMMATISCH RELEVANTE IDENTITÄT UND SEMANTISCHE FUNKTION

Ehe wir uns in Abschnitt 2 der besonderen grammatischen Erscheinung zuwenden, die uns in dieser Untersuchung vor allem beschäftigen wird, müssen wir kurz einiges über gewisse grundlegende Eigenschaften der grammatisch relevanten Identität (GRI) vorausschicken, die im Laufe der Entwicklung der generativen Grammatik zutage getreten sind.

Der den ersten transformationsgrammatischen Beschreibungen zugrunde liegende Begriff der einfachen Morphemkettenidentität erwies sich sehr bald als inadäquat. Es stellte sich nämlich heraus, dass auch die Struktur der Morphemketten, zwischen denen eine Transformation Identität fordert, berücksichtigt werden muss. So lässt sich z.B. (11)(a) auf die beiden in (b)

(11)   (a) Ich bereitete die Reise im Januar vor, aber auch meine Frau
        (b) Ich (bereitete) (die Reise im Januar) vor, aber auch meine Frau (bereitete) (die Reise im Januar) vor
        (c) Ich (bereitete) (die Reise) (im Januar) vor, aber auch meine Frau (bereitete) (die Reise) (im Januar) vor
        (d) Ich (bereitete) (die Reise im Januar) vor, aber auch meine Frau (bereitete) (die Reise) vor
        (e) Ich (bereitete) (die Reise) (im Januar) vor, aber auch meine Frau (bereitete) (die Reise im Januar) vor

und (c) angedeuteten Satzstrukturen zurückführen, in denen die zu tilgende Kette mit der Korrelatkette auch hinsichtlich ihrer Konstituentenstruktur übereinstimmt, nicht aber auf (d) oder (e).

Aber darüber hinaus musste der Identitätsbegriff hinsichtlich einzelner Konstituenten verfeinert werden. Eine adäquate Beschreibung der Unterscheide zwischen Sätzen wie

(12)   (a) Ich$_4$ hörte ihn$_5$ über ihn$_7$ reden
        (b) Ich$_4$ hörte ihn$_6$ über sich$_6$ reden

erfordert ja, dass eine Übereinstimmung zwischen referentiellen Elementen (hier den Pronomen) hinsichtlich ihrer Bezugnahme auf aussersprachliche Gegebenheiten berücksichtigt wird. Chomsky (1965) hat vorgeschlagen, diese für die GRI wesentliche Gleichheit bzw. Ungleichheit bei referentiellen Elementen mit Hilfe einer Kennzeichnung in der Tiefenstruktur durch

Indizes (wie in (12) angedeutet) zu erfassen. Nun ist eine entsprechende Unterscheidung jedoch auch in Fällen wie (13)–(14) nötig:

(13)   (a) Ich_5 hörte einen $Kritiker_8$ über einen $Kritiker_9$ reden
        (b) Ich_5 hörte einen $Kritiker_4$ über $sich_4$ reden

(14)   (a) Ich_5 hörte jeden $Kritiker_8$ über jeden $Kritiker_9$ reden
        (b) Ich_5 hörte jeden $Kritiker_4$ über $sich_4$ reden

Es handelt sich hier meiner Ansicht nach um die gleiche, für die GRI wesentliche Äquivalenzrelation zwischen referentiellen Elementen wie in (12). Nun sind (13) und (14) typische Beispiele für Sätze, die in der Prädikatenlogik mit Hilfe von Ausdrücken wiedergegeben werden, die Variable enthalten. In der Tat meine ich, dass die referentielle Äquivalenz, mit der wir es hier zu tun haben, im wesentlichen der Beziehung zwischen verschiedenen Stellen ein und derselben Variablen entspricht, und zwar nicht nur in Fällen wie (13) und (14), sondern auch in (12). Der Unterschied wäre dann etwa der, dass es sich in (13) und (14) um Variable handelt, die innerhalb des betreffenden Satzes mit Hilfe sprachlich-begrifflicher Mittel gebunden sind (durch den mit einer Existenzaussage verbundenen Ausdruck *einen Kritiker*, bzw. durch den mit einer Allaussage verbundenen Ausdruck *jeden Kritiker*), während die Variablen in (12) gewissermassen durch den Kontext, die Sprechsituation, gebunden sind. Soweit man Sätze wie (12) ausschliesslich als Beispiele linguistischer Strukturen betrachtet, scheint es mir demnach nicht ratsam, in solchen Fällen von Konstanten zu sprechen, wie es manchmal geschieht.[1] Da wir auf diese Fragen hier nicht näher eingehen können, begnüge ich mich mit dem Hinweis, dass nicht nur in (13) und (14), sondern auch in (12) jedenfalls nur die für die GRI wichtige Gleichheit oder Ungleichheit der Indizes Teil der linguistischen Struktur sein kann, nicht jedoch deren absolute Werte. Andernfalls ergäbe sich die unerwünschte Konsequenz, dass man es beispielsweise in (12)(a) mit ebenso vielen verschiedenen Sätzen der deutschen Sprache zu tun hätte, wie es verschiedene Indizierungen mit gleicher Äquivalenzstruktur gibt.

Diejenige Konstituentenkategorie, bei der eine derartige Kennzeichnung durch referentielle Indizes sich als nötig erwiesen hat, ist die Nominalphrase. Die Auffassung über die der NP zugrunde liegende Struktur hat in letzter Zeit eine Wandlung durchgemacht, die für die Beurteilung des Charakters der GRI Konsequenzen hat. McCawley (1967, 1969) und Bach (1968) haben gezeigt, dass es gute Gründe gibt, die referentiellen Indizes nicht als eine zusätzliche, zu der begrifflichen Charakterisierung der NP hinzu-

---

[1] So etwa anscheinend McCawley (1968), während z.B. Bach (1968) und Bierwisch (1970) eine ähnliche Auffassung zu vertreten scheinen wie die hier vorgetragene.

kommende Spezifizierung aufzufassen, sondern als das, was primär die Identität der NP ausmacht. Statt also etwa (15)(a) von einer Struktur wie (15)(b)

(15)   (a) Der Junge da ist mit sich zufrieden
         (b) (Der Junge da)$_5$ ist mit (dem Jungen da)$_5$ zufrieden

mit Hilfe von Pronominalisierungsregeln abzuleiten, setzt McCawley abstrakte Strukturen der in (16) angedeuteten Art an,

(16)   (x_5 is mit x_5 zufrieden) (der Junge da : x_5)

in denen also die begriffliche Charakterisierung *der Junge da* von den eigentlichen referentiellen Elementen getrennt ist und aus denen die entsprechenden Oberflächenstrukturen dadurch entstehen, dass die begriffliche Charakterisierung in Form von Substantiv bzw. restriktivem Relativsatz oder davon abgeleitetem Attribut auf Positionen der entsprechenden Indexziffer verteilt wird. Dieser Konzeption schliesse ich mich in den Grundzügen an und betrachte die NP der Tiefenstruktur (abgesehen von den aus einer Satzstruktur bestehenden NP, auf die wir noch zurückkommen) als referentielle Indizes, d.h., wenn man so will, als Variable, welche durch eine eventuell dazugehörende, wohl in Form von S-Strukturen vorliegende begriffliche Charakterisierung entweder eingeführt werden, wie in (13) und (14), oder, wo sie schon eigeführt, bzw. durch den Kontext gebunden sind, identifizierend präsentiert werden, wie im Falle von *der Beschenkte* in

(17)   Ich glaube nicht, dass du (jedem, der dich um Geld bittet)$_7$ so
         viel schenken kannst, dass (der Beschenkte)$_7$ daraufhin ein
         sorgenfreies Leben führen kann

und *der Junge da* in (15)(a). Aus einer solchen Vorstellung über die Tiefenstruktur der NP folgt, dass die Regeln, die die entsprechenden Oberflächenstrukturen ableiten, nur die referentielle Äquivalenz der NP zu berücksichtigen haben, und dass die Übereinstimmungen zwischen referentiell äquivalenten NP, die darüber hinaus in der Oberflächenstruktur auftreten (wie etwa Genuskongruenz, Gleichheit bei Pronomen wie *ich, du, man* etc.) nicht Reste einer ursprünglichen, für die Identitätsbedingungen der Regeln relevanten Identität, sondern vielmehr ein Ergebnis des Operierens dieser Regeln sind.

Nicht nur bei NP, sondern auch bei einzelnen lexikalischen Elementen machen die Identitätsbedingungen syntaktischer Regeln eine feinere Differenzierung nötig, da sie nämlich, wie sich am Beispiel polysemantischer Wörter zeigen lässt (vgl. (18)–(19)), über die Gleichheit der Lautgestalt hinaus auch

(18)   (a) Der Preis, den er gewinnen konnte, interessierte ihn weniger
             als der, den er nicht gewinnen konnte
        (b) *Der Preis, den er gewinnen konnte, interessierte ihn weniger
             als der, den er für die Zeitschrift bezahlen musste

(19)   (a) Der übervolle Koffer hielt erst dann nicht mehr, als der Zug
             hielt
        (b) *Der übervolle Koffer hielt erst dann nicht mehr, als der Zug
             es tat

semantische Übereinstimmung fordern.[2] Dies heisst, dass verschiedene
semantische Varianten in der Satzstruktur als verschiedene lexikalische
Elemente repräsentiert werden müssen.

Noch ein entscheidender Schritt zur Vertiefung des Begriffs der GRI muss
jedoch getan werden. Es zeigt sich nämlich, dass von syntaktischen Regeln
geforderte Identität zwischen Morphemketten sich nicht nur auf deren
derivierte Struktur, sondern auch auf ihre Tiefenstruktur bezieht.[3] Dies wird
deutlich, wenn man Ketten mit gleicher Oberflächenstruktur aber verschiedener Tiefenstruktur betrachtet:

(20)   Die Kritik der reinen Vernuft ist heute ebenso berechtigt $\begin{cases} \text{wie} \\ \text{wie} \end{cases}$

       $\left. \begin{array}{l} \text{sie es damals war} \\ \text{damals} \end{array} \right\}$

(21)   (a) Er will $\begin{cases} \text{(entweder) Bachs Violinsonaten oder Brahms'} \\ \text{irgendein Bachsches Orgelwerk} \end{cases}$

       $\left. \begin{array}{l} \text{Klarinettenquintett} \end{array} \right\}$ haben, und seine Frau auch

       (b) Er wünscht sich $\begin{cases} \text{Bachs Violinsonaten oder Brahms'} \\ \text{irgendein Bachsches Orgelwerk} \end{cases}$

       $\left. \begin{array}{l} \text{Klarinettenquintett (oder beides),} \end{array} \right\}$ und seine Frau auch

Der NP *die Kritik der reinen Vernunft* in (20) werden üblicherweise zwei
verschiedene Tiefenstrukturen zugeordnet, entsprechend den Bedeutungen
'die Kritik, die man an der reinen Vernunft übt' und 'die Kritik, die die reine
Vernunft an etwas übt'. Während man in diesem Fall die übereinstimmende

---

[2] Beispiele dieser Art hat schon Chomsky (1965) diskutiert, ohne sich einer bestimmten Erklärung anzuschliessen. McCawley (1968) befürwortet dagegen die gleiche Deutung wie die hier
vorgetragene.
[3] Wie ich erfahren habe, haben auch G. Lakoff und J. Ross diese Tatsache beobachtet, und zwar
schon 1966.

Deutung der nicht getilgten und der getilgten, bzw. als Pronomen auftretenden NP noch als Folge einer durch referentielle Indizes ausgedrückten
Äquivalenz in der Bezugnahme auf dieses oder jenes abstrakte Objekt
erklären kann, ist dies in (21) kaum möglich oder angebracht. Die Ambiguität der Sätze mit *oder* in (21) hängt mit Unterschieden hinsichtlich der
Einbettungsebene der Disjunktion zusammen (Dass es hier nicht um die
Distinktion zwischen 'vel' und 'aut' geht, ist daraus zu ersehen, dass ein in
der angedeuteten Weise hinzugefügtes *entweder* bzw. *oder beides* auf die
Doppeldeutigkeit keinen Einfluss hat). Das *oder* in (21)(a) kann in der dem
finiten Verb untergeordneten S-Struktur enthalten und somit Teil des
Wunsches sein, oder es kann dem finiten Verb übergeordnet und damit ein
oder des Sprechers sein. Entsprechendes gilt für (21)(b), was also zur Annahme
einer im Verb *sich wünschen* 'enthaltenen' untergeordneten S-Struktur
zwingt. Genau die gleiche Ambiguität wie *oder* zeigt (*irgend*) *ein*. Es handelt
sich hierbei in analoger Weise um Unterschiede hinsichtlich der Einbettungsebene der mit diesem Ausdruck verbundenen Existenzaussage.[4]
Welcher Art die Tiefenstrukturen der Sätze in (21) auch sein mögen, steht
jedenfalls fest, dass der getilgten Kette jeweils die gleiche Tiefenstruktur
zugrunde liegen muss wie der Korrelatkette.

Ehe wir jedoch hieraus auf die Relevanz der Tiefenstruktur für die GRI
schliessen dürfen, müssen wir zeigen, dass die Strukturunterschiede, die der
Ambiguität der Sätze in (20) und (21) zugrunde liegen, an dem Punkt der
Derivation nicht mehr erkennbar sind, an dem die Regeln ansetzen, welche
die Identitätsbedingungen enthalten. D.h., wir müssen uns fragen, ob die
Regeln, welche die verschiedenen als Ausgangspunkt denkbaren Tiefenstrukturen ein und derselben derivierten Struktur zuordnen, auf die
Morphemketten, zwischen denen Identität gefordert wird (oder wenigstens
auf eine von ihnen) schon angewendet worden sind, wenn diese Identitätsforderung gestellt wird. Wir wollen dabei die gegenwärtig wohl plausibelste
Konzeption des Transformationsteils zugrunde legen, welche mit zyklischen, postzyklischen und präzyklischen Transformationen rechnet.

Über die Regeln, die die betreffenden Ketten in (20) ableiten, ist mir
nichts Sicheres bekannt. In den Sätzen mit *irgendein* in (21) haben wir es
jedoch wahrscheinlich mit einer als 'Quantoreneinbettung' ('quantifier-
lowering') bekannten Regel zu tun, welche zyklisch operiert und (wohl in
Verbindung mit der Transformation, welche die begriffliche Charakterisierung referentieller Elemente auf die entsprechenden Indizes verteilt)
durch Einbettung des die Existenzaussage ausdrückenden Elements die NP

---

[4] Auf diese Erscheinung hat Bach (1968) anhand von Beispielen wie *She's trying to find a man with
a big bank account* und *She's looking for a man with a big bank account* hingewiesen.

irgendein Bachsches Orgelwerk ableitet. Wenngleich die adäquate Ableitung nebengeordneter Strukturen gegenwärtig ein im wesentlichen ungelöstes Problem zu sein scheint, ist doch zu vermuten, dass die NP mit *oder* in (21) entweder auf die gleiche Weise entstehen wie die mit *irgendein* oder durch eine Zusammenziehung nebengeordneter S-Strukturen ('conjunction reduction') abgeleitet werden, also durch eine Regel, die vermutlich ebenfalls zyklisch sein müsste, da sie im Falle einer dem Willensverb untergeordneten Disjunktion vor der Tilgung des Subjekts der eingebetten S-Struktur operieren müsste, um eine generelle Formulierung dieser (als 'equi-NP deletion' bekannten) zyklischen Subjektstilgung zu ermöglichen. Es ist also anzunehmen, dass wenigstens in (21) das Zusammenfallen der verschiedenen Tiefenstrukturen in ein und derselben derivierten Struktur durch zyklische Regeln bewirkt wird. Operiert nun die Tilgungstransformation in (21) zyklisch (oder nachzyklisch), so ist offensichtlich in dem Zyklus, in dem sie angewendet wird, keine Unterscheidung der zugrunde liegenden Strukturen mehr möglich. Eine solche wäre also nur denkbar, wenn die Tilgung präzyklisch erfolgte. Dies ist jedoch bei Tilgungen dieser Art nicht denkbar, da grundsätzlich die Schwierigkeit besteht, aus der durch eine präzyklische Tilgung entstehenden 'verstümmelten' Struktur die entsprechende Oberflächenstruktur abzuleiten. So benötigt man ja z.B. in

(22)   (a) Ich wurde gewählt, aber er nicht
        (b) Ich wurde gewählt, aber nicht von ihm

für die richtige Kasusmarkierung des Tilgungsrestes strukturelle Information, die erst nach der Anwendung der Passivtransformation vorliegt, also einer zyklisch und über vollständigen S-Strukturen operierenden Regel. Diese Überlegungen machen es also wahrscheinlich, dass die Berücksichtigung der Tiefenstruktur bei Tilgungen nicht auf eine frühe Anwendung der Tilgungstransformation zurückzuführen ist, sondern durch eine die GRI charakterisierende Bedingung erklärt werden muss.

In diesem Zusammenhang sei darauf hingewiesen, dass es Anzeichen dafür gibt, dass es sich bei den Regeln, die Identitätsbedingungen enthalten, in vielen Fällen um Operationen oder Restriktionen handelt, die nicht nur nicht präzyklisch sind, sondern vielmehr auf recht späten Derivationsstufen wirksam sind. So lässt sich an Beispielen wie

(23)   (a) $Karl_1$ versuchte, mir zu verheimlichen, dass er_1 krank war
        (b) *Er_1 versuchte, mir zu verheimlichen, dass $Karl_1$ krank war
        (c) Dass er_1 krank war, versuchte $Karl_1$ mir zu verheimlichen
        (d) Dass $Karl_1$ krank war, versuchte er_1 mir zu verheimlichen

zeigen, dass die endgültige Distribution von Pronomen und Korrelat nicht durch eine rein zyklisch operierende Regel erklärt werden kann. Eine solche müsste nämlich auf den Objektssatz von *versuchen* (d.h., vereinfacht ausgedrückt, auf *Karl₁ verheimlicht mir, dass er₁ krank ist*) angewendet werden, könnte also die notwendig später erfolgende Satzumstellung in (c) und (d) nicht berücksichtigen und würde deshalb nur (a) und (c), nicht aber (d) ableiten können.[5] Nun ist aber keineswegs sicher, dass auf der späten, postzyklischen Ableitungsstufe, auf der die betreffenden Bedingungen für das Auftreten von Pronomen anscheinend formuliert werden müssen, noch genügend Information zur Identifizierung von Korrelat und Pronomen vorhanden ist, zumal nicht in Beispielen wie

(24)   (a) Karl glaubt, dass ich Bachs Violinsonaten oder Brahms' Klarinettenquintett haben will, weil Peter es /= dass ich Bachs Violinsonaten oder Brahms' Klarinettenquintett haben will/ gesagt hat

(b) *Karl glaubt es /= dass ich .../, weil Peter gesagt hat, dass ich Bachs Violinsonaten oder Brahms' Klarinettenquintett haben will

(c) Weil Peter es /= dass ich .../ gesagt hat, glaubt Karl, dass ich Bachs Violinsonaten oder Brahms' Klarinettenquintett haben will

(d) Weil Peter gesagt hat, dass ich Bachs Violinsonaten oder Brahms' Klarinettenquintett haben will, glaubt Karl es /= dass ich .../

wo sich das Pronomen auf einen Satz bezieht. Es wird nämlich üblicherweise angenommen, dass das Pronomen in solchen Fällen auf eine volle S-Struktur zurückgeht und also im Gegensatz zu anderen Pronomen (vlg. S. 486) durch eine Pronominalisierungstransformation abgeleitet werden muss. Ganz gleich, ob diese Transformation schon angewendet worden ist oder nicht, ist also hier die relevante Tiefenstrukturidentität postzyklisch wohl nicht mehr zu erkennen. Auch bei manchen Tilgungsoperationen lässt sich ein postzyklischer Charakter wahrscheinlich machen. Vgl. etwa die Beispiele

(25)   (a) Karl versuchte, dem zweiten Arzt zu verheimlichen, dass der erste /= der erste Arzt/ ihn einen Simulanten genannt hatte

---

[5] Weitere, teilweise prinzipiell ähnliche Argumente gegen eine zyklische Pronominalisierungstransformation finden sich bei Postal (1970b) und Lakoff (1968). Die in (23)–(25) sich manifestierende Bedingung für 'Rückwärtspronominalisierung' diskutieren Ross (1967a, 1967b) und Langacker (1969).

(b) *Karl versuchte, dem zweiten /= dem zweiten Arzt/ zu verheimlichen, dass der erste Arzt ihn einen Simulanten genannt hatte

(c) Dass der erste /= der erste Arzt/ ihn einen Simulanten genannt hatte, versuchte Karl, dem zweiten Arzt zu verheimlichen

(d) Dass der erste Arzt ihn einen Simulanten genannt hatte, versuchte Karl dem zweiten /= dem zweiten Arzt/ zu verheimlichen

die denen in (23) genau entsprechen. Ergebnisse von Ross (1969), der Tilgungen in Fragesätzen wie in

(26)   Einer meiner Freunde will Bachs Violinsonaten oder Brahms' Klarinettenquintett haben, aber ich weiss nicht mehr wer

untersucht hat, deuten darauf hin, dass auch diese Operationen postzyklisch sind. Ross hat nämlich gezeigt, dass es im Englischen Anhaltspunkte dafür gibt, diese Tilgungstransformation erst nach der Fragewortumstellung operieren zu lassen. Nun scheint es Argumente für den späten, nichtzyklischen Charakter dieser Umstellung zu geben (vgl. Postal (1970b)). Sind diese stichhaltig, würde das also für eine (nichtzyklische, vermutlich) postzyklische Anwendung der betreffenden Tilgungsregel sprechen, wenigstens im Englischen.

Beispiele wie (24) legen den Gedanken nahe, dass bei den NP der Tiefenstruktur, die aus einem S bestehen, dieses S die gleiche Funktion hat, wie bei den übrigen NP der referentielle Index. Zwei NP der Tiefenstruktur wären demnach vom Gesichtspunkt der GRI dann als gleich zu betrachten, wenn sie aus dem gleichen Index oder der gleichen S-Struktur bestehen. Zwei S-Strukturen der Tiefenstruktur wiederum wären als gleich anzusehen, wenn sie auch hinsichtlich ihrer NP gleich sind. Diese Definition scheint in der Tat durch die in

(27)   (a) Ist es wahr, dass der Junge$_i$ krank ist und dass niemand$_j$ dem Arzt$_k$ das /= dass er$_i$ krank ist/ gesagt hat?

(b) Ich$_i$ glaube nicht, dass (jemand von uns)$_j$ jemanden$_k$ kennt, der$_k$ erfahren hat, dass er$_k$ krank ist, und der$_k$ sich darüber /= dass er$_k$ krank ist/ freut

(c) Ich$_i$ glaube nicht, dass (jemand von uns)$_j$ jemanden$_k$ kennt, der$_k$ erfahren hat, dass er$_j$ krank ist, und der$_k$ sich darüber /= dass er$_j$ krank ist/ freut

(d) Jeder$_i$ erzählte jedem$_j$, dass er$_i$ erfahren habe, dass er$_i$ mit ihm$_j$ verwandt sei, und dass ihn$_i$ das / = dass er$_i$ mit ihm$_j$ verwandt sei/ sehr freue

(e) Jeder$_i$ erzählte jedem$_j$, dass er$_i$ erfahren habe, dass er$_j$ mit ihm$_i$ verwandt sei, und dass ihn$_i$ das / = dass er$_j$ mit ihm$_i$ verwandt sei/ sehr freue

angedeuteten Zusammenhänge gerechtfertigt zu sein. Nun werden aber mit dieser Definition nicht Fälle wie

(28)   (a) Nicht nur Karl$_i$ war davon überzeugt, dass (fast jeder)$_j$ gesagt habe, dass er$_j$ mit sich$_j$ unzufrieden sei, sondern auch Peter$_k$ / = sondern auch Peter$_k$ war davon überzeugt, dass (fast jeder)$_l$ gesagt habe, dass er$_l$ mit sich$_l$ unzufrieden sei/

(b) Jeder$_i$ wird sagen, dass er$_i$ niemanden$_j$ vorgeschlagen habe, den$_j$ er$_i$ nicht persönlich gekannt hätte, und dass (jeder von uns)$_k$ das / = dass er$_i$ niemanden$_l$ vorgeschlagen habe, den$_l$ er$_i$ nicht persönlich gekannt hätte/ wissen müsse

(c) Karl$_i$ ist überzeugt, dass (fast jeder Schüler)$_j$ (fast jeden Hausaufsatz)$_k$, den$_k$ er$_j$ abgibt, selber geschrieben hat, aber ich$_l$ bezweifle das / = dass (fast jeder Schüler)$_m$ (fast jeden Hausaufsatz)$_n$, den$_n$ er$_m$ abgibt, selber geschrieben hat/

erfasst. Im Gegensatz zu (27) handelt es sich hier um Gleichheit zwischen S-Strukturen, welche in sich S-Strukturen enthalten, die sich auf Propositionalfunktionen, d.h. Begriffe oder Relationen, beziehen. Wie solche S-Strukturen, die Propositionalfunktionen entsprechen, von den übrigen exakt zu unterscheiden sind, hängt naturgemäss von der zugrunde gelegten Auffassung über die betreffenden Tiefenstrukturen ab. Andeutungsweise kann jedoch gesagt werden, dass es sich wohl im wesentlichen um S-Strukturen handelt, denen unmittelbar ein variableneinführender Ausdruck zugeordnet ist. Damit glaube ich u.a. auch S-Strukturen erfasst zu haben, die einer Existenz-oder Allaussage unmittelbar untergeordnet sind oder, wenn man so will, Argumente eines Existenz-bzw. Allaussageprädikats sind, oder die zur begrifflichen Charakterisierung von NP dienen. (Letztere Bedingung würde u.a. auch Fälle wie (6) und (25) erklären). Bei solchen S-Strukturen der Tiefenstruktur ist die Gleichheit dadurch gegeben, dass entsprechende Stellen entweder mit gleichen Indizes versehen sind oder mit Indizes, welche in der jeweiligen S-Struktur die gleiche Stellenverteilung aufweisen und durch einen der betreffenden S-Struktur unmittelbar zugeordneten oder in ihr enthaltenen variablenbindenden Ausdruck eingeführt sind. Diese Definition der Tiefenstrukturgleichheit von NP im allgemeinen und S im besonderen ist selbstverständlich sehr provisorisch und muss in mancher wesentlichen Hinsicht ergänzt und modifiziert werden. Mit einigen dieser notwendigen Ergänzungen werden wir uns in den folgenden Abschnitten näher zu befassen haben.

Die wesentliche Rolle der Tiefenstruktur für die GRI wirft die Frage auf, ob nicht vielleicht die Tiefenstruktur allein für die GRI entscheidend ist. Wenn dies der Fall wäre, müssten zwei Morphemketten, die auf die gleiche Tiefenstruktur zurückgehen, der Identitätsbedingung einer grammatischen Regel genügen, auch wenn sie sich an dem Punkt der Ableitung, an dem die Regel ansetzt, in ihrer derivierten Struktur unterscheiden. Folgende Abwandlungen der Beispiele (22) scheinen anzudeuten, dass es sich wenigstens nicht allgemein so verhält:

(29)

(a) Ich wurde genauso gewählt wie $\begin{cases} \text{er (gewählt wurde)} \\ \text{*ihn} \\ \text{man ihn wählte} \end{cases}$

(b) Man wählte mich genauso wie $\begin{cases} \text{man ihn wählte} \\ \text{ihn} \\ \text{*er} \\ \text{er gewählt wurde} \end{cases}$

Falls *man wählt x* und *x wird gewählt* auf die gleiche Tiefenstruktur zurückgehen (was allerdings nicht ganz sicher ist) müssen die Sätze in (29) damit erklärt werden, dass die durch die Passivtransformation bewirkten Unterschiede in der derivierten Struktur von der Identitätsbedingung der Tilgungstransformation berücksichtigt werden. Auch (10) deutet in diese Richtung. Da *gratulieren* und *beglückwünschen* so gut wie völlig synonym zu sein scheinen, ist es nicht sehr wahrscheinlich, dass in der Tiefenstruktur ein Unterschied hinsichtlich der Beziehung zum Objekt anzunehmen ist, der die unterschiedliche Verhaltensweise in (10)(d) und (e) erklären könnte. Es scheint also Anzeichen dafür zu geben, dass ausser der Tiefenstruktur auch gewisse Aspekte abgeleiteter Struktur für die GRI von Bedeutung sind. Da längst nicht alle Erscheinungen der Oberflächenstruktur von den syntaktischen Regeln, die Identitätsbedingungen enthalten, berücksichtigt werden, ist es eine interessante Frage, auf die wir noch zurückkommen werden, wie die Rolle derivierter Struktur für die GRI generell zu charakterisieren ist.

Die in diesem Abschnitt skizzierte Entwicklung des Begriffs der GRI ist deutlich durch eine immer stärkere Berücksichtigung der Inhaltsseite der sprachlichen Struktur gekennzeichnet. Es ist schwer, sich des Gedankens zu erwehren, dass die entscheidende Rolle, welche die referentielle Äquivalenz

bei NP, die semantischen Varianten polysemantischer lexikalischer Elemente und ganz allgemein die Tiefenstruktur von Sätzen für die GRI
spielen, auf das gemeinsame Prinzip zurückzuführen ist, dass die semantische
Funktion eines sprachlichen Elements für dessen syntaktische Identität, für
die Art, wie es von syntaktischen Regeln behandelt wird, wesentlich ist. Eine
solche Auffassung lässt sich gut mit den Ansichten der sog. generativen
Semantik vereinbaren, d.h. derjenigen in den letzten Jahren entwickelten
Grammatiktheorie,[6] welche die semantische Repräsentation eines Satzes
als die Eingabe des Transformationsteils betrachtet. Da sich meine Ergebnisse
auch im übrigen am besten in den Rahmen dieser Konzeption der generativen
Grammatik einfügen lassen, werde ich sie im wesentlichen der folgenden
Darstellung zugrunde legen. Ich fasse demgemäss die abstrakteste syntaktische Struktur des Satzes, die ich weiterhin Tiefenstruktur nennen will,
gleichzeitig als Form der semantischen Repräsentation des Satzes auf.

Wie wir sahen, benötigen Regeln mit Identitätsbedingungen grundsätzlich Information über die Tiefenstruktur, da die derivierte Struktur auf der
Ableitungsstufe, auf der sie angewendet werden, nicht generell die Feststellung der relevanten Identität erlaubt. Diese Zusammenhänge werden
von den ohnehin notwendigen, allgemeinen Prinzipien für die grammatisch
relevante Identität erfasst. Nun hat es sich aber gezeigt, dass auch in gewissen
anderen Fällen, wo es sich nicht um Identitätsbedingungen handelt, ein
ähnlicher, 'zurückblickender' Charakter der Transformationsbedingungen
angenommen werden muss und dass zudem eine Anzahl syntaktischer
Regularitäten gar nicht durch einzelne Transformationen oder Bedingungen
für deren Operieren erklärt werden können, sondern beispielsweise die
Feststellung einer Relation zwischen zwei weit auseinanderliegenden Ableitungsstufen oder einer Eigenschaft ganzer Folgen von Ableitungs-
schritten erfordern. Solche und andere Erscheinungen haben Lakoff (1969)
dazu veranlasst, grammatische Regeln ganz allgemein als Ableitungsbedingungen ('derivational constraints') aufzufassen, welche unter allen
endlichen Folgen von P-Markern diejenigen auslesen, die richtige Ableitungen darstellen. Transformationen sind dabei als diejenigen Ableitungsbedingungen aufzufassen, welche sich auf Paare unmittelbar aufeinanderfolgender P-Marker beziehen und somit den Charakter 'lokaler' Ableitungsbedingungen haben ('local derivational constraints' im Gegensatz zu
'global derivational constraints'). Diese Konzeption der transformationellen

---

[6] Vor allem in mehreren Arbeiten von Lakoff und McCawley. Ein besonders interessantes
Argument sowie genauere Hinweise auf einschlägige Literatur finden sich bei Postal (1970a).
Ross (1969b) bringt m.E. überzeugende Argumente gegen eine Erklärung des Zusammenhangs
zwischen semantischer Äquivalenz und syntaktischer Struktur mit Hilfe einer interpretativen
semantischen Komponente.

Ableitung wollen wir ebenfalls in der folgenden Diskussion voraussetzen.

2. INDIREKTE IDENTITÄT UND DERIVIERTE STRUKTUR

Wir wenden uns nun Beispielen folgender Art zu :[7]

(30)   (a) Der Schüler war ebenso unzufrieden mit sich wie der Lehrer
            (es war)

        (b) Karl ist nur dann gegen sich streng, wenn es die andern auch
            sind

        (c) Der Redner konnte sich auf dem Tonband hören aber der
            Diskussionsleiter (konnte es) nicht

        (d) Erkannte Karl sich auf den Bildern gleich wieder? – Nein,
            aber das tat Peter

        (e) Karl$_i$ weiss, wass er$_i$ zu tun hat, aber Peter (weiss es) nicht

        (f) Hast du Karl$_i$ gefragt, ob er$_i$ kommt? – Nein, aber seinen
            Bruder

        (g) Peter$_i$ hat mit dem Hund, den er$_i$ sich angeschafft hat, nur
            Ärger gehabt, und Karl auch

        (h) Peter$_i$ hat mit seinem$_i$ Hund nur Ärger gehabt, aber Karl
            nicht

Diese Beispiele sind offensichtlich doppeldeutig. So kann etwa in (30)(a)
entweder von der Unzufriedenheit des Lehrers mit dem Schüler die Rede
sein oder von seiner Unzufriedenheit mit sich selber, und Entsprechendes
gilt für die übrigen Sätze. Der Unterschied zwischen den jeweils zugrunde
liegenden beiden Strukturen scheint sich schematisch folgendermassen
darstellen zu lassen :

(31)   (a) $\underset{1}{X} - \underset{2}{/x_1/_{NP}} - \underset{3}{Y} - \underset{4}{/x_1/_{NP}} - \underset{5}{Z} - \underset{6}{/x_3/_{NP}} - \underset{7}{P} - \underset{8}{/x_1/_{NP}} - \underset{9}{R}$

        (b) $\underset{1}{X} - \underset{2}{/x_1/_{NP}} - \underset{3}{Y} - \underset{4}{/x_1/_{NP}} - \underset{5}{Z} - \underset{6}{/x_3/_{NP}} - \underset{7}{P} - \underset{8}{/x_3/_{NP}} - \underset{9}{R}$

Während in den (31)(a) entsprechenden Fällen die getilgte, bzw. pro-
nominalisierte Kette ein referentielles Element enthält (Term 8), welches, wie

[7] Obgleich unter Sätzen mit nebengeordneten Strukturen interessante Parallelen zu den Beispielen in (30) zu verzeichnen sind (vgl. I)

(I)   (a) Nicht nur Karl (selber), sondern auch Hans wusste, was ihm bevorstand
        (b) Entweder Karl (selber) oder Hans hat behauptet, dass er Krebs habe

können wir diese auf Grund der Unklarheit darüber, welche Rolle Regeln mit Identitätsbedingungen bei der Ableitung derartiger Strukturen spielen, leider nicht in die folgende
Diskussion mit einbeziehen.

zu erwarten, dem entsprechenden Element in der Korrelatkette (Term 4) referentiell äquivalent ist, scheinen die (31)(b) entsprechenden Fälle in erster Annäherung so zu charakterisieren zu sein, dass dort eine Kette getilgt, bzw. pronominalisiert wird, die ein referentielles Element (Term 8) enthält, das nicht mit dem entsprechenden Element der Korrelatkette (Term 4), sondern vielmehr mit einem anderen nicht-getilgten und in einem bestimmten Sinne übergeordneten Element (Term 6) identisch ist, zu dem es in der gleichen grammatischen Relation steht, wie das entsprechende Element (Term 4) zu einem mit diesem identischen Element (Term 2). Wir wollen in diesen Fällen vorläufig von einer Anwendung der Regeln auf Grund indirekter Identität (II) sprechen, im Gegensatz zu der normalen, direkten Identität (DI), mit der wir es offenbar in (31)(a) zu tun haben.[8]

Beispiele wie die in (30) stellen uns vor ein grundsätzliches, für das Verständnis der GRI entscheidendes Problem: Wie ist es zu erklären, dass ein und dieselbe Struktur Korrelat zweier verschiedener Strukturen sein kann und also von den syntaktischen Regeln als mit zwei verschiedenen Strukturen identisch betrachtet wird? Die Korrelatketten in (30) scheinen nämlich an sich keine durchgehende, mit den beiden Bedeutungen der ganzen Beispiele gekoppelte Ambiguität aufzuweisen, welche als Erklärung ihrer doppelten Funktion dienen könnte. Vielmehr scheint es so zu sein, dass die Identitätsbedingungen syntaktischer Regeln unter bestimmten Bedingungen von gewissen, normalerweise relevanten Aspekten der Satzstruktur absehen können, wodurch die Fälle mit II möglich werden. Es gilt also, die Bedingungen der II genau zu erfassen, um sie in Form einer möglichst generell formulierten Abschwächung des Identitätsbegriffs in die Charakterisierung der GRI aufnehmen zu können. Darin besteht das Hauptziel dieser Untersuchung.

Der Umstand, dass in den Beispielen in (30) bei II den indirekt identischen referentiellen Elementen 4 und 8 in (31)(b) in einer vollständigen Oberflächenstruktur gleiche Pronomen (*sich* in (a)–(d), *er* in (e)–(h)) entsprechen, könnte einen dazu veranlassen, diese Gleichheit der derivierten Strukturen

---

[8] Diese doppelte Tilgungsmöglichkeit in Sätzen wie (30), die ich erstmals in (Schiebe, 1967) etwas häher untersucht habe, hat auch Ross beobachtet und in (Ross, 1967b) und (Ross, 1969b) in einigen ihrer grundlegenden Bedingungen beschrieben. Die von ihm als 'sloppy identity' bezeichnete II definiert er so: "Constituents are identical... if they differ only as to pronouns, where the pronouns in each of the identical constituents are commanded by antecedents in the non-identical portions of the phrase-markers" (Ross, 1967b, §5.2. S. 190). Darüber hinaus erwähnt er (als eine Beobachtung von Anthony Naro) die Erscheinung, auf die sich Beispiel (33) bezieht, sowie (in Ross 1969b) die Notwendigkeit einer Gleichheit in der Beziehung der indirekt identischen Elemente zu ihrem jeweiligen Korrelat (vgl. die Beispiele (34)–(35)). Unsere Ergebnisse stimmen also in allen diesen Punkten gut überein, mit Ausnahme der Auffassung über die Rolle des Begriffs 'command', mit dem wir uns noch werden auseinandersetzen müssen (vgl. S. 520).

zur Erklärung der II heranzuziehen. Wenn man die Rolle der normalerweise notwendigen Tiefenstrukturidentität etwa in der Weise einschränken
würde, dass man annimmt, dass bei Pronomen, die in der gleichen Relation
zu ihrem jeweiligen Korrelat stehen, entweder die Tiefenstruktur zu berücksichtigen ist (= DI), oder, fakultativ, die Oberflächenstruktur (genauer:
eine oberflächennahe Struktur) (= II), so hätte man damit die Verhältnisse in (30) annähernd erfasst. So verlockend ein solcher Ansatz auf den
ersten Blick auch erscheinen mag, ist er leider nicht durchführbar, und zwar
aus einer ganzen Reihe von Gründen. Die wichtigsten seien hier angeführt.

Erstens ist die Erscheinung der II nicht auf Fälle beschränkt, in denen die
betreffenden Pronomen in der Oberflächenstruktur gleich wären. Folgende
Abwandlungen der Beispiele in (30) zeigen, dass Unterschiede zwischen den
Pronomen hinsichtlich Merkmalen wie Person, Genus, Numerus und
Reflexivität die Möglichkeit indirekter Identität nicht ausschliessen:

(32)   (a) Der Schüler war ebenso unzufrieden mit sich wie ich (es war)
        (b) Du bist nur dann gegen dich streng, wenn es die andern auch
            sind
        (c) Der Redner konnte sich auf dem Tonband hören, aber wir
            (konnten es) nicht
        (d) Erkannte Karl sich auf den Bildern gleich wieder? – Nein,
            aber das taten wir ja auch nicht
        (e) Wir wissen, was wir zu tun haben, aber du (weisst es) nicht
        (f) Hast du Karl$_i$ gefragt, ob er$_i$ kommt? – Nein, aber seine
            Schwester
        (g) Maria$_i$ hat mit dem Hund, den sie$_i$ sich angeschafft hat, nur
            Ärger gehabt, und Karl auch
        (h) Wir haben mit unserem Auto Ärger, aber die Mayers auch

Zweitens scheint es sich bei der II grundsätzlich nicht einmal um eine
Beziehung zwischen zwei Pronomen der derivierten Struktur zu handeln.
Nicht nur in (33)(a) ist II möglich,

(33)   (a) Dass er$_i$ krank war, verheimlichte Karl$_i$ mir, $\begin{cases} \text{genau wie} \\ \text{genau wie} \end{cases}$
            $\left.\begin{array}{l} \text{seinerzeit Peter} \\ \text{es seinerzeit Peter getan hatte} \end{array}\right\}$

        (b) Dass Karl$_i$ krank war, verheimlichte er$_i$ mir, $\begin{cases} \text{genau wie} \\ \text{genau wie} \end{cases}$
            $\left.\begin{array}{l} \text{seinerzeit Peter} \\ \text{es seinerzeit Peter getan hatte} \end{array}\right\}$

sondern anscheinend auch in (33)(b), wo eins der miteinander indirekt identischen Elemente (nämlich *Karl*) gar nicht als Pronomen auftritt. Es ist also offenbar nicht möglich, bei der Erklärung des Unterschieds zwischen DI und II in der oben angedeuteten Weise auf Unterschiede zwischen Tiefenstruktur und abgeleiteter Struktur zurückzugreifen.

Darüber hinaus gibt es Anzeichen dafür, dass die Bedingungen für die Möglichkeit indirekter Identität eher in der Tiefenstruktur als in der derivierten Struktur zu suchen sind. Wie schon angedeutet, müssen die indirekt identischen Elemente jeweils einem übergeordneten Element (nennen wir es kurz 'Hauptelement', da 'Korrelat', wie wir eben sahen, nicht ganz angebracht ist) referentiell äquivalent sein. Die Relation der indirekt identischen Elemente zu ihrem jeweiligen Hauptelement muss, wie wir ebenfalls schon erwähnten, in einem bestimmten Sinne gleich sein. Dies geht etwa schon daraus hervor, dass in

(34)   (a) Karl hat dich darum gebeten, dein Auto heilmachen zu lassen, $\left\{\begin{array}{l}\text{und Peter mich}\\\text{und Peter hat mich darum gebeten}\end{array}\right\}$

           (b) Karl hat dich darum gebeten, dein Auto heilmachen zu lassen, und Peter hat mich darum gebeten, mein Auto heilmachen zu lassen

           (c) Karl hat dich darum gebeten, dein Auto heilmachen zu lassen, und Peter hat mich darum gebeten, sein Auto heilmachen zu lassen

(35)   (a) Karl_i hat dich darum gebeten, sein_i Auto heilmachen zu lassen, $\left\{\begin{array}{l}\text{und Peter mich}\\\text{und Peter hat mich darum gebeten}\end{array}\right\}$

           (b) Karl_i hat dich darum gebeten, sein_i Auto heilmachen zu lassen, und Peter_j hat mich darum gebeten, sein_j Auto heilmachen zu lassen

           (c) Karl_i hat dich darum gebeten, sein_i Auto heilmachen zu lassen, und Peter hat mich darum gebeten, mein Auto heilmachen zu lassen

Beispiel (a) u.a. mit (b), nicht aber mit (c) gleichbedeutend sein kann. Genau das gleiche gilt nun aber auch beispielsweise für

(36)   (a) Du bist von Karl_i darum gebeten worden, sein_i Auto heilmachen zu lassen, während Peter mich darum gebeten hat

           (b) Du bist von Karl_i darum gebeten worden, sein_i Auto heilmachen zu lassen, während Peter_j mich darum gebeten hat, sein_j Auto heilmachen zu lassen

(c) Du bist von Karl$_i$ darum gebeten worden, sein$_i$ Auto heilmachen zu lassen, während Peter$_j$ mich darum gebeten hat, mein Auto heilmachen zu lassen

wo auf Grund der Anwendung der Passivtransformation in der Ableitung der Korrelatkette die Gleichheit der Relation zwischen den indirekt identischen Elementen und ihren Hauptelementen an der derivierten Struktur nicht mehr abzulesen ist, wohl aber an der Tiefenstruktur. Obgleich die genaue Charakterisierung dieser Gleichheit keineswegs unproblematisch ist (vgl. unten S. 518), ist also wohl anzunehmen, dass sie jedenfalls nicht anhand derivierter Struktur vorzunehmen ist.

Der Umstand, dass die zentrale Bedeutung der Tiefenstruktur für die GRI sich also offensichtlich auch im Zusammenhang mit der II bestätigt, legt es m.E. nahe, den Versuch zu unternehmen, die Bedingungen der II überhaupt anhand der Tiefenstruktur zu formulieren. Es ist sogar möglich, dass die II ausschliesslich als eine Beziehung zwischen Tiefenstrukturen zu definieren ist. Es ist nämlich wahrscheinlich, dass Unterschiede zwischen NP in derivierter Struktur, wie sie in (32) und (33)(b) zwischen den indirekt identischen Elementen auftreten, nicht nur bei II unberücksichtigt bleiben, sondern vielmehr zu jenen Aspekten abgeleiteter Struktur gehören, die überhaupt für die GRI keine Rolle spielen. Mir ist wenigstens kein klarer Fall einer Pronominalisierung oder Tilgung bekannt, dessen Erklärung eine Gleichheit zwischen NP erfordert, die sich nicht nur auf die Tiefenstruktur, sondern auch auf derivierte Merkmale bezieht. Im Gegenteil scheint es viele Fälle zu geben, wo auch bei DI derivierte Unterschiede zwischen NP vernachlässigt werden müssen, und zwar, wie

(37)   (a) Ich weiss, dass du mit jemandem über mich gesprochen hast.

$\left\{ \begin{array}{l} -\text{Weisst du auch, mit wem?} / = \text{mit wem ich über dich} \\ \text{gesprochen habe}/ \\ -\text{Woher weisst du das?} / = \text{dass ich mit jemandem über} \\ \text{dich gesprochen habe}/ \end{array} \right\}$

   (b) Ich begoss den Kaktus$_i$, aber die Pflanze$_i$ vertrug das / = dass ich sie$_i$ begoss/ nicht

   (c) Die betreffende Person$_i$ hat den Schlüssel zwar bekommen, aber das Kamel$_i$ hat vergessen, von wem / = von wem es$_i$ den Schlüssel bekommen hat/

   (d) Kommt Karl$_i$? – Ich weiss es / = ob er$_i$ kommt/ nicht

   (e) Ich vermute, dass Karl$_i$ kommt, aber ich weiss es / = ob er$_i$ kommt/ nicht

(f) Der Junge$_i$, dem$_i$ ich die Schlüssel gab, war darüber $/=$ dass ich ihm$_i$ die Schlüssel gab$/$ sehr erstaunt

andeutet, sowohl bei solchen NP, die auf referentielle Indizes, wie bei solchen, die auf S-Strukturen zurückgehen. Eine Gegenüberstellung von (37)(c) und den Sätzen in

(38)   (a) Das Kamel$_i$ hat vergessen, von wem es$_i$ den Schlüssel bekommen hat

   (b) Das Kamel$_i$ hat vergessen, von wem er$_i$ den Schlüssel bekommen hat

   (c) Das Kamel$_i$ hat vergessen, von wem sie$_i$ den Schlüssel bekommen hat

lässt überdies vermuten, dass derivierte Unterschiede zwischen NP, die in der Tiefenstruktur aus referentiellen Indizes bestehen, schon deswegen nicht berücksichtigt werden, weil die NP, die durch Tilgung eliminiert werden, hinsichtlich abgeleiteter Merkmale unspezifiziert sein müssen, d.h. auch in derivierter Struktur nur aus referentiellen Indizes bestehen dürfen, falls sie schon eingeführte Variable vertreten. Dies gilt jedenfalls dort, wo eine Kennzeichnung durch solche Merkmale mit einer begrifflichen Charakterisierung der entsprechenden Variablen verbunden wäre. Wie (38) zeigt, könnte (37)(c) an sich auch mit *er$_i$* oder *sie$_i$* statt mit *es$_i$* fortgeführt werden. Im Gegensatz zu *es* sind aber *er* und *sie* in solchen Zusammenhängen mit einer Charakterisierung des natürlichen Geschlechts verbunden. Da nun aber (37)(c) in dieser Hinsicht völlig unspezifiziert ist, kann (37)(c) nicht auf eine Satzstruktur zurückgehen, die (38)(b) oder (c) enthält. Und da diese Tatsache, wie etwa

(39)   (a) Diese Person$_i$ erfährt nicht, dass er sich auf $\left\{ \begin{matrix} \text{sie}_i \\ \text{*ihn}_i \end{matrix} \right\}$ beruft

   (b) Er beruft sich auf einen gewissen Karl Meyer$_i$, in der Hoffnung, dass diese Person$_i$ das $/=$ dass er sich auf sie$_i$ beruft$/$ nicht erfährt

andeutend zeigt, nicht durch die Annahme erklärt werden kann, dass die Identität der Tiefenstrukturen auch die Charakterisierung (bzw. Nicht-charakterisierung) der NP umfassen müsse, liegt es nahe, den Grund darin zu sehen, dass die betreffenden syntaktischen und semantischen Merkmale bei NP der Charakterisierung von Variablenstellen in der Oberflächen-struktur dienen und somit bei Variablenstellen, die an der Oberfläche gar nicht realisiert werden, selbstverständlich wegfallen. Ähnliches gilt auch bei

II und zeigt sich da vielleicht noch deutlicher. So kann etwa (40)(a) weder auf (40)(b) noch auf (40)(c) zurückgehen, da es im Gegensatz zu diesen

(40)   (a) Nicht ich bin es, der die Verantwortung trägt, sondern du
          /= du bist es, dX die Verantwortung trägt/

         (b) Nicht ich bin es, der die Verantwortung trägt, sondern du
          bist es, der die Verantwortung trägt

         (c) Nicht ich bin es, der die Verantwortung trägt, sondern du
          bist es, die die Verantwortung trägt

ebensowenig mit einer Voraussetzung über des Geschlecht des Angeredeten verbunden ist wie etwa der Satz *Du trägst die Verantwortung*. Der Tiefenstruktur von (40)(a) entspricht also offensichtlich überhaupt keine nichtreduzierte Oberflächenstruktur, da kein passendes, 'neutrales' Relativpronomen zur Verfügung steht. Ebenso scheint in

(41)   (a) Karl oder Peter oder Hans ist es, der da kommt

$$(b) \;^{*}\text{Karl oder Maria oder ihr Kind ist es,} \left\{ \begin{array}{l} \text{der} \\ \text{die} \\ \text{das} \\ \text{der bzw.} \\ \text{die bzw.} \\ \text{das} \end{array} \right\} \text{da kommt}$$

    (c) Nicht Hans ist es, der da kommt, sondern Karl oder Maria
        oder ihr Kind /= sondern Karl oder Maria oder ihr Kind
        ist es, dX da kommt/

ein Kongruenzkonflikt wie der in (b) durch eine Tilgung wie die in (c) vermieden werden zu können.[9]

Es ist wahrscheinlich, dass die Rolle der derivierten Struktur für die GRI noch weit über die besprochenen Aspekte hinaus einzuschränken ist. Da

---

[9] Obwohl die Verhältnisse bei nebengeordneten Strukturen wie gesagt höchst unklar sind, muss es doch als wahrscheinlich gelten, dass ein Satz wie (41) (c) durch eine Tilgung der angedeuteten Art entsteht. Auch wenn die nebengeordnete Struktur in (41)(c) mit Hilfe einer Zusammenziehungstransformation abgeleitet wird, muss nämlich diese Regel wohl zyklisch sein und also vor der Tilgungstransformation, die ja frühestens zyklisch operiert (vgl. S. 489) angewendet werden.

Man könnte meinen, gerade der Umstand, dass in (41)(b) im Gegensatz zu (a) ein Konflikt entsteht, deute darauf hin, dass bei Zusammenziehungen, anders als bei Tilgungen, Identitätsbedingungen im Spiele seien, die sich auf die betreffenden derivierten Merkmale der NP bezögen. Welche Rolle die Identität derivierter Strukturen bei Zusammenziehungen auch spielen mag, so handelt es sich doch bei den Bedingungen, die in (41)(b) nicht erfüllt sind, vermutlich nicht um Identitätsbedingungen, sondern eher um gewisse Verträglichkeitsbedingungen, da potentielle Kongruenzkonflikte nicht nur durch Tilgung, sondern auch z.B. durch eine 'Zusammenfassung' in Pluralformen verschiedener Art vermieden werden können. Vgl.:

eine eingehende Erörterung dieser Probleme hier zu weit führen würde, begnüge ich mich mit dem Hinweis, dass auch dort, wo es sich nicht nur um Gleichheit zwischen NP der derivierten Struktur handelt, so viel mehr Unterschiede irrelevant als relevant zu sein scheinen (z.B. sämtliche Wortstellungsunterschiede, aber auch manche andere, wie in

(42)   (a) $\begin{cases} \text{Ich habe mit dir darüber gesprochen} \\ \text{Mit dir habe ich darüber gesprochen} \end{cases}$ aber ich weiss nicht mehr, mit wem noch /= mit wem ich noch darüber gesprochen habe/

    (b) Er behauptet, mit jemandem darüber gesprochen zu haben und nicht mehr zu wissen, mit wem /= mit wem er darüber gesprochen habe/

    (c) Er muss mit jemandem darüber gesprochen haben, ohne dass seine Frau erfahren hat, mit wem /= mit wem er darüber gesprochen hat/

    (d) Er scheint dich nicht ebenso oft besuchen zu müssen wie mich /= (1) wie er mich besucht

           (2) wie er mich besuchen muss/

    (e) Karl brauchte niemandem etwas abzugeben, wohl aber Peter /= wohl aber musste (?) Peter jemandem etwas abgeben/

angedeutet), dass man sich eher die Frage zu stellen hat, welche Aspekte abgeleiteter Struktur denn überhaupt für die GRI wesentlich sind. In der Tat sind die einzigen mir bekannten Fälle, die für eine Berücksichtigung derivierter Unterschiede sprechen, Beispiele von der in (10) und (29) angeführten Art, wo also gewisse in Kasusunterschieden sich widerspiegelnde, abgeleitete Strukturunterschiede anscheinend nicht vernachlässigt werden dürfen. Aber auch diese Beispiele sind nicht ganz zuverlässig, da es nicht eindeutig klar ist, dass die betreffenden Unterschiede rein derivierter Natur

---

(I)   (a) Sowohl Karl wie Maria versuchten, ihre Aufmerksamkeit auf das Wesentliche zu konzentrieren

        (b) Sowohl Karl wie ich versuchten, unsere Aufmerksamkeit auf das Wesentliche zu konzentrieren

Den späten, 'oberflächlichen' Charakter solcher Kongruenzbedingungen zeigen, um nur ein Beispiel unter vielen zu nennen, Sätze wie

(II)   (a) Darüber haben $\begin{cases} \text{sich} \\ \text{*uns} \end{cases}$ sowohl meine Frau wie ich sehr gefreut

    (b) Darüber haben sowohl meine Frau wie ich $\begin{cases} \text{uns} \\ \text{*sich} \end{cases}$ sehr gefreut.

sind und nicht mit gewissen Unterschieden in der Tiefenstruktur in Zusammenhang stehen. Es ist also nicht ohne weiteres auszuschliessen, dass überhaupt nur die Tiefenstruktur für die Identitätsbedingungen syntaktischer Regeln relevant ist, zumindest was anaphorische Konstruktionen betrifft. Auf der Ableitungsstufe, auf der die betreffende Regel angewendet wird, würde dann für Korrelat und anaphorische Kette als einzige Identitätsbedingung gelten, dass sie auf gleiche Tiefenstrukturen zurückgehen. Bestätigt sich hingegen die Relevanz derivierter Struktur, sollte zunächst versucht werden, diese mit allgemeinen Prinzipien zu erklären, indem man etwa ihre Abhängigkeit von charakteristischen Eigenschaften der relevanten Strukturunterschiede (z.B.: 'von zyklischen oder postzyklischen Regeln eingeführt', 'vor oder nach der Anwendung der die Identität fordernden Regel eingeführt') oder von charakteristischen Eigenschaften der mit Identitätsbedingungen verbundenen Regeln untersucht, ehe man sie als idiosynkratische Eigenschaften dieser Regeln ansieht.

Wenn somit die bei II vernachlässigten Aspekte derivierter Struktur höchstwahrscheinlich durch eine ohnehin notwendige Charakterisierung der für die GRI irrelevanten abgeleiteten Strukturunterschiede mit erfasst werden, so hat sich die Auffassung, welche die II ausschliesslich als eine Beziehung zwischen Tiefenstrukturen definieren möchte, doch mit einer grossen Anzahl von Fällen auseinanderzusetzen, in denen Zusammenhänge zwischen Erscheinungen in der Oberflächenstruktur und der Möglichkeit indirekter Identität zu beobachten sind (vgl. nur etwa (43)). Eine solche

(43)   (a) Er$_i$ schickte seine$_i$ Kinder in die Schweiz, aber sein Freund tat das nicht /II möglich/

          (b) Seine$_i$ Kinder wurden von ihm$_i$ in die Schweiz geschickt, aber von seinem Freund nicht /II nicht möglich/

Auffassung der II setzt ja voraus, dass sich alle derartigen Erscheinungen auf Grund von ohnehin notwendigen Regeln mit Eigenschaften der Tiefenstruktur korrelieren lassen, welche ihrerseits die Möglichkeit indirekter Identität bedingen. Ehe wir jedoch beurteilen können, wieweit es aussichtsvoll ist, in allen diesen Fällen einen solchen Erklärungsweg einzuschlagen, müssen wir im folgenden versuchen, uns etwas genauer über die Grundzüge derjenigen Definition der II klar zu werden, die wir unsrer Analyse zugrunde legen wollen.

3. INDIREKTE IDENTITÄT UND THEMA-RHEMA-STRUKTUR. VERSUCH EINER DEFINITION DER NICHTSTRIKTEN IDENTITÄT

Bei dem Versuch, zu einer angemessenen Definition der II anhand der Tiefenstruktur zu gelangen, wollen wir von einer Erklärungsmöglichkeit ausgehen, auf die McCawley in (McCawley 1967) hinweist. Da ein Satz wie *John loves his wife* auf zweierlei Weise als eine Aussage über den als *John* Bezeichneten (etwa repräsentiert durch den Index x_1) aufgefasst werden könne, nämlich teils als Prädizierung der Eigenschaft '*x* loves *x*'s wife' ($= g(x)$), teils als Prädizierung der Eigenschaft '*x* loves x_1's wife' ($= h(x)$), so könnten, meint McCawley, die beiden Bedeutungen von *John loves his wife and so do I* durch semantische Strukturen der Form $g(x_1) \wedge g(x_2)$ (bei II) und $h(x_1) \wedge h(x_2)$ (bei DI) wiedergegeben werden (wobei x_2 Index von *I*). In beiden Fällen liege damit in der semantischen Repräsentation des Satzes eine Gleichheit vor (zwischen den beiden *g* bzw. *h*), die eine Tilgung ermögliche. Eine solche Erklärung der II scheint also vorauszusetzen, dass ein Satz wie *John loves his wife* auf verschiedene, semantisch äquivalente semantische Repräsentationen zurückgehen kann, die verschiedenen Zerlegungen der betreffenden Proposition in Konstanten und Propositionalfunktionen entsprechen. Eine derartige abstrakte strukturelle Ambiguität des die Korrelatkette enthaltenden Satzes wäre somit für die doppelte Tilgungsmöglichkeit in *John loves his wife and so do I* verantwortlich und die sog. II wäre dadurch als ein Sonderfall der DI erklärt, nämlich als ein Fall der oben (S. 492). erörterten Gleichheit zwischen Propositionalfunktionen.

Mir scheint, dass eine solche Auffassung der II einigen wesentlichen Aspekten dieser Erscheinung gerecht wird. Vor allem stellt sie eine Explikation des intuitiven Eindrucks dar, dass es sich, wenigstens in vielen Fällen, bei II um einen gleichbleibenden 'Rahmen' handelt, in dem ein Element an allen Stellen, an denen es auftritt, durch ein bestimmtes anderes Element ersetzt wird. Dennoch scheint mir eine solche Erklärung der II nicht ohne weiteres akzeptiert werden zu können. Meine Einwände betreffen vor allem folgende drei Punkte:

(1) Der relevante Unterschied zwischen den zu tilgenden Propositionalfunktionen bei II und DI (also $g(x)$ bzw. $h(x)$ im obigen Beispiel) ist nicht, wie McCawleys Darstellung anzudeuten scheint, der, dass an der Stelle, an der bei II eine Variable auftritt, bei DI eine Konstante erscheint.

(2) Die Annahme einer den Unterschied zwischen DI und II erklärenden strukturellen Ambiguität der Korrelatkette hat den Charakter eines Ad-hoc-Postulats, das einer blossen Definition der II nicht überlegen ist, solange die angenommene Ambiguität nicht mit weiteren Unterschieden hinsichtlich syntaktischer oder semantischer Eigenschaften korreliert und damit unabhängig von dem Unterschied zwischen DI und II motiviert werden kann.

(3) Der Unterschied zwischen DI und II lässt sich nicht in allen Fällen

durch eine entsprechende Ambiguität der Korrelatkette erklären; d.h., der McCawley'sche Ansatz löst nicht das vom Gesichtspunkt der GRI aus zentrale Problem bei Sätzen mit DI und II, nämlich wieso ein und dieselbe Struktur Korrelat zweier verschiedener Strukturen sein kann.

Punkt (1) lässt sich leicht belegen, indem man in Sätzen wie (30) das in Frage stehende Element durch ein anderes referentielles Element mit eindeutigem Variablencharakter ersetzt. So erhält man beispielsweise durch Abwandlung von (30)(a) und (e) die Sätze in

(44)   (a) Keiner der Schüler war so unzufrieden mit sich wie der Lehrer

(b) Jeder$_i$ behauptete, er$_i$ wisse, was er$_i$ zu tun habe, aber Peter nicht

die genauso doppeldeutig sind wie (30)(a) und (e). Die zu tilgenden Strukturen enthalten in solchen Fällen sowohl bei II wie bei DI nur Variable. Der wesentliche Unterschied scheint also eher darin zu bestehen, dass dort, wo die betreffende Struktur bei II eine NP enthält, die die Argumentvariable der entsprechenden Propositionalfunktion (oder Propositionalfunktionen) vertritt, bei DI eine NP auftritt, von der dies nicht gilt.

Was Punkt (2) betrifft, bin ich der Ansicht, dass strukturelle Unterschiede, die im wesentlichen der Herauslösung verschiedener Propositionalfunktionen aus einer Proposition entsprechen, tatsächlich für die uns hier interessierenden Erscheinungen von wesentlicher Bedeutung sind. Freilich glaube ich, dass es sich dabei um Strukturunterschiede handelt, die ohnehin postuliert werden müssen, um Zusammenhänge zu erklären, die von dem Phänomen der II an sich völlig unabhängig sind. Ich denke an Erscheinungen der Art, wie sie beispielsweise unter den Stichworten Thema-Rhema behandelt worden sind. In der Tat möchte ich die Hypothese aufstellen, dass die Aufteilung eines Satzes in Thema (Th) und Rhema (Rh) mit einer Zerlegung der Tiefenstruktur einhergeht, die im wesentlichen der Zerlegung von Propositionen in Argumente und Propositionalfunktionen entspricht, und dass in dieser Weise verstandene ThRh-Strukturen für Tilgungen im allgemeinen und II im besonderen von wesentlicher Bedeutung sind, ja, eine notwendige Voraussetzung für die Fälle mit II darstellen.[10]

Um die Rolle der ThRh-Struktur für die Erklärung der II diskutieren zu

---

[10] Auch Dahl (1969) vertritt die Auffassung, dass es sich bei der ThRh-Struktur um eine in der Tiefenstruktur zu repräsentierende, logische Beziehung handle. Seine Analyse unterscheidet sich jedoch wesentlich von der vorgelegten. Dahl hat auch gewisse Zusammenhänge zwischen ThRh-Struktur und II angenommen (in Dahl, 1970), ohne allerdings die ThRh-Struktur zur Erklärung des Wesens der II heranzuziehen.

können, muss ich meine Auffassung über den Charakter der ThRh-Distinktion etwas genauer darlegen. Da im Rahmen der vorliegenden Untersuchung eine eingehende Erörterung und Motivierung dieser Auffassung nicht möglich ist, (ich muss dazu auf Schiebe (in Vorbereitung) verweisen), begnüge ich mich damit, sie in ihren Grundzügen zu umreissen.

Wir wollen von den Beispielen in (45) ausgehen, in denen die ThRh-Aufteilung gewisser Sätze angedeutet ist (Thema kursiv, Rhema-Element in Klammer, mit Akzent):

(45)   (a) Ich möchte wissen, ob jemand mit Karl unzufrieden ist –
             (Háns) *ist mit ihm unzufrieden*

        (b) Ich möchte wissen, ob Karl mit jemandem unzufrieden
             ist – Das weiss ich nicht. Jedenfalls bezweifle ich, dass *er*
             (mit Háns) *unzufrieden ist*

        (c) Wer ist denn schon mit Karl unzufrieden! – (Háns) *ist mit
             ihm unzufrieden*

        (d) Nenne mir einen von denen, die mit Karl unzufrieden sind! –
             (Háns) *ist mit ihm unzufrieden*

        (e) Nenne mir den, der mit Karl unzufrieden ist! – (Háns) *ist
             mit ihm unzufrieden*

        (f) Wer ist es, der mit Karl unzufrieden ist? – (Háns) *ist mit ihm
             unzufrieden*

        (g) Ist Háns oder Péter mit Karl unzufrieden? – (Háns) *ist mit
             ihm unzufrieden*

        (h) Ist Hans mit Péter oder Kárl unzufrieden? – (Mit Kárl) *ist
             er unzufrieden*

Ohne den Anspruch erheben zu wollen, die mannigfaltigen Erscheinungen, die mit Ausdrücken wie Thema, Rhema, Emphase, Kontrast, topic, comment, focus, etc. bezeichnet worden sind, auch nur annähernd vollständig zu erfassen, glaube ich doch, auf einen wesentlichen und für unser Problem relevanten Aspekt dieser Phänomene hinzuweisen, wenn ich die in (45) gekennzeichneten Sätze als Aussagen über Begriffe deute, indem ich annehme, dass sie von einem bestimmten Begriff (etwa 'mit Karl unzufrieden zu sein' in (45)(a)) aussagen, dass er durch ein bestimmtes Individuum ('Hans') erfüllt sei, oder, mit anderen Worten, dass sie von einer gegebenen Propositionalfunktion ('x_1 ist mit x_2 unzufrieden', wo x_1 Argumentvariable der Funktion und x_2 Index von 'Karl' ist) aussagen, dass durch Einsetzen eines bestimmten Arguments (x_3 als Index von 'Hans') eine wahre Proposition entstehe. Vorbedingung für eine solche Aussage (nennen wir sie Rh-Aussage) über einen Begriff ist, dass dieser aus dem Zusammenhang gegeben ist. In dieser Vorgegebenheit besteht sein thematischer Charakter. Darüber hinaus kann der Begriff mit weiteren Voraussetzungen verschiedener Art verbunden sein, so vor allem mit der Voraussetzung, erfüllt zu sein (so in (45)(d) – (h), im Gegensatz zu (a) – (c)) und insbesondere einmalig erfüllt zu sein (so in (45)(e) – (h); in diesem Fall haben wir es im wesentlichen mit der gleichen Bedeutung zu tun wie in Sätzen wie *Hans ist es, der mit ihm unzufrieden ist*). Auch können Kombinationen der ThRh-Struktur mit anderen Voraussetzungen oder Aussagen durch Wörter wie *z.B., u.a., nämlich, und zwar, auch, sogar, nicht einmal, gerade, vor allem, besonders, höchstens, wenigstens, selber, nur* angedeutet werden, vor allem, wenn diese beim Rh-Element stehen. Die Art der Tiefenstrukturen, die m.E. bei Rh-Aussagen angenommen werden könnten, möge

(46) (a) Ích (Ich$_{x_3}$) *bin mit dir$_{x_2}$ zufrieden*
      (b)

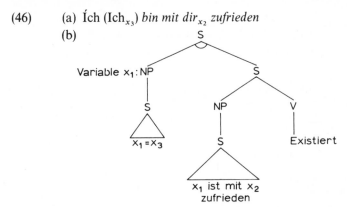

andeuten, wo jedoch manches, vor allem auch die Kennzeichnung der Vorgegebenheit des Themas sowei anderer eventuell damit verbundener Voraussetzungen, vernachlässigt ist. Der Struktur (46)(b) entspricht in traditioneller logischer Ausdrucksweise ungefähr die Aussage 'Es gibt ein t_1 aus der Menge der Elemente, die mit x_3 identisch sind, derart, dass x_1 mit t_2 zufrieden ist'. Die Einzelheiten dieser Analyse der ThRh-Struktur sind für die folgenden Ausführungen ohne Belang.[11] Wesentlich ist eigentlich nur, dass wir es mit Aussagen der Art 'Der Begriff, mit x_2 zufrieden zu sein,

---

[11] Zum besseren Verständnis sei jedoch folgendes angedeutet: Ich nehme an, dass jeder S-Struktur im Prinzip ein 'Voraussetzungsteil' zugeordnet sein kann, der seinerseits wieder aus S-Strukturen besteht. Dir Aufteilung in 'Voraussetzungsteil' und 'Aussageteil' ist durch die Konfiguration S angedeutet. Der Voraussetzungsteil dient u.a. auch zur Einführung und begrifflichen Charakterisierung von Variablen. *Variable x_1*:NP is die Abkürzung für einen S Ausdruck mit dieser Funktion, der also den referentiellen Bereich der Variablen definiert, dabei

ist durch x_3 erfüllt' zu tun haben und dass dabei in der Oberflächenstruktur die dem Element x_3 entsprechende, betonte Konstituente die betreffende Rh-Aussage in quantorenähnlicher Weise vertritt.

Es sei hinzugefügt, dass Sätze wie

(47)   (a) Was wolltest du mir von Hans sagen? – *Er ist* (unzufrieden mit Kárl)

(b) Wie steht Hans zu Karl? – *Er ist* (únzufrieden) *mit ihm*

in denen das Rh-Element offensichtlich einem Begriff oder einer Relation entspricht, sich vermutlich in analoger Weise deuten lassen. Ohne auf die weiteren damit verbundenen Probleme näher eingehen zu können, möchte ich andeutend sagen, dass ich also auch die Antworten in (47) als Aussagen über vorgegebene Begriffe auffasse, und zwar die in (a) als 'Der Begriff, ein Begriff zu sein, der von Hans gilt, ist durch den Begriff "unzufrieden mit Karl" erfüllt', und die in (b) als 'Der Begriff, eine Relation zu sein, die zwischen Hans und Karl besteht, ist durch die Relation "unzufrieden mit" erfüllt'.

Zum besseren Verständnis der folgenden Ausführungen sei zum Schluss noch auf die in

(48)   (a) (*Mit Kàrl*) IST (Háns) UNZUFRIEDEN

(b) (*Hàns*) IST (mit Kárl) UNZUFRIEDEN

angedeutete Erscheinung hingewiesen. Die Sätze in (48) können eine Bedeutung haben, die etwa wiederzugeben ist als 'Was Karl betrifft, so ist Háns mit ihm unzufrieden' bzw. 'Was Hans betrifft, so ist er mit Kárl unzufrieden'. Das durch (`) gekennzeichnete Element trägt dabei einen mit steigender Intonation kombinierten Nebenakzent. Man spricht in solchen Fällen zuweilen von Thema (topic) im engeren Sinne. Ich möchte dagegen von einem sekundären, untergeordneten Rh-Element sprechen und einen Satz wie (48)(a) so deuten, dass das Th der übergeordneten Rh-Aussage, also (*Mit Kàrl*) IST ( ) UNZUFRIEDEN seinerseits wieder aus einer Rh-Aussage mit dem Rh-Element (Mit Kàrl) und dem Th ( ) *ist* ( ) *unzufrieden* besteht. Diese Zusammenhänge zeigen sich vielleicht deutlicher bei einer Zusammenstellung mit entsprechenden Fragen, wie in

---

aber der Existenzaussage nicht unter- sondern vorgeordnet ist. Ein Grund für diese Analyse ist die dadurch ermöglichte einheitliche Beschreibung von Existenzaussagen, Allaussagen und dem, was man 'vorausgesetzte Quantoren' nennen könnte, z.B. generelles *ein* und manche Fälle des bestimmten Artikels. Ein schematisches Beispiel: Vorausgesetzt: Der referentielle Bereich der Variablen x_1 ist definiert durch den Begriff $f(x_1)$
$$\begin{cases} \text{Ausgesagt: Der Begriff } g(x_1) \text{ ist erfüllt /Existenzaussage/} \\ \text{Ausgesagt: Der Begriff } g(x_1) \text{ ist allgemein /erfüllt/Allaussage/} \\ \text{Ausgesagt: } g(x_1)/\text{generelles } ein/. \end{cases}$$

(49)   (a) Wer ist mit Kárl ǔnzufrieden?

            – (*Mit Kàrl*) IST (Háns) UNZUFRIEDEN

            (b) Mit wem ist Háns ǔnzufrieden?

            – (*Hàns*) IST (mit Kárl) UNZUFRIEDEN

wo ein betontes Element der Frage mit dem untergeordneten Rh-Element
der Antwort korrespondiert. Die Frage in (49)(a) setzt voraus, dass jemand
mit Karl unzufrieden ist. In erster Linie ist jedoch vorgegeben, dass es sich
um eine Frage handelt, die mit einer Voraussetzung der Form 'x_1 ist mit
x_2 unzufrieden' verbunden ist, und unter einer Anzahl denkbarer Voraussetzungen dieser Art wird ausdrücklich diejenige ausgewählt, die durch
Einsetzen von 'Karl' für x_2 entsteht. Die Antwort kann dann diesen stufen-
weisen Aufbau des Hauptthemas übernehmen. Eine denkbare Tiefenstruktur
solcher Sätze zeigt (50) (unter Vernachlässigung der Kennzeichnung der
thematischen Voraussetzungen):

(50)   (a) (*Mit Kàrl*$_{x_4}$) IST (Háns$_{x_2}$) UNZUFRIEDEN
            (b)

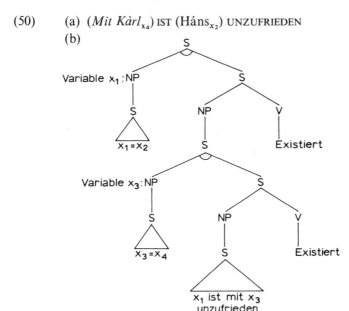

Dass zwischen ThRh-Struktur und Tilgungsoperationen enge Zusammenhänge bestehen, liegt auf der Hand. Es kann sicherlich angenommen werden,
dass eine notwendige Voraussetzung für die Tilgung eines Elements darin
besteht, dass es thematischen Charakter hat oder Teil einer thematischen
Struktur ist. Darüber hinaus scheint es mir, wenigstens was Tilgungen wie
die in (1) – (4) und

(51)   (a) Entweder ist Háns mit Karl unzufrieden oder $\begin{cases} \text{(Péter) } \textit{ist} \\ \text{Péter} \end{cases}$

          mit ihm unzufrieden $\Big\}$

          (b) Entweder ist Peter mit Háns unzufrieden, oder $\begin{cases} \textit{er ist} \text{ (mit} \\ \text{mit Kárl} \end{cases}$

          Kárl) *unzufrieden* $\Big\}$

          (c) Entweder ist Hàns mit Mártin unzufrieden oder
          (*Pèter*) ɪsᴛ (mit Kárl) ᴜɴᴢᴜꜰʀɪᴇᴅᴇɴ $\Big\}$
          Pèter mit Kárl

betrifft, sehr wahrscheinlich zu sein, dass das, was getilgt wird, genau einer
Th-Struktur entspricht, während das Rh-Element bzw. die Rh-Elemente
stehenbleiben. Den drei Tilgungsmöglichkeiten in (51) entsprechen z.B. genau
die drei verschiedenen möglichen Zerlegungen der Proposition 'Peter ist
mit Karl unzufrieden', durch die man die Propositionalfunktionen 'x ist
mit Karl unzufrieden', 'Peter ist mit x unzufrieden' und 'x ist mit y unzufrieden' erhält. Die Auffassung, dass es sich in solchen Fällen um Tilgungen
von Th-Strukturen handelt, erlaubt bei der zugrunde gelegten Analyse der
ThRh-Struktur also auch die Annahme, dass die Tilgung eine Anzahl von
Satzgliedern umfasst, die genau auf eine Konstituente der Tiefenstruktur
zurückgehen,[12] nämlich auf eine S-Struktur, die eine thematische Propositionalfunktion repräsentiert.

   Über solche Zusammenhänge mit Identitätsbedingungen enthaltenden
Regeln hinaus zeigt sich die Relevanz der ThRh-Struktur für das Problem
der II insbesondere in folgendem. Wenn Sätze wie (52)(a) und (53)(a) keine

(52)   (a) Karl ist mit sich unzufrieden
          (b) I'st ĕr nŭn mĭt sĭch ŭnzufrieden ŏder ni'cht? – *Er ist* (ni'cht)
          mit sich unzufrieden

          (c) $\begin{cases} \text{(Kárl)} \\ \text{(Karl sélber)} \end{cases}$ *ist mit sich unzufrieden*

          (d) Das kann ich nicht sagen. Jedenfalls bezweifle ich, dass
          (Kárl) *mit sich unzufrieden ist*

---

[12] Die Frage, auf welche Weise Elemente der derivierten Struktur Elemente früherer Ableitungsstufen, auf die sie zurückgehen, 'vertreten', spielt nicht nur für die uns hier interessierenden
Probleme eine Rolle, sondern scheint mir für eine Grammatiktheorie, die Ableitungsbedingungen
der Art fordert, wie sie die 'global derivational constraints' darstellen, überhaupt von wesent-
lichem prinzipiellen Interesse zu sein. Eine genaue Charakterisierung der betreffenden Prinzipien
steht m.W. noch aus.

      (e) Ist jemand mit sich unzufrieden?

      (f) Ist jemand mit Karl unzufrieden?

(53)   (a) $Karl_i$ weiss, was ihm_i bevorsteht

      (b) Wéiss ĕr$_i$, wăs ĭhm$_i$ bevŏrsteht, ŏder ni'cht? – *Er$_i$ weiss (ni'cht) was ihm$_i$ bevorsteht*

      (c) $\begin{cases}(Kárl_i)\\(Karl_i \text{ sélber})\end{cases}$ *weiss, was ihm$_i$ bevorsteht*

      (d) Das kann ich nicht sagen. Jedenfalls bezweifle ich, dass ($Kárl_i$) *weiss, was ihm$_i$ bevorsteht*

      (e) Weiss (irgendjemand von ihnen)$_i$, was ihm$_i$ bevorsteht?

      (f) Weiss (irgendjemand von ihnen)$_i$, was Karl bevorsteht?

ThRh-Aufteilung aufweisen, scheinen sie, soviel ich sehe, auch keinerlei Ambiguität zu zeigen (vgl. (52)(b) und (53)(b)). Sobald sie jedoch mit einer ThRh-Struktur wie die in den (c)- und (d)-Beispielen angedeutete verbunden sind, tritt eine Doppeldeutigkeit auf, deren Charakter bei der Verwendung der Sätze als Antwort auf die beiden Fragen (e) und (f) deutlich wird. (Bei der der (f)-Frage entsprechenden Bedeutung von (c) und (d) wird eine Verbindung des Rh-Elements mit *selber* vorgezogen). Das Th der in (52)(c) und (d) gekennzeichneten Sätze kann also im Prinzip teils dem Begriff 'unzufrieden mit sich', teils dem Begriff 'unzufrieden mit Karl' entsprechen. Dieser Strukturunterschied ist in (54) dargestellt:

(54)   (a) ($Kárl_{x_2}$) *ist mit sich unzufrieden*

      (b)

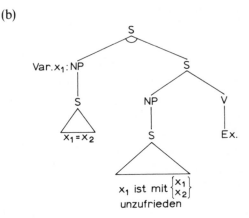

Ein Beispiel wie (55)(a) scheint sich demnach dadur ːh erklären zu lassen, dass man den Unterschied zwischen II und DI auf die Doppeldeutigkeit

(55)   (a) *Weiss* (Kárl$_{x_2}$) *was ihn erwartet?* – Nein, aber (Háns$_{x_3}$)

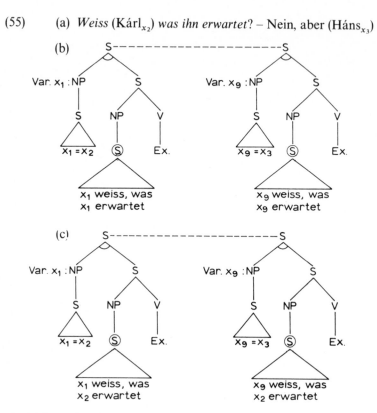

zurückführt, die die Frage in (55)(a) nach dem oben Gesagten aufweist. (55)(b) und (c) zeigen die relevanten Teile der anzusetzenden Tiefenstruktur von Frage und Antwort bei II ((b)) und DJ ((c)). In beiden Fällen werden Elemente getilgt, die auf eine S-Struktur zurückgehen (die eingekreiste S-Struktur der Antwort), die einer Propositionalfunktion entspricht. Als 'indirekt identisches Element' der Antwort in (b) tritt also an sich nicht der Index von 'Hans', sondern die Argumentvariable der betreffenden Propositionalfunktion auf. In beiden Fällen handelt es sich zudem um eine Tilgung auf Grund genauer Tiefenstrukturidentität zwischen zwei ganzen S-Strukturen (den eingekreisten). Diese Gleichheit ist von der Art, wie sie ohnehin für S-Strukturen angenommen werden muss, die sich auf Propositionalfunktion beziehen (vgl. oben S. 492).

Zusammenhänge dieser Art zwischen ThRh-Struktur, Tilgungen und II könnten die Hoffnung aufkommen lassen, der Unterschied zwischen DI und II liesse sich immer auf subtile Ambiguitäten in der ThRh-Struktur der Korrelatkette zurückführen. Dies ist, wie oben unter Punkt (3) schon erwähnt wurde, jedoch nicht der Fall. Bei einer genauen Überprüfung der

Beispiele mit DI und II bestätigt sich vielmehr die ursprüngliche Annahme, dass die Doppeldeutigkeit dieser Beispiele nicht allgemein durch irgendeine strukturelle Ambiguität der Korrelatkette erklärt werden kann, sondern dass es tatsächlich möglich sein muss, dass syntaktische Regeln ein und dieselbe Struktur als mit zwei verschiedenen Strukturen identisch betrachten. Vgl. die Beispiele

(56)   (a) Weiss er$_i$, was ihm$_i$ bevorsteht? – Er$_i$ weiss ni'cht, was ihm$_i$ bevorsteht – Aber sein Bruder doch wohl?

    (b) Ist Karl sehr unzufrieden mit sich? – Ja, er ist ebenso unzufrieden mit sich wie der Lehrer

    (c) Wenn jemand unzufrieden mit sich ist, sind seine Mitarbeiter es auch

(57)   (a) Wer$_i$ weiss nicht, was ihm$_i$ bevorsteht? – (Karl) *weiss nicht, was ihm bevorsteht*, allerdings weiss das seine Frau auch nicht

    (b) Wer ist mit sich unzufrieden? – (Karl) *ist mit sich unzufrieden*, und doch ist sein Lehrer das gar nicht

(58)   (a) Karl sieht ein, dass er dumm ist, aber Peter nicht, obwohl sogar seine Frau das tut /u.a. = x_1 sieht ein, dass x_1 dumm ist, aber x_2 sieht nicht ein, dass x_2 dumm ist, obwohl sogar x_3 einsieht, dass x_2 dumm ist/

    (b) Karl ist nicht unzufrieden mit sich, wohl aber Peter, und zwar mindestens ebenso sehr wie sein Lehrer /u.a. = x_1 ist nicht unzufrieden mit x_1, wohl aber ist x_2 unzufrieden mit x_2, und zwar ist x_2 mindestens ebenso unzufrieden mit x_2, wie x_3 mit x_2 unzufrieden ist/

In (56) zeigen die Korrelatketten keine ThRh-Aufteilung der Art, wie sie in (55) vorliegt (in Fällen wie (56)(c) ist eine solche Aufteilung überhaupt unmöglich), und lassen offensichtlich auch keine entsprechende Ambiguität erkennen. Trotzdem ist sowohl DI wie II möglich. In (57) zeigt die Korrelatkette zwar eine ThRh-Aufteilung der relevanten Art, aber diese ist durch den Zusammenhang so festgelegt, dass nur II möglich sein müsste. Trotzdem ist auch DI möglich. Den entscheidenden Beweis liefern jedoch Beispiele wie (58). Diese scheinen nämlich u.a. auch die angegebenen Bedeutungen haben zu können. Dann ist aber die Struktur, deren Subjekt *Peter* ist, auf Grund von II mit ihrem Korrelat getilgt worden, während sie gleichzeitig ihrerseits Korrelat einer zweiten, auf Grund von DI getilgten Struktur ist (in (58)(b) vermutlich durch Vermittlung einer weiteren getilgten Kette, die unmittelbar Hauptsatz des Vergleichssatzes ist).[13] D.h., ein und dieselbe Teilstruktur eines Satzes scheint gleichzeitig mit zwei anderen, eindeutig voneinander verschiedenen Teilstrukturen identisch zu sein. Derartige Beispiele schliessen, soviel ich sehe, jegliche Erklärung des Unterschieds zwischen II und DI als Reflex einer strukturellen Ambiguität der Korrelatkette aus, welcher Art diese Ambiguität auch sein möge. Wir müssen also offensichtlich darauf verzichten, die doppeldeutigen Beispiele mit II und DI grundsätzlich als Fälle genauer Tiefenstrukturidentität zu erklären, und uns mit dem ursprünglich aufgestellten Ziel begnügen, diese Erscheinungen durch eine Abschwächung des Begriffs der GRI zu erfassen. Allerdings zeigt sich uns der Unterschied zwischen DI und II auf Grund unsrer Analyse der ThRh-Struktur jetzt nicht mehr als ein Unterschied zwischen 'genauer' und 'ungenauer' Identität. So erscheinen uns einerseits manche Fälle, wo wir von II gesprochen haben, jetzt als Fälle genauer Tiefenstrukturidentität, etwa (55)(b), während wir andrerseits in Beispielen wie (57) und (58) Tilgungen auf Grund ungenauer Tiefenstrukturidentität antreffen, die wir als Fälle von DI angesprochen haben. Es erscheint deshalb ratsam, den Begriffen DI und II, die wir auch weiterhin auf die gleichen Fälle wie bisher anwenden wollen, eine Unterscheidung zwischen genauer, strikter Identität (SI) und ungenauer, nichtstrikter Identität (NSI) gegenüberzustellen. Unsre Aufgabe besteht dann darin, den Charakter dieser NSI, die uns in Beispielen wie (56)–(58) entgegentritt, zu definieren.

Angesichts der wichtigen Rolle, welche die ThRh-Struktur für die uns hier interessierenden Erscheinungen zu spielen scheint, neige ich der Auffassung zu, dass es sich in Beispielen wie (56)–(58) um einen Th-Wechsel handelt, dem zufolge das Th einer bestimmten Rh-Aussage, etwa 'x sieht ein, dass x dumm ist' in (Péter) *sieht ein, dass er dumm ist* in (58)(a) in ein anderes Th, 'x sieht ein, dass Peter dumm ist', umgedeutet wird. Es hat den Anschein, als repräsentiere eine S-Struktur gewissermassen gleichzeitig ihre verschiedenen möglichen ThRh-Aufteilungen, so dass die entsprechenden potentiellen Th-Strukturen anderen S-Strukturen als Korrelat dienen könnten. Ich möchte deshalb folgende, zugegebenermassen höchst provisorische Charakterisierung der NSI geben:

Eine S-Struktur S′ kann als Korrelat einer S-Struktur S″ fungieren, wenn S″ mit einer der Th-Strukturen identisch ist, die durch die verschiedenen ThRh-Aufteilungen von S′ entstehen, oder, falls S′ selber Th ist, wenn S″ mit der S-Struktur S‴ identisch ist, die durch Einsetzen des Rh-Elements

---

[13] Es sei darauf hingewiesen, dass (58)(a) und (b) ausserdem zu den Beispielen gehören, die zeigen, dass getilgte Strukturen Korrelatfunktion haben können, eine interessante Tatsache, auf die wir hier jedoch nicht eingehen können.

in die entsprechenden Variablenstellen in S' entsteht, oder mit einer der Th-Strukturen, die durch die verschiedenen ThRh-Aufteilungen von S''' entstehen.

Diese Definition ist vermutlich in mancher Hinsicht zu weit. So scheint eine Umdeutung wie die in

(59)   Peters Frau weiss, was ihm bevorsteht, aber Peter selber nicht, obwohl sogar Hans das tut /? $\neq x_1$ weiss, was x_2 bevorsteht, aber x_2 selber weiss nicht, was x_2 bevorsteht, obwohl sogar x_3 weiss, was x_3 bevorsteht/

aus einem mir unbekannten Grunde unmöglich oder wenigstens wesentlich schwerer zu sein als die in (58)(a), deren Umkehrung sie ja in gewissem Sinne ist. Dies ist um so eigenartiger, als in Fällen wie

(60)   Mit wem ist er unzufrieden? – Mit sich selber. – Das war sein Vater aber nie /u.a. = Mit wem ist x_1 unzufrieden? – x_1 ist mit x_1 unzufrieden – x_2 war aber nie mit x_2 unzufrieden/

eine Umdeutung anscheinend möglich ist.

Ich habe die NSI also als eine Beziehung zwischen S-Strukturen definiert. In der Tat glaube ich, dass die uns hier interessierenden Erscheinungen, vor allem auch die Fälle mit II, nur so richtig zu erfassen sind. Die Umdeutungen, mit denen wir es bei NSI anscheinend zu tun haben, haben nun jedoch in vielen Fällen den Charakter einer 'Verwechslung' miteinander identifizierter referentieller Elemente, die einer Einsetzung eines Arguments in Variablenpositionen der thematischen Propositionalfunktion entspricht. Es mag in diesem Zusammenhang von Interesse sein, dass derartige 'Verwechslungen' auch in anderen als den bisher behandelten Fällen vielfach eine Rolle zu spielen scheinen, so etwa in den verwandten Fällen in (61)(a)–(c), aber auch etwa in andersgearteten Beispielen wie (61)(d):

(61)   (a) Wer$_i$ ist es, der behauptet, dass er$_i$ Chinesisch könne?
            – Karl$_j$ (ist es, der behauptet, dass er Chinesisch könne), aber das /= dass er$_j$ Chinesisch kann/ ist natürlich nicht wahr

        (b) Wer ist es, der behauptet, Chinesisch zu können? – Karl$_j$ (ist es, der behauptet, Chinesisch zu können), aber das /= dass er$_j$ Chinesisch kann/ ist natürlich nicht wahr

        (c) Versuchte jemand zu fliehen? – Ja, Karl$_j$ (versuchte zu fliehen), aber Peter verhinderte es /= dass er$_j$ floh/

        (d) Keiner von denen, die sich geirrt hatten, wollte es /= dass er sich geirrt hatte/ zugeben

Auch scheinen z.B. manche Kongruenzerscheinungen bei Pronomen eine ungenaue referentielle Äquivalenz vorauszusetzen, eine Erscheinung, auf die wir zurückkommen werden (vgl. S. 522).

4. WEITERE PROBLEME

Wir wollen nun abschliessend kurz auf einige weitere Erscheinungen im Umkreis der II eingehen, um uns einen gewissen Überblick darüber zu verschaffen, welche Erklärungsmöglichkeiten uns durch die oben skizzierte Auffassung der NSI im allgemeinen und der II im besonderen als Beziehungen in der Tiefenstruktur zwischen S-Strukturen bestimmter Art gegeben sind.

Zu diesem Zweck müssen wir zunächst auf einen Aspekt der II hinweisen, den wir bisher stillschweigend übergangen haben. Wir haben in Fällen wie

(62)   (a) Nicht nur Karl$_i$ glaubt, dass er$_i$ krank sei, sondern auch Peter$_j$ (glaubt, dass er$_j$ krank sei)

(b) Nicht nur Karl$_i$ hat $\begin{cases} \text{den Hausaufsatz, den er}_i \text{ abgegeben} \\ \text{seinen}_i \text{ Hausaufsatz} \end{cases}$

hat $\Big\}$ ohne fremde Hilfe geschrieben, sondern auch Peter$_j$

(hat $\begin{cases} \text{den Hausaufsatz, den er}_j \text{ abgegeben hat,} \\ \text{seinen}_j \text{ Hausaufsatz} \end{cases}$ $\Big\}$ ohne fremde Hilfe geschrieben)

die indizierten Pronomen als indirekt identische Elemente angesprochen. Im Grunde sind aber auch die NP *dass er krank sei* in (a) bzw. *den Hausaufsatz, den er abgegeben hat* (*seinen Hausaufsatz*) in (b) indirekt identisch. Dies folgt in natürlicher Weise aus der Annahme, dass es sich bei II um Gleichheit zwischen S-Strukturen handelt, die ganze Propositionalfunktionen repräsentieren, wenn wir voraussetzen, dass wir es nicht nur in (62)(a), wo *dass er krank sei* gewissermassen der Name eines referentiellen Elements ist, sondern auch in (62)(b), wo *den Hausaufsatz, den er abgegeben hat* (bzw. *seinen Hausaufsatz*) ein referentielles Element begrifflich charakterisiert, mit S-Strukturen zu tun haben, welche notwendige Teile der jeweiligen Th-Strukturen sind und die Argumentvariablen der entsprechenden Propositionalfunktionen enthalten.[14] Wir können dann nämlich Tiefenstrukturen der in

[14] Eine solche Analyse wird etwa auch von Beispielen wie

(I)   (a) Karl$_i$ behauptet, dass nicht er$_i$ mit seinem$_i$ Chef verwandt sei, sondern Peter
        (b) Karl$_i$ behauptet, dass nicht er$_i$ mit seinem$_i$ Bruder verwandt sei, sondern Peter

(63) (a) Hat nur Karl$_{x_2}$ den Hausaufsatz, den er abgegeben hat, ohne fremde Hilfe geschrieben? – Nein, auch Peter$_{x_3}$

(b)

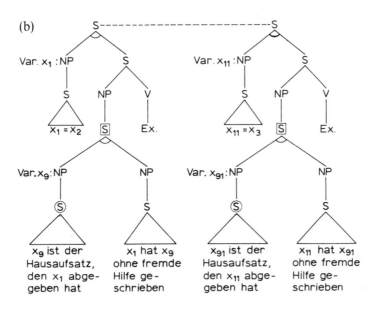

angedeuteten Art ansetzen, in denen die betreffenden Teilsätze Ⓢ auf Grund ihrer Eigenschaft, entsprechende Teile gleicher S-Strukturen [S], deren Identität ähnlicher Art wie die in (28)(c) ist) zu sein, als gleich angesprochen werden können. Diese Art der Gleichheit erklärt dann auch Fälle wie

(64) (a) Nicht nur Karl$_i$ glaubt, dass er$_i$ krank sei, sondern auch Peter$_j$ glaubt das / = dass er$_j$ krank sei/

   (b) Hat nur Karl$_i$ $\begin{cases} \text{den Hausaufsatz, den er}_i \text{ abgegeben hat,} \\ \text{seinen}_i \text{ Hausaufsatz} \end{cases} \begin{matrix} 1 \\ 2 \end{matrix}$
   ohne fremde Hilfe geschrieben? – Nein, auch Peter$_j$ hat
   ihn / = $\begin{cases} \text{den Hausaufsatz, den er}_j \text{ abgegeben hat,} \\ \text{seinen}_j \text{ Hausaufsatz} \end{cases} \begin{matrix} 1 \\ 2 \end{matrix}$ / ohne
   fremde Hilfe geschrieben

in denen wir es offenbar mit Pronominalisierungen zu tun haben, deren Identitätsforderung sich nur auf entsprechende Teilstrukturen gleicher

bestätigt. In (a) ist II nur dann möglich, wenn die Beschreibung *seinem Chef* Teil der Behauptung Karls ist. In (b), wo es naheliegt, *seinem Bruder* als eine Beschreibung aufzufassen, die auf den Sprecher zurückgeht, ist dementsprechend nur DI normal.

Propositionalfunktionen bezieht.[15] Wenn man mit Ross (1969a, 1969c) annimmt, dass es sich bei Ausdrücken wie *es sein, das sein, es tun, das tun* im Grunde um Satzpronominalisierungen handelt, lassen sich auch Beispiele wie

(65)　　(a) Nicht nur Karl$_i$ ist mit dir unzufrieden / = Karl$_i$ ist, (er$_i$) mit dir unzufrieden/, sondern auch Peter$_j$ ist es / = (er$_j$) mit dir unzufrieden/

　　　　(b) Nicht nur Karl$_i$ arbeitet daran / = Karl$_i$ tut, (er$_i$) daran arbeiten/, sondern auch Peter$_j$ tut das / = (er$_j$) daran arbeiten/

in analoger Weise deuten, nämlich im Prinzip wie (64)(a).

Wir wenden uns nun erneut der Frage zu, in welcher Hinsicht die Relation der indirekt identischen Elemente zu ihrem jeweiligen Hauptelement gleich sein muss. In Fällen, in denen eine ganze Th-Struktur getilgt wird, ist diese Gleichheit selbstverständlich dadurch gegeben, dass die indirekt identischen Elemente und die durch die Hauptelemente (d.h. normalerweise die Rh-Elemente) besetzten Variablenpositionen in der Th-Struktur und der mit dieser identischen Korrelatstruktur entsprechende Stellen haben. Auch in Fällen, in denen eine mit einer Identitätsbedingung verbundene Regel nur auf einen Teil des Themas angewendet wird, liegt die Identität der Th-Struktur mit ihrem Korrelat in der Tiefenstruktur und damit auch die Gleichheit der Relation zwischen den indirekt identischen Elementen und den Hauptelementen oft auf der Hand (so etwa in (64) und wohl auch in (36)). Beispiele wie

(66)　　Der èrste$_i$ ärgerte sich zwar darüber, dass man ihm$_i$ einen Spitznamen gab, aber den zwèiten$_j$ kúmmerte es / = dass man ihm$_j$ einen Spitznamen gab/ überhaupt nicht, der drìtte$_k$ machte sich sogar darüber / = dass man ihm$_k$ einen Spiznamen gab/ lústig, und der vièrte$_l$ erfúhr es / = dass man ihm$_l$ einen Spitznamen gab/ erst gar nicht

sind jedoch nicht so leicht zu deuten. Das, was hier in den vier Fällen gleich ist und als gemeinsames Th angesprochen werden könnte, scheint nicht viel mehr zu sein als die Voraussetzung, dass es sich um irgendeine Beziehung zwischen einer Person und der Tatsache, dass man dieser Person einen Spitznamen gab, handelt. Wir müssen also wohl annehmen, dass wir es mit einem untergeordneten Th der Form R (x, man gab x einen Spitznamen) zu

---

[15] In Fällen wie (64)(b), in denen die begriffliche Charakterisierung einer Variablen getilgt wird, kommen weitere, besondere Bedingungen hinzu, auf die wir hier nicht eingehen können.

tun haben, in das zunächst für x der Index der jeweiligen Person als unter-
geordnetes Rh-Element und dann für R die betreffende Relation als über-
geordnetes Rh-Element eingesetzt wird. Eine solche Analyse, die auch durch
die Betonungsverhältnisse bestätigt zu werden scheint, erlaubt es, die den
Pronominalisierungen zugrunde liegende Identität in (66) ebenso zu deuten
wie in (64). Noch problematischer sind nun aber Fälle wie

(67)   Nich nur (Kárl$_i$) *ist überzeugt davon, dass* er$_i$ *ein Genie sei,*
         sondern auch (Péter$_j$) *bildet sich das* /= dass er$_j$ ein Genie sei/
         ein

Um (67) ebenso erklären zu können wie (66), müssten wir eine weitere Aufteilung der angedeuteten Th-Strukturen annehmen, die einen gemeinsamen
'Rahmen' ergäbe. Ich möchte diese Möglichkeit nicht völlig ausschliessen,
bin mir aber keineswegs darüber klar, wie eine solche Aufteilung vorzunehmen wäre. Alternativ müssten für S-Strukturen, die eine Argumentvariable einer Propositionalfunktion enthalten, von der sie ein Teil sind,
besondere Identitätsbedingungen formuliert werden. Man beachte in
diesem Zusammenhang, dass die eingekreisten S-Strukturen in (63)(b) den
bisher angegebenen Identitätsbedingungen genügen, falls x_1 und x_{11} als
gleich angesehen werden, etwa auf Grund gleicher Voraussetzungen über
ihren referentiellen Bereich.[16]

[16] Ich bin der Überzeugung, dass die hier diskutierten Zusammenhänge für die Erklärung der
sog. Bach-Peters-Sätze (vgl. (I)) wesentlich sind. Sicherlich haben wir es nämlich in (I) und (II)–
(IV)

(I)   Derjenige$_i$, der ihn$_j$ verdiente, bekam den Preis$_j$, den er$_i$ haben wollte

(II)   Bekam jeder$_i$ den Preis, den er$_i$ haben wollte?

         – Nein, nur derjenige, der $\left\{{\text{den} \atop \text{ihn}}\right\}$ Preis, den er haben wollte, verdiente, bekam

         $\left\{{\text{den} \atop \text{ihn}}\right\}$ Preis, den er haben wollte

(III)   Derjenige$_j$, dessen Bruder$_i$ $\left\{{\text{wusste,} \atop \text{es wusste}}\right\}$ was er$_i$ zu tun hatte, wusste $\left\{{\text{selber nicht,} \atop \text{es selber nicht}}\right\}$

         was er$_j$ zu tun hatte

(IV)   Sowohl Karl wie Peter fanden einen Pilz, aber während Karl $\left\{{\text{den Pilz} \atop \text{ihn}}\right\}$ mitnahm,

         liess Peter $\left\{{\text{den Pilz} \atop \text{ihn}}\right\}$ stehen

mit Erscheinungen der gleichen Art zu tun, nämlich mit II. Die übliche Deutung der Bach-
Peters-Sätze, bei der eine normale, direkte Identität zwischen den indizierten NP in (I)
angenommen wird, versagt aber in (II)–(IV) völlig. Die übliche Deutung der Bach-Peters-Sätze
ist in ähnlicher Weise auch von Karttunen (1969) angezweifelt worden, der die besonderen
Eigenschaften dieser Sätze auf das Auftreten von 'non-referential pronouns' zurückführt, die
Frage nach der Art der Identität zwischen 'nichtreferentiell' gebrauchten NP allerdings
weitgehend offen lässt.

Eine weitere wichtige Frage, die wir bisher noch nicht erörtert haben, ist die nach der Abhängigkeitsrelation zwischen den indirekt identischen Elementen und ihren Hauptelementen. Einige der Auswirkungen der Bedingung, dass die Hauptelemente den indirekt identischen Elementen in einem bestimmten Sinne übergeordnet sein müssen, zeigen die Beispiele in

(68)   (a) (1) Er ist ebenso unzufrieden mit sich wie der Lehrer /II/
              (2) Mit sich (selber) ist er ebenso unzufrieden wie der Lehrer /II/

          (b) (1) Er ist ebenso unzufrieden mit sich wie mit dem Lehrer
              (2) Mit sich (selber) ist er ebenso unzufrieden wie mit dem Lehrer

          (c) (1) Er schickt seine Kinder ebenso oft in die Schweiz wie Peter (es tut) /II/
              (2) Seine Kinder schickt er ebenso oft in die Schweiz wie Peter (es tut) /II/

          (d) (1) Er schickt seine Kinder ebenso oft in die Schweiz wie Peters (Kinder)
              (2) Seine Kinder schickt er ebenso oft in die Schweiz wie Peters (Kinder)

          (e) (1) Seine Kinder wurden von ihm ebenso oft in die Schweiz geschickt wie von Peter
              (2) Von ihm wurden seine Kinder ebenso oft in die Schweiz geschickt wie von Peter

          (f) Er bat mich ebenso inständig darum, ihn nach Hause zu fahren wie Peter (es tat) /II/

          (g) Er bat mich ebenso inständig darum, ihn nach Hause zu fahren wie darum, dich nach Hause zu fahren

wo die Fälle, in denen II möglich ist, besonders gekennzeichnet sind. Ross (vgl. Anm. 8) hat angenommen, dass der Charakter dieser Abhängigkeitsrelation mit dem von Langacker (1969) eingeführten Begriff 'command' beschrieben werden könne, der dadurch definiert ist, dass ein Knoten A einem anderen Knoten B genau dann im Sinne von 'command' übergeordnet ist, wenn erstens keiner der Knoten den anderen dominiert und zweitens der S-Knoten, der als nächster A dominiert, auch B dominiert. Dass dieser Begriff nicht ohne weiteres, zumal nicht ohne Angabe der relevanten Ableitungsstufe, zur Erklärung der betreffenden Abhängigkeitsrelation herangezogen werden kann, zeigen jedoch schon Fälle wie (68)(b) und (d). Ich möchte annehmen, dass wir es statt dessen mit einer Hierarchie in der Tiefenstruktur zu tun haben, die u.a. NP innerhalb von S-Strukturen, die sich auf Propositionalfunktionen beziehen, derart einander überordnet, dass etwa eine NP = A einer anderen NP = B desselben Elementarsatzes übergeordnet ist, wenn A Subjekt ist, und dass eine NP = A einer anderen NP = B, die nicht im selben Elementarsatz steht, übergeordnet ist, wenn B in einer S-Struktur enthalten ist, die eine NP = C im selben Elementarsatz wie A entweder selber darstellt oder begrifflich charakterisiert. Fälle wie (68), sowie viele ähnliche Erscheinungen, sind nun m.E. auf Restriktionen zurückzuführen, welche die Möglichkeit referentiell äquivalenter NP, auf späteren Ableitungsstufen in anaphorische Beziehungen zueinander zu treten, u.a. eben auf Grund jener Tiefenstrukturhierarchie einschränken. Insbesondere scheinen mir Fälle wie (68) so erklärt werden zu können, dass die Argumentvariable der Propositionalfunktion, die der getilgten S-Struktur entspricht, bei II ja mindestens an zwei Stellen vorkommen muss und dass der variablenbindende Ausdruck in Form des Rh-Elements nur an der Stelle eingesetzt werden kann, die allen anderen im Sinne der genannten Hierarchie übergeordnet ist. Vermutlich sind auch noch weitere, strengere Bedingungen im Spiele. Obwohl ich auf diese im einzelnen sehr komplizierten Zusammenhänge nicht näher eingehen kann, glaube ich doch sagen zu können, dass es sich hier um Regularitäten handelt, die ohnehin angenommen werden müssen und bei der zugrunde gelegten Auffassung über das Wesen der II auch Fälle wie (68) mit erklären. Man vergleiche etwa Beispiele wie

(69)   (a) Wer ist unzufrieden mit sich?

(b) *Mit wem$_i$ ist er$_i$ unzufrieden?

(c) Wer$_i$ schickt seine$_i$ Kinder in die Schweiz?

(d) *Wessen$_i$ Kinder schickt er$_i$ in die Schweiz?

(e) *Von wem$_i$ wurden seine$_i$ Kinder in die Schweiz geschickt?

wo die genaue Übereinstimmung mit den Verhältnissen in (68)(a)–(e) darauf hindeutet, dass es sich um die gleichen Restriktionen handelt.

Das Fehlen indirekter Identität in (71) (im Gegensatz zu (32)(b) und (70))[17]

(70)   (a) (*Mit sich sèlber*) WAR (nicht nur Kárl) UNZUFRIEDEN, sondern (auch Péter)

[17] Auf Unterschiede dieser Art hat mich Östen Dahl anhand der schwedischen Beispiele *Sin fru älskar bara han* = Sein Frau liebt nur er/ und *Min fru älskar bara jag/* = Meine Frau liebe nur ich/ aufmerksam gemacht (vgl. Dahl (1970)). Seiner Erklärung dieser Beispiele schließe ich mich in dem wesentlichen Punkte an, dass es sich um ein Zusammenwirken von sekundärer Personalkongruenz und Oberflächenrestriktionen handelt.

> (b) (*Mit seinen Lèistungen*) WAR (nicht nur Kárl) UNZUFRIEDEN, sondern (auch Péter)
>
> (c) (*Was ihm bevòrsteht*) WEISS (nicht nur Kárl), sondern (auch Péter)

(71) (a) (*Mit mir sèlber*) WAR (nicht nur ĭch) UNZUFRIEDEN, sondern (auch Péter)

(b) *Mit meinen Lèistungen*) WAR (nicht nur ích) UNZUFRIEDEN, sondern (auch Péter)

(c) (*Was mir bevòrsteht*) WEISS (nicht nur ĭch), sondern (auch Péter)

lässt sich vermutlich mit Hilfe der Regeln erklären, die das Reflexivpronomen und die Personalpronomen der ersten und zweiten Person auf Grund ungenauer Variablenidentität ableiten. Wie wir schon sahen (vgl. (52) und (54)), kann ein Pronomen offensichtlich auch dann das Merkmal der Reflexivität erhalten, wenn es in der Tiefenstruktur an sich nicht direkt mit dem Subjekt identisch ist, sondern mit einem referentiellen Element, mit dem das Subjekt identifiziert wird. Entsprechendes gilt in den nahe verwandten Fällen

(72) (a) Wer ist es, der mit sich unzufrieden ist?
      – Karl ist es, der mit sich unzufrieden ist

(b) Wer ist es, der mit Karl unzufrieden ist?
      – Karl selber ist es, der mit sich unzufrieden ist

Auch andere Merkmale können auf Grund einer solchen 'Verwechslung' miteinander identifizierter Variablen auftreten. So tritt z.B. in

(73) (a) Wer ist mit sich unzufrieden? – (Ích) *bin mit mir unzufrieden*

(b) Wer ist mit seinen Leistungen unzufrieden? – (Ích) *bin mit meinen Leistungen unzufrieden*

(c) Wer weiss, was ihm bevorsteht? – (Ích) *weiss, was mir bevorsteht*

statt des zu erwartenden Reflexivpronomens bzw. Personalpronomens der 3. Person das Pronomen der 1. Person auf. Diese sekundäre Personal-kongruenz unterliegt nun jedoch anscheinend gewissen Beschränkungen. Teils tritt sie, im Gegensatz zu der sekundären Reflexivisierung, wohl nicht in Fällen wie

(74) (a) Wer ist es, der mit sich unzufrieden ist?
      – Ich bin es, der mit sich unzufrieden ist

(b) Wer ist es, der$_i$ mit seinen$_i$ Leistungen unzufrieden ist?
  – Ich bin es, der mit seinen Leistungen unzufrieden ist
(c) Wer ist es, der$_i$ weiss, was ihm$_i$ bevorsteht?
  Ich bin es, der weiss, was ihm bevorsteht

auf, teils scheint sie eher 'von links nach rechts' als 'von rechts nach links' wirksam zu sein, eine Annahme, für die u.a. auch Beispiele wie (II) in Anmerkung 9 sprechen. In Fällen, in denen ein referentielles Element der Th-Struktur dem Rh-Element vorausgeht, erfolgt die Kennzeichnung des referentiellen Elements wohl überhaupt eher auf Grund dessen, was durch das Th gegeben ist, als auf Grund der durch die Rh-Aussage hinzugefügten Information. Dies erklärt u.a. wohl auch, warum in (75)(a), im Gegensatz zu (b) und (c), keine II möglich zu sein scheint. Da auf Grund der durch *nicht*

(75)   (a) Was er zu tun hat, weiss nicht nur Karl, sondern auch seine
             Schwester

         (b) Was er zu tun hat, weiss nich nur Karl, sondern auch Peter

         (c) Nicht nur Karl weiss, was er zu tun hat, sondern auch seine
             Schwester

nur und *auch* ausgedrückten Voraussetzungsverhältnisse ein Th-Wechsel anscheinend ausgeschlossen ist, (wir werden gleich darauf zurückkommen) müsste nämlich das Pronomen *er* in (a) bei II die Argumentvariable der thematischen Propositionalfunktion vertreten. Die Wahl der maskulinen Form des Pronomens wäre dann aber (wie in (b)) mit einer Voraussetzung über den referentiellen Bereich dieser Variablen verbunden, die das Einsetzen eines Arguments wie 'seine Schwester' nicht zuliesse. Diesen Überlegungen zufolge kann also das Pronomen im übergeordneten Th in (71) das Merkmal der 1. Person nicht durch sekundäre Kongruenz mit dem Rh-Element erhalten haben, sondern dies Merkmal muss Kennzeichnung des Index der 1. Person in der Th-Struktur sein. Da ein Wechsel des übergeordneten Themas auch hier nicht möglich ist, ist somit II ausgeschlossen. Warum allerdings diejenige Form der Korrelatsätze, bei der nach dem oben Gesagten II möglich sein müsste, nämlich

(76)   (a) *Mit sich selber war nicht nur ich unzufrieden
         (b) *Mit seinen$_i$ Leistungen war nicht nur ich$_i$ unzufrieden
         (c) *Was ihm$_i$ bevorsteht, weiss nicht nur ich$_i$

ungrammatisch ist, ist mir nicht ganz klar. Vielleicht ist hier eine Oberflächenrestriktion im Spiele.

In einer ganzen Reihe von Fällen ist wider Erwarten die Möglichkeit direkter Identität ausgeschlossen und also nur II möglich. Wie wir eben bei Ausdrücken mit *nur* und *auch* sahen, können die Voraussetzungsverhältnisse derart sein, dass ein Th-Wechsel unnatürlich wirkt. Dies erklärt, dass in Beispielen wie

(77)   (a) Wer ist mit sich unzufrieden? Nur Karl$_i$? $\left\{ \begin{array}{l} - \text{Nein, auch} \\ - \text{*Nein, (auch} \end{array} \right.$

$\left. \begin{array}{l} \text{Peter}_j \\ \text{Péter}_j) \textit{ ist mit ihm}_i \textit{ unzufrieden} \end{array} \right\}$

(b) Nicht nur Karl$_i$ ist mit sich unzufrieden, sondern auch Peter$_j$,

$\left\{ \begin{array}{l} \text{ja, sogar dessen Frau} \\ ^{??}\text{ja, (sogar dessen Fráu)} \textit{ ist mit ihm}_j \textit{ unzufrieden} \end{array} \right\}$

im Gegensatz etwa zu (57) und (58), eine Umdeutung des Themas und damit DI bei der letzten Tilgung nicht gut möglich ist.

Beispiele wie

(78)   (a) Karl$_i$ hofft, dass er$_i$ gewählt wird, und Peter

$\left(\left\{ \begin{array}{l} \text{hofft} \\ \text{tut} \end{array} \right\} \text{das} \right) \text{auch}$

(b) Karl hofft, gewählt zu werden, und Peter $\left(\left\{ \begin{array}{l} \text{hofft} \\ \text{tut} \end{array} \right\} \text{das} \right) \text{auch}$

(79)   (a) Karl$_i$ hat in diesem Jahr ebensoviel verdient, wie er$_i$ im vorigen Jahr verdient hat, $\left\{ \begin{array}{l} \text{und Peter hat sogar noch mehr} \\ \text{und Peter sogar noch mehr} \end{array} \right.$

verdient$\left. \begin{array}{l} \\ \end{array} \right\}$

(b) Karl hat in diesem Jahr ebensoviel verdient wie im vorigen Jahr $\left\{ \begin{array}{l} \text{und Peter hat sogar noch mehr verdient} \\ \text{und Peter sogar noch mehr} \end{array} \right\}$

sind dagegen nicht so leicht zu erklären. Während in den (a)-Beispielen, in denen ein auf *Karl* sich beziehendes Pronomen auftritt, sowohl II wie DI möglich zu sein scheint, ist in den (b)-Beispielen, in denen das entsprechende referentielle Element getilgt worden ist, nur II denkbar. Man könnte zunächst meinen, dieser Unterschied wäre allein auf die Tilgung als solche zurückzuführen und wir hätten es nun doch mit einem Fall zu tun, in dem die derivierte Struktur eindeutig eine Rolle für die GRI spielt. Es scheint jedoch manches gegen eine solche Deutung zu sprechen, vor allem der Umstand, dass die durch Tilgungen herbeigeführten Unterschiede in der derivierten Struktur sonst an sich wohl nicht berücksichtigt werden, wie schon (61)(b) und (c) zeigen. Zudem zeigen die Konstruktionen in (78)(b) und (79)(b) gewisse Eigenschaften, die darauf schliessen lassen, dass wir es auch hier eher mit besonderen Voraussetzungsverhältnissen in der Tiefenstruktur zu tun haben. So scheinen die Tilgunsoperationen in (78)(b) und (79)(b), anders als etwa die Reflexivisierung, genaue Identität in der Tiefenstruktur zu fordern. Vgl.:[18]

(80)   (a) Wer hofft, dass Karl gewählt wird?

      – (Karl sélber z.B.) *höfft, dăss ĕr gewählt wĭrd*

      (b)[??] Wer hofft, dass Karl gewählt wird?

      – (Karl sélber z.B.) *höfft gewählt zŭ wĕrden*

(81)   (a) Wer hat in diesem Jahr ebensoviel verdient wie Karl im vorigen Jahr?

      – (Karl sélber) *hăt ĭn dĭesem Jăhr ĕbensoviel verdĭent wĭe ĕr ĭm vŏrigen Jăhr verdient hăt*

      (b)[??] Wer hat in diesem Jahr ebensoviel verdient wie Karl im vorigen Jahr?

      – (Karl sélber) *hăt ĭn dĭesem Jăhr ĕbensoviel verdĭent wĭe ĭm vŏrigen Jăhr*

Dies erklärt allerdings noch nicht, warum nicht auch in (78)(b) und (79)(b), wie in (78)(a) und (79)(a), eine Umdeutung und damit eine Tilgung auf Grund von NSI möglich ist. Obwohl mir keineswegs klar ist, wie dies zu verstehen ist, könnte hier vielleicht doch die Beobachtung weiterhelfen, dass in Fällen wie (78)(b) II anscheinend nur dann notwendig ist, wenn das übergeordnete Verb mit zum Th des nachfolgenden Satzes gehört. Man vergleiche etwa

(82)   (a) Karl will nach Italien reisen, aber Pèter will das ni'cht
      (b) Karl will nach Italien reisen, aber Pèter wi'll das nicht

wo nur in (a) II notwendig ist, während in (b) sogar nur DI möglich ist. Vielleicht lässt sich dies so deuten, dass in Fällen wie (78)(b) und (79)(b) diejenige Konstruktion, welche die S-Struktur mit dem getilgten referentiellen Element sowie dessen Tiefenstrukturkorrelat unmittelbar enthält,

---

[18] Beispiele wie (80) sind auch von Morgan (1970) im Englischen beobachtet worden. Er sieht ihre Erklärung darin, dass Equi-NP-Deletion nur Variable (im Gegensatz zu Konstanten) tilgen könne.

auf irgendeine Weise mit der Voraussetzung verbunden ist, dass die Positionen dieser beiden referentiellen Elemente durch die gleiche Variable besetzt sein müssen. Wenn diese Konstruktion dann im nachfolgenden Satz als thematische Struktur auftritt, wird die gennante Voraussetzung mit hinübergenommen und verhindert so DI.

Mit den Beispielen, die in diesem Abschnitt kurz behandelt wurden, haben wir selbstverständlich nur einen Bruchteil der zahlreichen und vielfach noch völlig ungeklärten Erscheinungen erfasst, die mit dem Problem der II und der NSI in Zusammenhang stehen. Trotzdem glaube ich sagen zu können, dass diese Übersicht hinreichend viele Erklärungsmöglichkeiten angedeutet hat, um ein weiteres Vordringen in der eingeschlagenen Richtung als einigermassen aussichtsreich erscheinen zu lassen.

5. ZUSAMMENFASSUNG

Im Laufe der Untersuchung haben sich u.a. folgende Annahmen ergeben, die mir einer weiteren Überprüfung wert zu sein scheinen:

(1) Die grammatisch relevante Identität ist in erster Linie eine Beziehung zwischen Konstituenten der Tiefenstruktur. Sofern derivierte Strukturen für die grammatisch relevante Identität überhaupt eine Rolle spielen, muss ihre Bedeutung für die Identitätsbedingungen syntaktischer Regeln weitgehend eingeschränkt werden, zumindest was Tilgungen und Pronominalisierungen betrifft. Die Konstituenten der Tiefenstruktur, zwischen denen bei Tilgungen und Pronominalisierungen Identität gefordert wird, scheinen teils Variable, teils S-Strukturen zu sein, d.h. also wohl Nominalphrasen.

(2) Die Strukturierung, die nach unsrer Auffassung mit der Zerlegung von Sätzen in Thema und Rhema einhergeht, ist wesentliche Voraussetzung für das Verständnis von Tilgungen im allgemeinen und von den Erscheinungen der indirekten Identität und der nichtstrikten Identität im besonderen.

(3) Die Bedingungen sowohl für die indirekte Identität wie für die nichtstrikte Identität sind vermutlich ausschliesslich durch die Tiefenstruktur gegeben.

Stockholms Universitet, Sweden

LITERATURVERZEICHNIS

Bach, E.: 1968, 'Nouns and Nounphrases', in Bach und Harms (1968).
Bach, E. und Harms, R.: (Hrsg.), 1968, *Universals in Linguistic Theory*, New York.
Bierwisch, M.: 1970, 'On Classifying Semantic Features', in Bierwisch, M. und Heidolph, K. E.: (Hrsg.), 1970, *Progress in Linguistics*, The Hague.

Binnick, R., Davison, A., Green, G., und Morgan, J.: (Hrsg.), 1969, *Papers from the Fifth Regional Meeting of the Chicago Linguistic Society*, Chicago.

Chomsky, N.: 1965, *Aspects of the Theory of Syntax*, Cambridge, Mass.

Dahl, Ö.: 1969, *Topic and Comment: A Study in Russian and General Transformational Grammar*, Göteborg.

Dahl, Ö.: 1970, *On Sloppiness*, University of Göteborg (Vervielf. durch: Outfit for Scandinavian Underground Linguistics Dissemination).

Karttunen, L.: 1969, 'Pronouns and Variables', in: Binnick *u.a.* (1969).

Lakoff, G.: 1968, *Pronouns and Reference* (Vervielf. durch: The Linguistics Club of Indiana University).

Lakoff, G.: 1969, 'On Derivational Constraints', in Binnick *u.a.* (1969).

Langacker, R.: 1969, 'On Pronominalization and the Chain of Command', in Reibel und Schane (1969).

McCawley, J.: 1967, 'Meaning and the Description of Languages', *Kotoba no uchū* (Tokyo) **2**, S. 10–18, 38–48, 51–57.

McCawley, J.: 1968, 'The Role of Semantics in a Grammar', in Bach und Harms (1968).

McCawley, J.: 1969, *Where Do Noun Phrases Come From?* (Vervielf.).

Morgan, J.: 1970, 'On the Criterion of Identity for Noun Phrase Deletion' (to appear in: *Papers from the Sixth Regional Meeting*, Chicago Linguistic Society) University of Chicago (Vervielf.).

Postal, P.: 1970a, 'On the Surface Verb "Remind",' *Linguistic Inquiry* **1**, S. 37–120.

Postal, P.: 1970b, 'On Coreferential Complement Subject Deletion', *Linguistic Inquiry* **1**, S. 439–500.

Reibel, D. und Schane, S.: (Hrsg.), 1969, *Modern Studies in English*, Englewood Cliffs, New Jersey.

Ross, J.: 1967a, 'On the Cyclic Nature of English Pronominalization', in *To Honor Roman Jakobson*, II, 1967, The Hague. (Abgedruckt in: Reibel und Schane (1969)).

Ross, J.: 1967b, *Constraints on Variables in Syntax*, Ph.D. Dissertation, MIT, 1967. (Vervielf. durch: The Linguistics Club of Indiana University).

Ross, J.: 1969a, 'Adjectives As Noun Phrases', in Reibel und Schane (1969).

Ross, J.: 1969b, 'Guess Who?' in Binnick *u.a.* (1969).

Ross, J.: 1969c, *Act*, MIT, (Vervielf.).

Schiebe, T.: 1967, *Vorstudien zu einer Abhandlung über das Reflexivpronomen im heutigen Deutsch*, Universität Stockholm, (Vervielf.).

Schiebe, T.: (in Vorbereitung), *Studien zur grammatisch relevanten Identität*.

PIETER A. M. SEUREN

THE COMPARATIVE

1. No idea is older in the history of linguistics than the thought that there is, somehow hidden underneath the surface of sentences, a form or a structure which provides a semantic analysis and lays bare their logical structure. In Plato's *Cratylus* the theory was proposed, deriving from Heraclitus' theory of explanatory underlying structure in physical nature, that words contain within themselves bits of syntactic structure giving their meanings. The Stoics held the same view and maintained moreover that every sentence has an underlying logical structure, which for them was the Aristotelian subject-predicate form. They even proposed transformational processes to derive the surface from the deep structure. The idea of a semantically analytic logical form underlying the sentences of every language kept reappearing in various guises at various times. Quite recently it re-emerged under the name of generative semantics.

This paper was written to support the theory that for every sentence its ultimate underlying structure, which is input to the grammar and is often called its deep structure, is what we want to regard as its semantic representation and has logical form. By logical form is meant the form which is required for any kind of formal logical argument. We are still far from knowing what the logical form of sentences exactly looks like. The assumption is that there is such a form: this has been the central assumption for the development of any branch or kind of logic. Although little is known about the semantic representations *cum* logical form *cum* deep structure of sentences, there is evidence that some such analysis is required as is found in predicate calculus. That is, we need quantificational structures in order to account for certain grammatical observations.

The point has been made by McCawley. In (1967) p.41 he gives as an example:

(1)   Those men saw themselves in the mirror.

which is ambiguous as between:[1]

---

[1] McCawley uses an unusual formalism to represent (2) and (3), involving 'restricted quantification', i.e., quantifiers over variables plus their domain. The reasons given for this are considerations of existential presupposition. I am not sure that this notation helps to overcome the problems connected with existential presupposition, but it is perhaps more convenient

F. Kiefer and N. Ruwet (eds.), Generative Grammar in Europe, 528–564. All Rights Reserved.
Copyright © 1973 by D. Reidel Publishing Company, Dordrecht-Holland.

(2)   For each man there was an event in which he saw himself in the mirror.

and:

(3)   There was a single event in which each of the men saw all of the men in the mirror.

We may give another example:

(4)   Planes are safer now than thirty years ago.

which is ambiguous as between the following two approximate readings:

(5)   For every plane there is an extent to which it is safe now but was not thirty years ago.

and:

(6)   There is an extent such that every plane is safe to that extent now but thirty years ago every plane was not safe to that extent.

The readings (5) and (6) are still far removed from what an adequate deep structure analysis will be. But it is clear that any adequate disambiguation requires at least the quantifying phrase 'there is an extent' or the like, which can occur in different positions, and some distinction between two groups of planes at different times for reading (6). If one proposes to analyze (4) as, for example:

(7)   Planes are safe to an extent to which they were not thirty years ago.

the ambiguity remains.[2]

2. Existing transformational accounts of comparative constructions do not do justice to the grammatical regularities that can be observed in connection with them. Among these accounts I reckon the following to be most prominent: Lees (1961), Smith (1961), Pilch (1965), Chomsky (1965, pp. 177–84), Huddleston (1967), Doherty and Schwartz (1967). All these treatments have one feature in common: in some form or other they take the comparative itself to be a primitive in the transformational component,

---

for the universal quantifier than the customary notation 'for all x, if x is a man, then . . .'. The important thing here, however, is that the ambiguity of (1) can only be made explicit with the help of quantifiers and variables, whether in some symbolic notation or in formalized English.
[2] It is to be noted that ambiguity arguments were among the earliest to be used, by Chomsky and others, for postulating underlying structures.

i.e., an unanalyzed deep structure term (in earlier treatments even with a different meaning). Chomsky, for example, gives for:

(8)   John is more clever than Bill.

the following underlying deep structure (1965, p. 178; I leave out details which are irrelevant for the present discussion):

(9)

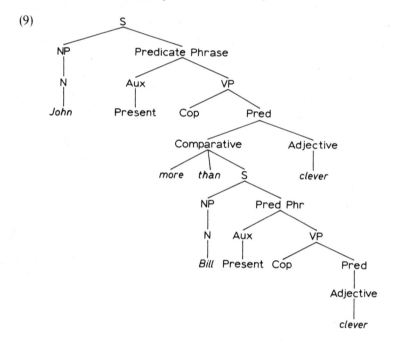

Although there are important differences between the linguistic analyses of the comparative found in the literature mentioned above, and the ways the logicians usually deal with it, they have in common that 'comparative' is taken as a primitive notion, not open to further analysis. Comparatives are described by logicians as transitive relations, and no further problems seem to arise. (See, for example, Russell (1940, pp. 64–5), Strawson (1952, pp. 202–3), Reichenbach (1947, pp. 251–3, 315–6).) I shall argue that, from the point of view of grammar, the comparative cannot be adequately described as a primitive. As a corollary it will follow that it must not be considered a primitive in logic either, but the logical aspects will receive no further attention.

Jespersen (1917, p. 80), relying on his acute feeling for grammatical analysis, intuited the presence of a negation element in comparatives. This idea was made explicit by Ross (1968, p. 294):

Notice first that words like *any* and *ever* may occur in *than*-clauses:

(10)　　He solves problems faster than any of my friends ever could.

But these words occur characteristically in negative sentences (and in questions and *if*-clauses), and are excluded in affirmative sentences:[3]

(11)　　(a)　*Any of my friends could ever solve those problems.
　　　　(b)　Could any of my friends ever solve those problems?
　　　　(c)　At no time could any of my friends ever solve those problems.
　　　　(d)　If any of my friends ever solve those problems, I'll buy you a drink.

Notice furthermore that negative elements cannot occur in *than*-clauses:

(12)　　(a)　*He is taller than nobody here.
　　　　(b)　*Bill ran faster than I couldn't.

These two facts strongly suggest that a negative element is present in the structure which underlies the *than*-clause.

He then proceeds to propose for:

(13)　　John is taller than that man (is).

as 'quite a plausible deep structure' the following:

(14)

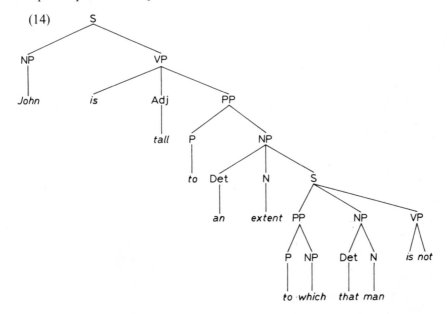

[3] There are, perhaps, grounds for analyzing *yes/no* questions as 'I question whether or not', and *if p* as 'or not *p*' (with (*then*) *q* for '(or *p* and) *q*'; *then* would thus be a pronoun-type replacement of a proposition). If these analyses are correct, the negation element provides the generalization for the occurrence of *any* and *ever*. Obviously, these problems cannot be gone into here.
　　Ross's examples have been renumbered in accordance with their occurrence in the present text.

(14) would also underly:

(15)   John is tall to an extent to which that man is not.

which is synonymous with (13).

The following rule for 'comparative introduction' is then proposed (p. 295):

(16)   *Comparative Introduction:*

$$X - \begin{Bmatrix} \text{Adj} \\ \text{Adv} \end{Bmatrix} - \textit{to an extent to} - \textit{which} - Y - \textit{not} - Z$$

1	2	3	4	5	6	7 ⇒ (optional)
1	2 + *er*	0	*than*	5	0	7

turning (14) into:

(17)

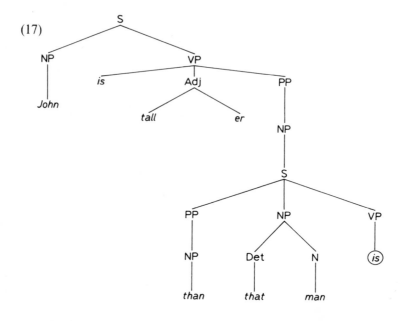

A further optional rule may then delete the circled node *is*, and consequently the vacuous VP above it.

Ross does not go into further details, the comparative not being his main concern in that paper.

3. Let us investigate the merits of (14) as an (not necessarily, *the*) underlying structure for (13). We can give further arguments for the assumption of a negation element in the *than*-clause.[4] There are certain grammatical features in English, whose occurrence is bound up with negation, and others that will not allow for negation. Baker lists some of them (1970, pp. 169–70). I partly draw on this material. He gives *already, rather, just as well, pretty* (as a degree adverb), *far* (with comparative), *still,* which preclude (or are peculiar with) sentence negation:

(18) *I haven't already eaten too much.

(19) *I wouldn't rather be at home.

(20) *I mightn't just as well take the train.

(21) *He didn't do pretty well on the exam.

(22) *He isn't far taller than his uncle.

(23) *John doesn't still play golf.

Now consider the following pairs:

(24) (a) You have already got less support than he has.
       (b) *He has got more support than you already have.

(25) (a) I would rather carry less than he does.
       (b) *He carries more than I would rather do.

(26) (a) I could just as well eat a bit more than you do.
       (b) *You eat a bit less than I could just as well do.

(27) (a) I would pretty much like to run faster than Bill.
       (b) *Bill runs slower than I would pretty much like to.

(28) (a) He would be far better off with less money than he has.
       (b) *He has more money than he would be far better off with.

(29) (a) John still wants to buy more books than he can afford.
       (b) *John can afford less books than he still wants to buy.

We see that the grammatical features that show positive polarity do not occur in the *than*-clause.

Conversely, 'negative polarity' features do occur in *than*-clauses, although no overt negation element is present. We have already seen *any* and *ever*. But there are many more. Baker mentions as 'negative polarity' items *much* (**He said much.*), *be all that* (**The colonel is all that bright.*), *bother V-ing* (**Bob will bother leaving a number.*), *lift a finger* (**George has lifted a finger lately.*), *care to* VP (**I care to go.*). We may add *be bothered V-ing* (**I can be*

---

[4] Ross gave some of the evidence presented below in an unpublished paper 'The Deep Structure of Comparatives', read at The First and Last Annual Harvard Spring Semantics Festival, May 16, 1969. I rely on the handout.

bothered doing that.), *far* (**We got far.*), *need* + infinitive (**You need leave.*), *can possibly* (**You can possibly mean that.*), *the slightest* (**I had the slightest intention of leaving.*), *budge* (**He would budge.*), *can help* (**I could help sneez-ing.*), *can stand/bear* (**I can stand/bear the sound of her voice.*), *at all* (**That is good at all.*), and there are no doubt others. All these 'negative polarity' items can occur in *than*-clauses:

(30)   (a)   The emperor was more inclined to amuse himself than to do *much* for his country.
       (b)   *The emperor was more inclined to do *much* for his country than to amuse himself.

(31)   That amount of spaghetti was more than I *was all that* keen to eat.

(32)   (a)   That's more than he will *bother* thinking of.
       (b)   That stuff was more than I could *be bothered* reading.

(33)   (a)   John's laziness was stronger than his willingness to *lift a finger*.
       (b)   *John's willingness to *lift a finger* was stronger than his laziness.

(34)   The fifth glass was more than I *cared to* drink.
(35)   I've solved lots of more difficult problems than he has got very *far* in even understanding.
(36)   John runs faster than he *need* run.
(37)   He was a greater bore than I *could possibly* put up with.
(38)   He went further than I had *the slightest* intention of going.
(39)   Given their characters, it is much easier for Bill to give in gracefully than for John to even *budge*.
(40)   My urge to steal was stronger than I *could help*.
(41)   The sound of her voice was more than I *could stand/bear*.
(42)   This is more serious than I would have believed *at all* possible.

This is strong evidence in favour of the assumption that there is a negation element in the underlying structure of comparatives. There is, however, also independent evidence in favour of this assumption. Joly (1967) observes that in a great many dialects of English *nor* is used instead of *than*:

(43)   He is richer nor you'll ever be.

If *nor* is analyzed as 'and not', and if we take the relative clause in (14) further back to *and*-conjunction – as we will do – this *nor* has a perfectly legitimate source in deep structure.

Joly furthermore provides Old-English þ *on-ne* as the etymology for *than*, which means 'by which not' (neuter pronominal relative in the instrumental case, followed by the negation element). *Than* would thus correspond directly, in Old-English, to a derivational stage such as given in (14).

We can, moreover, provide a natural explanation for the so-called '*ne* explétif' in French comparatives. There, the negative particle *ne* is obligatory in a *than*-clause if this clause contains a finite verb form:

(44)　　Jean est plus grand que je ne pensais.
　　　　(John is taller than I thought).

According to some, French *que* is derived from Vulgar Latin *quid*, which is derived from Latin *quo,* meaning 'by which'. The negation element has not been incorporated into the comparative particle, and crops up again under certain conditions. The same phenomenon is observed in Italian, where *non* + subjunctive is used in formal style:

(45)　　Giovanni è più alto che non pensassi.

Colloquial Italian prefers:

(46)　　Giovanni è più alto che pensavo.

Certain dialects of English, such as Cockney, have a negation-copying transformation, whereby the negative element is repeated for every following quantifying element:

(47)　　He has never been no good to no woman, not never.

Cockney also allows for the following:

(48)　　She did a better job than what I never thought she would.

The negation in *never* can be explained with the same negation-copying transformation, if we accept an underlying negation element in comparatives.

So far we can accept Ross's analysis. The assumption of an *extent*-phrase seems to be justifiable in the light of the so-called positive and negative connotations of gradable adjectives. Any grammar of English will have to explain the positive connotation in, e.g.:

(49)　　John is tall.

and the negative connotation in, e.g.:

(50)　　(a)　John is short.

    (b)   How short is John?
    (c)   John is not so short as Bill.
    (d)   John is that short.

It will have to explain the absence of either a positive or a negative connotation in, e.g.:

(51)   (a)   How tall is John?
        (b)   John is taller than Bill.
        (c)   John is shorter than Bill.
        (d)   The baby is too tall for the pram.
        (e)   John is too short for the basket-ball team.
        (f)   John is six feet tall.

It will have to explain the ungrammaticality of:

(52)   *John is five feet short.

and the ambiguity of:

(53)   (a)   John is that tall.
        (b)   John is not so tall as Bill.

No satisfactory analysis of these and similar data has been given so far in the literature. And no attempt will be made to give one here. But it is not unreasonable to expect that any adequate analysis will require an *extent*-phrase for all occurrences of gradable adjectives. Adverbials such as *how, so, that, -er than, six feet, too* can reasonably be expected to be derived from an underlying *extent*-phrase. Evidence for this expectation is that sentences such as (49) or (50a), which lack an overt *extent*-phrase, always have either a positive or a negative connotation, which could presumably be derived from an underlying general (i.e., recoverable) form of comparative, for example, 'more than one would expect'.

On the basis of the examples given in (49)–(53) we can distinguish between *neutral* gradables, which take a positive connotation when used without overt *extent*-phrase, and optionally in cases such as (53), and *negative* gradables, which are negatively marked when no overt *extent*-phrase occurs and in cases such as (50b–d). This distinction is further motivated by the fact that negative, but not neutral, gradables allow for 'negative polarity' items to occur with them:

(54)   (a)   It is difficult to ever get a straight answer from him.
        (b)   *It is easy to ever get a straight answer from him.

(55)   (a) It was unjust to ever start that war.
        (b) *It was just to ever start that war.

(56)   (a) It was impossible for him to lift a finger.
        (b) *It was possible for him to lift a finger.

We can even use this test to decide which of a pair of opposites is the negative one in cases where this is not immediately evident:

(57)   (a) It was nasty of him to think that I could do that at all.
        (b) *It was nice of him to think that I could do that at all.

(58)   (a) He is far from being prepared to admit that he has ever been wrong.
        (b) *He is close to being prepared to admit that he has ever been wrong.

It would go beyond the limits of this study, however, to explore the problems of positive and negative connotation any further here.

4. Ross's analysis, as given in (14), needs the obvious amendment that the predicate *tall* must be repeated in the structure underlying the *than*-clause, since we have, e.g.:

(59)   John is taller than that corridor is long.

where *long* cannot be deleted due to non-identity with *tall* in the main clause. That is, we clearly have to do with two sentences, or rather propositions. Parts of the second are deletable under certain identity conditions. In this respect Chomsky's analysis as given in (9) is correct.

A more serious objection, however, results from the ambiguity of (4) noted in Section 1. *Planes are safer now than thirty years ago.* As was pointed out there, there seems to be no other way to disambiguate this sentence than by introducing scope-bearing quantifiers. Predicate calculus provides a natural way of doing so:

(60)   (a) $\forall x$ $\exists e$ (now x is safe to e & not 30 years ago x was safe to e)

             x is a plane

        (b) $\exists e$ (now $\forall x$ (x is safe to e) & not 30 years ago $\forall y$ (y was safe to e))

             x is a plane y is a plane

(*e* is a variable ranging over extents; I use McCawley's notation of writing class inclusion below quantifiers – see note 1; a different treatment is suggested below).

In Ross's analysis, which corresponds to (7), the ambiguity is not resolved. The simple comparative:

(61)   John is taller than Bill.

can now be represented as:

(62)   ∃*e* (John is tall to *e* & not Bill is tall to *e*)[5]

or, more completely, as:[6]

(63)

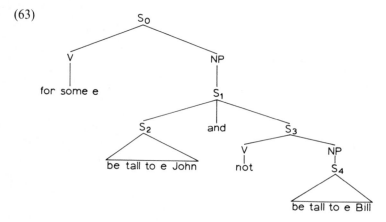

We can formulate the following tentative set of cyclical rules to transform structures like (63) into those like (61), or their near (shallow) equivalents (they apply in the order in which they are given):

(64)   (a)   *And*-Deletion
          (b)   Operator Incorporation
          (c)   *some/any* rule
          (d)   Subject-Verb Inversion
          (e)   *more than* rule

These rules have roughly the following characteristics:

(a) *And*-Deletion: The name has been chosen because of the similarity with ordinary *and*-Reduction, though not with further transposition rules which are typical of conjunction reduction. What is deleted must have an

---

[5] This analysis was proposed in Seuren (1969), p. 129.
[6] I disregard tense, as far as possible. I follow McCawley in letting the subject follow the verb (McCawley, 1970).

identical counterpart in the first clause. There are some further, more superficial, restrictions on *and*-Deletion in the comparative. Thus, for example, if
the predicate nominal remains undeleted, then the copula must remain so
too, together with a pronominalized form of the subject (except if the subject
is an original S):

(65)   (a)   John is heavier than *he* is fat.
        (b)   *John is heavier than fat.[7]
        (c)   The door is wider than is necessary.
        (d)   *The door is wider than it is necessary.

(b) Operator Incorporation: (This is sometimes called 'Quantifier Lowering'). An operator is any predicate with an embedded S as its subject-NP.
The embedded S is raised to replace the dominating S. The dominating predicate is incorporated into the original embedded S as one of its constituents.
(There are a number of constraints, some of which probably universal,
governing this process. For quantifiers and negation see Lakoff (1970)).

(c) *Some/any* rule: This rule converts *some* into *any* (*some time* into *ever*),
when, after (b), *not* precedes *some*.[8]

(d) Subject-Verb Inversion: This rule is discussed in McCawley (1970). It
turns VSO into SVO.

---

[7] (65b) is ungrammatical, at least in British English. We have, of course, *John is more heavy
than fat*. Note, however, that there is compulsory stress on *heavy* and *fat* here. There is also a
semantic difference between (65a) and this sentence: the former presupposes a relation between
exact measurements; the latter speaks about the greater or lesser adequacy of the expressions
John is heavy and *John is fat*. It seems that the sentence quoted here is a case of contrastive
stress. To deal with such cases satisfactorily would clearly go beyond the limits of this paper.
Generally, many particular problems related with comparatives are left out of account here.
Only such cases are discussed as might provide counterevidence to the analysis proposed here.

[8] As formulated in this way, this rule is too wide in at least two different ways. First, it should
apply only to cases of *some* which derive from an existential quantifier: *This isn't anything I
would like you to do*. Secondly, there are some curious exceptions. Assuming that there is a
negation element in questions and *if*-clauses (see note 3), it is still strange that we cannot say:

(1)   *Did he say anything again?
(2)   *Did he REALLY say anything?
(3)   *Is it true that he said anything?
(4)   *It wasn't very polite of you to say anything like that.
(5)   *He did NOT say anything.

Especially the predicate 'be true that' seems to block *any*. It is overt in (3), and may be taken to
underly (2) and (5). Robin Lakoff (1969) raises some interesting questions regarding this rule.
In most cases where *some* occurs in *if*-clauses, questions, or even after plain negation, the
higher verb 'be true that' seems to have been deleted. Compare:

> If you see somebody, you must tell me.
> If you see anybody, you must tell me.
> If it is true that you see somebody, you must tell me.
> *If it is true that you see anybody, you must tell me.

(e) *More than* rule:

(66)   Adj – to some e – X – and – Y – not – Z ⇒

               more – Adj – X – than – Y – Z

where e ranges over extents, X may be null, and either Y or Z, but not both, may be null.

Under certain phonological conditions a further rule applies, converting (stressed) *more + Adj* into *Adj + er*.

If applied to (63) the rules of (64) make for the following derivation:

S_4 – SV-Inversion –   Bill be tall to e
S_3 – Op-Incorporation – Bill not be tall to e
S_2 – SV-Inversion –   John be tall to e
S_1 – *And*-Deletion –   John be tall to e and Bill not
S_0 – Op-Incorporation – John be tall to some e and Bill not

   – *more than* –   John be taller than Bill.

(60a) corresponds to the following tree:

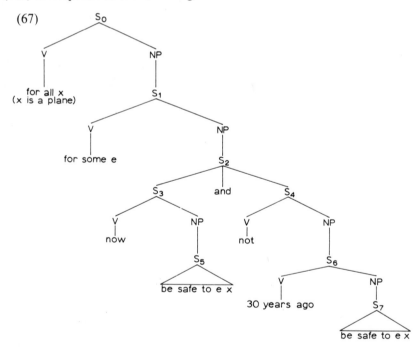

(67)

The rules will yield the following derivation:

S_7 – SV-Inversion – x be safe to e

S_6 – Op-Inc. –   30 years ago x be safe to e
S_4 – Op-Inc. –   30 years ago x not be safe to e
S_5 – SV-Inversion – x be safe to e
S_3 – Op-Inc. – x be safe to e now
S_2 – *And*-Deletion – x be safe to e now and 30 years ago not
S_1 – Op-Inc. – x be safe to some e now and 30 years ago not
      – *More than* – x be safer now than 30 years ago
S_0 – Op-Inc. –   all planes be safer now than 30 years ago.

(60b) has the following tree plus derivation:

(68)

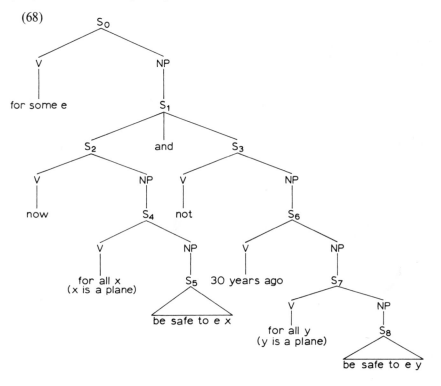

S_8 – SV-Inversion – y be safe to e
S_7 – Op-Inc. –   all planes be safe to e
S_6 – Op-Inc. –   30 years ago all planes be safe to e
S_3 – Op-Inc. –   30 years ago not all planes be safe to e
S_5 – SV-Inversion – x be safe to e
S_4 – Op-Inc. –   all planes be safe to e
S_2 – Op-Inc. –   all planes be safe to e now
S_1 – *And*-Deletion – all planes be safe to e now and 30 years ago not

S_0 – Op-Inc –   all planes be safe to some e now and 30 years ago not

– *More than* –   all planes be safer now than 30 years ago.

For:

(69)   John is taller than anybody.

the semantic representation will at least have the following structure:

(70) $\exists e$ (John is tall to e & not $\exists p$ (p is tall to e)) (where 'p' ranges over persons)

or:

(71)

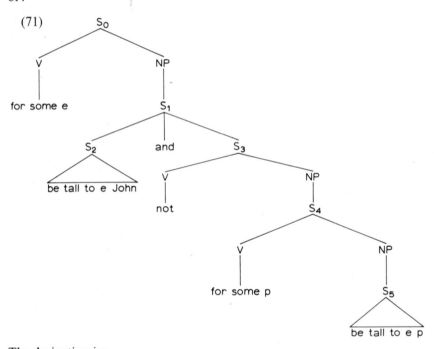

The derivation is:

S_5 – SV-Inversion – p be tall to e
S_4 – Op-Inc. –   some p be tall to e
S_3 – Op-Inc. –   not some p be tall to e
       – *Some/any* –   not any p be tall to e
S_2 – SV-Inversion –   John be tall to e
S_1 – *And*-Deletion –   John be tall to e and not any p
S_0 – Op-Inc. –   John be tall to some e and not any p
       – *More than* –   John be taller than any p.

The cyclic character of the *some/any* rule prevents problems for negative comparatives, such as:

(72)   John is not taller than Bill.

Here the uppermost *not* does not affect 'for some *e*', since the comparative treatment is completed before this *not* is incorporated: there is no *some* to be converted into *any* or to determine the position of *not*.

5. Let us now turn to a type of comparative discussed by Chomsky in *Aspects* (pp. 180, 234):

(73)   John is a more clever man than Bill.
(74)   I know several more successful lawyers than Bill.

In (73) it is understood that Bill is a man: we cannot replace *Bill* by *Mary*. In (74), on one reading, it is understood that Bill is a lawyer. On this reading (74) is equivalent to:

(75)   I know several more successful lawyers than Bill is.

On another reading it is equivalent to:

(76)   I know several more successful lawyers than Bill does.

(Note that (75) is bracketed as: *several* (*more successful*), but (76) as: (*several more*) *successful*. That is, *several* quantifies *lawyers* in (75), but in (76) it indicates how many more lawyers that are successful I know than Bill does. This point will be discussed in Section 6).

This ambiguity disappears in:

(77)   I know several lawyers more successful than Bill.

But in (77) it is no longer necessary to understand that Bill is a lawyer. Likewise, to take another example of Chomsky's (*Aspects,* p.234), we cannot say:

(78)   I have never seen a heavier book than this rock.

or, if we do, we must interpret *this rock* as referring to some kind of book. But there is no difficulty in:

(79)   I have never seen a book heavier than this rock.

There is no difficulty in (77) or (79). The comparative there is contained within a restrictive relative clause dependent on *lawyers* and *book* respectively. But there is a problem in (73), (74) and (78).

Let us consider (73). From the conditions on (64a), *And*-Deletion, it follows that (73) must be derived from:

(80)   John is a more clever man than Bill is a clever man.

or, rather, from:

(81)   ∃e (John is a clever to e man & not Bill is a clever to e man)

Let us assume there to be an optional rule, which can be called *Noun Raising*, which has the following effect:

the x (x is a house) is red ⇒ the x is a red house

More generally and precisely:

(82)   be – Adj – the x (x be Indef N) – X ⇒ be – Indef – Adj – N – the $x – X$

where 'x' ranges over variables, 'Adj' over adjectives including gradables plus their *extent*-phrases, 'N' over nouns, 'Indef' over underlying indefinite determiners (*a* or null); X may be null.

This rule is cyclic and precedes (64a).

(81) can thus be further reduced to:

(83)   ∃e (the x (x is a man & John is x) is clever to e & not the y (y is a man & Bill is y) is clever to e)

Let us assume a further optional rule, to be called *Relative Raising,* of essentially the following form:

(84)   be – NP – the x (... x ...) → ... NP ... ('x' is a variable ranging over variables)

(*NP*, being the predicate nominal, receives stress or focus of intonation. It keeps the stress all through the transformational treatment. This would imply that certain aspects of sentence intonation go back to very deep structure. Such aspects seem to override more superficial accentual rules: see, for example, note 10. We have to refrain, however, from going into problems of intonation more deeply here).

Relative Raising is cyclic and applies after Noun Raising but before (64a). Noun Raising finds support in the fact that in certain contexts expressions such as *It is a red house.* are preferred to *The house is red.* The evidence for Relative Raising is more plentiful and stronger. This rule accounts, in principle, for the meaning and the contrastive stress in, e.g.:

(85)   JOHN did not write the letter (PETER did).

which can be derived from:

(86)   not (be John the x (wrote x the letter))

By Relative Raising this will be transformed into:

(87)   not (wrote JOHN the letter)

and hence into (85).[9]

Relative Raising accounts for the stress on *whom* in, e.g.:

(88)   To whom did you write the letter?

which is to be derived from:

(89)   be who the x (wrote you the letter to x)

Relative Raising turns this into:

(90)   wrote you the letter to WHO

Wh-movement will then move the *who* to the front and, with all the necessary trimmings, the result will be (88).[10]

Strong evidence for Relative Raising comes from Tacitus, *Annals* 12.36:

(91)   Avebantque visere quis ille tot per annos opes nostras sprevisset.

The story is about Caratacus, the Britannic freedom fighter, who had been captured, after many years, by the Romans and was exhibited to the public in Rome. The sentence means: 'And they wanted to come and see who that man was who had scorned our power for so many years.' Literally, however, it says: 'And they wanted to come and see who that (man) had scorned our power for so many years.' The evidence consists in the word *ille* (demonstrative pronoun nominative singular masculine): had this not been present in the text, the sentence would not have been peculiar in any way. As it stands, however, it is strongly marked, stylistically: it is 'typical Tacitean'. Let us derive (91), roughly, from:

[9] Another possible derivation is to extrapose (*wrote x the letter*), so that we get: *not (the x be John (x wrote the letter)), after SV-Inversion; this will then become: It was not John who wrote the letter.* The derivation with Relative Raising seems to lead to difficulties in those cases where the stressed element is not an NP. These difficulties are only apparent, however, and can be solved by taking the stressed elements as quoted: quoted elements are always NP's.

[10] The stress on interrogative pronouns and adverbs seems to be universal. In Ancient Greek these words always have a rising tone on the first mora. If there is only one mora the rising tone is word final. There is a phonological rule in Ancient Greek which converts all word-final rising tones into flat tones before a single word boundary, but not in sentence-final position, or at the end of a major syntactic constituent. Interrogative pronouns and adverbs, however, do not obey this rule: those that have final rising tone keep it under all conditions, thereby overriding the general accentual rules of the language.

(92)   Avebantque visere (erat quis ille *x* (*x* tot per annos opes nostras
          spreverat))

Supposing that Relative Raising is the same in Latin as it is in English, it
would, strictly speaking, not apply, since the demonstrative pronoun *ille*
stands in the position of the weaker definite article (which has no overt
expression in Latin). Yet Tacitus, in his quest for brevity, forced the rule
to apply and left *ille* as a remnant of the underlying structure. In spite of
this irregularity the sentence is, strangely enough, immediately interpretable.

Let us now apply the rules to (83), or rather to its corresponding tree:

(93)

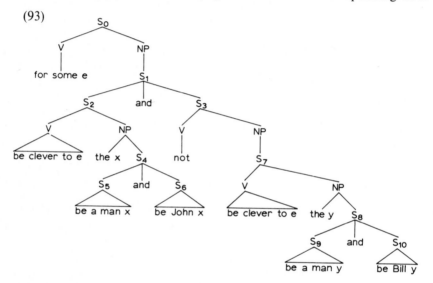

SV-Inversion operates on S_5, S_6, S_9 and S_{10}.

I take *be* + *NP* as verb. S_5 and S_9 now become *x be a man* and *y be a man*,
respectively. I assume furthermore (but this is a matter of slight importance
in the present context) that SV-Inversion operates on the predicate nominal
when this is a definite NP or a proper name. S_6 and S_{10} will then become
John be x and *Bill be y*, respectively. This blocks any form of *and*-Reduction
on S_4 or S_8. S_2 and S_7 now undergo Noun Raising. S_2 becomes:

(94)

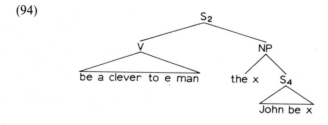

For S_7 the result is analogous, with y and *Bill* for x and *John* respectively.

Now Relative Raising applies to S_2 and S_7, yielding *John be a clever to e man* and *Bill be a clever to e man*. S_1 and S_0 undergo the standard treatment and the result is something near (73).

It must now be shown that (73) cannot be derived from, e.g.:

(95) $\exists e$ (the x (x is a man & John is x) is clever to e & not Bill is clever to e)

or:

(96)

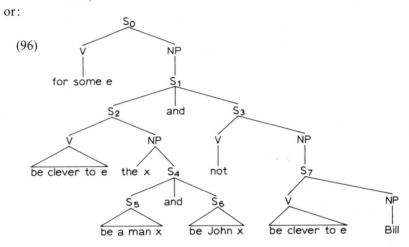

S_2 will become, as in the derivation of (93): *John be a clever to e man*. S_3, however, will be: *Bill not be clever to e*. Now *and*-Deletion does not apply to S_1, and (73) cannot be the output of (96). This explains why (73) cannot mean what (95) says. It does not explain what is wrong with:

(97)   *John is a more clever man than Bill is clever.

which is the expected output of the rules operating on (96). Instead we would wish to derive:

(98)   John is a man who is more clever than Bill.

Noun Raising and Relative Raising are both optional rules, and they are certainly not the only ones to deal with such structures as S_2 in (96). It may well be possible to develop S_2 into: *John is a man who is clever to e*. The deepest rules concerning noun phrases, adjectives and copula are still so unclear that any further elaboration here would rapidly develop into mere speculation. What does seem likely, however, is that there is some derivational constraint on *and*-Deletion in the comparative. The constraint would be such that a choice must be made among the available rules that maximum similarity is ensured of the two S's of the comparative *and*-conjunction. I shall not try to formulate this constraint more precisely here, but we will have occasion to refer to it more than once below.

6.   Let us now consider the two sentences:

(99)   John bought an older car than Bill (did).
(100)   John bought an older car than that Ford (is).[11]

There is an interesting difference between these two sentences. In (100) the indefinite article represents genuine quantification, but in (99) it does not. This appears from the fact that we can say:

(101)   John bought many older cars than that Ford (is).
(102)   John never bought any older car than that Ford (is).

but not:

(103)   *John bought many older cars than Bill (did).
(104)   *John never bought any older car than Bill (did).

We can say, however:

(105)   John bought older cars than Bill (did).

The same distinction between grammatical and ungrammatical as holds between (99) and (105) on the one hand, and (103) and (104) on the other, is observed in:

(106)   What John bought was an older car than what Bill bought.
(107)   What John bought was older cars than what Bill bought.
(108)   *What John bought was many older cars than what Bill bought.
(109)   *What John bought was never any older car than what Bill bought.

In (99) and (106), which are synonymous, it is presupposed, or implied, that Bill bought a car. (99) has the same structure as (73), which was discussed in Section 5. In fact, with the rules given so far we can derive both (99) and (106) in a way parallel to the derivation proposed for (73). Let us take as input structure (110). (99) is derived in the following way:

S_5 – SV-Inversion – x be a car
S_6 – SV-Inversion –   John buy x
S_9 – SV-Inversion – y be a car
S_{10} – SV-Inversion –   Bill buy y

---

[11] These examples are more suitable for this discussion than Chomsky's ambiguous (74). In fact, (99) and (100) correspond to the readings (76) and (75), respectively, of (74).

S_7	– Noun Raising –	be an old to e car the y (Bill buy y)
	–Relative Raising –	Bill buy an old to e car
S_3	– Op-Inc. –	Bill not buy an old to e car
S_2	–as S_7–	John buy and old to e car
S_1	– *and*-Deletion –	John buy an old to e car and Bill not
S_0	– Op-Inc. –	John buy an old to some e car and Bill not
	– *more than* –	John buy an older car than Bill.

(110)

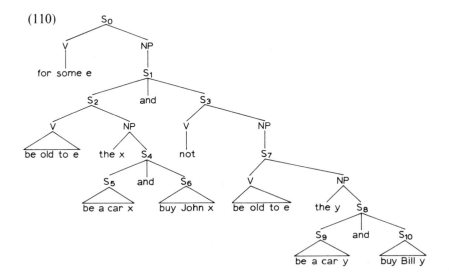

(106) is derived by not applying Relative Raising to S_7 and S_2. After Noun Raising S_7 will then become, by SV-Inversion:

the y (Bill buy y) be an old to e car

Not will subsequently be inserted before *be*. Similarly, S_2 will become:

the x (John buy x) be an old to e car

And-Deletion on S_1 will yield:

the x (John buy x) be an old to e car and the y (Bill buy y) not

Somewhere in the process the parts *the x (John buy x)* and *the y (Bill buy y)* will be converted into *what John buy* and *what Bill buy,* respectively. The *more-than* rule and further trimming will give (106). The same treatment can be given to (105) and (107). One notices again, as at the end of Section 5, that there is a tendency, if not a constraint, to ensure that there is maximum similarity between the two S's of the comparative *and*-conjunction.

It is clear from this analysis that the indefinite article in (99) and the null article in (105) do not represent quantification. What they represent is the indefinite article or determiner in the predicate 'be a . . .', which is a relation of class inclusion.

Let us now consider sentence (100). This sentence poses a new problem, for which only a tentative solution can be offered here. The sentence:

(111)   John bought a car.

can be derived from:

(112)   the x (John bought x) is a car.

by Relative Raising. This derivation is the proper one if *car* carries stress. On this interpretation the indefinite article does not represent quantification. If *car* is not stressed, however, we have to do with quantification.

The semantic representation can then be taken to be something correspon- ding to:

(113) $\exists x$ (John bought x & x is a car)[12]

We now assume as a principle that before Operator Incorporation can operate, the variable which is quantified by the operator must be made to occur only once within the brackets. In some cases Conjunction Reduction is a way of doing this. (In fact, *and*-Deletion was given above as preceding Operator Incorporation). In this case, however, Conjunction Reduction does not apply. But we can let another process apply, *Relativization*. This converts (113) into:

(114) $\exists x$ (John bought x, which is a car)

By Operator Incorporation this now becomes:

(115)   John bought an x, which is a car.

Let us assume a further rule, *NP-Reduction*, of roughly the following form:

(116)   Determiner – x – wh – be – Indef – NP $\Rightarrow$ Determiner – NP
         where 'x' ranges over variables.[13,14]

[12] It should be understood that there is a definite article for every variable under a quantifier. (113) is equivalent to: $\exists x$ (*John bought the x & the x is a car*). Since the status of the definite article in semantic representations is still unclear, I do not insist on its being expressed every- where in underlying structures. As a rule I only insert the definite article if the variable is not quantified.

[13] The variable e, which has been used so far as a variable ranging over extents, can now be treated in the same way. Instead of saying: $\exists e$ (*John is tall to e*) we can now say: $\exists e$ (*John is tall to e & e is an extent*). This will transform, through Relativization and NP-Reduction, to: *John is tall to an extent*.

[14] The NP-Reduction rule is nothing else than what has been proposed by Bach in *Nouns and Noun Phrases* (1968). There, as here, it is immaterial for the rule whether the relative clause is restrictive or non-restrictive.

The sentence:

(117)   John bought a red car.

is ambiguous. It is either derived from:

(118)   the x (John bought x & x is a car) is red

by Noun Raising and Relative Raising. Or we can derive it from:

(119) $\exists x$ (John bought x & x is a car & x is red)

Relativization may yield:

(120) $\exists x$ (John bought x & x, which is a car, is red)

which, by Noun Raising, will become:

(121) $\exists x$ (John bought x & x is a red car)

Further Relativization will give:

(122) $\exists x$ (John bought x, which is a red car)

and hence (117). Another possibility is:

(123) $\exists x$ (John bought x, which is a car, which is red)

which will lead to:

(124)   John bought a car which is red.

If this treatment is, at least in principle, correct, then (100) must be derived from:

(125) $\exists x$ (John bought x & x is an older car than that Ford)

The part *x is an older car than that Ford* will then have the same derivation as (73), discussed in Section 5. That is, (125) will be derived from:

(126) $\exists x$ (John bought x & $\exists e$ (x (x is a car) is old to e & not the y (y is a car & that Ford is y) is old to e))

in the same way as (73) was derived from (83). (126), in its turn, can be assumed to go back to:

(127) $\exists x$ (John bought x & x is a car & $\exists e$ (x is old to e & not the y (y is a car & that Ford is y) is old to e))

If the comparative treatment applies directly to the structure dominated by '$\exists e$', the result will be:

(128) x is older than the car which that Ford is

(127) will then become something like:

(129)   (a) John bought an older car than the car which that Ford is.

or: (b) John bought a car which is older than the car which that Ford is.

We feel, however, that (129a and b) sound quaint and unnatural. This is probably due to the principle, mentioned earlier, that there should be maximum similarity between the two constituent S's of the comparative. Such a derivation would not be unnatural for, e.g.:

(130) $\exists x$ (John bought x & x is a car & $\exists e$ (x is old to e & not the y (that table is y) is old to e))

which would result in:

(131)   John bought a car which is older than that table.

According to the principle of maximum similarity we relativize *& x is a car* in (127) under the x of *x is old to e*. The result is (126). Relativization would thus be outside the cycle and be allowed to apply wherever possible.

The fact that in (100) it is understood that a Ford is a car (so that it would be anomalous to replace *Ford* by, for example, *table*) is explained, in principle, by rule (116), NP-Reduction. From this rule it follows that (100) can only be derived from something like (125), which implies that a Ford is a car, as was shown in Section 5. If we give (130) the same treatment as (127), the derivation will block. (130) would then become:

(132) $\exists x$ (John bought x & $\exists e$ (x (x is a car) is old to e & not the y (that table is y) is old to e))

Now the comparative will be:

(133)   the car is older than that table

so that (132) will be:

(134) $\exists x$ (John bought x & the car is older than that table)

which makes no sense and cannot be further developed by any rule. If, on the other hand, we apply Noun Raising to (132), the result will be, for the comparative part:

(135)   ∃e (the *x* is an old to *e* car & not the *y* (that table is *y*) is old to *e*)

which does not allow for comparative treatment.

7. There is one category of comparative constructions which might seem to deal a fatal blow to the analysis given so far. Consider:

(136)   John is taller than six feet.

The *than*-clause cannot be derived from *than six feet is tall*. This is implausible not only on semantic grounds, but also for syntactic reasons. If (136) had the same underlying structure and the same derivation as (61) above:

(61)   John is taller than Bill.

we would expect the following to be grammatical:

(137)   (a) *Six feet is less tall than John.
         (b) *Six feet is as tall as John.
         (c) *John is not so tall as six feet.
         (d) *Six feet is smaller than John.
         (e) *Six feet is not so tall as John.

In fact, however, these are all ungrammatical. Yet we have:

(138)   (a) Six feet is less than John is tall.
         (b) Six feet is as much as John is tall.
         (c) Six feet is not so much as John is tall.
         (d) Six feet is more than John is tall.
         (e) John is more than six feet tall.

This suggests that what is compared in (136) is pure quantity. We can make this suggestion explicit by assuming that (136) is derived from:

(139)   John be tall to a greater extent than six feet (is).

If this is so, we have a case parallel to either (99) or (100). Let us see if (139) can be derived in a way analogous to either (99) or (100). A derivation according to the lines of (99) allows for a comparison with sentences such as:[15]

---

[15] This calls to mind Postal's analysis of comparatives: 'The degree to which John is tall exceeds the degree to which Bill is tall', which I found in Ross's handout (see note 4). Postal's analysis cannot be correct as it stands, since it does not take into account the negation element. But if we let *exceed* stand for 'be a greater extent than', we are close to our present proposal.

(140)   (a) The extent to which John is tall is greater than six feet.
          (b) What John is tall to is a greater extent than six feet.

More precisely, let us try to derive (139) in the following way, similar to (99):
    From (141), SV-Inversion will convert S_5 into: f be an extent; S_6 into: John be tall to f; S_9 into: g be an extent; S_{10} into: six feet be g.

    Noun Raising will convert S_2 into: be a great to e extent the f (John be tall to f); S_7 into: be a great to e extent the g (six feet be g).

    Now Relative Raising applies to S_7: six feet be a great to e extent, but not to S_2, under the principle of maximum similarity. After *and*-Deletion and SV-Inversion S_1 will be: the f (John be tall to f) be a great to e extent and six feet not.

(141)

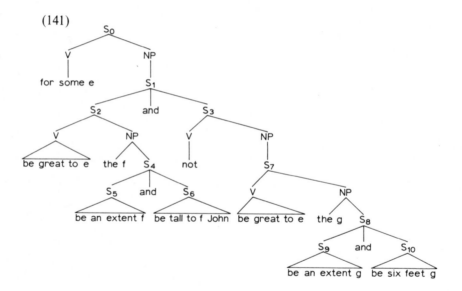

If Relative Raising now applies to S_0, we get: for some e (John be tall to a great to e extent and six feet not), which will then regularly become (139). But in reality the rule applies to S_1, which would violate the cyclical principle.

    It is preferable to derive (139) in a way analogous to (100). Now it will be derived from:

(142)   ∃e (John is tall to e & e is an extent & ∃f (e is great to f & not the g (g is an extent & six feet is g) is great to f))

or, more precisely, from:

(143)

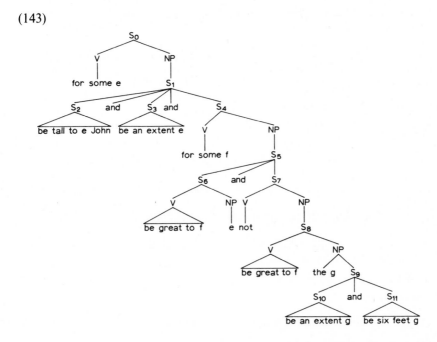

Relativization will now attach S_3 as a relative clause to the subject-NP of S_6, so as to ensure maximum similarity under S_5. S_5 will now become:

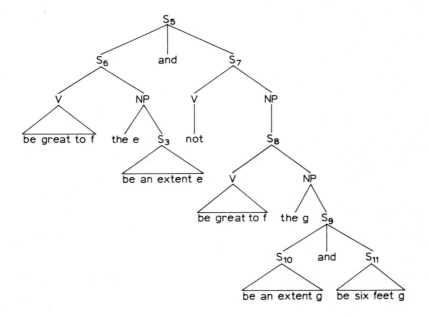

SV-Inversion and Noun Raising apply as usual. Relative Raising applies to S_8. The result will be:

e be a great to f extent and six feet not be a great to f extent

Comparative treatment will apply to S_4:

e be a greater extent than six feet

Relativization will reduce S_1 to:

John be tall to e, which be a greater extent than six feet

After Operator Incorporation on S_0, NP-Reduction will apply, yielding:

(139)   John be tall to a greater extent than six feet.

There seems to be no straightforward way of finding out whether the indefinite article a in (139) represents genuine quantification, as in (100), or class inclusion, as in (99). It is intuitively satisfactory to let (139) correspond with (100), and

(144)   John is tall to a greater extent than Bill.

with (99). The following observation might help to decide:

(145)   John is tall to some greater extent than six feet.

sounds more natural to me than:

(146) $^?$*John is tall to some greater extent than Bill.

We have concentrated our efforts, however, on (139), and not on (136), which was our point of departure. In order to derive the latter from the former we will need a rule:

(147)   Adj – to – a – greater – extent $\Rightarrow$ more – Adj.

In view of rule (64e), the *more-than* rule given above, this seems an *ad hoc* rule, too similar to (64e), which leads to the same result. We can avoid having the two rules (147) and (64e), however, by revising the treatment we gave to (61) (*John is taller than Bill.*). We take as the underlying structure for (61) not (63) given above, but rather:

(148) $\exists e$ (the $f(f$ is an extent & John is tall to $f)$ is great to e & not the g
         (g is an extent & Bill is tall to g) is great to e)

which corresponds exactly to (141), with *be tall to g Bill* for S_{10}. This comes close to Postal's proposal mentioned in note 15.

We now drop rule (64e) and introduce a new rule, which will operate after NP-Reduction:

(149)   a great to some e extent – X – and – Y – not – Z ⇒ more – X – than – Y – Z

where 'e' ranges over extents, 'X' may be null, and either 'Y' or 'Z', but not both, may be null.

(148) will now be developed into:

(150)   John is tall to a great to some e extent and Bill not.

By rule (149) this becomes:

(151)   John is tall to more than Bill.

This will be converted into:

(152)   John is more tall than Bill.

by the following rule:

(153)   Adj – $_{EP}$ [to – NP] ⇒ $_{EP}$ [NP] – Adj   ('EP': *extent*-phrase)

This rule also converts:

(154)   John is tall to six feet.

(derived, by Relative Raising, from:

(155)   the e (John is tall to e) is six feet)

into:

(156)   John is six feet tall.[16]

This proposal reduces all comparatives to comparatives of *much*: *more* or *less*. There are, in fact, independent grounds for regarding the word *much* as a lexical item representing something like 'a great extent' or 'a great amount', parallel to rule (149) for *more than*. There are a number of observations which show that *much* not only has features that classify it as a noun phrase, but has also adjective-like properties. On the one hand, we see *much* occurring in expressions such as *much milk, He didn't say much*, whereas *The milk is much.* is ungrammatical. On the other hand we find an adjectival quality in, for instance, *very much, too much, more*.

The derivation proposed for comparatives will generate (136) directly. (141) will now lead to (if we allow Relative Raising to apply to S_0):

[16] It will be noticed that Relative Raising, together with rule (153), predicts the correct stress on *more* and *six feet* in (152) and (156) respectively.

(157)   John be tall to a great to some *e* extent and six feet not

and hence to (136). (143) will become first:

(158)   for some *e* (John be tall to *e* and *e* be a great to some *f* extent
and six feet not)

Hence:

(159)   for some *e* (John be tall to *e* and *e* be more than six feet)

from which, by Relativization, Operator Incorporation and NP-Reduction:

(160)   John be tall to more than six feet.

and hence (136) (or (138e)). However, (139) cannot now be the result of
either (141) or (143). It will have to have an underlying structure of roughly
the following form:

(161)   John be tall to a great to a great to some *e* extent extent and six
feet not.

Although the derivation of (139) will be long, no new rules are needed for
it. Parallel to (143), we set up the following ultimate underlying structure:

(162)

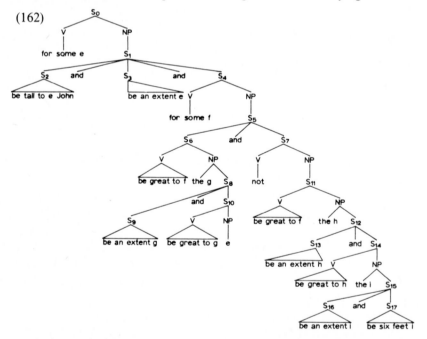

S_3 is attached as a relative clause to the subject-NP of S_{10}.

S_{14} – Noun Raising –   be a great to *h* extent the *i* (six feet be *i*)

	– Relative Raising –	six feet be a great to *h* extent
S_{11}	– Noun Raising –	be a great to *f* extent the *h* (six feet be a great to *h* extent)
	– Relative Raising –	six feet be a great to a great *f* extent extent
S_7	– Op.-Inc. –	six feet not be a great to a great to *f* extent extent
S_{10}	– Noun Raising –	be a great to *g* extent *e*
	– SV-Inversion –	*e* be a great to *g* extent
S_6	– Noun Raising –	be a great to *f* extent the *g* (*e* be a great to *g* extent)
	– Relative Raising –	*e* be *a* great to a great to *f* extent extent
S_5	– *and*-Deletion –	*e* be a great to a great to *f* extent extent and six feet not
S_4	– Op.-Inc. –	*e* be a great to a great to some *f* extent extent and six feet not
	– rule (149) –	*e* be a great to more extent than six feet
	– rule (153) –	*e* be a more great extent than six feet

Relativization of *e*, Operator Incorporation on S_0 and NP-Reduction will yield (139).

In the same way, the derivation of (99), *John bought an older car than Bill*, will remain essentially the same as that given in (110), but will involve a few more steps. Instead of (110) we give the following underlying tree:

(163)

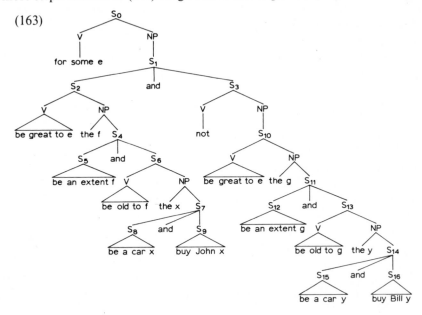

S_{13} will become: Bill buy an old to g car.
S_{10} will become: Bill buy an old to a great to e extent car.
S_2 will become: John buy an old to a great to e extent car.
S_0 will become: John buy an old to a great to some e extent
                            car and Bill not.

Hence, by rules (149) and (153):

John buy a more old car than Bill.

We conclude that the apparent counterexample:

(136)   John is taller than six feet.

far from disconfirming the analysis of the comparative given in previous sections, has led to a minor revision, which reduces all comparatives to forms of *more* (or *less*), and has in fact confirmed the analysis.

8.   If, as was proposed above, (61), *John is taller than Bill*, is analyzed as:

(148) $\exists e$ (the $f(f$ is an extent & John is tall to f)is great to e & not the g (g is an extent & Bill is tall to g) is great to e)

then the question arises how to analyze:

(164)   John is two inches taller than Bill.

In other words, what is the status of the constituent which indicates the degree of difference? The answer is not immediately obvious. Probably we have to do here with some sort of *for*-phrase, or 'extension phrase', placed before *not*:

'& for two inches it is not the case that the g . . .'

A *for*-phrase of this kind is comparable to durative phrases (which are, perhaps, a subspecies of extension phrases):

(165)   I haven't been in England for two years.

This sentence is ambiguous. It either means:

(166)   For two years it has not been the case that I was in England.

or:

(167)   It is not the case that for two years I have been in England.

But:

(168)   I haven't won a match for two years.

is not ambiguous; it only allows for an interpretation analogous with (166). Certain verbs, such as *not* or *be in England*, allow for a durative phrase. Other verbs, such as *win a match*, do not, which accounts for the non-ambiguity of (168). In the same way, it may be suggested, *not* freely allows for an extension phrase to be its immediate higher verb, but not, for example, *be great to an extent*. However, the matter is speculative.

General problems of underlying quantification and of tense and aspect are involved here, which cannot be disentangled now. The question of the status of the constituent *two inches* cannot be considered separately from the wider issue, not touched upon so far, why it is that, e.g.:

(169)   Bill is not so tall as John.

is synonymous with:

(170)   Bill is less tall than John.

and cannot mean that Bill is taller than John.[17]

An indication that we have to do with a *for*-phrase of extension, is:

(171)   But for two inches Bill is as tall as John.

which can be analyzed as:

(172)   For two inches it is not the case that Bill is as tall as John.

The same kind of *for*-phrase is found in, for example:

(173)   But for one town the army is in control of the country.

We do not have to be certain, however, as to the status of the constituent *two inches* in order to be able to derive the following sentence:

(174)   John is more taller than Bill than Peter.

with the help of the rules that have been proposed so far. In carrying out the derivation, let us assume that *two inches* is derived from a scope-bearing verb 'for two inches'. The precise form of this assumption, however, is not essential for the derivation. (174) can be paraphrased as:

(175)   The extent by which John is taller than Bill is greater than the extent by which Peter is taller than Bill.

---

[17] It is perhaps possible to account for this by considering $\exists e$ (x *be great to e*) as derived from:

$$\exists e \, \forall v \, (v \in e \supset x \text{ be great to } v) \qquad \text{where '}v\text{' stands for 'value'}$$

The comparative would then be analyzed as:

$$\exists e \, (\forall v \, (v \in e \supset x \text{ be great to } v) \, \& \, \text{not } \forall v \, (v \in e \supset y \text{ be great to } v))$$

which gives the correct interpretation. The matter cannot be pursued here, however.

In accordance with the assumptions hitherto adhered to, the deepest under-lying structure will be (176). The derivation will run as follows:

S_{29}	– Noun Raising –	be a great to i extent the h (Bill be tall to h)
	– Relative Raising –	Bill be tall to a great to i extent
S_{24}	– Op-Inc. (twice) –	for b Bill not be tall to a great to i extent
S_{23}	– as S_{29} –	Peter be tall to a great to i extent
S_{21}	– Comparative –	Peter be b taller than Bill
S_{18}	– Noun Raising –	be a great to e extent the b (Peter be b taller than Bill)
	– Relative Raising –	Peter be a great to e extent taller than Bill
S_3	– Op-Inc. –	Peter not be a great to e extent taller than Bill
S_2	– as S_{18} –	John be a great to e extent taller than Bill
S_1	– *and*-Deletion –	John be a great to e extent taller than Bill and Peter not
S_0	– Op-Inc. –	John be a great to some e extent taller than Bill and Peter not

Rule (149) converts this into:

John be more taller than Bill than Peter

which is close enough to (174).

The process is, of course, recursive: we can say how much more John is taller than Bill than Peter, and it may be the case that John is more more tall than Bill than Peter than Arthur.

9. We have tried to solve a number of problems by giving analyses and rules which have some explanatory value. The cases that have been dealt with seem to me to be central to the question what the essential grammatical structure of the comparative is. There are many aspects of this type of construction, however, that have not been touched upon. Thus, nothing has been said about 'negative' comparatives with *less than*; nor about the use of negative gradables (*young, new, short, small,* etc.) in comparatives; nor about the relations between comparatives and constructions such as *not so Adj as,* or *as Adj as,* or *too Adj to,* to mention just a few examples. There does not seem to be any reason to predict, however, that further investigation of these constructions would bring to light counterevidence to the analysis proposed here.

University of Oxford

(176)

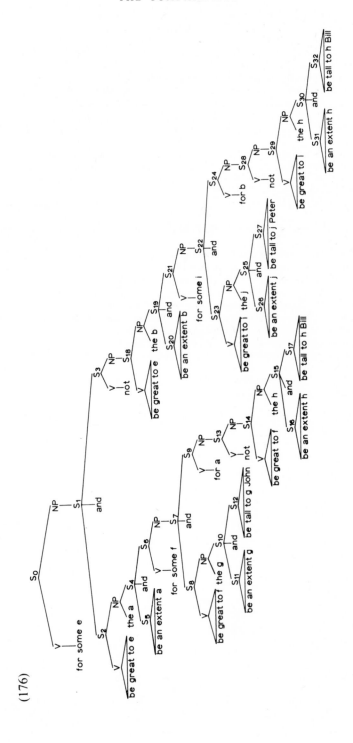

BIBLIOGRAPHY

Bach, E., 'Nouns and Noun Phrases', *Universals in Linguistic Theory*, E. Bach and R. T. Harms (eds.), New York (1968), pp. 91–122.

Baker, C. L., 'Double Negation', *Linguistic Inquiry* **1.2** (1970), pp. 169–86.

Chomsky, N., *Aspects of the Theory of Syntax* (1965), Cambridge, Mass.

Doherty, P. C. and Schwartz, A., 'The Syntax of the Compared Adjective in English', *Language* **43** (1967), pp. 903–36.

Huddleston, R., 'More on the English Comparative', *Journal of Linguistics* **3.1** (1967), pp. 91–102.

Jespersen, O., *Negation in English and Other Languages* (1917), Copenhagen.

Joly, A., *Negation and the Comparative Particle in English* (1967), Quebec.

Lakoff, G., 'On Derivational Constraints', *Selected Papers in Generative Semantics*, Tokyo (1970), pp. 120–42.

Lakoff, R., 'Some Reasons Why There Can't Be Any Some-any Rule', *Language* **45** (1969), pp. 608–15.

Lees, R. B., 'Grammatical Analysis of the English Comparative Construction', *Word* **17** (1961), pp. 171–85.

McCawley, J. D., 'Meaning and the Description of Languages', *Kotoba No Uchu* **2** (1967), No. 9: pp. 10–18; No. 10: pp. 38–48; No. 11: pp. 51–57.

McCawley, J. D., 'English as a *VSO*-Language', *Language* **46** (1970), pp. 286–99.

Pilch, H., 'Comparative Constructions in English', *Language* **41** (1965), pp. 37–58.

Reichenbach, H., *Elements of Symbolic Logic* (1947), New York.

Ross, J. R., 'A Proposed Rule of Tree Pruning', *Modern Studies in English*, D. A. Reibel and S. A. Schane (eds.), Englewood Cliffs (1968), pp. 288–99.

Russell, B., *An Inquiry into Meaning and Truth* (1940), London.

Seuren, P. A. M., *Operators and Nucleus, A Contribution to the Theory of Grammar* (1969), Cambridge.

Smith, C. S., 'A Class of Complex Modifiers in English', *Language* **37** (1961), pp. 342–65.

Strawson, P. F., *Introduction to Logical Theory* (1952), London.

EMANUEL VASILIU

SOME SEMANTIC AMBIGUITIES RELATED TO 'TENSE CATEGORY'

Rudolf Carnap, In Memoriam

1. INTRODUCTORY REMARKS

Understanding a sentence is but knowing *when* that sentence is to be asserted. Indeed, if I am given only a grammar of English and a list of English words (without their translation into another language I know), I can correctly construct an English sentence like

(1)   *the book is on the table*

but I am not able to make any assertion by means of this sentence because I am not aware of the *conditions* under which I could do it. We are allowed to consider that knowing these 'conditions' is equal to knowing that (1) is to be asserted if and only if:

(a)   there is exactly one object which, in a language like French is called *livre*;

(b)   there is exactly one object, which in the same language is called *table*;

(c)   between the two objects a definite spatial relation holds: they are *contiguous*, the first object occupies the place which is *over* the second one, and this spatial relation is indefinitely extended in time.

If I know (a)–(c) I am enabled to assert sentence (1) any time I see (or look at) a definite actual 'book' which actually 'lies' on a definite actual 'table'. In other words, if I know (a)–(c), I actually know which *facts* sentence (1) refers to. Moreover, by knowing (a)–(c) and listening to or uttering (1), I am enabled to say (1) does or does not correspond to the facts it is referring to: if (1) does correspond to these facts it is *true*, if it does not, it is *false*.

We can further say that (a)–(c) are the conditions under which (1) is to be considered *true*; if (1) fulfils these conditions it is to be considered true, if this is not the case, it is to be considered false.

The above explanations were intended to make clear what is understood here by *meaning*. In agreement with Carnap's view we consider that 'a

F. Kiefer and N. Ruwet (eds.), Generative Grammar in Europe, 565–581. All Rights Reserved.
Copyright © 1973 by D. Reidel Publishing Company, Dordrecht-Holland.

knowledge of the truth conditions of a sentence is identical with an understanding of its meaning' (Carnap (1958), p. 15). In other words, the meaning
of an expression S in a language L is the set K of truth conditions assigned to
S.

In agreement with this conception of 'meaning', *semantics* is meant as a
formal device by means of which a set of truth conditions, K_i, is assigned to
any definite sentence S_i of a language *L*.

Obviously, the above outlined conception about *meaning* and *semantics*
is very restrictive. It seems then to me to be worth discussing two points
closely related to this conception.

(1) Since natural languages do not contain only sentences making statements about the world, but also non-asserting sentences (like interrogative
sentences, and exclamative sentences, etc.), and sentences expressing emotion,
one might raise the question of whether the above defined concepts of
meaning and *semantics* can be taken as an adequate base for a semantic
description of natural languages. On the other hand, each speaker of a
natural language is allowed to make a definite selection among several
possibilities of *referring* to the same facts in terms of his language; sentences
resulting from these various allowed 'choices' are provided with a 'stylistic
value'; there are many linguists who consider that this 'stylistic value' of a
sentence belongs to its 'meaning'; that is, the 'meaning' of a sentence can be
divided into two parts: a 'cognitive' meaning and a 'stylistic' meaning. One
might ask, then, whether our conception of meaning and semantics can
account for the 'stylistic meaning'.

Both questions should be answered in the following way. Defining meaning and specifying the framework of semantics is a matter of *decision*. Accordingly, we have to say any sentence which is not a statement does not have
meaning (of course, in the sense discussed above); the information they
convey may concern the attitude of the speaker towards the expressions he
is using, and then, such information is of the same type as the information
conveyed by gesture, cry, etc. and is to be considered as para-linguistic
information associated with the purely linguistic one.[1] On the other hand, it
is to be noted that a large sub-class of non-assertive sentences, viz. interrogative ones, can be reduced, by means of a convenient device, to simple assertive sentences (see Vasiliu, 1970, pp. 181–184).

(2) For many scholars (linguists and/or logicians) the identification of
meaning with *truth conditions* might seem, perhaps, inconvenient because of

---

[1] Sentences called 'performative' in Austin's (1970, pp. 233–252.) terminology should be included in the same category. This kind of 'sentences' is to be viewed mostly as a part of an extra-
linguistic activity and not as a part of a language.

the ambiguity which to a very large extent characterizes natural languages. Indeed, since we assume that a sentence like

(2)   *I am leaving right now*

is true if I utter it at 4.30 p.m., Jan. 20, 71 and is false if uttered by somebody else at exactly the same time, or if I myself uttered it at 4.31 p.m., Jan. 20, 71, how are we to establish the truth conditions of such a sentence? Moreover, how are we to infer anything correctly from a sentence whose truth value can not be established in agreement with a set of explicit rules? Furthermore: since (2) does 'say' something about the world but what it 'says' is hopeless to express in terms of a set of 'truth conditions', it follows that the *meaning* of (2) (i.e. what 'is said' by (2)) is something different from the 'truth-conditions' of (2). Thus, describing exactly this kind of *meaning* which is not reducible to truth-conditions is the task of the semantics of natural languages.

Although in some respects this argument might look correct, in many others it is, to say the least, questionable, first, because it disregards the fact that any sentence like (2) may be said by any speaker (who knows the facts it refers to) to be true or false; furthermore, if it is accepted as a true sentence, its negation is considered false by any speaker (again who knows the facts the sentence refers to). In other words and in a more general way, I would say that the view under discussion here has no empirical support, because for *given sentence* (2), a speaker can, in principle, answer the question of whether (2) is true or false; and when he is unable to do this, he is able to explain *why* (because he does not know *whom I* refers to, because he does not know *when* (2) was uttered, and so on). That means the speaker is aware of the 'truth conditions' of a sentence like (2).

Secondly, to characterize (2) simply as *ambiguous* and further to say: since (2) is ambiguous it cannot be characterized either as true or as false and, accordingly, no inference can be made from (2) seems to me to be an oversimplified description. As a matter of fact, (2) *is* ambiguous, but its ambiguity is in some fashion limited because (2) obviously is not referring to *any* of the facts of the world: (2) could 'mean' many things but it cannot mean 'the cat eats the mice'; a more refined semantic description should account precisely for these 'limits' of the ambiguity of (2). On the other hand, if the range of the ambiguity of (2) is limited it follows that the class of facts (2) is referring to is also limited and we can then say that (2) should be asserted with respect to *these* facts. If such is the case, it follows that we can establish the conditions under which (2) may be asserted, that is, we can establish the truth conditions of (2). Furthermore, if such truth conditions are established, then one is enabled to make inferences from (2) about other sentences.

I think this view has the advantage of accounting for the empirical facts we just mentioned: the speaker's capability of characterizing (2) as true or false and the speaker's ability to make correct inferences from (2) to some other sentence(s).

The aim of this paper is to develop a formal device that accounts for some ambiguities related to the grammatical category of tense.

2. INFORMAL DESCRIPTION OF SOME AMBIGUITIES

In this paragraph I am going to consider some cases of ambiguity which, although not always obviously concerned with 'tense', may be reduced to ambiguities related to the tense, which will be described in terms of a formal device under Section 3.

Let us consider the following pairs:

(3)   (a) *I am leaving*
         (b) *I am staying*

(4)   (a) *I left*
         (b) *I stayed*

(5)   (a) *I am going to leave*
         (b) *I am going to stay*

(6)   (a) *I am leaving*
         (b) *I left*

(7)   (a) *I am leaving*
         (b) *I am going to leave*

(8)   (a) *I left*
         (b) *I am going to leave*

Since *to leave* and *to stay* are antonymous verbs, one is enabled to say sentences under (3)–(5) *contradict* each other (or, in other words, (3)–(5) are pairs of *incompatible* sentences).

However, this is not the only possibility for understanding these sentences; they may be understood as perfectly compatible if we assume either that:

(i) sentence (a) (from each of the pairs (3)–(5)) is uttered by one speaker, whereas sentence (b) (from each of the pairs (3)–(5)) is uttered by another one; or that

(ii) *the same speaker* utters sentences (a), (b) (from each of the pairs (3)–(5)) at two different times (let us say (a) at the time T_i and (b) at the time T_{i+1}).

Once the conditions under which the pairs under (3)–(5) are pairs of *compatible* sentences are established, we can more easily determine the conditions under which the same pairs should be understood as pairs of incompatible sentences. We should say (3)–(5) are pairs of incompatible sentences if we assume that:

(iii) both sentences (of the same pair) are uttered by *the same speaker* and each of them refers to the *same time* (T_i).

The pairs under (6)–(8) display a more complex ambiguity.

On the one hand, they can be understood as pairs of *contradictory* (or *incompatible*) sentences. Indeed, a sentence like (6)(b) asserts that the individual who is the 'agent' or the 'instigator' of the action is at a time T_i, the time T_i is *before* the time T_j, when sentence (6)(b) is uttered, and the action of 'leaving' is performed precisely at that time T_i, which can be neither the time when the sentence is uttered, nor the time *after* the sentence is uttered.

That is, if we make the assertion that the individual that '*I*' from (6)(b) refers to performs the action 'to leave' at a time which is *before* the time (6)(b) is uttered, this assertion precludes the possibility of asserting that the *same individual* performs the *same action* at a time which is either *simultaneous* with the moment (6)(b) is uttered or which is *after* the time (6)(b) is uttered.

On the other hand, sentences (6)(a) and (b) can be interpreted as *co-extensive* (that is referring to the same event) if we assume that the one individual, which '*I*' from (6)(b) refers to, utters (6)(a) 'in the past' (for example, in a sentence like: *He said*: '*I am leaving*', 'I am leaving' refers to a past event and this event may occur exactly at the same time as that to which a sentence like (6)(b) refers). In the same way, the pair (7) may be understood as referring to the same time location (that means (a) and (b) under (7) are *co-extensive*). Obviously, a similar understanding is not possible for (8).

3. The Formal Device Used in the Semantic Description

The following approach is to be viewed as derived from the theoretical principles developed in Vasiliu (1970). In agreement with this theory the following is assumed:

(1) There is a *semantic system* S_i of the form described in Vasiliu (1970), pp. 101–128, 194–195 (this system is similar to those constructed by Carnap (1958), Reichenbach (1966), etc.).

(2) There is a finite set of *translation rules* of the form specified in Vasiliu (1970), pp. 196–212, by means of which each kernel sentence generated by a '$[\varepsilon, F]$ grammar' of the form specified in Vasiliu (1970), pp. 184–189 is put into correspondence with one (or more) expressions in S_i, so that, if an ex-

pression E from S_i is a translation of a kernel sentence, 'E', from the natural language, L_i, E and E have the *same intension* (or, in other words, they are L-equivalent – in Carnap's (1958), sense – or they have the same meaning).

(3) If E is a translation of E, then, every semantic characterization which holds for E in S_i holds also for its corresponding in L_i expression, E.

(4) System S_i is a *coordinate-language* in the sense of Carnap (1958), pp. 161–164; (1960), pp. 74–75. We assume then that S_i refers to an ordered domain of space-time points. The *position* of each space-time point is determined with respect to the *time-axis* and to the *space-axis*. The *individual expressions of the standard form* of the system S_i show by their form the definite position within the ordered domain they refer to.

Once these general assumptions are made explicit, we may enter into some details that concern our specific topic.

The expressions of the standard form of S_i are of the type 'a_j^i'. The superscript i $(i = 1, 2, 3, \ldots)$ refers to the position of the individual 'a' with respect to the space-axis: a_j^i is located (with respect to this axis) AFTER a_j^{i-1} and BEFORE a_j^{i+1}. The subscript j refers to the position of the individual 'a' with respect to the time-axis: a_j^i is located (with respect to this axis) at a time which is AFTER 'a_{j-1}^i' and BEFORE 'a_{j+1}^i'. Thus, 'a_j^i' refers to that one and only one individual which has the *location i* at the time *j*. The following diagram is intended to show how various expressions of the standard form refer to the position one individual occupies within the ordered domain:

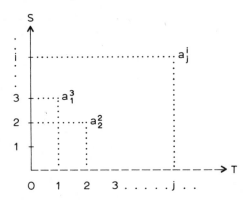

An expression like 'a_j^0' simply indicates a position on the time-axis, without respect to any space location; an expression like 'a_0^i' indicates the position on the space-axis, without respect to any time location; expression 'a_T^0' is meant to refer to *any* time-location.[2]

---

[2] Expression 'a_T^0' is used here instead of 'a_0^0' from Vasiliu (1970), p. 230, which, I think, has the disadvantage of being misleading.

An expression of the form 'H 'y' is an abbreviated form for an iota-expression:

3.1. DEFINITION: H '$y = {}_{Df} (\imath x) H (x, y)$

In agreement with 3.1. we may establish the following proposition:

3.2. PROPOSITION: $F(H'y) \equiv F[(\imath x)H x, y]$

The right-hand side of 3.2 is, obviously, an *individual description* (see Carnap (1958), pp. 142–146; (1960), pp. 32–35; Reichenbach (1966), pp. 256–266). An individual description should be defined as follows:

3.3. DEFINITION: $F[(\imath x) Hx, y] = {}_{Df} (\exists x) (z)[Hx, y \cdot (Hz, y \equiv Iz, x) \cdot Fx]$

(in 3.3. 'I' is a predicate whose intension is 'identical with'). A sentence like that from the right-hand side of 3.3. says that 'there is *exactly one* individual "x", which is in the relation "H"' with "y" and it also has the property (or: belongs to the class) "F".'

Expression '$(\exists x) (z)[Hx, y \cdot (Hz, y \equiv Iz, x) \cdot Fx]$' is to be divided into two parts; the first one, viz.: '$[\exists x)(z)[Hx, y \cdot (Hz, y \equiv Iz, x)]$' is said to assert the so called *uniqueness condition*, that is, it asserts that 'there is *exactly one* individual, x, which is in relation "H" with "y"'. An iota-expression (like '$(\imath x) Hx, y$' or its equivalent, 'H'y') always occurs as an *argument* of a *predicate*; moreover, such an expression may refer to the same individual to which an individual constant, like, for example, 'b', refers to. In such a case, we are allowed to write down:

(9) $(\imath x) Hx, y = b$

If (9) is true, then, we are allowed further to substitute 'b' for '$(\imath x) Hx, y$' in the left-hand side expression of 3.3.; from this substitution, we obtain:

(10) $F(b)$

On the other hand, by substituting an iota-expression for an individual variable within an expression like

(11) Fz

we obtain a well-formed expression in S_i:

(12) $F[(\imath x) Hx, y]$

However expression (12) is not logically implied by

(13) $(x) Fx$

whereas (10) is logically implied by (13).

The first and second person singular personal pronouns are usually said to refer to the *person uttering the message* (the first person) and to the person *receiving the message* uttered by the first person (the second person). This informal description of the meaning of the two personal pronouns suggests the following semantic interpretation:

Let us consider two predicates in S_i, i.e. 'EM' and 'RE' (both are two-place predicates). With respect to each of them we establish the following designation rules (for the concept of designation rules, see Carnap (1960), p. 4):

3.4. RULES OF DESIGNATION

(a) EMx, y = 'x' is *'emitent'* with respect to 'y'
(b) REx, y = 'x' is *'receiver'* with respect to 'y'

The relation referred to by the predicates 'EM', 'RE' are *antisymmetric, intransitive* and *irreflexive*; 'REx, y' is the *converse* of 'EMy, x'.

The so called 'absolute tenses' of the verb are usually defined by referring the time the action is performed to the time the message is uttered: then, the *past* is defined by the fact that the action is performed *before* the time of the message, the *present* is defined by the fact that the action is performed *at the same time* as the time of the message, the *future* is defined by the fact that the action is performed *after* the time of the message. This traditional description of the meaning of 'tenses' is described in terms of S_i as follows.

Let us establish the convention that the expression 'a_j' of the standard form refers to the time the message is uttered. Let us further assume that the lexicon of S_i contains predicates 'SIM', 'ANT' and 'POS' provided with the following rules of designation specifying their meaning:

3.5. RULES OF DESIGNATION

(a) SIMx, a_j^0 = 'x' is *simultaneous* with 'a_j^0'
(b) POSx, a_j^0 = 'x' *succeeds in time* 'a_j^0'
(c) ANTx, a_j^0 = 'x' *precedes in time* 'a_j^0'

In agreement with 3.4. and with the usual semantic description of the personal pronouns, we can say that the following relations hold between the formatives '*I*', '*you* (sing)' from English and the expressions 'EM 'y', 'RE 'x':

(14)   (a) T[EM'y, *I*]
        (b) T[RE'x, *you* (sing)]

In (14), the symbol T of the meta-language used here is meant to refer to a relation of *translation*; accordingly, (14)(a), (b) are to be read:

(15) (a) 'EM'y' is a *translation of* 'I'
    (b) 'RE'x' is a *translation of* '*you* (sing)'

Here T and '*translation of*' are understood as having the same meaning as that defined in Vasiliu (1970), pp. 189–195, especially theorem 49.4, p. 194, that is, they express an L-equivalence (see Carnap (1958), pp. 15–23; (1960), pp. 7–16, especially 13–16), or, in other words, they say that the two expressions (related by T) have the *same intension*.

In an analogous way, we may consider that the following relations hold, too:

(16) (a) $T[SIMx, a_j^0, Pres]$
    (b) $T[ANTx, a_j^0, Past]$
    (c) $T[POSx, a_j^0, Future]$

It is worth noting that the variable 'x' will be required by the further translation rules (which are not going to be mentioned here; see Vasiliu, (1970), pp. 208–209, RT24 and the explanations referring to it) to be *identical with the first argument* of the atomic sentence which translates the verb. In other words, since the *first argument* of such an expression corresponds to the 'subject' or, more precisely, to the 'agent' of the action we can say an expression like '$SIMx, a_j^0$' or '$ANTx, a_j^0$' is concerned with the time location of the 'agent' and not of the action itself. Since the individual which is the 'agent' is but a *term* of the relation expressed by the verb, it *must* be simultaneous with the relation expressed by the verb, it is reasonable to assume that expressions like those above mentioned express in an indirect way the location in time of the action itself. This 'indirect time-location' of the verb is required by expressions in S_i which are translations of copula sentences (in L_i): such sentences should be translated in S_i by implicational-expressions, where no atomic sentence corresponds to the copula, but only the implication sign '$\supset$' (see Vasiliu (1970), pp. 183–184, 204 rule RT17).

We assume, finally, that between the formatives (to) *leave*, (to) *stay* from English and the predicate constants 'LE', 'ST', from S_i the following relation holds:

(17) (a) $T[LE, leave]$
    (b) $T[ST, stay]$

According to the above explanations, the translations for (3)–(8) should be:

(3′) (a) $SIM\ [(EM\ 'y), a_j^0] \cdot LE(EM\ 'y)$
    (b) $SIM\ [(EM\ 'y), a_j^0] \cdot ST(EM\ 'y)$

$(4')$ (a) $\text{ANT}[(\text{EM 'y}), a_j^0] \cdot \text{LE}(\text{EM 'y})$
            (b) $\text{ANT}[(\text{EM 'y}), a_j^0] \cdot \text{ST}(\text{EM 'y})$

$(5')$ (a) $\text{POS}[(\text{EM 'y}), a_j^0] \cdot \text{LE}(\text{EM 'y}).$
            (b) $\text{POS}[(\text{EM 'y}), a_j^0] \cdot \text{ST}(\text{EM 'y})$

$(6')$ (a) $\text{SIM}[(\text{EM 'y}), a_j^0] \cdot \text{LE}(\text{EM 'y})$
            (b) $\text{ANT}[(\text{EM 'y}), a_j^0] \cdot \text{LE}(\text{EM 'y})$

$(7')$ (a) $\text{SIM}[(\text{EM 'y}), a_j^0] \cdot \text{LE}(\text{EM 'y})$
            (b) $\text{POS}[(\text{EM 'y}), a_j^0] \cdot \text{LE}(\text{EM 'y})$

$(8')$ (a) $\text{ANT}[(\text{EM 'y}), a_j^0] \cdot \text{LE}(\text{EM 'y})$
            (b) $\text{POS}[(\text{EM 'y}), a_j^0] \cdot \text{LE}(\text{EM 'y})$

4. THE FORMAL ACCOUNT FOR TENSE AMBIGUITIES

Since system S_i refers to an ordered domain and since S_i is a coordinate language, the *individuals* to which individual descriptions of S_i refer are various *positions* within the ordered domain. That is, expression 'EM 'y' is to be understood as referring to some definite position, 'a_k^i'.

An expression like 'a_k^i' stands for the pair of numbers $\{i, k\}$ (for example, if we have a_3^2, it stands for the pair $\{2, 3\}$; in other words, the couple $\{2, 3\}$ is taken as the *coordinate* of a position a which occupies the *next position in space after a_3^1* and the *next position in time after a_2^2*). Under such conditions the various pairs of numbers $\{_j^i\}$ may be interpreted as the possible *values* of the individual variables 'x', 'y', ...

In agreement with (9), (10) and the explanations under them, we are allowed, in principle, to make the substitution

(18) $\text{EM 'y}/a_k^i$

in a sentence like

(19) $\text{LE}(\text{EM 'y})$

and we obtain

(20) $\text{LE}(a_k^i)$

which is to be understood as 'the individual ($=$ position) having as coordinate the pair $\{i, k\}$ has the property of "leaving".'

Nevertheless it is worth to observe an identity like

(21) $\text{EM 'y} = a_k^i$

is always *factual* and, accordingly, does not *give* the extension of 'EM 'y' (in the sense of Carnap's book, (1960), pp. 73–81, especially definition 19.1). That means the extension of 'EM 'y'' is *not* logically determined by (21), but only *factually* determined.

The main consequence of this statement is that an expression like 'EM 'y'' may in principle refer to *any* of the positions within the ordered domain.

Since S_i is a coordinate language and, accordingly, since the values of the individual variables are pairs of numbers, we are enabled to use the *restricted quantifiers*. That is, between a quantifier and its operand we are going to insert a number expression, which should be understood as restricting the domain the preceding quantifier refers to. Then, an expression like:

(22) $(x)(^i_j)\,Fx$

is understood as saying "every number pair up to $\{^i_j\}$ has the property (or: belongs to the class) 'F' "; an expression like

(23) $(\exists x)(^i_j)Fx$

is understood as saying "there is at least one pair of numbers up to $\{^i_j\}$, such that it has the property (or: belongs to the class) 'F'."

We can now say the following expressions are *L*-TRUE and should be taken as postulates of the system S_i. Let us assume that expressions 'a^0_j' refers always to the time the message is uttered

4.1. POSTULATES

(a) $(\exists x)\,\mathrm{SIM}x, a^0_j \supset (x)(^i_{m=j})\,\mathrm{SIM}x, a^0_j \cdot (x)(^i_{m<j})\,\mathrm{ANT}x, a^0_j \cdot (x)(^i_{m>j})$
        $\mathrm{POS}x, a^0_j$

(b) $(x)(^i_{m=j})\,\mathrm{SIM}x, a^0_j \supset (x)(^i_{m\neq j}) \sim \mathrm{SIM}x, a^0_j$

(c) $(x)(^i_{m<j})\,\mathrm{ANT}x, a^0_j \supset (x)(^i_{m\geq j}) \sim \mathrm{ANT}x, a^0_j$

(d) $(x)(^i_{m>j})\,\mathrm{POS}x, a^0_j \supset (x)(^i_{m\leq j}) \sim \mathrm{POS}x, a^0_j$

The postulates (a)–(d) under 4.1. should be understood as follows:

(a) If there is at least one individual which is *simultaneous* with j (= the time of the message), then the following hold: every pair of numbers $\{i, m\}$ whose second member m is *equal with* j, is *simultaneous* with j; every pair of members $\{i, m\}$ whose second member, m, is *smaller than* j is *before* the time j; every pair of members $\{i, j\}$ whose second member, m, is *greater than* j is *after* the time j.

(b) If every pair of numbers $\{i, m\}$ whose second member, m, is equal with j is *simultaneous* with j, then every pair of numbers $\{i, m\}$ whose second member, m, is not equal with j *is not simultaneous* with j.

(c) If every pair of numbers $\{i, m\}$ whose second member, m, is smaller than

j is *before* the time j, then every pair of numbers $\{i, m\}$ whose second member, m, is greater than j or equal with j *is not before* the time j.

(d) If every pair of numbers, $\{i, m\}$, whose second member, m, is greater than j, *is after* the time j, then every pair of numbers $\{i, j\}$ whose second member, m, is smaller than j or equal with j *is not after* the time j.

The immediate consequence of 4.1. is the following lemma:

4.2. LEMMA:

(a) $(x)(^i_{m=j})(\text{SIM}x, a^0_j \supset \sim \text{ANT}x, a^0_j \cdot \sim \text{POS}x, a^0_j)$

(b) $(x)(^i_{m<j})(\text{ANT}x, a^0_j \supset \sim \text{SIM}x, a^0_j \cdot \sim \text{POS}x, a^0_j)$

(c) $(x)(^i_{m>j})(\text{POS}x, a^0_j \supset \sim \text{SIM}x, a^0_j \cdot \sim \text{ANT}x, a^0_j)$

Let us assume now that S_i is provided by a class of *meaning postulates* (in Carnap's (1960), pp. 222–229; see also Vasiliu (1970), pp. 213–238); let us further assume that among the other meaning postulates of S_i, the following one is to be found also:

4.3. MEANING POSTULATE: $(x)(\text{LE}x \supset \sim \text{ST}x)$

Let us turn back to examples (3')–(8'), in order to give them a semantic characterization.

We make the following assumptions with respect to (3')(a), (b)

(24)   *Assumption*
      (a) The time of the message is 'a^0_j'
      (b) In both (a), (b), for 'EM 'y' we have: EM '$y = x^i_j$'

In agreement with (24) we are allowed to replace 'EM 'y' by 'x^i_j' at any occurrence of 'EM 'y' within (3')(a), (b). We obtain:

(3'')   (a) $\text{SIM}(x^i_j, a^0_j) \cdot \text{LE}(x^i_j)$
      (b) $\text{SIM}(x^i_j, a^0_j) \cdot \text{ST}(x^i_j)$

It is obvious that (a), (b) under (3'') are *contradictory* (or *incompatible*), because of 4.3. It follows that sentences (3)(a), (b) are also *contradictory* (or *incompatible*). Let us now assume the following:

(25)   *Assumption*
      (a) The time of the message is 'a^0_j' in (3')(a) and 'a^0_k' in (3')(b).
      (b) For 'EM 'y' we have in both (3')(a), (b) EM '$y = x^i_j$'

If we again make the substitution EM 'y/x^i_j' in (3') and if we put (b) 'a^0_k' in (3') instead of 'a^0_j', we obtain:

(3''')   (a) $\text{SIM}(x^i_j, a^0_j) \cdot \text{LE}(x^0_j)$
       (b) $\text{SIM}(x^i_j, a^0_k) \cdot \text{ST}(x^0_j)$

In accordance with 4.1.(b), '$\mathrm{SIM}(x_j^i, a_k^0)$ is *L-false*, and then (3''')(b) is also *L*-false, whereas (3''')(a) is *factually true or false*. Since (3''')(a), (b) are translations of (3)(a), (b), respectively, we are allowed to say that if (25) holds, then (3)(b) is *L-false*, whereas (3)(a) is *factually true or false*.

Let us assume the following:

(25')   *Assumption*
    (a) The same as in (25)(a)
    (b) The same as in (25)(b)
    (c) EM '$y = x_k^i$ in (3')(b).

In agreement with (25') we may substitute 'x_k^i' for 'EM 'y' in (3')(b) and we obtain

(3''')   (c) $\mathrm{SIM}(x_k^i, a_k^0)\,\mathrm{ST}(x_k^0)$

It is obvious that (3''')(c) is *factually true or false* and (3''')(a) and (3''')(c) are *factually compatible*. That means (3)(a), (b) are *factually compatible* if (25') holds.

A similar procedure should be applied in determining the meaning of (4) and (5).

(26)   *Assumption*
    (a) The time of the message is 'a_j^0'
    (b) For 'EM 'y' from (4')(a), (b) the following holds:
        EM '$y = x_k^i$
    (c) $k < j$

In such a case, that is, if (26) holds, sentences under (4') become *contradictory* (or *incompatible*) and, then, sentences under (4) should be considered *contradictory* (or *incompatible*) too.

Let us assume that the following is true:

(26')   *Assumption*
    (a) The time of the message is still 'a_j^0'
    (b) For 'EM 'y' from (4')(b) we have:
        EM '$y = x_n^i$
    and
        $n \geqslant j$
    (c) For 'EM 'y' from (4')(a) we have EM '$y = x_k^i$
    and
        $k < j$

The conditions specified under (26') enable us to consider that (4')(a) is *factually true or false* and (4′)(b) is *L-false.* Thus (4)(a) is *factually true or false* and (4)(b) is *L-false.*

If we assume:

(26″)   *Assumption*
           (a) The time of the message is still a_j^0
           (b) For 'EM 'y' from (4′)(a) we have:
               $$EM \, 'y = x_k^i$$
           and
               $$k < j$$
           (c) For 'EM 'y' from (4′)(b) we have:
               $$EM \, 'y = x_n^i$$
           and
               $$n < j$$

Then the sentences under (4′) are *factually compatible* and so are the sentences under (4).

It is easy to see that the sentences under (5′) become *contradictory* if we modify (26)(c) by assuming that $k > j$; if we modify (26′) by assuming that $n \leqslant j$ (instead of $n \geqslant j$) and $k > j$ (instead of $k < j$), then sentence (5′)(b) becomes *L-false* and (5′)(a) becomes *factually true or false*; if we modify (26″) by assuming that $k > j$ (instead of $k < j$) and $n > j$ (instead of $n < j$), then the sentences under (5′) become *factually compatible.* The same semantic characterization is to be given to the sentences under (5).

Let us now make the following assumption:

(27)   *Assumption*
           (a) The time of the message is in (6′), (7′) a_j^0
           (b)   EM 'y = x_j^i
               in both (6′) and (7′)

If we replace 'EM 'y' by 'x_j^i' in (6′), (7′) at any occurrence of 'EM 'y', we obtain

(6″)   (a) SIM $x_j^i, a_j^0 \cdot LE(x_j^i)$
           (b) ANT$x_j^i, a_j^0 \cdot LE(x_j^i)$

(7″)   (a) SIM $x_j^i, a_j^0 \cdot LE(x_j^i)$
           (b) POS $x_j^i, a_j^0 \cdot LE(x_j^i)$

According to 4.2., if (6″)(a), (7″)(a) are true, then (6″)(b), (7″)(b) are both false. Their corresponding (6)(b), (7)(b) are *false* when (6)(a), (7)(a) are *true.*

Let us now assume the following

(27')   *Assumption*
  (a) The time of the message is still 'a_j^0'
  (b) For 'EM 'y' from (6')(b), (7')(b) we have
    EM '$y = x_k^i$
  (c) In (6')(b) we have
    $k < j$
  (d) In (7')(b) we have
    $k > j$

In agreement with (27') we obtain

(6'')   (a) SIM $x_k^i, a_j^0 \cdot \mathrm{LE}(x_k^i)$
    (b) ANT$x_k^i, a_j^0 \cdot \mathrm{LE}(x_j^i)$

(7'')   (a) SIM $x_k^i, a_j^0 \cdot \mathrm{LE}(x_k^i)$
    (b) POS $x_k^i, a_j^0 \cdot \mathrm{LE}(x_k^i)$

According to 4.2.(b), (c), if (6'')(b), (7'')(b) are *true*, then (6'')(a), (7'')(a) are *false*. Accordingly, if (6)(b), (7)(b) are true then (6)(a), (7)(a) are false.

Let us make the following assumptions:

(28)   *Assumption*
  (a) The time of messages of (6')(a) and (6')(b) is different:
    a_j^0 for (6')(a)
    a_m^0 for (6')(b)
  (b) $j < m$
  (c) EM '$y = x_j^i$ in both (6')(a) and (6')(b).

According to (28) we obtain from (6'):

(6''')   (a) SIM $x_j^i, a_j^0 \cdot \mathrm{LE}(x_j^i)$
    (b) ANT$x_j^i, a_m^0 \cdot \mathrm{LE}(x_j^i)$

The equivalence between (a) and (b), under (6''') is *provable*. However, the proof of this equivalence involves the *factual* requirements under (28), I think it is not convenient to say (a) and (b) are *L-equivalent* and, then, *synonymous*; accordingly they are not synonymous, but only *co-extensive*. The corresponding sentences (6)(a), (b) are, consistently, *co-extensive*, too.

In the same way, sentences (7)(a), (b) can be said to be *co-extensive* if the following factual assumptions hold:

(29)   *Assumption*
  (a) The same as (28)(a)

(b) $j > m$

(c) The same as (28)(c).

Applying a similar procedure, it can be shown that:

(i)   if (8′)(a) is true, then (8)(b) is L-false;

(ii)   if (8′)(b) is true, then (8)(a) is L-false;

(iii)   if 'EM 'y' from (8′)(a) refers to another position than 'EM 'y' from (8′)(b), then (8′)(a), (b) are factually compatible;

(iv)   (a) and (b) cannot be co-extensive.

Sentences (8)(a), (b) should be characterized in terms of (i)–(iv).

5. CONCLUDING REMARKS

We may conclude our semantic analysis by pointing out the following results:

(1) The ambiguity of sentences like (3)–(8) can be formally described in terms of the procedure of the type proposed.

(2) The ambiguity of these expressions can be reduced to a relatively small number of types. The formal device describing each type of ambiguity is the set of *factual requirements* expressed in terms of what we called *Assumptions*.

We can then say that the semantic interpretation of the sentences under (3) is determined by the factual requirements under (24), (25), (25′); the semantic interpretation of the sentences under (4) is determined by the factual requirements under (26), (26′), (26″); the semantic interpretation of the sentences under (5) is determined by the factual requirements obtained by modifying the form of (26), (26′), (26″); the semantic interpretation of the sentences under (6), (7) is determined by the factual requirements under (27), (27′), (28), (29). The sentences under (8) can also be semantically characterized in terms of four sets of factual requirements which we have to infer (i), (ii), (iii) or (iv) from. We might say that sentences under (3), (4), (5) are *three-ways ambiguous*, (6)–(8) are four ways ambiguous.

(3) The formalism developed in Sections 3 and 4 enabled us to describe in an exact way the semantic relations holding between sentences in spite of the fact that these sentences were ambiguous; indeed, in Section 4 various pairs of sentences were characterized as 'incompatible' (or 'contradictory'), 'factually compatible', 'co-extensive', etc. although each of those sentences was ambiguous.

We can then say that the formal device used in Sections 3 and 4 accounts for the following empirical 'datum', I was referred to in Section 1: in spite of the ambiguity that characterizes every natural language, we can and actually do infer one sentence from another sentence in every natural language; or, in spite of the same ambiguity, we can say whether any assertion made in a natural language, is true or false or, if we can not do it, we can say *why* we can not do it.

University of Bucharest

REFERENCES

Austin, J. L.: 1970, *Philosophical Papers*, Second Edition, Oxford University Press, London–New York, 1970.
Carnap, R.: 1958, *Introduction to Symbolic Logic and Its Applications*, New York, 1958.
Carnap, R.: 1960, *Meaning and Necessity*, Third Impression, Chicago, 1960.
Reichenbach, H.: 1966, *Elements of Symbolic Logic*, New York–London, 1966.
Vasiliu, E.: 1970, *Elemente de teorie semantică a limbilor naturale*, Bucureşti, 1970.

H. J. VERKUYL

TEMPORAL PREPOSITIONS AS QUANTIFIERS*

1. INTRODUCTION

In this article two logical expressions will be examined as for their relationship to the meaning of some Temporal Prepositions. These are the existential and the universal *quantifier*, which systematically occur in the structure of logical propositions. In analyzing Temporal Adverbials we encounter many facts allowing for generalizations in terms of these quantifiers. This poses the problem of whether or not the two logical operators are present in the structure of Temporal Adverbials. And if so, how we should account for them.

The present article has a limited scope and aims at the presentation of some generalizations which, in my opinion, should be expressed in our grammar. I shall demonstrate that Temporal Prepositions can be conceived of as quantifiers by analyzing Adverbials containing the Dutch Prepositions *tijdens* (during), *in* (at, in), *op* (on) and *gedurende* (for (the duration of), during). It is argued that the first three have a function corresponding to that of the logical expression 'there is at least an entity t such that...' in propositions and that the fourth Preposition corresponds to the expression 'for all t it is the case that...' in a certain class of Temporal Adverbials called 'Duration-Dating Adverbials'. In the course of the argument some points emerge as being of general interest for the question of how the description of Temporal Adverbials should be taken in hand:

(i)   the so-called 'Aspects of the Verb' are of a compositional nature;

(ii) it is necessary to distinguish between so-called Setting Prepositions i.e. the four above mentioned Prepositions, and Relational Prepositions like *sinds* (since), *vóór* (before). This distinction corresponds to the logical distinction between an open domain and a closed domain, to which quantifiers apply;

(iii) reasons can be found for dividing Temporal Nouns into two cate-

*This is a revised version of an article written in Dutch, entitled 'De relevantie van logische operatoren voor de analyse van temporele bepalingen', in *Studia Neerlandica* 2 (1970) pp. 7–32. I am very much indebted to Prof. Dr. A. Kraak and Dr. D. van Dalen for their valuable comments and criticisms on the earlier version and to Mr. J. H. J. Luif for some improvements in the present version. Any remaining errors are my own. I wish to express my gratitude to Mr. P. F. Vincent for correcting my English.

gories. The first category (Type I) contains such Nouns as *minuut* (minute), *uur* (hour), *week* (week); the second one (Type II) contains Nouns like *middag* (afternoon), *zomer* (summer), *vergadering* (conference), etc., the difference being expressed in terms of continuity and discontinuity respectively. This distinction partly underlies the classification of Temporal Adverbials.

In traditional Dutch grammar the most explicit proposal on the classification of Temporal Adverbials is Den Hertog's quadripartition. (Den Hertog, 1903, I, Sect. 46.) We find (a) Adverbials of Time: *gisteren* (yesterday), *tijdens de oorlog* (during the war), *in 1968*; (b) Adverbials of Duration: *urenlang* (for hours), *de hele dag* (the whole day), *gedurende de oorlog* (for the duration of the war, throughout the war); (c) Adverbials denoting an initial or a terminal point: *sinds gisteren* (since yesterday); and (d) Adverbials of Frequency: *vaak* (often), *drie keer* (three times). The term 'Temporal Adverbial' will be used here to cover members of (a)–(c).[1]

It will be argued that (a) can be retained, but that (b) should be split up into two categories, one of which is called *Duration-Dating Adverbials* (DDA), having a Definite Determiner, e.g. *gedurende de oorlog* (for the duration of/throughout the war), whereas the other category is called *Duration-Measuring Adverbials* (DMA), having an Indefinite Determiner, e.g. *urenlang* (for hours), *gedurende drie uur* (for three hours). Both categories will be referred to as Durational Adverbials. Members of (c) do not fall within our scope. It can be shown that they should be distributed over Adverbials of Time, DDA's and DMA's (See Verkuyl, forthcoming).

2. QUANTIFIERS AND PREDICATES

Quantifiers always occur with variables, i.e. terms which have no meaning in themselves. A proposition like:

(1) $(\exists x)$ $(x$ is sick$)$

can be paraphrased as: 'There is at least an x such that x is sick'. And the proposition:

(2) $(\forall x)$ $(x$ is sick$)$

asserts: 'for all x it is true that x is sick'. The quantifiers are said to bind the

---

[1] See also KVL (1969, p. 68) for the view that Adverbials of Frequency cannot be regarded as Temporal Adverbials because they do not refer to stretches or points of time. They pluralize Verb Phrases and are comparable with numerical elements in Noun Phrases. See also Verkuyl (1969, pp. 60–72) and McCawley (1968, p. 162).

variables; the two x's of (1) refer to the same entity. Proposition (1) expresses that there is *at least* an x who is sick. The quantifier determines the quantity of entities x the proposition relates to.

As it stands now, both paraphrases given are incomplete. Quantification is somewhat senseless if we do not determine the domain to which the proposition applies. The set to which x in our examples belongs is called the *Universe of Discourse* or *Domain of Discourse*. I shall speak of 'domain'. The exact paraphrase of (1) should read as follows: 'There is at least an entity x in our Domain of Discourse, such that x...'. Our paraphrase of (2) should be modified in the same way. Most normally the letters 'x', 'y', 'z', ... are used for objects. In the case of propositions concerning temporal entities we use the letter 't', often with subscripts: t_o (= Point of Speech), t_i, t_j, t_A, t_B, etc. Our claim that Temporal Prepositions should be conceived of as quantifiers amounts to saying that sentences like:

(3)   *Tijdens de vergadering* is de voorzitter flauwgevallen.
        During the conference the chairman fainted.
(4)   *Gedurende de vergadering* zat hij te lezen.
        Throughout the conference he sat reading.

should be represented in the same manner as (1) and (2). That is, if it is true that *tijdens* (during) corresponds to the existential quantifier, then we should be able to analyze (3) as:

(3a) $(\exists t) \, F(x_1, t)$

that is: there is at least a t such that the chairman fainted at t, where 'F' represents the Predicate 'to faint at', and 'x_1' is short for 'the chairman'. Likewise, sentence (4) should be represented as:

(4a) $(\forall t) \, R(y_1, t)$

that is, for all t it is true that he was reading, where 'R' represents the Predicate 'read at' and 'y_1' is short for 'he'. Indeed, (3a) and (4a) seem to represent (3) and (4) adequately. In both cases it is clear that *de vergadering* (the conference) refers to the domain containing the temporal entities to which the proposition applies. Much the same result can be obtained by analyzing (3) and (4) in another way. Consider the logical proposition

(3b) $D(X_1, Y_1)$

where 'D' represents 'during' and 'X_1' is short for 'the conference' and 'Y_1' for 'the chairman fainted'.

Now, the point is: (3b) expresses that the Preposition can be conceived of as a two-place Predicate, having as its arguments X_1 and Y_1. That is, (3b) represents the fact that sentence (3) relates two events viz. the event 'the conference' and the event 'the chairman's fainting'. The stretch of time referred to by *de vergadering* includes the points of time referred to by *de voorzitter viel flauw*. The title of this article suggests an option for analyzing sentences like (3) and (4) in terms of quantifiers. I do not think it is necessary to choose between (3a) and (3b), and, in fact, I did not. Quantifiers are translatable into Predicates. By analyzing such Prepositions as *tijdens* and *gedurende* in terms of quantifiers I simply hope to make some generalizations which would not be captured so easily if we were to turn immediately to representations like (3b).

3. OPEN AND CLOSED DOMAINS

The Domains of Discourse in sentences like (3) and (4) are located on the Time axis or may even be the Time axis itself; temporal domains can be said to be partially ordered by the relationship '$\leqslant$'. The entities belonging to a domain D_i are linearly ordered. D_i can be closed or open. By this, I mean to say that temporal entities belonging to D_i can constitute either a finite set or an infinite set. Sentences like:

(5)   Vanaf morgen *staan er minstens vijf maanschepen op de maan.*
         From tomorrow *there will be at least five spacecrafts on the moon.*

involve an open domain. That is, the durative event referred to by the italicized constituent of (5) holds virtually infinitely. An open domain is characterized by the fact that only one boundary is given explicitly.[2]

In sentences like:

(6)   Vorige week is hij overleden
         Last week he died

the referent of *vorige week* is a closed interval: the event 'his dying' has taken place within the boundaries of the interval 'last week'.

The Prepositions *tijdens*, *in*, *op*, and *gedurende* can only be used in sentences referring to closed domains. Prepositions like *sinds* (since, ever since), *na* (after), etc. are used in sentences referring to open domains, or to sentences where the missing boundary is indicated e.g. by the point of speech: *sinds de oorlog woont hij in Belgie* (since the war he has been living in Belgium) where the interval starting with the end of the war is 'closed' by t_o.

---

[2] An adverbial like *nooit* (never) may be an example of an open domain without boundaries.

Because the present analysis is restricted to the four Setting Prepositions, (3b) gives a clue to the organization of the remainder of this article. In 4 and 5 I shall deal with the internal structure of constituents occupying the place of Y_1 in (3b). It will be shown that there are reasons for distinguishing between Durative, Terminative, and Momentaneous *Verb Phrases*. In Section 6–11 I shall analyze Temporal Adverbials of the sort given in (3) and (4). Much attention will be paid to the internal structure of constituents occupying the place of X_1. In Sections 12 and 13 I shall discuss the setting function of the four Prepositions under analysis in terms of quantifiers.

4. TIME AND DURATION IN CHOMSKY (1965)

In his illustrative fragment of the base component Chomsky classified the Temporal Adverbials on the basis of their hierarchical status. The relevant rules introducing *Time* and *Duration* are:

$$(7) \qquad \text{(i)} \quad \text{S} \rightarrow \text{NP} \quad \text{Predicate-Phrase}$$

(ii)   Predicate-Phrase → Aux   VP (Place) (Time)

(iii)   VP → $\left\{ \begin{array}{l} be \text{ Predicate} \\ \text{V} \left(\left\{ \begin{array}{l} \text{(NP) (Prep-Phrase) (Prep-Phrase) (Manner)} \\ \text{Adj} \\ \text{S}' \\ (like) \text{ Predicate-Nominal} \end{array} \right\} \right) \end{array} \right\}$

(iv)   Prep-Phrase → Direction, Duration, Place, Frequency, etc. (p. 102)

Adverbials designated as *Time* are developed as sister-constituents of the VP as sister constituents. (See also Klooster and Verkuyl (1970), where type "can occur quite freely with various types of Verb Phrase, on the one hand, whereas many types of Prepositional-Phrase appear in much closer construction to Verbs" (p. 101). Some of Chomsky's examples are: *He laughed at ten o'clock* against *He laughed at the clown* and *He ran after dinner* against *He ran after John*. In the second of each pair of sentences Adverb Preposing is precluded: *at ten o'clock he laughed, after dinner he ran* against **at the clown he laughed, *after John he ran*.

Lakoff and Ross (1966) claim that *Duration* and *Frequency* do not belong to the VP. Their argument is based upon the fact that *do so* occurring in the second of two conjoined sentences replaces the VP of the first sentence and only this constituent. *Duration* is shown not to be replaced by *do so*. That is, in: *John [worked on the problem] for eight hours, but I [did so] for only two hours* the bracketed constituents are referentially identical. Were *Duration* (i.e. *for eight hours*) inside the VP, then replacement of this VP by *do so* would give **but I [worked on the problem for eight hours] for only two hours*, which is impossible.

Their test is not without difficulties, since it fails to deal adequately with sentences like *John brought us home in his Landrover and he preferred to do so because he knew that we would feel as if we were on safari* and *John worked for exactly three hours since he is an industrious person, but Peter did so since his boss was watching him* where *in his Landrover* and *for exactly three hours* fall inside the referential scope of *do so*, whereas they are supposed to be located outside. Some safety-valves are needed. In Verkuyl (forthcoming) it is argued that the difficulties raised by the above two counterexamples are due to the fact that Adverbials which can fall inside as well as outside the referential scope of *do so* are not generated by the base component as Adverbials, but are transformationally derived from higher structures and attached to the VP as sister constituents. (See also Klooster and Verkuyl (1972), where this claim is substantiated). In the next section additional support will be given for the view that Durational Adverbials should not be located inside the VP.

5. THREE TYPES OF VERB PHRASE

One of the immediate consequences of rejecting Chomsky's proposal with regard to the location of *Duration* is that we can deal adequately with such sentences as:

(6a)   *Vorige week *is* hij urenlang *overleden.*
         *Last week he died for hours.
(8)   Greetje *wandelde* urenlang *een kilometer.*
         Greetje walked a kilometre for hours.
(8a)   Greetje *wandelde* urenlang *van de Munt naar de Dam.*
         Greetje walked from the Mint to the Dam for hours.
(8b)   Greetje *wandelde* urenlang.
         Greetje walked for hours.
(9)   *De generaal *wurgde* wekenlang *zijn trouwe huishoudster.*
         *The general strangled his faithful housekeeper for weeks.

Only if we endorse McCawley's view that selectional restrictions cannot be said to account for such pragmatic factors as living just once and being able to strangle a person just once, can we remove the asterisk from (6a) and (9). The former sentence expresses the fact that he died repeatedly and (9) implies that the general's housekeeper had many lives. At any rate, in Chomsky's proposal, where (6a) and (9) are ungrammatical, as well as in McCawley's, any native speaker of Dutch would agree that there are restrictions between the italicized constituents of (6a), (8), (8a) and (9) on the one hand and the Durational Adverbial on the other which are not operative in (8b)[3]. The latter sentence asserts that Greetje had a single walk which lasted several hours. Greetje's walking is given as a continuous durative event, whereas the other sentences, if interpreted, imply a series of discrete events which either terminates necessarily as in (8), (8a) and (9), or which are moment-aneous as in (6a).

In order to account for the repetition in the above sentences, I shall postulate an element TERMINATIVE in the underlying structure of (8), (8a) and (9), and an element MOMENTANEOUS in the case of (6a). The continuity expressed by (8b) can be accounted for by the fact that an element DURATIVE can co-occur quite freely with *Duration*. In doing this, I am following trad-itional grammarians who dealt with the problem of how to describe the so-called 'Aspects' mainly discussed in the grammars of Slavonic languages. For a detailed study of Aspects in English I may refer to Poutsma (1926) who argued that the 'Aspects' are linguistic entities relevant to non-Slavonic languages as well. The prevailing view in the abundant literature on Aspects is that they should be assigned to the Verb.[4] According to this view there are Perfective (Nondurative) Verbs and Imperfective (Durative) Verbs. It is important to note that Chomsky's decision to restrict the presence of inherent syntactic features to Nouns, precludes the possibility of his adopting the traditional view of the 'Aspects' as inherent features of the Verb. Gruber (1967a) argued, convincingly to my mind, that Chomsky's system of syntac-tic features should be done away with anyhow. He designed a base component consisting of categorial nodes only, which represent syntactic as well as semantic information. According to Gruber "the language in which meaning is to be formalized must itself have a syntactic structure" (p. 19); in fact, "the base itself can be regarded as generating the very semantic elements that characterize meaning in language" (p. 19). This position led him to abrogate Chomsky's extremely intricate system of syntactic features collected in complex nodes upon which selectional rules and strict subcategorization rules operate. Instead, Gruber's base contains only categories. Thus e.g.

---

[3] See McCawley (1968, pp. 128–136). The question of which of the two views on selectional restrictions is correct does not affect the point at issue, and therefore I give both alternatives.
[4] 'Aspects' and 'Aktionsarten' were very much under discussion in the first quarter of this century, mainly in German studies, some of which appeared in *Indogermanische Forschungen*. Participants in the discussion were scholars like W. Streitberg, K. Brugmann, A. Leskien, B. Delbrück and many others. In English they are very briefly discussed in O. Jespersen, *The Philosophy of Grammar*, London, 1968, pp. 286–289, who included a list of the chief works and articles on the Aspects.

the feature '[+ Count]' in Chomsky (1965) becomes, in Gruber (1967a), a category 'COUNT'. This is not merely a terminological shift. One advantage is that the tree being generated can branch at a lower level than Chomsky's lexical categories NOUN, VERB and MODAL. (Chomsky, 1965, p. 74). Therefore, the information given by such elements as CONCRETE, MASS, PROPER, etc. can be ordered and given structure, whereas syntactic features are inherently unstructured and unordered (Gruber, 1967a, p. 22). Further, Verbs can be characterized inherently in terms of nodes like MOVEMENT, DURATIVE, etc. A third advantage is that lexical items can be attached to more than one category. This principle of polycategorial attachment makes it possible e.g. for the item *enter* to be attached to the underlying nodes GO + INTO, where GO represents a set of categories making up the characteristics of the Verb *go*.[5]

In Gruber's system traditional views concerning the Aspects of the Verb can be represented as in (Ia)–(Ic), where X is a variable which may be null.[6]

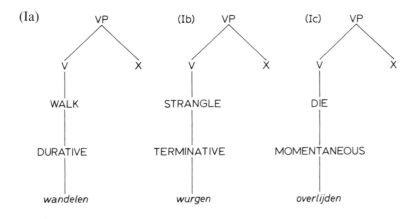

The nodes WALK, STRANGLE and DIE represent sets of categories character-

---

[5] See Gruber (1967a, p. 130). Notice that GO alone is Durative, whereas GO + INTO is Terminative. It should be stressed that in Gruber's view the lexicon is not part of the base component, as in Chomsky (1965). This enables him to abandon the interpretative Katz and Postal-*Projection rules* operating upon lexical items generated by the base in favour of rules generating trees of semantic categories to which lexical items can be attached after certain transformations have taken place.

[6] See Gruber (1967b) where *see* is analyzed as a Verb of Motion having the form [SEE + TO] where SEE is specified inherently as *Motional*. *Look and See* was written before Gruber developed his ideas about the syntactic and semantic unity of the base component. Structures like (Ia)–(Ic) are accommodated to his 1967a-position. In *Look and See* Gruber is very close to the ideas developed in the present section, presumably because both he and the present author have been influenced by Zeno Vendler's paper *Verbs and Times* (1957).

izing the Verbs *wandelen, wurgen* and *overlijden* and containing the categories
DURATIVE, TERMINATIVE and MOMENTANEOUS respectively.

However, a number of arguments suggest that the Aspects should not be
assigned to the Verb, but rather to the Verb Phrase. To begin with, it is
rather arbitrary to assign a (terminative) aspect to *wurgen* (strangle) as this
Verb cannot occur without a Direct Object. Intransitive Verbs like *wandelen*
and pseudo-transitive Verbs like *schrijven* (write) were taken to be unanalyzable into more fundamental complex structures. Therefore, they were
regarded as having an 'Aspect', this being a semantic primitive. Real transitive Verbs like *wurgen* were said to have Aspects owing to the inference that
if intransitive Verbs have 'Aspects', transitive verbs would have them either.
But there is no reason to say that *wandelen* is a Durative Verb because
wandelen in (8b) is also a VP, as X is null.

Now, let us consider the sentences (8)–(8c) and assume that *wandelen*
in (8b) indeed is a Durative Verb. Then we would be forced to say that there
are two Verbs *wandelen*, for if Aspects are assigned to Verbs then *wandelen*
in (8) and (8a) should be subcategorized as being TERMINATIVE. One way out
is to say that the element TERMINATIVE is inherent to *van de Munt naar de Dam*
and *een kilometer*. But this would not do for two reasons. Firstly, we would
need rules saying that the node TERMINATIVE is transferred from the complement to the Verb having the effect of neutralizing the node DURATIVE
inherent to the Verb. Secondly, it is clear that neither *van de Munt naar de
Dam* nor *een kilometer* can be said to have a node TERMINATIVE inherently.
There are sentences like:

(10)   *Van de Munt naar de Dam* stond urenlang een lange rij politiea-
         genten.
         From the Mint to the Dam a long row of policemen stood for
         hours.

(11)   De lengte van die tape is al jarenlang *een kilometer*.
         The length of that tape has been *a kilometre* for years.

in which no frequency is expressed at all. Apparently, the italicized constituents pertaining to spatial dimensions are temporalized by the fact that
wandelen is a Movement Verb whereas *staan* and *zijn* are Statives. (For the
term 'Stative', see Lakoff, 1966).

On the basis of these considerations we could say that the node TERMIN-
ATIVE in (8a) and (8b) represents semantic information scattered over lower
nodes such as MOVEMENT, and FROM . . . TO, or FINITE. The Verb Phrases of
(8a) and (8b) could therefore be represented as in (IIa) and (IIb):

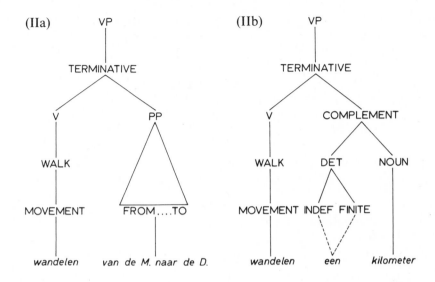

where V is characterized as a Nonstative Movement-Verb. *Een kilometer* in (8) is the Complement to the Verb *wandelen* and contains the node FINITE representing the information that the Complement pertains to a finite number of spatial units of measurement. For (10) and (11) the following representation would do:

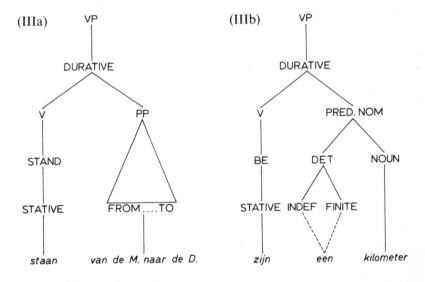

where both *staan* and *zijn* are characterized as Stative Verbs. Structure (Ia) can easily be changed: DURATIVE dominates nodes like V and MOVEMENT as well as *X* (which is null), and consequently we can account for the fact that PP in (IIa) apparently contributes to the category TERMINATIVE.

Consider also the sentences:

(12)   De aannemer bouwde wekenlang in Utrecht.
          The building contractor built in Utrecht for weeks.

(13)   De bas zong een hele avond.
          The bass sang (for) a whole evening.

The verbs *bouwen* and *spelen* are pseudo-transitive Verbs. They can occur with a Direct Object-NP. However, in that case we would obtain the sentences:

(12a)   ? De aannemer *bouwde* wekenlang *een huis*.
          ? The building contractor *built a house* for weeks.

(13a)   ? De bas *zong* een hele avond *een aria van Mozart*.
          ? The bass *sang a Mozart aria* for a whole evening.

which are both ungrammatical in my dialect, unless taken as expressing repetition. Neither *bouwen* and *zingen*, nor *een huis* in (12a) can be said to contain an element TERMINATIVE. For *bouwen* en *zingen* occur in (12) and (13) without causing repetition, and the Direct Object-NP *een huis* refers to an object rather than to temporal entities. Consequently, in (12a) and (13a) TERMINATIVE is present due to the combination of the italicized constituents, rather than to lexical meaning.

Consider now:

(12b)   De aannemer *bouwde* wekenlang *aan een huis*.
          lit.: The building contractor built at a house for weeks.
          The building contractor worked for weeks on the construction of a house.

(13b)   De bas *zong* een hele avond *uit een aria van Mozart*.
          The bass sang (passages) from a Mozart aria for a whole evening.

The italicized constituents of the b-sentences are Durative Verb Phrases. There are no restrictions with the Durational Adverbials. Apparently, there is no such node as TERMINATIVE in these sentences because of the presence of the Prepositions *aan* and *uit*. If we were to assign the Aspects to Verbs we would be forced to call *bouwen* and *zingen* in the a-sentences Terminative Verbs, and in (12) and (13) as well as in the b-sentences Durative Verbs. We would not be able to account for the fact that the difference between the a-sentences and the b-sentences is better explained in terms of the Prepositions *aan* and *uit* than in terms of two Verbs *bouwen* and *zingen*.[7]

Finally, consider the following sentences:

(14)   Zij aten urenlang.
        They were eating for hours.
(15)   *Zij aten urenlang een boterham.
        *They ate a sandwich for hours.
(16)   Zij aten urenlang boterhammen.
        They were eating sandwiches for hours.

Sentence (14) expresses that they were continuously involved in the process of eating something for hours. The same interpretation is possible for (16): their eating sandwiches went on for hours and this event may go on indefinitely. Sentence (15) is ungrammatical in my dialect. The sentence:

(15a)   Zij aten een boterham.
         They ate a sandwich.

concerns a terminative event. That is, eating a sandwich has a duration but necessarily comes to an end.

The difference between (15) and (16) is not a difference between the Verb *aten* in (15) and the Verb *aten* in (16), which would follow from the position that Aspects should be assigned to the Verb, but rather between the Plural NP in (16) and the Singular NP in (15). Likewise we can explain (14) in terms of an underlying unspecified dummy Pronoun corresponding to *iets* (something), which also allows for plural reference.

As far as the upper bound of the Aspects is concerned, it appears that there is no reason to assign them to the sentence. For if we replace the Plural Subject NP of (15) and (16) by a Singular NP *hij* (he), there is no difference whatsoever that would force us to analyze these sentences differently than we have done before. The same holds for the other sentences under discussion in this section.[8]

---

[7] H. Jacobsohn, in 'Aspektfragen', *Indogermanische Forschungen* **51** (1933), pp. 292–318, discussing German constructions like *ein Haus bauen* (build a house) and *an einem Haus bauen* observed: 'Ein Zeitwort wie *bauen* verhält sich zum Aspekt an sich neutral und wird erst durch die Art, in der das abhängige Nomen zu ihm tritt, als perfektiv oder durativ bestimmt' (p. 300). Jacobsohn here comes very close to assigning the Aspects to a higher level of constituency.
[8] Overdiep (1937, p. 57) argues that the Aspects should be assigned to the whole sentence, because there is a very close relationship between the Aspects and the Tenses. Further, they are characterized by intonation, rhythm and tempo. However, one of the consequences of this position is that we create new sentence types. It is unlikely, however, that they should be assigned to the upper S node.

I would conclude this section by stating that the above facts strongly suggest that the Aspects should not be assigned to the Verb and that they should not be regarded as semantic primitives. The above arguments give some evidence that they should be assigned to the VP as non-primitive semantic categories. In Gruber's system it appears to be possible to account for the Aspects by taking them as categorial nodes. That is, we can generate Durative, Terminative and Momentaneous VP's,[9] thus giving concrete form to Chomsky's loose allusion to "various types of Verb Phrase" in the above quotation below (7i)–(7iv). The tripartition into the three types of VP enables us to differentiate between Adverbials of Time and Durational Adverbials on the ground that they both occur outside the VP and that they stand in a different relation to the three types of VP. In Sections 12 and 13 these relations will be characterized.

6. SETTING PREPOSITIONS AND RELATIONAL PREPOSITIONS

As the scope of this article is restricted to non-sentential Temporal Adverbials like *tijdens de vergadering* (during the conference), *in het weekend* (in the weekend), *vanmiddag* (this afternoon), *toen* (then), etc., I shall take as a starting-point the Katz and Postal (1964)-position by saying that they should be regarded as Prepositional Phrases.[10] In fact, all Temporal Adverbials allow for a paraphrase in terms of a Prep Phrase. Thus, e.g. *toen* (then) can be analyzed either as *op dat moment* (at that moment) or *in die tijd* (at the time). If this point of departure is correct, the difference between sentences like

(17)   In die nacht is Marie op haar kamer gebleven.
          During that night Marie stayed in her room.

(17a)   Marie is die nacht op haar kamer gebleven.
          Marie stayed in her room that night.

boils down to a difference of surface structure configuration. The Preposition

---

[9] A detailed account of the principles underlying the composition of the Aspects is given in Verkuyl (forthcoming). It is argued that Aspects should not be regarded as categories as suggested by diagrams like (IIa)–(IIIb). Rather the term 'Aspects' applies to certain configurations of categories such as (IIa)–(IIIb) minus the Aspectival labels. There is some evidence that the surface subject-NP contains information determining the nature of the Aspects. Consequently, Aspects are a matter of underlying S-nodes rather than a matter of VP's. However, the main point concerning the relationship between the three Aspects under discussion and the Adverbials of Time cq. Durational Adverbials remains unaffected, as will be shown in Sections 12 and 13.

[10] Katz and Postal (1964, pp. 125 ff) argued that single-word Adverbials like *sometime* are generated as having a deep structure *Prep + NP*, where *Prep* is deleted. In Gruber (1967a) it is not necessary to delete *Prep*. The lexical item can be attached to PREP + NP as a whole.

need not appear in surface structure. I shall refer to this property as 'deletability of *prep*', where '*prep*' symbolizes the surface form of a Preposition.

Not all Temporal Adverbials have the property of 'deletability of *prep*'. Compare the following examples:

(18) Sinds Kerstmis woont hij in Engeland.
He has been living in England since Christmas.

(18a) *Kerstmis woont hij in Engeland.
*He has been living in England Christmas.

Prepositions like *sinds*, *na* (after), *voor* (before) are never deletable in surface structure. Or, in other words, it is only Adverbials containing Setting Prepositions like *tijdens*, *in*, *op* and *gedurende* which need not appear as *prep*, given certain conditions concerning the NP with which they occur. These conditions will be discussed in Section 11. The difference between the two categories of Prepositions can be demonstrated with the help of sentences containing Locative Prepositions, where the same distinction applies.

In *My wife is walking in the garden* the correct paraphrase is 'The garden is the place where my wife is walking'. That is, there is a binary relation between the event 'my wife's walking' and the place referred to as 'the garden'. Sentences like *My wife is walking beside the garden* allow for a paraphrase 'the place where my wife is walking is situated beside the place referred to as the garden'. That is, there is a ternary relation between the event 'my wife's walking', the place referred to as 'the garden' and the place where she is actually walking. Likewise we can paraphrase (18) in terms of 'In the period following Christmas he has been living in England', whereas (17) can be paraphrased as 'that night is the stretch of time in which she stayed in her room'; see KVL (1969, pp. 69ff).

Adverbials like *toen* (then), *vandaag* (to-day), etc. are always paraphrasable in terms of Setting Prepositions; they do not require that *prep* be present in their surface structure. By contrast, we see that Relational Prepositions are visible in one-word Adverbials like *sindsdien* (ever since), *daarna* (afterwards). Presumably this fact has general validity. *Daarna* in Hungarian is *miután*; *után* is the Relational Preposition *na* (after). Cf. also Persian *ba'd azan* (after that) where *ba'd* means *after*.

The setting function of *tijdens*, *in*, *op* and *gedurende* can be characterized as follows. They give the domain immediately. That is, the referent of the Noun Phrase is the domain of temporal entities to which sentences containing Setting Adverbials pertain. In the case of (18) the NP of the Relational Adverbial does not refer to the domain itself.

7. TEMPORAL NOUNS

Noun Phrases in Temporal Adverbials normally contain Nouns which "have something to do with time". These *Temporal Nouns* belong to the category of Abstract Nouns. NP's containing such Nouns as *uur* (hour), *middag* (afternoon), *zomer* (summer) can be said to refer directly to stretches of time, i.e. parts of the Time-axis which function in our calendar system. NP's with Nouns like *vergadering* (conference), *wedstrijd* (game), *afwezigheid* (absence) refer indirectly to stretches of time because their referents are events and not temporal units belonging to a system which is used to order events with respect to each other. Nouns like *tel* (second), *moment, ontploffing* (explosion), *botsing* (collision) allow for the same distinction between direct or indirect reference to parts of the Time-axis. For reasons given below in Section 8 they will not be very much under discussion in this article.

Though cases like *Tijdens Johnson* (lit: During Johnson), *tijdens de soep (melk)* (during the soup (milk)) are interesting border-line cases it is not possible to discuss them here. In Verkuyl (1969) they are analyzed as having an underlying node EVENT which need not occur in surface structure. Consequently, *Johnson* and *soep* or *melk* should not be regarded as Temporal Nouns.

Temporal *Setting* Adverbials are characterized by the fact that their NP necessarily refers to a limited stretch of time. We can best demonstrate this point with the help of nominalized Temporal Nouns of durative origin. Consider:

(19)   Tijdens het bestaan van het heelal draait de aarde.
        During the existence of the universe the earth rotates.

(19a)   Tijdens het lopen van de robot zal de computer hier gereserveerd
        blijven voor noodgevallen.
        During the walking of the robot this computer will be set aside
        for emergency cases.

Sentence (19) restricts the earth's rotation to a period during which the universe exists. The presupposition connected with (19) is that the universe's existence is finite. It is interesting to observe that the use of the Preterite in (19) would imply that the universe in question had ceased to exist. Notice also that we do not find **Tijdens het eeuwig bestaan van het heelal...* (*During the eternal existence of the universe...), unless we change the meaning of *eeuwig* (eternal). And though a robot may walk for ever, sentence (19a) implies that its walk will be limited to a certain stretch of time.

8. TIJDENS AND GEDURENDE

The setting function of Prepositions can be demonstrated with the help of the differences between *tijdens* and *gedurende* which unlike *in* and *op* can only occur in Temporal Adverbials. The following analysis will prepare the ground for a classification of Temporal Adverbials corresponding to the distinction between the existential and universal quantifier respectively.

Both *tijdens* and *gedurende* require a NP which refers to a stretch of time. Consequently, the sentences:

(20)   *Tijdens de knipoog van Marie werd haar vriend boos.
        *During Marie's wink her boy-friend became angry.

(21)   *Gedurende de knipoog van Marie was haar vriend boos.
        *Throughout Marie's wink her boy-friend was angry.

are ungrammatical, unless we as it were protract the wink in time, which would introduce the feature in question.

Nominalized constructions of the type:

(20a)   Tijdens het knipogen van Marie werd haar vriend boos.
        During Marie's winking her boy-friend became angry.

(21a)   Gedurende het knipogen van Marie was haar vriend boos.
        Throughout Marie's winking her boy-friend was angry.

include the information that Marie produced a series of rapid eye movements, which again introduces 'duration'. Notice that *het knipogen van Marie* can refer either to one wink or to a series of winks. The same ambiguity can be found in *hoesten* (cough), *boeren* (belch), *slikken* (swallow). *Tijdens* and *gedurende* disambiguate suchlike constituents. If we paraphrase *tijdens* in terms of 'there is at least a *t* in the domain, such that . . .' and *gedurende* as 'for all *t* in the domain it is true that . . .', then the relevance of the feature both Prepositions have in common, comes out quite clearly: an analysis in terms of quantifiers would be of no significance if the domain contained only one *t*. Consider now the following sentences:

(22)   Tijdens de operatie brandde het rode lampje een uurlang.
        During the operation the red lamp burned for an hour.

(22a)   *Gedurende de operatie brandde het rode lampje een uurlang.
        *Throughout the operation the red lamp burned for an hour.

In (22a) a conflict arises: the meaning of *gedurende de operatie* is 'for the duration of the operation' whereas *een uurlang* concerns a part of that period. The same difference comes out in sentences with Momentaneous VP's.

(3a)   *Gedurende de vergadering viel de voorzitter een keer flauw.
         *Throughout the conference the chairman fainted once.
(17b)   *Gedurende die nacht is Marie bevallen.
         *Throughout that night Marie gave birth.

If we omit *een keer* we can interpret (3a) only as asserting that the chairman fainted repeatedly during the meeting. And any interpretation of (17b) would require Marie's superhuman fertility. If we substitute the Terminative VP *een verhaal vertellen* (to tell a story) for *is bevallen*, (17b) will still express repetition.[11]

Another difference between *tijdens* and *gedurende* is illustrated by the following sentences:

(23)   Tijdens een receptie heeft hij me verschrikkelijk verveeld.
         During a reception he was a terrible nuisance to me.
(23a)   *Gedurende een receptie heeft hij me verschrikkelijk verveeld.
         *For a reception he was a terrible nuisance to me.
(24)   *Tijdens een uur heeft Piet over zijn vogels verteld.
         *During an hour Piet talked about his birds.
(24a)   Gedurende een uur heeft Piet over zijn vogels verteld.
         For an hour Piet talked about his birds.
(25)   Tijdens een uur pauze heeft Piet over zijn vogels verteld.
         During an hour's break Piet talked about his birds.
(26)   *Gedurende een uur pauze heeft Piet over zijn vogels verteld.
         *For an hour break Piet talked about his birds.

which illustrate that *receptie* and *uur pauze* behave differently from *uur* in their relationship to the two Prepositions.

9. TYPE I- AND TYPE II-NOUNS

Nouns like *uur* (hour), *receptie* (reception), *pauze* (intermission), *middag* (afternoon), etc. are Temporal Nouns. They are also Count Nouns, and pertain to stretches of time. However, there are important differences between them. Hours follow each other continuously in time, whereas afternoons and parties cannot or do not in most cases do so. That is, an

---

[11] In this connection it is not without importance to point out that newspaper captions give a clue to the difference between *tijdens* and *gedurende*. For instance, in the caption *Cees Verkerk tijdens de 10000 m race* (Cees Verkerk during the 10000 m. event), *tijdens* cannot be replaced by *gedurende* (throughout) without giving the peculiar reading that Verkerk skated the 10000 metres in the position recorded by the picture. *Gedurende* could be substituted for *tijdens* if the sentence would be used to announce the complete film of the 10000 metres event. Film-flashes require *tijdens*.

hour H_i is followed without any interruption by its successor H_{i+1}. An afternoon A_j and its successor A_{j+1} are necessarily separated by an interjacent interval. Reception R_{k+1} can immediately follow R_k but need not necessarily do so.

The above three possibilities can be represented as in (27).

(27)

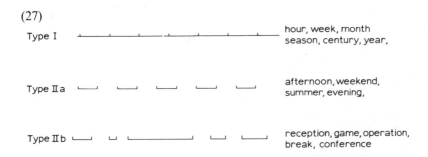

Nouns like *uur, week, maand* (month) will be called 'Temporal Nouns of Type I'. The temporal units of (27-I) constitute a set of continuous identical temporal units which form the basic elements of the system that is used in natural language to order events in terms of the Time-axis. The other Nouns in (27) are called 'Temporal Nouns of Type II'. The bipartition does not apply to Non-Count Nouns. The reason for this will gradually become clear in the following sections.

The need for a distinction between Type I- and Type II-Nouns emerging from the contrast between (23) and (24) on one hand, and (23a) and (24a) on the other will be elucidated below. The bipartition brings out some crucial differences between Adverbials of Time and Durational Adverbials.

The following paradigms quite clearly illustrate the point at issue:

(28)   We overbruggen nu een periode van drie *jaar* (*weken, eeuwen*).
        lit.: We will pass over a period of three *years, weeks, centuries*.
        We will now go back three *years, weeks, centuries* in time.

The italicized constituents cannot be replaced by Type II-Nouns. Consider also:

(29)   We wachtten *urenlang* op haar.
        We waited for her *for hours*.

Uren in (29) cannot be replaced by the Plural of Type II-Nouns without causing frequency: *We wachtten weekenden lang op haar* (we waited for weekends) says that we waited repeatedly, i.e. not continuously as in (29).

10. The function of the determiner in dating events

In this section I shall also discuss Adverbials containing the Prepositions *in*, and *op* so far as the latter occurs with NP's referring to stretches of time. There is some reason to believe that *tijdens*, *in* and *op* are complementary. That is, we have *op vrijdag* (on Friday) but not* *in vrijdag* (*in Friday) or *tijdens vrijdag (*during Friday). On the other hand, we find *in het weekend* (at the weekend) and *tijdens het weekend* (during the weekend). I shall not pay much attention to these idiosyncracies, but rather to what the three Prepositions have in common. In referring to all three of them and overlooking the above differences in co-occurrence, I shall use the symbol TIJDENS, representing an underlying non-terminal Preposition.

Consider the following examples in which the Adverbials contain an Indefinite Article:

(30)   *Ik heb tijdens een maand in Den Haag gewerkt.
         *I worked in the Hague during a month.

(30a)   Ik heb tijdens een zomervakantie in Den Haag gewerkt.
         I worked in The Hague during a summer vacation.

Sentences like (30) and (24) show that Type I-Nouns cannot occur with TIJDENS, Likewise *op een uur (on an hour), *in een jaar (at a year) are ungrammatical. Sentences like (23) and (30a) indicate that Type II-Nouns quite freely occur with an Indefinite Determiner: *op een middag* (on an afternoon), *in een lesuur* (in a lecture hour).

I shall briefly discuss some apparent counter-examples. They will illustrate the point at issue.

Firstly we find sentences like:

(31)   Hij vertrok naar Amerika in een jaar waarin drie maanreizen
         werden gemaakt.
         He went to America in a year in which three lunar missions
         were carried out.

This sentence contains a Relative Clause, which is obligatorily Restrictive. Years in which three lunar missions are carried out do not necessarily follow each other continuously (see Section 11, sentence (37)).

Secondly, there are sentences such as:

(32)   Ik heb Jan in een maand niet gezien.
         I haven't seen Jan for/in a month.

Sentences like (32) are only grammatical if they are negative:

(32a)   *Ik heb Jan in een maand gezien.
         *I saw Jan in a month.

The Adverbial in (32) means a period beginning a month ago and ending at the Point of Speech. Such periods are irrepeatable. Therefore, rather than being a counter-example it simply escapes from the bipartition in the same way as the Modified Adverbial in (31).

Thirdly, consider:

(33)   In een uur kan er veel gebeuren.
        A lot can happen in an hour.

(34)   In een jaar vallen er duizend druppels op die steen.
        In a year a thousand drops fall on to that stone.

These sentences are general statements: in (33) we have a Modal Auxiliary, in (34) neutral Tense. *In* means 'within' or 'per' and does not correspond to TIJDENS.

Fourthly, the Noun *dag* (day) can be used as a Type I-Noun and means 'natural day' (in Dutch *etmaal*), but seems to occur as a Type II-Noun in opposition to *nacht* (night) as well. Cf. *op een etmaal* (*on a natural day) as opposed to *op een nacht* (on a night). However, sentence

(35)   Op een dag stond ik naar de sterren te kijken.
        lit.: On a day I was watching the stars.
        One day I stood stargazing.

is perfectly normal and indicates that *dag* in (35) is not a Type II-Noun. Note that the question *Wanneer zag je hem?* (When did you see him?) cannot be answered with *op een dag* (one day) whereas *op een nacht* is perfectly acceptable. *Op een dag* in (35) does not give factual information and seems to have the function of introducing a neutral time coordinate comparable with *once* in *Once upon a time there was a king*. The examples (32)–(34) do not allow for the question *Wanneer?* (When?).

Finally, we do not find *in een zomer* (in a summer), *tijdens een winter* (during a winter) which runs counter to the general pattern we have met up to now, namely that Type II-Nouns can take an Indefinite Determiner in Adverbials with TIJDENS. I cannot at present find an explanation for this fact. Presumably, we have to relate seasons to the meteorological year in which they occur. That is, *in een winter van 1966/67*, *in een zomer van 1968* are ungrammatical because any construction of the form *een X van Y* (an X of Y) is ungrammatical if the referent of Y contains just one member. However, there are no solid arguments to confirm this view.

Adverbials with *gedurende* and (-) *lang* can occur freely with any Type I-Noun when having an Indefinite Article as is illustrated by (24a), (12b), (14) and some other examples. The class of Duration-Measuring Adverbials will contain this sort of Adverbial, as will be argued in section 13.

We can now turn to the Definite Article. In TIJDENS-Adverbials Type I-Nouns cannot occur with *de* or *het*:

(30b)   *Ik heb tijdens de maand in Den Haag gewerkt.
         *I worked in The Hague during the month.
(24b)   *In het uur heeft Piet over zijn vogels verteld.
         *In the hour Piet talked about his birds.

An apparent counter-example is *Jan verdient 900 gulden in de maand* (lit.: Jan earns 900 guilders in the month). However, *in de maand* here means 'per month, a month, every month'. Type II-Nouns can occur freely with the Definite Article:

(30c)   Ik heb tijdens de zomervakantie in Den Haag gewerkt.
         I worked in The Hague during the summer vacation.
(24c)   In het weekend heeft Piet over zijn vogels verteld. (Present Perfect)
         At the weekend Piet talked about his birds.

Sentences like (24c) give a clue to a better understanding of the role of Tense. It can only mean that Piet talked about his birds at *one* particular weekend, most probably last weekend. By contrast, sentences like:

(24d)   In het weekend vertelde Piet over zijn vogels. (Preterite)
         At the weekend Piet talked about his birds.

are ambiguous. In one reading *het weekend* refers to one particular weekend; in the other (24d) says that Piet was in the habit of talking about his birds at the weekends. A correct paraphrase of the habitual reading would be: 'when it was weekend Piet told us about his birds'.

As far as Adverbials with *gedurende* (or with (-) *lang*) are concerned, they cannot occur with Noun Phrases of the form [DEF. ARTICLE + TYPE I-NOUN] *gedurende het uur* (for the hour), *het jaar lang* (for the year), *het kwartier lang* (for the quarter of an hour). This fact as well as the fact that *gedurende* can occur with NP's of the form [DEF. ARTICLE + TYPE II-NOUN], e.g. *gedurende de vergadering* (throughout the conference), *gedurende de wedstrijd* (throughout the game), are of prime importance. Add to this that we do not find *de vergadering lang* (lit.: the conference long, for the conference), then we are nearly set for a classification of Durational Adverbials based upon a distinction between two Prepositions *gedurende*, one equivalent to (-) *lang* and taking only Indefinite Articles, the other occurring with Definite Determiners. However, before we make this step (in Sections 12 and 13) we have to pursue the main line of argument of this section.

The distinction between Type I- and Type II-Nouns appears to be neutralized if the Determiner is developed into a Demonstrative Pronoun:

(24e)   In dat uur heeft Piet over zijn vogels verteld.
         In that hour Piet told us about his birds.
(35c)   Ik heb gedurende dat uur naar hem geluisterd.
         I listened to him for the duration of/during that hour.
(30c)   Ik heb tijdens die zomervakantie in Den Haag gewerkt.
         I worked in The Hague during that summer holiday.

I shall discuss the consequences of this fact in the next section.

11. DATING OF EVENTS

Temporal Adverbials containing Demonstrative Pronouns seem to have the primary task of providing for unique reference to stretches of time. However, the term "unique reference to something" is by no means unambiguous, as becomes clear if one studies the logical and philosophical literature on reference, i.e. on the set of problems connected with an accurate description of the relationship between language and (non-linguistic entities in) the world. Both Quine (1960) and Strawson (1968) point out that such constituents as *the lion, the captain, Pegasus,* etc. need not have unique reference since either more than one subject or none can be involved. Strawson, elaborating suggestions made by Quine (1960, pp. 100–1), says that constituents like *that lion, Mama,* and the above mentioned ones are "used for the purpose of *identifying* the object, of bringing it about that the hearer . . . knows which or what object is in question", and "The identificatory task is characteristically the task of the definite singular terms" (pp. 74–5).[12]

Both Quine and Strawson restricted themselves to reference to objects. Applied to Temporal Adverbials Strawson's quotation amounts to saying that such constituents as *de vergadering* (the conference), *deze week* (this week), *die maand* (that month) identify stretches of time. The task of Setting

[12] It would carry me too far to explain the term 'singular term' in detail. Suffice it to say that the above examples are called 'singular terms'. Strawson (1968, p. 80) says: 'The position of a singular term in general can be directly explained as position accessible to quantifiers and variables of quantification or to those expressions of ordinary language to which quantifiers and variables correspond'. Their counterparts, the so-called *general terms,* 'complement quantifiers (or other occupants of singular-term position) to yield sentences'.

Prepositions is to relate events to these identified stretches of time; in other words Temporal Setting Adverbials containing the above NP's date certain events.

Notice that identification of stretches of time and uniqueness of reference coincide as in *deze week* (this week), *die zomer* (that summer). But NP's like *die maand* (that month) in *Die maand geeft hij college in Leuven* (that month he lectures in Louvain) can refer to his giving lectures say every October. In general, if one can ask *In welk jaar was dat?* (in which year was that?) with respect to an Adverbial, the Adverbial in question does not restrict the reference to one single irrepeatable stretch of time.

It goes without saying that I cannot venture into the Quine/Strawson-discussion here, since this would carry us too far from the main theme. However, by summarizing the analysis of Section 11 I shall have the opportunity to indicate that their theory of reference is not adequate to deal with certain aspects of reference to temporal entities, due to their having confined themselves to reference to objects.

We have seen that Type I- and Type II-Nouns impose different conditions on the way in which Adverbials can date events. Type I-Nouns require a more 'powerful' Determiner than Type II-Nouns. The Adverbial *in het uur* (in the hour) is ungrammatical, *in het weekend* (in the weekend) is grammatical and is, moreover, capable of unique reference (cf. (24c)). *Op een middag* (on an afternoon) presupposes the existence of an afternoon (admitting the possibility of identification), which is absent in *op een uur* (on an hour). Apparently the existence of entities requires that they have some individuality. Thus we can say that Nouns have their own contribution to reference as far as identification is concerned. Neither Quine nor Strawson was able to make this observation because Nouns pertaining to objects behave like Type II-Nouns.

Only in structures of the form PREP + DEMONSTRATIVE PRONOUN + PRONOUN and in cases like (36) and (37) does the difference between the two types disappear, because the Determiner here delimits the bounds of the stretch of time referred to, i.e. the domain, so that it becomes possible to identify this domain. The difference in conditions for dating becomes clear when we realize that we are concerned with identification of an interval on the Time-axis for which the presence of an initial and a terminal point is essential. The Type I- intervals follow upon each other without interruption in time, and consequently they cannot be identified so easily as Type II-intervals.

Apart from Adverbials containing Demonstrative Pronouns, there are those that date by virtue of the Modifying constituents they contain. I have in mind those cases which have already been touched upon in connection with ungrammatical Adverbials like *in een jaar (in a year) and *in het uur (in the hour), see sent. (31); consider also:

(36)   In de week voor Pasen worden in Zandvoort veel germanismen gebruikt.
         In the week before Easter many germanisms are used in Zandvoort.

(37)   Hij was in Amerika in het jaar waarin Eisenhower overleed.
         He was in America in the year in which Eisenhower died.

Voor Pasen (before Easter) and waarin Eisenhower overleed cancel out the ungrammaticality of *in de week (in the week) and *in het jaar (in the year). Note that the Adverbial of (36), though identifying, does not provide for uniqueness of reference, for every year there is a week before Easter. We could say that in (36) the conditions for uniqueness of reference are present but are not completely realized. Their realization may be due to Tense (e.g. Present Perfect in (36) would give uniqueness of reference) or to adding other modifying constituents e.g. dit jaar (this year), etc. The presence of these conditions, however, determines the possibilities for identifying stretches of time.

The subdivision of the category of Type II-Nouns into Type IIa and Type IIb-Nouns is motivated by syntactic considerations, as appears in sentences like:

(38)   *Ik heb tijdens mijn weekend in Loosdrecht gezeild. (IIa)
         *I sailed in Loosdrecht during my weekend.

(39)   Ik heb tijdens mijn zomervakantie in Den Haag gewerkt. (IIb)
         I worked in The Hague during my summer holiday.

Nouns like weekend, avond (evening), zomer (summer) either do not or only rarely allow a Possessive Pronoun. An explanation for this fact might be that the underlying structure of in het weekend contains an S of the form [IT BE WEEKEND] whereas tijdens mijn zomervakantie would contain something like [I HAVE SUMMER VACATION].

In Adverbials with Non-Count Nouns like afwezigheid (absence), ziekte (illness), presidentschap (presidency), jeugd (youth), where these words cannot occur with the Definite Article, Possessive Pronouns can occur:

(40)   *Tijdens het presidentschap viel Johnson erg tegen.
         *During the presidency Johnson did not come up to expectations.

(41)   Tijdens zijn presidentschap viel Johnson erg tegen.
         During his presidency Johnson did not come up to expectations.

Likewise we do not find *tijdens de jeugd* (*during the youth).

If we summarize the cases where the identification of the domain is possible, then we get:

(a) DEM. PRONOUN + TYPE I or TYPE II-NOUN.
(b) DEF ARTICLE + TYPE I or TYPE II-NOUN.
(c) POSSESSIVE PRONOUN + NON COUNT-NOUNS or TYPE IIb-NOUNS.
(d) DEF ARTICLE + TYPE II-NOUN.
(e) INDEFINITE ARTICLE + TYPE II-NOUN.

Finally, a few remarks about the conditions which govern the deletability of *prep* in surface structure. In general, it can be said that a necessary condition for deleting *prep* is that the NP of the Temporal Adverbial should make unique reference to the domain possible. This point can be illustrated as follows:

(42)   Piet zeilde het weekend in Loosdrecht. (Preterite)
        lit.: Piet sailed the weekend in Loosdrecht.
        Piet spent the weekend sailing in Loosdrecht.
(43)   Piet heeft het weekend in Loosdrecht gezeild. (Present Perfect)
        lit.: Piet sailed the weekend in Loosdrecht.
        Piet spent the weekend sailing in Loosdrecht.

Sentence (42) is ungrammatical when it is a matter of a series of weekends: in that case we would expect to find *de weekenden* (the weekends) or *elk weekend* (every weekend); the perfective sentence (43) which is as such more predisposed to unique reference, is grammatical.

The following sentences contain an interesting difficulty concerning the deletability of *prep*:

(44)   *Zij heeft het weekend een kilometer gewandeld (Term. VP).
        lit.: She walked the weekend a kilometer.
(45)   *Hij is het weekend vermoord (Mom. VP).
        He was killed the weekend.
(46)   Hij is het weekend bij ons gebleven (Dur. VP).
        He stayed the weekend with us.

Sentences (44) and (45) are ungrammatical because Terminative and Momentaneous VP's cannot take *het weekend*. The deleted *prep* appears to be GEDURENDE. *Het weekend* in (46) is a Duration-Dating Adverbial.

12. THE SETTING FUNCTION OF 'TIJDENS'

As far as Setting Prepositions in Temporal Adverbials are concerned there is an obvious distinction to be made between *tijdens*, *in* and *op* on the one hand and *gedurende* on the other – a distinction which is clearly expressible in terms of the existential and universal quantifier discussed in Section 2. I shall draw on the following sentences for a closer definition of the function of the first three prepositions:

(47)   Tijdens de wandeling hadden Piet en Teun het uitvoerig over schaatsen. (Dur. VP)
        During the walk Piet and Teun had a detailed discussion about skating.

(48)   Op die vergadering hield Karel een korte toespraak. (Term. VP)
        At the conference Karel gave a short speech.

(49)   In het weekend heeft Albert zijn been gebroken. (Mom. VP)
        At the weekend Albert broke his leg.

These sentences illustrate the meaning of TIJDENS quite clearly. In sentence (47) it is neither necessary nor impossible that Piet and Teun spent the whole of their walk on the subject of skating. In sentence (48) the speech takes up a number of successive moments which fall within the event 'conference'. In sentence (49) we are concerned with one moment among many constituting the interval 'weekend'.

This threefold reference falls completely within the paraphrase of the existential quantifier given in (3a). The expression 'there is at least a temporal entity *t* such that ...' explicitly states the presence of a *t* in the domain, but it does not preclude the presence of more than one *t* for which the Predicate of the proposition holds as well. Compare the proposition *some men are politicians* which is analyzed in logic as 'there is at least an *x* such that *x* is a man and *x* is a politician'. It is obvious that the proposition may concern more than one man, but the quantifier involved is explicit as far as the minimum is concerned.

In this connection it might be illuminating to make use of the notion 'mapping onto' used in set theory. Sentence (48) can be regarded as the expression of a relation between a Terminative event 'Karel's giving a short speech', represented as $(C.D)$, and an event 'that conference', represented as (A,B), in terms of the Time-axis:

(IV)

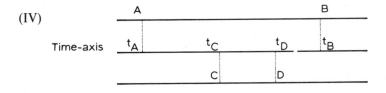

The interval (A,B) is mapped onto the interval (t_A, t_B). i.e. there is a one-to-one correspondence between all elements of (A,B) and of (t_A, t_B). It will be clear that the interval (t_A, t_B) is the representation of what has been called *the domain* throughout this article. On the basis of the previous analysis in Section 10 it might be argued that the Determiner plays a role in the bringing about of this mapping of (A, B) onto (t_A, t_B). The interval (C, D) representing a Terminative event is mapped onto the interval (t_C, t_D). If the above contention that the Determiner plays role in the 'mapping'-function is true, it could be equally well maintained that Tense plays a corresponding role.[13]

As is shown above, the setting function of TIJDENS shows similarities with that of *gedurende*. The crucial difference is to be found in the relation between the domain (t_A, t_B) and the intervals having a one-to-one correspondence with Terminative, Momentaneous and Durative events. The setting function of TIJDENS admits the following relations:

(50)   (i) $(t_C, t_D) \subset (t_A, t_B)$

         (ii) $(t_C, t_D) \subseteq (t_A, t_B)$

         (iii) $\{t_C\}$ $\subset (t_A, t_B)$

where the symbol '$\subseteq$' indicates the relationship 'is included by' and where the symbol '$\subset$' indicates the relationship 'is a proper subset of'. In the latter case it cannot be true that $(t_C, t_D) = (t_A, t_B)$ or that $\{t_C\} = (t_A, t_B)$. The sets of (50i)–(50iii) are subsets of the infinite set called 'Time-axis'. The setting function of TIJDENS determines the possible relations between these sets.

The representation of the setting function of TIJDENS in (50) can without further ado be translated in terms of quantifiers. The existential quantifier is another way of expressing the relations specified in (50) with the help of set theoretical notions.

The relations expressed in (50ii) and (50iii) bring up the question of where within the domain (t_C, t_D) and $\{t_C\}$ should be located. Sentences like:

(51)   *Tijdens de terugkeer naar de aarde landde de Apollo-8 in de Stille Oceaan.

        *During the return to earth the Apollo-8 landed in the Pacific Ocean.

(52)   *Tijdens haar zwangerschap kreeg Emilia een veelbelovende dochter.

        * During her pregnancy Emilia got a daughter full of promise.

[13] See for the relationship between Tense and Determiner, Verkuyl (1969), where it is argued that they relate to each other transformationally. Such a relationship would explain why nominalized constructions with a Definite Determiner cannot occur in sentences with a so-called *Irrealis*.

containing Momentaneous Verb Phrases provide a clear argument that the Preposition sets $\{t_C\}$ within the bounds of (t_A, t_B) and not at its end, whereas in *Tijdens de Franse overheersing ontplofte er een kruitschip in Leiden.* (During the French rule a powder-ship exploded in Leyden) neither initial point nor terminal point come into consideration. There is a fundamental tendency to set Momentaneous and also Terminative events 'somewhere in the middle' of (t_A, t_B). This vagueness which is inherent to the meaning of the existential quantifier can also be demonstrated with the help of (48). We would be surprised to hear that Karel's speech terminated the conference. It may be noted in passing that in such sentences as:

(53)   Tijdens de wandeling is hij te water geraakt en verdronken.
          During the walk he fell into the water and drowned.

(54)   Tijdens de huwelijksinzegening is de bruid weggelopen.
          During the marriage ceremony the bride ran away.

intentional factors play a role. Logically speaking, the walk and the wedding ceremony finished as soon as the Momentaneous and Terminative events occur; psychologically speaking we can still talk of the interval (t_A, t_B) as the image of (A, B) on the Time-axis. Presumably we have to account for this fact by saying that there is some kind of 'norm' in operation.

The meaning of TIJDENS should be characterized as follows: in the interval (t_A, t_B) there is at least a t for which it is the case that the Predication holds at t. In this meaning description three elements are of importance: (i) a *durational* aspect: TIJDENS requires a domain consisting of more than one temporal entity; (ii) an *existential* aspect: the taking place of an event is expressed, i.e. it is realized in time; (iii) a *quantificational* aspect: the information is given that the Predication concerns at least one t.[14]

13. THE SETTING FUNCTION OF 'GEDURENDE'

The setting function of *gedurende* appears to present no difficulties in description. In a similar way to (50) we can represent the referent of the NP of the Adverbial and the Durative event on the Time-axis in such a way that

[14] Essentially the formal description of the meaning of TIJDENS boils down to deriving a pre-lexical structure having roughly the form AT + SOME + MOMENTS + OF + THE + INTERVAL + $_S[X]_S$, where X is a variable representing a tenseless sentential structure of an abstract nature. The Preposition *tijdens* can be attached polycategorially to the non-S part of this structure. DDA's have ALL instead of SOME. The $_S[X]_S$-part of the underlying structure must be nominalized, if *tijdens* and *gedurende* are attached to its non-S part. If Nominalization does not take place, the temporal conjunction *toen* (when) can be attached to AT + SOME + MOMENTS + OF + THE + INTERVAL plus the Complementizer *that*. Hence we can account for the synonymity between the phrase *tijdens zijn ziekte* (during his illness) and the clause *toen hij ziek was* (when he was ill).

their images coincide. Instead of the three relations in (50) we can make do
with:

(55) $(t_C, t_D) = (t_A, t_B)$

The facts accounted for in this analysis are, however, more complicated
than in the case of TIJDENS and deserve discussion.

I shall take as my starting-point the following sentences:

(56)   *Gedurende een uur* had ik hem aan de telefoon.
           For (the duration of) an hour I had him on the telephone.
(56a)   Mijn telefoongesprek met hem *duurde een uur*.
           My telephone conversation with him *lasted an hour*.
(57)   **Gedurende het uur* had ik hem aan de telefoon.
           *For the hour I had him on the telephone.
(57a)   *Mijn telefoongesprek met hem *duurde het uur*.
           *My telephone conversation with him *lasted the hour*.
(58)   *Gedurende dat uur* had ik hem aan de telefoon.
           For that hour I had him on the telephone.
(58a)   *Mijn telefoongesprek met hem *duurde dat uur*.
           *My telephone conversation with him *lasted that hour*.

The agreement in terms of grammaticality that we find between the members
of the pairs (56)/(56a) and (57)/(57a) is absent in (58)/(58a), a remarkable
discrepancy which demands explanation.

In *mijn telefoongesprek duurde een uur* (my call lasted an hour) *een uur* is
a Specifying Complement to the Verb, like *vijftien gulden* (fifteen guilders),
een kilo of twee (a kilogram or two), *vijf man* (five men) in respect to the Verbs
in *Dat boek kost vijftien gulden* (that book costs fifteen guilders), *Die lamsbout
weegt een kilo of twee* (that leg of lamb weighs a kilogram or two), *De
Noorse schaatsploeg telde vijf man* (the Norwegian skating team numbered
five men). The Definite Article and the Demonstrative Pronoun cannot occur
in a VP with a specifying complement, witness the ungrammatical sentences
(57a) and (58a) and **Dat boek kost de vijftien gulden* (*that book costs the
15 guilders), **Die lamsbout weegt deze kilo of twee* (*that leg of lamb weighs
this kilogram or two), **Die tafel meet de meter* (*that table measures the
metre), etc. The sentences at issue here can be paraphrased as follows: *Dat
boek heeft een prijs; die prijs is vijftien gulden* (that book has a price; that
price is fifteen guilders). Likewise (56a) can be paraphrased as *Mijn telefoongesprek had een duur; die duur was een uur* (My call had a duration;
that duration was one hour). This paraphrase reflects the ungrammaticality
of (58a): measurement of duration assumes that it is possible to quantify

the units of measurement, here 'hours', whereas the Demonstrative Pronoun (and the Definite Article) indicate uniqueness of reference or (the possibility of) identification. Hence the conflict in *Mijn telefoongesprek had een duur; die duur was dat uur* (*My call had a duration; that duration was that hour).[15]

In view of the analysis in Sections 10 and 11 which brought out the fact that Type I-Nouns cannot occur in *gedurende*-Adverbials together with the Definite Article, I would like to discuss Specifying complements with *duren* in some detail because they appear to be the most 'natural' environment for Type I-Nouns in comparison to Type II-Nouns. There are many arguments for assuming that (56) and (56a) relate to each other transformationally and therefore a closer analysis of Specifying Complements may help us.

It is striking that the Noun in Specifying Complements can be singular even if more than one unit of measurement is being referred to:

(59)   Het schip meet 50 000 ton.
       lit. *The ship measures 50 000 ton.
       The ship is 50 000 tons.

(60)   Mevrouw Jansma weegt nauwelijks honderd pond.
       lit.: Mrs. Jansma weighs scarcely a hundred pound.
       Mrs. Jansma weighs scarcely a hundred pounds.

(59a) *Het schip meet 50 000 tonnen.
       lit.: The ship measures 50 000 tons.

(60a) *Mevrouw Jansma weegt nauwelijks honderd ponden.
       lit.: Mrs. Jansma weighs scarcely a hundred pounds.

There are some names of units of measurement that have to appear in the Plural, like *kwartje* (twenty-five cents) and *dubbeltje* (ten cents). Of the Temporal Nouns-Type I *minuut* (minute) and *maand* (month) require the Plural in most dialects of Dutch; *kwartier* (quarter of an hour) can only occur in the Singular. *Jaar* (year) and *uur* (hour) can appear in the Singular or Plural:

(61)   De receptie van Jan en Greetje duurde drie uur.
       lit.: The reception of Jan and Greetje lasted three hour.

(62)   De receptie van Jan en Greetje duurde drie uren.
       lit.: The reception of Jan and Greetje lasted three hours.

There is, however, a difference of meaning that corresponds to a difference in evaluation of the reception: in (62) the hours that the reception lasted have a

[15] See KVL (1969, pp. 50–2); Klooster (1972, pp. 250–265): the term 'Specifying Complement', introduced by Klooster, is preferable to the traditional term 'Adverbial of Quantity'. If we were to consider the above Measure Phrases as Adverbials then, apart from sentence Adverbials, they would be the only class that did not allow for a paraphrase in terms of a Prepositional Phrase.

certain amount of individuality. That is, (62) rather than (61) would be used to express that the reception was experienced by the speaker as being an awfully protracted affair: every hour counted.[16] Cf. also *Cees Verkerk heeft nu drie jaar geschaatst* (lit.: Cees Verkerk has now been skating for three year) as against *Cees Verkerk heeft nu drie jaren geschaatst* (lit.: Cees Verkerk has now been skating for three years). In connexion with this I refer to the un-grammaticality of *De ober rekende op drie receptie* (lit.: the waiter counted on three reception) and *de bespreking duurde drie weekend* (lit.: the discussion lasted three weekend). Temporal Nouns of Type II pertain to stretches of time which have individuality by virtue of their nature. Type I-Nouns like *uur* and *jaar* can individualize by occurring in their Plural form. Adopting Klooster's terminology we could call such Nouns as *kilo, ton, uur, jaar* 'integer-independent' Nouns, because they are not covered by the general rule that the number of Nouns depends on the Numerical element occurring with it (Klooster, personal communication).

If we represent diagrammatically what is expressed by means of VP's with a Specifying Complement, then we get something like:

(63)

	h	h	h	h	h	h	h		
duren	0	1	2	3	4	5	6	7	(*h* = hour)

	k	k	k	k	k	k	k		
wegen	0	1	2	3	4	5	6	7	(*k* = kilo)

for Verbs like *wegen* (weigh), *meten* (measure), *duren* (last). For *tellen* (count, number), *kosten* (cost), etc. other representations are necessary which are not relevant, except for their being discontinuous. The striking thing about (63) is that it shows so much similarity with the representations that did service for the characterization of Temporal Nouns-Type I (See 27)). By means of VP's with Specifying Complement the result of a measurement is given: with *duren, wegen* and *meten* every specification of the number of units of measurement implies that they are continuously ordered. Therefore the bounds of the given quantity are sufficient and the quantity can be given undifferentiated. In other words, in *dat pakje weegt drie kilo* (that parcel weighs three kilograms) the points '0' and '3' are important as limits. The points '2' and '1' are implied by point '3'.

---

[16] Notice that we do not find sentences like *... duurde ettelijke uur* (lit: ... lasted several hour). *Ettelijke* and *verscheidene* (several) differentiate owing to their lexical meaning. For a deteiled analysis see Verkuyl (1969, pp. 44–7). See for the notion 'differentiation' Klooster and Verkuyl (1970).

W. G. Klooster (personal communication) drew my attention to the fact that we do not find *de helft van drie uren* (lit: the half of three hours), whereas we have *de helft van drie uur* (lit: the half of three hour).

In sentences like:

(64)   De operatie duurde vier uur.
        The operation lasted four hours.
(65)   De terugreis naar de aarde duurde drie dagen.
        The return to earth lasted three days.

the total *number* of hours and days is relevant, as is the case with:

(66)   Gedurende vier uur stond Jan op de markt.
        For three hours Jan stood on the market.
(67)   Drie dagen lang verbleven ze in het ruimteschip.
        For three days they stayed in the space-ship.

where the result of measurement is expressed by the Adverbials. We can paraphrase *duurde vier uur* in (64) and *gedurende vier uur* in (66) with 'the number of temporal units "hour" is four'. Note also that *hun verblijf in het ruimteschip duurde drie dagen* (their stay in the space-ship lasted three days) is synonymous with (67). Only by implication i.e. because the units of measurement are continuously ordered as in (63), do these sentences tell us that for all moments of the relevant period the Predication held.

If we compare with this the sentences:

(66a)   Gedurende die vier uur stond Jan op de markt.
        For those four hours Jan stood on the market.
(67a)   Gedurende die drie dagen verbleven ze in het ruimteschip.
        For those three days they stayed in the space-ship.

then from the analysis of the function of the Determiner in sections 10 and 11 it can be seen that *die vier uur* (those four hours) and *die drie dagen* (those three days) refer to identified intervals on the Time-Axis. Recall that *hun verblijf in het ruimteschip duurde die drie dagen* (their stay in the space-ship lasted those three days) is ungrammatical. The dating took place because the NP provided for identification and because *gedurende* is a Setting Preposition. The two a-sentences should be paraphrased as follows: *for all moments of the period dated it is true that* ... rather than as: *the number of those hours/days was four/three*. In the former paraphrase the universal quantifier is not implicitly as in the paraphrase of (66) and (67), but explicitly present, i.e. running through the whole identified domain.

The complications which I saw arise in connection with sentences like (56)–(58a) in the analysis of Adverbials containing *gedurende* appear to have something to do with different types of variable involved. In (66) and (67) we are concerned with the quantification of units of measurement 'hour' and 'day', in the a-sentences it is the quantification of moments constituting an identified interval. In the first case we can think of the presence of an operator related to some extent to the *numerical quantifier*.[17]

If we analyze the syntactic phenomena described here in terms of the difference between quantifiers and the difference in the nature of the variables, then it becomes possible to clarify the complicated relationship between (56) and (56a): temporal measurement excludes the use of the Demonstrative Pronoun, whilst in a Temporal Adverbial as in (58) the presence of the Demonstrative Pronoun is one of the conditions for dating. A formal description of the transformational relationship between sentences like (56) and (56a) is given in Klooster and Verkuyl (1972).

It will become clear that Den Hertog's analysis which categorized *urenlang* (for hours) and *gedurende de/deze oorlog* (for the duration of), throughout the/this war) under the same heading, is in need of revision. Adverbials like *urenlang* (for hours), *gedurende drie uur* (for three hours) are Duration-Measuring Adverbials; Adverbials like *gedurende die drie uur* (throughout those three hours), *gedurende de oorlog* (throughout, for the duration of the war), *het weekend* (this weekend), etc. are Durational-Dating Adverbials.

14. CONCLUSION

The above observational facts as well as the generalizations made with respect to the different types of Temporal Adverbial indicate that logical principles underlie the organization of our temporal experiences by means of natural language. There are reasons to assume that the underlying structure of Temporal Adverbials should be represented in terms of quantifiers. That is, if it is correct to say that the meaning and function of TIJDENS corresponds to the meaning and function of the existential quantifier, then these correspondences should be expressed in our description of sentences containing Adverbials of Time. The same holds *mutatis mutandis* for the other quantifiers discussed here.

Since at present too little is known of the exact nature of Adverbials, Prepositions, the Determiner and Tense, it is not possible to give an explicit description of the Adverbials under discussion in such a short scope.

The study of Temporal Adverbials is still in its heuristic stage and therefore this article aimed at the presentation of some generalizations which, in my opinion, are not only Dutch-specific but of a more general validity.

University of Amsterdam

[17] See for the characterization of the numerical quantifier, and in general of the existential and universal quantifier, e.g. A. Tarski (1954).

BIBLIOGRAPHY

Chomsky, N.: 1965, *Aspects of the Theory of Syntax*, Cambridge, Mass.

Gruber, J. S.: 1967a, *Functions of the Lexicon in Formal Descriptive Grammars*, Technical Memorandum 3770/000/00, System Development Corporation, Santa Monica.

Gruber, J. S.: 1967b, 'Look and See', *Language* **43**, 937–47.

Hertog, C. H. den: 1903², *Nederlandsche Spraakkunst. Handleiding ten dienste van aanstaande (taal)onderwijzers*, Vol. I, Amsterdam.

Katz, J. J. and Postal, P. M.: 1964, *An Integrated Theory of Linguistic Descriptions*, Cambridge, Mass.

Klooster, W. G.: 1972, *Reduction in Dutch Measure Phrase Sentences*, in this volume, p. 243.

Klooster, W. G. and Verkuyl, H. J.: 1972, 'Measuring Duration in Dutch', *Foundations of Language* **8**, 62.

Klooster, W. G., Verkuyl, H. J., and Luif, J. H. J.: 1969, *Inleiding tot de Syntaxis*, Culemborg/ Keulen (abbreviated in KVL).

Lakoff, G.: 1966, 'Stative Adjectives and Verbs in English', *Mathematical Linguistics and Automatic Translation, Report NSF-17*, The Computation Laboratory of Harvard University, Cambridge, Mass.

Lakoff, G., and Ross, J. R.: 1966, 'Criterion for Verb Phrase Constituency', *NSF Report*-17, Cambridge, Mass.

McCawley, J. D.: 1968, 'The Role of Semantics in a Grammar', *Universals in Linguistic Theory* (Emmon Bach and Robert T. Harms, eds.), New York.

Overdiep, G. S.: 1937, *Stilistische grammatica van het moderne Nederlandsch*, Zwolle.

Poutsma, H.: 1926, *A Grammar of Late Modern English*, Vol. IV, Groningen, 285–314.

Quine, W. V. O.: 1960, *Word and Object*, Cambridge, Mass.

Strawson, P. F.: 1968², 'Singular Terms and Predication', *Philosophical Logic,* Oxford, 69–88. From *Journal of Philosophy* **58** (1961, 393–412).

Tarski, A.: 1954⁶, *Introduction to Logic and to the Methodology of Deductive Sciences*, New York.

Vendler, Z.: 1957, 'Verbs and Times', *Philosophical Review* **66**, 143–60. Also in: *Linguistics in Philosophy*, Ithaca/New York, 1967.

Verkuyl, H. J.: 1969, 'De constituentenstatus van tijdsbepalingen', Internal Publication, Instituut voor Neerlandistiek, Amsterdam.

Verkuyl, H. J., (forthcoming), *On the Compositional Nature of the Aspects*.

ANNA WIERZBICKA

IN SEARCH OF A SEMANTIC MODEL OF
TIME AND SPACE

For what is time? Who can easily and briefly explain it? Who can even comprehend it in thought or put the answer into words? Yet is it not true that in conversation we refer to nothing more familiarly or knowingly than time? And surely we understand it when we speak of it; we understand it also when we hear another speak of it. What then, is time? If no one asks me, I know what it is. If I wish to explain it to him who asks me, I do not know.[1]

A occurred at time *t*.

A occurred at the same time as *B*.

A occurred before *B*.

A occurred earlier than *B*.

A began at time *t*.

A ended at time *t*.

A stopped at time *t*.

A lasted from t_1 to t_2.

A lasted *N* hours longer than *B*.

What do these sentences mean? It is clear that the meanings of the particular words used in these sentences intermesh, that they are related to one another. The object of the present paper is to explain the meanings of the main words relating to time (and space) in such a way as to make their interrelations explicit. An attempt will be made to paraphrase sentences of the type exemplified above by means of a minimal number of words which are held to be indefinables. These paraphrases shall be formulated in ordinary language and therefore it is necessary that the primary indefinable words should be common words used in everyday speech. This task may appear formidable, if not totally infeasible. It is submitted, however, that the difficulties are not insurmountable. The central problem appears to be the finding of the right set of indefinables. After a lengthy process of discussion and trial and error, the following three elements emerged which seem to be crucial for the interpretation of all concepts connected with both time and space: 'to become', 'to be a part of', 'world'.[2]

In 622 Mahomet fled from Mecca to Medina.

[1] St. Augustin, 'Confessions', Book Eleven, Chapter XIV, 17.

[2] The semantic element of 'becoming' has been suggested as an indefinable by A. Bogusławski (in a lecture delivered at Warsaw University in June 1970). The present paper owes much to the ideas put forward in that lecture.

F. Kiefer and N. Ruwet (eds.), Generative Grammar in Europe, 616–628. *All Rights Reserved.*
Copyright © 1973 *by D. Reidel Publishing Company, Dordrecht-Holland.*

This sentence suggests to our minds a world called 'the year 622'. In this world an infinite number of different parts can in principle be singled out. One such part is a man by the name of Mahomet fleeing from Mecca to Medina. That man in the process of fleeing is (was) a part of the world called 'the year 622'.

> Mahomet fled from Mecca to Medina *in 622*
>> = The world of which Mahomet fleeing from Mecca to Medina was a part, was the world called 'the year 622'.

> John played the piano *on Monday*
>> = The world of which John playing the piano was a part was the (a) world called 'Monday'.

> Socrates lived *in the 5-th century B.C.*
>> = The world of which the living Socrates was a part was the world called 'the 5-th century B.C.'

The explications suggested above presuppose a certain model of the world. It is inevitable that this should be so. The demonstration of a certain model of the world is one of the essential goals that the explications of words and phrases of natural language aim towards. The model which it is sought to detect and explicitly formulate is the one which inheres in the common intuition of all language users. By the nature of things, this model differs from the one suggested by science. It may be briefly characterized as follows.

'A' world – is 'everything', but everything that can be pointed at, therefore 'everything at particular time'. This 'particular time' may be a second, a month, a year, a century – this does not matter. What matters is that that world has no time dimension – it is not space-time, but just space, space filled with something. Thus, a world of common intuition is one time-crosssection of space-time, or 'everything-at-a-particular-time'. This 'everything-at-a-particular-time' – a world – changes incessantly, thus becoming a different 'everything'.

In a world i.e. in an 'everything-at-a-particular-time' various parts can be distinguished. These parts are not parts of space-time either – they have no 'time dimension'. They participate in one world's becoming different worlds, and even form the basis of this becoming: what 'worlds' differ from one another in, is their content.

Whenever we mention some event, we predicate something of a certain 'world': namely that among its parts was such-and-such, in such-and-such a state. The very word 'world', may very well be dispensed with (and usually is dropped): instead of saying 'the world designated by the name "the year 1970"' we say, briefly, 'the year 1970'. Instead of saying 'the worlds designated by the names "the year 1970", "the year 1971",' etc., we say briefly 'the seventies'. But in actual fact, we are describing *worlds*.

Contemporary philosophers like to say that the world in general and particular objects within it have not only spatial, but also temporal parts, and that there is no reason why one should not speak of those temporal parts in the *same* way as one does of the spatial ones. Quine, for example, says:

Each specific time or epoch, of say an hour's duration, may be taken as an hour-thick slice of the four-dimensional material world, exhaustive spatially and perpendicular to the time axis.[3]

And Richard Taylor maintains that:

The notion of length, in turn, leads to that of parts, both spatial and temporal. Distinctions between the spatial parts of things are commonplace, but it is no less significant to reason that things have temporal parts too, often quite dissimilar to each other – for instance, widely separated parts of a man's history.[4]

There is little doubt that this conception is alien to common intuition. When referring, for example, to different parts of one human body one means hands, legs, head, etc. contemporary to one another and not a baby body, a boy body, a grown-up body, a senile body. Although a human body – or any other object – is something that is limited both in space and time the concept of 'part' in ordinary language is reserved for portions of reality coexistent in time, and not following one another.

It is commonly said that a man's life consists of babyhood, childhood, youth, maturity and old age – but it is not said that a man consists of a baby, a child, a young man and an old man. We do say, on the other hand, that a child becomes a boy, a boy becomes a young man, and so on. Similarly, it cannot be said that the world consists of worlds following one another. But we do say that the world changes – that is to say, one world becomes a different world. The objects distinguished by common thought are always parts of a three-dimensional world. This three-dimensional world keeps becoming a different world – a world which contains different parts.

> Buddha lived before Socrates.
> Christ lived after Socrates.
> Mahomet lived after Christ.

[3] W. V. Quine, 'Time', in: *Problems of Space and Time* (ed. by J. J. Smart), New York (1964), p. 372.
[4] R. Taylor, 'Spatial and Temporal Analogies and the Concept of Identity', in: *Problems of Space and Time*, p. 382.

There was a world of which a living man Buddha was a part. There was a world of which a living man Socrates was a part. There was a world of which a living man Mahomet was a part. Between those various worlds there is a relation which can be expressed by a single word: 'becoming'. The living Buddha was a part of a certain world which was becoming a world of which the living Socrates was a part and this world in its turn was becoming a world of which the living Christ was a part, etc. The course of events, transition, time: a world shaped in a certain way (containing a specific configuration of parts) becomes a different world (worlds). This seems to be the basic model inhering in the common intuition: whenever we 'look' at the world, we perceive in it certain parts with certain properties; the properties (and configurations) of these parts change, that is to say something happens; therefore every world that we fix our sight on becomes worlds with different and/or differently arranged parts. Changes, occurrences, the course of events are all reducible to the simple concept of 'becoming'. Ethnological research has pointed out that the one-way linear model of time, characteristic of western civilization, is not universal and that thinking in terms of eternal returns prevails in various archaic cultures.[5] Nonetheless it seems that the concept of 'becoming' does not in itself necessarily presuppose a linear model, and therefore it can claim the status of a universal category.

> X played *after* Y
> > = The world-of-which-the-playing-X-was-a-part was a world that the world-of-which-the-playing-Y-was-a-part was becoming.

> Y played *before* X
> > = The world-of-which-the-playing-Y-was-a-part was a world that was becoming the world-of-which-the-playing-X-was-a-part.

> Buddha lived *before* Socrates
> > = The world-of-which-the-living-Buddha-was-a-part, was a world that was becoming the world-of-which-the-living-Socrates-was-a-part.

> Christ lived *after* Socrates
> > = The world-of-which-the-living-Christ-was-a-part, was a world that the world-of-which-the-living-Socrates-was-a-part was becoming.

---

[5] See M. Eliade, *Traite d'histoire des religions*.

X played *before* 6 o'clock
  = The world-of-which-the-playing-*X*-was-a-part was *a* world that was becoming the world of 6 o'clock.

X played *before 6 o'clock*
  = The world-of-which-the-playing-*X*-was-a-part, was *the* world that was becoming the world of 6 o'clock.

X played between 5 and 6
  = The world-of-which-the-playing-*X*-was-a-part, was a (the) world that the world of 5 o'clock was becoming and that itself was becoming the world of 6 o'clock.

When Saint Augustine pondered the mystery of time, what puzzled him even more than the problem of relative and absolute chronology was that of measuring time. Let us consider the questions that he raised: what do the expressions 'for a long time', 'for a longer time', 'as long as' mean?

Plato lived for a long time.
Plato lived longer than Socrates.

Perhaps these sentences mean: 'The living Plato was becoming a part of many different worlds', 'The living Plato was becoming a part of a greater number of various worlds than the living Socrates'.

This interpretation seems unacceptable. Worlds, like moments, cannot be counted or even quantitatively estimated, their objective temporal thickness being indeterminate. In order to make worlds – or anything else – countable, one must impose on them some discrete scale, and single out some border points.

It is well known that the common speech of many peoples makes explicit use of a discrete scale for measuring time. American Indians indicate a man's age in terms of the number of winters he has lived, Polish peasants – in terms of the number of springs. In the speech of some American Indian tribes the duration of a journey is indicated in terms of the number of sleeps ('in the distance of so many sleeps'), or the number of moons. Many peoples reckon time in terms of the ripening of particular crops.[6]

But what discontinuous scale do we commonly apply when estimating duration in an unspecified way, without using exact measures; what, in other words, do we actually mean by the expressions 'for a long (short) time', 'for a longer (shorter) time than'?

---

[6] See J. H. Breasted, 'The Beginnings of Time. Measurement and the Origins of Our Calendar', in: *Time and Its Mysteries,* New York, 1962.

One possible answer might be the following: the general discrete scale that we impose on 'everything' in order to be able to count different 'worlds' (i.e. to estimate time), is that which stems from the limited capacities of the human observer. That is to say, although the number of worlds is theoretically uncountable, a man can speak of the maximum number of worlds which he would be able to distinguish within one world. He may take as a determinant of the number of worlds that of observable sunrises, or a number 24 times as great or 1400 (24 × 60) times as great, or 8640 (24 × 60 × 60) times as great, or still greater – but always a finite, countable one. Since the notion of duration implies also a direct succession of worlds (what is meant are *successive* worlds), the explication has to take into account this aspect as well, that is to say it has to 'connect' the counted worlds. I would submit the following explications.

> Plato lived for a long time
> > = One can think of the world of which the living Plato was a part as of many worlds.

> Plato lived longer than Socrates
> > = One can think of the world of which the living Plato was a part as of more worlds than the worlds of which the living Socrates was a part.

Thus, to say that something happened at a certain time means that an object (or objects) in a certain state *was* (*were*) a part of a certain world; to say that something lasted for so long means that one can think of the world of which a certain object (or objects) in a certain state *was* (*were*) a part as of so many worlds.

The concept of length of time seems to be closely connected with those of beginning and end. Beginning and end, and temporal boundaries in general, imply duration, and therefore – in our terms – refer to *worlds* (not *a world*), a part of which something *becomes* (not *is*).

> X started playing at 5 o'clock
> > = The first of the worlds of which the playing X was a part was the world of 5 o'clock
> > = The world of which the playing X was a part and which was becoming all the other worlds of which the playing X was becoming a part, was the world of 5 o'clock.

> X finished playing at 6 o'clock
>> = The last of the worlds of which the playing X was a part, was the world of 6 o'clock
>> = The world of which the playing X was a part and which all the other worlds of which the playing X was becoming a part were becoming, was the world of 6 o'clock.

> X played until 6 o'clock
>> = The worlds of which the playing X was a part, were the worlds which were becoming the world of 6 o'clock.

> X played from 5 o'clock (on)
>> = The worlds of which the playing X was a part were the worlds which the world of 5 o'clock was becoming.

> X played from 5 o'clock to 6 o'clock
>> = The worlds of which the playing X was a part were the worlds that the world of 5 o'clock was becoming and which themselves were becoming the world of 6 o'clock.

> X stopped playing at 6 o'clock
>> = The world that the worlds of which the playing X was a part were becoming and that itself was not becoming any worlds of which the playing X was a part, was the world of 6 o'clock.

The above explications seek to capture both the closeness and the differences of meaning between such notions as 'finish' and 'stop', 'start' and 'after', 'finish' and 'before', 'from . . . to' and 'between'.

Another interesting relationship worth modelling is that of 'before/after' and 'earlier/later'. At first glance the two may seem completely synonymous. However, such sentences as 'He came today later than yesterday', in which 'after' could not be introduced, make it clear that 'after' and 'later' should not be identified. Moreover, 'later' ('earlier') in contradistinction to 'after' ('before') seems to imply a certain measure of time:

'A happened later than B' suggests not only that 'A happened after B', but also that 'more time had passed before A happened than before B happened'. The following solution is submitted:

> X played after Y
>> = The world-of-which-the-playing-X-was-a-part was a world that the world-of-which-the-playing-Y-was-a-part, was becoming.

X played later than Y

= One can think of more worlds which were becoming the world-of-which-the-playing-X-was-a-part than worlds which were becoming the world-of-which-the-playing-Y-was-a-part.

'Later' is usually short for something like 'later in the day' or 'later in the year' or 'later in life'. Therefore, 'more worlds' means here 'more worlds within the day (year, life etc.)'.

On the basis of the suggested analysis we can construct explications for all kinds of temporal notions. By way of example, I will submit explications of one group of words, designating units of time.

DAY = a world a part of which is a Sun enabling people to see;

NIGHT = a world that a Sun enabling people to see is not a part of;

MONDAY = day called 'Monday';

HOUR = one of the twenty four worlds which together are thought of as one day and night;

MINUTE = one of the sixty worlds which together are thought of as one hour;

WEEK = seven days and nights one of which becomes the others;

MONTH = one of the twelve worlds which together are thought of as one year;

JANUARY = month called 'January';

YEAR = a world which can be thought of as four worlds: spring, summer, autumn, winter;

SUMMER = a world a part of which is a Sun causing creatures on earth to be warm;

WINTER = a world that a Sun causing creatures on earth to be warm is not a part of;

SPRING = a world that winter becomes and that itself becomes summer;

AUTUMN = a world that summer becomes and that itself becomes winter;

5 o'clock (P.M.) = the last of the worlds which can be thought of as the fifth hour after noon;

NOON = a world which becomes half of the worlds that can be thought of as a day, and which the other half of the worlds that can be thought of as a day become;

MOMENT = a world which cannot be thought of as many worlds;

PERIOD = a world which can be thought of as many worlds;

TIME = the world thought of as worlds one of which becomes the others.

For some time now, people have been drawing attention to the very characteristic polysemy of words referring to spatial and temporal relations. In
many, if not all, languages, such words as 'before', 'long', 'beginning', 'end'
refer to both time and space. The question arises how the temporal and
spatial meanings of the same words are interrelated.

Let us begin with absolute statements of time and place. In the case of
time an attempt has been made to reduce them to a predicate of 'being a part
of a certain world' which is ascribed to objects (not events) characterized in
some way. Now we shall consider the meaning of the word 'place' or rather
the expression 'to be somewhere (in some place)'.

> Socrates spent his whole life in Athens.
> Mahomet taught in Mecca and Medina.
> Kaaba, the holy stone of the Moslems, is in Mecca.
> The Parthenon is in Athens.

Kaaba is simply a part of Mecca, the Parthenon a part of Athens. But were
Mahomet-teaching-in-Mecca or Socrates-talking-in-Athens *parts* of Mecca
and Athens? One would hardly say so, and if one did, one would transgress
against the normal usage of language. Socrates was not a part of Athens –
and at the same time he 'as if was'.

> X is now at the place P
> = X is now as if a part of P.

> Where was Socrates at that time?
> = What was Socrates as if a part of at that time?

Sentences of the form 'X is in P' are often ambiguous. They can be meant
either to indicate that X is simply a part of P, or that X, not being a part of
P, is as if a part of P. Actually only sentences of the second kind refer to
place, because a 'place' in common usage remains the same place irrespective
of what is found there, that is to say, it is not defined by its contents. A sentence like 'X is in P' only indicates place if X could be outside P. A sentence
like 'Mecca is in Arabia' is not meant to indicate a place: its function is to
identify something that is called 'Mecca' as a part of Arabia. But a sentence
like 'Mahomet was then in Mecca' is not meant to indicate one of the parts
of the Mecca of that time. It is meant to indicate the *place* where Mahomet
was. The difference between the sentences 'Mecca is in Arabia' and 'Mahomet
was then in Mecca' is not less striking than their similarity. The suggested
explication 'to be as if a part' seems to account for both the similarity and
the difference.

> X is moving (in M)
> = X becomes as if a part of various parts (of M).

The type of movement which occupies a prominent place in our thought is movement in a certain direction. The semantic formula which corresponds to it would read:

> X was moving in the direction D (by road R)
> = X was becoming as if a part of the parts of R which were closer to D (closer than the previous ones).

The words 'closer', 'farther', 'far', 'near' have to be explained independently.

> It is closer from A to B than from A to C (by road R).

Closer: less far, a smaller distance. Before we consider the words 'far' and 'distance', we must explain the key word 'smaller' ('bigger', 'equal').

> A is smaller than B
> = A is such that it could be as if a part of B.

> B is bigger than A
> = B is such that A could be as if a part of it.

> A and B are equal
> = A and B are such that neither A could be as if a part of B nor B could be as if a part of A.

Now we can try to reduce the complex notion of 'distance' ('how far') to the elementary concepts of 'part' and 'becoming'.

> It is closer from A to B than from A to C (by road R)
> = All those parts of R whose as if part anything becomes that is first as if a part of A then as if a part of B, could be as if a part of all those parts of R whose as if part anything becomes that is first as if a part of A, then – as if a part of C.

> X walked from A to B (by the road R).
> X began walking in A.
> X finished walking in B.

Explicating:

> The walking X was first becoming as if a part of A
> = The first part of the road R whose as-if part the walking X was becoming, was A.

> The walking X was at the end becoming as if a part of B
>   = The last part of the road whose as-if part the walking X was
>   becoming, was B.

We have introduced into the explications of the words 'beginning' and 'end' ('finish') the expressions 'first part' and 'last part'. These latter two expressions are obviously based on the notions of 'before' and 'all'.

The first part = that part whose as-if part anything becomes before it becomes an as-if part of all the other parts.

The last part = that part whose as-if part anything becomes after it becomes an as-if part of all the other parts.

The expressions 'first part' and 'last part' allow us to account for the content of sentences which define boundaries in space[7]:

> This is where X's property begins
>   = This is the first part of X's property
>   = This part of X's property is the one whose as-if part anything
>   becomes before it becomes an as-if part of all the other
>   parts of X's property.

And, correspondingly:

> This is where X's property ends
>   = This is the last part of X's property. = This is the part of
> X's property whose as-if part anything becomes after it
>   becomes an as-if part of all the other parts of X's property.

> Poland from the Baltic to the Świętokrzyskie Mountains is
>   almost totally flat. = The part of Poland whose first part is
>   the Baltic and whose last part is the Świętokrzyskie Moun-
>   tains, is almost totally flat.

> X walked for a long time.
> A long time ago.
> A long journey.
> A long way.
> A long stick.

It has been suggested that 'length' in the temporal sense can be interpreted as a number of distinguishable worlds whose part such and such an object was. Now the question arises whether 'length' in the spatial sense should be treated in the same or in some different way.

---

[7] At the time when I am reading the proofs of this article I consider the analysis of boundaries in space suggested here incorrect. I am unable, however, to present a revised version right now.

The first problem which presents itself in this connexion is how to distinguish 'length' from other spatial dimensions: 'width', 'height', 'depth', 'thickness', none of which has – in contradistinction to 'length' – a temporal counterpart. This problem has recently attracted the attention of several semanticists, particularly following on the publication of Manfred Bierwisch's study of 'spatial adjectivals'.[8]

Rather than entering into any polemical discussions of the different interpretations that have been proposed, I will restrict myself to putting forward my own suggestion, whose main advantage seems to be the reduction of the number of indefinables required for explaining spatial concepts. The explications that I postulate are as follows:

LENGTH = the distance between the beginning and the end;
HEIGHT = the distance between the top and the bottom;
DEPTH = the distance between the surface and the part furthest from it;
WIDTH = the distance between the right and the left side;
THICKNESS = the distance between the opposite surfaces.

The word 'distance' means, naturally, 'how far'; the word 'far' and also 'beginning' and 'end' have been explained previously.

The hypothesis of the presence of the elements of 'beginning' and 'end' in the semantic structure of the word 'long' is corroborated by the fact that of all the dimensional concepts 'length' alone has both temporal and spatial reference: the words 'top', 'bottom', 'side' and 'surface'. And in general the use of the notions of 'length', 'height', 'depth', 'width' and 'thickness' seems to be fully predictable on the basis of the use of the words 'beginning' and 'end', 'top' and 'bottom', 'right' and 'left' etc. That is to say we speak of the length of an object only if we speak of its beginning and end, the concept of height is applicable only to those objects in which we distinguish a top and a bottom, the concept of width – to those which we usually face in a definite way (that is to say in a way which enables us to discern their right and left side) etc.

Needless to say, the hypothesis of the semantic structure of dimensional words sketched in above requires that the words 'side', 'top', 'bottom', 'surface', 'left', 'right' and 'opposite' be independently explained. I would suggest the following explications for these words:

TOP = that part which all the other parts are under;
BOTTOM = that part which is under all the other parts;

[8] M. Bierwisch, 'Some Semantic Universals of German Adjectivals', *Foundations of Language* **3** (1967).

DIETER WUNDERLICH

VERGLEICHSSÄTZE

Eine der hervorstechendsten Eigenschaften des Menschen ist seine Fähig-
keit, Dinge und Ereignisse seiner Erfahrungswelt in Klassen einteilen zu
können, sie miteinander zu vergleichen und endlich quantitative Konzepte
zu entwickeln. Hierauf gründet sich jede wissenschaftliche Tätigkeit. Wir
begegnen ihren Vorstufen aber schon in der Weise, wie alltägliche Erfahrung
organisiert und kommuniziert wird. Die Struktur der natürlichen Sprachen
erlaubt es, Klassenzuordnungen, Vergleiche und schließlich auch Messungen
auszudrücken: *dies ist ein Nagetier* drückt einen klassifikatorischen Gesichtspunkt, *es ist dunkler als jenes* einen komparativen und *es ist 20 cm lang*
einen quantitativen Gesichtspunkt aus; die zuhilfegenommene Struktur ist
die der Prädikatssätze, die der Vergleichssätze (welche vor allem Adjektivphrasen enthalten) und die der Maßausdrücke. Es gibt Adjektive, die nur
klassifikatorisch gebraucht werden können (etwa *tot*, *fertig*), andere, die
dazu auch komparativ verwendet werden (etwa *klug*, *blau*) und dann dritte,
die auch Maßausdrücke zulassen (etwa *lang*, *groß*). Jede neue Stufe der
Erfassung von Erfahrungen geht einher mit einer Erweiterung der sprachlichen Möglichkeiten: eine Sprache mit Prädikaten ermöglicht Klassifikat-
ionen, eine Sprache mit Relationen ermöglicht Vergleiche, eine Sprache mit
Funktoren (d.h. Ausdrücken für Funktionen, die numerische Werte haben)
ermöglicht, quantitative Merkmale einzuführen. In den Sprachen der
Wissenschaft werden solche Ausdrucksmöglichkeiten systematisch angelegt,
in den natürlichen Sprachen sind sie bereits vorhanden. Wir müssen nur
versuchen, sie freizulegen und ihre Funktionen zu klären.

   Große Bereiche unserer Erfahrung im Alltag bleiben qualitativ, dennoch
lassen sie komparative Begriffe zu. Hierzu gehören Urteilsbildungen über
Wahrnehmungen, über das Verhalten von Personen und Institutionen, über
ihre Leistungen, Meinungen usw., die fast immer im Vergleich zu anderen
Wahrnehmungen, Verhaltensweisen, Leistungen, Meinungen oder zu bestimmten normativen Prinzipien und Erwartungen erfolgen. Für Wissenschaften wie die Soziologie und die Psychologie ist die Analyse von vergleichenden Urteilen grundlegend. Eine Urteilsanalyse setzt immer auch
die Kenntnis voraus, wie solche Urteile sprachlich gefaßt werden. Deshalb
scheint es eine nützliche Aufgabe, gerade die Struktur und die Bedeutung
von Adjektivphrasen zu klären. Hierzu soll ein kleiner Beitrag geleistet

F. Kiefer and N. Ruwet (eds.), Generative Grammar in Europe, 629–672. *All Rights Reserved.*
Copyright © *1973 by D. Reidel Publishing Company, Dordrecht-Holland.*

werden. Er fällt geringer aus, als meine Bemerkungen bisher vielleicht erwarten lassen. Dies ist nicht zuletzt auch eine Folge davon, daß erst wenige Arbeiten vorliegen, an die angeknüpft werden kann. Einen willkommenen Ausgangspunkt gibt mir hier der Aufsatz von Monika Doherty 'Zur Komparation antonymer Adjektive'. Deshalb werde ich mit einer Kritik ihrer Darlegungen beginnen.

Monika Doherty hat das semantische Verhalten von Adjektiven wie *groß* versus *klein*, *fleißig* versus *faul* in Form McCawley' scher Baumstrukturen dargestellt. Sie hat außerdem eine Anzahl von Transformationsregeln angegeben, die die von ihr angenommenen semantischen Strukturen in wohlgeformte syntaktische Oberflächenstrukturen überführen sollen.[1] Gegenüber beiden Teilen ihres Vorschlags ist Kritik angebracht. Im Teil I meines Aufsatzes will ich einige Einwände formulieren gegen die Form der semantischen Strukturen, die Doherty annimmt, bzw. gegen die zugrundeliegende semantische Analyse. Da sich aus dieser Kritik eine Möglichkeit zur Umformulierung der semantischen Strukturen ableiten ließe, müßten gleichzeitig auch einige der vorgeschlagenen Transformationen verändert werden. Unabhängig hiervon ergeben sich auch sonst Einwände gegen die von Doherty gegebene Formulierung der Transformationen, auf die ich in diesem Zusammenhang aber nicht eingehen will.

In einem zweiten Abschnitt möchte ich dieselben Fakten, die Doherty behandelt hat, im Rahmen einer etwas konservativeren Theorie darstellen: ich bediene mich dafür eines Systems von syntaktischen Basisregeln und syntaktischen Merkmalen (ungefähr auf der Linie Chomsky, 1968; Bowers, 1970). Die Merkmalkombinationen erhalten sowohl eine phonologische Interpretation (Lexikon) wie auch eine semantische Interpretation. Die letztere liefert zwanglos (in einer etwas korrigierten Form) diejenigen semantischen Zusammenhänge, die Doherty zum Ausgang genommen hat.

Neben einfachen Vergleichssätzen wie

(1)   (a)   *Peter ist nicht weniger groß als Paul*
        (b)   *Peter ist fast so faul wie Paul*

gibt es zahlreiche weitere Arten von Vergleichsbildung, z.B.

---

[1] Prädikathebung; Lexikalisierung; Übertragung von phonologischen Repräsentationen auf prälexikalisch identische semantische Repräsentationen; Normeliminierung; Komparationsreduktion, zugleich Einführung von *wie* oder *als*; Komparativbildung (= Einführung des Komparativmorphems – *er*); Regeln zur logischen Bewertung (z.B. Feststellung von Kontradiktionen, ebenfalls Ableitung von Paraphrasen oder Konsequenzen).

(2)   (a)   *Peter ist genauso faul wie gefräßig*

(b)   *Peter ist größer als das Bett lang ist*

(c)   *Peter ist genau so groß wie ich vermutet habe*

(d)   *Peter läuft schneller als Paul*

(e)   *Peter ist ein besserer Schüler als Paul*

(f)   *Peter liebt kürzere Röcke als Paul*[2]

(g)   *Peter liebt kürzere Röcke mehr als Paul*[2]

(h)   *Peter liebt mehr Rindfleisch als Paul*[2,3]

(i)   *Peter liebt Rindfleisch mehr als Paul*[2]

Diese sollen in explorativer Weise im Abschnitt 3 behandelt werden.

Im 4. Abschnitt schließe ich eine Betrachtung über (implizite oder explizite) positive und negative Normen an. Dabei werden z.T. Ergebnisse des 2. Abschnitts wieder aufgenommen, jedoch sind gegenüber der Darstellung von Doherty noch weitere Fakten einbezogen. Als Beispiel mögen Sätze stehen wie

(3)   (a)   *Peter ist mir zu faul*

(b)   *das Reck ist nicht niedrig genug für Peter*

(c)   *Peter ist zu groß für das Bett*

(d)   *Peter hat zu lange Haare*

Der 5. Abschnitt befaßt sich mit Superlativformen wie

(4)   (a)   *Peter ist am faulsten*

(b)   *Peter ist der Lustigste in der Klasse*

Einige 'uneigentliche' Formen des Vergleichs werden im 6. Abschnitt erörtert. Hierunter verstehe ich Konstruktionen wie

(5)   (a)   *Peter fuhr so schnell, weil die Polizei ihn jagte*

(b)   *Peter ist so faul, daß er wahrscheinlich sitzen bleibt*

(c)   *Peter ist ein so guter Schachspieler, daß er 5 Partien simultan spielen kann*

I

1.1.   Doherty hat, im Anschluß an Bierwisch (1967) und mit den neuen Darstellungsmitteln, die vor allem von McCawley (1968) und Lakoff (1969) inauguriert worden sind, einige interessante Verhaltensweisen von antonymen Adjektiven präzisieren können.

---

[2] Diese Beispielsätze verdanke ich Utz Maas, Berlin.
[3] Die Konstruktion dieses Satzes wird nicht von allen Sprechern des Deutschen akzeptiert. Sie ist analog zu der des Satzes (2f) zu verstehen.

In den Sätzen

(6)   (a)   *Peter ist (eben) so groß wie Paul*
        (b)   *Peter ist größer als Paul*
        (c)   *Paul ist kleiner als Peter*
        (d)   *Peter ist nicht größer als Paul*
        (e)   *Paul ist nicht kleiner als Peter*

wird lediglich eine Relation zwischen der Größe von Peter und derjenigen von Paul verstanden, unabhängig davon, ob Peter und Paul – absolut gesehen – groß oder klein sind.

In den folgenden Sätzen ist jedoch ein Durchschnitts- oder Erwartungswert (= Norm) impliziert, in Bezug auf den die absoluten Größen zu verstehen sind.

(7)   (a)   *Peter ist groß*
        (b)   *Peter ist klein*
        (c)   *Peter ist (eben) so klein wie Paul*
        (d)   *Peter ist nicht so groß wie Paul*[4]
        (e)   *Peter ist weniger groß als Paul*
        (f)   *Peter ist noch größer als Paul*

Diese Sätze sind zu interpretieren als

(a) 'Peter ist größer als normal/erwartet'[5]
(b) 'Peter ist kleiner als normal/erwartet'
(c) 'Paul ist kleiner als normal, und Peters Größe ist gleich Pauls Größe, also ist auch Peter kleiner als normal' usw.

In der Interpretation von (7c) bis (7f) können unterschieden werden:
– die Präsupposition (Voraussetzung) des Satzes, z.B. 'Paul ist kleiner als normal',
– die explizit ausgesagte Bedeutung, z.B. 'Peters Größe ist gleich Pauls Größe',

---

[4] In der Interpretation dieses Satzes unterscheide ich mich von Doherty. Ich interpretiere 'Paul ist groß, und Peter ist kleiner als Paul'. Allerdings ist folgender Satz ohne einen Normbezug zu verstehen: *Peter ist nicht einmal so groß wie Paul*, wie sich durch eine Fortsetzung *und der ist schon klein* testen läßt. Aber auch hier wird 'Peter ist kleiner als Paul' verstanden, und nicht etwa 'Peter ist kleiner oder größer als Paul'.

[5] Wie bereits Leisi (1953), Abschnitt IV F, und auch Bierwisch (1967) ausgeführt haben, kann sich die infrage kommende Norm auf verschiedene Weise konstituieren: – 'Peter ist größer als die Durchschnittsgröße von Personen einer gewissen Gruppe beträgt, zu der er gehört' (der Umfang dieser Gruppe hängt vom Kontext ab, oder er bleibt unbestimmt), (ein Elefant, der klein ist, ist – absolut gesehen – immer noch größer als eine Fliege, die groß ist, weil die Minimalgröße von Elefanten die Maximalgröße von Fliegen übersteigt), – 'Peter ist größer als seine sonstigen Körperabmessungen dies erwarten lassen', – 'Peter ist größer als ich dies erwartet habe', – 'Peter ist groß genug, um eine (im Kontext genannte) bestimmte Tätigkeit ausführen zu können'.

– die aus beiden resultierende Konsequenz, im Beispiel 'Peter ist kleiner als normal'.

Daß es sich hier in der Tat um eine Präsupposition handelt, zeigt der Negationstest, bei dem zwar die explizite Aussage negiert wird, nicht aber die Präsupposition:

Peter ist nicht (eben) so groß wie Paul

ist zu interpretieren als 'Paul ist groß, und Peters Größe ist nicht gleich Pauls Größe'.

Hinsichtlich der Konsequenz für die Beziehung von Peters Größe zur Norm sind die Sätze (7d) und (7e) – im Unterschied zu (7c) und (7f) – nicht eindeutig: 'entweder auch Peter ist größer als normal, oder er ist nicht größer als normal'. Deutlich wird dies an möglichen Fortsetzungen:

Peter ist nicht so groß wie Paul, er ist sogar ziemlich klein

aber

*Peter ist noch größer als Paul, trotzdem ist er ziemlich klein

Beim Gebrauch von wertenden Adjektiven wie *fleißig, faul* wird aber in jedem Fall der Bezug auf eine Bewertungsnorm impliziert:[6] z.B. bedeuten die Sätze

(8) *Peter ist so fleißig wie Paul*
    Peter ist fauler als Paul:

'Paul ist fleißig, auch Peter ist fleißig, und ihr beider Fleiß ist gleich',
'Paul ist faul, auch Peter ist faul, und Peters Faulheit übersteigt Pauls Faulheit (bzw. Peters Fleiß ist noch geringer als Pauls Fleiß)'

---

[6] Diese Norm bezieht sich normalerweise niemals auf eine vorausgesetzte durchschnittliche Bewertung, sondern darauf, ob eine gesetzte Norm (= 'Soll' bei Doherty) erfüllt wird, oder nicht erfüllt wird. Das Erfüllen der Norm kann darin bestehen, ein gewisses Maß mindestens zu erreichen (= 'positive Norm') oder umgekehrt gerade nicht zu erreichen (= 'negative Norm'). Vgl. hierzu die Beispielsätze (3) und die Ausführungen im Abschnitt 4. Die Interpretation von Doherty in Bezug auf negative Normen kann ich freilich nicht teilen. Ihr zufolge wäre der Satz *Paul ist faul* zu interpretieren als 'der Fleiß von Paul genügt einem negativen Sollwert von Fleiß', während ich aber interpretieren würde: 'der Fleiß von Paul genügt nicht der aufgestellten Norm von Fleiß, bzw. ist kleiner als diese'. Unter negativer Norm will ich deshalb etwas anderes verstehen als Doherty, illustrierbar z.B. durch den Satz *Paul ist zu fleißig*, nämlich etwa angesichts der Gruppennormen innerhalb einer Schulklasse, in der sich ein Schüler durch zu deutlichen Fleiß isoliert. Daß Faulheit nicht eine eigene, vom Fleiß unabhängige Normskala bildet, zeigt die Abweichung solcher Imperative wie **sei faul!* gegenüber *sei fleißig!, sei nicht so fleißig!* Eine mögliche Berechtigung erhielte Dohertys Behauptung erst angesichts von Konstruktionen wie *Peter ist dümmer als dumm* ('Peter ist dümmer als der Normalfall eines Dummen', 'Peter ist noch dümmer, als ich ihm bestenfalls an Dummheit zugestehen würde'), welche ich hier aber als idiosynkratische Wendungen ausschließen will. Vgl. Anm. 29.

1.2. Dem satz

(9)   *Peter ist so klein wie Paul*

gibt Doherty die folgende semantische Repräsention:

$$\text{GEN}(\text{GROSS}(a_i(\text{Peter} \cap \text{NEG}(\text{GEN}(\text{GROSS}(a_i(\text{Peter})),\text{GROSS}(D(x)))))),$$
$$\text{GROSS}(a_j(\text{Paul} \cap \text{NEG}(\text{GEN}(\text{GROSS}(a_j(\text{Paul})),\text{GROSS}(D(x)))))))$$

mit GEN für GENÜGT, D für Durchschnittswert; bzw. graphisch:

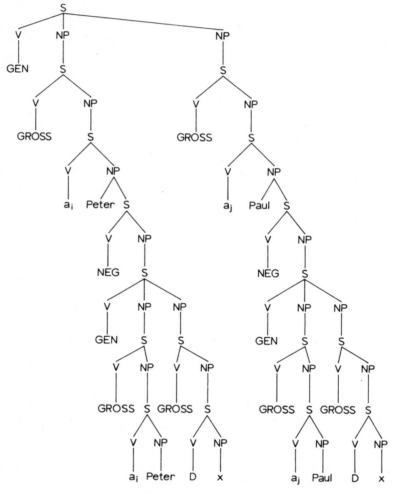

Fig. 1.   (Doherty, S.9)

Gegen diese Darstellung läßt sich folgendes einwenden: (Bei der prädikaten-
logischen Deutung der Kategorien S,V und NP folge ich der üblichen

Konvention, die auch Doherty (S.5) benutzt: die NP werden als Argumente, die V als Prädikate, die S als Propositionen verstanden. Die a_i und a_j sind als Variable für den Größenwert anzusehen, d.h. als Variable über dem reellen Zahlenbereich, die mit einer beliebigen Maßeinheit, wie z.B. m, cm, verbunden werden können).[7]

(1) Vernünftigerweise müssen wir GROSS als Maßfunktion verstehen, d.h. etwa als Funktion auf der Menge X von Personen mit Werten im positiv reellen Zahlenbereich R^+. Jede Maßfunktion ist eine rechtseindeutige Relation, die Elementen aus der Definitions- oder Argumentmenge (hier: X) Elemente aus einer Wertmenge zuordnet (hier: GROSS$(X) \subseteq R^+$). Der Größenwert $a_i = $ GROSS(x_i) für $x_i \in X$ ist daher nicht ein Prädikat zu x_i, sondern ein Funktionswert zu x_i, und GROSS ist nicht ein Prädikat zu $a_i(x_i)$, sondern GROSS ist die Maßfunktion, die einem x_i ein a_i zuordnet.

(2) Wenn der Satz *Peter ist groß* als 'Peter ist größer als normal' verstanden wird, und 'normal' im Sinne eines (erwarteten) Durchschnittswerts für die Größe einer Personengruppe genommen wird, so kann dieser Wert nicht durch D = GROSS(x) symbolisiert werden. Dies würde voraussetzen, daß es tatsächlich ein einzelnes x gibt, dessen Maßwert genau D entspricht. Der Durchschnittswert kann nur über die ganze infragekommende Menge X definiert werden. Die Durchschnittsgröße einer gegebenen Menge $X = \{x_i\}$ ergibt sich als

$$\text{GROSS}_D(X) = \frac{\sum_j a_j \cdot \text{card}(X_j)}{\sum_j \text{card}(X_j)}$$

mit $X_j = \{x_i / \text{GROSS}(x_i) = a_j\}$
$X_j \subset X$
$\sum_j \text{card}(X_j) = \text{card}(X)$
card = Kardinalzahl (bzw. Umfang) einer Menge

Die Bedeutung von *Peter ist groß* wäre also darzustellen als

Peter$\in X \wedge (E$ GROSS$(X))($GROSS $\subset$ MASS $\wedge$ GROSS(Peter) $>$
GROSS$_D (X))$

mit Peter $\in X$. 'GROSS $\subset$ MASS' ist zu lesen als 'GROSS ist eine Maßfunktion'.[8]

---

[7] Bei anderen Adjektiven (wie z.B. *fleißig*), für die Maßausdrücke, die eine lineare Skala verwenden, nicht existieren, müßte man auf a_i, a_j entweder ganz verzichten und sich auf die Darstellung der komparativen Relationen beschränken, oder man müßte einräumen, daß die a_i, a_j auch als Variable über einem komplexen Zahlenbereich oder über beliebige Punktmengen eines mehrdimensionalen Raums verstanden werden können.

[8] Für die Relation $>$ läßt sich auch ÜB verwenden, so daß abkürzend

ÜB(GROSS(x_1), GROSS$_D(X)$)

mit $x_1 = $ Peter zu schreiben ist, anstelle Dohertys

ÜB(GROSS$(a_i(x_1))$, GROSS$(D(x))$).

Sehr oft ist die infragekommende Menge X aber auch im Kontext eines Satzes nicht explizit gegeben. Damit wird die angegebene Berechnungsvorschrift für $\text{GROSS}_D(X)$ hinfällig. Stattdessen muß von einem Erwartungswert für die Größe der möglichen Elemente von X ausgegangen werden (der evtl. in Ausdrücken der induktiven Logik präzisierbar ist). In unserem Beispiel ist $\text{GROSS}_D(X)$ zu ersetzen durch $\text{GROSS}_{ERW}(\text{Peter})$ bzw. $\text{GROSS}_{ERW}(x_i)$ mit Peter $\in \{x_i\}$.

Ein Sollwert ist in jedem Fall keine Eigenschaft einer Menge X, sondern ein Wert, der für jedes einzelne Element von X verlangt wird. *Peter ist fleißig* ist also zu charakterisieren als

$$\text{GEN}(\text{FLEISS}(\text{Peter}), \text{FLEISS}_{SOLL}(x_i))$$

mit Peter $\in \{x_i\}$ und GEN als Abkürzung für GENÜGT.

(3) Die Interpretation der von Doherty verwendeten Relation GEN ist unklar. So charakterisiert Doherty *Peter ist so groß wie Paul* durch

$$\text{GEN}(\text{GROSS}(\text{Peter}), \text{GROSS}(\text{Paul})),$$

worin GEN für die Relation = stehen müßte, andererseits aber *Peter ist klein* durch

$$\text{NEG}(\text{GEN}(\text{GROSS}(\text{Peter}), \text{GROSS}_D(X))),$$

worin NEG GEN die Relation $<$ bedeutet, d.h. GEN müßte als $\geq$ verstanden werden. Dieselbe Interpretation wäre nötig für *Peter ist fleißig*: 'Peters Fleiß ist größer oder gleich dem verlangten Fleiß', Die Verwendung der Relation $\geq$ anstelle von GEN setzt hier allerdings voraus, daß im Prinzip eine Bezugnahme auf lineare Maßskalen möglich ist (vgl. Anm. 7).

(4) Die Struktur in Figur 1 könnte (mit einigem Wohlwollen) paraphrasiert werden durch 'die Größe von Peter, der klein ist, entspricht der Größe von Paul, der (ebenfalls) klein ist'. Doherty versteht den Relativsatzanschluß, dargestellt durch Verzweigungen wie NP, offenbar als Teil

einer semantischen Repräsentation. Dieser Auffassung kann ich nicht folgen: Relativsatzanschluß ist ein typisch syntaktisches Phänomen, dem semantisch (man denke etwa an die Unterscheidung von restriktiven gegenüber nichtrestriktiven Relativsatzanschlüssen) durchaus unterschiedliche Repräsentationen entsprechen können. In unserem Beispiel wäre eine konjunktive Form vorzuschlagen: z.B. 'Peter ist klein, und Paul ist klein, und die Größe von Peter ist gleich der Größe von Paul'

GROSS(Peter $<$ GROSS$_D(X)$ $\wedge$ GROSS(Paul) $<$ GROSS$_D(X)$
$\wedge$ GROSS(Peter) $=$ GROSS(Paul)
mit Peter $\in X$, Paul $\in X$.

Andere mögliche syntaktische Realisierungen dieses Ausdrucks sind

(10)   *Peter und Paul sind beide klein, aber sie sind gleich groß*
         Peters Größe, welche unter dem Durchschnitt liegt, entspricht
         Pauls Größe, die gleichfalls unter dem Durchschnitt liegt

Sie können aus Figur 1 nur abgeleitet werden, wenn man recht komplizierte Umordnungstransformationen annimmt.

Jedoch sind meiner Auffassung nach die Sätze (10) nicht bedeutungsgleich mit (9): in (9) wird vorausgesetzt, und nicht explizit ausgesagt, daß Paul klein ist, und es ergibt sich die Konsequenz, die ebenfalls nicht explizit ausgesagt wird, daß Peter klein ist – in (10) wird aber beides explizit ausgesagt. Ein weiterer Nachteil der Darstellung von Doherty und meiner oben vorgeschlagenen Verbesserung ist demnach, daß zwischen Präsupposition, expliziter Aussage und Konsequenz kein Unterschied gemacht wird.

1.3 Am Schluß ihres Aufsatzes führt Doherty Markierungen der Adjektive bezüglich einer Norm ein. Es überrascht, daß diese Maßnahme nicht systematischer ausgebaut und diskutiert wird. Dohertys Argumentation erweckt den Anschein, als wäre eine Markierung von Adjektiven wie *groß*, *klein* nur deswegen sinnvoll, weil sich damit ihr Verhalten zusammen mit *weniger* und *noch* besser beschreiben läßt.[9] In meinem Alternativvorschlag (Abschnitt 2) werde ich von Anfang an mit Markierungen arbeiten, die zur Syntaxsprache gehören, aber entsprechende Interpretationen ermöglichen.

1.4. Doherty diskutiert die Notwendigkeit einer gesonderten logischen Komponente (S.26ff). Ihre Aufgabe soll es sein, Kontradiktionen innerhalb eines Satzes festzustellen und entsprechend zu bewerten. Außerdem hat sie die Funktion, zu einer gegebenen semantischen Struktur die Menge der implizierten und der äquivalenten Strukturen anzugeben. Dies läßt sich ausnutzen zur entsprechenden Umformung einer gegebenen Struktur (sprich: Ersetzung durch eine ihrer Paraphrasen), die dann zu einer semantisch äquivalenten Verbalisierung führt. Die Forderung nach eine *gesonderten* logischen Komponente muß allerdings im Rahmen einer vorausgesetzten generativen *Semantik* überraschen: man sollte annehmen, daß die Semantik-Komponente, von der ausgegangen wird, die Aufgabe der logischen Bewertung bereits leistet. Freilich ist der Grund für das Vorgehen von Doherty

---

[9] Die Markierung ergibt sich bei Anwendung der Normeliminierung, Doherty, S.30.

ersichtlich: er liegt in der inkonsequenten Vereinigung von Semantik- und Syntaxbeschreibung: Doherty formuliert eine syntaktische Basis (enthaltend die Kategorien S, V, NP), die gleichzeitig semantisch verstanden wird. In dieser Basis kommen aber z.B. Relativsatzkonstruktionen vor, die keine direkte semantische Übersetzung finden können. Andererseits ist diese Basis (weil syntaxorientiert) zu eng, sie umfaßt nicht Definitionen für äquivalente und implikative Ausdrücke (welche normalerweise in einer Semantiksprache enthalten sind), so daß diese in einer zusätzlichen Komponente vereinigt werden müssen. Für uns ist diese Inkonsequenz Anlaß, eine strikte Trennung von Syntax- und Semantikbeschreibung anzunehmen.[10]

II

Meine Beschreibung von antonymen Adjektiven in Kopulasätzen umfaßt drei Teile:

(1) eine syntaktische Basis;

(2) eine Lexikon-Auswahl (ich beschränke mich auf die Adjektive *groß*, *klein*, *fleißig*, *faul* und auf die phonologische Interpretation der eigeführten syntaktischen Merkmale);

(3) Regeln der semantischen Interpretation der Merkmale (die Adjektive selbst werden nicht interpretiert; daß sie semantisch keineswegs Grundterme sind, hat Bierwisch (1967) gezeigt).

Anschließend dokumentiere ich Beispiele.

2.1 SYNTAKTISCHE BASIS

Verzweigungen

$$S' \rightarrow (NEG\ -)S$$
$$S \rightarrow NP_i - VP$$
$$VP \rightarrow Kop - AP$$
$$AP \rightarrow (Spez_A -)\ A$$
$$Spez_A \rightarrow \begin{Bmatrix} Pos \\ Komp \end{Bmatrix} - NP_j\ ^{11}$$

[10] Vgl. die ausführliche Argumentation in Wunderlich (1970), Abschnitt 1.1.1. Während ich dort in die Syntaxbeschreibung aber zahlreiche Terme (sprich: syntaktische Merkmale) aufgenommen habe, die nur dazu dienten, die Übersetzung in die semantische Beschreibung möglichst einfach zu gestalten, und damit im Grunde die semantische Interpretation schon vorweggenommen haben, so glaube ich, daß es mir hier im Abschnitt 2 gelungen ist (mithilfe von einfachen Markierungsmerkmalen $m, u, +, -$) die syntaktische Beschreibung von schon unmittelbar semantisch bedeutsamen Termen weitgehend freizuhalten.

[11] Im nächsten Abschnitt wird sich zeigen, daß mindestens alternativ zu NP_j (wenn nicht gar an Stelle von NP_j) S eingeführt werden muß, dieses S normalerweise ebenfalls eine Kopula + Adjektivphrase enthält, wobei $AP \rightarrow A$ gelten muß. Außerdem gelten gewisse Identitätsbedingungen für die NP.

Zwischen NP_i und A gelten dieselben Selektionsbeschränkungen wie zwischen NP_j und A.

Ersetzung durch Merkmale

$$Pos \rightarrow [Pos, \begin{Bmatrix} 0 \\ - \\ + \end{Bmatrix}]$$

$$Komp \rightarrow [Komp, \begin{Bmatrix} 0 \\ - \\ + \end{Bmatrix}]$$

$$A \rightarrow [A, \begin{Bmatrix} Rel \\ Abs \end{Bmatrix}]$$

Merkmalerweiterung

$$[Rel] \rightarrow \begin{Bmatrix} [u, +] \\ [u, -] \end{Bmatrix}$$

$$[Abs] \rightarrow \begin{Bmatrix} [m, +] \\ [m, -] \end{Bmatrix}$$

Ummarkierungen

$$[u] \rightarrow [m]/ \begin{Bmatrix} Spez_A = \varnothing \\ [\begin{Bmatrix} Pos \\ Komp \end{Bmatrix}, \begin{Bmatrix} + \\ - \end{Bmatrix}] - Y - [A, Rel, \underline{}] \end{Bmatrix} \quad \begin{matrix} \text{vg. Sätze (11)} \\ \text{vgl. Sätze (17) bis (24)} \end{matrix}$$

$$[u, -] \rightarrow [m, -]/[Pos, 0] - Y - [A, Rel, \underline{}] \qquad \text{vgl. Satz (13b)}$$

$$[u, +] \rightarrow [m, +]/NEG - Z - [Pos, 0] - Y - [A, Rel, \underline{}]$$

vgl. Satz (14a)

mit Y und Z als Variable über Konstituentenketten.

2.2 LEXIKON-AUSWAHL

$$\begin{Bmatrix} [Spez, Pos, 0] & : \begin{Bmatrix} eben \\ genau \end{Bmatrix} \\ [Spez, Pos, -] & : \begin{Bmatrix} fast \\ beinahe \end{Bmatrix} \\ [Spez, Pos, +] & : mindestens \end{Bmatrix} \quad so\ \Delta\ wie$$

$$\begin{Bmatrix} [Spez, Komp, 0] : & \overset{\Delta}{[K]} \\ [Spez, Komp, -] : & weniger\ \Delta \\ [Spez, Komp, +] : & noch\ \overset{\Delta}{[K]} \end{Bmatrix} \quad als$$

$[K]$ ist das Komparitivmorphem; Δ ist Platzhalter für A.

Umgangssprachlich können *wie* und *als* auch als Alternanten vorkommen

$$\left.\begin{array}{l}[A, \text{Rel}, \ldots, +]:gro\beta \\ [A, \text{Rel}, \ldots, -]:klein\end{array}\right\}\text{Antonym}\,(gro\beta,\,klein)$$

$$\left.\begin{array}{l}[A, \text{Abs}, \quad m, +]:flei\beta ig \\ [A, \text{Abs}, \quad m, -]:faul\end{array}\right\}\text{Antonym}\,(flei\beta ig,\,faul)$$

NEG : *nicht, kaum*, . . .

2.3. SEMANTISCHE INTERPRETATIONSREGELN

NP_i, NP_j bezeichnen verschiedene Objekte x_i, x_j einer Klasse X. Über X existiere eine Maßfunktion $\mathfrak{A}$, die durch A bezeichnet wird. Es soll gelten $\mathfrak{A}(x_i) = a_i$, $\mathfrak{A}(x_j) = a_j$.

N sei die Abkürzung für $\mathfrak{A}_{\text{D}}(X)$, $\mathfrak{A}_{\text{ERW}}(x_i)$ oder $\mathfrak{A}_{\text{SOLL}}(x_i)$ mit $x_i \in X$.

$$[m, +]: \rightarrow \left\{\begin{array}{l}\left.\begin{array}{l}a_i > \text{N}/[A, \text{Rel}, \underline{\quad}\,] \\ a_i \geqslant \text{N}/[A, \text{Abs}, \underline{\quad}\,]\end{array}\right\} \,/\text{Spez}_A = \varnothing \\ \left.\begin{array}{l}\langle a_j > \text{N}\rangle/[A, \text{Rel}, \underline{\quad}\,] \\ \langle a_j \geqslant \text{N}\rangle/[A, \text{Abs}, \underline{\quad}\,]\end{array}\right\}/\text{Spez}_A \neq \varnothing\end{array}\right\}$$

$$[m, -]: \rightarrow \left\{\begin{array}{l}a_i < \text{N} \,/[A, \ldots, \underline{\quad}\,] \quad /\text{Spez}_A = \varnothing \\ \langle a_j < \text{N}\rangle/[A, \ldots, \underline{\quad}\,] \quad /\text{Spez}_A \neq \varnothing\end{array}\right\}$$

Die Spitzklammerung $\langle\;\rangle$ symbolisiert eine Präsupposition, die definitionsgemäß von der Negation nicht erfaßt wird.

$$[\text{Pos},0]: \rightarrow \left\{\begin{array}{l}\left.\begin{array}{l}a_i < a_j/[A, \ldots, +] \\ a_i > a_j/[A, \ldots, -]\end{array}\right\}/\text{NEG-}Z\underline{\quad} \\ a_i = a_j \text{ sonst}\end{array}\right\}$$

$$[\text{Pos}, -]: \rightarrow \left\{\begin{array}{l}a_i < a_j \wedge a_j - a_i \leqslant \delta/[A, \ldots, +] \\ a_i > a_j \wedge a_i - a_j \leqslant \delta/[A, \ldots, -]\end{array}\right\}$$

$$[\text{Pos}, +]: \rightarrow \left\{\begin{array}{l}a_i \geqslant a_j/[A, \ldots, +] \\ a_i \leqslant a_j/[A, \ldots, -]\end{array}\right\}$$

$$[\text{Komp},0]: \rightarrow \left\{\begin{array}{l}a_i > a_j/[A, \ldots, +] \\ a_i < a_j/[A, \ldots, -]\end{array}\right\}$$

$$[\text{Komp}, -]: \rightarrow \left\{\begin{array}{l}a_i < a_j/[A, \ldots, +] \\ a_i > a_j/[A, \ldots, -]\end{array}\right\}$$

$$[\text{Komp}, +]: \rightarrow \left\{\begin{array}{l}a_i > a_j/[A, \ldots, +] \\ a_i < a_j/[A, \ldots, -]\end{array}\right\}$$

2.4. Beispiele

Ich kürze ab: a für a_i, b für a_j

TABELLE I

	Syntakt. Merkmale	Semant. Interpretation
(11) *Peter ist groß*	[Rel, m, +]	$a > N$
klein	[Rel, m, −]	$a < N$
fleißig	[Abs, m, +]	$a \geqslant N$
faul	[Abs, m, −]	$a < N$
(12) *Peter ist nicht groß*[12]	NEG [Rel, m, +]	$a \leqslant N$
klein	NEG [Rel, m, −]	$a \geqslant N$
fleißig	NEG [Abs, m, +]	$a < N$
faul	NEG [Abs, m, −]	$a \geqslant N$
(13) *Peter ist so groß wie Paul*	[Pos, 0] [Rel, u, +]	$a = b$
klein	[Pos, 0] [Rel, m, −]	$a = b$
fleißig	[Pos, 0] [Abs, m, +]	$\langle b < N \rangle \wedge a = b$
faul	[Pos, 0] [Abs, m, −]	$\langle b \geqslant N \rangle \wedge a = b$
(14) *Peter ist nicht so groß wie Paul*	NEG [Pos, 0] [Rel, m, +]	$a = b$
klein	NEG [Pos, 0] [Rel, m, −]	$a = b$
fleißig	NEG [Pos, 0] [Abs, m, +]	$\langle b < N \rangle \wedge a = b$
faul	NEG [Pos, 0] [Abs, m, −]	$\langle b \geqslant N \rangle \wedge a = b$
(15) *Peter ist größer als Paul*	[Komp, 0] [Rel, u, +]	$a > b$
kleiner	[Komp, 0] [Rel, u, −]	$a < b$
fleißiger	[Komp, 0] [Abs, m, +]	$\langle b \geqslant N \rangle \wedge a > b$
fauler	[Komp, 0] [Abs, m, −]	$\langle b < N \rangle \wedge a > b$
(16) *Peter ist nicht größer als Paul*	NEG [Komp, 0] [Rel, u, +]	$a \leqslant b$
kleiner	NEG [Komp, 0] [Rel, u, −]	$a \geqslant b$
fleißiger	NEG [Komp, 0] [Abs, m, +]	$\langle b \geqslant N \rangle \wedge a \leqslant b$
fauler	NEG [Komp, 0] [Abs, m, −]	$\langle b < N \rangle \wedge a \geqslant b$

[12] Hieraus folgt z.B., daß *Peter ist nicht groß und nicht klein* ein korrekter Satz ist: $a \leqslant N \wedge a \geqslant N \supset a = N$, während **Peter ist nicht faul und nicht fleißig* abweicht: $a < N \wedge a \geqslant N \supset$ Widerspruch.

Tabelle I (kontinuiert)

		Syntakt. Merkmale		Semant. Interpretation
(17)	Peter ist weniger groß als Paul	[Komp, −]	[Rel, m, +]	$\langle b > N \rangle \wedge a < b$
	klein	[Komp, −]	[Rel, m, −]	$\langle b < N \rangle \wedge a > b$
	fleißig	[Komp, −]	[Abs, m, +]	$\langle b \geq N \rangle \wedge a < b$
	faul	[Komp, −]	[Abs, m, −]	$\langle b < N \rangle \wedge a > b$
(18)	Peter ist nicht weniger groß als Paul	NEG [Komp, −]	[Rel, m, +]	$\langle b > N \rangle \wedge a \geq b$
	klein	NEG [Komp, −]	[Rel, m, −]	$\langle b < N \rangle \wedge a \leq b$
	fleißig	NEG [Komp, −]	[Abs, m, +]	$\langle b \geq N \rangle \wedge a \geq b$
	faul	NEG [Komp, −]	[Abs, m, −]	$\langle b < N \rangle \wedge a \leq b$
		Die Adjektiv-Merkmale und die Interpretation in Bezug auf die Norm entsprechen überall denen in den Sätzen (17) und (18)		
(19)	Peter ist noch größer als Paul	[Komp, +]		$a > b$
	kleiner	[Komp, +]		$a < b$
	fleißiger	[Komp, +]		$a > b$
	fauler	[Komp, +]		$a < b$
(20)	Peter ist nicht noch größer als Paul	NEG [Komp, +]		$a \leq b$
	kleiner	NEG [Komp, +]		$a \geq b$
	fleißiger	NEG [Komp, +]		$a \leq b$
	fauler	NEG [Komp, +]		$a \geq b$
(21)	Peter ist fast so groß wie Paul	[Pos, −]		$a > b \wedge a - b \leq \delta$
	klein	[Pos, −]		$a < b \wedge b - a \leq \delta$
	fleißig	[Pos, −]		$a > b \wedge a - b \leq \delta$
	faul	[Pos, −]		$a < b \wedge b - a \leq \delta$
(22)	Peter ist nicht fast so groß wie Paul[13]	NEG [Pos, −]		$a < b \wedge b - a > \delta$
	klein	NEG [Pos, −]		$a > b \wedge a - b > \delta$
	fleißig	NEG [Pos, −]		$a < b \wedge b - a > \delta$
	faul	NEG [Pos, −]		$a > b \wedge a - b > \delta$

[13] Diese Interpretation ist nicht voll gesichert. Wenn den Sätzen aber überhaupt eine Interpretation gegeben wird, dann normalerweise die, daß nicht nur als Negation zu fast verstanden wird (vor allem beim Akzent auf fast).

Tabelle I (kontinuiert)

	Syntakt. Merkmale	Semant. Interpretation
(23) *Peter ist mindestens so groß wie Paul*	[Pos, +]	$a \geqslant b$
klein	[Pos, +]	$a \leqslant b$
fleißig	[Pos, +]	$a \geqslant b$
faul	[Pos, +]	$a \leqslant b$
(24) *Peter ist nicht mindestens so groß wie Paul*[14]	NEG [Pos, +]	$a < b$
klein	NEG [Pos, +]	$a > b$
fleißig	NEG [Pos, +]	$a < b$
faul	NEG [Pos, +]	$a > b$

[14] Diese Sätze sind kaum akzeptabel. Wenn sie aber interpretiert werden, dann wie angegeben.

Hieraus ergeben sich z.B. die folgenden Sätze als Paraphrasen:

Peter ist nicht so groß/klein/fleißig wie Paul
   ≡ *Peter ist weniger groß/klein/fleißig als Paul*

Peter ist fleißiger/fauler als Paul[15]
   ≡ *Peter ist noch fleißiger/fauler als Paul*

Peter ist mindestens so groß wie Paul
   ≡ *Peter ist nicht weniger groß als Paul*

Peter ist größer als Paul
   ≡ *Paul ist kleiner als Peter*

Peter ist nicht so faul wie Paul
   ≡ *Peter ist weniger faul als Paul*
   ≡ *Paul ist fauler als Peter*

Als Implikationen ergeben sich z.B.:

Peter ist nicht so fleißig/faul wie Paul
   ⊃ *Peter ist nicht fleißiger/fauler als Paul*

Peter ist noch fleißiger/fauler als Paul
   ⊃ *Peter ist nicht weniger fleißig/faul als Paul*

Peter ist größer als Paul
   ⊃ *Peter ist nicht so groß wie Paul*

Peter ist weniger groß als Paul
   ⊃ *Paul ist größer als Peter*

III

Der bisher behandelte Ausschnitt aus der Grammatik von Vergleichssätzen muß in mehrerer Hinsicht erweitert werden.

3.1.   Wir betrachten zuerst Sätze wie

(25)   (a)   *Peter ist genauso faul wie gefräßig*
         (b)   *Peter ist genauso groß wie ich (es) vermutet habe*
         (c)   *Peter ist größer als das Bett lang ist*

Offenbar sind (25a) und (25b) aus Sätzen her zu erklären, die vollständig lauten

[15] Während sich bei den relationalen Adjektiven *groß, klein* durch Zufügung von *noch* ein Bedeutungsunterschied ergibt, scheint dies bei den absoluten Adjektiven nicht der Fall. Dies ist aber nur eine Folge unserer noch unvollständigen Beschreibung. Zu *Peter ist noch fleißiger als Paul* gehört die Präsupposition 'Paul ist sehr fleißig', zu *Peter ist fleißiger als Paul* lediglich die Präsupposition 'Paul ist fleißig'.

(26)　　(a)　*Peter ist genauso faul wie er gefräßig ist*

　　　　(b)　*?Peter ist genau so groß wie ich vermutet habe, daß er groß ist*

Analog ließe sich dann auch

(15)　　(a)　*Peter ist größer als Paul*

auf

(27)　　*?Peter ist größer als Paul groß ist*

zurückführen.[16]

Die Generalisierung gegenüber den Regeln in 2.1. ist leicht zu formulieren: die Ko-Konstituente von Pos bzw. Komp lautet S und nicht NP; S ist entweder ebenfalls ein Satz mit Kopula und AP,[17] oder S ist ein Satz, dessen Objektsatz diese Struktur hat (und darüberhinaus bis auf Spez identisch ist mit dem obersten Matrixsatz). Es besteht allerdings der Unterschied, daß (27) kaum akzeptabel ist, sondern wohl notwendig reduziert werden muß, während jedenfalls (26a) gut akzeptiert wird. Die Reduktionsbedingungen sind wahrscheinlich ähnliche wie bei der Koordination: die identischen Teile, d.h. entweder *A* (in (27)) oder NP (in (26a)) oder S insgesamt (in (26b)) werden getilgt.

Damit überhaupt akzeptable Sätze zustandekommen, muß für beide vorkommende A außerdem dieselbe bzw. eine kompatible Maßfunktion existieren: dies gilt für *groß* und *lang* (für die beide ein Längenmaß existiert) und wohl auch für *faul* und *gefräßig* (die beide keine Maßausdrücke erlauben, weswegen ihre Maßfunktionen kompatibel sind);

(28)　　**Peter ist größer als das Bett schwer ist*

ist dagegen strikt abweichend. Allerdings können

(29)　　*?Peter ist genauso faul wie groß*
　　　　Peter ist ebenso dumm wie lang

eher akzeptiert werden (vielleicht deswegen, weil *faul*, *dumm*, für die es keine Maßausdrücke gibt, deshalb mit allen möglichen Maßfunktionen kompatibel sind?), während

(30)　　**Peter ist genau so faul wie Paul groß ist*

wieder völlig abzulehnen ist.

---

[16] Genau in dieser Weise wird der Satz von Doherty abgeleitet und später einer Komparationsreduktion unterworfen.

　　Auf der Basis eines solchen Vorschlags erklären sich auch die Interpretationsregeln für $[m, +]$ und $[m, -]$ in 2.3.: die ausgesagte Bedeutung des in (27) eingebetteten Satzes *Paul ist groß*, nämlich GROSS(Paul) > N, hat für den gesamten Satz die Funktion einer Präsupposition.

[17] Diese AP enthält keine Teilkonstituente Spez, da Sätze wie **Peter ist größer als das Bett länger ist als das Sofa* (oder ähnlich) strikt ungrammatisch sind.

Bei den Adjektiven müssen zusätzlich die Markierungen übereinstimmen:
akzeptabel sind

(31)   (a)   *Peter ist kleiner als das Bett lang ist*
                      u   u

          (b)   *Peter ist noch kleiner als das Bett kurz ist*
                          m   m

hingegen abweichend sind

(32)   (a)   **Peter ist größer als das Bett kurz ist*
                      u   m

          (b)   **Peter ist noch kleiner als das Bett lang ist*
                          m   u

Auch

(33)   (a)   ?*Peter ist genauso faul wie klug*
                              m, −   m, +

          (b)   ?*Peter ist genauso fleißig wie Paul faul ist*
                              m, +   m, −

sind wahrscheinlich als abweichend einzustufen: hier wird ein negativ
markiertes zusammen mit einem positiv markierten Adjektiv verwendet.

   Bei einem Satz wie

(25)   (a)   *Peter ist genauso faul wie gefräßig*

bereitet die Interpretation zunächst Schwierigkeiten: hier werden verschiedene, aber offenbar doch kompatible Maße miteinander verglichen.
Was sich entspricht, ist ihre relative Differenz zur Norm. Formal ließe sich
dieser Sachverhalt vielleicht wie folgt angeben:

$$\text{FAUL}(\text{Peter}) - \text{FAUL}_N(x_i) = \text{GEFRÄSSIG}(\text{Peter}) - \text{GEFRÄSSIG}_N(x_i)$$
$$\text{mit Peter} \in \{x_i\}.$$

3.2.   Eine andere Erweiterung unserer Grammatik muß Sätze umfassen
wie [17a]

(34)   (a)   *Peter läuft schneller als Paul*

          (b)   *Peter denkt schneller als er spricht*

(35)   (a)   *Peter arbeitet hier genauso gut wie zuhause*

          (b)   *Peter arbeitet schnell genauso gut wie langsam*

[17a] Wir betrachten nur Sätze, die einen Gradvergleich enthalten; alle sog. Analogievergleiche
bleiben unberücksichtigt, z.B.

(a)   *Peter ist wie Paul*
(b)   *Peter läuft wie Paul*
(c)   *Peter schwimmt wie ein Fisch*

Satz (b) z.B. könnte durch eine Struktur ähnlich Figur 3 wiedergegeben werden, mit Adv = ϕ
und Komp durch Pos ersetzt. Spez müßte wahrscheinlich S direkt dominieren.

(36)   (a) *Peter ist ein besserer Schüler als Paul*
        (b) *Peter ist ein ebenso konservativer Vater wie Lehrer*

(37)   *Peter ist ein besserer Schüler als ich (es) erwartet habe*

(38)   *Peter ist ein besserer Handwerker*

In allen diesen Sätzen werden die Adjektivformen nicht prädikativ gebraucht, sondern entweder adverbial oder attributiv. Wie bisher sind Positiv-und Komparativformen möglich, in Verbindung mit einfachen NPn (wie *Paul*) oder mit S (wie *er spricht* . . . , *ich habe erwartet* . . .).

Die semantische Interpretation wird derjenigen beim prädikativen Gebrauch in großen Teilen gleichen, sie ist allerdings mit der Schwierigkeit verbunden, daß hier wahrscheinlich eine Prädikatenlogik 2. Stufe vorausgesetzt werden muß.

Die geeignete syntaktische Beschreibung wird davon abhängen, wie überhaupt Adverbien und attributive Adjektive in unserer Grammatik beschrieben werden.

So könnte für (34a) und (34b) etwa davon ausgegangen werden, daß *schnell* zur VP in einem höheren Satz gehört:

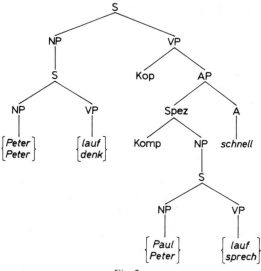

Fig. 2.

'Peters Laufen ist schneller als Pauls Laufen'
'Peters Denken ist schneller als Peters Sprechen'

Eine andere Lösung entspricht der von Bowers (1970) anvisierten:

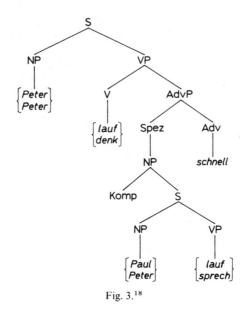

Fig. 3.[18]

Die Entscheidung, ob hier Figur 2 oder Figur 3 vorzuziehen ist, möchte ich offenlassen.

In beiden Darstellungen wird aber (34a) auf den Satz

(39)   *Peter läuft schneller als Paul läuft*

bezogen. Um die Parallele zur Darstellung von

(15)   (a)   *Peter ist größer als Paul*

als Reduktionsform aus

(27)   ʾ*Peter ist größer als Paul groß ist*

zu ziehen, müßte jedoch von

(40)   **Peter läuft schneller als Paul schnell läuft*

ausgegangen werden, einem Satz, der gegenüber (39) zwar deutlich als abweichend zu kennzeichnen ist.[19] dafür aber das Adverb, auf das sich die Maßfunktion bezieht, auch in Spez explizit enthält.

Es ergeben sich die Beschreibungsalternativen:

(1) Spez wird in jedem Fall direkt zu S expandiert; die Möglichkeit also,

---

[18] Es ist problematisch, ob Spez hier direkt NP dominiert oder nicht vielmehr S. Vgl. weiter unten.

[19] Bei der prädikativen Verwendung von Adjektiven ist **Peter ist schneller als Paul ist* (also die Parallele zu (39)) strikt abweichend, ʾ*Peter ist schneller als Paul schnell ist* (d.h. die Parallele zu (40)) wesentlich leichter zu akzeptieren. Vielleicht ist dieser Unterschied lediglich in den Bedingungen für die Tilgung identischer Terme zu beschreiben: wenn ein prädikatives Adjektiv getilgt wird, muß notwendig auch die zugehörige Kopula getilgt werden.

daß Spez direkt NP dominiert, wird ausgeschlossen. Hiermit wird ein Gewinn an Generalisierung erreicht. Dafür wird aber in Kauf genommen, daß das Adjektiv oder das Adverb in dem von Spez dominierten S immer getilgt werden muß, sofern es sich von dem Adjektiv oder Adverb, das als Ko-Konstituente von Spez auftritt, nicht unterscheidet. (Es bleibt also nur erhalten in Fällen wie

(25)   (c)   *Peter ist größer als das Bett lang ist*
(26)   (a)   *Peter ist genauso faul wie er gefräßig ist*.)

Die Tilgung der identischen NP und V ist hingegen fakultativ.

(2) Spez wird alternativ zu S oder NP expandiert. Dieses NP ist in seiner Form identisch mit der Subjekts-NP des Satzes[20] (entspricht der Lösung Figur 2), oder es enthält außer AdvP und AP dieselben Konstituenten wie der Matrixsatz (entspricht der Lösung Figur 3). Diese Beschreibung ist weniger generell, hat aber den Vorteil, daß eine obligate Tilgung des identischen Adjektivs oder Adverbs überflüssig ist.

Welche Beschreibung insgesamt vorteilhafter ist, kann ich nicht beurteilen. Provisorisch entscheide ich mich für die Möglichkeit (2). Hierfür spricht z.B., daß mir kein Beispiel bekannt ist, wo unter Spez ein anderes *Adverb* auftreten könnte als das in Schwesterposition zu Spez.

Satz (35a) zeigt, daß sich der Vergleich auch auf ein freies Adverbial beziehen kann. Bei einer Lösung entsprechend Figur 2 müßte *gut* zu einer VP in einem höheren Satz gehören als *hier*:

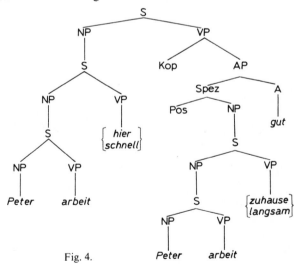

Fig. 4.

---

[20] Dies meint identische Konstituenten, aber wahrscheinlich auch identische syntaktische Merkmale.

Es gilt auch hier wieder die Bedingung, daß der unter Spez eingebettete Satz von gleicher Struktur ist wie der unter der Subjekts-NP.

Ganz entsprechend ist die Struktur des Satzes (35b) anzunehmen.

Für die Beschreibung der Sätze mit attributiven Adjektiven bieten sich wiederum zwei Möglichkeiten an.

(1) Das Adjektiv wird aus einem Relativsatz her erklärt (so die übliche Auffassung, z.B. Motsch (1964)), cf. Figur 5.

(2) Das Adjektiv wird unter Spez, das zu einer NP gehört, entwickelt (Vorschlag Chomsky (1968), Bowers (1970)), cf. Figur 6.

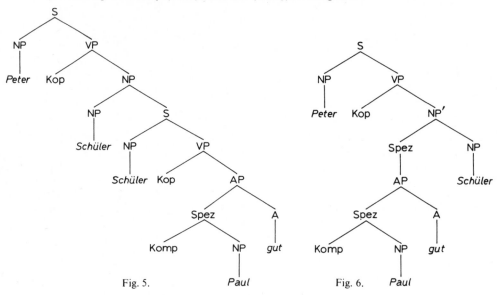

Fig. 5.   Paul   Fig. 6.   Paul

Ich will auch hier offenlassen, welche dieser beiden Beschreibungsalternativen zu wählen ist.[21]

Um die Struktur eines Satzes wie (36a) darzustellen, ist es offenbar vorzuziehen, unter Spez eine NP und nicht ein S anzunehmen. Denn alle folgenden Sätze sind stark ungrammatisch:

(41)   *Peter ist ein besserer Schüler als Paul ein Schüler ist
        *Peter ist ein besserer Schüler als Paul ein guter Schüler ist
        *Peter ist ein Schüler, der besser als Paul ein Schüler ist
        *Peter ist ein Schüler, der besser als Paul ein Schüler ist, der gut ist

---

[21] Über die Darstellung von Relativsätzen und Attributen in der Syntax besteht bisher noch keine Einigkeit. Keiner der gemachten Vorschläge kann wirklich voll überzeugen. (Zur Diskussion des hiermit verwandten Problems der Darstellung von Nominalisierungen vgl. Wunderlich (1969)). Es gibt außerdem Adjektive, die nur attributiv (z.B. *rechter Idiot, ziemlicher Dummkopf, gewisse Leute, werter Herr*) und andere, die nur prädikativ (z.B. *entzwei, flügge, schuld*) gebraucht werden können.

Allerdings ist dieser Satz akzeptabel:

(42)   *Peter ist als Schüler besser als Paul als Schüler ist*

Wie er aber aus Figur 5 oder Figur 6 abgeleitet werden könnte, ist mir unklar. Umgekehrt ist auch (36a) wohl kaum aus der (42) zugrundeliegenden Struktur abzuleiten.

Satz (36b) ist durch

(43)   *Peter ist ein ebenso konservativer Vater wie er ein konservativer Lehrer ist,*

aber nicht durch

(44)   **Peter ist ein Vater, der ebenso konservativ ist wie Peter ein Lehrer ist, der konservativ ist.*

paraphrasierbar, ein Sachverhalt, der eher die Annahme von Figur 6 unterstützt. Spez unter AP wird hier zu Pos und S entwickelt:

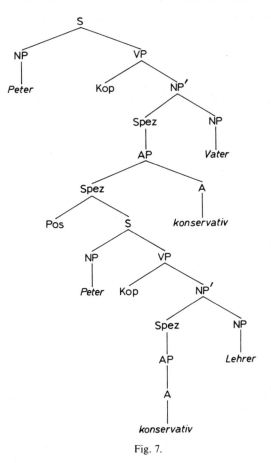

Fig. 7.

Satz (37) bereitet Schwierigkeiten: die Frage ist, wie der Objektsatz von *ich habe erwartet* lauten muß. Nach den bisherigen Konventionen müßten wir entweder paraphrasieren

> (45)   *Peter ist ein Schüler, der besser ist als ich erwartet habe, daß er gut ist

oder

> (46)   *Peter ist ein besserer Schüler als ich erwartet habe, daß er ein guter Schüler ist

Beide Sätze sind abweichend. Erst wenn in (45) *gut* und in (46) *ein guter Schüler* getilgt wird, könnten die Sätze akzeptiert werden.

Satz (38) ist *ohne* Akzentkennzeichnung vierdeutig: beim Primärakzent auf *Peter* und Sekundärakzent auf *besserer* wird ein fehlendes Vergleichsglied aus dem Kontext ergänzt, z.B. *Peter ist ein besserer Handwerker als Paul*, beim Primärakzent auf *besserer* versteht man entweder dasselbe, oder, daß Peter besser ist als der durchschnittliche Handwerker, oder aber, daß Peter zu den sog. besseren Leuten gehört (= die besser gestellt sind als der Durchschnitt). Beim Akzent auf *Handwerker* wird der Satz pejorativ verstanden, durch ein Vergleichsglied ließe er sich etwa ergänzen zu *Peter ist ein besserer Handwerker denn Wissenschaftler*. Wir erkennen, daß das Fehlen eines expliziten Vergleichsglieds zu den verschiedensten Interpretationen in Bezug auf eine vorausgesetzte Norm Anlaß geben kann (vgl. auch Abschnitt 4).

3.3. Die Sätze

> (47)   (a) *Peter liebt kürzere Röcke mehr als Paul*
>   (b) *Peter liebt kürzere Röcke als Paul*

haben sehr verschiedene Bedeutungen. Wenn im Satz (47a) das Adjektiv ausgespart wird, ergibt sich trotzdem ein grammatischer Satz, im Satz (47b) aber nicht:

> (48)   (a) *Peter liebt Röcke mehr als Paul*
>   (b) *Peter liebt Röcke als Paul*

Die Bedeutung des Satzes

> (49)   *Peter liebt kürzere Röcke*

ist Bestandteil der Bedeutung von (47a), aber nicht der Bedeutung von (47b). (47b) besagt nicht einmal, daß Peter Röcke liebt, sondern vielmehr, daß Peter es liebt, daß Röcke ein gewisse Eigenschaft haben.

Das Vergleichsglied, auf das sich *kürzer* bezieht, ist in (47b) explizit angegeben (deswegen kann *kürzer* auch nicht getilgt werden), während es in (47a) und (49) implizit bleibt (deswegen kann *kürzer* dort getilgt werden). *ein kürzerer Rock* meint einen Rock, der weniger lang ist als die durchschnittliche (bzw. normalerweise erwartete) Rocklänge beträgt; er ist jedoch länger als ein kurzer Rock.

Formal: *ein langer Rock$_1$, ein längerer Rock$_2$, ein kürzerer Rock$_3$, ein kurzer Rock$_4$*: $\rightarrow$ LANG(Rock$_1$) > LANG(Rock$_2$) > LANG$_D$({Rock$_i$}) > LANG(Rock$_3$) > LANG(Rock$_4$)

In (47a) kann *Paul* auch durch *Hosen* ersetzt werden, in (47b) nicht ohne weiteres:

(50) (a) *Peter liebt Röcke mehr als Hosen*
      (b) ?*Peter liebt kürzere Röcke als Hosen*

Allerdings sind die Sätze

(51) (a) *Peter liebt Röcke kürzer als Hosen*
      (b) *Peter liebt, daß Röcke kürzer sind als Hosen*

wieder voll akzeptabel.

Wir können (47a) wie folgt paraphrasieren:

(52) (a) *Peter liebt Röcke, die kürzer als normal sind, mehr als Paul Röcke liebt, die kürzer als normal sind*
      (b) *Peters Liebe zu kürzeren Röcken ist größer als Pauls Liebe zu kürzeren Röcken*

Da wir einen impliziten Normbezug auch bisher nicht in der syntaktischen Struktur dargestellt haben, sondern durch Markierungsmerkmale, scheidet (52a) als direkte Verbalisierung der anzunehmenden Tiefenstruktur aus.

Der Vergleich von (48a) und (50a) zeigt, daß das Vergleichsglied S enthalten muß: sonst ließe sich (48a) nicht wie *Peter liebt Röcke mehr als Paul sie liebt* und (50a) nicht wie *Peter liebt Röcke mehr als er Hosen liebt* verstehen. Das Wörtchen *mehr* drückt nicht einen Vergleich zwischen Maßen aus, die ein Individuum charakterisieren, sondern zwischen Maßen, die eine Proposition charakterisieren. Wir können deshalb das Wörtchen *mehr* durch *größer als* ersetzen, wenn gleichzeitig die beiden Teilsätze in Satznominale verwandelt werden (entsprechend der Paraphrase (52b)).

Als Tiefenstruktur des Satzes (47a) nehme ich die in Figur 8 dargestellte Struktur an. Problematisch bleibt freilich, ob *Peters Liebe zu* und *daß Peter liebt* ... aus derselben Form hergeleitet werden dürfen, was hiermit behauptet ist (Vgl. die Diskussion in Wunderlich (1969)). Um die Oberflächenform (47a) abzuleiten, könnte etwa die VP des eingebetteten Subjektsatzes an den obersten S-Knoten gehängt werden; gleichzeitig muß *K groß* durch *mehr*

ersetzt werden. Anschließend findet Permutation innerhalb der AP statt.
Das Ergebnis bildet Figur 9 ab. Die Rechtfertigung dieses Vorschlags steht
noch aus, da mir die Einzelheiten der notwendigen Prozesse unklar sind.
Entsprechend den Sätzen (51a) und (51b) kann auch der Satz (47b) paraphrasiert werden:

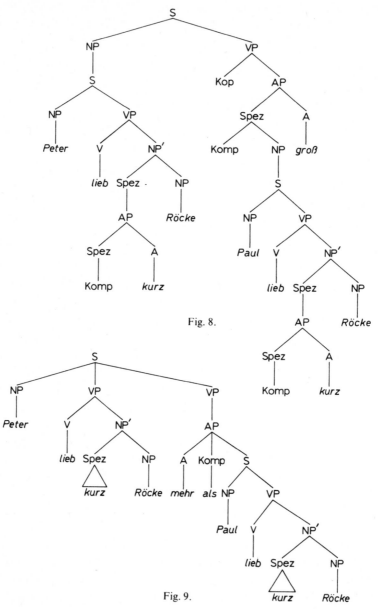

Fig. 8.

Fig. 9.

(53)   (a) *Peter liebt Röcke kürzer als Paul*

        (b) *Peter liebt, daß Röcke kürzer sind als Paul liebt, daß Röcke
             sind*

Satz (53a) ist sicherlich als abgeleitet zu verstehen, und zwar aus einer
Struktur, die (53b) zugrundeliegt.[22] Für diese will ich Figur 10 annehmen:

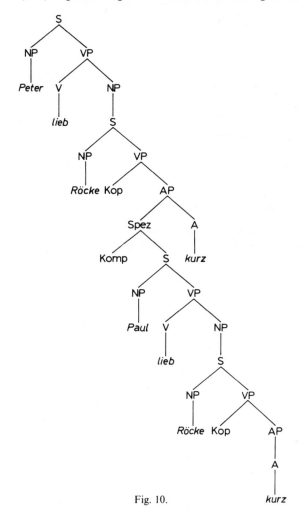

Fig. 10.

Wir betrachten nun noch Satzpaare, die sich entsprechend (47a) und (47b)
in ihrer Bedeutung stark unterscheiden:

[22] Vgl. dazu *Peter liebt, daß die Suppe warm ist* ⇒ *Peter liebt die Suppe warm.* Die Transformation, die dies leistet, entspricht derjenigen, die *Peter sieht den Vater kommen* auf *Peter sieht, daß
der Vater kommt* bezieht.

(54)   (a)   *Peter liebt Rindfleisch mehr als* $\left\{\begin{array}{l} Paul \\ Schweinefleisch \end{array}\right\}$

        (b)   *Peter liebt mehr Rindfleisch als* $\left\{\begin{array}{l} Paul \\ Schweinefleisch \end{array}\right\}$

(54a) ist genauso wie (47a) zu paraphrasieren:

(55)   *Peters Liebe zu Rindfleisch ist größer als*

                $\left\{\begin{array}{l} Pauls\ Liebe\ zu\ Rindfleisch \\ seine\ Liebe\ zu\ Schweinefleisch \end{array}\right\}$

In (54b) hat *mehr* eine andere Funktion, es gehört zu einer Komparation innerhalb des Objektsatzes nach *lieb*, zu ergänzen ist jeweils *Menge*:

(56)   (a)   ?*Peter liebt, daß die Menge Rindfleisch größer ist als die Menge Rindfleisch, wie sie Paul liebt*

        (b)   *Peter liebt, daß die Menge Rindfleisch größer ist als die Menge Schweinefleisch*

Das interne Verhalten von Nominalphrasen wie *Menge Rindfleisch, Pfund Tomaten, Glas Wasser*, usw. ist bisher erst ungenügend geklärt worden, weswegen ich hier auf eine weitere Erörterung verzichten will.

Möglich wäre auch eine andere Lösung, die *mehr* als Komparativform von *viel* behandelt: Dann wäre für (54b) als Tiefenstruktur Figur 11 anzunehmen

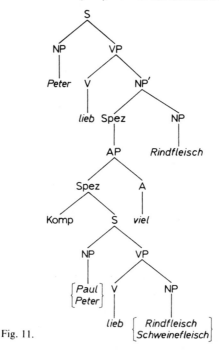

Fig. 11.

IV

Nach diesen sehr skizzenhaften Bemerkungen über eine Erweiterung der syntaktischen Beschreibung von Vergleichssätzen soll hier noch einmal auf die semantische Beziehung zur Norm eingegangen werden.

4.1. Zur vorläufigen Klärung verwende ich die Sätze (57), die ich zu synonymen Paaren angeordnet habe:

(57)　　*Peter ist groß genug – Peter ist nicht zu klein*
　　　　Peter ist zu klein – Peter ist nicht groß genug
　　　　Peter ist klein genug – Peter ist nicht zu groß
　　　　Peter ist zu groß – Peter ist nicht klein genug

Zunächst ist festzustellen, daß $[A, \ldots, \pm]$ – *genug* synonym ist mit *nicht-zu*-$[A, \ldots, \mp]$ und *zu*-$[A, \ldots, \pm]$ synonym ist mit *nicht*-$[A, \ldots, \mp]$ *-genug*.

Die intensionale Interpretation von *genug* ist: 'die Norm wird erfüllt', die von *zu*: 'die Norm wird nicht erfüllt', während die Negation durch *nicht* diese Interpretation umkehrt: *nicht-genug*: → 'die Norm wird nicht erfüllt', *nicht-zu*: → 'die Norm wird erfüllt'.

Die Adjektive *groß* und *klein* werden hier durchweg relational verstanden. Das zeigt sich daran, daß die Sätze

(58)　　$Peter\ ist\ (zwar) \begin{Bmatrix} klein \\ gro\beta \end{Bmatrix}, aber\ er\ ist \begin{Bmatrix} gro\beta \\ klein \end{Bmatrix} genug$

　　　　$Peter\ ist\ (zwar) \begin{Bmatrix} gro\beta \\ klein \end{Bmatrix}, aber\ er\ ist\ zu \begin{Bmatrix} klein \\ gro\beta \end{Bmatrix}$

ohne Schwierigkeit akzeptiert werden. Die Norm, auf die sich *Peter ist klein* bezieht, ist deshalb offenbar eine andere als die Norm, auf die sich *Peter ist klein genug, Peter ist zu klein* beziehen. Die erstgenannte Norm konstituiert sich durch die für Peter erwartete Größe bzw. durch die Durchschnittsgröße einer Gruppe von Personen, zu der Peter gehört. Die letztgenannte Norm – sie allein soll uns hier weiter beschäftigen – gehört zu einem momentanen Kontext. Der Kontext ist entweder durch bestimmte Zustandskonstellationen, Vorgänge oder Handlungen gegeben, an denen Peter sich beteiligt (diese Konstellationen können wechseln und damit auch die Norm, die an die Größe von Peter gelegt wird),[23] oder der Kontext ist durch Individuen gegeben (Sprecher oder Angesprochener von Sätzen, oder in Sätzen erwähnte Personen oder Institutionen), die sich durch Vorlieben,

---

[23] Leisi (1953) hat diese Norm 'Tauglichkeitsnorm' genannt (2. Aufl. 1961, S.101).

Vorurteile, Vorschriften, Annahme von gruppenspezifischen Normen usw. in Bezug auf die Größe von Peter gegenüber anderen Individuen auszeichnen (solche Normen können also von Sprecher zu Sprecher wechseln). Mit der absoluten Größe haben alle diese Normen nichts zu tun.

Jeder der aufgezählten Typen von Normen kann auch explizit ausgedrückt werden. Die folgenden Sätze machen deutlich, daß sich bei einem anderen Kontext der Bezug zur Norm genau umkehren kann.

(59) *Peter ist zu groß für das Bett, aber er ist zu klein, um rüber-zuspringen*

   der Schrank ist klein genug, um ihn ins Auto zu kriegen, und groß genug, um alles Notwendige darin unterzubringen

(60) *dieses Mädchen ist mir zu klein und meinem Freund zu groß*

   Peters Haare waren dem Lehrer zu lang, ihm selbst aber nicht lang genug

Die Gegenüberstellung von zwei Normbezügen verschiedenen Typs ist abweichend:

(61) **Peter ist zu groß für das Bett und mir zu klein*

Ein anderer Typ von Abweichung entsteht, wenn die Erfüllung der Norm vorschreibt, daß ein gewisses Maß erreicht oder überschritten (bzw. unterschritten) wird, der Adjektivausdruck *zu-A* bzw. *A-genug* aber gerade eine umgekehrte Norm voraussetzt:

(62) (a) *?Peter ist klein genug, um an das Reck zu reichen*
            $-N$ $+N$

   (b) *?der Schrank ist zu groß, um alles Notwendige*
            $-N$
                              darin unterzubringen
                              $+N$

   (c) *?der Schrank ist zu klein, um ihn ins Auto zu kriegen*
            $+N$ $-N$

In (62a) und (62b) wird durch den Kontext eine $+$Norm aufgestellt, durch den Adjektivausdruck aber eine $-$Norm vorausgesetzt. (Ich verwende '$+$' statt 'positiv' und '$-$' statt 'negativ'). In (62c) verhält es sich umgekehrt. Unter $+$Norm verstehe ich, daß das Erfüllen der Norm bedeutet, daß ein gewisses Maß überschritten oder höchstens erreicht wird, unter $-$Norm verstehe ich, daß das Erfüllen der Norm bedeutet, daß ein gewisses Maß unterschritten oder höchstens erreicht wird.

In der Syntax werden die Regeln eingeführt:

$$\text{Spez} \rightarrow \text{Part} - \left\{ \begin{array}{l} \text{S} \\ \text{PP} \end{array} \right\}$$

$$\text{Part} \rightarrow \left\{ \begin{array}{l} [\text{Part}, +] \\ [\text{Part}, -] \end{array} \right\}$$

mit Part für Normvergleichspartikel.

Lexikon: [Part, +]: *genug*

[Part, −]: *zu*

Für jedes infragekommende Adjektiv gilt (nach den Regeln im Abschnitt 2)

$$A \rightarrow [A, \ldots, \{\pm\}]$$

Damit sind 4 Kombinationen möglich.

TABELLE II

Spez	Phonologische Realisierung	A	Semantische Interpretation	Präsupposition	Konsequenz
Part, +	*A genug*	+	Norm erfüllt	+ Norm	$a_i \geqslant a_{+N}$
Part, +	*A genug*	−	Norm erfüllt	− Norm	$a_i \leqslant a_{-N}$
Part, −	*zu A*	+	Norm nicht erfüllt	− Norm	$a_i > a_{-N}$
Part, −	*zu A*	−	Norm nicht erfüllt	+ Norm	$a_i < a_{+N}$

a_i ist der Wert der Maßfunktion für das durch die Subjekts-NP beschriebene Objekt. a_N ist der Wert der Maßfunktion, der von der Norm festgelegt ist.

Beispiele: *Peter ist groß genug*

Peter ist klein genug

Peter ist zu groß

Peter ist zu klein

Aus der Tabelle wird klar, daß z.B. *nicht groß genug* und *zu klein* Synonyme sind, denn es gelten die Konsequenzen non ($a_i \geqslant a_{+N}$) bzw. $a_i < a_{+N}$, jeweils auf eine + Norm bezogen, und diese Ausdrücke sind äquivalent.

Aus manchem Kontext geht die Art der Norm (ob + Norm oder − Norm) nicht klar hervor. Dann können Inkompatibilitäten wie in (62) nicht auftreten. Die Interpretation der Sätze ist aber immer, was den Typ der Norm betrifft, eindeutig; hierfür brauchen wir nur die Tabelle heranzuziehen: *zu* mit einem − markierten Adjektiv und *genug* mit einem + markierten Adjektiv setzen eine + Norm voraus, *zu* mit einem + markierten Adjektiv und *genug* mit einem − markierten Adjektiv setzen eine − Norm voraus. Betrachten wir die Sätze

(63) (a) *der Bogen ist zu klein für das Paket*
      (b) *der Bogen ist zu groß für das Paket*

a_N ist hier durch die Ausmaße des Pakets gegeben. (63a) kann nur so interpretiert werden: $a_i < a_{N+}$, z.B. 'der Bogen ist zu klein, um das Paket darin einzuwickeln', (63b) kann nur so interpretiert werden: $a_i > a_{N-}$, z.B. 'der Bogen ist zu groß, um im Paket Platz zu finden'.

Mithilfe der semantischen Interpretation läßt sich auch ohne Schwierigkeit die Klasse der möglichen Paraphrasen herleiten:

(64) *Peter ist zu groß für das Bett*

Für *Peter* gilt das Maß a_1, für *Bett* das Maß a_2.
Interpretation $a_1 > a_{2(-N)}$
Äquivalente Ausdrücke:
(a) $non(a_1 \leqslant a_{2(-N)})$; (b) $a_2 < a_{1(+N)}$; (c) $non(a_2 \geqslant a_{1(+N)})$.
Verbalisierung:

(65) (a) *Peter ist nicht klein genug für das Bett*
      (b) *das Bett ist zu klein für Peter*
      (c) *das Bett ist nicht groß genug für Peter*

Statt (65b) und (65c) könnten auch gebildet werden:

(66) (b) *das Bett ist zu kurz für Peter*
      (c) *das Bett ist nicht lang genug für Peter*

Für den Satz

(67) *Peter ist zu klein für das Reck*

ergibt sich als eine der Paraphrasen

(68) *das Reck ist zu hoch für Peter*

(und normalerweise nicht:

(69) *das Reck ist zu groß für Peter*)

Welches Adjektiv jeweils zu wählen ist, ergibt sich aus der semantischen Beschreibung, einmal der Substantive, die räumlich ausgedehnte Objekte bezeichnen (wie *Mensch* und alle Eigennamen für Personen, *Bett, Schrank*), und zum andern der Adjektive, die räumliche Dimensionen angeben (wie *groß, dick, hoch, breit*, usw.). Hierbei können wir uns weitgehend auf die

Analyse von Bierwisch (1967) stützen, einschließlich gewisser Ergänzungen durch Teller (1969).

Bei dem Versuch, Bierwischs Merkmalanalyse anzuwenden, ist mir allerdings ein Problem aufgefallen, das Bierwisch unzureichend gelöst hat; es handelt sich um die Einführung des Merkmals (+ Haupt) bzw. (− Haupt). Bierwisch schreibt: 'Das Merkmal (− Haupt) bestimmt das Verhalten von *dick*. (+ Haupt) spezifiziert alle Dimensionen, die beim Gebrauch von *groß* involviert sind' (dt. 1970, S. 293).

das Bett ist dick ist abweichend; also müssen alle drei Dimensionen von 'Bett' mit (+ Haupt) gekennzeichnet werden.

das Bett ist groß kann aber nur hinsichtlich zweier Dimensionen verstanden werden (der Länge und der Breite), nicht hinsichtlich der Höhe; also dürfen bei 'Bett' auch nur zwei Dimensionen (+ Haupt) gekennzeichnet werden.

Peter ist dick: es ist im wesentlichen nur eine Dimension gemeint; sie müßte (− Haupt) gekennzeichnet werden, die beiden andern Dimensionen (+ Haupt).

Peter ist groß: hier wird ebenfalls nur eine Dimension verstanden; diese wäre (+ Haupt) zu kennzeichnen, die beiden andern Dimensionen dann notwendigerweise (− Haupt).

Es bleibt also unklar, sowohl für *Bett* wie für *Mensch* und alle Personennamen, wie die Kennzeichnung der drei involvierten Dimensionen durch (± Haupt) vorzunehmen ist.

Ganz provisorisch wähle ich folgenden Ausweg: es gibt eine erste Merkmalszerlegung (± Haupt$_1$) in Bezug auf das Verhalten gegenüber *dick*, eine zweite Merkmalszerlegung (± Haupt$_2$) bei (+ Haupt$_1$) in Bezug auf das Verhalten gegenüber *groß*.

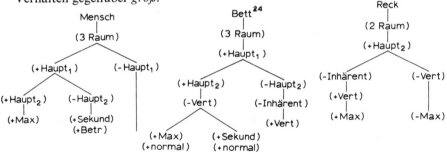

---

[24] Da Sätze wie *das Bett ist breiter als lang* keineswegs ausgeschlossen werden sollten, jedoch für diesen Fall (− normal) gelten könnte, wähle ich ein zusätzliches Merkmalspaar (± normal) entsprechend dem Vorschlag von Teller (1969), S.207 ff.

Mit diesen Festlegungen, zusammen mit den semantischen Eintragungen
für die Adverbien (vgl. Bierwisch (1970), S. 313), erklärt sich, daß in dem
Satz

(64)   *Peter ist zu groß für das Bett*

die Dimension $(+ \text{Haupt}_2)$ $(+ \text{Max})$ des *Peter* genannten Objekts mit der
Dimension $(+ \text{Haupt}_2)$ $(+ \text{Max})$ $(+ \text{normal})$ des *Bett* genannten Objekts
verglichen wird, und daß die Sätze

(66)   (a) *Peter ist zu lang für das Bett*
         (b) *das Bett ist zu kurz für Peter*

mögliche Paraphrasen zu (64) sind. Ebenfalls erklärt sich, daß die Paraphrase zu

(67)   *Peter ist zu klein für das Reck*

nicht

(69)   *das Reck ist zu groß für Peter*

lauten wird, sondern

(68)   *das Reck ist zu hoch für Peter*,

da die Dimension $(+ \text{Haupt}_2)$ $(+ \text{Max})$ des *Peter* genannten Objekts mit
der Dimension $(+ \text{Haupt}_2)$ $(+ \text{Vert})$ $(+ \text{Max})$ des *Reck* genannten Objekts
verglichen wird (und nicht etwa mit der Dimension $(+ \text{Haupt}_2)$ $(- \text{Vert})$
$(- \text{Max})$).

4.2.   Bisher habe ich mich ganz auf Adjektive beschränkt, die Maße für
Raumdimensionen benennen. Komplizierter ist die Sachlage bei Wertungs-
adjektiven wie *fleißig, faul*.
Wir bilden parallel zu (57) die folgenden Sätze

(70)   *Peter ist fleißig genug   – Peter ist nicht zu faul*
         Peter ist zu faul   – Peter ist nicht fleißig genug

(71)   *Peter ist faul genug   – Peter ist nicht zu fleißig*
         Peter ist zu fleißig   – Peter ist nicht faul genug

Wir erinnern uns, daß *fleißig* und *faul* in allen Fällen bezüglich einer Norm
markiert waren. Das gilt auch hier, denn Sätze wie

(72)   *?Peter ist zwar fleißig, aber er ist faul genug*
         ?Peter ist zwar fleißig, aber er ist zu faul

sind abweichend. Die Unterscheidung zweier verschiedener Typen von

Normen, zum einen in Bezug auf einen Erwartungs oder Durchschnittswert, zum andern zu einem momentanen Kontext gehörend, scheint bei den Adjektiven *fleißig*, *faul* nicht möglich zu sein; die Norm, um die es sich hier handelt, gehört stets zum momentanen Kontext.

(73)   *Peter ist faul, aber mir ist er fleißig genug*

ist genauso wie (72) abweichend.[25] Jedoch ist

(74)   *der Lehrer hält Peter für zu faul, aber mir ist er fleißig genug*

ein völlig korrekter Satz, da die Normen zu zwei verschiedenen Kontexten gehören.

Wie bei den Adjektiven *groß* und *klein* ist zwischen + Normen und − Normen zu unterscheiden: die Sätze (70) werden in Bezug auf eine + Norm verstanden (die etwa von einem Lehrer aufgestellt sein mag), die Sätze (71) in Bezug auf eine − Norm (die etwa von den Mitschülern aufgestellt sein mag). Problematisch bleibt dabei aber z.B. die Interpretation von *Peter ist faul genug*: man könnte diesen Satz so verstehen, daß eine negativ *bewertete* Norm erfüllt wird (etwa im Sinne von *Peter ist faul genug,* $\left\{ \begin{matrix} um\ bestraft\ zu\ werden \\ um\ sitzenzubleiben \end{matrix} \right\}$; andererseits könnte man auch sagen, daß es eine Norm gibt, die verlangt, daß ein gewisses Maß an Fleiß nicht überschritten werden soll (diese Norm habe ich − Norm genannt), und diese Norm wird erfüllt. Diese zweite Interpretation ist sicher nötig für den Satz

(75)   *Peter ist den Initiatoren des Bummelstreiks faul genug,*

ebenfalls für den Satz

(76)   *Peter ist seinen Arbeitskollegen zu fleißig; sie befürchten eine Heraufsetzung der Arbeitsnorm*

(lediglich, daß *zu fleißig* bedeutet: die von den Arbeitskollegen verstandene Norm wird nicht erfüllt, d.h. ein gewisses Maß wird *über*schritten). Bei der ersten Interpretation würde ein Erfüllen der Norm bedeuten, daß eine Sanktion ausgeübt wird; bei der zweiten Interpretation gilt genau das Umgekehrte: bei Nichterfüllen der Norm könnte eine Sanktion ausgeübt werden.

Nun ist es gewiß widersinnig, daß bei Erfüllen einer Norm eine Sanktion ausgeübt wird. Ich vermute, daß die erste Interpretation, so wie sie oben gegeben wurde, fallengelassen werden kann. Die allgemeine Konvention wäre: Bei Erfüllen der Norm wird von der normsetzenden Person (Gruppe,

---

[25] Dies ist einleuchtend, denn *Peter ist faul* enthält schon implizit einen Bezug auf den Sprecher des Satzes, der hier nämlich seine eigenen Normvorstellungen anwendet.

Institution) überhaupt nicht oder mit einer Belohnung reagiert (etwa wenn die absolute Differenz zwischen erreichtem Maßwert und Normmaßwert einen gewissen Betrag übersteigt), bei Nichterfüllen der Norm wird von der normsetzenden Person (Gruppe, Institution) ebenfalls entweder gar nicht oder aber mit einer Sanktion reagiert (etwa wenn, genau wie oben, die absolute Differenz zwischen erreichtem Maßwert und Normmaßwert einen gewissen Betrag übersteigt). Linguistisch gesehen verhält sich das Erreichen des Sanktionsbereiches bei einer + Norm wie eine − Norm, und umgekehrt. Die folgende Figur soll die Verhältnisse illustrieren:[26]

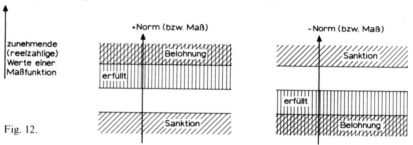

Fig. 12.

Wir haben jetzt zwei verschiedene Normbegriffe verwendet: der erste bezog sich auf die linguistisch erschließbaren Präsuppositionen + Norm bzw. − Norm, die der Deutlichkeit halber nunmehr durch + Maß bzw. − Maß ersetzt werden sollen, der zweite bezog sich auf die Wertsetzung, auf die mit Belohnung oder Sanktion reagiert werden kann, d.h. entweder + Maß oder − Maß wird zur Norm erklärt (welches von beiden jeweils gilt, ergibt sich aus dem Komplement von Part oder aus dem weiteren Kontext).

Unsere Tabelle II läßt sich dan wie folgt erweitern zur Tabelle III: (S.665)

Die + und − Merkmale sind jetzt so gewählt, daß folgendes gilt: Sei π das Produkt der drei Vorzeichen aus den Spalten Spez, A und Normfestsetzung, dann

TABELLE IV

π	Spez	Semantische Interpretation
+	+	Norm wird erfüllt
−	+	Sanktionsbereich wird erreicht
+	−	Norm wird nicht erfüllt
−	−	Satz ist abweichend

[26] Dabei bin ich mir im Klaren, daß es sich hier um eine starke Vereinfachung handelt. Normalerweise brauchen die Werte nicht reellzahlig zu sein und Belohnungs- und Sanktionsbereich könnten auch anders abgegrenzt werden. Von einer + Norm her gesehen würde *Peter ist zu faul, um ihn zu bestrafen* etwa bedeuten: 'es lohnt sich nicht, durch Strafe etwas erreichen zu wollen'. Jedenfalls würde der Maßwert außerhalb des Sanktionsbereichs liegen. Vgl. auch Anm. 27.

TABELLE III

Spez	Phonolog. Realisierung	A	Semantische Interpretation	Präsupposition	Wenn	Dann
Part, +	A genug	+	Maß wird erreicht	+Maß	+Maß die Norm ist	Norm wird erfüllt
Part, +	A genug	−	Maß wird erreicht	−Maß	+Maß die Norm ist	Sanktionsbereich wird erreicht[27]
Part, −	zu A	+	Maß wird nicht erreicht	−Maß	+Maß die Norm ist	Satz ist abweichend[28]
Part, −	zu A	−	Maß wird nicht erreicht	+Maß	+Maß die Norm ist	Norm wird nicht erfüllt
Part, +	A genug	+	Maß wird erreicht	+Maß	−Maß die Norm ist	Sanktionsbereich wird erreicht
Part, +	A genug	−	Maß wird erreicht	−Maß	−Maß die Norm ist	Norm wird erfüllt
Part, −	zu A	+	Maß wird nicht erreicht	−Maß	−Maß die Norm ist	Norm wird nicht erfüllt
Part, −	zu A	−	Maß wird nicht erreicht	+Maß	−Maß die Norm ist	Satz ist abweichend

[27] Aus der Figur 12 ist bereits ersichtlich, daß aus 'der Sanktionsbereich wird erreicht' folgt: 'die Norm wird nicht erfüllt'. Jedoch gilt nicht das Umgekehrte. So erklärt sich, daß *Peter ist faul genug, um bestraft zu werden* bedeutet: 'der Bereich für die im Kontext genannte Sanktion (= Bestrafen) wird erreicht'. Der Satz *Peter ist zu faul, um bestraft zu werden* kann eine solche Interpretation nicht erhalten; er drückt gerade aus, daß Peter nicht bestraft wird. Aber selbstverständlich drücken beide Sätze aus, daß Peter die Norm nicht erfüllt (wenn wir als Norm ein + Maß voraussetzen).

[28] Da sich die Sanktionsspezifikation auf nicht ganz einfache Weise aus dem Kontext konstituieren muß, kann, strenggenommen, nicht gesagt werden 'dieser Satz ist abweichend', sondern nur 'in diesem Kontext ist dieser Satz abweichend'. Was darunter zu verstehen ist, möge folgender Text verdeutlichen, der abweichend ist:

*Peter sollte fleißig sein. Da er aber zu fleißig ist, wird er bestraft
    + Maß   A +

Wenn wir im ersten Satz aber *fleißig* durch *faul* substituieren, wird als Norm ein −Maß aufgestellt,   und der entstehende Text ist akzeptabel:

Peter sollte faul sein. Da er aber zu fleißig ist, wird er bestraft
    − Maß   A +

(71a)   *Peter ist faul genug*

kann nun bedeuten: bei einem + Maß als Norm wird der Sanktionsbereich erreicht (= 1. Interpretation); oder: ein − Maß als Norm wird
erfüllt (= 2. Interpretation).
Hingegen

(77)   *Peters Haare sind zu lang*

kann nur bedeuten: ein − Maß als Norm wird nicht erfüllt.
Bei der Negation wird die soeben aufgeführte Interpretation negiert.

(78)   *Peter ist nicht faul genug*

kann bedeuten: (1) bei einem + Maß als Norm wird der Sanktionsbereich
nicht erreicht. Dies könnte zweideutig sein (die Norm ist erfüllt oder nicht),
da aber *faul* die minus − markierte Form des Adjektivs ist, ist zu schließen,
daß die Norm nicht erfüllt wird.

(2) ein − Maß als Norm wird nicht erfüllt.

(78) ist deshalb nicht notwendig eine Paraphrase zu *Peter ist zu fleißig*,
denn dieser Satz kann nur bedeuten: ein − Maß als Norm wird nicht erfüllt.

(79)   *Peters Haare sind nicht zu lang*

kann nur bedeuten: ein − Maß als Norm wird erfüllt. Deswegen ist (79)
nicht notwendig eine Paraphrase zu

(80)   *Peters Haare sind kurz genug*,

denn dieser letzte Satz könnte auch bedeuten: bei einem + Maß als Norm
wird der Sanktionsbereich erreicht (etwa in dem Satz *Peters Haare sind
kurz genug, um ihn als Vertreter der herrschenden Moral aus unserer Gruppe
auszuschließen*, so unwahrscheinlich die Äußerung eines solchen Satzes auch
sein mag.[29])

Verallgemeinernd kann gefolgert werden, daß die einzelnen Satzpaare,
die in (70) aufgezählt wurden, zwar in spezifischen Kontexten Paraphrasen-
paare sein können, im allgemeinen Fall jedoch nicht. Insbesondere weisen
aber die Sätze *Peter ist nicht zu faul*, *Peter ist nicht zu fleißig* auch eine
adversative Nuance auf. Als normaler Kontext könnte sich beispielsweise
anschließen . . . *sondern zu ungeschickt/zu wenig kameradschaftlich.*

[29] Während einige Normen und die zugehörigen Sanktionsandrohungen innerhalb einer
Sprachgemeinschaft explizit formuliert werden (meistens durch Autoritätspersonen, z.B. 'die
Haare sollen kurz sein'), bleiben andere Normen (die häufig zunächst in der Negation autorita-
tiver Normen bestehen) inexplizit und konstituieren sich in einem stillschweigenden Gruppen-
konsensus. Dies ist der Grund, warum Sätze wie der eben erwähnte, der die Explikation einer
gewissen Gegennorm zur Voraussetzung hätte, sehr unwahrscheinlich sind.

V

Wir wollen uns jetzt kurz den Superlativformen zuwenden.

(81)   (a)   *Peter ist am fleißigsten*
          (b)   *Peter ist am faulsten*

In (81a) wird ausgedrückt, daß sich Peter innerhalb einer (vom Kontext her bestimmten) Gruppe durch einen Maximalwert an Fleiß auszeichnet, in (81b), daß er sich durch einen Minimalwert an Fleiß auszeichnet. Dies läßt sich formal wie folgt darstellen:

$$\text{Peter} \in X \wedge (A\,x_i)\,(x_i \in X \wedge x_i \neq \text{Peter}$$
$$\supset \text{FLEISSIG (Peter)} \left\{ \begin{smallmatrix} > \\ < \end{smallmatrix} \right\} \text{FLEISSIG}\,(x_i))$$

Äquivalent dazu ist die Formulierung

$$\text{Peter} \in \{x_i\} \wedge \text{FLEISSIG (Peter)} = \left\{ \begin{matrix} \text{Max} \\ \text{Min} \end{matrix} \right\} (\text{FLEISSIG}\,(x_i))$$

Der Umfang der Menge $X = \{x_i\}$ kann auf verschiedene Weise ausgedrückt werden:

(82)   (a)   *Peter ist von allen meinen Freunden am fleißigsten*
          (b)   *Peter ist in seiner Klasse am fleißigsten*
          (c)   *Peter ist der Fleißigste seines Jahrgangs*

In (82b) und (82c) wird 'von den Schülern in seiner Klasse' bzw. 'von den Personen seines Jahrgangs' mitverstanden, da *Klasse* und *Jahrgang* noch nicht unmittelbar als Bezeichnungen für Personen dienen. Die Konstruktion $am - [A, S]$ (mit $[S]$ für das Superlativmorphem) kann in die substantivierte Form $d - [A, S]$ verändert werden. Während $am - [A, S]$ nur zusammen mit Präpositionalphrasen mit *von*, *in*, *unter* vorkommt, kann $d - [A, S]$ auch zusammen mit einem Genitivattribut verwendet werden.

Von den Sätzen

(83)   (a)   *Peter ist in Englisch am faulsten*
          (b)   *Peter ist in Englisch der Faulste*

ist (83a) zweideutig, (83b) aber eindeutig. Die eine Bedeutung von (83a) ist identisch mit der von (83b), etwa 'Peter ist von den Schülern seiner Klasse in Englisch am faulsten;' 'in Englisch' muß hierbei als zusätzlicher Index für die Menge $X = $ 'Schüler in Peters Klasse' verstanden werden. Die andere Bedeutung von (83a) kann umschrieben werden 'Peter ist, wenn er Englisch treibt, am faulsten' oder 'Peters Tätigkeit in Englisch ist von allen seinen Tätigkeiten diejenige, bei der am faulsten ist'. Wie eine formale semantische

Notation aussehen könnte, ist mir noch unklar. Man könnte versuchen, Peter durch eine Menge $\{Peter_{y_i}\}$ darzustellen, wobei jedes Element dieser Menge Peter in einer seiner möglichen Tätigkeiten y_i ist. ($\{y_i\}$ ist also eine Indexmenge, die auf die Einermenge $\{Peter\}$ abgebildet wird). Sei $Peter_{y_i}$ = Peter treibt Englisch. Dann würde gelten

$$(A\ Peter_{y_i})\ (y_i \neq y_1 \supset \text{FLEISSIG}\ (Peter_{y_1}) < \text{FLEISSIG}\ (Peter_y\ ))$$

In den Sätzen (83) ist *in Englisch* syntaktisch anders darzustellen als *in seiner Klasse* in (82b); dies wird schon daraus deutlich, daß sich diese Ausdrücke nicht gegenseitig ausschließen:

(84)   *Peter ist in seiner Klasse in Englisch am faulsten*

Einen Hinweis mag die Möglichkeit der *wenn*-Paraphrasierung geben, die in einigen Fällen möglich ist:

(85)   (a)   *Peter ist im Weinrausch am lustigsten*
          (b)   *Peter ist am lustigsten, wenn er einen Weinrausch hat,*

für (84) ist sie allerdings zwar akzeptabel, aber nicht unbedingt gleichbedeutend:

(86)   *Peter ist in seiner Klasse am faulsten, wenn sie Englisch treibt*

Die Superlativformen sind auch in adverbialer und in attributiver Stellung möglich:

(87)   (a)   *Peter spricht am schnellsten*
          (b)   *die schnellsten Schwimmer Europas treffen sich in Barcelona*

In der letzteren ist wiederum – wie bei der substantivierten Form $d - [A, S]$ – ein Genitivattribut möglich zur Benennung des Bereichs, in dem der Maximal- bzw. Minimalwert gebildet wird.

Ein Satz wie (87b) mit einer Pluralform ist in semantischer Hinsicht nicht voll bestimmt: es könnten sich mehrere Schwimmer durch gleiche maximale Schnelligkeit auszeichnen, und diese treffen sich, oder es könnten sich mit dem schnellsten Schwimmer der zweitschnellste, der drittschnellste, usw. treffen, oder es könnten sich die schnellsten Schwimmer Ungarns mit den schnellsten Schwimmern Hollands, usw. treffen.[30] Diese Unbestimmtheit ist aber keineswegs als Mehrdeutigkeit zu verstehen; dies ist in der formalen Notation zu berücksichtigen. Etwa:

---

[30] Der Satz ist sogar noch weiter unbestimmt: die schnellsten Brustschwimmer sind immer noch langsamer als relativ langsame Kraulschwimmer, die 1500 m – Schwimmer sind langsamer als die 100 m – Schwimmer, usw.

$X = \{x_i\}$ = die Schwimmer in Europa

MAX-SCHNELL = Menge von Maximalwerten als Teilmenge aus $\{$SCHNELL $(x_i)\}$ (wie sie im einzelnen konstituiert wird, bleibt unbestimmt)

$X_1 = \{x_j/$SCHNELL $(x_j) \in$ MAX-SCHNELL$\}$

X_1 = die schnellsten Schwimmer Europas; $X_1 \subset X.$[31]

Für die syntaktische Darstellung der Superlativformen kann die Grammatik aus Abschnitt 2 wie folgt erweitert werden:

$$\text{Spez} \rightarrow \text{Sup} - \left\{ \begin{matrix} \text{PP} \\ \text{S}_\text{K} \end{matrix} \right\}^{32}$$

phonologische Interpretation:

Sup: $am - \dfrac{\Delta}{[S]}$ mit $[S]$ für das Superlativmorphem

$am - \dfrac{\Delta}{[S]} \Rightarrow d - \dfrac{\Delta}{[S]} /\underline{\qquad}$ PP fakultativ

$\begin{array}{cccc} d - \dfrac{\Delta}{[S]} & - P & - NP \\ 1 & 2 & 3 & 4 \\ \Rightarrow 1 & 2 & \phi & 4 \text{ fakultativ} \\ & & & \text{[Genitiv]} \end{array}$

Im allgemeinen, wenn nicht ein anderer Normbezug dagegen gesetzt wird, ist auch mit den Superlativformen ein impliziter Normbezug verbunden. So wird aus

(81) (a) *Peter ist am fließigsten*

normalerweise gefolgert, daß Peter fleißig ist. Aber aus

(88) *Peter ist noch am fleißigsten*

wird gerade umgekehrt gefolgert, daß Peter eher faul ist, und das Adjektiv wird rein relational verstanden. Dies gilt auch für Sätze wie

(89) (a) *Peter ist faul, aber doch noch am fließigsten*
      (b) *Peter ist der Kleinste, aber trotzdem groß*

---

[31] Wie diese oder die vorhergehenden semantischen Darstellungen in Form McCawley' scher Baumstrukturen wiederzugeben wären, ist vollkommon unklar. Solange nicht das Problem der Quantifikation und der Wiedergabe von Mengen in natürlichen Sprachen näher geklärt ist, bleibt McCawleys Anspruch lediglich ein Postulat, das nicht erfüllt werden kann.

[32] S_K steht hier z.B. für Konditionalsätze, die mit *wenn* anschließen.

VI

In den folgenden Sätzen

(90)   *Peter fuhr so schnell, weil die Polizei ihn jagte*

(91)   (a) *Peter ist so faul, daß er wahrscheinlich sitzenbleibt*
          (b) *Peter ist ein so guter Schachspieler, daß er 5 Partien simultan spielen kann*

ist es das Vorkommen des Wörtchens *so*, das mich veranlaßt hat, die mit ihnen exemplifizierten Konstruktionstypen hier überhaupt kurz zu diskutieren.

Satz (90) enthält einen impliziten Vergleich, der auf einer Tautologie beruht. Wir müssen einen (sprachlichen oder außersprachlichen) Kontext voraussetzen, aus dem hervorgeht, daß Peter schnell ist. Dann läßt sich (90) paraphrasieren durch

(92)   *Peter fuhr so schnell wie er fuhr, weil die Polizei ihn jagte*

Der Nebensatz (hier mit *weil* angeschlossen) hat stets die Funktion einer Begründung.

In den Sätzen (91) wird durch den *daß*-Satz eine Folgerung ausgedrückt, die sich darauf bezieht, daß ein gewisser Maßwert erreicht oder unterschritten (bzw. überschritten) wird. Der Folgerungssatz kann oft ein Modaladverbial enthalten, woraus folgt, daß er sich in dieser Hinsicht wie ein oberer Satz verhält:

(93)   *Peter ist so faul, daß er* $\begin{Bmatrix} wahrscheinlich \\ sicher \\ so\ nehme\ ich\ an \end{Bmatrix}$ *sitzenbleibt*

In den Sätzen (91) kann *so* durch *derart* (oder *in einem solchen Maße*) substituiert werden, aber nicht durch *genauso* oder *ebenso*, während in den Komparativsätzen jedes *so* durch *genauso* oder *ebenso* substituiert werden kann, aber nicht durch *derart*

(94)   *Peter ist* $\begin{Bmatrix} so \\ derart \\ *genauso \end{Bmatrix}$ *faul, daß er wahrscheinlich sitzenbleibt*

(95)   *Peter ist* $\begin{Bmatrix} so \\ *derart \\ genauso \end{Bmatrix}$ *faul wie Paul*

Hieraus geht die syntaktische Verschiedenheit der Konstruktionen klar hervol.[33] Nach dem Vorschlag von Bowers (1970) kann man auch in den Sätzen (91) *so* . . . , *daß*-S unter Spez entwickeln; für (91a) wäre dann die Tiefenstruktur Figur 13 anzunehmen.

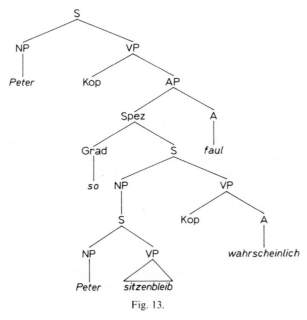

Fig. 13.

Das Wörtchen *so* läßt sich hier unter einer Konstituenten Grad einführen (die ebenfalls benötigt wird, um *sehr, besonders,* usw. abzuleiten). Dies läßt sich dadurch rechtfertigen, daß *so* auch isoliert vorkommen kann: z.B.

(96)   *Peter ist so faul,*

wobei es bei einer Äußerung des Satzes entweder durch eine Geste begleitet wird (beispielsweise in *die Stullen waren so dick*) oder emotionale Betonung erhält (vgl. dazu *Peter ist so schrecklich faul*).
Wir können also annehmen:

Spez → Grad (− S)
phonologische Realisierung:
Grad: *so*

Zusammenfassend ergeben sich für die Spezifikation eines Adjektivs die folgenden Möglichkeiten:

---

[33] In (90) kann *so* ebenfalls nicht durch *genauso* substituiert werden, aber auch nicht durch *derart*. Wenn wir annehmen, daß (90) aus der (92) zugrundeliegenden Struktur abgeleitet werden kann, müßte gefordert werden, daß mit Tilgung des Vergleichsglieds auch ein vorkommendes *genau* oder *eben* getilgt wird.

$$\mathrm{Spez}_A \rightarrow \left\{ \begin{array}{l} \mathrm{Grad}(-S) \\ \mathrm{Sup} - \left\{ \begin{array}{l} \mathrm{PP} \\ S_K \end{array} \right\} \\ \left\{ \begin{array}{l} \mathrm{Pos} \\ \mathrm{Komp} \end{array} \right\} - \left\{ \begin{array}{l} \mathrm{NP} \\ S \end{array} \right\} \\ \mathrm{Part} - \left\{ \begin{array}{l} S \\ \mathrm{PP} \end{array} \right\} \end{array} \right\}$$

Zweifellos ist die Analyse damit noch nicht abgeschlossen. Neben den detaillierteren Betrachtungen in den Abschnitten 2 und 4, die einen relativ umgrenzten Phänomenbereich erfaßt haben, habe ich in den anderen Abschnitten einige notwendige Erweiterungen skizzieren wollen. Die günstigste Notation kann erst bestimmt werden, wenn dieser größere Phänomenbereich mit derselben Ausführlichkeit untersucht ist.

Technische Universität, Berlin

LITERATUR

Bierwisch, Manfred: 1967, 'Some Semantic Universals of German Adjectivals', *Foundations of Language* 3, 1–36 (1970 in: Hugo Steger, Hrsg., *Vorschläge für eine strukturale Grammatik des Deutschen*, Darmstadt, Wiss. Buchges., pp. 269–318.)

Bowers, John: 1970, 'Adjectives and Adverbs in English', MIT (= mimeogr.).

Chomsky, Noam: 1968, 'Remarks on Nominalization', MIT (= mimeogr.).

Doherty, Monika: 1970, 'Zur Komparation antonymer Adjektive', *ASG-Bericht* Nr. 6, Berlin.

Lakoff, George: 1969, 'On Generative Semantics', demn. in: D. D. Steinberg, L. A. Jakobovits, (eds.), *Semantics – An Interdisciplinary Reader in Philosophy, Linguistics, Anthropology and Psychology*, London, Cambridge Univ. Press.

Leisi, Ernst: 1953, *Der Wortinhalt. Seine Struktur im Deutschen und Englischen*. (2. Aufl. 1961) Heidelberg, Quelle & Meyer.

McCawley, James D.: 1968, 'Lexical Insertion in a Transformational Grammar without Deep Structure', *Papers from the 4th Regional Meeting*, Chicago Ling. Soc., pp. 71–80.

Motsch, Wolfgang: 1964, *Syntax des deutschen Adjektivs*, Berlin, Akademie.

Teller, Paul: 1969, 'Some Discussion and Extension of Manfred Bierwisch's Work on German Adjectivals', *Foundations of Language* 5, 185–217.

Wunderlich, Dieter, 1969, 'Warum die Darstellung von Nominalisierungen problematisch bleibt', in: D. Wunderlich (ed.), *Probleme und Fortschritte der Transformationsgrammatik*, München, Hueber 1971, pp. 189–218.

Wunderlich, Dieter: 1970, *Tempus und Zeitreferenz im Deutschen*. München, Hueber.

W. U. WURZEL

DIE FLEXION DER VERBEN UND DAS ABLAUTSYSTEM*

1. FLEXIONSKLASSEN UND MERKMALE

Auch die morphologische Klassifizierung der Verben geht auf J. Grimm zurück, der die Verben, die so 'stark' sind, daß sie ohne 'äußere Unterstützung' die verschiedenen Zeitstufen bilden können, als 'stark flektierend', die anderen, d.h. die mit *t*-Flexiv im Präteritum, dagegen als 'schwach flektierend' klassifizierte. Unter den schwachen Verben gibt es eine im Nhd. sehr zusammengeschmolzene Subklasse, die, zusätzlich zum *t*-Element, eine Art sekundär entstandenen 'Ablaut' *e-a* aufweist, der historisch eigentlich ein unterbliebener Umlaut ist und von Grimm aufgrund eines historischen Irrtums 'Rückumlaut' gennant wurde. Hierzu gehören nur noch die Verben auf *-ennen* (*brennen, kennen, nennen, rennen*), die Präteritum und Partizip Perfekt obligatorisch mit Vokalwechsel bilden, die auf *-enden* (*senden, wenden*), bei denen daneben normale schwache Formen existieren und die vollständig unregelmäßigen Verben *bringen* und *denken*. Eine besondere Verbklasse stellen die Modalverben dar, die sich als einzige morphologische Klasse übrigens nicht nur morphologisch, sondern auch syntaktisch einheitlich verhalten. Morphologisch gehört in die Klasse auch das Vollverb *wissen*. Diese Verben stehen faktisch zwischen starken und schwachen, da sie sowohl über *t*-Präterita als auch über ablautende Formen verfügen. Nimmt man allerdings das Vorkommen von *t*-Formen zum Kriterium, wie wir es tun wollen, kann man sie mit gutem Grund als schwach einstufen. Auf diese Weise lassen sich die Flexionsregeln einfacher formulieren. Wichtig ist, daß diese in historischen Grammatiken meist 'Präteritopräsentien' gennanten Verben auch im Präsens besondere Flexionsendungen haben oder, genauer gesagt, nicht die gewöhnlichen Endungen bekommen.

Wenn wir davon ausgehen, daß aus syntaktischen Gründen ein Merkmal [± Mod] ('Modalverb') ohnehin vorauszusetzen ist, so benötigen wir noch zwei weitere Merkmale, um die morphologischen Klassen der deutschen Verben voneinander unterscheiden zu können. Zu diesem Zwecke wählen wir [± Stark] und [± Regulär]. Damit ergibt sich das folgende System morphologischer Merkmale:

*Aus: W. U. Wurzel: *Studien zur deutschen Lautstruktur*, *Studia Grammatica* VIII, Berlin, 1970.

F. Kiefer and N. Ruwet (eds.), Generative Grammar in Europe, 673–690. *All Rights Reserved.*
Copyright © 1973 *by D. Reidel Publishing Company, Dordrecht-Holland.*

(1)

	Starke Verben	Regelmäßige schwache Verben	'Rückumlautsverben'	Modalverben
Mod	(−)	(−)	−	+
Stark	+	−	−	(−)
Reg	(+)	+	−	(−)

In der Tabelle sind dabei die redundanten Merkmale eingeklammert. Die Merkmaleinsparung durch aufzustellende Redundanzregeln erweist sich als eine rein technische Lösung, jedenfalls dann, wenn man die Natürlichkeit der Flexionsklasse mit den im Lexikon notwendigen Merkmalspezifikationen in Beziehung setzt: Für die starken Verben und sogar die systemperiphären Modalverben ist je ein Merkmal weniger notwendig als für den Haupttyp der deutschen Verbalflexion, die schwachen, der zugleich der Zielpunkt aller Klassenveränderungen innerhalb des deutschen Verbsystems ist (vgl. die ehemaligen Präteritopräsentien *gönnen* und *taugen*, die 'Rückumlautsverben' *senden* und *wenden*, und solche ehemals starke Verben wie *nagen* und *schrauben*) und die einzige produktive Klasse darstellt.

Auch hier scheint uns folglich die morphologische Markiertheit die beste der möglichen 'Redundanzlösungen' darzustellen. Unter ihrer Voraussetzung brauchen die schwachen Verben für keines der morphologischen Merkmale mehr im Lexikon spezifiziert zu werden, hier genügt einfach die syntaktische Information 'Verb'. Das interpretiert recht gut die Tatsache, daß jedes neu ins Lexikon aufgenommene Verb (gleich welcher Herkunft) automatisch die Charakterisierungen eines (einfachen) schwachen Verbs erhält. Von diesen 'normalsten' Verben unterscheiden sich die starken Verben nur eben darin, daß sie stark sind und auch die 'Rückumlautsverben' nur in einem Merkmal, nämlich [± Reg]. [+ Stark] und [− Reg] sind also weniger natürlich als die entgegengesetzten Werte. Bei den Modalverben genügt im Lexikon die syntaktische Information [+ Mod], die nur diese Verben haben. Der normale, unmarkierte Fall (denn [+ Mod] ist ja faktisch als [m Mod] zu werten) ist hier [− Mod]. In Abhängigkeit von diesem Merkmal ist schießlich bei den Modalverben noch [u Reg] als [− Reg] zu spezifizieren. Die Modalverben erhalten den negativen Wert, denn ihre Präteritalbildung funktioniert im Grunde ebenso wie die der 'Rückumlautsverben'.

Damit nehmen wir für die Verben die folgenden morphologischen IR (= Interpretationsregeln) an:

Morphologische Interpretationsregeln für Verben

(MIR 1)   [u Mod] → [− Mod]

(MIR 2)   [u Stark] → [− Stark]

(MIR 3)   [u Reg] → $\left\{\begin{matrix} [-\text{ Reg}] & / & \overline{[+\text{ Mod}]} \\ [+\text{ Reg}] & & \end{matrix}\right\}$

Das Lexikon enthält also nunmehr die Spezifizierungen, wie sie in (2) auf-
geführt sind:

(2)

	Starke Verben	Regelmäßige schwache Verben	'Rückum-lautsverben'	Modalverben
Mod				+ (m)
Stark	m			
Reg			m	

Neben den eben diskutierten Merkmalen spielen selbstverständlich noch
eine Reihe syntaktischer Merkmale eine Rolle in der Verbmorphologie. Es
sind dies:

(3)   (a) die Personenmerkmale [± 1.Ps], [± 2.Ps] und [± 3.Ps];

        (b) die Tempusmerkmale [± Präs], [± Prät] und [± PP]
('Partizip Perfekt');

        (c) Die Modusmerkmale [± Konj] ('Konjunktiv') und [± Imp]
('Imperativ'), der Indikativ hat [− Konj] und spezifizierte
Personenmerkmale (die dem Imperativ fehlen);

        (d) das Merkmal [± Pl].

Ein Verb, das in der 3. Person Plural des Präteritum Indikativ steht, hat
also beispielsweise die folgenden Merkmalspezifizierungen:

(4) $\begin{bmatrix} + \text{ V} \\ + \text{ Prät} \\ - \text{ Konj} \\ + \text{ Pl} \\ + \text{ 3.Ps.} \end{bmatrix}$

Möglicherweise müssen die soeben konstatierten Merkmale etwas
modifiziert werden. Das könnte der Fall sein, wenn aufgrund innersyntak-
tischer Vorgänge andere Merkmale sich als zweckmäßiger erweisen sollten.
Solche Veränderungen wären jedoch nicht sehr problematisch, da die
Substanz der folgenden Flexionsregeln die gleiche bleibt und diese nur
aufgrund anderer, ähnlicher Merkmale operieren müßten.

2. FLEXIONSREGELN

Die Konjugation geschieht am besten in vier Schritten durch vier auf-
einanderfolgende Regelschemen, die untereinander konjunktiv geordnet
sind und ihrerseits, wenigstens z.T., aus disjunktiv geordneten Einzelregeln
bestehen.

Zuerst führen wir die Tempus- (bzw. PP-) Kennzeichnung ein. Alle Verben
mit dem Merkmal [− Stark], d.h. auch die Modal- und 'Rückumlauts'
verben erhalten in der Umgebung [+ Prät] oder [+ PP] das Flexiv /t/, alle
davon nicht erfaßten Verbstämme mit dem Merkmal [+ PP], also die
starken, das Flexiv /n/. In den Präteritalformen der starken Verben wird
dagegen kein Tempusflexiv eingeführt, dafür aber später ein Ablautvokal
erzeugt.

Der nächste Schritt ist, den zu erzeugenden Partizipialformen das Präfix
/ge/ zuzuweisen. Die einfachste Lösung für Fälle, wo in den Endketten im
Partizip Perfekt kein /ge/ auftritt (*berichtet*, *übersétzt*, *zerstört*; *schmarótzt*,
marschiert), besteht darin, auch diesen das /ge/ zuerst zuzuweisen und nach
Anwendung von bestimmten Akzentregeln zu eliminieren, da andernfalls
die Bedingungen für die /ge/-Einführung nur in höchst komplizierter Weise
zu formulieren sind und die Grammatik sehr stark belasten, die Elimi-
nierungsregel (die zugleich auch für /be/ gilt) aber sehr einfach als vor un-
betonter Silbe wirkend gefaßt werden kann.

Das /ge/ kann nicht im gleichen Regelschema angefügt werden wie die
Flexive /t/ und /n/, da ja innerhalb von Regelschemen disjunktive Ordnung
zwischen den Einzelregeln herrscht und bei Zusammenfassung beider
Vorgänge in einem Schema nur entweder /t/ bzw. /n/ oder /ge/ an einem
Verbstamm erscheinen könnte. Wir nehmen also die beiden morphologi-
schen Prozesse wie folgt auseinander:

(F1)   *Präterital- und PP-Flexiv*

$$\varnothing \rightarrow \begin{cases} \text{(a)} & t/ \begin{bmatrix} - \text{Stark} \\ \begin{Bmatrix} + \text{Prät} \\ + \text{PP} \end{Bmatrix} \end{bmatrix} \\ \text{(b)} & n/[+ \text{PP}] \end{cases} \underline{\quad}]_V$$

(F2)   *PP-Präfigierung*

$$\varnothing \rightarrow \text{ge}/ \,_V[\underline{\quad}[+ \text{PP}]$$

Obwohl der Konjunktiv, wenigstens morphologisch, in der gegenwärtigen
Sprache keine bedeutende Rolle mehr spielt, wollen wir auch seine speziellen
Formen erzeugen. Abgesehen von den umgelauteten Präteritalformen, mit

denen wir uns später noch zu beschäftigen haben werden, und dem Mangel des Personalflexivs /t/ in der 3. Persons Präsens Singular (*er schreibe, arbeite* vs. *er schreibt, arbeitet*) unterscheiden sich die konjunktivischen Verbformen durch das Vorhandensein eines *e* vor bestimmten Flexiven von den indikativischen: *du kommst*, aber *kommest, du kamst*, aber *kämest* und *ihr schreibt*, aber *schreibet, ihr schriebt*, aber *schriebet*. Bei den schwachen Verben (mit /t/ im Präteritum) gibt es diesen Unterschied nur im Präsens: *du fehlst*, aber *fehlest*, dagegen nur: *du fehltest*. Es ist also, wenigstens für bestimmte Fälle, ein Konjunktivelement /e/ vorzusehen, das zwischen Verbstamm und Personalendung steht: /kom + e + st/ vs. /kom + st/ und /kam + e + st/ vs. /kam + st/.

Wie früher bereits erwähnt wurde, ist aus mehreren Gründen in der Phonologie des Deutschen eine Geminatenvereinfachungsregel notwendig. Diese Regel gestattet uns auch hier eine einfache und angemessene Lösung: Das Konjunktivelement /e/ braucht nicht durch belastende Merkmale auf die 2. Person Singular und Plural eingeschränkt zu werden, sondern wird statt dessen in allen Personen eingeführt, so daß sich z.B. für das Verb *kommen* im Präsens die folgenden Ableitungen ergeben, die wir den Indikativformen gegenüberstellen.

(5)

	Konjunktiv			Indikativ		
	ich komme	*du kommest*	*er komme*	*ich komme*	*du kommst*	*er kommt*
Konjunktiv	kom + e	kom + e	kom + e			
Personalfl.	kom + e + e	kom + e + st	kom + e	kom + e	kom + st	kom + t
e-Epenthese	kom + e + e	kom + e + est	kom + e	kom + e	kom + est	kom + et
e-Eliminierg.	kom + e + e	kom + e + st	kom + e	kom + e	kom + st	kom + t
Geminatenverschmelzung	kom + e	kom + e + st	kom + e	kom + e	kom + st	kom + t

	Konjunktiv		Indikativ	
	wir, sie kommen	*ihr kommt*	*wir, sie kommen*	*ihr kommt*
Konjunktiv	kom + e	kom + e		
Personalfl.	kom + e + en	kom + e + t	kom + n	kom + e
e-Epenthese	kom + e + en	kom + e + et	kom + en	kom + et
e-Eliminierg.	kom + e + en	kom + e + t	kom + en	kom + t
Geminatenverschmelzung	kom + e + n	kom + e + t	kom + en	kom + t

Die Konjunktivregel ist sehr einfach zu formulieren:

(F3)   *Konjunktivelement*

$$\emptyset \rightarrow e/[+ \text{Konj}]\underline{\hspace{1cm}}]_V$$

Nach einem Verbstamm mit dem Merkmal [+ Konj] wird das Konjunktiv-element /e/ angefügt. Das Dentalsuffix braucht wieder in der Regel nicht explizit zu erscheinen. Für die phonetischen Endketten der schwachen Präterita hat dieses /e/ allerdings keine Bedeutung, da die *e*-Epenthese-Regel zwischen dem Präterital-/t/ und den Personalflexiven in allen Fällen ein [e] einführt. Ähnlich wie bei einigen Fällen des Beispiels (5) unter-scheiden sich hier also Konjunktiv- und Indikativformen nur in den zugrun-deliegenden Strukturen, vgl. *ich suchte* (Konj. /zūx + t + e + e/, Ind. /zūx + t + e/ und *wir suchten* (Konj. /zūx + t + e + n/, Ind. /zūx + t + n/). Es wäre auch eine andere, weniger generelle Lösung möglich, bei der schwache Konjunktiv Präteritum kein /e/ erhalten würde.

Es verbleibt nur noch, den Verben die korrekten Personalflexive zu-zuweisen. Ihre Anzahl ist nicht groß: /n/ erscheint in der 1. und der 3. Person Plural, /st/ in der 2. Person Singular und /t/ in der 2. Person Plural aller Flexionsklassen in beiden Zeiten und beiden Modi. Das /t/ tritt weiterhin im Imperativ Plural und in der 3. Person Präsens Indikativ auf, im letzteren Fall allerdings nicht bei den Modalverben (vgl. *er arbeitet, schreibt* vs. *er muß, will*). Das vierte Personalflexiv /e/ kommt schließlich vor in dem noch morpholo-gisch unflektierten Formen des schwachen Präteritums, d.h. der 1. und 3. Person Singular (wo die starken Verben kein Personalaffix erhalten), im Imperativ Singular (bei Imperativen wie *gib* und *lies* wird diese /e/ später wieder eliminiert) und in der 1. Person Präsens der Nichtmodalverben. Zwischen dem Verbstamm und dem Personalflexiv kann das /t/ des Präteri-tums und /oder das /e/ des Konjunktivs stehen.

(F4)   *Personalflexive* (S. 679)

Das Merkmal [− 2.Ps] gibt eine Zusammenfassung der 1. und der 3. Person. Nachdem im (b) die 2. Person Singular abgearbeitet ist, erfaßt (c) automatisch nur noch die 2. Person Plural. Einzelregel (f) braucht keine detailliertere Einschränkung, weil an diesem Punkt der Ableitung nur noch die 1. und 3. Person Singular Präteritum noch kein Flexiv haben. Das gleiche gilt auch für (h). Unter Voraussetzung der disjunktiven Ordnung kann sich [+ Präs] nur noch auf die 1. Person Singular beziehen. Morphologisch unflektiert bleiben neben der 1. und 3. Person Präsens Singular der Modalverben auch

$$\varnothing \to \left\{ \begin{array}{ll} \text{(a)} & \text{n/} \begin{bmatrix} - \text{2.Ps} \\ + \text{Pl} \end{bmatrix} \\[2ex] \text{(b)} & \text{st/} \begin{bmatrix} + \text{2.Ps} \\ - \text{Pl} \end{bmatrix} \\[2ex] \text{(c)} & \\ & \text{t/} \left\{ \begin{array}{l} [+ \text{2.Ps}] \\[1ex] \begin{bmatrix} + \text{Imp} \\ + \text{Pl} \end{bmatrix} \\[2ex] \begin{bmatrix} - \text{Mod} \\ + \text{Präs} \\ - \text{Konj} \\ + \text{3.Ps} \end{bmatrix} \end{array} \right. \\ \text{(f)} & \\ & \text{e/} \left\{ \begin{array}{l} \begin{bmatrix} - \text{Stark} \\ + \text{Prät} \end{bmatrix} \\[2ex] [+ \text{Imp}] \\[1ex] \begin{bmatrix} - \text{Mod} \\ + \text{Präs} \end{bmatrix} \end{array} \right. \end{array} \right] _V$$

die 1. und 3. Person Präteritum Singular der starken Verben (*ich, er schrieb* vs. *ich, er suchte*).

Mit Anwendung der Flexionsregel (F4) haben wir allen Verben die notwendigen Flexive zugewiesen. Bei einem Teil der Formen entsprechen die erzeugten Ketten schon genau den phonetischen Strukturen, bei einigen anderen müssen auf die Output-Ketten der Verbalflexion noch bestimmte, phonologische Regeln angewandt werden, die Elemente einführen, eliminieren und vereinfachen, wie es in (5) demonstriert wurde. Dennoch haben wir noch nicht alle bei der Verbformbildung auftretenden Regularitäten beschrieben. Während wir bei den schwachen Verben neben den zugrundeliegenden Präsensformen wie /zūx + st/ korrekte Präteritalformen wie /zūx + t + st/ erzeugt haben, sind diese Formen bei den starken Verben weitgehend phonologisch nicht distinkt und /zing + st/ wäre sowohl die Repräsentation für *du singst*, als auch für *du sangst*. Wir benötigen also noch eine Reihe von Regeln, die die 'innere Flexion' des deutschen Verbalsystems, also den Ablaut, darstellen und beispielsweise aus dem lexikalischen Morphem /zing/ aufgrund der Informationen [+ Stark] und [+ Prät] die abgelautete Form *sang* erzeugen. Den damit im Zusammenhang stehenden Problemen wollen wir uns im nächsten Abschnitt zuwenden.

3. DAS ABLAUTSYSTEM

Es gibt im Deutschen drei Muster von ablautenden Verben, die sich darin unterscheiden, wieviel unterschiedliche Vokale in den drei Formen (lexikalischer) Stamm, Präteritum und Partizip Perfekt auftreten. In diesen Formen können drei oder auch nur zwei unterschiedliche Vokale erscheinen, wobei, wenn es nur zwei sind, der Vokal des Partizips entweder mit dem des Stammes oder aber mit dem des Präteritums übereinstimmt. Die Verben unterscheiden sich ferner im Verhalten der 2. und 3. Person Präsens Singular zum Umlaut (einschließlich der 'Hebung' *e-i*), was allerdings mit dem Ablaut nichts zu tun hat. Insgesamt treten die folgenden Ablautmuster auf, wobei wir die Quantität des Stammvokals zunächst vernachlässigen wollen:

(6)

(a)   *Vokal des PP ist mit dem des Stamms identisch*:

    (1)   *e-a-e*.   *lesen, las, gelesen*; stets Umlaut: *liest*

    (2)   *i-a-e*:   *liegen, lag, gelegen*

    (3)   *a-i-a*:   *halten, hielt, gehalten*; stets Umlaut: *hält*

    (4)   *o-i-o*:   *stoßen, stieß, gestoßen*; stets Umlaut: *stößt*

    (5)   *u-i-u*:   *rufen, rief, gerufen*; nie Umlaut: *ruft*

    (6)   *a-u-a*:   *fahren, fuhr, gefahren*; stets Umlaut: *fährt*

(b)   *Vokal des PP ist mit dem des Präteritums identisch*:

    (1)   *e-o-o*:   *schmelzen, schmolz, geschmolzen*; mit Umlaut: *schmilzt*
               heben, hob, gehoben; ohne Umlaut: *hebt*

    (2)   *i-o-o*:   *fliegen, flog, geflogen*

    (3)   *ä-o-o*:   *erwägen, erwog, erwogen*; nie Umlaut: *erwägt*

    (4)   *ö-o-o*:   *erlöschen, erlosch, erloschen*; mit Umlaut: *erlischt*
               schwören, schwor, geschworen; ohne   Umlaut: *schwört*

    (5)   *ü-o-o*:   *lügen, log, gelogen*; nie Umlaut: *lügt*

    (6)   *ei-i-i*:   *reiten, ritt, geritten*

    (7)   *au-o-o*:   *saufen, soff, gesoffen*; mit Umlaut: *säuft*
               saugen, sog, gesogen; ohne Umlaut: *saugt*

(c)   *Vokal des PP ist weder mit dem des Stamms noch mit dem des Präteritums identisch*:

    (1)   *e-a-o*:   *werfen, warf, geworfen*; stets Umlaut: *wirft*

    (2)   *i-a-o*:   *sinnen, sann, gesonnen*

    (3)   *i-a-u*:   *finden, fand, gefunden*

    (4)   *ä-a-o*:   *gebären, gebar, geboren*; mit Umlaut: *gebiert*

Daneben gibt es eine unbedeutende Anzahl von Sonderfällen, die uns hier noch nicht interessieren sollen.

Zur Unterscheidung der drei Bildungsmuster führen wir die beiden Merkmale [± PP = St] und [± PP = Prät] ein. (a) ist dann [+ PP = St], (b) [+ PP = Prät] und (c) [− PP = St, − PP = Prät].

Innerhalb der drei soeben konstituierten Klassen (a), (b) und (c) lassen sich leicht bestimmte generelle Regularitäten erkennen. Nehmen wir uns zunächst die Klasse (c) vor, die die wenigsten Gruppen beinhaltet. Alle Verben in (c) haben einen vorderen Stammvokal und im Präteritum ein *a*. Während drei Gruppen von Verben im PP ein *o* zeigen, erscheint einmal *u* und zwar vor der Verbindung 'Nasal plus Konsonant'. Viele der Verben mit *o* im PP haben jedoch Nominalisierungen, in denen ebenfalls ein *u* vorhanden ist. Es heißt nicht nur *Fund, Schwung* und *Trunk* (wie *gefunden, geschwungen, getrunken*), sondern auch beispielsweise *Bruch, Drusch, Spruch, Wurf* und *Geburt* (neben *gebrochen, gedroschen, gesprochen, geworfen* und *geboren*). Wir können also auch hier, d.h. bei (1), (2) und (4) einen Ablaut 'vorderer Vokal-*u*' ansetzen und später unter bestimmten Bedingungen das *u* in ein *o* verwandeln, so daß Formen wie *geworfen, gesonnen* usw. richtig entstehen.

Die Klasse (b) besteht aus zwei verschiedenen Gruppen von starken Verben. In (1) bis (5) wird ein vorderer Stammvokal (es kann jeder einzelne der im Deutschen vorkommenden sein!) in der Umgebung [+ Prät] oder [+ PP] offenbar in *o* verwandelt. Doch auch hier ergibt sich, daß daneben Nominalisierungen mit *u*-Formen existieren und demzufolge eine Zwischenstufe *u* anzusetzen ist, vgl. *Hub, Flug, Genuß, Schub, Schwur, Lug* und *Trug*.

Evidenzen für das Vorhandensein einer Vokalsenkung *u-o* in der Grammatik liefern auch die dipthongischen Stämme. Wir wollen die deutschen Dipthonge als Folgen 'Vokal plus Glide' analysieren, wobei an dieser Stelle nicht darauf eingegangen werden soll, weshalb und wie das im einzelnen geschieht. Wichtig für unsere gegenwärtige Analyse des Ablautsystems ist nur, daß die zweiten Bestandteile von *ei* und *au* die Glides /j/ und /w/ sind. Die Veränderung bei (6) und (7) kann dann so gefaßt werden, daß im Präteritum und im PP der erste Bestandteil von Dipthongen getilgt und der zweite vokalisiert wird. So werden dann auch korrekte Formen wie *ritt, geritten, der Ritt; schmiß, geschmissen, der Schmiß* usw. erzeugt werden. Dagegen entstehen bei *au* Formen wie **suff, *gesuffen, der Suff*, von denen nur die letzte, wieder eine Nominalisierung, richtig ist. Die wirklichen Präterita und PP können auch hier wieder durch die Vokalsenkungsregel abgeleitet werden, die für Nomina nicht gilt.

Auch (a) besteht aus Gruppen von Verben, die sich in den Prinzipien ihrer Präteritalbildung (denn nur diese ist ja hier relevant) unterscheiden. Die

Verben aus (1) und (2) zeigen die gleichen Präteritalformen wie die aus (c), mit denen sich auch das Merkmal – PP = Prät gemeinsam haben. Die Verben (a3) bis (5) weisen ebenfalls wiederum den gleichen Ablauttyp auf, nämlich 'hinterer Vokal -*i*'. Dieser Regularität entziehen sich jedoch die Verben der Gruppe (6), in denen mit dem hinteren Vokal (*a*) des Sammes ein *u* wechselt. Es gibt also zwei Gruppen von starken Verben mit dem Stammvokal /a/, die sich durch unterschiedliche Präteritalbildung (*i* vs. *u*) ergeben. Die Information über die Präteritalbildung läßt sich in keiner sinnvollen und generellen Weise aus anderen vorhandenen, etwa syntaktischen oder phonologischen Informationen ermitteln, so daß wir zur Abgrenzung der starken Verben mit *i*-Präteritum von denen mit *u*-Präteritum noch ein besonderes Merkmal brauchen, das wir [± i-Prät] nennen wollen, und das nur für die Verben mit hinterem Stammvokal relevant ist. Es ist jetzt relativ unkompliziert, die von uns bei der Auswertung der einzelnen Ablauttypen festgestellten Regularitäten und Zusammenhänge in Regelform zu bringen. Zuerst stellen wir die eigentlichen Ablautvorgänge in einem Regelschema zusammen.

Es ist ein Schema morphologischer Regeln und enthält als ein solches Einzelregeln, die *per conventionem* untereinander disjunktiv geordnet sind.

(A1)   *Ablaut bei starken Verben*

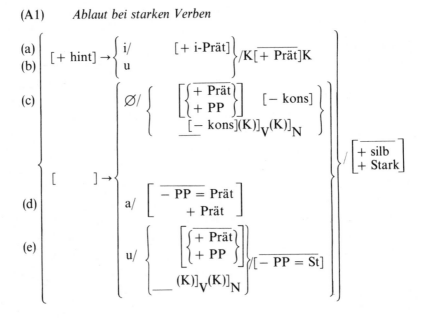

Die Regeln (a) und (b) erzeugen die Präteritalformen der starken Verben mit

einem hinteren Stammvokal. Dieser wird in Abhängigkeit vom Vorhanden-
sein/Nichtvorhandensein des Merkmals [+ i-Prät] in /i/ bzw. /u/ überführt. Die Konsonanten vor und hinter dem Stammvokal (in der Verbindung
/K [+ Prät]K/) sind notwendig, damit hintere Vokale als Bestandteile von
Dipthongen nicht mit erfaßt werden. Die Dipthonge werden durch die
Regel (c) abgelautet, indem die ersten Bestandteile (das *e* in *ei* und das *a* in
au) getilgt werden. Diese Ablautregel gilt nicht nur für die Flexion der Verben,
sondern auch bei Nominalisierungen wie *Biß, Pfiff, Suff* und *Trieb* (das
fakultative *K* zwischen der verbalen und der nominalen Kategorisierung
steht für das mögliche /t/, vgl. *Verzicht* und *Schrift*).

Die Regel (d) erfaßt alle noch nicht gebildeten Präteritalformen von
Verben mit dem Merkmal [− PP = Prät], d.h. den Verben, die im Präteritum
und PP unterschiedliche Vokale haben. Das sind die Verben aus (6a), *lesen*
und (c), *werfen*.

Schließlich erzeugt Regel (e) alle präteritalen, partizipialen und nominalen
u-Formen (die dann später größtenteils in *o* überführt werden). Sie gilt nur
für die Verben mit dem Ablautmerkmal [− PP = St] und leitet demzufolge
die PP-Formen von (6c) (hier haben wir *a*-Präterita!) und die PP- und
Präteritalformen von (6b) ab, vgl. *werfen, warf, geworfen* vs. *schmelzen,
schmolz, geschmolzen*. Das Merkmal [− PP = St] verhindert, daß von (A le)
Partizipien wie **gelosen* und **gelogen* anstelle von *gelesen* und *gelegen*
generiert werden. Noch einmal zurück zur Regel (A 1c). Diese besteht in der
Eliminierung der ersten, d.h. der silbischen Bestandteile der Dipthonge, so
daß als 'Ablaut-vokale' die Segmente /j/ und /w/ übrigbleiben, die jedoch
keine Vokale, sondern unsilbische Glides sind. Diese müssen also noch
vokalisiert werden, damit nicht z.B. statt *blieb* die Präteritalform [bljb]
erzeugt wird. Um das zu erreichen, wollen wir – wenigstens vorläufig – eine
Vokalisierungsregel annehmen, die einem nichtkonsonantischen Segment
das Merkmal [+ silb], die Charakterisierung der Vokale, zuweist, wenn es
hinter einem Konsonanten steht:

(7)   [− kons] → [+ silb]/K _____

Insgesamt erzeugt (A1), unter Voraussetzung von (28), die folgenden Vokale:

(8)   e $\begin{Bmatrix} a \\ a \end{Bmatrix}$ (d)   e
           i   e

           a $\begin{Bmatrix} i \\ i \\ i \end{Bmatrix}$ (a)   a
           o   o
           u   u

           a   u   (b)   a

$$
\begin{array}{l}
\left.\begin{array}{l}
\text{e} \\ \text{i} \\ \text{ä} \\ \text{ö} \\ \text{ü}
\end{array}\right\{
\begin{array}{ll}
\text{u } (= \text{o}) & \text{u } (= \text{o}) \\
\text{u } (= \text{o}) & \text{u } (= \text{o}) \\
\text{u } (= \text{o}) & \text{u } (= \text{o}) \\
\text{u } (= \text{o}) & \text{u } (= \text{o}) \\
\text{u } (= \text{o}) & \text{u } (= \text{o})
\end{array}
\Big\}(\text{e}) \\[2mm]
\left.\begin{array}{l}
\text{ei} \\ \text{au}
\end{array}\right\{
\begin{array}{ll}
\text{i} & \text{i} \\
\text{u } (= \text{o}) & \text{u } (= \text{o})
\end{array}
\Big\}(\text{c}) \\[2mm]
\begin{array}{l}
\text{e} \\ \text{i} \\ \text{i} \\ \text{ä}
\end{array}
\left\{\begin{array}{l}
\text{a} \\ \text{a} \\ \text{a} \\ \text{a}
\end{array}\right\}(\text{d})
\quad
\left\{\begin{array}{l}
\text{u } (= \text{o}) \\ \text{u } (= \text{o}) \\ \text{u} \\ \text{u } (= \text{o})
\end{array}\right\}(\text{e})
\end{array}
$$

Wir wollen als nächstes die Bedingungen für die Senkung von *u* zu *o* untersuchen. Wie uns die Übersicht (8) zeigt, bleibt das *u* im Ablautsystem des Verbs nur in ganz wenigen Fällen erhalten, nämlich erstens im Präsens und PP von *rufen*, zweitens im Präteritum der Verben vom Typ *fahren* und drittens vor Nasal und Konsonant (*gefunden*). Dazu kommen dann noch die von uns schon diskutierten Nominalisierungen. Wir müssen also die Vokalveränderung auf das Präteritum und das PP einschränken und vor Nasal und Konsonant generell ausschließen. Verben wie *rufen, fahren, graben* usw. sind durch das Merkmal [+ PP = St] gekennzeichnet, so daß, um auch sie auszuschließen, nur das Merkmal [– PP = St] in der Regel vorhanden sein muß. Obwohl die *u*-Senkung primär mit dem Ablaut im engeren Sinne nichts zu tun hat, wollen wir sie hier behandeln, da sie im Grunde nur für das Ablautsystem Bedeutung hat.

(P1)   *u-Senkung*

$$
\begin{bmatrix} + \text{ silb} \\ + \text{ hoch} \end{bmatrix}
\rightarrow [(_a\text{hoch}_a)]/
\begin{bmatrix}
+ \text{ hint} \\
- \text{ PP} = \text{St} \\
\left\{\begin{array}{l} + \text{ Prät} \\ + \text{ PP} \end{array}\right\}
\end{bmatrix}
(_b\text{NK}_b)
$$

$C: a = b$

Die Bedingung *C* gibt an, daß *a* und *b* stets die gleichen Werte haben müssen, entweder 1, so daß '[+ hoch]...NK' (d.h. der Vokal bleibt hoch, wenn das Cluster 'NK' folgt) oder 0, so daß '[– hoch]...NK' (d.h. der Vokal wird nicht hoch, also *o*, wenn das Cluster nicht folgt) gilt. Im zweiten Fall tritt genau die notwendige Veränderung ein, während sie im ersten Fall unterbleibt. Die Regel erzeugt u.a. die folgenden korrekten Formen: *schmolz/ geschmolzen, flog/geflogen, erwog/erwogen, erlosch/erloschen, log/gelogen, soff/gesoffen, geworfen, gesonnen, geboren.*

Wir haben bisher nur die Veränderungen in der Qualität der Verbvokale in unsere Betrachtung einbezogen, während wir die Veränderungen in der Gespanntheit dieser Vokale nicht überprüft haben. Dieses Vorgehen ist auch insofern berechtigt, als meist die Präterital- und PP-Vokale denen des Präsens in der Quantität gleich sind, vgl. *lēsen/lās/gelēsen, schmĕlzen/ schmölz/geschmölzen* und *wĕrfen/wărf/gewŏrfen*. Es gibt aber auch andere Fälle. Unter den Verben mit dem Ablaut 'hinterer Vokal -i/u' sind einige, bei denen einem ungespannten Präsensvokal ein gespannter im Präteritum entspricht: *făllen/fiel, hălten/hielt, lăssen/ließ, schăffen/schūf, wăchsen/wūchs* und *wăschen/wūsch*. Das gleiche gilt auch für die Verben *ĕssen, frĕssen* *-gessen* und *mĕssen* (vgl. *āß, frāß* usw.). Beide Verbgruppen haben das Merkmal [+ PP = St], und wenn wir die gesamten Verben mit diesem Merkmal überprüfen, zeigt es sich, daß sie stets, ungeachtet ihres Präsensvokals, im Präteritum einen gespannten Vokal aufweisen. Wir können also eine Regel formulieren, die bei Anwesenheit der Merkmale [+ PP = St] und [+ Prät] einem Vokal das Gespanntheitsmerkmal zuweist. Weiterhin stehen neben Verben wie *wĕrfen/wărf/gewŏrfen* solche wie *sprĕchen/sprăch/gesprŏchen/* und *trĕffen/trăf/getrŏffen*. Letzteres sind genau die, bei denen ein Obstruent folgt, während die ersteren nach dem Vokal einen Sonoranten haben. Die Verbklasse ist mit den Merkmalen [− PP = St, − PP = Prät] gekennzeichnet und die Umwandlung des ungespannten Vokals kommt wiederum nur im Präteritum vor, so daß auch hier die Regel relativ leicht zu formulieren ist.

Anders in der Verbklasse, bei der im Präteritum und im PP der gleiche Vokal vorliegt. Eine Reihe von Verben behält hier den gespannten Stammvokal auch in den ablautenden Formen, vgl. *biegen/bōg, fliegen/flōg*, während andere in diesen Formen ungespannte Vokale haben, vgl. *fließen/flŏß, gießen/gŏß* und *reichen/rŏch*. Mit einer einzigen Ausnahme (*bieten/bōt* statt *bŏtt*) werden die Vokale immer vor stimmlosen Konsonanten ungespannt. Das gilt übrigens auch für Nominalisierungen wie *Flŭß, Gŭß, Gerŭch* vs. *Flūg* und *Schūb*. Wichtig ist, daß die hier diskutierte Regel den in der Verbflexion vorkommenden Konsonantenveränderungen folgt, denn es heißt *Bŭcht* (zu *biegen*), *Flŭcht* (zu *fliehen*) und *sŏtt* (zu *sieden*). Das Verb *bieten* wird als Ausnahme zu der Regel markiert. Ebenso wie die starken Verben mit /i/ verhalten sich die mit einem Dipthong in der Basisform, denn auch bei ihnen muß die Gespanntheit des Vokals in den ablautenden Formen aufgrund der Gespanntheit des folgenden Konsonanten ermittelt werden. So stehen *bĭß, rĭtt* und *strĭtt* neben *blieb, schien* und *schwieg*. Für die Einordnung nach den Konsonantenveränderungen sprechen die Formen *schnĭtt* und *lĭtt* (zu *schneiden* und *leiden*) sowie die Nominalisierungen *Schrĭft* und

Tríft (zu *schreiben* und *treiben*). Es existiert auch hier eine Ausnahme, nämlich *hieß*, das ohnehin nicht das Merkmal [+ PP = Prät] (vgl. *geheißen*) hat. Sowohl bei den Verben mit /i/ als auch bei denen mit Dipthong spielt also der Präsensvokal für die Gespanntheit bzw. Nichtgespanntheit der abgeleiteten Vokale des Präteritums und des PP keine Rolle. Diese ist nur abhängig von dem unmittelbar folgenden Segment.

Auch die eben verbal formulierten Regularitäten gehören nicht zu den Ablautregeln selbst. Wie die *u*-Senkung gehören sie zu den Regeln der Phonologie, nicht zuletzt, da sie nach bestimmten konsonantischen Alternationen eingeordnet werden müssen. Sie sehen, zusammengefaßt und formalisiert, wie folgt aus:

(P2)   *Gespanntheit der Ablautvokale*

$$
[+ \text{silb}] \rightarrow
\begin{cases}
\begin{aligned}
\text{(a)}\\
\text{(b)}
\end{aligned}
\quad [+ \text{gesp}] /
\left\{
\begin{array}{l}
[\overline{+ PP = St}] \\[2pt]
\left[\begin{array}{l} - PP = St \\ - PP = \text{Prät} \end{array}\right] [+ \text{obstr}]
\end{array}
\right\}
/ [\overline{+ \text{Prät}}] \\[20pt]
\text{(c)} \quad [\alpha \text{ gesp}] /
\left[
\begin{array}{l}
\overline{+ PP = \text{Prät}} \\
\left\{ \begin{array}{l} + \text{Prät} \\ + PP \end{array} \right\} \\
\underline{\qquad} (K)]_V (K)]_N
\end{array}
\right] [\alpha \text{ sth}]
\end{cases}
$$

Die Einzelregeln sind in der Reihenfolge (ihrer optimalen) gegeben, in der sie von uns diskutiert worden sind. (c) ist dabei wieder eine Zusammenfassung zweier Regeln: Wenn der folgende Konsonant stimmlos ist, ist der Vokal ungespannt, und wenn der folgende Konsonant stimmhaft ist, ist der Vokal gespannt.

Mit den diskutierten Regeln werden alle korrekten Formen der von uns als [+ Reg] charakterisierten Verben erzeugt, ausgenommen die Flexionsformen mit Umlaut und *e-i*-Wechsel, denen wir uns später zuwenden werden. Es müssen nun lediglich noch die vom Infinitiv abweichenden Vokale der Modalverben (Präteritopräsentia) und der 'Rückumlautsverben' abgeleitet werden. Wir stellen die dafür notwendigen Regeln auf, obwohl diese nur für wenige Fälle gelten.

Das folgende Regelschema erzeugt alle im Vokalismus vom Infinitiv bzw. Präsens Plural abweichenden Vokale des Präteritums, des PP und des Präsens Singular außer den Präsens-Singular-Formen *weiß* und *will*, die wohl nur als idiosynkratisch aufgefaßt werden können. Einen weiteren Einzelfall, das Präsens Singular von *müssen*, *muß*, beziehen wir in die Regel ein, da zu seiner Erzeugung nur ein Merkmal mehr notwendig ist.

(A2)   *Ablaut bei Modal- und "Rückumlauts" verben*

$$
(a)\ \ \left.\begin{array}{l}
\\
\left[-\ \text{hint}\right]\ \to\ \left\{\begin{array}{l}
\begin{bmatrix}+\ \text{hint}\\+\ \text{ndr}\end{bmatrix}\Big/\begin{bmatrix}-\ \text{hoch}\\-\ \text{rund}\end{bmatrix}\\[6pt]
\begin{bmatrix}+\ \text{hint}\\+\ \text{rund}\end{bmatrix}
\end{array}\right\}\Big/\left[\left\{\begin{array}{l}+\ \text{Prät}\\+\ \text{PP}\end{array}\right\}\right]\\[24pt]
(c)\ \begin{bmatrix}-\ \text{hint}\\+\ \text{rund}\end{bmatrix}\ \to\ \begin{bmatrix}+\ \text{hint}\\\alpha\ \text{rund}\\\sim\!\alpha\ \text{ndr}\end{bmatrix}\Big/\ \_\_[\sim\!\alpha\ \text{sth}]/[-\ \text{Pl}]
\end{array}\right\}\Big/\begin{bmatrix}+\ \text{silb}\\+\ \text{Reg}\end{bmatrix}
$$

C: (a) ist fakultativ für Verben auf /nd/.

Die Regel (a) leitet die Präterital- und PP-Vokale der 'Rückumlauts-verben' ab (obligatorisch z.B. *brannte/gebrannt*; *sandte/gesandt* neben *sendete/gesendet*). (b) der Modalverben (*durfte/gedurft, konnte/gekonnt, mochte/gemocht, mußte/gemußt, wußte/gewußt*). (c) faßt zwei Einzelregeln zusammen: Vor stimmlosen Segment tritt im Präteritum ein /u/ auf (einziger Fall: *muß*), vor ungespanntem ein /a/ (*darf, kann, mag*). (b) kann die Präterital- und PP-Formen der Verben *sollen* und *wollen* nicht ableiten, da diese Verben keinen vorderen Basisvokal haben. Desgleichen erfaßt (c) nicht die Singular-formen *soll* (hier bleibt der Vokal) sowie *will* und *weiß*, die völlig idiosyn-kratisch sind.

Es folgen noch einige Bemerkungen zu starken Verben mit von den normalen Regularitäten abweichenden Ablautformen.

Wir haben bei den Verben des Typs (6c) das Merkmal [+ PP = St] vorausgesetzt, obwohl hier die Präsensformen *bitten, liegen* und *sitzen* die PP-Formen dagegen *gebeten, gelegen* und *gesessen* lauten. Es gibt, wie wir gesehen haben, auch keinen Ablaut '*i-e*', da innerhalb des Ablautsystems die vorderen Vokale völlig gleich funktionieren und das entscheidende Merkmal [±hint] ist. Der Basisvokal /ĭ/ bzw. /ī/ scheidet also aus, da aus ihm durch Ablaut das /e/ bzw. /ē/ des PP nicht zu gewinnen ist. Dagegen muß die Grammatik ohnehin eine '*e-i*'-Regel enthalten, die solche Alternationen wie *schmelzen – schmilzt* und *Berg – Gebirge* beschreibt. Diese Regel muß also so erweitert werden, daß sie nicht nur regelmäßige Alternationen der erwähnten Art beschreibt, sondern auch aufgrund eines Regelmerkmals funktioniert. Die entsprechenden Verben, zu denen sich noch das 'Rückumlautsverb' *bringen* gesellt, erhalten also den Basisvokal /e/ bzw. /ē/ und die Markierung für die erwähnte Regel im gesamten Präsens. Bei *bitten* ist weiterhin der gespannte Stammvokal des PP idiosynkratisch, während der Wechsel vom ungespannten im Präsens zum gespannten im Präteritum durch (A 2a) vollzogen wird.

Ähnlich den diskutierten Verben gehört *hängen* in die gleiche Klasse wie *halten, fallen, braten* usw. Es muß im Präsens für das Umlautregelschema markiert werden, das dann wiederum ein Regelmerkmal enthalten muß. Das Verb *sein* hat im Präsens (und Imperativ) eine sehr abweichende Flexion, die auf mehrere suppletive Stämme zurückgeht. Die übrigen Formen lassen sich auf eine Basisform /vēz/ (vgl. mhd. *wesen*) zurückführen, die im Präteritum das /z/ in ein [r] verwandelt und sonst wie *lesen* funktioniert.

Ebenso wie *gefunden* ist das PP von *schinden* gebildet, während das Präteritum abweichend *schund* heißt. Das Verb *schinden/schund/geschunden* hat einfach im Lexikon das Merkmal [+ PP = Prät], das die Anwendung von (A 1d) nicht zuläßt (*schand*), und die Präteritalform wird durch (A 1e) erzeugt.

Von *werden* gibt es neben dem systematisch vollkommen regulären, aber etwas archaischen *ward* das gebräuchlichere *wurde*, während der Plural des Präteritums stets *wurden* lautet. Es sind hier also, möglicherweise abhängig von bestimmten stilistischen Charakterisierungen, zwei Arten der Flexion vorzusehen. Für *werden/ward/wurden/geworden* sind dabei die folgenden Lexikoneintragungen vorzunehmen: [− PP = St, Singular: − PP = Prät, Plural: + PP = Prät]. Dann wird das Präteritum Singular durch (A 1d) erzeugt, das Präteritum Plural und das PP durch (e). Für das Präteritum *wurde/wurden* sind die Lexikonangaben [− PP = St, − PP = Prät], so daß nur (A 1e) angewandt werden kann. Im Präteritum Singular ist dann ein Flexiv /e/ wie bei den schwachen Verben einzuführen, und in jedem Fall ist das Präteritum von (P3), der *u*-Senkung, durch ein Regelmerkmal auszunehmen.

Das Einzelverb *kommen* hat die für Verben mit hinterem Stammvokal gewöhnlichen Merkmale [+ PP = St, − PP = Prät] und dazu das Regelmerkmal [m Regel (A 1b)], das aufgrund der Interpretationsregel (IKR) in '−' überführt wird. Da diese Regel also nicht anwendbar ist, wird die Form *kăm* durch (d) erzeugt, die ganz regulär von (P 4a) gespannt wird: *kām*.

Das *i*-Präteritum von *laufen* ist wohl nur zu gewinnen, wenn wir für das Verb eine Basisform $/1 \begin{bmatrix} + \text{silb} \\ + \text{hint} \end{bmatrix} f/$ annehmen, aus der dann unter Voraussetzung von [+ i-Prät] *lief* zu erzeugen wäre. Der hintere Vokal wäre dann (im Präsens und PP) zu 'dipthongieren', damit das *au* entsteht. Ein unregelmäßiges, wohl sinnvoll nur als suppletiv zu fassendes Präsens liegt auch in *gehen* vor, dessen übrige Formen in normaler Weise von der Basisform

/gang/ (vgl. mhd. *gangen*, dial. Präsens *ich gang*) abgeleitet werden können, wenn das Verb die Merkmale [− PP = St, − PP = Prät, + i-Prät] hat. Das Präteritum wird von (A 1a) gebildet, und [− PP = St] verhindert die Anwendung von (P 4a), so daß nicht *gieng entstehen kann, sondern gĭng (wie sằng).

Ganz unregelmäßig ist *stehen/stand/gestanden*, wo sich ganz einfach empfiehlt, auch die Form des Präteritums/PP ins Lexikon aufzunehmen.

Wir wollen den Abschnitt über den Ablaut im deutschen Verbalsystem mit einer kurzen Diskussion der Realisierung der einzelnen Ablautklassen im Lexikon und damit im Zusammenhang stehenden Fragen abschließen. Die von uns oben vorgenommene Klassifizierung der ablautenden Verben geht von der Art des Stamm- bzw. Basisvokals aus. Es ergeben sich drei große Klassen: Verben mit hinterem Stammvokal, solche mit vorderem und solche mit einem Dipthong, wobei es irrelevant ist, welcher Dipthong auftritt. Die Verben mit einem hinteren Stammvokal zerfallen in zwei Klassen, die i-Präterita und die u-Präterita. Bei den Verben mit hellem Stammvokal gibt es drei verschiedene Klassen. Die erste zeichnet sich dadurch aus, daß die zu ihr gehörigen Verben drei verschiedene Ablautvokale zeigen. Im Präteritum erscheint /a/, im PP /u/. In der zweiten Klasse erscheint dagegen /u/ im Präteritum und im PP und in der dritten unterscheidet sich der Vokal des PP nicht von dem des Präsens und im Präteritum steht /a/. Die einzelnen Klassen haben die folgende Merkmalspezifikation:

(9)	Hinterer Stammvokal		Vorderer Stammvokal			Diphthong
	Prät. mit /i/	Prät. mit /u/	/a/ − /u/	/a/	/u/ − /u/	/u/ − /u/
PP = St	(+)	(+)	−	+	(−)	(−)
PP = Prät	(−)	(−)	−	(−)	+	(+)
i-Prät	+	−	(−)	(−)	(−)	(+)

Von den Merkmalen ist allerdings eine große Zahl redundant; sie wurden in der Übersicht eingeklammert. Auch bei verbleibenden Merkmalen sind wieder einige einzusparen, wenn wir, wie bei anderen morphologischen Prozessen, mit Hilfe der morphologischen Markiertheit arbeiten wollen. So gibt es mehr Verben mit hinterem Stammvokal und i-Präteritum als solche mit u-Präteritum. Weiterhin ist, wie leicht anhand des empirischen Materials zu überprüfen ist, die Übereinstimmung der Vokale von Stamm und PP bei allen Verben mit Dipthongen und vorderen Vokalen der unnormalere Fall gegenüber der Nichtübereinstimmung, während bei den Verben mit hinterem Stammvokal die Nichtübereinstimmung gar nicht vorkommt. Für die dipthongischen Verben ist charakteristisch, daß die Vokale von Präteritum und PP generell übereinstimmen, während das bei Verben mit hinteren Vokalen überhaupt nicht vorkommt und bei den Verben mit vorderem Stammvokal den weniger üblichen und natürlichen Fall darstellt. Wir nehmen die folgenden Interpretationsregeln an, die das soeben Konstatierte ausdrücken:

Morphologische Interpretationsregeln für den Ablaut

$$(\text{MIR 11}) \, [\text{u i-Prät}] \quad \rightarrow \quad \begin{cases} [+ \text{ i-Prät}]/\text{K} & \begin{bmatrix} + \text{ silb} \\ + \text{ hint} \end{bmatrix} \text{K} \\ [- \text{ i-Prät}] \end{cases}$$

$$(\text{MIR 12}) \, [\text{u PP} = \text{St}] \quad \rightarrow \quad \begin{cases} [+ \text{ PP} = \text{St}]/\text{K} & \begin{bmatrix} + \text{ silb} \\ + \text{ hint} \end{bmatrix} \text{K} \\ [- \text{ PP} = \text{St}] \end{cases}$$

$$(\text{MIR 13}) \, [\text{u PP} = \text{Prät}] \quad \rightarrow \quad \begin{cases} [+ \text{ PP} = \text{Prät}]/[\overline{- \text{ kons}}] \\ [- \text{ PP} = \text{Prät}] \end{cases}$$

Wenn wir diese IR annehmen, vereinfachen sich die Lexikoneintragungen wie in (10) angegeben:

(10)

	Hinterer Stammvokal		Vorderer Stammvokal			Diphthong
	Prät. mit /i/	Prät. mit /u/	/a/–/u/	/a/	/u/–/u/	
notwendige Spezifizierung	—	m i-Prät	—	m PP = St	m PP = Prät	—

Deutsche Akademie der Wissenschaften, Berlin

FOUNDATIONS OF LANGUAGE

SUPPLEMENTARY SERIES

Edited by Morris Halle, Peter Hartmann,
K. Kunjunni Raja, Benson Mates, J. F. Staal,
Pieter A. Verburg, and John W. M. Verhaar